LEARNING TO TEACH IN THE SECONDARY SCHOOL

'Well-structured and well-written, with the emphasis on the student teacher throughout' *Student Teacher's response to the first edition*

Learning to teach may sound easy enough, but the reality involves a lot of hard work and careful preparation. To become an effective classroom teacher requires good subject knowledge, a knowledge of your pupils and the confidence to respond to dynamic classroom situations.

This very practical text is a revised edition of the highly successful first edition. The latest legislation is incorporated and even more useful ideas and strategies are included. The importance of ICT is dealt with in a new chapter and throughout the book. This text guides you through your school experience by giving a sound and practical introduction to the teaching skills needed to gain Qualified Teacher Status, but it also helps you to develop those qualities that lead on to good practice and a successful future in education.

The book is divided into units, each covering a key concept or skill, including:

- classroom management
- discipline
- planning lessons and schemes of work
- differentiation and grouping pupils
- assessment
- special educational needs
- using ICT in teaching and learning
- getting a job

The book offers advice on how to write assignments which link theory to practice. It is the core text that supports each of the subject-specific texts in the *Learning to Teach* series, also published by Routledge. It is also a companion text to *Starting to Teach in the Secondary School* by the same authors. It is an essential buy for every student teacher.

Susan Capel is Reader in Education and Director of the Academic Standards Unit at Canterbury Christ Church University College. **Marilyn Leask** is Principal Lecturer in Education at De Montfort University, Bedford. **Tony Turner** is Senior Lecturer in Education at the Institute of Education, University of London.

Learning to Teach Subjects in the Secondary School Series

Series Editors
Sue Capel, Canterbury Christ Church College; Marilyn Leask, De Montfort University, Bedford and Tony Turner, Institute of Education, University of London.

Designed for all students learning to teach in secondary schools, and particularly those on school based initial teacher education courses, the books in this series complement *Learning to Teach in the Secondary School* and its companion, *Starting to Teach in the Secondary School*. Each book in the series applies underpinning theory and addresses practical issues to support students in school and in the higher education instituion in learning how to teach a particular subject.

Learning to Teach Art and Design in the Secondary School
Lesley Burgess and Nicholas Addison

Learning to Teach Design and Technology in the Secondary School
Gwyneth Owen-Jackson

Learning to Teach English in the Secondary School
Jon Davison and Jane Dowson

Learning to Teach Modern Foreign Languages in the Secondary School
Norbert Pachler and Kit Field

Learning to Teach Geography in the Secondary School
David Lambert and David Balderstone

Learning to Teach History in the Secondary School
Terry Haydn, James Arthur and Martin Hunt

Learning to Teach Mathematics in the Secondary School
Sue Johnston-Wilder, Peter Johnston-Wilder, David Pimm and John Westwell

Learning to Teach Music in the Secondary School
Pauline Adams and Chris Philpott

Learning to Teach Physical Education in the Secondary School
Susan Capel

Learning to Teach Religious Education in the Secondary School
Andrew Wright

Learning to Teach Science in the Secondary School
Tony Turner and Wendy DiMarco

Learning to Teach using ICT in the Secondary School
Marilyn Leask and Norbert Pachler

LEARNING TO TEACH IN THE SECONDARY SCHOOL

A COMPANION TO SCHOOL EXPERIENCE
2nd edition

Susan Capel, Marilyn Leask and Tony Turner

London and New York

The ideas in this book have been influenced by the pupils, student teachers, teachers and lecturers with whom we have worked over the years. As it is impossible to thank them all individually, we take this opportunity to acknowledge their influence on our thinking.

Our families and close friends too have contributed to this book through their unwavering support, without which the book could not have been written. For her unfailing encouragement, we also thank Helen Fairlie from Routledge.

First edition published 1995
by Routledge
Second edition published 1999
by Routledge
11 New Fetter Lane, London EC4P 4EE

Simultaneously published in the USA and Canada
by Routledge
29 West 35th Street, New York, NY 10001

Routledge is an imprint of the Taylor & Francis Group

Selection and editorial matter © 1995, 1999 Susan Capel, Marilyn Leask and Tony Turner; individual chapters © their authors

Typeset in Palladia by Solidus (Bristol) Limited
Printed and bound in Great Britain by
TJ International Ltd, Padstow, Cornwall

British Library Cataloguing in Publication Data
A catalogue record for this book is available from the British Library

Library of Congress Cataloging in Publication Data
Learning to teach in the secondary school : a companion to school
    experience / [edited by] Susan Capel, Marilyn Leask, and Tony
    Turner. — 2nd ed.
        p. cm.
    Includes bibliographical references (p.) and index.
    1. High school teaching–Handbooks, manuals, etc.   2. Classroom
management–Handbooks, manuals, etc.   I. Capel, Susan Anne, 1953–
. II. Leask, Marilyn, 1950– .   III. Turner, Tony, 1935– .
LB1737.A3L43   1999
373. 1102–dc 21   98-51546
                                                                              CIP

ISBN 0–415–19937–9

CONTENTS

ILLUSTRATIONS

FIGURES

TABLES

LIST OF TASKS

The Task Number identifies the Chapter (first number) and Unit (second number)

NOTES ON CONTRIBUTORS

Diana Burton is Principal Lecturer and Head of Secondary Teacher Education at the Crewe School of Education, Manchester Metropolitan University. She has taught Education Studies to students and serving teachers and has been involved in the re-design of school-based teacher education courses, leading developments in mentor training and researching the subsequent changes in the role of university tutors. She taught humanities and social science in an urban comprehensive school for twelve years, developing a particular interest in pastoral care and educational psychology. She has a PhD from Birmingham University, the subject of which was the potential of cognitive style for developing differentiated approaches to learning. Current research interests include the application of learning-style measurements to aspects of pupil behaviour and learning.

Susan Capel is Reader in Education and Director of the Academic Standards Unit at Canterbury Christ Church University College. She was previously programme director for the Secondary PGCE at Bedford College of Higher Education. Prior to working in higher education she taught physical education and geography in the UK and Hong Kong. She has a PhD in physical education and has published widely in a range of areas, including the development of physical education students as teachers and factors influencing physical education initial teacher education. She was co-author of *Starting to Teach in the Secondary School: A Companion for the Newly Qualified Teacher* and was responsible for *Learning to Teach Physical Education in the Secondary School: A Companion to School Experience*, both of which are companions to this book.

Jon Davison is Head of the Department of Secondary Education at Canterbury Christ Church University College. He is director of the PGCE (Secondary) programme. Previously, he taught English and media studies in inner London for seventeen years, and became an advisory teacher at the English and Media Centre, London. His research includes language and gender issues, media literacy and popular culture. He edited *After the Bomb*, which won the Times Educational Supplement School-book Award 1991. Other publications include *Subject Mentoring in the Secondary School* and *Learning to Teach English in the Secondary School: A Companion to School Experience*, a companion to this book.

Jane Dowson is Senior Lecturer in Language and Literature at De Montfort University, Bedford. She co-ordinates the secondary PGCE and BEd English courses. She has taught in an upper secondary school. She was a member of the East Midlands Flexible Learning Project and was part of the De Montfort University Evaluation Team for the National Shakespeare Project in Leicestershire schools (1992–1994). She is joint editor, with Jon Davison, of *Learning to Teach English in the Secondary School* (Routledge, 1998). Her publications include *Women's Poetry of the 1930s* (Routledge, 1996) and *Selected Poems of Francis Cornford*'(Enitharmon, 1996).

Graham Haydon is a Lecturer in Philosophy of Education at the Institute of Education, University of London. He has experience of initial teacher education at the Institute over many years and through several changes in the format of teacher training: at the receiving end as a student there himself; as a course tutor in professional studies and in optional courses; and for several years as co-ordinator of the Issues in Education component of the Institute's PGCE. He now runs an INSET course at Masters level in Values in Education. Much of his research and publication has been on the political and moral aims of education, including values education, in a plural society.

David Lambert is a Senior Lecturer in Education at the Institute of Education, University of London and formerly Head of Geography and acting Deputy Headteacher at a comprehensive school in Hertfordshire. He was a member of the SEAC geography committee and helped establish the Assessment and Examinations Working Group of the Geographical Association. His present responsibilities include being PGCE course tutor for geography and PGCE Co-ordinator for East London.

Marilyn Leask is a Principal Lecturer at De Montfort University. As TVEI co-ordinator she had email in her classroom in 1985. She has since worked on a number of educational projects focused on the use of IT and more recently the INTERNET in education. She co-ordinates the pedagogical research on the EU-funded European Schoolnet Multimedia project. She is also the chair of TeacherNetUK. She has published a number of texts in initial teacher education, management and quality issues. She is joint series editor of the Routledge *Learning to Teach in the Secondary School* series. Recent texts include editing *Issues related to using ICT in Schools* and, with John Meadows, *Teaching and Learning with ICT in the Primary School*.

David Lines is a Lecturer in Business Education at the Institute of Education. He has been involved with external examination for fifteen years, both as examiner and syllabus developer. For the past eight years he has served as Chief Examiner at Advanced Level for the Associated Examination Board, and latterly for the University of London Examinations and Assessment Council. He has acted as consultant for the School Curriculum and Assessment Authority and the National Council for Vocational Qualifications, and is currently undertaking research for the Employment Department on GNVQ assessment.

Gill Nicholls is currently a Senior Lecturer in Education at the University of Surrey. She is responsible for the Centre of Professional Development and Education and the Convenor of the PhD and EdD research programme. She previously worked at Canterbury Christ Church University College on the PGCE (Secondary) course. She is actively involved in curriculum development and professional development in secondary schools and currently working on a research project related to satellite science and the school curriculum. Her other professional interests include the use of prior conceptions and cognition in the development of computer software for the teaching of science; and the issues related to pupils in transition from Keystage 2 to Keystage 3. Her most recent publication is *Pupils in Transition* (Routledge).

Norbert Pachler works at the Institute of Education, University of London, as a Lecturer with responsibility for the Secondary PGCE in Modern Foreign Languages and the MA in Modern Languages in Education. His research interests include modern foreign languages teaching and learning, comparative education as well as the application of new technologies in teaching and learning. In 1997 *Learning to Teach Modern Foreign Languages in the Secondary School*, which he wrote with Kit Field, was published by Routledge. The sequel, *Teaching Modern Foreign Languages of Advanced/Advanced Subsidiary Level*, is forthcoming. He has also contributed to the generic titles in this series *Learning to Teach in the Secondary School* and *Starting to Teach in the Secondary School*.

David Pollak is a Lecturer in Learning Support and Dyslexia Studies at De Montfort University. He is a member of the Learning and Training Support Service team. He has 25 years' experience of teaching in compulsory and higher education, having taught pupils and students of all ages in maintained, independent and special schools. In 1993 he completed his MA by action research, investigating social and emotional factors at the special school for dyslexic teenagers at which he was Head of English. David has worked as a learning support tutor at the Universities of Sussex and Brighton. He is currently studying for a PhD the subject of which is 'Learning life histories of higher education students who are dyslexic'.

Roger Strangwick is a Principal Lecturer at De Montfort University, Bedford. After studying maths and physics at University, he lived for a while in Spain. He learnt Russian during National Service then spent some time in advertising before qualifying as a teacher. He worked in schools in Liverpool, Lincolnshire, Swindon and Hitchin. While teaching, he took an external degree in English. He is co-author of two text books and has also written plays and poems. In 1975 he took an MA in Education at the University of East Anglia and an MA in Linguistics at the University of Westminster.

Tony Turner is a Senior Lecturer in Education at the Institute of Education, University of London, in the Science and Technology Group. During that period he has been involved in teaching and research. He has been involved with planning, organising and running new school-based PGCE courses, including the Secondary Articled Teacher Scheme. Previously he was Research Fellow on a Nuffield Science Teaching Project at the Centre for Science Education, Chelsea College, and before that worked on school science curriculum development at the University of the West Indies. Current research interests include issues of recruitment to teach science in a culturally diverse society. He is co-author of *Learning to Teach Science in the Secondary School* (Routledge, 1998).

Margaret Whitehead is Head of Quality, Faculty of Health and Community Studies at De Montfort University, Bedford. She trained as a physical education teacher and subsequently studied philosophy of education, writing her PhD on the implications of existentialism and phenomenology to the practice of physical education. In 1980 she was appointed Head of Professional Studies for Secondary Initial Teacher Education at Bedford College of Higher Education and has since been instrumental in devising and teaching courses related to developing students' teaching skills and strategies. She has lectured widely on in-service courses, running sessions on topics such as 'Teaching: craft into art' and 'Using teaching strategies to achieve learning objectives'. As president of the Physical Education Association of the United Kingdom (PEAUK 1999–2001) she takes an active role in the development of her subject nationally.

Barbara Wynn is Headteacher of the Willink School in Berkshire. She was previously Deputy Head at Cheney School, Oxfordshire where she was responsible for developing a very successful staff development scheme involving both teaching and non-teaching staff. She was involved in the development of the Oxford Internship Scheme in schools run by Oxford University, then became a teacher–examiner in that scheme. She has written two school text books and has contributed to a number of education books on teacher education, sexism in education and staff development.

FOREWORD

There are may differences between the programme of teacher education that I entered as a PGCE student nearly half a century ago and that which intending teachers follow today. But the similarities are more important than the differences. Then, as now, we were soon brought to realise that there are no quick fixes to acquiring the knowledge and skill necessary for success in the classroom. Despite all the advances made in understanding how the brain works and personality develops, we are no nearer to devising sure-fire ways of motivating learners and achieving high standards. Even with electronic access to far larger quantities of information than even the best equipped libraries could offer, we have to acquire the arts of analysis and interpretation and face to face communication by practice and experience, just as we have always done.

The ability to engage young people in the enterprise of learning, to share with them the excitement of commitment to a discipline, to help them to experience the satisfactions of study in depth – these are not reducible to formulae to be acquired from books or from unstructured observation of even the most gifted teachers. Both are necessary, neither are sufficient. Induction into a profession takes time. It is best conducted within institutional partnerships that offer strong personal support, ample resources and generous opportunities to work in real school settings.

Learning to Teach in the Secondary School recognises both what is new and what is enduring in teacher education. During the five years since its first publication many thousands of students and teachers have benefited from the ideas, insights and experience that its authors bring from their work in classrooms in schools, colleges and universities. But as in any professional field, knowledge, technique and relevant legislation continue to develop and must be reflected in the content and organisation of courses. Hence the need for this second edition.

In undertaking revisions, the authors have been attentive not only to new regulations and curriculum prescriptions, such as the switch from *Competences* to *Standards* in England and Wales, but also to the reviews of teacher educators and their students. All this had led to the inclusion of a chapter on ICT, significant revisions to those on Special Educational Needs and How Pupils Learn, and a new section on preparing and writing coursework for the Post Graduate Certificate in Education.

The basic approach remains that of developing professionalism, strengthening partnerships and encouraging teachers to make a commitment to their own learning as well as that of their students, throughout their careers. This second edition, like the first, will make an important contribution to the continuing improvement of teacher education.

Professor Sir William Taylor CBE

ACKNOWLEDGEMENTS

Acknowledgement is gratefully expressed for material from the following publications:

Unit 3.3, OFSTED (1993) Working papers for the inspection of secondary initial teacher training, London: Office of Her Majesty's Chief Inspector.

Unit 5.4, DES (1988) Notes from DES Conference N213, London: DES.

Unit 6.1, DES/Welsh Office (1988). *National Curriculum. Task Group on Assessment and Testing (TGAT Report)*, London: DES.

Unit 7.3, DES (1989) *From Policy to Practice*, London: DES.

Unit 8.1, Humphrys, G. (1993) *Getting a Teaching Job*, University of Greenwich: sponsored by TASC.

Unit 8.3, OFSTED (1994a) *Handbook for the Inspection of Schools, Part 6: The Statutory Basis for Education*, London: Office of Her Majesty's Chief Inspector.

Appendix 3, DES (1989) *Discipline in Schools. Report of the Committee of Enquiry Chaired by Lord Elton (The Elton Report)*, London: HMSO.

Appendix 4, DFE (1994) *Code of Practice on the Identification and Assessment of Special Educational Needs*, London: DFE.

Unit 8.2, p. 467. OFSTED (1993) *The New Teacher in School: a Survey by Her Majesty's Inspectorate in England and Wales, 1992*, London: HMSO.

Chapter 7 and Unit 6.3. Patten, J. (1994) 'Educational outputs', *Schools Update* (summer), London: DFE.

Crown copyright is reproduced with the permission of the Controller of HMSO.

The publisher and the authors wish to state that every effort was made prior to publication to secure permission for the reproduction of extracts on pages 26 and 415.

INTRODUCTION

Teaching is both an art and a science. In this book we show that there are certain essential elements of teaching that you can master through practice that help you become an effective teacher. However, there is no one correct way of teaching, no one specific set of skills, techniques and procedures that you must master and apply mechanically. Every teacher is an individual and brings something of their own unique personality to the job. We hope that this book helps you to develop skills, techniques and procedures appropriate for your individual personality and style and provides you with an entry to ways of understanding what you do and see. An effective, reflective teacher is one who can integrate theory with practice. We also hope that it provides the stimulus for you to want to continue to learn and develop throughout your career as a teacher.

DEVELOPING YOUR PHILOSOPHY OF TEACHING

There have been many changes in initial teacher training over recent years and the most significant of these has been the shift from higher education to more school-based training. We would argue that an initial teacher training course provides not merely **training** but also the further **education** of intending teachers. What we mean by this is that teacher training is not an apprenticeship but a journey of personal development in which your skills of classroom management develop alongside an emerging understanding of the teaching and learning process. This is a journey of discovery which begins on the first day of your course and may only stop when you retire. Thus, we should refer to initial teacher **education** rather than initial teacher training. We use the term initial teacher education throughout this book.

The advantage of a school-based course is the opportunity it gives for the student teacher to appreciate at first hand the complex, exciting and contradictory events of classroom interactions without the constant immediacy of having to teach all the time. It should allow the student time to make sense of experiences, both in the classroom and the wider school, that demand explanations. Providing such explanations requires you to have a theory of teaching and learning.

By means of an organised course which provides for practical experience, structured observation and reflective activity suitably interwoven with theoretical inputs, student teachers can begin to develop their own theory of teaching and learning. Theoretical inputs can come from tutors and teachers, from lectures and from libraries and we hope from using this book. Theory also arises from practice, the better to inform and develop practice.

Everyone who teaches has a theory of how to teach effectively and of how pupils learn. The theory may be implicit in what the teacher does and the teacher may not be able to tell you what their theory is. For example, a teacher who is a disciplinarian is likely to have a different theory about the conditions for learning than a teacher who is very liberal in their teaching style. Likewise, some teachers may feel that they do not have a philosophy of education. What these teachers are really saying is that they have not examined their views, or cannot articulate them. What is your philosophy? For example, do you consider that your job is to transfer the knowledge of your subject to pupils? Or are you there to lead them through its main features? Are you 'filling empty vessels' or are you the guide on a 'voyage of discovery'? On the other hand, perhaps you are the potter, shaping and moulding pupils.

It is recognised that an initial teacher education course only allows a start to be made on developing your own personal understanding of the teaching process. There are a number of different theories about teaching and learning. You need to be aware of what these are, reflect on them and consider how they help you to explain more fully what you are trying to do and why. Through the process of theorising about what you are doing, reflecting on a range of other theories as well as your own, you understand your practice better and develop into a reflective practitioner, i.e. a teacher who makes conscious decisions about the teaching strategies to employ and who modifies their practice in the light of experiences.

An articulated, conscious philosophy of teaching emerges only if a particular set of habits are developed. In particular, the habit of reviewing your own teaching from time to time. It is these habits which need to be developed from the start of your initial teacher education course. This is what is meant by many authors when they refer to 'the reflective practitioner'. This is why we (as well as your course tutors) ask you to evaluate your own teaching, to keep a diary and to develop a professional portfolio to record your development and carry that forward from your initial teacher education course to your first post. Part of this reflection will be included in your career entry profile.

HOW TO USE THIS BOOK

Structure of the book

The book is laid out so that elements of appropriate theory introduce each issue. This theory is interwoven with tasks designed to help you identify key features of the behaviour or issue. A number of different inquiry methods are used to generate data, e.g. reflecting on the reading and observation or on an activity you are asked to carry out, asking questions, gathering data, discussing with a tutor or another student teacher. Some of the tasks involve you in activities that impinge on other people, e.g. observing a teacher in the classroom, or asking for information. If a task requires you to do this, **you must first of all seek permission of the person concerned.** Remember that you are a guest in school(s), you cannot walk into any teacher's classroom to observe. In addition, some information may be personal, or sensitive and you need to consider issues of confidentiality and professional behaviour in your inquiries and reporting.

The main text is supported by a number of appendices that provide further guidance to you as a student teacher. The glossary of terms is included to help you interpret the jargon of education. An appendix on writing and reflection is included to help you with the written assignments on your initial teacher education course. There are also extracts from two documents which are referred to in the main body of the book and some useful addresses.

Developing your competence

The range and type of competences/standards you are expected to become aware of and develop during your initial teacher education course will have been derived from those for student teachers in the country in which you are learning to teach. The units in this book are designed to help you work towards developing these competences. Your tutors in school and in your institution help you identify levels of competence appropriate to your status as a student teacher and as a newly qualified teacher. We ask you at appropriate points in the text to relate the work directly to the specific competences standards to which you are working.

In addition to these competences/standards required of newly qualified teachers, there are competences that are unlikely to be developed until into your first post, e.g. developing and sustaining working relationships with pupils at Key Stage 4, as they are unlikely to be achieved adequately without more experience than school experience can give. You will develop such competences as you gain experience in your first post.

Your diary of reflective practice

As you read through the book and complete the tasks, we ask you to keep a reflective diary. This diary can be used to record the outcomes of tasks and your thoughts on the reading, analyses undertaken as part of that reading, or other activities that arise as part of your course. The diary can also be used to record your reactions to events, both good and bad, as a way of letting off steam! It provides a record of your development which will be very useful in developing your professional portfolio and writing the relevant sections of your career entry profile.

Your professional portfolio

Your professional portfolio provides a selective record of your development as a teacher and is something that you continue to develop throughout your teaching career. At the end of your initial teacher education course it contributes directly to your career entry profile. It is likely that your institution has a set format for a professional portfolio, in which case you will be told about it. If not, you should develop your own. You can use any format and include any evidence you think appropriate.

This portfolio should contain selective evidence of your development, your strengths as well as areas for further development. At a minimum this can be provided through evidence of completion or otherwise of the competences required as part of your course. However, to be truly beneficial, it should contain much other evidence. This further evidence could be work of value to you, a response to significant events, extracts from your diary of reflective practice, good lesson plans, evaluations of lessons, teaching reports, observations on you made by teachers, outcomes of tasks undertaken, assessed and non-assessed coursework.

Try to develop your portfolio during your course, using evidence from learning experiences on the course. At the end of your course you can use your portfolio as the basis for completing your career entry profile. To help with this you might write a personal statement describing aspects of your development as a teacher during your initial teacher education course. This would include reference to your teaching reports written by teachers, tutors and yourself. The portfolio can be used to enable you to reflect on your learning and achievements; to help you complete applications for your first post; and to take to interview. It can help provide the basis of your continued professional development as it enables you to identify competences in need of development and thus targets for Continuing Professional Development (CPD) in your first post, first through your career entry profile then as part of the appraisal process you will be involved with as a teacher. It describes strengths and weaknesses, hopes for the future and identifies elements of your emerging personal philosophy of teaching. Thus, we strongly recommend that you start to keep a diary of reflective practice now to form the basis for this professional portfolio.

Ways you might like to use this book

With much of your course being delivered in school, you may have limited access to a library, to other students with whom to discuss problems and issues at the end of the school day and, in some instances, limited access to a tutor to whom you can refer. There are likely to be times when you are faced with a problem in school which has not been addressed up to that point within the course you are following and you need some help immediately, e.g. before facing a class the next day or next week. This book is designed to help you address some of the issues or difficulties you are faced with during your period of initial teacher education, by providing supporting knowledge interspersed with a range of tasks to enable you to link theory with practice.

The book is designed to be used in a number of ways. It is designed more for you to dip in and out of, to look up a specific problem or issue that you want to consider, rather than for you to read from cover to cover (although you may want to use it in both ways of course). You can use it on your own as it provides background information and supporting theory about a range of issues you are likely to face during your initial teacher education course. Reflecting on an issue faced in school with greater understanding of what others have written and said about it, alongside undertaking some of the associated tasks, may help you to identify some potential solutions. The book can also be used in association with your tutors (higher education and/or school staff responsible for overseeing your learning and development). The tasks are an integral part of the book and most of them can be completed by you individually. Most tasks do, however, benefit from wider discussion, which we would encourage you to do whenever possible. However, some tasks can only be carried out with other student teachers and/or with the support of a tutor. You will need to select those that are appropriate to your circumstances.

However, this book will not suffice alone; we have attempted to provide you with guidance to further reading by two methods. The first, by references in the text, the details of which appear at the end of the book. The second, by the readings related to the units. These further readings, to direct and develop understanding, appear at the end of the units. Addresses are also given to provide easy access to further information. In addition, you should use this book alongside your course handbook which outlines specific course requirements, agreed ways of working, roles and responsibilities.

If you see each unit as a potentially open door leading to whole new worlds of thought about how societies can best educate their children, then you will have achieved one of our goals – to provide you with a guide book on your journey of discovery about teaching and learning. Finally, we hope that you find the book useful and of support in school. If you like it, tell others; if not, tell us.

We have tried to mix and balance the use of gender terms in order to avoid clumsy he/she terminology. We call school children 'pupils' to avoid confusion with students, by which we mean people in further and higher education. The important staff in your life are those in school and higher education institution; we have called all these people tutors. Your institution will have its own way of referring to staff.

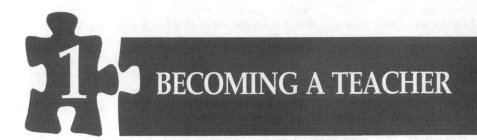

BECOMING A TEACHER

Through the units in this chapter, the complexity and breadth of the teacher's role and the nature of teaching are explored. You are posed questions about your values and attitudes because these influence the type of teacher you become. Learning about **teaching and learning** is, we suggest, a lifelong process for the teacher which is aided by regular reflection on practice and continuing education, e.g. through continuing professional development.

Each unit in this chapter examines different facets of the work of student teachers and experienced teachers.

Unit 1.1 covers wider aspects of the teacher's role, including academic and pastoral roles and we consider the necessity for continual curriculum review.

In unit 1.2 we discuss the expectations which your higher education and school tutors will have of you. The meaning of professionalism is discussed and the idea that you will have your own philosophy of teaching is introduced. Phases which mark your development as a teacher are identified. We suggest that as your confidence and competence in managing the classroom grow, you can expect the focus of your work to move from your self-image and the mechanics of managing a lesson, to the learning taking place generally and, as you become more experienced, to the learning for the individual pupil.

Unit 1.3 provides advice for managing time, both inside and outside the classroom, and for preventing stress. There are a variety of competing demands made on your time and if you learn to use your time effectively, you will have more time to enjoy your work as a teacher and more leisure time.

Unit 1.4 provides an introduction to ways in which information and communications technology can be used to support teaching and learning.

To become a teacher you need to supplement your **subject knowledge** with **professional knowledge** about teaching and learning and to develop your **professional judgement**, e.g. about managing situations which arise with pupils. Ways of developing your professional knowledge and judgement provide themes running throughout the book.

You may come to recognise your situation in the following poem called 'Late'.

You're late, said miss
The bell has gone,
dinner numbers done
and work begun.

What have you got to say for yourself?

Well, it's like this, miss.
Me mum was sick,
me dad fell down the stairs,
the wheel fell off me bike
and then we lost our Billy's snake
behind the kitchen chairs. Earache
struck down me grampy, me gran
took quite a funny turn.
Then on the way I met this man
whose dog attacked me shin –
look, miss, you can see the blood
it doesn't look too good,
does it?

Yes, yes sit down –
and next time say you're sorry
for disturbing all the class.
Now get on with your story,
fast!

Please miss, I've got nothing to write about.

Judith Nicholls in Batchford, R. (1992)
Assemblies for the 1990s

1.1   WHAT DO TEACHERS DO?

The answer to this question depends on where and when the question is being asked. You will be teaching in the twenty-first century. We'd like to take you back in time, just for a moment, to English schools in the Middle Ages.

Curtis (1967, pp. 23–24) writes that in England in the twelfth century,

> theology was considered the queen of studies, to which philosophy served as an introduction. The studies which led to the supreme study of theology were known generally as the Seven Liberal Arts. The Arts (or sciences) were termed liberal from *liber*, free and constituted the course of study suitable for the freeman as contrasted with the Practical and Mechanical Arts which were learned and practised by slaves in the classical period. The arts were divided into the Trivium and Quadrivium. . . . The subjects of the Trivium consisted of Grammar, Rhetoric and Dialectic (logic); and of the Quadrivium, Arithmetic, Geometry, Astronomy and Music – the subjects of the Trivium were taught to younger pupils and the Quadrivium to older pupils. There were grammar schools (providing preparation for university work), song schools (for teaching singing in Latin at church services) and reading and writing schools (effectively providing a primary education). The three schools were often housed under the one roof and the language of instruction changed with political changes – from Latin to Norman-French to the vernacular.

Can you imagine teaching in this way today? Whom would we consider the freemen and whom the slaves? Clearly what teachers teach reflects the times in which they live so change is essential in education. Without change, we would have a fossilised, out-of-date curriculum – what Peddiwell (1939 cited in Goddard and Leask, 1992) called the 'sabre-toothed curriculum'. Peddiwell describes a prehistoric community which successfully taught its youngsters how to deal with sabre-toothed tigers. Unfortunately, the curriculum wasn't updated when the sabre-toothed tigers died out, with the result that the children's education didn't prepare them for the new challenges facing the community. This illustrates the necessity for regular review of the curriculum and, for similar reasons, teachers' knowledge and skills should be regularly updated. So what teachers do depends on what is happening in the wider community. The way society develops an appropriate curriculum is discussed in more detail in Chapter 7.

OBJECTIVES

By the end of this unit you should:

- be aware of the range of skills and forms of knowledge which a teacher uses in planning and giving lessons;
- have considered the relationship between subject knowledge and effective teaching;

- have an understanding of various aspects of a teacher's role and responsibilities including academic and pastoral roles, administration and health and safety;
- be developing your own philosophy of teaching.

CLASSROOM PRACTICE – AN INTRODUCTION TO HOW TEACHERS TEACH

The teacher's job is first and foremost **to ensure that pupils learn**. To a large extent, **what** (i.e. the lesson content) pupils should learn in maintained (state) schools in England and Wales is determined through legislation and the requirements are set out in various National Curriculum documents. Parents, through governors, can, however, have a say about sex education. On the other hand, **how** you teach so that the pupils learn effectively (i.e. the methods and materials used) is left to the professional judgement of the individual teacher, department and school.

> **Task 1.1.1   FOCUSING ON COMPETENCES/STANDARDS**
> It may help you to understand what is expected of newly qualified teachers if you find out about the competences/standards you are required to reach by the end of your course. These can be found in your course handbook and other documentation provided by your institution.

Teaching is a very personal activity and while certain teaching styles and strategies might suit one teacher, they might not be appropriate for another. However, although there exists a core of good practice to which most teachers would subscribe, there are differences between teachers which relate to personality, style and philosophy. Moreover, observers of the same teacher might well disagree about the strengths and weaknesses of that teacher. In your first days in school, it is likely that you will spend time observing a number of experienced teachers. It is highly unlikely that you will see two teachers who teach identically. Perhaps you will see teaching styles which you feel more at home with, while others do not seem as appropriate to your own developing practice. Of course, there is no one way to teach. Provided effective teaching and learning takes place, a whole range of approaches from didactic (formal, heavy on content) to experiential (learning by doing) is appropriate – often in the same lesson. Unit 5.3 provides more details about teaching styles.

Learning to manage the classroom is similar in many ways to learning to drive. At the outset there seems so much to remember. How do you manage to: depress the clutch; brake; change gear; be aware of oncoming traffic and cars following you; look in the mirror; indicate; obey the speed limit; observe traffic signs and signals; be aware of and sensitive to, changing road and weather conditions; anticipate problems and steer simultaneously? After a short time, however, such skills become part of subconscious patterns of behaviour.

Much of what many experienced teachers do to manage their classes has become part of their unconscious classroom behaviour. Their organisation of the lesson so that pupils learn is implicit in what they do rather than explicit. So much so, that often teachers find it hard to articulate exactly what it is they are doing or why it is successful. This situation, of course, does not help the student teacher. It also gives weight to the spurious notion that teachers are born rather than made and that nobody can tell you how to teach.

Undoubtedly some teachers may well begin teaching with certain advantages such as a 'good' voice or organisational skills. Nevertheless there are common skills and techniques to be learned that, when combined with an awareness of and sensitivity to, the teaching and learning contexts, enable student teachers to manage their classes effectively.

Teaching is a continuously creative and problem-solving activity. Each learner or each group of learners has their own characteristics which the experienced teacher takes into account in planning the relevant learning programme. For example, if there has been recent controversy over environmental issues in the local area or the school has taken refugees fleeing from civil war, an effective teacher will adapt their approach to the discussion of such matters to make lessons more relevant and to allow the pupils to draw on their experience. Although lessons with different groups may have similar content, a lesson is rarely delivered in the same way twice. Variations in interactions between the pupils and the teacher affect the teaching strategy chosen.

THE WORK IN THE CLASSROOM – THE TIP OF THE ICEBERG

On the surface, teaching may appear to be a relatively simple process – the view that the teacher stands in front of the class and talks and the pupils learn appears to be all too prevalent. (Ask friends and family what they think a teacher does.)

The reality is somewhat different.

Classroom teaching is only the most visible part of the job of the teacher. The contents of this book are designed to introduce you to what we see as the invisible foundation of the teacher's work: **professional knowledge** about teaching and learning and **professional judgement** about the routines, skills and strategies which support effective classroom management. Your **subject knowledge** comes from your degree and from your continuing professional development. An effective teacher draws on these three factors in planning each and every lesson; and the learning for a particular class is planned ahead – over weeks, months and years – so that there is **continuity and progression** in the pupils' learning. Each lesson is planned as part of a sequence of learning experiences.

The following analogy may help you understand what underpins the work in the classroom. Think of a lesson as being like an iceberg – 70% to 80%, the base, is hidden (Figure 1.1.1). The work in the classroom represents the tip of the iceberg. Supporting this tip, but hidden, are many elements of the teacher's professional expertise. These include:

- evaluation of previous lessons;
- preparation for the lesson;
- planning of a sequence of lessons to ensure learning progresses;
- established routines or procedures which ensure that the work of the class proceeds as planned;

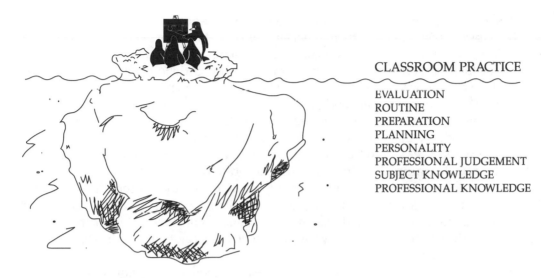

Figure 1.1.1 The work in the classroom – the tip of the iceberg
Acknowledgement: Simon Beer

- personality – including the teacher's ability to capture and hold the interest of the class, to establish their authority;
- subject knowledge;
- professional knowledge about effective teaching and learning;
- professional judgement built up over time through reflection on experience.

During your course, you will often see experienced teachers and student teachers teaching. But what are you really seeing? You need to learn to 'read the classroom' – to train yourself to look beyond what is readily visible so that you come to understand the variety of skills and strategies which the teacher brings to bear in order to maximise the learning taking place. Some of these skills and strategies are easily identifiable, others require you to observe more carefully. Any classroom observation you undertake must have a purpose, be focused, generate information and should provoke thought. We hope to sensitise you to what happens behind the classroom scene so that you can build on that knowledge in your own classroom work.

Throughout your course, you should expect to develop confidence and new levels of competence in all these areas.

SUBJECT KNOWLEDGE AND EFFECTIVE TEACHING

A common misunderstanding about teaching is that if you know your subject then you automatically can teach it well. In the same way that delivering milk to the doorstep provides no guarantee that it will be taken into the house, so too is it with the subject content of a lesson. You cannot assume that pupils will automatically take in what you had hoped to teach them. The fact that you are an expert in a subject is no guarantee that you can help others learn that subject.

It is usually assumed that students on a one year post-graduate course have a certain level of subject knowledge and their initial teacher education course usually concentrates on subject application to the classroom. These students often find they have to relearn aspects of their subject which they may not have thought about for years as well as material which is new to them. You can expect to have to widen your knowledge base so that you have a deeper understanding of the subject than is required by the syllabus. Wider knowledge enables you to develop differentiated tasks much more easily and gives you confidence that you will be able to answer questions.

Teaching requires you to transform the knowledge you possess into suitable tasks which lead to learning. Acquiring appropriate up-to-date knowledge requires some effort on your part and this is just part of the work of the teacher. The National Curriculum provides a useful starting point for student teachers and most subject associations produce relevant materials and run annual conferences which help you keep up with developments. Addresses of subject associations can be found in *The Education Year Book* (published annually).

However, to teach effectively, you need more than good subject knowledge.

Task 1.1.2   SUBJECT KNOWLEDGE COMPETENCES/STANDARDS

Identify the competences/standards in Subject Knowledge required by your course. You will see that some of these relate to the National Curriculum. Now look at the National Curriculum for your subject. Analyse it to identify the areas of knowledge that you can cope with now, those you could cope with with some effort and those areas which require totally new learning. Where there are areas which are unfamiliar to you, set yourself goals for improving this aspect of your knowledge. You may find it helpful to discuss these goals with more experienced colleagues. Make sure to check your progress regularly, e.g. before school experience and after your final school experience. A personal profile of your developing knowledge of subject matter could be included in your Career Entry Profile, which you will take to your first post. Your knowledge needs may be able to be further addressed in your first post as a newly qualified teacher through in-service education, for example.

As already indicated, **personality and personal style** do influence your effectiveness as a teacher but many skills and strategies can be learned and practised until they become part of your professional repertoire. We introduce you to theories underpinning educational practice and ideas which can provide a foundation for your development as an effective teacher whatever your subject. But what do we mean by effective teaching?

Effective teaching occurs where the learning experience structured by the teacher matches the needs of the learner, i.e. tasks develop the individual pupil's knowledge, skills, attitudes and/or understanding in such a way that the pupil is applying past knowledge as appropriate and laying the foundation for the next stage of learning. A key feature of effective teaching is balancing the pupils' chance of success against the level of difficulty required to challenge them. Effective teaching depends on complex inter-relationships of a whole range of factors, a major one of which is the teacher's understanding of the different ways in which pupils learn. Chapter 5 provides further

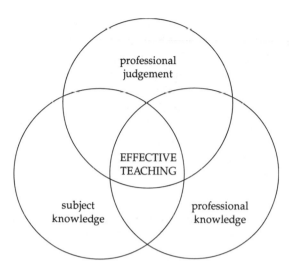

Figure 1.1.2 Subject knowledge is part of the effective teacher's professional tool kit

information about pupil learning. Understanding about the ways in which learning takes place is essential to your work as a teacher of a subject and this understanding provides the foundations on which to build your professional knowledge about teaching and learning. The more closely the teaching method matches the preferred learning style of the pupils the more effective the teaching will be. The content covers various aspects of the teaching and learning process which influence a teacher's effectiveness.

As a student teacher you have the opportunity to develop a repertoire of teaching styles and strategies and to test these out in the classroom. The information in various chapters should help you in this process. It may take you considerable time before you can apply the principles of effective teaching to your classroom practice but you can monitor your development through regular evaluation of lessons (see Unit 5.4). We aim to provide a basic introduction to what are complex areas and it is up to you to develop systematically your professional knowledge and judgement through analysing your experience (i.e. through reflection) and wider reading. Figure 1.1.2 illustrates what we see as the interconnections between effective teaching, subject knowledge, professional knowledge and professional judgement.

THE WIDER ROLE

The success of a school depends on the qualities and commitment of the staff as well as the pupils. A teacher's work is very varied and probably no one teacher's job is exactly the same as another's.

Most staff have responsibilities beyond their subject specialism: they may become involved in cross-curricular issues; personal, social and health education; school development planning; work experience; liaison with primary schools; careers advice; links with industry; planning educational trips and social events; curriculum planning and development; assessment; planning and implementing school policies; extra-curricular activities. In addition, teachers have a role to play in supporting the school ethos by reinforcing school rules and routines, e.g. on behaviour, dress and in encouraging pupils to develop self-discipline so that the school can function effectively and pupils can make the most of opportunities available to them.

Under the 1988 Education Reform Act, teachers in England and Wales have responsibility for implementing the National Curriculum and for the spiritual and moral welfare of their pupils (Unit 8.3 sets out statutory duties) so most teachers have both a specialist academic role and a pastoral role. Both roles encompass administrative as well as teaching responsibilities.

Table 1.1.1 Some of the activities which teachers undertake in their academic and pastoral roles

The academic role	The pastoral role and spiritual and moral welfare
The academic role of the teacher encompasses a variety of activities including: • subject teaching • lesson preparation • setting and marking of homework • assessing pupil progress in a variety of ways including marking tests and exams • writing reports • recording achievement • working as part of a subject team • curriculum development and planning • undertaking visits, field courses • reporting to parents • keeping up to date (often through work with the subject association) • implementing school policies • extra-curricular activities • examining for GCSE and A level boards	Pastoral duties vary from school to school. They often include: • working as part of a pastoral team • teaching personal, social and health education • taking part in the daily act of worship required by legislation • getting to know the pupils as individuals • helping pupils with problems • being responsible for a form: registering the class, following up absences • monitoring sanctions and rewards given to form members • reinforcing school rules and routines, e.g. on behaviour • writing reports, ensuring records of achievement and/or profiles are up to date • house/year group activities (plays/sports) • liaising with parents • ensuring school information is conveyed to parents via pupils • giving careers and subject guidance • extra-curricular activities

There are a number of administrative responsibilities which are part of a teacher's job: for example, record keeping (marks for homework, tests, classwork, attendance), marking, producing pupils' profiles and helping with records of achievement and pupil profiles, writing references, attending meetings and planning. From the beginning of your school experiences, it is worth trying to develop efficient ways of dealing with this administration otherwise you will waste a lot of time. Developing your word processing skills may be useful. Unit 1.3 on time management provides further advice. Later units provide more detailed information on a variety of aspects of the academic and pastoral roles.

HEALTH AND SAFETY

All teachers are responsible for the health and safety of the pupils in their charge. Legally, as a student teacher you cannot take on that responsibility. Whenever you are teaching, the ultimate responsibility lies with the class teacher.

Nevertheless in planning your lessons you must take into account the health and safety of your pupils by appropriate planning, e.g. identifying activities that do not endanger pupils, e.g. climbing on chairs; or for science and related subjects following the COSHH (Control Of Substances Hazardous to Health) regulations. Sharing your lesson plans in advance with your class teacher is an essential feature of your responsibility to both the pupils and your teachers. If you have any doubts about the safety of the lesson, ask for advice. If advice is not available, then don't use that strategy.

Whilst you are teaching, an experienced teacher must always be available in the classroom or nearby. If the lesson has special safety considerations, e.g. in PE or science, then if the class teacher or a suitably qualified teacher is not available, you must not proceed as if they were. Have an alternative lesson up your sleeve which does not require specific subject specialist support but could be carried out with the support of another teacher. Sometimes you may have to cancel your planned lesson.

It follows from this situation that, legally, you cannot act as supply teacher to fill in if the regular teacher is absent.

Task 1.1.3	**HEALTH AND SAFETY PROCEDURES**

Find out who is responsible for health and safety in your school experience school. Find the school and departmental policies on health and safety. Check the procedures you will be expected to apply – for example, in science, find out how you should check the safety of the chemicals or other equipment you may use, locate the eyewash bottle and gas, water and electricity isolating taps/switches; in PE check that you know how to test the safety of any apparatus pupils might use. Find out the names of the First Aiders in the school, where the first aid box is, what you are permitted to do if an incident occurs and what forms have to be filled in to record any accident.

We suggest that you take a first aid course and find out particularly how to deal with, faints, nose bleeds, fits, asthma attacks, epilepsy, diabetic problems, burns, bleeding and common accidents. But you should not administer first aid yourself unless qualified and even then, only the minimum necessary. You should report any incident and make a written record. There will usually be a record book in school for this purpose. Your subject association should be able to provide you with subject specific safety information and local branches of the British Red Cross or St John Ambulance have information about first aid courses. St John Ambulance produces a first aid text for schools (details are provided at the end of this unit).

Teachers also have a wide range of statutory duties which are further discussed in Unit 8.3.

> **Task 1.1.4   HEALTH AND SAFETY – WHAT SHOULD YOU KNOW?**
> What should you know and be able to do if you are to discharge your duties as a student teacher and as a teacher in your subject area? Discuss this with your tutor and other student teachers in your specialist area. To what extent do school and department rules help staff and pupils understand their duties in the area of safety?

⁝ Summary and key points

In the UK, while the curriculum is to a large extent centrally determined, the choice of teaching methods and materials is largely in the hands of the individual teacher. Your own philosophy of teaching affects the way you approach your work – this philosophy should develop over time as you acquire further professional knowledge and your professional judgement develops.

Clearly there are certain skills which the effective teacher possesses and you can identify many of these by skimming through the contents of each chapter. As a student, you have to move from knowing about these skills to being able to exercise them flexibly so that the planned learning can take place. The lists of competences for newly qualified teachers are best regarded as highlighting areas for development in which you will improve your capability. There are no ready-made patterns for success in teaching. Key elements in becoming a successful teacher, i.e. teaching effective lessons, include:

- adequate, secure subject knowledge
- attention to planning
- awareness of pupil needs
- concern for the welfare of pupils.

A range of different solutions can be employed in most situations and different strategies succeed with different pupils.

FURTHER READING

Hargreaves, D.H. and Hopkins, D. (1991) *The Empowered School: The Management and Practice of Development Planning*, London: Cassell.

Chapter 9 contains a discussion of the nature of professional judgement which describes four dimensions to the development of a teacher's professional judgement: making intuitive professional judgements; making considered professional judgements; refining professional judgements; complementing professional judgements with evidence. This work makes interesting reading for those who wish to consider this aspect of professionalism more closely.

Kyriacou, C. (1995) *Essential Teaching Skills*, Cheltenham: Stanley Thornes.

Kyriacou, C. (1997) *Effective Teaching in Schools: Theory and Practice (2nd edition)*, Cheltemham: Stanley Thornes.

These books are aimed at student teachers and more experienced teachers who wish to examine and develop their practice. They cover the key areas which student teachers should understand.

Marland, M. (1997) *The Art of the Tutor: Developing your Role in the Secondary School*, London: David Fulton.

Marland, M. (1993) *The Craft of the Classroom (2nd Edition)*, Oxford: Heinemann.

Both texts provide practical advice for the beginning teacher.

St John Ambulance (1994) *Emergency Aid for Schools (5th edition)*

This is obtainable from St John Supplies, Priory House, St John's Lane, London WC1M 4DA. A useful text for all teachers providing basic information about incidents and accidents which many teachers come across.

1.2   THE STUDENT TEACHER'S ROLE AND RESPONSIBILITIES

INTRODUCTION

The school-based experiences of the student teacher depend on a three-way partnership between the school, the student and higher education institution, except in those cases where the school is undertaking teacher education on its own. These experiences include the periods of whole class teaching as well as those occasions when direct class teaching is not the main purpose of the exercise.

In most partnerships between the school and the student teacher, roles and responsibilities have previously been agreed and worked out. It is important that the student teacher is aware of what those are. The same principle applies when two institutions are in partnership with the student. Agreed roles and responsibilities can often be found in the handbook for the course.

In this unit we discuss your tutors' expectations of you and open up the notion of professionalism. We then go on to discuss the phases of development through which a student teacher is likely to pass.

OBJECTIVES

By the end of this unit you should:

- have clarified your own role and that of your tutors in the partnership;
- have an understanding of your working role within the school;
- be aware of your responsibilities and your tutors' expectations of you;
- have developed an understanding of the professional responsibilities and behaviour required of a newly qualified teacher;
- recognise the phases of development you are likely to be going through in the transition from student to effective teacher, including taking on a pastoral role.

THE SCHOOL TUTOR

Schools identify members of staff to support and advise student teachers, often from the student's subject department. Increasingly schools are appointing a general school tutor or mentor to oversee the work of student teachers in the school. You can expect to meet regularly with school staff to discuss your progress, any lessons observed and wider school issues.

ARRANGEMENTS FOR SCHOOL EXPERIENCE

What is expected of you in school?

Your school-based work is usually built up through a series of structured activities:

- detailed observation of experienced teachers: where you look at specific aspects of teaching in a lesson, e.g. how teachers use questions to promote learning;
- team teaching: where you share the lesson with others – planning, giving the lesson and evaluating together;
- micro-teaching: this is a short teaching episode where you teach peers or small groups of children – it can be useful to video-tape your micro-teaching so that an analysis of different aspects of your teaching can be carried out;
- whole class teaching with the class teacher present; and finally
- whole class teaching on your own. (As a student, you should always have an experienced teacher nearby.)

An important issue for students on school experience is the way feedback is given on lessons. The amount of feedback students get from teachers watching their lessons varies. In any case, some student teachers like to have feedback on every lesson and feel deprived if they don't get it. Some students prefer a small amount of very focused feedback, others can cope with a page or more of comments. Written feedback is essential because it provides a record of your progress and ideas for your development. In practice, your course will have agreed conventions governing this aspect of your work. These take into account how you are to achieve the competences/standards required in Scotland, Northern Ireland and England and Wales.

You will probably find comments on your teaching divide into those relating to **tangible** technical issues which can be worked on relatively easily and those relating to **less tangible** issues relating to pupils' learning. Technical problems such as your use of audio-visual aids, the quality and clarity of your voice, how you position yourself in the classroom, managing transitions from one activity to another in a lesson are easy to spot, so you may receive considerable advice on these issues. Problems with these aspects of your work are usually resolved early in your course, whereas less tangible issues which are directly related to the quality of pupil learning require ongoing reflection, attention and discussion, e.g. your approach to the explanation of lesson content, your style of questioning, your evaluation of pupil learning. More detailed advice related to the teaching of your specific subject is given in the subject specific texts in this series.

THE STUDENT TEACHER ROLE

You are expected to play a full part in the life of the school – taking on as many aspects of a teacher's work as possible – and you should take advantage of any opportunities to extend your experience. As well as the **structured teaching activities** identified above, you can expect to undertake a wide range of activities. Table 1.1.1 provides a full list.

Teachers have other roles and responsibilities such as planning the curriculum and liaising with outside agencies but these are not usually undertaken by student teachers.

However, you may have the opportunity to help to write course materials if your department is developing new areas of work.

In addition to these general responsibilities, staff have expectations relating to:

1   your organisation and teaching approach
2   your professionalism
3   your social skills.

Table 1.2.1 Summarises expectations staff may have of you in these areas.

Table 1.2.1 The school's expectations of the student teacher

(i) Organisation and teaching approach
You will be expected to:
- be well organised
- arrive in plenty of time. And that doesn't mean arriving just as the bell goes. It means arriving considerably earlier in order to arrange the classroom; check the availability of books and equipment; test out equipment new to you; talk to staff about the work and the children's progress; and clarify any safety issues.
- plan and prepare thoroughly. Be conscientious in finding out what lesson content and subject knowledge are appropriate to the class you're teaching. In many cases, you will be teaching material which is new to you or which you last thought about many years ago. Staff will expect you to ask if you're not sure but to work conscientiously to improve your subject knowledge. They will not be impressed if you frequently show you have not bothered to read around the subject matter of the lesson.
- keep good records: have your file of schemes of work and lesson plans, pupil attendance and homework records up to date. Your evaluations of your lessons are best completed on the same day as the lesson.
- know your subject
- try out different methods of teaching. Teaching practice is your opportunity to try out different approaches without having to live with the results of failures, but you have a duty to the class teacher not to leave chaos behind you.

(ii) Professionalism
You will be expected to:
- act in a professional manner, e.g. with courtesy and tact; and to respect confidentiality of information
- be open to new learning: seek and act on advice
- be flexible
- dress appropriately (different schools have different dress codes)
- become familiar with and work within school procedures and policies. These include record keeping, rewards and sanctions, uniform, relationships between teachers and pupils.
- accept a leadership role. You may find imposing your will on pupils uncomfortable but unless you establish your right to direct the work of the class, you will not be able to teach effectively.
- recognise and understand the roles and relationships of staff responsible for your development
- keep up to date with your subject
- take active steps to ensure that your pupils learn
- discuss pupil progress with parents.

(iii) Social skills
You will be expected to:
- develop good relationships with pupils and staff
- keep a sense of humour
- work well in teams
- be able to communicate with children as well as adults
- learn to defuse difficult situations.

PROFESSIONAL ATTITUDES AND RESPONSIBILITIES

Part ii of Table 1.2.1 provides some guidance about professional behaviour but professionalism extends beyond personal behaviour.

What does it really mean to be a professional?

There is some debate about whether teaching is a profession and, over the years, you will come to your own conclusions. However, we would suggest that the hallmarks of a profession are that there is a substantial body of knowledge which the professional needs to acquire, that substantial training is required before an individual can be accepted into the profession and that the profession is self-governing as well as publicly accountable. On the basis of this definition, for you, becoming a member of the teaching profession means that you make the following commitments. That you will:

- **reach an acceptable level of competence and skill** in your teaching by the end of your course. This includes acquiring knowledge and skills which enable you to become an effective teacher and which enable you to understand the body of knowledge about how young people learn and how teachers can teach most effectively.
- **continuously develop your professional knowledge and professional judgement** through experience, further learning and reflection on your work.
- **be publicly accountable for your work**. Various members of the community have the right to inspect and/or question your work: the head, governors, parents, inspectors. You have a professional duty to plan and keep records of your work and that of the pupils. This accountability includes implementation of school policies, e.g. on behaviour, on equal opportunities.
- **to set personal standards and conform to external standards** for monitoring and improving your work.

There is a professional code of ethics which is currently unwritten in the UK but which you are expected to uphold. For example, you are expected to treat information about individuals with confidentiality; provide equal opportunities for the pupils in your care; deal with pupils in an objective, professional manner regardless of your personal feelings; keep up to date in your subject; reflect on and develop your teaching; adopt appropriate language and a professional demeanour. From time to time, there is debate in the profession about adopting a code of ethics but no code has been accepted in the UK.

In some countries (e.g. Scotland, Australia and parts of Canada) teachers must have their qualifications accepted and registered with a national or state teachers' council before they are allowed to teach. Their names may be removed from this register if, for example, they are found guilty of professional misconduct. In England and Wales recognition of qualifications by the Department for Education and Employment (DFEE) is required before you can teach in government-funded schools but the DFEE does not have a professional role as do teaching councils in other countries. The role of the General Teaching Council for England and Wales can be expected to take some time to become established. But it has the potential for raising the professional status of teachers in England.

Task 1.2.1   **PROFESSIONAL ACCOUNTABILITY**
As a teacher, you are held professionally accountable for your own work. What does this mean in practice? Discuss this question with other student teachers and make a note of the standards which you would wish to govern your own professional conduct.

As a student teacher you gradually take on the responsibilities of a teacher and develop as a professional. To do this you go through three main phases of development. In the following section, we discuss these so that you can get a sense of how you may achieve the goals you are setting yourself.

PHASES OF DEVELOPMENT

Initially most student teachers are concerned with how they come across as teachers (self-image), how they are going to control the pupils, if there is sufficient material for the lesson and whether the pupils will ask difficult questions. It is only when you have achieved some confidence in your classroom management skills that you are able to focus on whether the learning outcomes you've planned for have been generally achieved. Your initial focus is the self, after which the needs of pupils begin to emerge.

In becoming an effective teacher ready to take up your first post, you can expect to pass through three broad overlapping stages which we identify as:

- Phase 1: focus on self-image and class management
- Phase 2: focus on whole class learning
- Phase 3: focus on individual pupil's learning.

Many students are six or eight weeks into their school experience before they feel a level of confidence about their image and the management of the class (phase 1). They can then start to focus on whether the learning taking place is what was intended (phase 2). Once a student teacher feels reasonably competent in classroom management and in achieving global objectives, they should be able to shift their focus to the needs of individuals (phase 3).

Figure 1.2.1 shows how the focus of your work may change over time as you become more effective as a teacher.

As you move to phase 3 we would expect you to become aware of your pupils' personal development as well as their academic development. On school experience you can initially expect to assist the form tutor, who introduces you to this area of work.

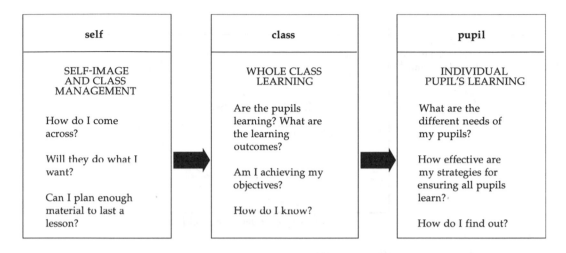

Figure 1.2.1 Phases of development of a teacher

PHASE 1: SELF-IMAGE AND CLASS MANAGEMENT

How do I come across?

Do you see yourself as a teacher? Student teachers can find it quite hard to change their self-image from that of learner, in which they may have had a passive role, to the active, managing, authoritative image of a teacher. Up until now, you may have been a learner in most classrooms you've been in and now you have to make the transition from learner to teacher. This requires a change in self-image. Teaching is sometimes likened to acting and thinking of this comparison may enable you to assume a new role more easily. Accompanying this role is a need to change your perspective. As a learner, the teachers were 'them in charge', as a student teacher, teachers and tutors are also 'them in charge' of you, but as a class teacher, you now become 'one of them in charge'. Your role and your perception of it change during your school experience.

As your experience increases, your professional judgement should develop along-side your store of professional knowledge but confidence and self-belief are also needed to help you carry off the part. Figure 1.2.2 illustrates the interdependency of these different aspects.

There has been much research on what makes teachers effective and the various texts on teaching skills and classroom management listed throughout this book provide a wide range of perspectives on effectiveness (e.g. the subject specific texts in this series, Kyriacou, 1995, 1997; Wragg, 1997, 1994; Marland, 1993, 1997; Robertson, 1989, 1996). A summary of the attributes of effective teachers drawn from these texts is listed in Table 1.2.2.

When pupils' perceptions of teachers were researched as part of a wider study on discipline in Scotland (Munn *et al.*, 1990), pupils identified over 75% of their teachers as

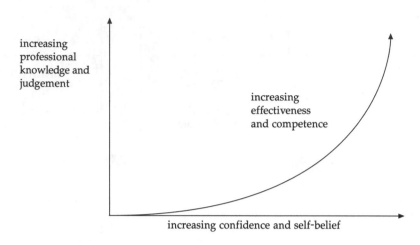

Figure 1.2.2 Becoming an effective teacher

being effective in terms of getting the class to work well, although as the authors point out, getting the class to work well is not the same as ensuring that the pupils learn what was intended. Humour as well as use of sanctions and threats were perceived by pupils as important characteristics of the effective teacher. The amount of talk between pupils in lessons is usually of concern to staff. Yet pupil comments about the effect of the level of talk were mixed, i.e. some felt a high level of talk was a sign that the teacher wasn't in control, while others did not suggest this link. Making it clear to pupils about the types of talk which you allow in the classroom can be helpful to pupils. 'Partner talk' is an example of what you might allow when pupils are working together, i.e. a soft voice which only one other person can hear.

It is unlikely that any one teacher will have all the attributes listed below. In any case, you could probably have many of the attributes listed below but still lack authority in the classroom. Neither the attributes themselves nor relationships between teachers and pupils can be developed by checking off attributes on a checklist. However, you can monitor and evaluate their development. We have included this list in order to give you ideas to consider when you are undertaking your own self-evaluation.

Table 1.2.2 Attributes of effective teachers

humorous	enthusiastic	enjoys the subject
relaxed	organised	makes the work relevant
imaginative	supportive	is active in helping pupils learn
warm	cheerful	uses a variety of methods
firm	flexible	has high expectations
listens	encourages	explains clearly
fair	sympathetic	gives praise
friendly	responsive	applies sanctions fairly and doesn't make empty threats

> **Task 1.2.2**
>
> **WHAT KIND OF TEACHER DO YOU WANT TO BE?**
> What image do you want to create? What role do you see yourself assuming? How would you like others to see you as a teacher? If you are at the beginning of your course, write a profile for the 'sort of teacher I want to be' in about 500 words. Base this on your own education and educational experiences.
>
> Repeat the activity at the end of the course when you've had experience. You might use this to write a summary statement for your career entry profile at the end of your course. The purpose of a career entry profile is described in the introduction.

Will they do what I say? Classroom management and control

Controlling adolescents is one of the biggest worries student teachers have initially. Unit 2.3 provides a considerable amount of information to prepare you for this aspect of your work and Unit 2.1 contains guidelines about observing teachers and classrooms. Developing an aura of authority takes time, effort and reflection on what has happened in order to modify your behaviour. The tasks in Unit 2.1 are designed to help you analyse the routines and expectations which appear to be operated, often effortlessly, by the teachers whose classes you take.

To see how these routines and expectations are established you would have to shadow a teacher new to a school from the beginning of the school year. The early weeks that teachers new to a school spend with their classes are crucial to setting up the working relationship as is the way new teachers conduct themselves in the corridors and play-ground. The pupil grapevine is a powerful means of spreading a teacher's reputation. Teachers who have been at the school for some time are automatically treated in a certain way by pupils because their reputation has gone before them. So you need to work at establishing your reputation.

PHASE 2: WHOLE CLASS LEARNING

Teaching is not the same as learning, nor is telling pupils the same as them learning. Teaching means organising experiences and activities which cause pupils to engage actively with the material and thus learn. Copying notes, for example, does not, in our experience, lead to active engagement, whereas constructing notes with help and guidance is good practice. The teacher's role is then to monitor the outcomes from these experiences and activities. Chapter 5 provides further details about learning.

As you become more competent in classroom management, your concerns shift from asking 'Will I survive?' to 'Are the pupils learning anything from me?' The way you present your lesson and explain the material (the exposition) and the methods you use for asking questions about it become the focus of your attention as you try to improve the learning taking place for the whole class. In Unit 2.2 on lesson planning, the importance of setting clear objectives for each lesson is stressed. These identify the learning outcomes which you expect from that lesson such as skill development, mastery of content, development of attitudes, understanding of processes. However, what is important is that the objectives are clear enough for you to identify when the pupil has achieved those objectives, by action or other behaviour. Individual lesson objectives give a cumulative picture of the outcomes that you expect your class to achieve. Assessment is then based on the achievement (or otherwise) of outcomes.

Your lesson evaluations help you monitor the learning of the class. They provide an analysis of what went well and what could have been improved. You can expect your class teachers and tutor to discuss your evaluations. In this second phase of your development, such post-lesson discussions focus more on the learning taking place rather than on the image and management issues which will have preoccupied you initially.

PHASE 3: INDIVIDUAL LEARNING

Later, as your analytical and planning skills develop and you build your confidence and professional knowledge about learning, you become able to design your lessons so that the **academic needs of individual pupils** are better catered for, i.e. you can more easily build differentiation into your teaching.

Effective teachers help individual pupils to grow. If a teacher can manage, in spite of the pressures of time, to give individuals a sense of achievement and self-worth then their pupils' motivation is usually increased. The converse is also true.

Task 1.2.3   **'THE AVERAGE CHILD'**

Reflect on the poem below 'The Average Child'. Think about the implications for your own teaching. In your classroom observations and evaluations, focus on an 'average child' for a number of sessions. Plan your interactions with a small group of these pupils so that you leave them feeling 'special'. Discuss your perceptions with other student teachers.

The Average Child
I don't cause teachers trouble, my grades have been okay.
I listen in my classes and I'm in school everyday.
My parents think I'm average, my teachers think so too.
I wish I didn't know that cause there's lots I'd like to do.
I'd like to build a space rocket, I've a book that shows you how.
Or start a stamp collection, well no use trying now.
Cause since I've found I'm average, I'm just not smart enough you see
I know there's nothing special that I should expect of me.
I'm part of that majority that hump part of the bell*,
who'll just spend all his life in an average kind of hell.

Buscemi (date unknown)

*This refers to the bell shape of a 'normal distribution' curve.
Source: Reeve, P. (1992) 'The Average Child', unpublished dissertation, De Montfort University, Bedford

Whilst student teachers are expected to analyse their effectiveness in achieving their lesson objectives, the skills and experience required to be able to provide differentiated work usually take longer to develop and opportunities should arise to develop this understanding further after your initial teacher education course. Differentiated work is work which is designed to allow pupils with different abilities to achieve preset goals, i.e. it provides the opportunity for pupils to undertake different tasks or to achieve different outcomes depending on ability. Unit 4.1 provides further information about how you may differentiate work.

Task 1.2.4	**WHAT HAVE THE PUPILS LEARNED?**

Towards the end of your school experience, arrange to interview individual pupils before you teach them about what they know about a topic. Have specific questions in terms of knowledge and understanding that you expect them to achieve through their work on the topic. Then interview them after the lesson to find out what they understand about it after being taught. Consider the implications of the findings for your teaching.

❖ Summary and key points

In this unit we have introduced you to some of the complexities of your role as a student teacher. The role of a teacher is diverse but with practice, support, increasing experience and ongoing learning, you can expect your level of competence to rise and with it satisfaction.

Because of the dynamic nature of educational practice you should expect to go on learning throughout your career. Your initial teacher education course only provides a foundation on which to build your professional knowledge and your professional judgement.

In becoming a teacher, you can expect to move through the three phases (self-image and class management, class learning, individual learning) as your experience, confidence and competence increase. We hope, by identifying each phase, that we have helped you understand the task ahead of you. Evaluation through critical reflection is one of the tools in your professional tool kit which you can use to analyse your effectiveness in helping pupils learn (see Unit 5.4). The professional knowledge and judgement of the experienced teachers with whom you work also provide a rich resource on which to draw in developing your own knowledge and judgement about how to support pupil learning effectively.

FURTHER READING

Allsop, T. (1994) 'The language of partnership', in M. Wilkin and D. Sankey (eds) *Collaboration and Transition in Initial Teacher Course*, London: Kogan Page, pp. 42–55.

This article contains an interesting discussion of the arrangements for looking after student teachers, expectations and some school responses in the Oxford Internship schemes. It identifies 'language' as an important factor in identifying and setting roles. By language, the authors mean the definitions of roles and expectations written into the agreements between the school and college or school and student.

BBC (September 1994) 'Simple minds' video – Education Special: Understanding Science Series.

This video has some interesting material which shows how transient learning can be, even for graduates.

Kyriacou, C. (1995) *Essential Teaching Skills*, Cheltenham: Stanley Thornes.

Kyriacou, C. (1997) *Effective Teaching in Schools: Theory and Practice (2nd edition)*, Cheltenham: Stanley Thornes.

Extend the advice in this unit.

Marland, M. (1997) *The Art of the Tutor: Developing your role in the Secondary School*, London: David Fulton.

Marland, M. (1993) *The Craft of the Classroom (2nd edition)*, Oxford: Heinemann.

Both provide very practical advice for the student teacher.

Munn, P., Johnstone, M. and Holligan, C. (1990) 'Pupils' perceptions of effective disciplinarians', *British Educational Research Journal*, 16, 2: 191–198.

This article provides interesting data from a three-year research project on discipline in schools in Scotland. The pupils' perceptions of the characteristics of the effective teacher are interesting to consider in the light of your own teaching experience.

Robertson, J. (1996) *Effective Classroom Control (3rd edition)*, London: Hodder and Stoughton.

Robertson, J. (1989) *Effective Classroom Control: Understanding Teacher–Pupil Relationships*, London: Hodder and Stoughton.

Robertson provides advice and strategies for students to use in developing good relationships with pupils. He focuses particularly on analysing and dealing with unwanted behaviour and establishing and expressing authority.

1.3   MANAGING YOUR TIME AND PREVENTING STRESS

INTRODUCTION

Although teaching can be rewarding and exciting, it can also be very stressful and demanding. You may be surprised by the amount of time and energy you use while on school experience (and later as a teacher), inside and outside the classroom and outside the school day. There is little time within a school day in which you can relax. Even your breaks are often disrupted. This means that you must plan the use of your time and energy effectively over the week. You must not spend so much time preparing one lesson that you do not have time to prepare the others well (there are, of course, times when you want to take extra time planning one particular lesson, e.g. for a difficult class with whom the last lesson did not go well or if you are less familiar with the material). Likewise, you must use your energy wisely, so that you have enough energy to teach each lesson well.

Undoubtedly you will be tired. Many student teachers have told us that they are so tired when they get home from school that they have to force themselves to stay awake to plan and prepare lessons in the evening. If your teaching commitment is not to take over your whole life, you need to use your time and energy to advantage. You also need to manage stress associated with your school experience and teaching.

Although you are unlikely to find competences/standards related to time and stress management on your course, if you can put the ideas in this unit into practice, you are more likely not only to survive your school experience and teaching itself, but also to enjoy the job and develop as a teacher.

OBJECTIVES

By the end of this unit you should be able to:

- identify ways you can use your time more effectively in the classroom;
- develop ways to manage your time more effectively;
- identify factors that may cause you stress;
- develop methods for coping with stress.

MANAGING YOUR TIME

Managing your time in the classroom

Waterhouse (1983) indicated that by prioritising activities, teachers are able to use classroom time most effectively and economically. The following list of ways of managing your time in the classroom is adapted from Waterhouse (1983, p. 46):

- devise simple, fast procedures for routine events and dealing with recurring problems;
- eliminate unnecessary routines and activities from your own performance;
- delegate (to classroom assistants or pupils) responsibilities and jobs that are within their competence;
- regularly review the conduct of lessons in terms of effective use of your own and pupils' time;
- maintain a good balance in the use of time on teaching, supervisory and organisational activities;
- allocate a high proportion of available time for academic work;
- spend a high proportion of time in 'substantive interaction' with pupils (i.e. explaining, questioning, describing, illustrating).

This should enable pupils to:

- spend a high proportion of their time actually engaged on their tasks; and
- experience a high degree of success during their engaged time.

These time management principles can be applied in many ways in the classroom. For example,

- using classroom assistants or pupils to help give out and collect textbooks, pupils' books, equipment, to mark straightforward homework tests in class, make sure the classroom is left ready for the next class with the chairs tidy, floor clear, board clean and books tidied away;
- carrying a marking pen with you as you move around the class checking the work that is going on. As you skim pupils' work and comment to them, you can make brief notes on the work. It is easier to pick up mistakes and check work when it is fresh in your mind. This saves you having to go back to the work at a later stage which, in itself, wastes time;
- collecting in books which are open at the page where you should start marking;
- ensuring that work is dated and that homework is clearly identified so that it is easy for you to check what work has been done and what is missing. Ruling off each lesson's work helps you to check this;
- keeping one page of your mark book for comments about progress (folding the page over ensures that comments are not seen inadvertently by pupils). As you see pupils' work in class or when you are marking, you can make brief notes which are then immediately at hand for discussions with parents, head of year, report writing, etc.

You can spend a lot of class time on discipline. Establishing rules for behaviour in the classroom early in your first few lessons with a class can save time later on (see Unit 3.3 on managing pupil behaviour).

> **Task 1.3.1 HOW YOU SPEND YOUR TIME IN LESSONS**
> Write in your diary other ways you may use time effectively and economically in the classroom. Observe how several experienced teachers use their time effectively and economically in lessons, using a series of checklists, each with something specific to look for, e.g. how they divide time between teaching, supervisory and organisational activities, how much time is spent disciplining pupils, how much time they spend explaining and questioning, procedures for routine events such as collecting in homework or giving back books or which responsibilities and jobs are delegated to classroom assistants or pupils that are within their competence. Ask another student teacher or your tutor to observe how you use time in the classroom in one lesson or over a series of lessons. Discuss with the observer the findings and possible ways of using yours or the pupils' lesson time more effectively and economically. Record these in your diary and try them out systematically in your teaching.

Task 1.3.1
Planning outside the classroom

Careful planning for a lesson and series of lessons outside the classroom enables lesson time to be used most effectively. It is helpful to allocate time for each activity in a lesson (e.g. use a time line in your lesson plan, as described in Unit 2.2). This enables you to see what you have planned to do in each lesson and to evaluate the lesson later. It is important that you plan for such things as pupils moving from one part of the school to another for the lesson, changing time for physical education or getting the class settled, particularly at the beginning of the day, after a break or lunch. You may find that initially you under- or overestimate the time tasks take to accomplish. At the end of each lesson you can compare the time taken for each activity with that allocated. In this way you gradually become realistic about how long different activities in a lesson take.

You also need to plan for a series of lessons. You have a certain amount of work to cover over a given period of time. If you do not plan the time effectively, you may find yourself taking too long over some of the content and not leaving yourself with enough time to complete everything required in the time available. Pupils' knowledge and understanding develop over a period of time; therefore if they do not complete the content required, their learning may be incomplete. Unit 2.2 provides more information about lesson planning and schemes of work.

> **Task 1.3.2 PLANNING HOW TO USE LESSON TIME**
> When planning your lessons, deliberately think about how best you can use the available time, determine what proportion of time to allocate to each activity and indicate, next to each activity, the amount of time to be allocated to it. When you evaluate the lesson and each activity in it, look specifically at how the time was used. Ask yourself how you can organise pupils and establish routines to make more time available for teaching. Include these in future lesson plans.

Managing your own time effectively

However well you use time in the classroom, you may not be using the time you put into your work and your own time to best advantage. Some people naturally use their time more effectively than others. Some people always seem to work long hours but achieve little, whereas others achieve a great deal but still appear to have plenty of time to do things other than work. One explanation for this could be that the first person wastes time, through, for example, being unsystematic in managing time or handling paper-work, putting off work rather than getting on and doing it, trying to do it all rather than delegating appropriately or not being able to say no to jobs, whereas the second person uses time well by, for example, having clear objectives for work to be done, prioritising work and completing urgent and important jobs first and writing lists of jobs to achieve during the day. Which of these descriptions fits you?

Fontana (1993) stressed that if we could use our time effectively at work we would be more efficient and more productive, be better able to plan long term, be more satisfied with our work and our job, be less stressed, have more time for ourselves and more opportunity to switch off out of work. There are many different techniques you can use to manage your time effectively. Figure 1.3.1 highlights some of these.

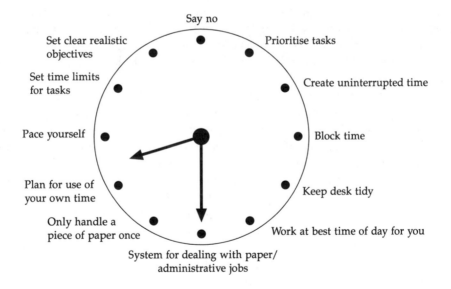

Figure 1.3.1 How to avoid working around the clock

PREVENTING STRESS

Studies of stress in student teachers (Capel, 1992, 1993, 1996, 1997, 1998; Hart, 1987) have shown that major causes of stress for student teachers include:

- control and discipline;
- motivating pupils and maintaining pupils' interest;
- conflict with pupils;
- coping with the ability range of pupils within a class;
- practical skills of teaching and techniques of lesson preparation;
- disagreement with the tutor;
- personality disagreement with the tutor;
- observation, evaluation and assessment of teaching by the supervisor, particularly receiving the supervisor's or class teacher's opinion of classroom competence;
- role overload, role conflict and role ambiguity.

It may be that stressors outside work, e.g. tensions of home and family, are brought to and add to stress at work and make a person more vulnerable to stressors at work. Job stress may vary during the year according to the demands of a job, personal circumstances and/or other factors at any one time. A significant stressor at a particular time could account for differences in stress experienced by people at different times of a school year.

There are, of course, many other aspects of your teaching that may cause you stress or anxiety, e.g. delivering material with which you are not very familiar or reprimanding a pupil. Later units in this book identify practical ways to help you overcome many of these concerns. The last two on the list above are considered briefly here.

Role overload can occur because there are so many things for you to do as a teacher and too little time in which to do them. This can mean working very long hours to get the job done and not having enough time mentally and physically to relax for work the following day or week.

> **Task 1.3.3** **BALANCING YOUR WORK AND LEISURE TIME**
> Over the course of a week on school experience, list the time you spend on school-related activities other than teaching your classes and the amount of leisure time that you have. Why is the balance as it is? Is this balance acceptable? If not, is it because of, for example, inefficiency, lack of experience or overload? How can you improve it? Discuss the balance of work and leisure with other student teachers.

Role conflict can result from doing a number of different activities within your job, each requiring different responsibilities, demands and skills, e.g. teaching, form tutoring, talking to parents, administration (clerical work and committee duties), other jobs within the department, in-service training and professional development (inter-role conflict) or from trying to meet the different expectations of a number of people with whom you are working, e.g. pupils, your tutor, other teachers, head of department, senior managers, parents, OFSTED (intra-role conflict). Often you are not quite sure how to perform in the role of a student teacher as your role is ambiguous.

Role overload and conflict may affect student teachers more than qualified teachers for a number of reasons, e.g. student teachers take longer to prepare each lesson than more experienced teachers, student teachers may be unsure of their role in a lesson, a department or the school as a whole (role ambiguity) and they may, at any one time, be answering to and trying to please a number of people, who expect different things.

When you are being observed, evaluated and assessed, you are 'on show'. You are vulnerable because your developing skills are analysed and constructively criticised. This may be exacerbated by school teachers' taking on the role of tutors in teacher training. Pateman (1994) indicated that the role of teachers in assessing the teaching competence of student teachers means that many student teachers feel unable to talk freely and openly to teachers about other concerns. Thus, the role of the teacher–tutor in assessment does not take account of student teachers' needs for friendship, counselling and tutoring. This may cause stress for student teachers. This finding is supported in other research on stress in student teachers, e.g. Capel (1994).

Task 1.3.4

CAUSES OF STRESS FOR STUDENT TEACHERS

In your diary write a list of factors that cause stress for you in your role as a student teacher. Compare these with causes of stress identified by another student teacher. Discuss similarities and differences. After reading the next section of this unit identify ways you can prevent or alleviate the stress. Try out methods of prevention as soon as you can.

Task 1.3.5

SYSTEMATIC OBSERVATION OF ASPECTS OF YOUR TEACHING

You should be getting regular feedback on your teaching from your tutor. However, you may want to ask your tutor to focus specifically on one aspect of your teaching that is causing you anxiety and then give you feedback on this, along with ideas about how you might be able to improve in this area, e.g. giving feedback to pupils, giving praise, working with individuals in the class. It may help to develop an observation schedule for each specific aspect. Examples of lesson observation schedules can be found in the *Learning to teach (subjects) in the secondary school* series edited by Capel, Leask and Turner which are listed in the front of this book. Plan your next lesson taking these points into account. Ask your tutor to observe another lesson a couple of weeks later to see if there is any difference in your performance. Try this again with another aspect of your teaching.

How can you cope with your stress?

Many different strategies to prevent or alleviate stress have been identified. However, as there are different causes of stress for different people and for the same person at different times, there is no one way to cope with stress; you have to find out what works for you or for you in particular situations. Different ways of preventing and/or alleviating stress, therefore, are appropriate for different people.

Those identified below have been drawn from a number of sources (e.g. D'Arcy, 1989; Dean, 1993; Kyriacou, 1989). The strategies listed for managing your time may also be useful, as not using your time effectively may cause stress. These lists are by no means exhaustive and you may find other strategies useful.

- **Prepare for stressful situations when you are not under pressure**, e.g. prepare lessons before the day on which you are teaching them.
- **Role-play a situation which is causing you anxiety and/or visualise what you can do to overcome the problem**. This helps you to focus on the problem and can be used to rehearse how you are going to cope.
- **Actively prepare** for the situation, e.g. prepare a lesson more thoroughly than normal for a class which is causing you anxiety. Plan thoroughly how you can reduce the likelihood of the problem occurring or deal with a particular problem. This strategy can help you to identify the reasons for the problem and to focus on possible ways of preventing or dealing with it.
- **Develop effective self-management techniques**, e.g. establish routines so that you can do things automatically, particularly when you are tired.
- **Recognise and try to develop your strengths as well as your weaknesses** so that you can rely on your strengths as you work on improving any weaknesses.
- **Do not worry about incidents that have happened in school and keep problems in proportion**. Try not to take problems home.
- **Identify where you can get help**. You should get regular feedback on your teaching, but identify other people who may be able to help.
- **Develop support systems which provide a network of people with whom you could talk through problems**, e.g. other student teachers, your tutor, other teachers, a partner or friend. You may want to talk to different people for help with different problems. You may form a group with other student teachers to provide mutual support, talk about your concerns, develop a shared understanding of the problem and provide possible alternative solutions and practical help to address the problem, e.g. through another student teacher observing a lesson and discussing it afterwards.
- **Take account of the amount and variety of work you are doing to reduce both role overload and conflict**. This may mean, for example, that you need to try to take work home less often or take on fewer extra-curricular activities. You may need to work on this over a period of time.

Summary and key points

We would be very surprised if you, as a student teacher on school experience, are not tired. Likewise, we would be very surprised if you were not anxious when someone comes in to watch your lessons, particulary if that person has a say in whether you become a qualified teacher, or if you were not worried about other aspects of your school experience. It may help to know that you are not going to be alone in being tired or feeling anxious or worried about your school experience and many of the causes of tiredness and stress are the same for other student teachers. Where you are alone is in developing effective techniques for managing your time and for coping with stress. There are no ready answers for managing time or preventing or alleviating stress. Other people can help you with this, but nobody else can do it for you because they are complex processes and what works for someone else may not work for you. Finally, you must work at managing your time and stress over time; there are no short-term, one-off solutions to these problems.

FURTHER READING

Adair, J. (1988) *Effective Time Management: How to Save Time and Spend it Wisely*, London: Pan Books.

This book looks at what things people do that waste time and provides useful tips about how they may manage their time better. It should help you to consider how you use your time and how you may manage your time better.

Cole, M. and Walker, S. (eds) (1989) *Teaching and Stress*, Milton Keynes: Open University Press.

This book is a compilation of articles about stress and burnout in teachers. Together they provide good background on many issues from a number of different perspectives.

Dunham, J. (1995) *Developing Effective School Management*, London: Routledge.

This book is designed to help teachers to identify and develop knowledge and skills to become effective middle managers. It includes chapters on time management and stress management, which should be helpful to you as student teachers.

Fontana, D. (1993) *Managing Time*, Leicester: British Psychological Society Books.

This book is based on the premise that good time management can be learned. It combines text and a series of exercises to help you better understand different aspects of time management, including the qualities of a good time manager, determining how you currently use your time and planning how you can use your time better.

Handy, C. (1993) *Understanding Organizations (4th edition)*, London: Penguin.

This book includes a section on stress, which provides a broader perspective of stress than that found when looking only at stress in teachers.

1.4   TEACHING AND LEARNING WITH ICT: AN INTRODUCTION

INTRODUCTION

In this unit we introduce you to ways in which Information and Communication Technology (ICT) can be used in your teaching to support your pupils' learning and for your own professional development. (The term ICT is now widely used instead of the term IT to indicate that the communication technologies of Internet and email are included.) Teacher Training Agency documentation defines ICT as including 'computers, the Internet, CD-ROM and other software, television, radio, video, cameras and other equipment' (TTA, 1998, p. 1).

The ideas in the unit are based on practice in innovative schools. If you are just starting to learn to use a computer, then you may find the ideas in this chapter daunting. Although student teachers in the UK are required to demonstrate competence in the basic skills in word processing, databases, spreadsheets, email and Internet use we do not cover basic skills here. If you are just beginning to use computers, there are many texts providing this information, for example, Hogg (1998), Warren (1998). You may wish to take your 'European Computer Driving License.[1] This provides a structured way of developing your skills supported by material freely available from the British Computing Society. Details can be found on http://www.bcs.org.uk/ecdl/.

We focus deliberately on pedagogical applications of ICT because the new knowledge about curriculum applications being created by innovative teachers in schools is not yet widely disseminated.

The rapid pace of development in ICT software and hardware is forcing everyone who uses the technology to undergo a process of continual learning and regular adjustment of working practices. 'Just-in-time learning' where the learner learns just enough to go to the next stage and 'experiential learning' (learning through doing) are familiar patterns of learning for those working with ICT. A working environment where staff are mutually supportive and can work collaboratively to solve ICT challenges is essential if teachers are to keep up with change. It is likely that the National Curriculum in England and Wales and assessment procedures will have to be more flexible if the demands of government for an ICT literate teaching profession and ICT literate pupils are to be accommodated.

In this chapter you will find references to software and to web sites which are recommended by teachers as well as references to texts which may provide you with further ideas. But these ideas only provide starting points. Web sites change regularly with new ones developing and old ones disappearing daily. The resources we reference are those which we consider are providing a professional service and are likely to have a permanent presence on the Internet. The situation with regard to the quality and type of equipment available in schools is also rapidly changing. Some schools and LEAs already have useful web sites and intranets (closed networks) well established. If you work in organisations with these resources then you will be able to integrate Internet and email applications easily into your teaching programme. For example, you may be able to ask for web sites which you want to use for your teaching to be downloaded and hosted on the school or LEA server (a computer dedicated to Internet/intranet work). This means that access to the materials is reliable and not limited by the slowness of Internet connection. Or you may be able to join in existing initiatives running in your department. Some teachers have access to 'electronic white boards' where images and texts stored in or accessed using the computer can be projected on to a large screen and manipulated by the teacher to emphasise points made during the lesson, e.g. in English literature lessons snippets of video recordings of plays can be projected alongside the text.

OBJECTIVES

By the end of this unit you should:

- understand a range of ways in which ICT can be deployed for educational purposes;
- have explored a number of these options through visiting various educational web sites;
- have identified specific applications relevant to your subject area and used those available to you;
- have audited your skills and knowledge in this area against those demanded by your course and developed an action plan for improving these.

BACKGROUND

Computers became widely available in schools in the mid-1980s. Initially these offered basic word processing, spreadsheet and database capabilities. Whilst electronic networking was available between some schools at this time, such a resource did not become widely accessible to all schools until the middle to late 1990s when access to the Internet (through a world wide web of networked computers) became available at prices individual schools could afford. In the meantime CD-ROM technology also developed together with software[2] which made it easy for pupils and teachers to make multimedia and from this, using low-cost CD-ROM writers, to produce inexpensive CD-ROMs. However, it was access to the Internet in particular which changed computers from being machines which were used for quite specific purposes in specialist rooms to machines which provided a medium which combined the attributes of video machines, telephones, television and radio and which could be employed for a range of purposes in all classrooms.

In countries around the world, teachers are under increasing pressure to demonstrate that they can use ICT for teaching and learning as well as for professional development. Acquiring knowledge about the educational applications of ICT is therefore not an optional activity. Traditional approaches to teaching, where teachers often taught their pupils in the ways they had been taught themselves, must be reviewed in the light of what technology can now offer. However, as with any changes in classroom practice, the question must always be asked 'What is the most effective approach to take to achieve the desired learning outcomes?' ICT should only be used where its use is justified as a method of achieving the stated learning outcomes for any lesson.

THE SKILLS AND KNOWLEDGE REQUIRED OF STUDENT TEACHERS

Teacher Training Agency documentation (TTA, 1998) states that student teachers in England must demonstrate that they have acquired a range of ICT competences. These include **word processing, desktop publishing, spreadsheet or database software** as well as being able to demonstrate that they understand how ICT can support their own **professional development** as well as **teaching and learning in their subject area** and for **pupils with particular special educational needs**. They must also demonstrate an understanding of **ethical issues** (e.g. children's personal details such as names and photographs should not be placed on the web), **health and safety legislation** (e.g. children should not be required to use workstations which are poorly designed) and legal issues such as **data protection and copyright** (e.g. that the strict limits on the reproduction of materials authored by others includes placing such material on school web sites and personal details of individuals are not held on computer without appropriate authorisation). Students in other parts of the UK must also demonstrate similar competences.

As a useful starting point, we suggest that you audit your strengths and weaknesses then establish an action plan to ensure that you work on your weaknesses and become familiar with the ways that ICT can support the work in your own subject.

> **Task 1.4.1**
> ### AUDITING YOUR SKILLS AND KNOWLEDGE
> Your school or higher education institution will provide you with the criteria you have to satisfy in terms of ICT competence. We suggest you use these to identify the areas in which you are competent and those in which you need to develop further competence. When you have undertaken task 1.4.2 we suggest you draw up an action plan which identifies the areas on which you are going to work, the ways in which you are going to develop competence and the timescales you set yourself.

Table 1.4.1 illustrates ways the various facets of ICT, as defined by the English National Curriculum for IT (applications, communicating information, modelling, handling data, control and measurement) can be applied in different subjects.

There are many courses and programmes which individuals can undertake if they wish to learn how to use word processing, desktop publishing, spreadsheet or database software and, increasingly, training will become available in the application of the communicative aspects of the technology to particular subjects. Earlier in this chapter we discussed the international context in which you will be working as a teacher and the

Table 1.4.1 Elements of ICT in various subject areas (with thanks to Dave Maguire)

Maths
- Applications – Space programme,
- Communicating – Multimedia, email projects
- Modelling – Number patterns, algebra
- Handling data – Class database, graph work
- Control – Programming language, e.g. Turtle, Logo
- Measurement – Accurate short/long, period measurements

Modern Foreign Languages
- Applications – Internet, Teletext, translation services
- Communicating – Multimedia, DTP, Word processing, email
- Modelling – Cafe bills
- Handling data – Class surveys, topic database

Physical Education
- Applications – Recording, timing
- Communicating – Events leaflets, posters
- Handling data – Personal/group performance database/spreadsheet
- Measurement – Accurate timing, recording

Technology
- Applications – Industrial production, engineering, electronics
- Communication – Health and safety posters, design (logos, packaging)
- Handling data – Product survey/comparisons
- Modelling – Building design
- Control – Lathes, textiles/embroidery

Science
- Applications – Nuclear power stations
- Communication – Safety posters, word-lists
- Modelling – Experiment modelling
- Handling data – Graph work, data logging
- Control – Experiment control
- Measurement – Accurate short/long period measurements

Art and Design
- Applications – Commercial art
- Communicating – Multimedia for students' portfolios
- Modelling – Spread sheet to model designs specs.
- Handling data – Surveys
- Control – Embroidery

Business and Commercial Studies
- Applications – Commercial packages, administration systems
- Communicating – Business letters, email, Internet
- Modelling – Business modelling
- Handling data – Pay packages, databases

Drama, Dance and Music
- Applications – Ticket booking, lighting control, recording studios
- Communicating – Multimedia for students portfolios, Internet and email projects, sound files
- Modelling – Lighting sequences
- Control – Lighting sequences, MIDI interfaces

English
- Applications – Publishing, news services, advertising
- Communicating – Word processing, multimedia, email, Internet
- Handling Data – Class surveys, database of books/reading

Humanities (Geography, History, RE)
- Applications – Weather stations, archiving, museums
- Communicating – Multimedia, word processing, posters, projects related to culture and beliefs
- Modelling – Spread sheet modelling, building design packages, simulations
- Handling data – Surveys, database, Internet
- Measurement – Weather, wind speed, rainfall

Source: adapted from Leask and Litchfield (1999)

> **Task 1.4.2**
>
> **IDENTIFYING ICT RESOURCES FOR YOUR SUBJECT AREA**
> Find out what ICT resources are available to you in your school/higher education institution to support your subject area. Discuss the application of these to the lessons you are taking with your tutor and fellow students. Use these resources in lessons and evaluate your success in achieving the learning objectives you set. Draw up and implement the action plan described above which sets out a strategy for ensuring your weaknesses are addressed.

pressure on teachers to be ICT literate. The requirements of teachers listed above are demanding and need you to take an active role in your own professional development. In the UK, the new Labour government elected in 1997 took this sufficiently seriously to divert lottery funding into teacher education. This national priority is likely to remain so for a number of years. There is research evidence which indicates that when ICT is effectively deployed, student motivation and achievement is raised in a number of respects. This evidence is introduced in the next section.

WHY USE ICT?

Research carried out for the National Council for Educational Technology (NCET) in the mid-1990s provided evidence of the following positive reasons for using IT in schools. (Note: this work was done before the opportunities offered by ICT were widely available so the term IT is used). Table 1.4.2 summarises these findings.

Table 1.4.2 Evidence from research about the way IT supports teaching and learning

1	Children who use a computer at home are more enthusiastic and confident when using one in school
2	Video games can be educational if they are well managed
3	IT can provide a safe and non-threatening environment for learning
4	IT has the flexibility to meet the individual needs and abilities of each student
5	Students who have not enjoyed learning can be encouraged by the use of IT
6	Computers give students the chance to achieve where they have previously failed
7	Computers can reduce the risk of failure at school
8	IT allows students to reflect on what they have written and to change it easily
9	Using a computer to produce a successful piece of writing can motivate students to acquire basic literacy skills
10	IT gives students immediate access to richer source materials
11	IT can present information in new ways which help students to understand, assimilate and use it more readily
12	IT removes the chore of processing data manually and frees students to concentrate on its interpretation and use
13	Difficult ideas are made more understandable when information technology makes them visible
14	Interactive technology motivates and stimulates learning
15	Computing programs which use digitised speech can help students to read and spell
16	IT gives students the power to try out different ideas and to take risks
17	Computer simulations encourage analytical and divergent thinking

18   IT is particularly successful in holding the attention of pupils with emotional and behavioural difficulties
19   IT can often compensate for the communication and learning difficulties of students with physical and sensory impairments
20   Pupils with profound and multiple learning difficulties can be encouraged to purposeful activity and self-awareness by IT
21   Using IT makes teachers take a fresh look at how they teach and the ways in which students learn
22   Computers help students to learn when used in well-designed, meaningful tasks and activities
23   Students make more effective use of computers if teachers know how and when to intervene
24   IT offers potential for effective group working
25   Giving teachers easy access to computers encourages and improves the use of IT in the curriculum
26   Head teachers who use computers raise the profile of IT in their schools
27   Management Information Systems can help save money and time in schools

Source: NCET (1994)

Task 1.4.3   HOW DOES ICT HELP TEACHING AND LEARNING?
Consider the list above in the light of your experiences in schools. What evidence have you come across of the potential of computer supported activity, as outlined in this table, being realised. Is there any scope within your school situation for testing some of the findings listed in this table and examining how various forms of ICT could support teaching and learning in your subject area?

It is worth noting that a number of the points in the table relate specifically to the support that IT provides for pupils with special educational needs. Glendon Franklin (1999) provides detailed advice about particular forms of ICT which support pupils with SEN. He recommends that teachers interested in special educational needs issues join the on-line forum run within the Virtual Teacher Centre by the British Educational Communications Technology Agency (BECTA).[3] BECTA also produce a number of publications providing detailed advice, including subject specific advice, to teachers about ICT issues. Much of this information is available on their web site including reviews of CD-ROMs.[4]

Motivation and classroom management

Cox (1999) provides a detailed examination of motivational theories and their application to ICT. She also gives the following advice on the teaching of word processing which you may wish to use as a checklist against your own practice when using computers.

In planning a series of lessons using word-processing there are a number of pitfalls to avoid which are too commonly seen in classrooms. The following is a list of **don'ts** which applies to many uses of ICT which provide no motivation and very little learning benefit either:

- don't devise a task which has no relevance to anything else in school or at home;
- don't assign pupils to computers before preparing them for the task they will be doing;
- don't let the pupils sit at computers while you are talking to them at the introduction of the lesson;
- don't leave the pupils for the whole lesson just working on their task with no intervention to remind them of the educational purpose;
- don't expect the pupils to print out their work at the end of every lesson;
- don't end the lesson without drawing them together to discuss what they have achieved;
- don't rely on the technology to run the lesson.

As mentioned earlier in this chapter, the rapid development of technology means that it may be hard for any individual to claim expert status across a whole range of software and hardware. Selinger (1999) suggests the following solution to the problem of pupils knowing more than you do yourself:

> Classroom dynamics with ICT alters considerably especially when teaching takes place in a computer room. There will be an increase in noise level and pupils may need to move freely around the classroom. It is also not always easy to be sure pupils are on task or not, and you have to find ways of ascertaining this through questions and summing up sessions at the end of the lesson. You may well find yourself in the unusual position of knowing less than your pupils about hardware or software. There is no need to feel threatened by this situation; use it as an opportunity to increase your own knowledge, and to give pupils an opportunity to excel. Some software requires independent learning, but do not feel as though you are no longer teaching, your role as a mediator between the pupils and the machine is often crucial in developing their understanding. Questioning pupils about what they are doing, and why they are doing it in that way, demands that they have to articulate their understanding and in so doing can consolidate their learning.

Selinger also provides advice about how to manage ICT in the classroom with varying numbers of machines (Leask and Pachler, 1999).

PEDAGOGIC AND PROFESSIONAL APPLICATIONS OF THE INTERNET

Ways of using the capability of the Internet for pedagogic and professional purposes are still developing. The Internet provides educators with the following:

1 Access to a huge range of **free and high quality information** sources including the rapid and inexpensive publication of the *latest research findings*[5] from researchers around the world in all disciplines, as well as access to *museums, galleries, newspapers, radio stations*[6] and *libraries*. These resources are often available in a variety of languages. In the UK, the National Grid for Learning[7] and the Virtual Teacher Centre within it are intended to provide resources to support teachers. DFEE[7], OFSTED[7] and TTA[8] sites all have information of potential use to teachers. Unfortunately information of dubious

quality and information inappropriate for school pupils is also easily available. Teaching strategies and procedures in schools related to access to the Internet need to take these issues into account by considering the location of computers and rules for access and use.

2 For teachers and schools **the opportunity to publish information** about their work. *School web sites*[9] provide opportunities for publishing material for a range of purposes. For example, pupils are sometimes set projects to publish material about their school and LEA curriculum which they have researched themselves. In doing this, both pupils and teachers are developing their knowledge about the use of this technology. Parents can be kept informed more fully about the work their children are doing through web site publications and, of course, parents who are seeking schools for their children may find such sites of value in guiding their choice. In addition, the school web site can provide a useful departmental resource as colleagues pool ideas and use the web site as a form of departmental filing cabinet for resources.

3 **Synchronous (e.g. video conferencing and on-line chat/discussion groups) and asynchronous communication (e.g. email)** with single or multiple audiences, e.g. with other teachers, pupils, parents and experts in particular fields regardless of their location. Some schools tap the expertise of parents and local companies to provide *experts on line* for short periods. These are specialists who are able to answer children's questions in areas relevant to their expertise. Teachers are using these facilities for a range of purposes both curriculum based and for professional development. For example, joint *curriculum projects* with classes in other countries can be easily maintained through the use of email. Results of such collaboration can also be posted on the school web site for participants in both countries to see. The European School Net site (http://www.eun.org)[10] provides a partner finding service. (If you go to this web site you will find a map of Europe surrounded by the logos of national educational web sites. Clicking on the map provides access to EUN, clicking on the logos gives access to sites in different countries.) If you are interested in undertaking such projects then starting with something small and achievable will enable you to develop strategies which work for you in your particular subject. For example, survey work carried out by pupils in two countries can be done over a very short time span, perhaps a couple of weeks. This enables you to avoid problems with clashes of holidays. Table 1.4.3 provides some guidelines for the running of email projects. But these ideas are just a beginning, there are many other possibilities. For example, Lord Grey School in Bletchley has undertaken sustained ICT curriculum projects across subjects and involving many countries. Holy Cross Convent School in Surrey has undertaken innovative cross-curricular video conferencing projects with a school in Japan. This work is described further by Lawrence Williams the director of studies (Pachler and Williams, 1999). Further examples of projects with other schools, e.g. Virtual field trips,[11] Virtual art galleries, are given in Leask and Pachler (1999). Others are listed on the Mirandanet[12] site. TeacherNet UK is a teachers' organisation which is working on ways of developing on-line provision which supports professional development.[13]

FINDING PARTNERS FOR EMAIL/VIDEO-CONFERENCING/INTERNET-BASED PROJECTS

There are a number of ways of finding partners. These include the following:

- by using existing contacts, through exchanges for example or through the local community and teachers in the school;
- by emailing schools direct. Various sites provide lists of schools emails e.g. European Schoolnet (http://www.eun.org);
- by advertising your project e.g. by registering it on a site such as those mentioned below;
- by searching sites listing school projects and finding projects which seem to fit with your curriculum goals.

Sites such as the Global School House[14] in the USA, OzteacherNet[15] in Australia, European Schoolnet, Internet Scuola in Italy,[16] provide all three options. The Central Bureau for Exchanges and Visits[17] may also be able to help (adapted from Leask and Pachler, 1999). Table 1.4.3 provides advice about issues to consider when setting up such projects.

Table 1.4.3 Check-list for planning ICT projects with other schools

1 What learning outcomes do you want the pupils to achieve in terms of: knowledge/concepts, skills, attitudes?
2 What is the time scale of the project and how does that fit with school holidays and other events in the partner school?
3 What languages can you work in? (Don't forget that parents, other schools and the local community may be able to help here.)
4 What resources – staff, equipment, time – are involved?
5 Does anyone need to give their permission?
6 How are you going to record and report the outcomes?
7 Do staff need training?
8 Can you sustain the project within the staff, time and material resources available to you?
9 What sorts of partners are you looking for?
10 How are you going to find the partners?
11 How are you going to evaluate the outcomes?

It is too early to predict the extent to which teaching processes are likely to change in response to the opportunities discussed above. In the UK at secondary level, change would accelerate if the examination boards incorporated ICT-based work into assessment requirements. Clearly pupils have to be taught skills of critical appraisal of material but good teachers will be doing this already. Issues related to plagiarism as pupils download sections of text and incorporate these into assignments are likely to be more problematic for teachers. Whilst teacherless classrooms are unlikely to occur, certainly the positive motivation which some learners feel when using technology is not to be underestimated but this does depend on the context for learning which the teacher establishes.

Task 1.4.4 **EXPLORING THE POTENTIAL OF THE INTERNET TO SUPPORT THE WORK IN THE CLASSROOM**

If you have not already done so, we suggest you take this opportunity to find out how teachers of your subject are using the Internet to support teaching and learning. You may, for example, ask other teachers for ideas in a chat area. You may wish to undertake a general search for curriculum projects in your area using the general search engines such as Excite or Yahoo. It may be of use to know that the term K–12 (kindergarten to year 12) is used on web sites in the USA to refer to the years of compulsory schooling. Ideas are sometimes published on school web sites. If you are going to be looking for jobs shortly it may be useful to explore the local education authority web site for those areas in which you wish to work as well as the inspection and league table information on maintained schools which is available on the DFEE and OFSTED sites accessible through the VTC (Virtual Teacher Centre).

Summary and key points

In this chapter, it has only been possible to touch on some of the classroom practice and professional development opportunities available through ICT. We recommend that you extend your understanding beyond the guidance here by reading more widely in this area, by experimenting with different types of software of particular use in your subject, by spending some time surfing the Internet to identify high-quality resources and educational web sites which are specifically relevant to your interests and by talking to teachers and student teachers who are themselves exploring the possibilities offered by new technologies. However, it is important to remember that ICT use in the classroom should be directly related to the achievement specified learning outcomes. As Cox (1999) points out, using ICT in your classroom provides no guarantee that learning takes place.

FURTHER READING

The subject specific texts in this *Learning to Teach* series all contain chapters about the use of IT or ICT in the specific subject area. You may find further ideas for the application of ICT in your subject area in these texts. The Routledge text *Teaching and Learning with ICT in the Secondary School* (Leask and Pachler, 1999) provides detailed guidance and the web site linked to this book lists a number of sites recommended by the teachers and other contributors to that book.

Warren, A., Brunner, D., Maier, P. and Barnett, L. (1998) *Technology in Teaching and Learning: An Introductory Guide*, London: Kogan Page.

This text provides detailed guidance on basic ICT terminology and use.

OTHER READINGS

Collins, J., Hammond, M. and Wellington, J. (1997) *Teaching and Learning with Multimedia*, London: Routledge.

Cox, M. (1997) *The Effects of Information Technology on Students' Motivation*, Final Report, NCET/King's College London.

Crook, C. (1994) *Computers and the Collaborative Experience of Learning*, London: Routledge.

Leask, M. (1999) *Issues in the use of ICT in schools*, London: Routledge.

NCET, (1994) *Information Technology Works! Stimulate to Educate*, Coventry.

Papert, S. (1993) *The Children's Machine: Rethinking School in the Age of the Computer*, New York: Basic Books.

Papert, S. (1996) *The Connected Family: Bridging the Digital Generation Gap* (includes CD-ROM and Web-site links), Atlanta, Georgia: Longstreet Press.

Sandholtz, J.H., Ringstaff, C. and Dwyer, C.D. (1996) *Teaching with Technology: Creating Pupil-Centred Classrooms*, New York: Teachers College Press.

Somekh, B. and Davis, N. (eds) (1997) *Using Information Technology effectively in Teaching and Learning*, London: Routledge.

WEB ADDRESSES

Many of these web addresses have been recommended by Ed Baines, Glendon (Ben) Franklin, David Litchfield, Norbert Pachler and Christina Preston who all contributed to Leask and Pachler (1999). Their contribution is gratefully acknowledged.

1 The European Computer Driving Licence is supported by the British Computing Society and details can be found on http://www.bcs.org.uk/ecdl/.
2 Hyperstudio is software which is very easy for pupils to use to produce multimedia presentations. Free demonstrations are available from TAG Developments Ltd, 25 Pelham Road, Gravesend, Kent DA110HU.
3 Specific information relating to Special Education Needs is scattered across the web so a starting point that gathers many of them together is useful. Such a site is http://www.becta.org.uk/SENCO/. This site will lead you inevitably to the SENCO forum in the VTC. Further help and advice for teachers working with gifted children can be obtained from the National Association for Gifted Children at http://www.rmplc.co.uk/orgs/nagc/. BECTA, formerly NCET, is at the Science Park, Milburn Park Road, Coventry, tel: 01203 416994.
4 See e.g. BECTA CD-ROM reviews available at: http://www.becta.org.uk/info-sheets/cdrom.html.

5 The British Educational Research Association provides access through 'web sites' to research papers from conferences around the world (http://www.bera.ac.uk). It is now common practice for papers presented at conferences to be put on the web site so that at the touch of a couple of buttons, you can find out the latest research news.

6 Searching through the news and media categories in the Yahoo search engine on the web provides access to thousands of news sites around the world. Ones you may find useful include http://www.reuters.com, http://www.bigissue.com, http://www.telegraph.co.uk, http://www.guardian.co.uk. The BBC news site is excellent: http://www.bbc.co.uk. If you have Realplayer on your computer (available free from http://www.realplayer.com, the g2 version is best, Realplayer plus is better (but costs) you can access radio and video news of the day.

7 National Grid for Learning can be found by clicking on the NGFL symbol on the European Schoolnet, http://www/eun/org or on http://www/nglf.gov.uk. The UK Government Funded Virtual Teacher Centre can be found through the NGFL as can the DFEE and OFSTED web sites.

8 TTA is at http://www.teach-tta.gov.uk.

9 See, for example, the Lord Grey School web site at Holy Cross Convent School web site.

10 Access to European government supported educational web sites is easily found through the European School Net on http://www.eun.org. Clicking on the symbols for each country takes you through to their networks, clicking on the map of Europe takes you to the heart of the European Schoolnet. This initiative had, at its foundation in 1998, the support of eighteen ministries of education across Europe.

11 Virtual field trips http://www.field-guides.com/.

12 Mirandanet is on http://www.mirandanet.com.

13 TeacherNetUk is on http://teachernetuk.org.uk.

14 Global School House http://www.gsh.org/. Projects are on http://www.gsh.org/pr/index.html.

15 OzTeacherNet http://www.owl.qut.edu.au/oz-teachernet. Projects are on http://www.owl.qut.edu.au/oz-teachernet/projects/projects.html.

16 Internet Scuola http://www.quipo.it/internetscuola/homeing.html.

17 See e.g. 'ePALS Classroom Exchange' available at http://epals.com/ and 'Windows on the Worlds' by the Central Bureau for Educational Visits and Exchanges available at http://www.wotw.org.uk/.

Note The Office of the Data Protection Registrar is at Wycliffe House, Water Lane, Wilmslow, Cheshire SK9 5AF, tel: 01625 545700.

2 BEGINNING TO TEACH

The last chapter was concerned with the role and responsibilities of the teacher and how you might manage those. In this chapter, we look first at how you might learn from observing experienced teachers and then move on to consider aspects of planning and preparing lessons.

For most students there is a period during which you observe other teachers working, take part in team teaching and take part of a lesson before taking on a whole lesson. During this period, you use observation and critical reflection to build up your professional knowledge about teaching and learning and your professional judgement about managing learning. Unit 2.1 is therefore designed to focus your attention on how to observe the detail of what is happening in classrooms.

It is also difficult for a student teacher to become fully aware of the planning that underpins each lesson as planning schemes of work (long-term programmes of work) is usually done by a team of staff over a period of time. The scheme of work will then usually stay in place for some time. The extent of the actual planning for each lesson may also be hidden – experienced teachers will have internalised their planning so their notes for a lesson will usually be brief in comparison with those that a student teacher will need. Unit 2.2 explains planning processes. Unit 2.3 combines much of the advice of the first two chapters in an analysis of the issues you will probably need to be aware of before taking responsibility for whole lessons.

The quality of lesson planning is crucial to the success of a student teacher in enabling the pupils to learn. Defining clear and specific objectives for the learning in a particular lesson is one aspect of planning that many student teachers initially find difficult. The following story (from Mager, 1990, p. v) reinforces this need to have clear objectives for lessons:

> Once upon a time a Sea Horse gathered up his seven pieces of eight and cantered out to find his fortune. Before he had travelled very far he met an Eel, who said,
>
> 'Psst. Hey, bud. Where 'ya goin'?'
>
> 'I'm going out to find my fortune,' replied the Sea Horse, proudly.
>
> 'You're in luck,' said the Eel. 'For four pieces of eight you can have this speedy flipper and then you'll be able to get there a lot faster.'
>
> 'Gee, that's swell,' said the Sea Horse and paid the money and put on the flipper and slithered off at twice the speed. Soon he came upon a Sponge, who said,
>
> 'Psst. Hey, bud. Where 'ya goin'?'
>
> 'I'm going out to find my fortune,' replied the Sea Horse.
>
> 'You're in luck,' said the Sponge. 'For a small fee, I will let you have this

jet-propelled scooter so that you will be able to travel a lot faster.'

So the Sea Horse bought the scooter with his remaining money and went zooming thru the sea five times as fast. Soon he came upon a Shark, who said,

'Psst. Hey, bud. Where 'ya goin'?'

'I'm going to find my fortune,' replied the Sea Horse.

'You're in luck. If you take this short cut,' said the Shark, pointing to his open mouth, 'you'll save yourself a lot of time.'

'Gee, thanks,' said the Sea Horse and zoomed off into the interior of the Shark and was never heard from again.

The moral of this fable is that if you're not sure where you're going, you're liable to end up someplace else.

We hope that by the end of this chapter, you will be able to plan lessons in which both you and the pupils know exactly what they are meant to be learning.

2.1 READING CLASSROOMS

INTRODUCTION

The following true story appears in 'Teachers' first encounters with their classes' (Wragg, 1984).

> A chemistry graduate once arrived at his school experience school in January. Before commencing his own teaching he watched a third year class's regular chemistry teacher take a double period of practical work. After a brief exposition delivered whilst seated on the front bench, one or two shared jokes and asides, the experienced chemistry teacher signalled the start of the practical phase with 'Right 3C you know what to do, so get the gear out and make a start.' The class dispersed quickly to the cupboards and far recesses for various pieces of equipment and an hour of earnest and purposeful experimental work ensued.
>
> The following week the chemistry graduate took the class himself and began by lolling on the front bench in imitation of the apparently effortless and casual manner he had witnessed only seven days earlier. After a few minutes of introduction he delivered an almost identical instruction to the one given by the experienced man the week before 'Right 3C, get the gear out and do the experiment.' Within seconds pupils were elbowing their fellows out of the way, wrestling each other for Bunsen burners, slamming cupboard doors. He spent most of the practical phase calling for less noise and reprimanding the many pupils who misbehaved.

The point of this story is that observation should not be used to identify role models for your own practice; mimicry is an inadequate basis for building a professional career. By January of that academic year, this experienced teacher would have moulded the class to his own way of working. The pupils and teacher know how to respond to each other; they know the boundaries of behaviour and work within them, most of the time. What the student teacher had not seen was the process which had led to this situation. Consequently attempting to copy the practice of another, albeit successful, teacher failed because there was no shared background of expectation or understanding.

In this unit you are introduced to ways of observation and suggestions of how to focus on important teaching skills. You will find subject specific support as well in the series 'Learning to Teach (Subjects) in the Secondary School' (see p. ii). You should take every opportunity throughout your period of training in school to watch teachers, focusing on your current needs. We hope this introduction gives you confidence to develop your own strategies for observation, encourages you to reflect on your own and others' practice and to monitor your progress in relation to the competences and standards for your course of initial teacher education.

OBJECTIVES

Watching other teachers teach is an important part of developing your own teaching skills. This is true of all teachers, student, newly qualified or experienced. At the end of this unit you should have:

- considered ways of observing teachers and pupils in classrooms with a purpose in mind;
- learned to recognise and record information from observations so that analysis can take place;
- begun to evaluate your own teaching as well as that of others' against the competences and standards expected for a newly qualified teacher;
- gained some insights into the complex nature of teaching and learning.

See also Unit 1.1.

WHY OBSERVE?

The situation described in the introduction to this unit suggests that copying the skilful practice of other teachers is not enough. However, watching experienced teachers informs your own teaching especially if you observe skilful ones and are able to identify practices and behaviours which are of use to you. The range of what counts as good teaching is wide, encompassing a range of personalities, strategies and methods contributing to style. You should endeavour to watch teachers from many subject areas in the course of your school experiences. Through reflection, discussion , reading and experimentation what it means for you to teach well emerges and develops. However, watching other people do things you want to do yourself can be frustrating. Quite rightly the beginner wishes to get stuck in and learn how to do it 'on the job'. This is well and good but, although practice makes perfect, bad practice consolidates imperfection. It would be wise to watch competent teachers, alongside 'hands-on' experience.

At the start of school experience your main concerns include such things as whether you can stand in front of the class and make them listen to you, control the pupils' behaviour or remember enough of the subject matter to get through the lesson. A first essential before your first lesson with a class is to see them being taught by their regular teacher. So what do you look for in that lesson? How do you behave? What can you do to ensure that the experience of observing and being observed (by the pupils) is to your advantage?

GETTING STARTED

One of the first jobs of a teacher is to get the class into the room, settled and on to task as quickly as possible, the preparing and beginning phases of a lesson. How do different teachers do that?

Task 2.1.1

WATCHING THE START OF A LESSON
You are about to watch a class being taught and it is one you haven't seen before. You know the teacher having met her once already. Read through all sections of this task before embarking on it.

Preparing yourself

1 Write a list of questions that interest you about how she will start the lesson. Do this on your own for about five minutes.
2 If possible, share your ideas with another student teacher. Agree a set of questions – use about ten minutes for this exercise.
3 Categorise the questions by using these features of beginning a lesson:

1 Outside the classroom	2 Entrance and settling	3 Introducing the lesson

You should now have a list of questions of interest and importance to yourself. They may include the following or ideas related to them:

- were the children left outside until the teacher came or did they have entry without the teacher?
- did they enter quietly, in silence or in what manner?
- did the teacher stand at the door or did she get on sorting out her own books and materials while the pupils came in?
- do pupils have their own seats or do they sit anywhere?
- did the teacher take a register?
- what were the pupils expected to do during registration?
- how many pupils did the teacher speak to before the lesson started?
- was it public conversation or was it small group/single conversation?
- what was the talk about?
- at what point did the lesson proper begin? How did the pupils know; what was the signal?
- did pupils bring bags and coats into the lesson? What did they do with them? Who organised this?
- at what point did the pupils know what the lesson was about?
- how long from the time of entry did it take for the lesson proper to start?

For each lesson you watch note the background details of the class, e.g. year group, stream, etc., to help subsequent discussion and to understand the strategies used by the teacher. See the checklist at the top of Figure 2.1.1.

Observer . . . .   Date . . . .

Class name . . . .   Time(s) . . . .   Room . . . .   Year group . . . .

Class teacher . . . .   Boys/girls/mixed   Subject of lesson . . . .

Real time	Place	Pupil actions	Teacher action	Pupil talk	Teacher talk	Notes

Figure 2.1.1 Classroom observation guide

Checking with the teacher

Agree with the class teacher when and where you can observe the class. Tell the teacher what you are going to do and the sort of data you are planning to collect. Ask if you can talk with her for a short while after the lesson or later the same day, in order to share what you have seen and to clarify the information you have collected. For example, ask why a particular strategy was used.

Arrive at least five minutes before the lesson is due to start. Identify where you can sit during the lesson. If you intend to observe the start of the lesson, beginning from the corridor outside the classroom, check where you can stand, decide whether you are going to write notes as you wait and what you are going to say to pupils if they ask what you are doing. It may be more sensible to keep a mental note of these outside events and record them later inside the classroom.

You need a notepad, pencil, watch and a copy of the pro forma, Figure 2.1.1.

Making use of the data

1 Relate your data to the three categories of questions as suggested above. How does the teacher deal with the pupils in the corridor outside the classroom and get them into the classroom? Compare your notes with that of other student teachers.
   • Did the pupils line up in silence and enter in a formal manner? Or was entry to the room a casual affair? How did the teacher gain quiet? What did she say? Was

it something like 'come in 3B, bags on the side and stop chewing, Billy'?
What advantage is there to either mode of entry? Which mode would you adopt in this school?

- Once in the classroom what did the teacher say to the class? Was it about the pupils themselves; about the work in hand; or about outside events?
  What atmosphere does she create?
- Are any pupils praised or reprimanded? What words or phrases were used for reprimand; for praise?
  List these remarks.
- How was the transition from the informal part of the lesson to formal handled? How did the pupils know when this change of focus took place? What was said or done? Was it change of language or voice; of body language? Perhaps it was to do with where the teacher stood?
- Was a register taken?
  Was registration used as control exercise? Was talking allowed? Did this event mark the transition from informal to the formal part of the lesson (i.e. when teaching began)?
  How will you use the registration time in your lessons?

2   What other issues arise from this observation task? Discuss these with your tutor and other student teachers.

The flow of a lesson

It is sometimes helpful to draw together a sequence of a lesson – a flow diagram of what happened. The opening of the lesson may have gone like this:

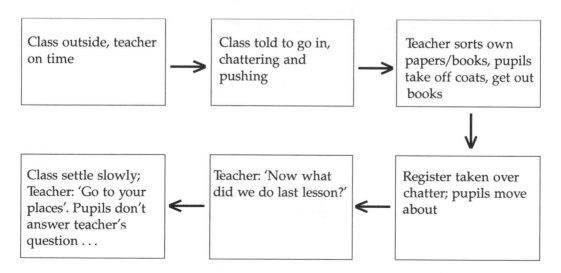

Draw up your own sequence; keep it to between four to five boxes. Put in key actions/ activities and compare your sequence with other student teachers' or your tutor's.

USING OTHER PEOPLE'S DATA

Information about classroom behaviour and practice can be gained very quickly by most visitors to a classroom, provided they are primed in advance. An example of data collected by observation of teacher talk is shown in Figure 2.1.2. The purpose of the observation was to identify for the observer the talking going on at the beginning of the lesson. Information was collected about who did the talking and what the talk was about. The lesson was the beginning of a practical activity in which the teacher was preparing the class for working in groups. Incidental events were noted that may have affected the lesson.

The data in Figure 2.1.2 shows some information gained over a period of twenty minutes. Each item of information was collected at minute intervals. (This represents a twenty minute snapshot of a classroom; it may or may not reflect their overall style of teaching or the teachers' view of practical activities.)

Task 2.1.2   **TEACHER–PUPIL TALK (see Figure 2.1.2)**

The purpose of your task is to infer from the data some information about the nature and purpose of the lesson. Use the following questions to interrogate the data. You may wish to address other issues as well.

- What is the talk about?
- Who initiates the talk?
- Who does the most talking?
- What is the nature of the talk?
- How effective was the introduction? How would you decide?

When discussing your responses bear in mind the limited amount of information you have about the class, teacher and subject. Discuss the observations in terms of:

1 Ownership of a lesson. Is the lesson one that pupils have a hand in designing and carrying out or is it a directed task? What may this have to do with commitment to the task and understanding of any subject matter?
2 Identify occasions when this approach could be used. Does it arise out of necessity, such as behaviour issues; from the nature of the work or subject; or may it reflect a preferred teaching style?
3 We are not told how the latecomers were dealt with, except that they were not allowed to interfere with the proceedings. How would you deal with latecomers?

Adapting the enquiry technique to other situations

How might the technique explained in Task 2.1.2 be used to gather different information about classrooms? Some suggestions are given below. Identify the objectives of your task and agree them with the class teacher first. Then draw up an observation schedule for yourself. Make sure you keep notes of events that allow you to interpret your findings. After the observation period, immediately or as soon as possible afterwards, share your information with the class teacher. He may be very interested in your data and may be able to explain some events.

Useful enquiries might include:

1 Transitions: for example, the change from pupil-centred activity to teacher-led summary. Observe an **end of lesson period**, in which the teacher might be bringing together what has been learned. Try to find out about:
   • Who does most of the talking?
   • Is there a summarising discussion?
   • Is the summary recorded by pupils in any way?
   • What evidence is there whether the learning is successful?
   • Did the teacher check if pupils had learned anything? How did she do this?
   • Were the aims of the lesson achieved?
   • Is homework set?
   • If yes, was the homework related to the lesson?
   • How was the class dismissed and in what manner did pupils leave the room?
2 Listen to **pupil conversation** when they are working in groups and find out:
   • how much time they spend talking to each other;
   • how much time is given to 'on task' talk;
   • if the on-task talk is about procedure (how) or about concepts (why);
   • if the pupils understand what they are doing and why they are doing it;
   • how they resolve difficulties in the group;
   • who, if anyone, is left out.
3 Where is the teacher positioned during the lesson? See Task 2.1.6 for details and discussion.

Discuss your findings with other student teachers or with your tutor.

Investigating the displays in classrooms

A feature of some schools is the lively attractive displays of children's work, either from a project, a school event or classwork. The best work often greets you in the foyer entrance as you enter the school. Are the classrooms equally as attractive?

Class around teacher at front of the classroom

Time	Who initiates				Purpose
	Teacher (T)	Pupil	Discipline	Give info.	Seek info.
1.45	✓		✓		
1.50	✓				✓
1.52	✓			✓	
1.53	✓	✓			✓
1.54	✓				✓
1.55	✓			✓	
1.56	✓			✓	
1.57					
1.58	✓			✓	
1.59	✓			✓	
2.00					
2.01	✓				
2.02	✓		✓		
2.03	✓	✓		✓	
2.04	✓				
2.05	✓			✓	
2.06	✓			✓	
2.07	Practical	work	underway		
Totals	15	2	2	8	3

Figure 2.1.2 Classroom talk
The task was to gain information about who initiates the interaction between pupils and teacher, how many people are involved and how long it goes on. We took evidence at minute intervals, identifying who was talking and the purpose.

			Comment
Give instructions	Seek clarification	Checking understanding	
Some info. might be interpreted as instructions			Settling in. Needed three–four minutes
			One phrase reply by pupil to T. question
			Late pupil arrives
			Another late pupil. T. writes table on board
			Pupils copy from board
			Two more pupils arrive late
			Pupils copy from board
			Fifth late pupil. T. helps latecomers
			Mild disciplinary control
			Response to questions
		✓	
			Note: five pupils late; were not allowed to disrupt discussion. Dealt with efficiently
		1	

Task 2.1.3 WHY DISPLAY THE WORK OF PUPILS?

What advantages does displaying pupils' work have for the teacher? Discuss with other student teachers the advantages of this practice. It is prominent in primary schools, less so in secondary schools. Why might this be so?

Task 2.1.4

WHAT DO CLASSROOMS LOOK LIKE?

What is the impression that classrooms convey as you look about you? Pupils spend most of their time in classrooms and this may affect the way they view and value what is taught in them. In this activity try to find out what is visible in the room, what it is for and if and how, it supports teaching and learning.

What to do

You need plain A4 paper, folded to make two facing A5 pages. Draw a rectangle on one side leaving a margin of 2–4 cm all round. On one side sketch one wall and mark on the diagram what is on the wall. On the margin of the sketch add other points of interest such as plants, aquarium, statue, notice board. Annotate the sketch on the facing A5 side, to help interpret what you see. Repeat for as many walls as you have time for. For each item consider the following features:

origin	other teachers, class teacher, pupil, commercial, other
purpose	decoration, relevant to lesson, left over from previous lessons, information, e.g. fire exit, purpose not clear
is it looked after?	new, old, dusty, defaced, tatty and soiled (look for dates)
attractively presented?	yes, no, care taken; colourful, eye catching
been there ages?	yes, no, can't tell
technical	name it, does it look used?
made reference to?	yes, no, not sure
notice board	does it have notices; recent/for pupils; for other teachers?
safety/conduct	purpose clear, obscure; clear instructions
language used	suitable for school use; recognises ESL or SEN pupils?

What to do with the observations

Share your findings with other student teachers in the school or your HE institution and together discuss the image of the school revealed by this information. Discuss your findings in terms of:

• who 'owns' the classroom; and who teaches in there; and how many teachers use this room?
• what encouragement the classroom environment gives to pupils (to look, read, engage, play, interact);
• the cultural diversity of the school;
• how the images of boys and girls are portrayed;
• valuing pupils' work;
• the effect on the learning environment.

You might like to consider the question 'is the rest of the school like this classroom?' This type of activity could be developed by comparing classrooms or comparing classroom displays with those in corridors. Several; student teachers could, as a group, study these aspects of the school. A short report could be made for the school; check with your school tutor about the best way to do this.

FURTHER ENQUIRIES AND OBSERVATIONS; SOME SUGGESTIONS

Many other aspects of teaching can be observed; some examples are given below. You should be able to adapt these for your own use.

Task 2.1.5

TEACHERS' QUESTIONS

What types of question do teachers ask? Are they simple questions with one word answers or are they more complex involving explanation? Investigate the frequency of different types of questions. You could classify questions into recall of fact and using prior knowledge to speculate about events or anticipate new ideas. Many writers refer to these sorts of questions as 'closed' and 'open'; see Unit 3.1 for further information about 'questioning'.

Do teachers:

- ask mainly closed questions?
- ask both open and closed questions according to purpose and circumstance?
- accept only right answers?
- dismiss wrong answers?
- give enough time for pupils to give an answer?
- encourage pupils to frame a reply?

Explore the way teachers respond to right and wrong answers given by pupils.

Task 2.1.6

WHERE IS THE TEACHER DURING A LESSON?

The movement of teachers in the classroom may say a lot about their relationship with pupils, about how they keep an eye on activity and behaviour and about their interest in the pupils.

Draw an A4 map of the classroom in which you are observing. Mark on it key points, teacher's desk, pupil desk, blackboard, OH projector, etc. Have several copies of the blank available. Throughout the lesson at designated times mark on your map where the teacher stands and where she has moved from. Do this at regular intervals, e.g. one minute and so build up a picture of position and movement. At the same time record the time and what is going on in the lesson. This will enable you to relate teacher movement to lesson activity.

Analyse your map and discuss:

- Where is the teacher most likely to be found during the lesson? What reasons can you offer for this: writing on the board; explaining with an overhead projector; helping pupils with written work?
- Does the teacher keep an eye on all the events in the room and, if so, how?
- Is it done by eye contact from the front or does the teacher move about the room?
- How did the teacher know that pupils were on task for most of the lesson?
- Were some pupils given more attention than others? What evidence do you have for this? What explanations are there for this pattern of observations?
- Was the teacher movement related to pupil behaviour in any way? Examine this idea and look for the evidence.
- Did the nature of the subject matter dictate teacher movement? How might movements change in different subject lessons? Give an example.

Share your information with other student teachers. What information does your 'map' give you about 'pupil territory' and 'teacher territory'?

Some teachers use their desk and board and equipment as a barrier between them and the pupils; others get in among the pupils and the desks. Are there 'no-go areas' which the teacher does not invade? Are there similar spaces for teachers which the pupil does not invade? See Unit 3.3 on managing pupil behaviour.

Task 2.1.7   HANDLING DISRUPTIVE PUPILS

Identify examples of disruptive behaviour, record its immediate causes and how the pupil was dealt with. How did the rest of the class react to the situation; how was the delivery of the lesson affected? Were other staff involved, head of department, senior teacher, technical staff? Try to record what was said by the teacher, what action was taken and how the problem was prevented from recurring in this lesson.

Are there formal procedures in school to document such incidents? Do not attempt to deal with the problem yourself or to make hasty judgements about the rights and wrongs of the situation. Afterwards, you may wish to discuss the lesson and the incident with the teacher.

After the lesson try to find out if there is a history of such behaviour and how the teacher and school are dealing with it. What advance preparation do you need to make in your early lessons on school experience to deal with such pupils?

Task 2.1.8   USING A VISUAL AID

Devise a way of investigating how a visual aid is used by a teacher with a class, e.g. video clip, CD-ROM, internet, wall chart. You should seek permission to watch the teacher in this way and tell the teacher your purpose in carrying out this task, and what you intend to do with your findings. Before the lesson, identify the important points and key ideas to be conveyed through the use of the resource; view the resource yourself. Record:

- what advanced planning takes place;
- why this resource is selected;
- how the resource is used in the lesson – how the material is introduced to the pupils; is advice given to pupils about what to do while they are watching it; is there advance warning about how the viewing will be followed up; is the material shown straight through or given in stages; is there a seating plan;
- how the material was followed up and its connection with the topic or unit of work; what were the pupils asked to do (write, draw, read a text, make notes)?
- the response of pupils – interest, understanding, appropriate level, want to know more, no interest, seen it before;
- how the visual aid portrayed people. Was there bias in the presentation, e.g. about men and women? Were any assumptions made that you might wish to challenge, about events, cultural stereotypes, causes of events, etc.? Record your evidence for discussion with the teacher or other student teachers.

At the end of the lesson, ask pupils what they thought about the presentation. For example:

1 Did they understand the key ideas? Were any ideas beyond most pupils?
2 Was the presentation or flow difficult to understand or follow?
3 Was the language understood and appropriate for this class?
4 Identify words or ideas about which pupils were unsure?

Similar tasks can be developed to observe the way teachers use transparencies on the overhead projector; or how teachers demonstrate how to use a machine; or demonstrate a process. These skills contribute towards your repertoire of teaching methods.

Summary and key points

You have discovered that teachers and pupils have set up a working relationship in which both parties know the rules, the codes of behaviour and their boundaries. You have seen many teachers working smoothly with a class in which the boundaries are kept, apparently without great effort; beneath that order you may have realised that there is a history of carefully nurtured practice involving much hard work by the teacher in establishing an appropriate atmosphere.

On occasions you may have seen these boundaries being broken and seen ways in which the teacher restores the working atmosphere. Each and every teacher has their own way of dealing with this problem. Watching the ways other teachers deal with such problems helps you widen your own repertoire of skills. You should find it helpful if you focus on how teachers handle behavioural problems for at least one of your classroom observation tasks.

The class you work with during school experience is someone else's; you are unlikely to break the relationship set up between them. In this respect your job of learning to teach is made more difficult; do you break the established pattern of behaviour or not? It is useful to remember that the school experience is a learning exercise and not one in which you are expected to take on the whole class as if it is yours for the year.

The observations have taken in a number of activities designed to help you organise a number of enquiries and get the most out of observation; more importantly, this should enable you to organise other enquiries of interest to you as you seek solutions to problems arising in your own teaching.

Observing can include looking, listening, recording, analysing and selecting; after evaluation some of what you have seen and heard may be incorporated into your own teaching. Unless observing moves on from you merely being in the classroom, letting the events wash over you, observation becomes boring and more importantly, of little value. So you need to focus on events, strategies, circumstances and observe those; and then do something with the results. Watching other people's lessons is also about feelings: your own because of the task ahead of you; the teachers' because they are under scrutiny and the pupils' because they are wondering what you are there for and what you might be like next week! So the observer is observed, too.

What we see and hear we have to interpret. You need to remember that, as a student teacher, you are likely to be familiar with classrooms. You have spent many years of your life, literally hundreds of hours, in classrooms as a pupil and student and you have a good idea of what you think makes a good classroom. The first point to recognise is that you are biased because of that experience. You are a not a neutral observer or one that brings a fresh eye to teaching.

You need to unlearn most of what you know about the classrooms of your adolescence and of undergraduate days before you can start to understand today's classrooms. Your experience then was that of a learner but that is only half the story; your experience was probably that of a successful learner otherwise you would not be in the position you are now. In addition you were probably a keen learner, not a reluctant one. All these features of your background may have to be carefully examined and their usefulness evaluated for the task in hand – teaching today's children in today's classrooms.

Observation activities are part of the transition from student teacher to experienced teacher. It is important to help you to see classrooms and teachers as you haven't seen them before and how you are unlikely to see them as a practising teacher. You bring bias to your observations and you may exercise bias in your judgements. Your observations of the lesson of a classroom teacher should be different from those made by the classroom teacher. You each bring a different purpose to the task. The class teacher is looking for quality of learning and is concerned for his performance. At this stage you are not so much concerned with quality but what was done to achieve it and make the lesson run smoothly.

Observation is in one sense a research exercise. It enables you to gather data on teacher performances and pupil learning. By analysing that data, you can begin to identify factors that contribute to effective teaching and learning and so place them in the framework of your own emerging skills. One way of establishing your own framework is to refer to your checklist of competences or standards required of Newly Qualified Teachers.

Observing other teachers working should be a continuing exercise; as your own teaching develops you need to refine and widen your skills and watching others with purpose can aid that development. We have suggested that:

- all teachers have their own style. An initial teacher education course aims to help you find your own style.
- your observation and interpretation of teachers and pupils in classrooms is affected by your own past experience. You need to be aware of this bias when you analyse the work of others and in your own teaching.
- when teachers interact with the class then each pupil in the class responds differently to the teacher. Learning and teaching, although carried out in groups, is an intensely personal activity.
- you can learn a lot about aspects of teaching and learning by focusing on particular tasks, events or happenings in the classroom. Understanding those events in terms of the interactions between teacher and pupils and the effect those interactions have on learning allows you to make decisions about your own approaches to teaching and learning.
- you need to evaluate your emerging teaching skills regularly over the course, setting your views against those of staff supporting you and your course requirements.
- your teaching skills develop throughout your career. You can rarely say 'I can do that' but you should be able to describe your development against the background of new challenges and widening experiences.

FURTHER READING

Hopkins, D. (1993) *A Teachers' Guide to Classroom Research (2nd edition)*, Buckingham: Open University Press.

Contains practical ideas for teachers wanting to investigate their own classroom practice.

Stoll, L. and Fink, D. (1996) *Changing our Schools*, Buckingham: Open University Press. See 'Teachers as Learners' *et seq*. pp. 152–7.

A discussion about the role of teachers in the 'learning community' and the need for teachers to be learners throughout their teaching career.

Wragg, E. (1994) *An Introduction to Classroom Observation*, London: Routledge.

Contains useful perspectives of life in the classroom and how to record and analyse observational data.

2.2   SCHEMES OF WORK AND LESSON PLANNING

INTRODUCTION

If your time with the pupils is to be used effectively, you need to plan carefully for each lesson – taking account of how pupils learn, the requirements of the curriculum, the most appropriate methods of teaching the topic and the resources available as well as the evaluations of previous lessons.

There are two levels of planning particularly appropriate to your work in the classroom – the **scheme of work** and **the lesson plan**. You will quickly gain experience of planning as you plan lessons and schemes of work on your school experience. However, planned activities do not have to be followed through rigidly and at all costs. Because planning is integrally linked to evaluation and development, evaluation of plans for a specific situation may point to the need to change or develop your plans.

OBJECTIVES

By the end of this unit, you should be able to:

- explain what is meant by the terms: 'aims', 'objectives', 'progression', 'differentiation';
- construct schemes of work (also known as programmes or units of work);
- construct effective lesson plans.

Check the competences/standards for your course which relate to lesson planning and schemes of work to make sure you understand what is required of you.

PLANNING WHAT TO TEACH

What should you teach and how should you teach it?

The factors influencing **what** should be taught (lesson content) are discussed in Unit 1.1, but how much you teach in each lesson and **how** you teach it (teaching methods) are the teacher's own decisions.

Lesson content

Recall the 'sabre-toothed curriculum' of the stone age and the 'queen of studies' from medieval times (Unit 1.1). Similarly, the knowledge, skills, understanding and attitudes appropriate for a young person entering the world of work in the twenty-first century are vastly different to those which were considered appropriate even fifteen years ago. Ideas about what teachers should teach change over time and the curriculum is under constant scrutiny by those responsible for education.

As a student teacher, you are usually given clear guidelines about what to teach and the goals for pupils' learning within your subject. These goals are in part usually set out in government produced documents, e.g. the National Curriculum documents, school documents and syllabuses prepared by examination boards. If you teach in England and Wales, you will of course need to become familiar with the National Curriculum requirements and the terminology (see Chapter 7). However, before you plan individual lessons you need an overall picture of what learning is planned for the pupils over a period of time. This overall plan is called a **scheme of work** and you will find departmental schemes of work cover between half a term's work and a couple of years' work.

Teaching methods

However constraining the guidelines on content are, the decision about which teaching methods to use is usually yours. As you become more experienced as a teacher, you acquire your own personal approach to teaching. But as people learn in different ways and different teaching methods are suitable for different types of material, you should become familiar with a range of ways of structuring learning experiences in the classroom. For example, you might choose to use discussion, rote learning, discovery learning, role play and so on. Chapter 5 gives you detailed advice on teaching styles and strategies appropriate to different approaches to learning.

> **Task 2.2.1**
>
> **HOW DO YOU LEARN?**
> Spend a few minutes making notes of the methods which you use to help you learn and the methods of teaching used by teachers from whom you felt you had learned a lot. Then make notes about those situations from which you did not learn. Compare these notes with those of other student teachers. People learn in different ways and different areas of learning require different approaches. You need to take account of such differences in planning your lessons and to demonstrate that you can use a range of teaching methods in order to take account of such differences.

SCHEMES OF WORK AND LESSON PLANS

There are two main stages to planning for pupil learning:

1 Preparing an outline of the work to be covered over a period – **the scheme of work**.
2 Planning each individual lesson – **the lesson plan**.

A number of formats for both schemes of work and lesson plans are in use. We suggest you read the advice given for the teaching of your subject in the subject specific texts in this series. However, whilst the level of detail may vary between different approaches, the purpose is the same – to provide an outline of the work to be done either over an extended period (scheme of work) or in the lesson (lesson plan) so that the planned learning can take place. The best plans are ones which support you in your teaching so that your pupils learn what you intend them to learn. Try different approaches to planning in order to find those most appropriate to your situation. The illustrations in this unit are intended to provide examples with which you can work and later modify.

The scheme of work

This might also be called the 'programme of work' or the 'unit of work'. Different terms may be used in your school or in your subject but the purpose is the same – to devise a long term plan for the pupils' learning. So a **scheme of work** sets out the long-term plans for learning and thus covers an extended period of time – this could be a period of years, a term or half a term or weeks, e.g. for a module of work. A scheme of work should be designed to build on the learning which has gone before, i.e. it should ensure **continuity** of pupil learning.

Schemes of work should be designed to ensure that the knowledge, skills, understanding and attitudes of the pupils are developed over a particular period in order to ensure **progression** in learning. The term 'progression' means the planned development of knowledge, skills, understanding or attitudes over time. In some departments, the schemes of work are very detailed and include teaching materials and methods as well as safety issues.

Using a scheme of work

Usually, you are given a scheme of work. In putting this together, the following questions have been considered:

1 what are you trying to achieve? (Aims for the scheme of work and objectives for particular lessons – see the definitions following.)
2 what has been taught before?
3 how much time is available to do this work?
4 what resources are available?
5 how is the work to be assessed?
6 how does this work fit in with work pupils are doing in other subjects?
7 what is to be taught later?

The scheme itself may be quite brief (Figure 2.2.1 shows a proforma used by student teachers on one course) but it will be based on the above information.

Each of these areas is now discussed in turn. To start with think about what learning should be taking place.

Scheme of work for x topic

Area of work	Ref:

Class	No. in class	Age	Key stage
No. of lessons	Duration	Dates	

Aims (from the National Curriculum programmes of study)

(Objectives are listed in each lesson plan)

Framework of lessons	NC reference

Assessment strategies

Other notes (safety points)

Figure 2.2.1 Scheme of work proforma

1 What are you trying to achieve? The **aims** of a scheme of work are general statements about the learning that should take place over a period.

Objectives are specific statements which set out what pupils are expected to learn from a particular lesson in a way that allows you to identify if learning has occurred.

Objectives are prepared for each lesson and further detail is included under lesson planning later in this unit.

In devising each scheme of work a small aspect of the whole curriculum will have been taken and a route planned through this which provides the best opportunities for pupils to learn. **Progression** in pupil learning should be considered and built into schemes of work.

2 What has been taught before?   This information should be available from school documentation and from staff. In the case of pupils in their first year of secondary education, there is usually a member of staff responsible for liaising with primary schools who may have this information.

3 How much time is available to do this work?   The length of lessons and the number of lessons devoted to a topic are decided by the department or school in which you are working. Don't forget that homework has a valuable role to play in enhancing learning and that not all the lessons you expect to have will be available for teaching. Time will be taken up by tests, revision, fire drill, special events, lateness.

4 What resources are available?   Resources include material resources as well as human resources and what is available depends on the school where you are working. You need to find out the procedures for using resources in the school and what is available. You may find there are resources outside the school to draw upon – parents, governors and charities. Many firms provide schools with speakers on current topics. There may be field studies centres or sports facilities nearby. You need to check if there are any safety issues to consider when choosing appropriate resources.

5 How is the work to be assessed?   Teaching, learning and assessment are interlinked. Most of the work you are doing with pupils is teacher assessed although some will be assessed by outside agencies. A main purpose of teacher assessment is formative – to check pupils' progress, e.g. in relation to lesson objectives. In any case, you should keep good records of the pupils' progress (homework, classwork, test results) in your own record book as well as providing these in the form required by the school or department. Chapter 6 focuses on assessment issues.

Task 2.2.2	RECORD KEEPING AND ASSESSMENT

RECORD KEEPING AND ASSESSMENT
Ask staff in your department how they expect pupil assessment records to be kept and what forms of assessment you should use for the work you are doing.

6 How does this work fit in with work the pupils are doing in other subjects?   There are many areas of overlap where it is useful to discuss the pupils' work with other departments. For instance, if pupils are having difficulty with measurement in technology, it is worth checking if and when the mathematics department teaches these skills and how they teach them. Cross-curricular dimensions to the curriculum (see Units 7.2 and 7.3) will have been considered by the school and responsibilities for different aspects shared out among departments. Ask staff in your department what responsibilities the department has in this area.

7 What is to be taught later? Progression in pupil learning has to be planned for and a scheme of work has to be drawn up for this purpose. From this scheme of work you know what work is to come and the contribution to pupil learning that each lesson is to make.

> **Task 2.2.3** **DRAWING UP A SCHEME OF WORK**
> In consultation with your tutor, draw up a scheme of work to last about six to eight lessons. Focus on one particular class which you are teaching. Use the format provided for your course (or the one we provide in Figure 2.2.1) or one which fits in with the planning methods used in the department.

The lesson plan

The **lesson plan** provides an outline of one lesson within a scheme of work. In planning a lesson, you are working out the detail required to teach one aspect of the scheme of work. To plan the lesson you use a framework and an example of a lesson planning framework is given in Figure 2.2.2.

Date:............................. Class:...............................

Area of Work:...

Aim:..

Objectives:..
....

Time	Teacher activity	Pupil activity	Notes/Equipment needed
0–5 min	Class enter and settle	Coats and bags put away	
5–10 min	Homework discussed/ recap of work so far/task set/new work explained		
10–25 min	Teacher supports groups/individuals	Pupils work in individual groups to carry out the task	
. . . and so on			
Ending	Teacher summarises key points/sets homework		

Evaluation: Were objectives achieved? What went well? What needs to be addressed next time? How are individuals responding?

Figure 2.2.2 Planning a lesson: one possible approach

The following information is required for you to plan effectively.

1 Overall aim(s) of the scheme of work and the specific objectives for this lesson   Defining objectives which clarify exactly what learning you hope will take place is a crucial skill for the effective teacher. It helps you to be clear about exactly what the pupils should be achieving and it helps the pupils understand what they should be doing. However, drawing up effective objectives requires thought.

At this stage in your career, if you can ensure that your lesson objectives focus on what should be achieved from the lesson in terms of pupils' learning, then you will have made a good start.

Listing objectives after the following phrase **By the end of this lesson, pupils will be able to . . .** may help you to devise clear goals and to understand the difference between aims (general statements) and objectives (specific goals).

Words that help you be precise are those such as **state**, **describe**, **list**, **identify**, **prioritise**, **solve**, **demonstrate an understanding of**. These words force you to write statements which can be tested. If you think your objectives are vague, ask yourself whether the objective makes it clear what the pupils must achieve. If you tell the pupils what your objectives are will they understand what is expected of them? Objectives may be related to knowledge, concepts, skills, behaviours and attitudes.

> **Task 2.2.4   WRITING OBJECTIVES**
> You will find different terminology in use – some people refer to behavioural objectives, some to learning objectives. These are the same things and they refer to the observable outcomes of the lesson, i.e. to what pupils are expected to be able to do. Discuss the writing of objectives with other student teachers and your tutor. Choose a particular lesson and, as a group, devise appropriate objectives which relate to changes in pupils' learning or behaviour. Pay particular attention to the quality and type of objectives you are setting – are they focused on the pupils' learning?

2 Range of abilities of the pupils   As you develop as a teacher, you are expected to incorporate **differentiation** into your planning. This refers to the need to consider pupils' individual abilities when work is planned so that both the brightest pupils and those with lesser ability are challenged and extended by the work. Differentiation can be achieved in different ways depending on the material to be taught. Differentiation may, for example, be achieved by **outcome**, i.e. different types or qualities of work may be produced, or by **task**, i.e. different tasks may be set for pupils of differing abilities. (Unit 4.1 provides further information.) You provide **continuity** of learning for the pupils by taking account of and building on their existing knowledge, skills and attitudes.

3 Time available   On the examples of a lesson plan provided, a time line is drawn on the left hand side. If you refer to this in the lesson, you are quickly able to see if it is necessary to adapt the original plan to fit the time available.

4 Resources available   Staff usually go out of their way to help students have the appropriate resources. But don't forget that others may be needing them so ask in good time for the resources you require. Check how resources are reserved in your department.

5 Approaches to classroom management   These should be suitable to the topic and subject (see Chapters 3 and 4).

6 Teaching strategies and the learning situations   These should be set up as appropriate to the work being covered (see Chapter 5). Explaining and questioning are two key skills which you should work to improve. It is a good idea to write out questions in advance which you may want to use to test the pupil's grasp of the topic and which develop thinking. Until you are more experienced, you may find it difficult to phrase appropriate questions (Unit 3.1 has further details).

7 Assessment methods   Decide which ones you will use in order to know whether your objectives have been achieved (see Chapter 6).

8 Any risks associated with the work   Safety is an important issue in schools. In some subjects, the assessment of risk to the pupils and incorporation of strategies to minimise this risk are a necessary part of the teacher's planning. Departmental and national guide-lines are provided to ensure the safety of the pupils and should be followed. Student teachers should consult their head of department or tutor for guidance on safety issues. If you are in doubt about an activity and you cannot discuss your worries with your tutor, do not carry out the activity.

9 What do the pupils know now?   As your experience of the curriculum and of pupils' learning develops, you will find it easier to answer this question. You need to consider what has been taught before as well as the experience outside school which pupils might have had. It may be appropriate to do some form of testing or analysis of knowledge, skills and understanding or to have a discussion with pupils to discover their prior experience and attitudes to the work in question. As a student teacher you should seek advice from the staff who normally teach your classes.

  Lessons have a structure and a rhythm to them. As you read this next section, think about the overall pattern to a lesson and the skills you use at each stage.

Constructing a lesson

Initially, you might find it difficult to see exactly how teachers manage their classes. In order to help you see the underlying structure of a lesson, we have divided the lesson and its planning into five key areas: preparation; beginning; moving on; ending, evaluation. Figure 2.2.3 (The structure of a lesson) illustrates this rhythm.

Preparation   The most successful lessons are thoroughly planned and structured

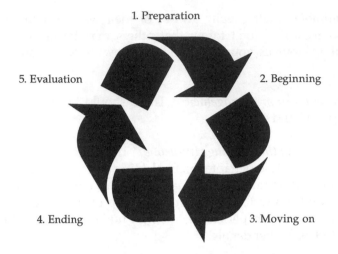

1. Preparation

5. Evaluation

2. Beginning

4. Ending

3. Moving on

Figure 2.2.3 The structure of a lesson
Acknowledgement: Chris Kettle

Task 2.2.5

PLANNING AND GIVING LESSONS
As you read about each stage, make notes in your diary to remind you of key points to pay attention to when you are planning and giving lessons. Unit 2.3 provides more details.

beforehand and you manage a class more effectively if you carefully consider how you will organise yourself and the pupils beforehand.

Make sure you have enough of the necessary materials, equipment and resources. Know the exact number of the items you are using so that you know if something has been lost and can take steps to find it immediately. Most departments have developed their own systems of stock control, but a useful technique for textbooks is to number them and when you give them to pupils, record the textbook number in your mark book.

Ensure that you know how to operate any equipment you plan to use (e.g. television monitors, videos, computers or subject-specific equipment) and that it is in working order. If you are carrying out a science experiment, you should do it yourself before the lesson. This enables you to anticipate problems pupils might encounter.

Plan a variety of appropriate teaching and learning activities (see Chapter 5). Remember, the concentration span of adults is about twenty minutes and that of most pupils is shorter. Plan extra, related activities in case your chosen approach does not work or pupils complete tasks more quickly than you anticipate.

Give advance warning to pupils of any books, materials, etc., that they need for the lesson. If you have asked them to collect particular items or materials, don't rely on them remembering – bring enough yourself in order for the lesson to proceed just in case.

Beginning   A good beginning is a crucial part of a successful lesson as it sets the tone, motivates pupils and establishes your authority. There are a number of key points to be kept in mind when you think about beginning your lessons.

Be in the classroom before the pupils arrive and, where possible, have the board prepared with notes, diagrams, etc. Undoubtedly, the school you are in will have established rules about pupil movement around the school and entry to classrooms. However, in the lower years in particular, it is advisable to line up pupils outside your teaching room and to usher them inside in an orderly manner.

Settle the class as quickly as possible and ensure that all pupils are facing you – even when they are seated in groups around tables – and are listening in silence before you begin the lesson. Do not begin the lesson when any pupil is talking, but wait calmly, confidently and expectantly for quiet. You will get it! Do not press on until you have established quiet. It is worth taking the time to do so.

Class management is much easier when you know the pupils by name. So make a determined effort to learn their names as quickly as possible. It does not happen by osmosis, so you have to work at it. Seating plans are useful, as is the practice in the early stages of asking pupils to raise their hands when you register them. Although it might appear time consuming, giving out exercise books to pupils individually quickly allows you to put a face to a name.

If you are unable to address pupils by name address them by their class/form designation. For example, 'Right 7G, I want everyone looking this way.' This is far better than 'Right girls/boys/ladies/lads etc.' Never resort to 'Oi you, blondie!' or some equally rude outburst. Similarly, impersonations of deflating a balloon through continued 'Sshh-sshh-ing' do nothing to enhance your authority. Unfortunately, the practice seems all too common in the classroom.

Pupils like to know what is expected of them. They relax and have a far more positive approach if you explain what you plan to do in the lesson, with a brief rationale of how it fits in with previous and future work and if you let them know what you want them to achieve in the lesson.

Establish a crisp, but not rushed, pace from the beginning. Never stand in one place in the room for more than a matter of a few minutes and some teachers suggest that you don't sit at the teacher's desk during the lesson except *in extremis*. Use eye contact, vary the pace and tone of your voice (see Unit 3.1) and monitor pupil reaction continually.

Moving On Smooth, seamless transitions between one part of the lesson and the next are vital if there is to be overall continuity and coherence. Having introduced the lesson, you need to explain the purpose of the first (and thereafter any subsequent) pupil task. Be very clear about what you want the pupils to do and tell them exactly how long they are to spend on the activity. They then have an idea of the pace they need to work at and how much you expect them to 'produce'.

Before they begin the activity, check that all pupils understand exactly what they are expected to do. Deal with any queries before the class begins work. This saves endless repetition of the task to individuals.

Have a definite routine for distributing books and materials. Will you give out equipment? Will pupils come out to collect it row by row, table by table? Will one pupil per table/row collect it? In any event, it is essential that this activity is carried out in a controlled and orderly manner in any classroom. Moreover, if you are teaching a physical education or science subject, the safety aspect of this area of class management is of unequalled importance.

When the pupils are engaged in the activity, move around the room monitoring pupil progress and dealing with questions; but do not interfere unnecessarily. Let them get on with the task. Even when the whole class is engaged in a task, it is rarely appropriate to sit at the teacher's desk and 'switch off'. Effective class management depends upon your active involvement. Key skills are: circulation; monitoring progress; the use of proximity to pupils; sensitivity to and awareness of, pupil needs.

Give one or two minutes' warning of the end of the activity. Be vigilant about keeping to the time limit you imposed at the beginning of the activity. Do not let things 'slide'. Be aware that not every pupil will finish the task set. Use your judgement in assessing that, while a few may not have finished within your deadline, most are ready for the next stage. If, however, it becomes clear that the whole class needs longer than you anticipated for an activity, be flexible enough to adjust your planning.

At the end of the activity, settle the class and expect all pupils to be sitting quietly, facing you before you proceed to the next stage of the lesson. Be sure to maintain your business-like manner and the crisp pace you established earlier.

Ending   It is important that any learning experience is rounded off, that pupils experience a sense of completion. Similarly, pupils need some mental space between lessons. They need to 'come down' from one lesson in order to prepare themselves for the next. Remember, depending upon the timetable, pupils may need to negotiate the conceptual intricacies of between four and eight subjects in a day. Your lesson, therefore, needs to be completed in an organised manner.

Plan enough time at the end of the lesson to: sum up what has been achieved; set homework where appropriate; give a brief idea of what the next lesson will comprise and (if necessary) explain what pupils will need to bring to it.

As with the distribution of materials (see the section on beginning), have a definite, orderly routine for collection.

Before pupils leave, make sure the classroom is neat and tidy and remember that the pips or bell are signals for you, not the pupils. Dismiss the pupils by table or row and ensure that they leave the room in a quiet, controlled fashion. Enforcing a quiet orderly departure also adds to the pupils' experience of the standards you expect, i.e. that your classroom provides an orderly and calm learning environment. Take a well-earned ten second breather before beginning the whole process again with the next class!

Evaluation and planning future lessons   As soon as you can after the lesson, evaluate its success. What went well? What didn't go well? What evidence do you have which allows you to answer with some degree of certainty? (See Unit 5.4.) What should you change next time on the basis of this evaluation and how will this fit in with the scheme of work? If you develop the practice of reflecting on your work as a matter of course, then modifying future practice on the basis of this reflection becomes second nature. In this way, you use your experience systematically to build up your professional knowledge and to develop your professional judgement.

> ## ❗ Summary and key points
>
> You should now be able to explain the following terms, aims, objectives, progression, differentiation and have considered how to construct schemes of work and lesson plans which are comprehensive and useful.
>
> At this point, you may like to reflect on criteria used by the Office for Standards in Education (OFSTED) inspectors for judging teaching quality. Although teaching methods vary, the criteria to judge a teacher's effectiveness which are used by OFSTED are standard.
>
> Teaching quality is to be judged by the extent to which
> - teachers have clear objectives for their lessons
> - pupils are aware of these objectives
> - teachers have a secure command of the subject
> - lessons have suitable content
> - activities are well chosen to promote learning of that content
> - activities are presented in ways which will engage and motivate and challenge all pupils, enabling them to make progress at a suitable pace.
>
> (from OFSTED (1993a) *The Handbook for the Inspection of Schools*, Part 2, p. 27)
>
> These criteria represent goals to which you might aim.

FURTHER READING

Cohen, L., Manion, L. and Morrison, K. (1996) *A Guide to Teaching Practice (4th edition)*, London: Routledge.

A useful, comprehensive book dealing with central issues of classroom practice. Readable and aimed specifically at those with no teaching experience.

Kyriacou, C. (1995) *Essential Teaching Skills*, Cheltenham: Stanley Thornes.

An excellent and readable overview of the key skills which underpin effective teaching.

Mager, R. (1990) *Preparing Instructional Objectives (2nd edition)*, London: Kogan Page.

Although this book is focused on skills-based objectives nevertheless the exercises in it will help you develop your skills in setting objectives. Mager has written may other texts dealing with these issues.

2.3   TAKING RESPONSIBILITY FOR WHOLE LESSONS

INTRODUCTION

This unit draws attention to issues which have particular relevance to you when you are just starting to take responsibility for whole lessons.

Recall the iceberg image of a teacher's work from Unit 1.1. The delivery of the lesson in the classroom represents the tip of the iceberg, whilst the bulk of the teacher's work for a lesson – routines, preparation, subject knowledge, professional knowledge and judgement, previous lesson evaluations – is hidden. This unit focuses on particular aspects of planning and teaching which initially cause many student teachers problems.

OBJECTIVES

By the end of this unit, you should have considered the following:

- routines for good class management;
- how your personal attributes contribute to your effectiveness;
- lesson preparation;
- how to avoid common problems.

Concerns common to student teachers who are beginning to teach are also discussed.

ROUTINES FOR CLASS MANAGEMENT

Routines for class and lesson management provide a structure so that learning can take place within a classroom where the rules are understood by all. In time, these routines become instinctive for you. Establishing rules decreases the likelihood of having to waste lesson time disciplining pupils at a later stage.

But your routines are not established in a vacuum. The pupils you teach have been in schools for at least seven years – they expect the teacher to establish 'norms' for classroom work, talk and movement and most pupils are conditioned to accept such classroom routines. This doesn't mean that they won't resist you when you insist on certain types of behaviour but it does mean that they have certain expectations that you will set the rules. Three types of routines in operation are:

- for managing work and movement;
- for managing relationships and reinforcing expectations of attitudes and behaviour;
- for gaining attention – for both the pupils and the teacher.

Routines for managing work and movement

For your early lessons, one of your main goals is to get the pupils down to work fairly promptly by providing them with clear tasks and clear instructions. Even if these tasks are not the most intellectually demanding at this stage, your concern is to establish yourself as an organised teacher who sets clear objectives for a lesson and provides work which allows students to achieve those objectives. These lessons will probably go more easily if you can fit in with established routines.

> **Task 2.3.1 CLASSROOM NORMS**
>
> Make a list of your expectations for the presentation of work, talk and movement for pupils in your classroom. Find out through observation and discussion what the expectations of experienced teachers are, especially the teachers of the classes you are taking. Update and amend your list as you gain experience with what works for you.

Routines for managing relationships and reinforcing expectations

Adopting a **firm, fair, friendly** approach may help you develop good relationships with pupils. Pupils have certain expectations of you. They expect the teacher to be consistent and fair in applying rules. They expect those who do well to be rewarded and/or acknowledged, e.g. through praise, even just a quiet word or by letting them go first at the end of the lesson. Those who don't abide by your rules expect to be reprimanded. A quiet individual reprimand at the end of a lesson may be sufficient to establish your authority with many pupils. Confrontations in front of the whole class are to be avoided. Remember, the role of routines is to make your lessons run smoothly – everyone should know what your expectations are for classroom behaviour.

It takes time for the student teacher and for any teacher new to a school, to find out about influences on classroom relationships which come from the community. Information about the range of group 'norms' of behaviour for teenagers in the local area and background information about other social relationships (e.g. which pupils are cousins, stepsisters or brothers) may help you understand more easily your pupils and their expectations.

Experienced teachers can often anticipate when trouble is brewing between pupils and defuse the situation. They use their voice sparingly – drawing on a range of other controls, e.g. placing themselves near pupils who need more encouragement to stay on task and using non-verbal gestures to remind pupils to keep working. If needed, there are a number of sanctions which all teachers can use. Beware of giving pupils detentions as a first step. Time is precious to you so don't waste it and in any case establishing your authority can be just as easily achieved by using one of a range of other sanctions: for example,

- the pupil is required to apologise (or face sanctions);
- a verbal warning is given – a brief reprimand or keeping the pupil for a moment at the end of the lesson to indicate your displeasure;
- a couple of pupils tidy up after the others have gone (teachers are wise to protect their professional reputations by not remaining alone in closed classrooms with individual pupils);
- additional work is given.

Task 2.3.2	**SANCTIONS AND REWARDS**

Find out about the policies on sanctions and rewards at the school where you are teaching. Make notes of the key issues which affect your work. Check your understanding of the application of these policies with experienced staff.

Routines for gaining attention

Getting the attention of the whole class at points during the lesson is a skill which experienced teachers practise effortlessly. Firstly, act as though you believe the pupils will obey you. One pattern teachers often practise is to call for attention ('Stop what you're doing and just look here for a minute'). They then follow this with a focus on an individual ('Paul, that means you too') which acts as a reminder to all pupils that if they don't want to be the focus of the teacher's attention they need to stop what they're doing. The time to call the class to attention is not when they're all working well but when the work is flagging and they need to be spurred on or they've come to a difficult point – unless, for example, you wish to draw their attention to a point on safety.

One of the fundamental rules of the classroom is that pupils should not speak when the teacher is speaking. Spending a few minutes in a lesson waiting for silence until you speak will save a lot of time later as pupils know what you expect. Pupils may need reminding of your expectations and you probably need to reinforce the idea that this is one of your basic rules. You must be able to get the class's attention when you require it. When observing classes, the following questions may help you see some of the strategies used by teachers to establish this aspect of their authority.

- **What verbal cues does the teacher use to establish quiet?** Key phrases such as 'Right then', 'Put your pens down now' establish that the teacher requires the class to listen. Some students make the mistake of thinking the words 'quiet' or 'shush' repeated over and over will gain the required effect. Experienced teachers tend to use more subtle or strident methods, e.g. QUIET! – said once with great emphasis. Units 3.2 and 3.3 provide further advice.
- **What non-verbal cues does the teacher use to gain attention?** Look at the way teachers use gestures – eyes, face, arms, hands – to establish that they require the class to listen. They may stand still and just wait. Their pupils will know that if they keep their teacher waiting they will be penalised. Unit 3.1 contains more ideas.

There are also routines related to the way pupils gain the teacher's attention. The usual routine is that the pupil puts up their hand and doesn't call out. Again, we suggest you find out what the current practice is for the classes you are teaching. If you decide to change established practices then you have to put in considerable effort to establish the new rules.

YOUR PERSONAL ATTRIBUTES

Body language plays an important role in your communication with others and is an aspect of the way you present yourself which you should consider. Some personal attributes which may interfere with your teaching may only reveal themselves once you are teaching. For this reason, it is worth keeping this aspect of your interaction with pupils and staff under review.

Try to establish early in your teaching experience:

- whether your voice can be heard at the back of a classroom;
- whether you have any particular habits which will interfere with the developing of a relationship with a class, e.g. do you rattle coins in your pocket as you speak; do you play with your hair; are you able to use facial expressions effectively to indicate enthusiasm; do you speak in a monotone; do you look at people when you speak to them; what do you communicate through your smiling (some people inadvertently smile when they are angry)?
- what messages your posture and your movement in classrooms and corridors convey;
- what gestures you normally use when speaking.

We suggest you ask for feedback occasionally on these aspects in order to check whether you are inadvertently presenting yourself in an unfavourable manner. Unit 3.1 on communication provides more detail.

LESSON PREPARATION

> I spent days preparing my first lesson on my first teaching experience – Geography with a group of 15 year olds who weren't exactly enamoured with the subject. Educationally it was a disaster! I was so nervous that I rushed through my carefully prepared 40 minute lesson and at the end of 10 minutes I had nothing more to say. I panicked and told them to draw a map – any map – for the rest of the lesson.

This true story, from a (now) very successful teacher, highlights the nervousness which many student teachers experience when faced with their first lessons. Such nervousness is natural. You are assuming an unfamiliar role – as a teacher – but there are no set lines which you can learn to carry you through the scene. Over time, you build your professional knowledge about teaching and learning and your professional judgement about how to manage the work in the classroom so that the situation described above does not arise. In the meantime, you are having to learn from each situation you face.

When you are spending hours planning for your first lessons, you may wonder whether you've made a sound choice of career but recall the learner driver mentioned in Unit 1.1. In time, many aspects of driving become automatic; so it is with some features of teaching. In your first lessons, it is a good idea not to try to do anything too ambitious. Limited success is better than unlimited disaster!

It is, of course, possible for a teacher to be in a classroom with a class and for no effective teaching or learning to take place! Effective teaching requires some planned learning to occur in those being taught. Therefore, for your pupils to learn effectively, you must plan carefully.

We suggest you skim through Units 2.2, 5.2 and 5.3 of this book as they provide ideas about the basic teaching skills and planning approaches which you need to employ in your first lessons. You should, of course, be building on your experience of group work, micro-teaching and on the observations you have made.

Following the steps outlined below should ensure that you start your first lessons from a position of being well prepared.

1 Plan the lesson and ask for advice about your plan

> **Task 2.3.3**
>
> **CHECKING YOUR LESSON PLAN**
> Look at your plan for one of your lessons. Are you making your expectations of the pupils clear at each stage? Are the pupils actively engaged at each point or are they wasting time waiting for you to organise books or equipment? Are you expecting them to concentrate on you talking for too long; to take in too much new information without the chance to discuss it and assimilate it? Is there scope for pupils to feed back to you what they've learned this lesson, e.g. through question and answer? As a trial run, try to explain the main points of the lesson to another student teacher. The quality of explanation you are able to give affects the learning which takes place as does the nature of questions you ask. Ask another student teacher, your tutor or the teacher whose class you are teaching to keep these points in mind when they observe the lesson and to give you feedback afterwards.

2 Check that you have adequate extension and alternative work   Anticipate that additional work may be needed. You may find that equipment you had planned to use stops working or the specialist in your subject is not available to supervise you.

3 Know the class if possible through your observations and have a strategy for using and learning names   Try to learn names quickly – making notes beside the names in the register may help you remember. Drawing up a seating plan can help; pupils may always, or at least usually, sit in the same places. In any case, you can ask them to sit in the same seats until you know their names.

Tony Buzan (1984, 1995) writes extensively on developing memory and he suggests a number of strategies for remembering faces:

- try to link the faces or characteristics of people new to you with existing friends with the same names;
- try to use images to make a mental link between the name and the face of the new person;
- try to repeat the person's name several times during your conversation with them. ('That's an interesting piece of work, David. David, what do you enjoy most about . . .?')

Unit 2.2 provides additional advice on learning names.

If you have the opportunity to observe the class beforehand, look at how the teacher deals with the potentially noisy or the very quiet pupils.

AVOIDING COMMON PROBLEMS

By this point, you know the routines you will use, your lesson is planned. You have also given some thought to where you will stand, when and how you will move around the room. You know to keep scanning the class and, when you talk to children, not to have your back to most of the class.

Judging the timing during a lesson is one of the most difficult problems initially and following a time line on your lesson plan can help you see at a glance how the lesson is progressing in relation to the time allowed.

Unavoidable incidents will occur to interrupt the flow of your carefully prepared lesson but other incidents can be anticipated or at least dealt with effectively if you are prepared. It is as well to anticipate problems so that you are not too distracted from the lesson you planned to deliver. We discuss below some of the more common incidents and possible solutions so that you are not taken by surprise.

1 One or more pupils won't settle to the work   When some pupils are being disruptive, it is essential to get the bulk of the class working, preferably on work which requires less input from you than normal. This allows you time to deal quietly and firmly with those resisting your authority and thus to establish your authority over them. Ignoring deliberately provocative remarks ('This is boring') can help you avoid confrontation. Try to motivate uninterested pupils by linking the work with their interests if possible. Letting them feel you are interested in them as people can promote positive relationships but you still should expect them to work. Ask your experienced colleagues for advice if particular pupils constantly cause you trouble. It is likely that they are also causing some other staff difficulties.

2 You are asked a question and you don't know the answer   This is bound to happen. You can admit you don't know – 'What an interesting point, I've not thought of it that way'; 'I just can't remember at the moment' – but make arrangements for the answer to be found. The pupil can follow it up for homework, use the library to look for the answer or write to those who might know. You may also be able to find out from other teachers, student teachers or your subject association.

3 You are asked personal questions   At some point you'll be asked 'Have you got a boyfriend/girlfriend? Are you a student (ask the school if you are to be introduced as a member of staff or a student)? Have you ever done this before? How old are you?' – or comments may be made about your car (or lack of one) or what you are wearing.

Don't allow yourself to be distracted from the work in the lesson. You can choose whether or not to answer personal questions but set boundaries beyond which you won't go. Often a joke deflects the questioner – 'Mine is the Rolls parked around the corner'. Offering to answer the question in the pupils' time, after the lesson, can lead to loss of interest on the part of the questioner.

4 A pupil swears   As a student teacher, you cannot solve all the problems of the pupils and the school. Usually if a pupil is asked to repeat what they said, they will omit the offensive word and will feel sufficiently rebuked. You will have indicated that swearing is unacceptable.

What you do need to do is to establish a line about what is acceptable and stick to it. Make it clear to your classes what your rule is and link it to school policy which should be 'no swearing'.

However, swearing at teachers or abusing other pupils are serious offences and you must take action. There are different ways in which you might react – depending on the pupils, the context, the school. You may require an apology or you may wish to take the matter further. Take advice from experienced teachers. Act in haste and repent at leisure is good advice for a student teacher. Take a little time to decide on the response. Letting a pupil know an act was unacceptable and that you are thinking about how to respond can be more effective than an ill-considered response from you at the time. Consistency in your approach to discipline is an important facet of establishing your reputation. You want the pupils to know that if they do X, which is unacceptable, some form of action, Y, will always follow. (This approach is an application of behaviourist learning theories (Unit 3.2) – you are teaching the pupils to understand that a certain negative action on their part **always** gets a certain negative response from you. Thus it is perfectly clear to them how to avoid a negative response.)

Task 2.3.4   **SWEARING**
Discuss the following two scenarios with the teachers with whom you're working. What is an appropriate response for you in each case?

1 You overhear a pupil use swear words in conversation with another pupil. The word is not used in an abusive way.
2 A child swears at another child or at you!

What are the routine responses for dealing with these incidents in your school?

---

5 Pupils are not properly equipped to do the work – they lack PE kit, pens, books, maths equipment   You should aim to get most of the class working so that you can then direct your attention to those who require individual attention. Many departments have systems in place for dealing with pupils' lack of kit and equipment. In the early days of your teaching, it can be less disruptive to your lesson for you simply to supply the missing item (pencil/paper) so you can keep the flow of the lesson going. But make sure you retrieve what you have loaned and indicate firmly that you expect pupils to provide their own.

Task 2.3.5	**PROCEDURES FOR DEALING WITH POORLY EQUIPPED PUPILS**

Find out whether there is a system in the department in which you are working for dealing with pupils who are not properly equipped. Plan how you can avoid this problem interfering with the smooth running of your lesson.

6 Equipment doesn't work   You must check equipment beforehand and, in any case, have an alternative lesson planned if your lesson is dependent on equipment working.

7 You have too much material   Pupils have to get to their next lesson on time and to have their break on time. So you must let them go on time! Five minutes or so before the end of a lesson (more if they have to change or put equipment away), pull the lesson together, reminding them of what's been achieved and what's expected in the way of homework, perhaps what's coming next. They then pack away and are ready to go at the correct time.

8 The pupils finish the work earlier than you had anticipated   Inevitably there will be occasions when you have time with a class which you didn't expect. The work may have been finished early or changes in arrangements meant you couldn't do what you had planned. This can be a worrying experience for a student teacher; however, such time can be used to educational advantage in a number of ways:

1 Have questions prepared relating to recent work in the area under study.
2 Do a quick test of the issues covered in the lesson or a spelling test of new words.
3 Use your lesson objectives to devise questions about the work.
4 Ask pupils to work in pairs or teams to devise questions to be put to the rest of the class or to other teams. Answers can be written in rough books with the pupils swapping books to mark them.
5 Work coming up in subsequent lessons can be introduced so that pupils can see the purpose in what they are doing now – remember repetition is an aid to learning. Introducing concepts briefly in one lesson means they will be more familiar when you go over them in depth later.
6 Pupils' existing knowledge on the next topics could be ascertained by question and answer. (Learning is more certain where you, as the teacher, build on pupils' existing knowledge and experience.)
7 You may take the opportunity to check the pupils' ability to apply a range of study skills. There are excellent books on this topic available through the major newsagents.

Plan together with the pupils ways of learning the work you've been covering, e.g. developing a spider diagram for summarising the key points in a topic in history or geography, producing a mnemonic to aid the recall of key issues (see Unit 5.2 for more ideas).

8   Homework (either past or just set) can be discussed in more detail. You may allow the pupils to discuss this together.

Or, in practical subjects:

9   You may ask pupils to repeat a sequence they've been working on in PE, perhaps extending it to incorporate another skill; to observe each other performing the sequence and to comment on the performance; or to demonstrate what is coming up in the next lesson.

10 Alternatively, if the class is new to you, you may take the opportunity to learn their names.

With experience, you acquire the skill of fitting work to the time available so the problem ceases to cause you anxiety.

MORE GENERAL CONCERNS

There are a number of more general concerns which most students feel at some point or another. We discuss these here so that by anticipating problems and posing solutions, you may be better prepared for dealing with them.

1 Maintaining good behaviour   This is cited as an area of concern by student teachers more often than any other area and Units 3.2 and 3.3 provide more detailed guidance. Various books listed in the Bibliography (Kyriacou, Cohen and Manion, Marland, Wragg, Robertson) also provide valuable advice. Pupils are influenced by your confidence, the material, the demands of the work and your ability to enforce rules. The first lesson may be a honeymoon period, where the pupils are sizing you up or on the other hand, they may test you out. If you insist (in a quiet firm way) that you are in charge of what happens in the classroom, then the vast majority of pupils will give way – as long as you are seen as fair and reasonable. Whilst it is important not to see the class as 'them' against 'you', adopting a 'divide and rule' strategy can pay dividends: praise those who work well and reward them – for example, with privileges or house points or merit slips – using the systems established within the school. Do not expect to win over all pupils immediately; some may take months; a few may never be won over. Discuss any difficulties you have with other teachers – it may be that they have effective strategies for dealing with the pupils who are giving you concern.

2 Defusing situations   Inexperienced teachers tend to reprimand pupils much more frequently than experienced teachers, probably because they have less well developed subtle control mechanisms (e.g. body language).
    Techniques used by teachers to defuse situations include:

- Anticipating changes of mood and concentration and moving the lesson on and perhaps increasing the pace of the lesson, e.g. 'Right, let's see what you've understood already . . .'.
- Scanning the class regularly, even when helping individuals or groups so that potential problems are prevented: 'That's enough, Julia' or 'Have you got a problem over there?' is usually sufficient to remind pupils to keep on task. Pupils will be impressed if you can see what they are doing without them realising you are looking at them. Standing in position at a pupil's desk perhaps towards the back of the room allows you to monitor the work of pupils close to you as well as to scan the rest of the class without them seeing you.
- Using humour to keep pupils on task – a knowledge of adolescent culture and local activities is useful: 'You're too busying thinking about what you'll be doing on Friday night to concentrate.'
- Using a whole range of non-verbal cues: posture, facial expressions, gestures, positioning in the classroom to reinforce your authority. The children will recognise these and you need to recognise them too (see Unit 3.1).

Notice that none of these techniques require the teacher to shout or to be angry in order to keep the children on task.

Task 2.3.6	**DEFUSING DIFFICULT SITUATIONS**

DEFUSING DIFFICULT SITUATIONS
We suggest that when you are observing experienced teachers you look specifically at how they defuse situations so that reprimands are not required. Note these in your diary.

3 Retrieving situations   You may have a poor lesson with a class. This doesn't mean that all lessons with that class will be like that. What it does mean, however, is that you must analyse the situation and put into place strategies for ensuring that the next lesson is better. Experienced colleagues should be able to give you advice. Observing an experienced teacher, even if in another discipline, teaching a group that you have difficulty with can be eye opening and can provide you with ideas for the way forward. Discuss what you've seen with the teacher. Ask someone to watch you teach the class with whom you are having difficulty and ask for suggestions about how you can improve.

4 Personal vulnerability, lack of self-belief and confidence   In becoming a teacher, you are more vulnerable than when being educated for many other professions as you are exposed to a discerning audience (the class) early on. So much of your performance in the classroom depends on your own personal qualities and your ability to form good relationships with pupils from a wide range of backgrounds. Your performance is analysed and commented on by those who observe your teaching. You are forced to face your own strengths and weaknesses as a result of this scrutiny. This can be stressful particularly when you may be given apparently conflicting advice from different observers. As you become more experienced and you develop more analytical skills for use in appraising your performance, you should build your self-belief and confidence.

5 *Dealing with your feelings*   Incidents will occur which leave you feeling deflated, unsure or angry. Try to adopt a problem-solving reflective approach to your work so that you maintain some objectivity and can learn from any difficult experiences you have. One group of PGCE students was asked, at the end of their year of initial teacher education, what advice they would give new student teachers. Above all else, they said, keep in touch with other students so that you can discuss your concerns with others in the same situation. It is likely that your concerns will also be the concerns of other student teachers.

6 *The challenge to your own values*   Most people mix with people who hold similar values and attitudes. As a teacher, you are dealing with children from different backgrounds and with different expectations about education and different values to your own. You need to consider how you can best provide equal opportunities in your classroom and what strategies you might use to motivate disaffected pupils. Chapter 4 provides further advice in these areas.

7 *Loss of books or equipment and breakages*   Schools have different approaches to dealing with loss and breakage of equipment by pupils should it occur. Seek advice from those with whom you are working. Anticipating and thus avoiding problems will make your life easier. The simple strategy of managing your lesson so that there is sufficient time at the end to check that equipment and books are returned saves you time in the long run.

8 *Having a ready answer*   There are a number of routine situations which can throw you off balance in the lesson, e.g. 'Someone's taken my pen/book', 'Sir, she did it too', 'Miss, he started it', 'But Miss, you let her go to the toilet', 'Do you like . . .' (and here they name a pop group about which they all know but of which you've never heard). Discuss these situations with other students and make notes for yourself about how you might deal with them. See how other teachers deal with these.

9 *Time and stress management*   These are important enough issues that unit 1.3 is devoted to them. Here we want to raise three points:

- giving the lesson is only one part of a teacher's job;
- preparing your first lessons takes you a long time;
- if you skimp on lesson preparation, then the stress level you experience in the lesson will be high as you will not feel in control.

Summary and key points

Your first encounters with the pupils are important in setting the tone for your relationships with them. It is worth carefully considering the image you wish to project in these early lessons and planning your work to help reinforce this image. If you want to create the image that you are a disorganised teacher who doesn't know what the lesson is about any more than the pupils do, then this is relatively easy to achieve. Your image is something you should create deliberately and not just allow it to happen.

Most student teachers have to work on controlling their nerves and developing their self-confidence. Covering the following points in your preparation should prevent some of the difficulties you would otherwise encounter:

- set clear, simple objectives for the lesson that are likely to be achieved;
- plan the lesson carefully and have extension work ready;
- know the class and obtain pupil lists;
- check the room layout: are things where you want them? What about safety issues?
- know the school, class and lesson routines;
- be on time;
- prepare board work beforehand if possible (check that it won't be rubbed off if there is a lesson before yours) or use a pre-prepared overhead projector transparency or worksheet;
- act as though you are in charge although you probably won't feel that you are;
- know the subject or make crib notes and put key points on the board or an overhead transparency if you're unsure;
- plan the rhythm of the lesson to give a balance between teacher talk and pupil activity;
- include a time line in your lesson plan so that you can check during the lesson how the plan is working. Try not to talk too quickly.
- be prepared to clamp down on misbehaviour. It is easier to reprimand one pupil who is misbehaving than to wait until they have goaded other pupils into following suit or retaliating.
- visualise yourself being successful;
- have a fallback plan for the lesson.

From the observations you've done, you should have established how other teachers deal with minor infringements of school rules – remember there are a number of types of reprimand you can use before you give out detentions.

One of your major problems may be believing that you are indeed a teacher. This is a mental and emotional transition which you need to make. The pupils, parents and staff usually see you as a teacher, albeit a new one and expect you to behave as such.

FURTHER READING

Buzan, T. (1984, 1995) *Use Your Memory*, London: BBC Books.

This is just one of Tony Buzan's books which are packed with ideas for improving memory. Why not draw them to the attention of your pupils?

The subject specific texts in the Learning to Teach series will provide you with further advice.

Some teachers join chat rooms or discussion groups or the Internet to discuss issues related to their teaching. We suggest you take care when using these as the discussions may be public and may be archived – hence what you say may be used for purposes you hadn't intended.

3 CLASSROOM INTERACTIONS AND MANAGING PUPILS

Effective classroom management is essential to effective learning. Classroom management refers to arrangements made by the teacher to establish and maintain an environment in which learning can occur, e.g. effective organisation and presentation of lessons so that pupils are actively engaged in learning. Classroom management skills and techniques are addressed throughout this book in a number of different chapters and units. This chapter includes three units about different aspects of classroom management related to interacting with pupils. Together they give an insight into the complex relationships which are developed between teachers and pupils, and emphasise the need for well-developed skills and techniques that you can adapt appropriately to the demands of the situation. They reinforce the fact that, although you must plan your lessons thoroughly, not everything you do in the classroom can be planned in advance, as you cannot predict how pupils will react in any situation on any given day.

Classroom interactions are based on verbal and non-verbal communication. Unit 3.1 is designed to help you communicate effectively in the classroom. It considers verbal communication, including listening skills and then non-verbal communication, both on its own and how it enhances or detracts from verbal communication. Non-verbal communication is addressed largely by considering how teachers present themselves to pupils.

In Unit 3.2 we consider aspects of motivating pupils. The unit starts by asking what motivation is and presents a number of theories of motivation. It then considers factors affecting motivation in the classroom, concentrating on the use of praise and punishment, feedback, and finally, motivating individuals.

We recognise student teachers' concerns about managing behaviour and misbehaviour. Our objective in Unit 3.3 is to help you address these concerns by focusing on managing pupils' behaviour. The unit emphasises the importance of preventing misbehaviour as far as possible (recognising that teachers cannot prevent all misbehaviour), but also being prepared to deal with misbehaviour that does occur. Thus, the unit also includes sections on managing behaviour problems and developing effective classroom management skills to prevent misbehaviour. We also consider the Elton Report *Discipline in Schools* (DES/WO, 1989) as this important document contains much valuable information and recommendations about all aspects of behaviour in schools.

3.1   COMMUNICATING WITH PUPILS

INTRODUCTION

> A teacher opens up unknown or only half suspected areas of skill or knowledge; he makes things clear; he makes things as simple as possible. He enables pupils to do more things and to do them better, to understand more things and to understand them better.
>
> (Marland, 1993, p. 11)

We can all think of teachers who achieved this and from whom we have learned a lot. These teachers may have been very different as people and as teachers, with different personalities and styles. Whatever their differences, they all had in common the ability to communicate effectively with pupils.

Communication is a two-way process involving the mutual exchange of information and ideas. This unit focuses on communication between the teacher and pupils. However, classroom communication can also be between pupil and pupil. Communication between pupils is also very important, as it can enhance or hinder learning in the classroom. Pupils can learn from communicating with each other, e.g. by talking about a task. Equally, such communication can be irrelevant to the lesson and may interfere with the progress of the lesson, therefore detracting from pupils' learning.

Most of us tend to think we communicate well. However, we may never have analysed our communication skills and when we study them systematically, most of us can find room for improvement. You cannot predict how pupils will react to an activity, a conversation or a question asked. In order to respond appropriately you need well-developed communication skills and techniques, combined with sensitivity and judgement. Your response, both verbally and non-verbally, in any classroom situation influences the immediate and, possibly, long-term relationship with the class.

Communication is a complex process which can occur in many different ways, e.g. written, verbal and non-verbal. In this unit we consider both verbal and non-verbal communication. First we consider aspects of verbal communication, including using your voice (volume, projection, pitch, speed, tone, clarity and expressiveness), the language you use and the importance of active listening. We then consider aspects of non-verbal communication, e.g. appearance, gesture, posture, facial expression and mannerisms, particularly in relation to how you present yourself as a teacher.

OBJECTIVES

By the end of the unit you should be able to:

- appreciate the importance of effective verbal and non-verbal communication skills;

- vary your voice consciously to enhance your teaching;
- appraise your use of language and use questioning more effectively as a teaching tool;
- understand the relationship between verbal and non-verbal communication;
- be aware of and have control over, your own self-presentation in order to present yourself effectively.

By meeting these objectives you will have addressed those course competences/ standards related to communication. Identify in your course handbook those competences/standards associated with communicating effectively and refer to these as you work through this unit.

VERBAL COMMUNICATION

Gaining attention

You need to establish procedures for gaining pupils' attention at the beginning of a lesson and also when you want the class to listen again after they have started an activity. This latter skill is especially important if there is a safety risk in the activity or lesson. Before you start talking to a class, make sure that all pupils can see and hear you, that you have silence and that they are paying attention. Establish a means of getting silence, e.g. say 'quiet please', clap your hands, blow a whistle in physical education or bang on a drum in music and use this with the class each time. Some teachers wait for quiet and do not speak until it is calm. Once you are talking, do not keep moving around because this distracts the pupils, who may pay more attention to the movement than to what you are saying.

Using your voice

A teacher's voice is a crucial element in classroom communication. It is like a musical instrument and if you play it well, then your pupils will be an appreciative and responsive audience. Some people have voices that are naturally easier to listen to than others. However, you can change the way you talk. Certain qualities are fixed and those give your voice its unique character, but there are many variations available and those variations lend impact to what you say. It is important to stress that you can change the way you talk. There are many different aspects of your voice that you can alter in order to use it more effectively, including volume, projection, pitch, speed, tone, clarity and expressiveness of the voice. You can practise each of these.

The most obvious way you can vary your voice is by altering the **volume**, by talking very quietly or very loudly. It is useful to have the whole volume range available but it is rarely a good thing to be loud when it is not needed. Having achieved silence, do not shout into it. Loud teachers have loud classes. If you shout too much, you may get into the habit of shouting all the time. It happens and sometimes people know somebody is a teacher because of their loud voice. Also, if you shout too much, you may lose your voice every September! Of course, you have to be heard, but this is done by projection more than by volume.

You **project** your voice by making sure it leaves your mouth confidently and precisely. This needs careful enunciation and breath control. If your voice is projected well, you are able to make a whisper audible at some distance. Equally, good projection brings considerable volume to your ordinary voice without resort to shouting or roaring.

Everybody varies the **pitch** of their voice naturally. Each group of words spoken has its own 'tune' which contributes to the meaning. A person may have a naturally high or low voice but that 'natural' pitch can be varied with no pain. Generally speaking, deep voices sound more serious and significant; high voices are more exciting and lively. To add weight to what is being said the pitch should be dropped; to lighten the tone the pitch should be raised. A lower voice can create a sense of importance. A voice with a lower pitch comes across as more authoritative and confident than a high-pitched voice. It can also be raised more easily to command attention, whereas raising a naturally high-pitched voice may result in something similar to a squeak, which does not carry the same weight.

Speed variations give contrast to delivery. You can use pause to good effect. It shows confidence if you can hold a silence before making a point or answering a question. Equally, have the patience to wait for a pupil to respond. Research suggests that three seconds is a reasonable time for any such pause. Speaking quickly can be a valuable skill on occasion. You need concentration and careful enunciation to speak quickly.

Task 3.1.1	THE QUALITY OF YOUR VOICE

Record your voice. You may want to read from a book or a newspaper or to record yourself in natural monologue or conversation. Play the recording back and listen to it with a friend or another student teacher. If you have not heard yourself before, the experience may be a little shocking! Your voice may sound different from the way you hear it and a common response is to blame the recording equipment. This is probably not at fault. Remember that you hear your voice coming back from your mouth. Most of your audience hear it coming forward. As you become used to listening to yourself, try to pick out the good points of your voice. Is it clear? Is it expressive? Is the basic pitch pleasant? When you have built up your confidence, consider areas for improvement. Do you normally speak too fast? Is the tone monotonous?

Repeat the task, but this time trying to vary your voice. For example, try reading at your normal speed, then faster, then as quickly as you can. Remember to start each word precisely and to concentrate on what you are saying. Then try varying the pitch of your voice. You will be surprised how easy it is. Ask another student teacher to listen to the tape with you, comment on any differences and provide any helpful advice for improving.

To use your voice effectively you need to consider the factors above together. For example, you do not communicate effectively if the pitch of your voice is right, but you are not speaking clearly or the volume is wrong, e.g. you are shouting at the group or pupils at the back cannot hear what you are saying. It is also important to put feeling into what you say. Often, pupils respond to HOW you say something rather than WHAT you say. If you are praising, sound pleased; if you are disciplining, sound firm. If you deliver all talk in the same way, do not be surprised if pupil response is undifferentiated.

Language of the teacher

A teacher's language must be accessible. There is no point in talking to pupils in language they do not understand. That does not mean subject vocabulary cannot be introduced, only that you must not assume that everybody knows the words or constructions that you do. All teachers are teachers of language; you gradually introduce your class to the language of the subject but to do this you must start with a simple direct language which makes no assumptions. Do not assume that pupils understand simple connecting phrases, e.g. 'in order to', 'so that', 'tends to', 'keep in proportion', etc.

It is easier for pupils to understand a new concept if you make comparisons or use examples or references to which they can relate. As a teacher your language must be concise. When you are speaking, you stress or repeat important words or phrases. That is important in teaching too. If they help learning, repetition and elaboration are valuable, but filling silence with teacher talk is generally unproductive. It is too easy for you to inflict your increasing eloquence on a captive audience. You take longer to deliver the same information and also pupils' time may not be used most effectively.

However, it is generally accepted that pupils understand something and learn it better if they hear it a number of times, therefore, as the Chinese proverb says, you should

*   tell them what you are going to tell them,
*   tell them,
*   then tell them again what you have told them.

Task 3.1.2	THE LANGUAGE OF YOUR SUBJECT

Write down a list of specialist words and phrases used in your subject or in a particular topic in your subject that you may be teaching. Think how many of these might be in the normal vocabulary of an average pupil at your school. Consider this aspect of your lesson planning carefully. How might you introduce and explain these words and phrases? How might you allow pupils opportunities to practise their use of the words in the lesson? Tape the lesson that you are teaching. After the lesson replay the tape and consider your use of language in the lesson, particularly those aspects identified above. It can be particularly helpful to listen to this with a student teacher learning to teach another subject who does not have the same subject knowledge and language that you are using and who therefore may be nearer to pupils' experience of the subject. Then consider whether you could have given the pupils the same information in a shorter time and whether you could have used the pupils' time more effectively.

A teacher's language is not just used to convey the subject. It is also used to create individual relationships with pupils which make them more interested in learning. Using pupils' names; showing interest in their lives outside the classroom; valuing their experience; all these are important in building a positive atmosphere for classroom learning (see Unit 3.2 on motivating pupils for further information).

Teachers also use language to impose discipline. Often, negative terms are used for this. This is not inevitable and a positive approach may have more success. For example, how about suggesting a constructive activity rather than condemning a destructive one? Could earlier praise or suggestion have made later criticism unnecessary? It is also important when disciplining a pupil to consider who else can hear, as a rebuke in public can have a negative influence on the pupil concerned (see Unit 3.3 on managing pupils' behaviour).

Types of communication

There are many different ways in which verbal communication is used in teaching. Three of these, explaining, questioning and discussion, are briefly considered below.

Explaining

Teachers spend a lot of time explaining to pupils. In some teaching situations it can be the main form of activity in the lesson. Explaining provides information about what, why and how, it describes new or clarifies the meaning of, terms or gives reasons.

Being able to explain something effectively is an important skill for teachers to acquire because pupils expect teachers to explain things clearly and become frustrated when they cannot understand an explanation. A good explanation is clear and well structured. It takes account of pupils' previous knowledge and understanding, uses language that pupils can understand, relates new work to concepts, interests or work already familiar to the pupils. A good explanation actively engages pupils in learning and therefore is able to gain and maintain the pupils' attention. Use of analogy or metaphor can also help an explanation. Pupils learn better if they are actively engaged in the learning process. You must plan to involve pupils, e.g. mix an explanation with tasks, activities or questions, rather than relying on long lectures, dictating notes or working out something on the board.

Task 3.1.3	**EXPLAINING**

EXPLAINING
Observe an experienced teacher and another student teacher explaining a subject to a group of pupils. Write down in your diary the techniques they use, e.g. relating the new work to something pupils have learned previously, using analogies or metaphors or by actively involving pupils by such techniques as questioning. Also write down how pupils respond to the explanation. Compare the outcomes of the two observations and discuss your notes with the teacher and student teacher.

Questioning

One technique for actively involving pupils in their learning is questioning. Teachers use a lot of questions in their teaching. Research suggests that it may be as many as 400 in an average day, which can be as much as 30% of teaching time (Wragg, 1984).

Asking questions effectively   In order to use questioning effectively in your classes you need to plan for this in your lessons and prepare the questions beforehand (see Unit 2.2 on lesson planning). To use questioning effectively you need to consider:

- why you are asking a question(s);
- what type of question(s) you are going to ask;
- when you are going to ask questions;
- how you are going to ask questions;
- of whom you are going to ask a question, how you expect the question answered, how you are going to respond if the pupil does not understand the question or gives an inappropriate answer and how long you are going to wait for an answer.

However, you cannot plan this rigidly; you must be flexible, adapting your plan during the lesson to take account of pupils' responses.

Asking questions is not a simple process. Questions are asked for many reasons, e.g. to get pupils' attention or check that they are paying attention, to check understanding of an instruction or explanation, reinforce or revise a topic, increase understanding, encourage thinking or develop a discussion. Perrott (1982) indicated that questions are asked to develop the six levels of thought processes described by Bloom (1956, see Perrott, 1982), i.e. knowledge, comprehension, application, analysis, synthesis or evaluation.

Questions can be categorised in different ways. One common way of categorising them is into open and closed questions.

Closed and open questions   The most common reason for asking questions is to check that pupils have learnt what they are supposed to have learnt or that they have memorised certain facts or pieces of information. These are questions like: What is the capital of Peru? What is the atomic weight of nitrogen? How many people are in a netball team? What do we call the main artery leading from the heart? How do you spell 'geranium'? These are called **closed** questions. There is only one correct answer to each of those questions. The pupil either knows the answer or not. No real thought is required. Pupils recall information rather than think about the answer. Closed questions might be given to the whole class, with answers coming instantaneously. A short question–answer session like that might reinforce learning, refresh pupils' memories or make a link to new work.

On the other hand, **open** questions may have several possible answers and it may be impossible to know if an answer is 'correct'. These questions are often used to develop understanding. Examples of open questions are: How could we reduce vandalism in cities? What sort of man is Hamlet? Why did the Roman Empire decline and fall? How might you defeat the offside trap in soccer? What words could you use to describe a wood in spring?

These questions are much more complex than the first set. The respondent has to think and manipulate information, e.g. reason or apply the information and use knowledge, logic and imagination to answer them. Open questions cannot usually be answered quickly. Pupils probably need time to gather information; sift evidence; advance hypotheses; discuss ideas; plan answers.

You can ask closed or open questions or a combination of the two as **a series of questions**. The questions in the series can start with a few relatively easy closed questions and then move onto more complex open questions. A series of such questions is designed to extend pupils' understanding of a topic. Such a series of questions take time to build up if they are to be an integral part of the learning process and therefore they must be planned as an integral part of the lesson. If they are put at the end of the lesson as a time filler, their effect is lost. Questions at the end of the lesson are much more likely to be closed–recall questions to help pupils remember what they have been taught in the lesson.

Questions can be asked to the whole class; to specific named individuals; or to groups. The questions can be spoken; written on a board; or given out on printed sheets. The answers can be spoken or written. They can be given at once or produced after deliberation. For example, you may set a series of questions for homework and either collect the answers in to mark or go through them verbally with the class at the start of the next lesson.

Effective questioning is a skill you must develop as a teacher. It requires you to be able to ask clear, appropriate questions, use pause to allow pupils to think about an answer before responding, use prompting to help pupils who are having problems to answer a question and use follow-up questions to probe further, encourage pupils to develop their answers, extend their thinking, change the direction of the questioning and involve the whole class by distributing questions around the class. Your non-verbal communication, e.g. eye contact, manner, tone of voice, is important in being able to question effectively.

Wragg (1984, p. 116) studied errors in questioning by student teachers. Errors of presentation, e.g. not looking at pupils when asking a question, talking too fast, at the wrong volume or not being clear, were identified by teachers as the most common errors. He considered that the ease of detection and of improvement of these errors may have contributed to them being identified as the most common errors. The second most common type of error was the way student teachers handled replies to questions, e.g. they only accepted answer(s) which they wanted or expected. You must avoid the guessing game type of question and answer session where the teacher has a fixed answer in mind and is not open to possible alternative answers. Pupils then spend their time guessing what the teacher wants. Other errors identified by teachers in this study were pupils not knowing why particular questions were being asked, student teachers not giving enough background information to enable pupils to answer questions, asking questions in a disjointed fashion rather than a logical sequence, jumping from one to the other without linking them together and tending to focus on a small group of pupils and ignoring the rest of the class. Teachers tended to focus on those pupils sitting in a V-shaped wedge in the middle of the room. Some aspects of questioning were not identified as common errors, but Wragg felt that this may be because they are difficult to detect and to correct, e.g. whether the vocabulary is appropriate for the pupils' level of understanding or whether they are too long, complex or ambiguous. It is as important to think about and develop these aspects of questioning as it is those which are more

> **Task 3.1.4**
>
> **QUESTIONING**
>
> Plan a lesson that incorporates a series of questions as described above, i.e. why, what, when, how, of whom you are going to ask the question, how you expect the question to be answered (write down as many appropriate and inappropriate answers as you can), how you are going to respond if the pupil does not understand the question or gives an inappropriate answer and how long you are going to wait for an answer. Ask your tutor to observe the lesson when you teach it, looking particularly at the effectiveness of the questioning. You may want to devise a list of questions for the observer, e.g. did the pupils understand the questions? Did a number of different pupils respond? Did the questions lead the pupils to a deeper level of understanding? Discuss the lesson with your tutor afterwards. Try to take account of that discussion when planning your next series of questions.

obvious.

The use of questioning in a lesson should not be considered in isolation; rather it should be considered in relation to the use of other teaching techniques. For example, you can encourage pupils to participate actively in questioning by listening and responding appropriately to answers, praising good answers, being supportive and respecting answers and not making pupils feel they will be ridiculed if they answer a question incorrectly (see Unit 3.2 on motivating pupils for further information).

Discussion

Questioning and discussion overlap and questioning may lead naturally into discussion in order to explore a topic further. The teacher is still in control of a discussion but, as pupils generally have some control over the direction of a discussion, they have more control over the material to be included than in many teaching situations. The relatively less structured atmosphere of a discussion can be used to encourage pupils to contribute more freely, as can suggestions or questions interjected by the teacher as appropriate. Again, the atmosphere of the class and the response of the teacher and other pupils all contribute to the success or otherwise of a discussion. To develop an effective discussion in a lesson takes planning, e.g. of seating arrangements, questions to stimulate discussion and how you are going to respond to different potential developments of the discussion so that as many pupils as possible should be able to make a contribution. Before you use discussion in your classes, it is wise to observe another teacher use this technique in their teaching. See also the Appendix to 4.5 called 'Handling Discussion' on p. 210.

Listening

Communication with pupils is not effective if you do not listen to and take account of the response. **Being able to listen effectively** is as important as being able to send the message effectively. Learn to recognise and be sensitive to whether or not a message has been received properly by the other person, e.g. you get a bewildered look or an inappropriate answer to a question. Be able to react appropriately, e.g. repeat the same question or rephrase the question. However, also reflect on why the communication was not effective, e.g. was the pupil not listening to you? If so, why? For example, the pupil had 'switched off' in a boring lesson or the question was worded poorly. It is all too easy to blame a pupil for not listening properly, but it may be that you had a large part to play in the breakdown of the communication. Do not assume that pupils have your grasp of meaning and vocabulary.

It is too easy to ask a question and then 'switch off' or think about the next question or the next part of the lesson while an answer is being given. This lack of interest conveys itself to the person speaking. It is distracting to know that the person you are talking to is not listening and not responding to what is being said. Good listening is an active process, with a range of non-verbal and verbal responses that convey the message to the person speaking that you are listening to what is being said. These include looking alert, looking at the person who is talking to you, smiling, nodding and making verbal signals to show you have received and understood the message or to encourage the person to continue, e.g. 'yes', 'I see what you mean', 'go on', 'Oh dear', 'mmmm', 'uh-huh'.

NON-VERBAL COMMUNICATION

Much teacher–pupil communication is non-verbal. Non-verbal communication includes your appearance, gestures, posture, facial expression and mannerisms. Non-verbal communication supports or detracts from verbal communication, depending on whether or not verbal and non-verbal signals match each other; for example, if you are praising someone and smiling and looking pleased or if you are telling them off and looking stern and sounding firm, you are sending a consistent message and are perceived as sincere. On the other hand, if you are smiling when telling someone off or are looking bored when praising someone, you are sending conflicting messages that cause confusion and misunderstanding. Robertson (1989, pp. 70–71) expresses this very well:

> When non-verbal behaviour is not reinforcing meaning, . . . , it communicates instead the speaker's lack of involvement. Rather than being the message, it becomes the message about the messenger.

Effective communication therefore relies not only on appropriate content, but also on the way it is presented.

Non-verbal communication can have a considerable impact without any verbal communication, e.g. by looking at a pupil slightly longer than you would normally, you indicate your awareness that they are talking or misbehaving. This may be enough to make the pupil stop. You can indicate your enthusiasm for a topic by the way you use gestures. You can probably think of a teacher who stands at the front of the class leaning against the board with arms crossed waiting for silence, the teacher marching down between the desks to tell someone off or the teacher who sits and listens attentively to the problems of a particular pupil. The meaning of the communication is very clear and there is no need to say anything. Thus, non-verbal communication is important for good communication, classroom management and control.

Task 3.1.5	**IMPROVING YOUR VERBAL AND NON-VERBAL COMMUNICATION**

Develop two lists, one of matching verbal and non-verbal communications, the other of ones that do not match. There are some examples given above to help you start on this list. Practise those that are matching and then ask your tutor or another student teacher to observe whether your verbal and non-verbal communication match in your teaching. You can give the observer the list generated above as a starting point. After the lesson discuss the outcome with the observer and then try to identify areas where you can overcome problems of non-matching verbal and non-verbal communication. Practise these and then ask the observer to observe another lesson to see if you have improved.

PRESENTING YOURSELF EFFECTIVELY

There might seem to be some contradiction in including this section as it could indicate that there is a correct way to present yourself as a teacher. However, the title clearly refers to you as an individual, with your own unique set of characteristics. Herein lies one of the keys to effective teacher self-presentation: while there are some common constituents, it is also the case that every teacher is an individual and brings something of their own unique personality to the job.

Initial impressions are important and the way you present yourself to a class on first meeting can influence the class and their learning over a period of time. A teacher's appearance is an important part of the impression created, as pupils expect all teachers to wear clothes that are clean, neat and tidy and certain teachers to wear certain types of clothes, e.g. it is acceptable for a physical education teacher but not a history teacher to wear a tracksuit. Thus, first impressions have as much to do with non-verbal as with verbal communication, although both are important considerations.

How teachers follow up the first impression is equally important, e.g. whether you treat pupils as individuals, how you communicate with pupils, whether you have any mannerisms such as constantly flicking a piece of hair out of your eyes or saying 'er' or 'OK' frequently when you are talking, which reduce or prevent effective communication (pupils tend to focus on any mannerism rather than on what is being said and they may even count the number of times you do this!). It is generally agreed that effective teaching depends on and is enhanced by self-presentation that is **enthusiastic**, **confident** and **caring**. Why are these attributes important? How can you work towards making these part of your self-presentation as a teacher?

Enthusiasm

One of the tasks of a teacher is to enable pupils to learn to do or understand something. Before many young people will make an effort to get to grips with something new, the teacher needs to 'sell' it to them as something interesting and worthwhile. Your enthusiasm for your subject is very infectious.

Task 3.1.6	CONVEYING ENTHUSIASM 1

CONVEYING ENTHUSIASM 1
Think back to teachers you have worked with and identify some whose enthusiasm for their subject really influenced your learning. Discuss your recollections with another student teacher and consider how these teachers' enthusiasm was evident. Try out some of these teachers' strategies with classes you are teaching.

There are perhaps three principal ways in which you can communicate enthusiasm. These include both verbal and non-verbal communication. The first is via **facial expression**. Robertson (1989, p. 64) described this as:

> An enthusiastic speaker will be producing a stream of facial expressions which convey his excitement, disbelief, surprise or amusement about his message. Some expressions are extremely brief, lasting about one fifth of a second and may highlight a particular word, whereas others last much longer, perhaps accompanying the verbal expression of an idea. The overall effect is to provide a running commentary for the listener on how the speaker feels about the ideas expressed. In contrast, a speaker who is not involved in his subject shows little variation in facial expression. The impression conveyed is that the ideas are brought out automatically and are failing even to capture the attention of the speaker.

The second is via the **use of your voice**. The manner in which you speak as a teacher gives a very clear indication of how you feel about the topic under debate and is readily picked up by pupils. See the section above about using your voice.

A third way to convey enthusiasm is via your **poise and movement**. An enthusiastic speaker has an alert posture and uses gestures in an animated fashion.

| Task 3.1.7 | CONVEYING ENTHUSIASM 2 |

CONVEYING ENTHUSIASM 2

Ask your tutor or another student teacher to observe a lesson and grade you A, B or C for enthusiasm in self-presentation, looking at facial expression, voice, poise/movement in turn. You may like to use an observation table as shown in the example below:

	Facial expression	Voice	Poise/Movement
e.g. Welcome to the class	B	B	C
Lesson introduction	C	C	C
Instructions for first task	B	B	C

Remember that your enthusiasm should be evident at all times, not only when you are presenting material but also when you are commenting on a pupil's work, particularly perhaps when the pupil has persevered or achieved a goal. Enthusiasm should be sustained throughout the lesson. Discuss the results and try to improve your rating in two or three further lessons.

Confidence

It is of paramount importance that as a teacher you present yourself with confidence. This is easier said than done because confidence relates both to a sense of knowledgeable mastery of the subject matter being worked on and to a sense of assurance of being in control over the classroom conduct of the pupils.

There is an irony in pupils' response to teacher confidence. For pupils this expression of authority is part of the role they expect of a teacher, and where this confidence is in evidence, pupils feel at ease and reassured. In fact, pupils prefer the security of a confident teacher. However, it is in young people's nature to attempt to undermine authority if they sense at any time that a teacher is unsure or apprehensive.

The key to confident self-presentation is to be well planned, both in respect of material and in all areas related to organisation (see Unit 2.3 on taking responsibility for whole lessons for further information). Of course, in many cases it is experience that brings confidence but sadly pupils seldom allow that to influence their behaviour. Without the benefit of experience it is of course true that all your excellent plans may not work, for one reason or another and you may have no alternative 'up your sleeve'. Whatever happens you need to cultivate a confident exterior, even if it is something of an act and you are feeling far from assured inside.

How is confidence conveyed? Confidence can be conveyed verbally and non-verbally. Verbally it is displayed in clear, purposeful instructions and explanations that are not disrupted by hesitation. Instructions given in a direct and business-like manner, such as 'John, please collect the scissors and put them in the red box', convey a sense of confidence. On the other hand, put in the form of a question, such as 'John will you collect the scissors and put them in the red box?' can convey a sense of your being less assured, not being confident that, in fact, John WILL co-operate. There is also the possibility of the pupil saying 'No'! Your voice needs to be used in a firm, measured manner. A slower, lower, well-articulated delivery is always more authoritative and displays more confidence than a fast, high-pitched method of speaking. Use of voice is particularly important in giving key instructions, especially where safety factors are involved and in taking action to curtail inappropriate pupil behaviour. This is perhaps the time to be less enthusiastic and animated and more serious and resolute in your manner.

Task 3.1.8	CONFIDENCE

CONFIDENCE
Tape-record a lesson in which you are involved in a variety of verbal inputs. After the lesson, listen to the tape yourself and decide if you sound confident and enthusiastic and if your voice is appropriate. Discuss with a colleague whether the principal message you are giving on the tape is one of confidence and enthusiasm. Remember also that there could be a danger of 'going over the top' when showing enthusiasm. If you are overexcited it can give the episode a sense of triviality, so the enthusiasm has to be measured.

Non-verbally confidence is expressed via tone of voice, posture, movement and eye contact, both in their own right and as an appropriate accompaniment to verbal language. There is nothing agitated about the movement of confident people. They tend to stand still and to use their arm gestures to a limited extent to reinforce the message being conveyed.

Eye contact is a crucial aspect of conveying confidence to pupils. A nervous person avoids eye contact, being somehow afraid to know what others are thinking, not wanting to develop a relationship that might ultimately reveal their inability or weakness. It is clearly your role as a teacher to be alert at all times to pupil reaction and to be striving to develop a relationship with pupils that encourages them to seek your help and advice. Steady, committed eye contact is usually helpful for both of these objectives. You must also recognise that the use of eye contact is regarded differently by people of different cultures, e.g. some members of some cultures avoid use of eye contact (this also applies to other aspects of non-verbal communication, such as proximity to another person). You should therefore take into account cultural sensitivities. Take advice from your tutor, a staff member of that culture, staff at the local multicultural centre or the Commission for Racial Equality (see the address in Appendix 5).

USING EYE CONTACT
During one day of teaching make a conscious effort to look pupils in the eye while you are giving whole class instructions or explanations, taking account of cultural differences in eye contact. Ask your tutor or another student teacher to observe only this aspect of your teaching and give you feedback as to how successful you are being.

Caring

It is perhaps not surprising that young people feel that a **caring** approach is important in developing an effective relationship with teachers. In a piece of research reported in Wragg (1984, p. 82) children were found to favour teachers who were 'understanding, friendly and firm'. Many more pupils indicated that this was their preference over 'efficient, orderly and firm' and 'friendly, sympathetic and understanding'. It is interesting to note that firmness is also a preferred characteristic.

Notwithstanding young people's preferences, interest in pupils as individuals and in their progress is surely the reason most teachers are in teaching. Your commitment to pupils' well-being and learning should be evident in all aspects of your manner and self-presentation. While this attitude goes without saying, it is not as straightforward as it sounds as it demands sensitivity and flexibility. In a sense it is you as the teacher who has to modify your behaviour in response to the pupils (rather than it always being the pupil who has to fall into line with everything asked for by the teacher). There is obviously a potential conflict between firm confidence and flexible empathy. It is perhaps one of the challenges of teaching to find the correct balance between these two and to be able to display each at the appropriate time.

A caring approach is evident from a range of features of teaching, from efficient preparation through to sensitive interpersonal skills such as listening. Those teachers who put the interests of the pupils above everything have taken the time and trouble to prepare work thoroughly in a form appropriate to the class. Similarly the classroom environment shows thoughtful design and organisation.

In the teaching situation, caring teachers are fully engaged in the task at hand, observing, supporting, praising, alert to the class climate and able to respond with an appropriate modification in the programme if necessary. Above all, however, caring teachers know the pupils by name, remember their work, problems and progress from previous lessons and are prepared to take time to listen to them and talk about personal things as well as work. In other words, caring teachers show a real sensitivity to pupils' individual needs.

⁞ Summary and key points

As teachers you can improve your ability to communicate, as the techniques and skills can be learned and practised. Good communication is essential for developing good relationships with pupils, a positive classroom climate and effective teaching. This unit has aimed to help you identify both the strengths and weaknesses in your communication and provide the basis for further development. Your developing professional knowledge and judgement should enable you to use these skills sensitively and to best advantage.

FURTHER READING

Kyriacou, C. (1986) *Effective Teaching in Schools*, Oxford: Basil Blackwell. Chapter 4.

This chapter looks at setting up the learning experience, including giving an explanation, questioning and discussion as part of teacher exposition.

Perrott, E. (1982) *Effective Teaching*, London: Longman. Chapters 4 and 5.

Chapter 4 looks at lower order questions which require pupils to recall information and higher order questions which require pupils to manipulate information for some purpose. Chapter 5 builds on this by looking at a questioning strategy needed to help pupils develop skills in higher order thinking.

Robertson, J. (1989) *Effective Classroom Control: Understanding Pupil–Teacher Relationships (2nd edition)*, London: Hodder and Stoughton.

This book looks at relationships between teachers and pupils. It considers this in different ways, but includes sections on expressing your authority, establishing authority in first meetings and conveying enthusiasm. The sections consider effective non-verbal communication in these relationships.

3.2   MOTIVATING PUPILS

INTRODUCTION

Pupils' attitudes to school and motivation to learn are a result of a number of factors, including past experiences, future expectations, family background, peer group, teachers, school ethos, culture and class. The link between motivation and educational performance is complex.

Some pupils have a more positive attitude to school and to learning, e.g. it is valued at home or they see a link between education and a job. These pupils are therefore more likely to work hard, behave in the classroom and succeed in education. Many pupils want to learn but depend on teachers to get them interested in a subject at school. Even though some pupils may not be inherently motivated to learn, the school ethos, teachers' attitudes, behaviour, personal enthusiasm (see Unit 3.1 on 'Communicating with Pupils'), teaching style and strategies in the classroom can increase their motivation to learn. Pupils not motivated to learn are more likely to misbehave. If the teacher does not manage the class and their behaviour effectively, the learning of all pupils in the class can be negatively affected.

Thus, a central aim for a teacher is to motivate pupils to learn. There are a range of techniques you can use to increase pupils' motivation to learn, for example:

- showing your enthusiasm for a topic, subject or teaching;
- treating each pupil as an individual;
- providing quick feedback by marking work promptly;
- rewarding appropriate behaviour.

In order to use such techniques effectively you need to understand why each technique is used. A study of motivation is therefore crucial to give you some knowledge and insight into ways of motivating pupils to learn. There is a wealth of material available on motivation. This unit tries to draw out some of the material we feel is of most benefit to you as a student teacher.

OBJECTIVES

By the end of the unit you should be able to:

- understand the role and importance of motivation for effective teaching and classroom management;
- appreciate some of the key elements of motivation for effective teaching;
- understand how to motivate pupils effectively.

By completing this unit you will have addressed some of the competences/standards expected of you as a newly qualified teacher. Refer to the competences/standards for your course now and identify those implicitly or explicitly related to motivation of pupils.

WHAT IS MOTIVATION?

Child (1993, p. 35) said that motivation comprises 'internal processes which spur us on to satisfy some need'. Motivation can be intrinsic (motivation from within the person rather than from someone else, e.g. a sense of achievement at having completed a difficult piece of work) or extrinsic (motivation from someone else, e.g. praise from a teacher for good work). Research has shown that intrinsic motivation is generally more motivating than extrinsic motivation and is therefore to be encouraged in learning.

A teacher's job would certainly be easier if all pupils were motivated intrinsically. However, pupils are asked to do many activities at school which are new to them, which are difficult, at which they may not be immediately successful or which they may perceive to be of little or no relevance to them. In order to become intrinsically motivated, pupils need encouragement along the way, e.g. written or verbal praise for effort, making progress or success, feedback on how they are doing or an explanation of the relevance of the work. Teachers can deliberately plan such extrinsic motivators into their lessons. Developing motivation is part of good formative assessment (see Units 6.1 and 6.2).

What motivates people?

The activities that people start and continue and the amount of effort they put into those activities at any particular time are determined by their motivation. Pupils may be motivated by a number of factors. These include:

- achievement (e.g. completing a piece of work which has taken a lot of effort);
- pleasure (e.g. getting a good mark or praise from a teacher for a piece of work);
- preventing or stopping less pleasant activities (e.g. avoiding getting a detention);
- satisfaction (e.g. feeling that you are making progress);
- success (e.g. doing well in a test).

It is often very difficult for a teacher to identify what is motivating a particular pupil at a particular time or indeed for a pupil to identify exactly what is motivating her. As a teacher you can often only infer whether or not pupils are motivated by observing their behaviour; for example, a pupil who is not motivated may not be listening to what you are saying, is talking, looking bored or staring out of the window. Low motivation may result from a number of factors, e.g. boredom or a task being too difficult.

Theories of motivation

There are a number of theories of motivation. In addition, we adopt our own, often unconscious, theories. Examples of theories of motivation, along with some of their implications for you as a teacher in determining learning activities, are given in Table 3.2.1.

Below are several tasks to help you think about the application of these theories. Record the outcomes in your diary so that you can compare these theories of motivation.

Table 3.2.1 Theories of motivation and their implications for you as a teacher

Theory	Author and date	Main points	Implications for teachers
Theory *x* and theory *y*	McGregor, 1960	*Theory x* managers assume that the average worker is lazy, lacks ambition, is resistant to change, self-centred and not very bright.	You may treat pupils differently, depending on whether you inherently believe in theory *x* or theory *y*.
		Theory y managers assume that the average worker is motivated, wants to take responsibility, has potential for development and works for the organisation. Any lack of ambition or resistance to change comes from experience.	A *theory x* teacher externally motivates pupils by directing, controlling their actions, persuading, rewarding and punishing them to modify their behaviour.

A *theory y* teacher encourages intrinsic motivation by allowing pupils to develop for themselves. |
| Achievement motivation | Atkinson, 1964 McClelland, 1961 | Motivation to perform an achievement-orientated task is related to (i) the need to achieve on a particular task, (ii) expectation of success on the task and (iii) the strength of the incentive after the task has been successfully completed. | Plan tasks that are challenging but attainable with effort. Work should be differentiated according to individual needs. Tasks on which pupils expect to achieve approximately 50% of the time are the most motivating. Also need to plan for the loss of motivation if pupils fail (up to 50% of time). |
| Attribution theory | Weiner, 1972 | Success or failure is attributed to ability, effort, difficulty of task or luck, depending on (i) previous experience of success or failure on the task, (ii) the amount of work put in or (iii) a perceived relationship between what is done and success or failure on the task. | Reward effort as well as success, as pupils are more likely to try if they perceive success is due to effort, e.g. can give two marks for work, one for standard of the work, the other for effort. Use teaching and assessment which is individualised rather than competitive. |

Expectation theory	Rogers, 1982	Teachers' expectations of pupils' performance can influence the way pupils perform, their motivation to learn and how they attribute success or failure. Pupils perform in the way they are expected to perform by teachers.	Pupils perform according to expectations of them. Do not prejudge pupils on their past performance so that you convey your expectations (high or low) of them. Rather, encourage pupils to work to the best of their ability all the time.
Hierarchy of needs theory	Maslow, 1970	Hierarchy (highest to lowest): 1 Self-actualisation (need to fulfil own potential) 2 Self-esteem (need to feel competent and gain recognition from others) 3 Affiliation and affection (need for love and belonging) 4 Need for physical and psychological safety 5 Physiological needs (e.g. food, warmth) Energy is spent meeting the lowest level of unmet need.	If basic needs, e.g. sleep, food, warmth, are not met, a pupil concentrates on meeting that need first and is unlikely to benefit from attempts by teachers to meet higher level needs. Try to create a classroom environment to fulfil basic needs first, e.g. rules for using dangerous equipment provide a sense of physical safety, routines give a sense of psychological security, group work can give a sense of belonging (affiliation) (Postlethwaite 1993).
Behavioural learning theories	Skinner, 1953	Activity or behaviour is learned and maintained because of interaction with the environment. An activity or behaviour reinforced by a pleasurable outcome is more likely to be repeated.	Positive reinforcement (reward), e.g. praise, generally increases motivation to learn and behave. This has a greater impact if the reward is relevant to the pupils, they know how to get the reward and it is given fairly and consistently.

Task 3.2.1   THEORY *x* AND THEORY *y*

In two columns, write down your general assumptions about (i) people you work with and (ii) pupils in classes you teach, using assumptions from theory *x* and theory *y* in Table 3.2.1. Do you have the same assumptions for both sets of people? Which theory do you tend towards? Write down in the same two columns anything you can about your approach to people you are working with or to your teaching. Reflect on these as you read through this unit to see if you are using the most appropriate and effective methods of motivation.

| Task 3.2.2 | **ACHIEVEMENT MOTIVATION** |

Discuss with your tutor how you can differentiate work so that all pupils in a mixed ability class can perceive that they can succeed approximately 50% of the time in line with achievement motivation theory. How is the work modified to enable each pupil to be able to succeed? What can you do to prevent loss of motivation if pupils are not successful in this work?

| Task 3.2.3 | **ATTRIBUTION THEORY OF MOTIVATION** |

Reflect on one aspect of your educational performance in which you have had success and one in which you were not as successful. In relation to attribution theory, for each of these, reflect on (i) to what you attribute your success or not, (ii) whether you expect certain grades from assignments and (iii) to what you attribute unexpected grades: ability, effort, difficulty of the task or luck.

It is generally accepted that pupils are more likely to try harder if they can see a link between the amount of effort they put in and success in the activity. Therefore, as a teacher you should design activities which encourage pupils to attribute success or failure to effort. However, this is not always easy. Postlethwaite (1993) identified the difficulty of determining how much effort a pupil has put into a piece of work (especially that done at home) and hence the problems of marking the work. You can no doubt think of occasions where one person has put in a lot of effort on a piece of homework, but missed the point and received a low mark, whereas another person has rushed through the homework and managed to achieve a good mark. In 'norm-referenced' marking a mark is given solely for the level of performance on a piece of work in relation to the level of performance of the rest of the group. A certain percentage of the class get a designated category of mark, no matter how good each individual piece of work. This encourages success or failure to be attributed to ability or luck. In 'criterion-referenced' marking, pupils' work is not compared to allocate marks. Rather, pupils are given a mark which reflects how closely the criteria for the assessment have been met, irrespective of the performance of other pupils. Thus, all pupils who meet stated criteria for a particular category of mark are marked in that category. Although this overcomes some of the disadvantages of norm-referenced marking, it does not reflect how much effort the pupil has put into the work (see also Units 6.1 and 6.2 on assessment).

Postlethwaite went on to say that effort can best be judged by comparing different pieces of the same pupils' work, as the standard of work is likely to reflect the amount of effort put in. Effort can be encouraged by giving two marks for the work, one for content and standard of the work and one for effort and presentation. Thus, even if the content and standard are poor, it may be possible to praise the effort. This praise can motivate the pupil to try harder, especially if the mark for effort is valued by pupils. He suggested that another way of encouraging pupils to attribute success to effort is to ask them to write about the way they tackled the task.

Expectation theory says that a teacher forms an impression of a pupil on which expectations of that pupil are based; the teacher's verbal and non-verbal behaviour is based, consciously or unconsciously, on those expectations; the pupil recognises, consciously or unconsciously, the teacher's expectations of them from the teacher's behaviour; and responds in a way that matches the teacher's behaviour and expectations of them (Rogers, 1982). It is generally accepted that if a teacher expects high achievement and good behaviour, pupils perform to the best of their ability and behave well. If, on the other hand, teachers have low expectations of pupils' work and behaviour, pupils achieve little and behave badly. In the same way, teachers can develop stereotypes of how different groups of pupils perform or behave; stereotypes can direct expectations (see Gillborn and Gipps, 1996, Chapter 4).

One aspect of the organisation of a school that may particularly influence teachers' expectations of pupils is the way pupils are grouped. If pupils are streamed by ability they remain in the same group throughout the year, whatever their ability in different subjects. Whatever the labels attached to each stream, pupils are perceptive and judge their abilities by the stream they are in. This may be partly because teachers' verbal and non-verbal behaviour communicates clearly their expectations. Teachers expect pupils in the 'top' stream to do well; therefore they behave accordingly, e.g. actively encouraging pupils, setting challenging work. Teachers expect pupils in the 'bottom' stream not to do as well; therefore they behave accordingly, e.g. constantly nagging pupils, setting easy work (or none at all). Both groups of pupils tend to fulfil the expectations of teachers. No doubt many of you have heard of the notorious 'bottom' stream in a school. Problems of streaming can be overcome by setting pupils for different subjects, i.e. recognising pupils' ability in different subjects and changing the grouping of pupils according to their ability

Task 3.2.4   EXPECTATION THEORY AND YOUR TEACHING
Reflect on whether your expectations of, and behaviour towards, pupils have been influenced by previous knowledge (given to you by the teacher) about the ability or behaviour of particular pupils in a class you are teaching. Ask someone to observe a class you are teaching, looking specifically to see if your behaviour indicates that you might have different expectations of pupils. Discuss their observations.

Task 3.2.5   HIERARCHY OF NEEDS THEORY
Consider some of the home and school conditions likely to leave pupils with unmet needs when they come to school which prevent effective learning (according to the hierarchy of needs theory (Maslow, 1970)). Discuss with your tutor or another student teacher what you can do in your lessons that may help pupils to meet these basic needs to provide a foundation for effective learning. Discuss when and to whom you should report if you suspect pupils' most basic needs are not being met, as this may require the skills of other professionals.

in a specific subject. The problems can also be overcome by grouping pupils in mixed ability classes and providing differentiated work within the class to enable pupils of different abilities to work alongside each other (for further information about this see Unit 4.1 on differentiation).

Rewards

Four types of **reward** (positive reinforcements) have been identified (Bull and Solity, 1987). These are listed below in the order in which they are most often used:

- social rewards (social contact and pleasant interactions with other people, including praise, a smile to recognise an action or achievement or to say thank you, encouraging remarks or a gesture of approval);
- token rewards (house points, grades, certificates);
- material rewards (tangible, usable or edible items);
- activity rewards (opportunities for enjoyable activities).

Task
3.2.6

USING REWARDS
Develop an observation schedule which has sections for the four types of reward listed above. Observe a class and mark in the appropriate category any reward used by the teacher in the class. Discuss with the teacher the variety and frequency of use of the different possible methods of reward. Ask your tutor or another student teacher to undertake the same observation on one of your lessons. Discuss the differences in variety and frequency of reward used. As you plan your lessons consider how you might use reward in the lesson. Ask the same person to observe a lesson a couple of months after the first one and see if you have changed your use of reward in your lessons. Relate this to what you know about behavioural learning theories.

Factors influencing motivation to learn

Success

Success is generally motivating in itself. Some pupils struggle to succeed, whereas others succeed much more quickly. There are many ways to help pupils succeed, e.g. using a technique often called whole–part–whole teaching. In this, pupils are shown the whole activity first so that they know what they are trying to achieve. The activity is then broken down into small, self-contained, achievable parts, which allow pupils to receive reinforcement for each small, successful step. Pupils gradually build up the whole from these small steps; therefore when they attempt the whole, they are most likely to succeed. You may relate to this by thinking about when you learned (or tried to learn) front crawl in swimming. You probably practised your arms, legs and breathing separately before you tried to put it all together. What other techniques can you use to help pupils succeed?

> **Task 3.2.7**   **WHOLE–PART–WHOLE TEACHING**
> As part of your normal lesson planning with a class, select one activity which you can break down into small, self-contained, achievable parts, which can be put together to build up gradually to the whole. Ask your tutor or another student teacher to observe you teaching this activity. Show the class the whole activity first and then gradually teach the separate parts of the activity, giving pupils appropriate feedback at each stage (see below for more information about giving feedback), until you have built up the whole activity. At the end of the lesson discuss how this went with some of the pupils. Discuss with the observer how the pupils responded and how well they learned the task.

Praise

Research findings show that pupils generally respond more positively to praise and positive comments about their work or behaviour than to criticism and negative comments. This, in turn, may produce a more positive atmosphere, in which pupils work harder and behave better. If pupils do misbehave in such an atmosphere, Olweus (1993, p. 85) suggested that the use of praise makes pupils feel appreciated and relatively well liked, which may make it easier for them to accept criticism of inappropriate behaviour and to attempt to change.

Research has also shown that teachers give relatively little praise. OFSTED (1993) reported that teachers' vocabulary is generally more negative than positive. Praise is given more often for academic than social behaviour and social behaviour is more likely

> **Task 3.2.8**   **THE LANGUAGE OF PRAISE**
> Draw up an observation schedule that has categories for praise given to an individual, a group or the whole class and negative comments to an individual, a group or the whole class, for both academic work and social behaviour. Observe a class taught by an experienced teacher. Sit in a place where you can hear everything that is said. Record the number of times praise is given and the number of times negative comments are made in each of the categories given above. Observe the same experienced teacher in another lesson. This time write down the different words, phrases and actions the teacher uses to give praise and negative comments in each of these categories and the number of times each is used.
>
> Ask someone to conduct the same observations on your lessons. You might be surprised to find that you use a phrase such as 'good' or 'OK' very frequently in your teaching. Discuss the differences with your tutor and develop strategies to help you improve the amount of praise you give, the range of words, phrases and actions you use to give praise, if appropriate. Record these strategies in your diary and gradually try to incorporate them into your teaching.

to be criticised than praised, maybe because teachers expect pupils to behave appropriately in the classroom.

Some teachers use very few different words to praise pupils, e.g. 'good', 'well done', 'OK'. What other words can you use to praise someone or give feedback? Try to develop a list of such words because if you use the same word to praise pupils all the time, the word loses its effect. The range of words must be accompanied by appropriate non-verbal communication signals (see Unit 3.1 on communicating with pupils for more information about non-verbal communication).

Although it is generally accepted that praise aids learning, there are dangers in using praise. There are times when it may not be appropriate to use praise. For example, pupils who become lazy about their work as a result of complacency may respond by working harder if their work is gently criticised on occasion. If praise is given automatically, regardless of the work, effort or behaviour, pupils quickly see through it and it loses its effect. Praise should only be used to reward appropriate work, effort or behaviour.

Some pupils do not respond positively to praise, e.g. they are embarrassed by praise, especially if they are praised in front of their peers. Others perceive praise to be a form of punishment, e.g. if they are teased or rejected by their peers for 'being teacher's pet' or for behaving themselves in class. Other pupils do not know how to respond to praise because they have not received much praise in the past; for example, because they have continually received low marks for their work or because they have been in the bottom stream, they have therefore learned to fail. Some of these pupils may therefore want to account for their failing as a result of not caring or not trying to succeed. One way they may do this is by misbehaving in the classroom.

Thus, pupils respond differently to praise. In the same class you may have some pupils working hard to get praise from the teacher or a good mark on their homework, whilst others do not respond well to praise or are working hard at avoiding praise. You have to use your judgement when giving praise; for example, if you praise a pupil who is misbehaving to try to encourage better behaviour, you may be seen to be rewarding bad behaviour, thereby motivating the pupil to continue to misbehave in order to get attention. If you are not immediately successful in your use of praise, do not give up using praise, but consider whether you are giving it in the right way, e.g. would it be better to have a quiet word, rather than praise pupils out loud in front of their peers? As your professional knowledge and judgement develop you become able to determine how best to use praise appropriately to motivate pupils in your classes.

Punishment

Teachers use both praise and punishment to try to change behaviour. However, reward, most frequently in the form of praise, is generally considered to be more effective because it increases appropriate behaviour, whereas punishment decreases inappropriate behaviour. If pupils are punished they know what behaviour results in punishment and therefore what not to do, but may not know what behaviour avoids punishment.

However, there are times when punishment is needed. At such times, make sure that you use punishment to best effect; for example, avoid punishing a whole class for the behaviour of one or a few pupil(s), always make it clear which pupil(s) are being punished for what behaviour, always give punishment fairly and consistently and in proportion to the offence. Do not make idle threats to pupils, by threatening them with punishment that you cannot carry out. In order to increase appropriate behaviour, identify to the offender any positive aspects of the behaviour being punished and explain the appropriate behaviour. Unit 3.3 provides further information on reprimanding pupils and managing behaviour problems.

Feedback

It may be that pupils who do not respond positively to praise are underperforming and have been doing so for a long time. You may be able to check whether they are underperforming by referring to the standard assessment data held on pupils when they enter the school. Such pupils and others benefit from being given feedback on how they are doing, as it helps pupils to know whether they are on the right track when learning something. Feedback gives pupils information about how they are doing and motivates them to continue. A pupil is more likely to learn effectively or behave appropriately if feedback is used in conjunction with praise. A sequence in which feedback is sandwiched between praise, i.e. praise–constructive feedback–praise, is designed to provide encouragement and motivation, along with information to help the pupil improve the activity. Giving praise first is designed to make pupils more receptive to the information and, afterwards, to have a positive approach to try again. Try combining feedback with praise in your teaching.

Feedback can be used effectively with the whole–part–whole teaching method described above. If you give feedback about how a pupil has done on each part, this part can be improved before going on to the next part. If you give feedback immediately (i.e. as an attempt is being finished or immediately after it has finished, but before another attempt is started), pupils can relate the feedback directly to the outcome of the activity. Thus, pupils are more likely to succeed if they take small steps and receive immediate feedback on each step. This success can, in turn, lead to increased motivation to continue the activity.

One problem with giving immediate feedback is how you can provide feedback to individual pupils in a class who are all doing the same activity at the same time. There are several methods which you can use to provide feedback to many pupils at the same time, e.g. getting pupils to work through examples in a book which has the answers in the back, setting criteria and letting pupils evaluate themselves against the criteria or having pupils assess one another against set criteria (see the reciprocal teaching style of Mosston and Ashworth (1994) in Unit 5.3 for more information about this and other teaching styles). Pupils are generally very sensible and constructive when responsibility for giving feedback is placed on them, if they have been properly prepared for it.

Not all feedback comes from another person, e.g. the teacher or another pupil; feedback also comes from the activity itself. The feedback from the activity may be easier to identify for some activities than others; for example, a pupil gets feedback about their success if an answer to a maths problem matches that given in the book or the wicket is knocked down when bowling in cricket. In other activities, right or wrong, success or failure, is not as clear cut, e.g. there is often no right or wrong answer to an English essay. In the early stages of learning an activity pupils find it hard to use the feedback from the activity, e.g. they may notice that they were successful at the activity, but not be able to identify why. Normally, therefore, they need feedback from another person. This immediate, external feedback can be used to help pupils become more aware of what they are doing and how they are improving and to identify why they were successful or not at the activity and therefore to make use of feedback from the activity. Later in the learning, e.g. when refining an activity, pupils should be able to benefit from feedback from the activity itself and therefore it is better not to give immediate feedback.

Finally, to be effective, feedback should be given about pupils' work or behaviour, not about the pupils themselves. It must convey to the pupils that their work or behaviour is satisfactory or not, not that they are good (or bad) *per se*.

You need to observe pupils very carefully in order to spot small changes or improvements. This allows you to provide appropriate feedback. See Unit 2.1 on reading classrooms for more information about observation techniques and Units 6.1 and 6.2 on formative assessment. Your developing professional knowledge and judgement will help you to know when and how to use feedback to best effect.

Task 3.2.9   **TEACHING STYLES**

As an integral part of your lesson planning, select one activity where pupils can observe each other and provide feedback. Devise a handout with the main points to be observed. Plan how you are going to introduce this activity into the lesson. Discuss the lesson plan with your tutor. Ask your tutor to observe the lesson. Discuss the effectiveness of the strategy afterwards, determining how you can improve its use. Also try to observe teachers who use this strategy regularly. Try the strategy at a later date in your school experience. Think of other ways in which you can get more feedback to more pupils when they are doing an activity. Include these, as appropriate, in your lesson plans.

Motivating individuals

As the discussion above has highlighted, there is no one correct way to motivate pupils to learn. Different motivation techniques are appropriate and effective in different situations, e.g. pupils of different ages respond differently to different types of motivation, reward, punishment or feedback. Likewise, individual pupils respond differently. Further, any one pupil may respond to the same motivator differently at different times and in different situations.

Pupils need to feel that they are individuals, with their needs and interests taken into account, rather than just being a member of a group. If pupils are not motivated, do not let them avoid doing the task, but try to find other ways of motivating them; for example, if pupils are bored by work that is being done, try to stimulate their motivation by relating it to something in which they are interested. You can motivate pupils most effectively by using motivation techniques appropriate for a particular pupil in a particular situation.

Thus, you need to try to find out what motivates each pupil in your class. As a student teacher you are at a disadvantage here because you can only know what motivates each pupil and what rewards they are likely to respond to if you know your pupils well and know something about their needs and interests. As a student teacher, you do not usually spend enough time in one school to get to know the pupils very well and therefore you can only try to motivate individual pupils by using your knowledge and understanding of pupils of that age. Learning pupils' names quickly gives you a start in being able to motivate pupils effectively (see Unit 2.3 on taking responsibility for whole lessons, for strategies you can use to learn pupils' names). As you get to know pupils, you can identify what motivates them by finding out what activities they enjoy, what they choose to do and what they try to avoid, what types of reward they work for and to what they do not respond (e.g. by observation, talking to pupils, discussing a pupil with the form tutor or other teachers). The sooner you can relate to pupils individually, the sooner you can manage a class of individuals effectively. However, this does not occur at an early phase in your teaching (see phases of development in Unit 1.2).

Summary and key points

This unit has identified some general principles and techniques for motivation. However, you need to be able to use these appropriately. For example, if you praise a group for working quietly while they are working you may negatively affect their work. It is better in this situation to let the group finish their work and then praise them. In addition, pupils are individuals and therefore respond differently to different forms of motivation, reward, punishment and feedback. Further, the same pupil responds differently at different times and in different situations. To motivate each pupil effectively therefore requires that you know your pupils so you can anticipate how they will respond. Motivation is supported by good formative assessment techniques. Your developing professional knowledge and judgement will enable you to combine theory with practice to motivate pupils effectively in your classes, which raises the standard of their work.

FURTHER READING

Child, D. (1993) *Psychology and the Teacher (fifth edition)*, London: Cassell.

Chapter 3 provides in-depth consideration of motivation in education. It starts by considering three broad types of theories of motivation, then looks specifically at how motivation applies in education and finally describes how some of the theories of motivation impact on you as a teacher.

Entwistle, N. J. (1993) *Styles of Learning and Teaching*, 3rd ed., London: David Fulton .

Chapters 5 and 9 contain extended discussion about the relationship between personality and motivation and styles of learning.

Kyriacou, C. (1986) *Effective Teaching in Schools*, Oxford: Basil Blackwell.

This book contains chapters on lesson management and classroom climate, both of which consider aspects of motivation, e.g. whether lesson management helps to maintain pupils' motivation and whether the opportunities for learning are challenging and offer realistic opportunities for success.

3.3 MANAGING CLASSROOM BEHAVIOUR

INTRODUCTION

'Good behaviour and discipline in schools are essential to successful teaching and learning' (DFE, 1994a, p. 1). Misbehaviour prevents pupils learning effectively. It is easier to prevent misbehaviour in the classroom than it is to deal with it afterwards. There is no easy answer to preventing misbehaviour. However, there is less misbehaviour and more effective teaching and learning in classes in which there is effective class management. The Elton Report (DES/WO, 1989, p. 69) concluded that:

> teachers' group management skills are probably the single most important factor in achieving good standards of classroom behaviour; . . . those skills can be taught and learned.

Thus, behaviour in the classroom is directly affected by the quality of your classroom management skills. However, behaviour may also be influenced by other factors, e.g. demotivated pupils are more likely to misbehave than motivated pupils. The demotivation may be the result of a number of factors, only one of which is classroom management. There are some principles on which effective classroom management techniques are based and these principles identify ways of coping with any misbehaviour that does occur, although you must adapt these according to your preferred teaching style, the class and the circumstances.

This unit is designed to enable you to reflect on whether your management is contributing to the incidence of misbehaviour in the classroom and to identify some possible strategies for improving this; and consequently to help you manage your classroom to prevent misbehaviour and to enable effective teaching and learning to take place. As you cannot prevent all misbehaviour in class, we also consider ways of dealing with misbehaviour. In this unit we also consider briefly misbehaviour outside the classroom.

The Elton Report (DES/WO, 1989), *Discipline in Schools*, is considered to be a key text, providing valuable insight into behaviour and recommendations about how to improve discipline in schools. We therefore look at aspects of this report in this unit. The key recommendations related to you as a student and newly qualified teacher are reproduced in this book as Appendix 3 but we recommend that you also look at the full report to develop further understanding about this area. This should be in the library in your institution.

OBJECTIVES

By the end of this unit you should be beginning to:

- understand common causes of misbehaviour in the classroom;

- develop a variety of class management skills designed to prevent misbehaviour;
- develop techniques to deal with behavioural problems that you might encounter.

By doing this you address competences/standards related to managing behaviour and discipline required on your course. Refer to your course competences/standards at this point and identify the specific competences/standards you are addressing.

What is misbehaviour?

Misbehaviour is usually defined as behaviour which causes concern to teachers (Elton Report, DES/WO, 1989). There are many types of pupil misbehaviour, ranging from minor irritation or disruption such as talking in class or not settling down to work, to major confrontations or disruption in the class or school, including bullying and racial harassment.

Teachers' perceptions vary as to what constitutes misbehaviour. While teachers generally agree about types of misbehaviour, there is less agreement about what constitutes minor and major disruption and how any misbehaviour should be dealt with.

Task 3.3.1

MISBEHAVIOUR 1

Spend a few minutes brainstorming the types of pupil misbehaviour that you believe might occur in the classroom. You may recall misbehaviour which occurred in classes you have taught or observed or classes in which you were a pupil. Try to group these into categories of misbehaviour (you may want to start with the four main sources of misbehaviour given by Francis (1975, in Smith and Laslett, 1993, p. 34): noise, equipment, movement and chatter. Then try to list these in rank order of misbehaviour, from very minor disruption to major confrontation. Ask another student teacher to do this activity at the same time and then compare your notes. See if you can agree the rank order. As you gain experience, write down how you plan to deal with each type of misbehaviour.

Task 3.3.2

MISBEHAVIOUR 2

Discuss with your tutor the types of misbehaviour which are inappropriate in the classroom, e.g. talking and how the behaviour is controlled, e.g. by the teacher, by school rules and expectations. If you teach a practical subject, e.g. design technology, physical education or science, discuss with your tutor the implications of misbehaviour in relation to safety in the lesson and how behaviour is controlled. Consider these in relation to the types of misbehaviour identified in Task 3.3.1 above.

These differences are mainly due to differences in personality, e.g. some teachers are more tolerant and some more strict than others. However, there should be some guidelines in your school experience school as to what is considered appropriate behaviour and what is not.

Misbehaviour in the classroom

Causes of misbehaviour

The three most common causes of misbehaviour in the classroom are: boredom; an inability to do the work a teacher has set; and effort demanded for too long a period without a break. Misbehaviour can also be a means of seeking attention. Clearly, these factors can be anticipated and avoided by careful lesson planning and considered class management. Another factor to be borne in mind is that school life for pupils is as much (some argue more) a social experience as an academic one and the complex web of social interaction between pupils undoubtedly underpins classroom interaction. Pupils come into the classroom continuing conversations begun on the way to school, in the playground or corridors. This is not to say that the social nature of a pupil's school life should be allowed to dominate the classroom, rather that it should be acknowledged and kept in mind.

Some pupils are more predisposed to misbehave than others, e.g. low academic self-esteem sometimes affects pupils' behaviour in the classroom. Much can be done if you anticipate this factor and plan the lesson to take account of it. The few pupils that you encounter with real emotional difficulties (as opposed to those 'difficulties' which are part of adolescence) and pupils whose sets of values are completely different from those of the school, may cause you problems. However, they will have been identified by the school and you should discuss these problems with colleagues to identify the support you might be offered and successful strategies which others use with particular pupils.

Class management skills designed to prevent misbehaviour

Remember that the best judges of teachers are pupils. They are experts because they spend at least five hours a day for eleven years observing them. What a pupil thinks is a 'good teacher' might not conform with your model, but pupils do have certain expectations of teachers. Pupils expect teachers to **establish and conform to certain routines**, e.g. going in and sitting down quietly when they arrive, collecting and returning books, getting equipment out or moving around the classroom. They know what they have to do and that there are not going to be any surprises; therefore it makes them feel safe. See Unit 2.3, 'Taking responsibility for whole lessons', for further information about establishing routines.

Pupils 'test out' any new teacher, however experienced, for example, they may test the routines you try to establish. Your response to this is very important. If you over-react, are too harsh or respond in a way that rewards pupils, e.g. you become flustered or angry, the pupils continue to try to find out how far they can go. If, however, you do not rise to any bait given by pupils, but respond coolly, calmly, firmly and fairly, the pupils soon become bored with testing you out and get on with the task of learning.

Perhaps the key skill to develop concerning general class management is the ability to **anticipate problems before they arise**. As with health care, where the most positive and successful form is preventative medicine, the most successful way of managing pupil behaviour is to prevent misbehaviour. If you cannot prevent misbehaviour entirely, the next best thing is to try to contain it as much as possible, to prevent minor disruptions from escalating into major confrontations.

Whatever teaching style you begin to adopt in the classroom, the key to teaching effectively is to **establish your authority**. If you do not establish your authority, e.g. because you are anxious or tense, the atmosphere in the class may be affected and your attempts to manage the class undermined. Your authority in the classroom is founded upon four main aspects, which are:

- conveying your status;
- teaching competently;
- effective class management;
- effectively dealing with pupil misbehaviour.

In Unit 1.2, the section on phases of development considers establishing your authority in greater depth. In addition, Robertson (1989) considers authority in great detail in his book *Effective Classroom Control* and you may wish to refer to this for further information.

Laying the ground rules

Perhaps the most important factor in classroom management in the prevention of misbehaviour is **the establishment of ground rules to prevent misbehaviour**.

Any school in which you teach has its set of rules and code of conduct to which pupils are expected to conform. Similarly, it has a clearly defined system of rewards and punishments. The pupils are aware of these facts. It is essential that you are very clear about these systems too and that you enforce and employ them equably, even if you personally disagree with some aspects of them. Do not try to court favour with pupils by expressing disagreement. It is unlikely to earn their respect.

Even if the school has rules about classroom behaviour, it is worth spending some time with a new class establishing an agreed set of rules for behaviour in your classroom. The rationale for these rules needs to be established. You may be surprised at how sensible pupils are when engaging in this exercise. Once you and the class have drawn up your rules, display them in the classroom. At the first sign of a minor infringement, draw attention to the agreed set of rules. Likewise, give positive reinforcement to those pupils who keep the rules, by, for example, remembering to raise a hand rather than calling out (see Unit 3.2 on motivation which looks in more detail at reinforcement).

Wragg (1984, adapted from p. 67) lists the following as the most common rules to be found in the classroom:

Task
3.3.3 **SCHOOL RULES**
Obtain a copy of the rules and code of conduct to which pupils are expected to conform, both inside and outside the classroom and the system of rewards and punishments available to teachers to maintain these rules or deal with breaches of them. If these are not written down, discuss with your tutor what these are and make sure you are clear about them. Compare similarities and differences between these rules and code of conduct and those collected by a student teacher from another school. Observe lessons taught by experienced teachers to see how these rules operate in the school. If there were some rules which you did not see during your observation, ask each teacher how they would deal with this. Compare how different teachers interpret and operate the rules. Do teachers interpret them in the same or their own way? Do teachers develop their own sets of rules for their own classrooms? Discuss your findings and the implications for your teaching with your tutor .

- rules for entering, leaving and moving around the classroom;
- rules to do with safety;
- pupils do not talk when the teacher, or another pupil, is addressing the class;
- pupils must raise a hand to speak – not shout out;
- pupils must not challenge the teacher's authority;
- pupils should not make disruptive noises;
- work must be completed in a specified way;
- pupils should ask if they do not understand what they are to do;
- pupils should make a positive effort in their work;
- pupils must not interfere with the work of others;
- respect should be shown for property and equipment.

Smith and Laslett (1993) described four rules of effective classroom management: get them in (greeting, seating, starting); get them out (concluding, dismissing); get on with it (content, manner); and get on with them (who's who; what's going on?). These 'rules' may help you to remember the broad range of activities you need to address in order to manage your classroom effectively to prevent misbehaviour. Sections in Unit 2.2 on thorough planning (preparation of schemes of work and lesson planning, having enough of the needed equipment), an effective beginning to the lesson, smooth, seamless transitions and a successful completion of the lesson address these issues in more detail. We suggest that you refer to these sections at this point and consider these particularly in relation to pupil behaviour in class.

Managing behaviour problems

Effective class management, then, comprises a variety of skills and techniques used with awareness and sensitivity. A well-managed class is much less likely to cause behaviour problems. However, you cannot stop all misbehaviour through effective class management, so how do you cope when pupil behaviour does give cause for concern?

As you may have discovered in the discussion with another student teacher while attempting Task 3.3.1 above, one teacher might regard a particular behaviour as trivial, while another deems it as serious. Of course, any pupil misbehaviour might be regarded as being in some way serious if it interferes with the smooth flow of a lesson or with the pupil's or another pupil's work. However, it is interesting to note that in the Elton Report (DES/WO, 1989), HMI reported the following to be the most frequently cited forms of misbehaviour:

- arriving late for the lesson;
- not paying attention to the teacher;
- excessive talking – talking out of turn;
- being noisy – both non-verbally and verbally;
- not getting on with the work;
- pupils being out of their own seats without good reason;
- hindering others.

Your own list of misbehaviour developed in Task 3.3.1 may have included the violent or indeed homicidal, so it is comforting to note that all examples of the most common misbehaviour are, in effect, trivial. This is not to say that serious misbehaviour does not occur but, like violent crime, it is in reality extremely rare – it is just that it makes the headlines. There is also some comfort to be drawn from the fact that if thirty pupils wish to stand up and walk out of the classroom, there is nothing that even the best teacher in the world can do to stop them. We have never known it to happen.

Task 3.3.4	**COPING WITH MISBEHAVIOUR**

Write down how incidents of the most frequently cited forms of misbehaviour from the Elton Report (DES/WO, 1989) above have been dealt with by you if they have occurred in your classroom and by experienced teachers you have observed. How did your handling of these compare with that of experienced teachers? Try to identify specific areas where you need to improve your class management techniques to deal with misbehaviour and discuss with your tutor what you can do to improve in these areas.

Strategies to prevent misbehaviour

It is important to be vigilant in class and constantly monitor the mood, atmosphere, attitude and behaviour of any class you are teaching. Even if you are reading aloud to a class, it is necessary to scan the class frequently to gauge from, say, body language, the pupils' level of attention with your reading. Make eye contact with pupils. Eye contact held just slightly longer with a pupil who is whispering to another is usually enough to silence the miscreant without the need to stop reading.

Circulate around the classroom even when reading. It is not necessary to wander continually like a lost soul, but spending a few minutes in each part of the room ensures that the pupils are very aware of your presence quite close to them. Again, if a pupil is misbehaving as you are addressing the class, your moving towards them and standing by them is often enough to quieten them without the need to break your flow or even to mention their behaviour.

Being very aware of the class enables you to notice pupil misbehaviour. Noticing misbehaviour and responding calmly, quickly, effectively and good-humouredly prevents such behaviour from escalating. The same is true of pupils' disrespect. If pupils do not experience negative consequences, they continue to push the boundaries of accepted behaviour.

Changing the pace of a lesson by providing a variety of tasks and activities does much to prevent boredom, which is, perhaps, the major cause of misbehaviour. If you become aware that a pupil is experiencing difficulty with a task, be on hand to give academic help. Of course, you are not there to do the work for them, but you are there to facilitate their learning; for example, a pupil may misbehave because of frustration at not being able to do the work set and therefore you must help the pupil to understand the work and solve the problem, thus reducing the frustration. You must not let the pupil avoid doing the work because they find it difficult. Such action compounds the problem later when the pupil cannot do the next piece of work because it is based on the current work.

If a pupil continues to misbehave, move her. You need to have articulated your intention to do so to the whole class at the laying down of the ground rules and to have warned the pupil that this action might be a consequence of her current behaviour. Warning miscreants clearly gives them an opportunity to avoid sanctions. In doing this you allow them not to lose face. However, always do what you have promised or threatened to do. Never make idle threats because pupils soon learn that you do not follow through with your threats and therefore they take no notice of them. Not only do the threats lose their effect but also you lose your credibility. Empty threats create a downward spiral in which it becomes continually more difficult to prevent misbehaviour.

Reprimanding pupils

Your main objective in noticing misbehaviour or in reprimanding a pupil must be to allow the class to continue in a productive manner. Therefore, you should express concern and, possibly, disappointment, as this may cajole the pupil into responding appropriately. At all costs avoid anger: **the throbbing, protruding veins and bulging eyes of an angry teacher make a highly entertaining diversion for even the most well-motivated pupil**.

A major objective in reprimanding a pupil should be to avoid confrontation. The use of private rather than public reprimands negates the need for a pupil to save face in her social sphere. Do not enter into a debate with a pupil, but firmly inform her that you will discuss the matter at a time convenient to you, such as after the lesson. Then immediately carry on with the lesson.

Avoid unfair comparisons and never insult or criticise a pupil; rather, criticise the behaviour. For example, 'Stop being so stupid, Michael!' can be guaranteed to prompt a face-saving response, whereas 'All right Michael, it's time to be getting on with the work' makes the same point. However, do avoid the 'You wouldn't do that at home, would you Michael?' as it allows even the slowest of wits to reply 'Yes, I would!' and raise a laugh at the teacher's expense.

Direct your comments to the work, as in 'Is there a problem with this piece of writing, Michael?', to show that you are aware of his misbehaviour, but allows him to reply 'No' and then get on with the task. It also allows you to emphasise what is required of a pupil rather than dwelling on the negative. Following up such an interchange by looking through what has been produced thus far also allows the teacher to praise some aspect of the work and reinforce a pupil's positive behaviour.

Remember that a correctly targeted reprimand delivered firmly, fairly and without anger is effective. Try to avoid reprimanding the whole class, as it is guaranteed to be unfair to some and may well alienate those who were thus far sympathetic towards you. For similar reasons never denigrate pupil(s) in public or belittle an individual or a whole class.

It is essential that you are seen to be consistent and fair in your reprimands. Pupils possess a finely tuned sense of justice. A punishment should be in proportion to the offence committed. Do not make empty threats and resist the temptation to 'up the stakes' from sanctions such as 100 to 1000 lines or a detention to detention every night for a week – you destroy any credibility you might have. All schools have their own systems of sanctions, but if you do have recourse to detentions, remember that you are normally required to give parents at least twenty-four hours' notice of your intention. You need to check with the school the policy on detentions.

It should not need to be said, but never, under any circumstance, even in the face of the severest provocation, physically punish a pupil. That way lies litigation and a very short career in teaching.

If, despite all efforts, a pupil's behaviour is impossible, seek support. Avoid classroom confrontation with the pupil at all costs. Be very aware of the school support system and obtain the necessary support from a colleague. Most schools operate some system of 'parking' extremely difficult pupils in order that a teacher might get on with the job of teaching a class. For example, pupils may be 'parked' at the head's or deputy head's office or sent to the head of year. Check if such a system operates in your school experience

---

Task 3.3.5

ANALYSING MISBEHAVIOUR

This task invites you to reflect upon an incident that may have occurred in your own classroom, in the light of what you have learned from this unit. You may have experienced an example of pupil misbehaviour towards you, however trivial. Briefly note down details of what happened. In the light of what you now understand about management of pupil misbehaviour record in your diary:

- what you believe were the causes of the misbehaviour;
- how this misbehaviour might have been anticipated and prevented;
- how you would deal with such misbehaviour now.

school. Remember, if you have effective class management skills, have made every attempt to pre-empt and deal effectively with misbehaviour, have avoided anger and confrontation and the pupil is still extremely difficult – then the problem lies elsewhere.

The Elton Report (DES/WO, 1989, p. 13) concluded that the most effective schools seem to be those in which there is a positive atmosphere. This is based on consensus about

> standards of behaviour among staff, pupils and parents. Staff, pupils and parents should have clear guidance about these standards and their practical application; staff should be encouraged to recognise and praise good behaviour as well as deal with bad behaviour. Pupils should be clear about the distinction between the punishment given for minor and more serious misbehaviour and these punishments should be applied fairly and consistently.

Misbehaviour outside the classroom

Teachers have a key role to play in maintaining standards of behaviour in school. You have the major responsibility for control and discipline in your classroom. In addition, you must do your part to prevent or deal with, if they should occur, other serious incidents of misbehaviour in the school, including bullying and racial harassment. The Elton Report (DES/WO, 1989, p. 26, recommendation 28) recommended that

> headteachers and staff should be: alert to signs of bullying and racial harassment; deal firmly with all such behaviour; and take action based on clear rules which are backed by appropriate sanctions and systems to protect and support victims.

The report then indicated that schools should not allow such behaviour to occur and everyone (including pupils) must take responsibility to prevent it or deal with it when it does occur. In order to do this effectively a whole school approach to dealing with such problems is needed. Some schools have constructed a whole school approach to discipline which centres on the reinforcement of the positive aspects of pupil behaviour. *Assertive Discipline* (see Canter and Canter, 1977) described one such whole school approach.

The Elton Report (DES/WO, 1989) also highlighted the need for concerted action at classroom, school, community and national levels, i.e. a concerted effort by a number of professionals working as a team, plus governors, LEAs and government (as well as teachers and parents) in influencing the effectiveness of discipline in schools. The school policy should recognise the need for the school to work as part of the wider community and to call on other professionals such as counsellors, educational welfare officers, educational psychologists or education social workers, as appropriate. The Elton Report (DES/WO, 1989, p. 13, recommendation 15) emphasised 'the importance of the pastoral role of class teachers and form tutors and the need for the school to maintain regular contact with the education welfare service and other agencies rather than calling them in as a last resort'. See Chapter 4 in Capel, Leask and Turner (1997) for more information about the role of the education social worker and educational psychologist.

An effective whole school policy supports teachers in their responsibility for control and discipline in their classroom, in the wider school and in their pastoral role. One

> **Task 3.3.6**
>
> **THE WHOLE SCHOOL BEHAVIOUR POLICY**
> One of the recommendations of the Elton Report (DES/WO, 1989) was that headteachers and teachers, in consultation with governors, develop whole school behaviour policies which are clearly understood by pupils, parents and other school staff. Ask your tutor for a copy of this policy. Study it carefully and discuss its origins, implementation and effectiveness with your tutor and other school staff. Compare this policy with one from another school collected by another student teacher or the examples of behaviour policies contained in the Elton Report. Record the differences in your diary and reflect on these in the light of your continued development as a teacher.

purpose of the pastoral role is to ensure that there is a member of staff who has an overview of an individual pupil's progress and is able to provide support. One aspect of pastoral work which may be of immediate concern is bullying, which, as indicated above, is a major factor affecting pupils' ability to learn at school. It was recognised in the Elton Report (DES/WO, 1989, p. 107) that often pupils are aware of serious bullying and racial harassment before staff because they occur outside the classroom, in corners of the playground, on the way home from school or in other out of the way places. It is important that pupils feel able to tell staff about such incidents because, beyond any physical injury, the misery caused to individual pupils can be very damaging to their self-esteem, motivation and their achievement. The school's behaviour policy should also make it clear that pupils have a responsibility to share this knowledge with staff in confidence. An effective pastoral system should enable this to operate effectively.

In their pastoral role, teachers have a range of responsibilities for the individual pupil. Haydon and Lambert (1992, p. 35) identify three dimensions of pastoral care:

> *pastoral casework:* work with individual pupils on any aspect which affects their development and achievement;
>
> *pastoral curriculum:* all aspects of work with groups (not just tutorial groups) which contribute to their personal and social development;
>
> *pastoral management:* the planning, monitoring, reviewing and communication systems required amongst the various teams and individuals. This supports the overall orderly climate required for pupils' learning and development.

The importance of the pastoral role in influencing pupil behaviour was specifically mentioned in the Elton Report (DES/WO, 1989). The committee stressed 'the importance of personal and social education as a means of promoting the values of mutual respect, self discipline and social responsibility which underlie good behaviour'. They recommended 'that personal and social education should be strengthened both inside and outside the National Curriculum' (Elton Report, DES/WO, 1989, p. 13, recommendation 14).

Task 3.3.7

THE PASTORAL ROLE
Discuss with your tutor the pastoral role undertaken by teachers in your school, especially in relation to discipline in the school. How is pastoral care organised? What is the role in pastoral care of the individual teacher as a class teacher and as a form tutor? What support is there for them in these roles? Observe teachers working with a form. Discuss their role with your tutor and compare this with the role of a form tutor recorded by another student teacher working in another school.

Task 3.3.8

BULLYING
Discuss with your tutor what you can do to prevent bullying in your school. Who can you turn to for help? How does the whole school policy for behaviour, rules and codes of conduct both inside and outside the classroom support teachers in this task? Is bullying covered as an issue in pastoral work? If so, how? When? Discuss this with your tutor.

Task 3.3.9

YOUR PERSONAL VALUES
Your personal values and beliefs on politics, marriage, family life, gender roles, for example, may be at odds with those of some pupils and could influence your responses to the demands of the pastoral role. Consider situations where your personal values and beliefs might be different from those of pupils. What do you say to a pupil who complains about another member of staff being a poor teacher? Or who argues about conforming to school rules which you yourself do not feel are vitally important? Discuss these issues with other student teachers and your tutor and identify what might be appropriate responses to situations in which pupils' actions contradict your personal values and beliefs.

Task 3.3.10

IMPLICATIONS OF THE ELTON REPORT (DES/WO, 1989)
Discuss with another student teacher what the information in Appendix 3 means for your work in school, in terms of your work in the school as a whole, your classroom and your pastoral role.

> ## ⁞ Summary and key points
>
> The key to managing classroom behaviour effectively is effective class management. Well-planned, well-prepared and well-managed lessons are far less likely to promote behaviour problems in pupils. Likewise, an awareness of and sensitivity to, pupil mood and motivation prevents much problem behaviour about which student teachers are most concerned. Active participation in lessons minimises disruption (see also Unit 5.2 on Active Learning).
>
> To maintain effective learning in your classroom you need to read this unit in conjunction with others that relate to managing your classroom and work on developing effective classroom management techniques. Also remember that you are part of a team and can draw on the support and advice of the team as and when you need it.
>
> Also, you have responsibility for pupils' behaviour beyond your classroom. You have a pastoral role, but, further, a role across the school. In effective schools, teachers are supported in managing behaviour by school policies and procedures. In return, the teachers must support fully the school policies and procedures.

FURTHER READING

Canter, L. and Canter, M. (1977) *Assertive Discipline*, Los Angeles: Lee Canter Associates.

This is a training pack including video and work book. Although the materials were designed for INSET purposes to facilitate a school-wide approach to discipline, there is much to be gained from an investigation of the use of positive reinforcement in class management. Available *only* from Behaviour Management Ltd, UK (see TES, 1994, 18 March, Review Section, pp. 1–2).

Department for Education (1994b) *Bullying: Don't Suffer in Silence. An Anti Bullying Pack for Schools*, London: DFE.

This pack is part of a series of measures by the government to combat bullying. It contains a video which shows the steps some schools have taken to combat bullying. The video is accompanied by a training pack. This should be available in all schools.

Department of Education and Science and the Welsh Office (1989) *Discipline in Schools. Report of the Committee of Enquiry Chaired by Lord Elton* (The Elton Report), London: HMSO.

This report is the outcome of an enquiry into discipline in schools in response to concern about the problems facing the teaching profession. It covers a wide range of aspects of the problem and contains examples of behaviour policies from schools.

OFSTED (1993c) *Achieving Good Behaviour in Schools: A Report from the Office of Her Majesty's Chief Inspector of Schools*, London: HMSO.

This is a short booklet which reports on 'the evidence of inspection to examine some of the means by which schools with high standards of behaviour and good discipline achieve them' (p. 1) in order to identify some principles of good practice and suggest a possible code of practice for schools.

Smith, C.J. and Laslett, R. (1993) *Effective Classroom Management: A Teacher's Guide*, London: Routledge.

This book considers many aspects of discipline in the classroom, from minor disruption to confrontation. It includes some very good case studies of how confrontations can occur and how they can be managed well or, alternatively, how they can get out of hand. It includes a section on working with pupils with emotional and behavioural difficulties in mainstream classrooms.

4 PUPIL DIFFERENCES

This chapter invites you to consider several aspects of the development of the individual. The responses of individuals to teaching and learning are unique, partly because of the physical environment in which they have been nurtured and partly through their genetic features. In some cases, children need particular support; thus Unit 4.6 discusses the provision of Special Educational Needs. In addition, cultural influences provide them with a set of practices and values, which together interact with both the teacher and the curriculum and affect learning.

This chapter contains six units, each of which seeks to focus on one aspect of development. It is not intended to be a thorough discussion of each feature of development; we should need six books to do that.

Unit 4.1 addresses differentiation and recognises that pupils learn in different ways and at different rates. It addresses immediately the task of planning work to take account of differences. You may need to return to this unit after dipping into the other units. This unit focuses on the teaching of a wide range of pupils whose performance lies in the middle ground, i.e. the needs of most pupils. The teaching of pupils with special educational needs who are statemented or are gifted or have disabilities such as dyslexia, is introduced in Unit 4.6. We suggest that such studies are best met in the NQT year and beyond.

Unit 4.2 focuses on physical characteristics of pupils as they develop and mature into adolescence and adulthood. An important feature of this unit is the attempt to discuss subject choice at 13+ in this context.

In Unit 4.3 intellectual development is addressed; you are invited to look specifically at the cognitive differences in performance between pupils of different ages. As with many other units in this book, there are numerous opportunities for you to work with pupils and we suggest you see for yourself how pupils respond to different intellectual tasks and reflect on implications for your teaching.

In Unit 4.4 the cultural background of pupils is considered: this unit includes aspects of class, gender and ethnicity while, at the same time, acknowledging that other characteristics contribute to cultural identity, e.g. belief systems. Providing the same educational opportunities for all is not a guarantee that all pupils can take advantage of them. Equal opportunities policies must go beyond 'provision' to consider 'access', whereby pupils are enabled to take advantage of the curriculum.

Unit 4.5 invites you to look at opportunities in school to guide the moral development of your pupils, by means of examples which use day-to-day events and touches on values education. While not stressing differences, the focus of the chapter, it does acknowledge the range of values and beliefs in our society.

Finally, Unit 4.6 addresses the ways in which the special needs of pupils may be met and how schools must now respond to the 1994 Code of Practice.: see Appendix 4

4.1   DIFFERENTIATION, PROGRESSION AND PUPIL GROUPING

INTRODUCTION

In this unit we explore ways in which differentiated learning methods are used to take account of pupil differences. Schools have traditionally sought to cope with differences in pupils through setting, banding and streaming. Streaming places the best performers in the top stream for all subjects, the least able performers in the bottom stream, with graded classes in between. Banding on the other hand places pupils in broad bands of ability for all subjects. Banding avoids producing classes comprising only pupils of low ability or those unwilling to learn. Setting describes the allocation of pupils to classes by ability in each subject.

Differentiation is about raising the standards of all pupils in a school, not just those underachieving. It can be conceived of as within a whole school policy, as set out in *Better Schools* (DES, 1985). Differentiation is a planned process of intervention in the classroom learning of the pupil. Its purpose is to maximise the potential of the pupil. A central aspect of any strategy to improve standards is the teacher's expectation of pupils and pupils' opinions about themselves; see Units 2.2 and 3.2.

This unit discusses differences between pupils and invites student teachers to consider how best to provide appropriate learning environments for them. Strategies for developing differentiated units of work are provided, building on the subject specialist focus of the reader.

OBJECTIVES

You should be able to:

- discuss teaching methods which allow for differentiation;
- apply principles of differentiated learning and progression to lesson planning;
- evaluate mixed ability grouping as an approach to differentiated learning;
- appreciate that strategies adopted for teaching and learning reflect fundamental views about the purpose of education;
- identify teaching methods for differentiation in terms of teacher competences;
- relate your progress in planning and teaching for differentiation to the standards expected of an NQT.

LEARNING AND PROGRESSION ACROSS ABILITIES

By far the greatest challenge to teachers is to maintain progression in the learning of all pupils in their class. Each pupil is different. This is true of pupils in both streamed and mixed ability classes. The teacher has to take account of personal interest, ability and motivation, to set work which challenges and interests pupils but, at the same time, ensures for each a measure of success. Differentiating the work for pupils, depends on teachers knowing their pupils, being secure in their own subject knowledge and having access to a range of teaching strategies. There is no one right way to differentiate the work for pupils.

Each pupil brings to school unique knowledge, skills and attitudes formed by interaction with parents and peers, through their everyday experience of their world and through the media. They are not blank sheets on which new knowledge is to be written. Many pupils have skills of which the school is not aware: some pupils care for animals successfully; others play and adapt computer games; yet others may work with parents in the family business and know far more arithmetic than we dream of, as the following parody of stock market practice applied to a mathematics lesson suggests:

> Teacher: 'What is two plus two, Jane?'
> Jane: 'Am I buying or selling, Sir?'

All pupils bring a view based on the acceptance of particular cultural values; such values may represent a recognised religious faith or humanistic principles. Yet others may bring a set of values from home related to immersion in a commercial atmosphere or farming life. Others may reflect a background which owes less to an organised response to life but is born of pragmatism and a common-sense response to immediate needs.

Such diversity of background is found in your classrooms; planning for differentiation has to take account of differences in culture, expectation, knowledge and experience. This 'cultural inheritance' that each child has interacts with their 'potential for learning', i.e. the capacities with which the pupil is born. Each child responds to the curriculum in a different way. It is the teacher's job to make the curriculum interesting, relevant and cognitively digestible. We know little about the potential of each child; mixed ability grouping is one way of promoting learning for all, while avoiding labelling pupils, providing that ways and means can be found to ensure progression. Progression becomes the task of guiding the pupil from where they are towards a number of possible goals. Each step in that progression needs some guarantee of success, a recognised goal, understood and agreed by the pupil. Progress must be monitored by assessment tasks purpose-built into the curriculum.

Developing differentiated work

The curriculum involves the syllabus, the objectives, methods, resources and assessment tools; feedback from assessment should direct the next learning experience taking account of ways children learn. It is unrealistic to expect one teacher to plan differentiated work separately for each pupil; it is better perhaps to identify groups of pupils who can

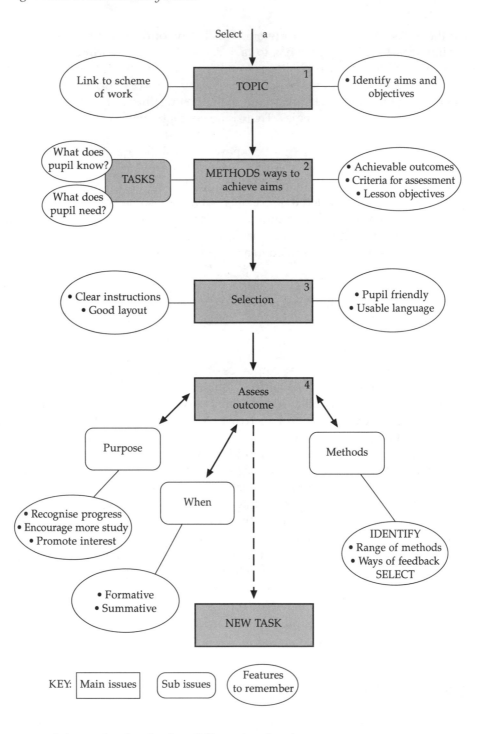

Figure 4.1.1 Scheme for developing differentiated tasks

work to a given objective using methods suitable to those pupils and the topic in question. Assessment tells you whether objectives are met, e.g. by marking books, talking to pupils, setting and marking a test or checking pupils' written work and guide further task setting.

It is helpful to some teachers to have a framework in which to plan work. One such plan is shown in Figure 4.1.1. The diagram assumes that you know what you want to teach – the Topic – and its place in the school's scheme of work. The diagram then draws attention to factors to be considered in preparing lesson plans (see Unit 2.2). The aims and short-term objectives must be broad enough to apply to most pupils in your class. There are often a number of ways of achieving the same goal; Step 2 requires you to consider the tasks to be set pupils, relating those tasks to pupil readiness and anticipated outcomes. Achievable outcomes are one way of ensuring motivation. By identifying achievable outcomes for different groups of children, the process of differentiation is set in motion. The final selection, Step 3, reminds you of some practical issues to consider in selecting or preparing resources, again reflecting another feature of differentiation. Step 4 finally addresses assessment issues in more detail. At this point the objectives of the work need to be recalled. If you have different objectives for different pupils, the assessment must reflect those differences.

Thus aims concerning the knowledge gained by pupils need a different assessment from aims directed at how they did the task; or if communication skills were the focus of the lesson these require yet a different approach and timing. Some aspects of learning can be tested after submission of the work, others require monitoring throughout. Step 4 draws attention to purpose, timing and methods.

Task 4.1.1 **LESSON PLANNING FOR DIFFERENTIATION 1**
Select a topic for a class you are teaching. Use Figure 4.1.1 to develop a general outline of a lesson for your class. Prepare notes for Steps 1, 2, 3 and 4 identified in Figure 4.1.1. Identify whether your plan has recognised a common task for all pupils, thus differentiating by outcome; or whether you have differentiated by selecting different tasks for pupils or groups of pupils.

This task could be done either:

- in a group of subject specialists, sharing ideas as they evolve; or
- personally, but later sharing your plan with other student teachers, especially those who know the school and pupils in your class.

Now go on to adapt your plan for particular pupils in your classes. First, however, read the case histories of some other pupils and respond to Tasks 4.1.2 and 4.1.3. Then proceed to Task 4.1.4.

Case studies of pupils

Read through these case studies of pupils and use them to do Tasks 4.1.2 and 4.1.3.

PETER   Peter is a popular member of his group and has an appealing sense of humour. He can use this in a disruptive way to disquiet teachers while amusing his peers.

He appears very bright orally but when the work is of a traditional nature, i.e. teacher led, he often avoids the task in hand; it is at such times that he can become disruptive. His disruption is not always overt; he employs a range of elaborate avoidance tactics when asked to settle to work and often produces very little. His written language and numeracy attainments are significantly lower than those he demonstrates orally.

When given responsibility in groups, Peter can sometimes rise to the challenge. He can display sound leadership ability and, when he is motivated and interested in a group project, can encourage his peers to produce a good team effort. His verbal presentations of such work can be lively, creative, humorous and full of lateral thinking. At such times Peter displays an extensive general knowledge.

Peter's tutor is concerned about Peter's progress. He fears that Peter will soon begin to truant from those subjects in which teaching is traditional in style. He is encouraging Peter's subject teachers to provide him with as much problem solving work as possible.

TINA   Tina is underachieving across the curriculum in her written work, although orally she appears quite bright. Her concentration span on written work is short. In basic skills she is getting behind her peers. In lessons she can appear quite demanding, as she often appears to need work to be individually set and she finds it difficult to get started and then to sustain and complete pieces of work. She can appear to spend significant amounts of lesson time disrupting the work of other learners. She seems to have a knack of knowing just how to provoke and 'wind up' other learners, so disputes are not unusual. She has been known to be rather con-frontational towards teachers, who perceive this to happen when Tina feels threatened.

At the same time, Tina has got what some people describe as 'charm'. Others describe this as being good manipulation. This makes her quite difficult to deal with in school, different teachers develop very different approaches and boundaries in relation to her.

She has a clique of peers who seem to follow her lead. She has a paradoxical relationship with others in the class, who seem to be wary of her, yet also rather courteous towards her.

FILIMON   Filimon arrived a year ago from Ethiopia via the Sudan. He had not been at school for at least a year due to his country's war. He speaks Sunharic at home, as well as some Arabic, but knew no English on arrival. Eight months of the year he has spent at school here have been a 'silent period' during which time he was internalising what he was hearing. Now he is starting to speak with his peers and his teacher. He has a reading partner who reads to him every day and now Filimon is reading these same stories himself.

JOYCE   Joyce is a very high achiever. She always seems to respond to as much extension activity as she can get. She puts in a lot of effort and produces very well presented work (capably using IT, for example), and amply demonstrating her ability to understand, evaluate and synthesise. Joyce's achievements are maximised where she is able to work on her own or in a pair with one of a couple of other girls in the class. In other groups she tends to keep herself to herself. Some teachers are concerned that she is not developing her social and leadership potential.

Joyce's parents put a lot of pressure on her and are keen for Joyce to follow an accelerated programme wherever this is possible. Should she achieve her ambitions for higher education, Joyce will not be the first in her family to make it to Oxbridge.

(Adapted from Greenhalgh, 1994)

Use these case studies to respond to Tasks 4.1.2 and 4.1.3.

Task 4.1.2	**CASE STUDIES OF PUPILS**

Identify the skills and abilities of each pupil. Identify those factors that you think you need to take account of in planning lessons generally in your subject. Share your analysis with other student teachers.

Task 4.1.3	**USING CASE STUDIES TO GUIDE LESSON PLANNING**

Consider ways in which the work prepared in Task 4.1.1 would need to be modified to be suitable for one or more of the pupils identified by the case studies.

Developing and using your own case studies   The following task is designed to focus your attention on one or two pupils in your class and on their learning needs, subsequently to redesign the lesson.

Task 4.1.4	**WRITING YOUR OWN CASE STUDY**

If you have the opportunity, write case studies for two pupils in the class you teach, e.g. the class identified in Task 4.1.1. You should keep the pupils anonymous for this purpose. When collecting the information talk to the regular class teacher about your task; ask for their contribution and comment on your case study. Then either: on your own,

- consider how the topic in Task 4.1.1 might be appropriate for these two pupils;

or: with a group of student teachers in your school,

- share your case studies and identify some learning characteristics or needs of these pupils;
- select those needs which you can take account of when preparing class work for these pupils and discuss ways of using them to set achievable goals, select learning materials and appropriate assessment methods.

More about differentiation: 'stimulus–task–outcome' flow diagrams

The outcome of any particular task depends on the way it is presented to the pupil and how they respond. Teaching methods can be restricted by our own imagination, by presenting a task in only one way with one particular outcome in mind, rather than looking for different ways to get to similar goals or for a range of acceptable responses to a task.

A traditional teaching goal is to ensure pupils know facts. One such task is to learn by heart Mark Antony's speech on the death of Caesar.

This may be represented by:

STIMULUS	TASK	OUTCOME
Play the role of Mark Antony in a class presentation of excerpts from *Julius Caesar*.	Learn by heart the relevant text	Complete oral recall

Or as a **flow diagram**:

$$ X \longrightarrow X \longrightarrow X $$

Stimulus   Task   Outcome

Many topics lend themselves to recall methods: learning the names of element symbols in science; preparing vocabulary in a modern language lesson; recalling formulae or tables from mathematics; and learning to spell. Such methods are necessary, if unexciting.

Task 4.1.5   **RECALL**
Select two recall tasks for your own subject area, identifying the appropriate age or level. Suggest ways of helping different groups of pupils accomplish these tasks.

Active learning   Figure 4.1.1 suggested looking for different methods of achieving the same ends (see Step 2). For example, to stimulate pupils to punctuate a piece of text for parts of speech you could:

• Engage in a three-minute discussion with them, tape it and ask them to transcribe it.
• Use an interview from a newspaper report; read it out loud and discuss it with the class; give out a report with the punctuation removed and ask for the punctuation to be inserted.

- Ask pupils to gather opinions about a topic of interest and write a report which includes verbatim examples of opinion, e.g. interviewing other pupils about proposed new school uniforms.
- Get them to write their own play.

Suggest other ways of teaching punctuation.

Does the following flow diagram represent the way this piece of work was set?

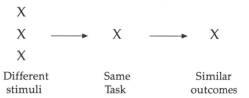

You might like to go on and consider circumstances when different outcomes arise from the same stimulus. Again select a class you are teaching and pupils you know.

Task 4.1.6 LESSON PLANNING FOR DIFFERENTIATION 2

Imagine you have a set of photographs showing the interiors of domestic kitchens covering the period 1850 to the present. Describe two or more ways in which you could use these photographs to teach your subject. Confine your discussion to a class you teach and to a single lesson.

For each use you describe identify:

- how you use the photographs;
- the task(s) set for your pupils;
- the expected outcome(s);
- how you assess outcomes;
- in which ways the task(s), outcomes and assessment are differentiated.

Analyse your plans in terms of stimulus, task and outcome. If you can't think of ways to use this set of photographs choose another stimulus; for example, video clip of astronaut working in space lab; a Salvador Dali painting such as *Persistence of Memory*.

Beyond task and outcome

The discussion of differentiation in terms of setting tasks or assessing outcomes suggests that work is given to pupils and they get on with it. In practice, of course you support pupils while they are working. Thus differentiation also takes place at the point of contact with the group or individual. Differentiation is not simply a case of task or outcome.

Your **response to pupils** working in class includes:

- checking that they understand what they are supposed to do;

- listening to a discussion and prompting or questioning when needed;
- helping pupils to brainstorm an idea or problem;
- asking questions about procedure or techniques;
- suggesting further action when difficultires arise or motivation flags;
- giving pupils supporting worksheets or other written guidance appropriate to the problem in hand. The guidance might explain the topic in simpler terms or simpler language;
- checking pupils' notebooks and noting progress;
- marking pupils' work;
- encouraging pupils by identifying success;
- setting targets for improvement;
- increasing the demand of an existing task;
- noting unexpected events or achievements for a plenary session.

You could discuss this list with other students and identify those elements appropriate to the teaching of your subject. You may wish to add to the list of responses above.

The different ways in which you respond to your pupils' activities affects the quality of their performance; your response to pupils is an important feature of a differentiated approach and knowing how to respond is part of the repertoire of all good teachers. Thus the dichotomy of differentiation, discussed above as a simple 'task vs. outcome' issue, hides a host of other ways by which you support your pupils. And knowing how to set such tasks depends on how well you know your pupils.

Identifying different tasks around the same theme requires some ingenuity. The task needs to be challenging yet within a pupil's capability. The ways in which a task can be differentiated include:

- the degree of open-endedness of the task;
- the degree of familiarity with the resources;
- whether the task is a complete piece of work or a contributory part of a larger exercise;
- the amount of information you give pupils;
- the language level at which the task is presented;
- whether the task is set orally or by means of written guidance;
- degree of familiarity with the concepts needed to tackle the task;
- the amount of guidance given to pupils; for example, in science lessons, the guidance given on making measurements, recording data or drawing a graph.

You may wish to discuss this list and rewrite it in terms of tasks appropriate to your subject and the context of your teaching.

Differences in outcome may be recognised by the amount of help given and by the:

- extent to which all aspects of a task have been considered;
- adoption of a suitable method of approaching a task;
- use of more difficult concepts or procedures in planning;
- recognition of factors involved in the task and limiting the choice appropriately;
- thoroughness and accuracy of recording data in a quantitative exercise;
- appropriateness and selection of ways to present information and the thoroughness and depth of analysis;

- use of appropriate theory to explain work;
- accuracy and understanding of conclusions drawn from a task, e.g. are statements made appropriate to the content and purpose of the task;
- distinction between statements supported by evidence from speculation or opinion;
- way the report is written up, the selection of appropriate style for the target audience;
- the ability of pupils to express themselves in an increasingly sophisticated language;
- the selection of appropriate diagrams, sketches or pictures;
- sensible use of ICT to support a task;
- recognition of the limitations of a task and awareness of ways to improve it.

Differentiation requires that you know your pupils. You have to judge the extent to which pupils have given a task their best shot. If left to their own devices, pupils may settle for the easy option. Your role is to push the pupil, or group of pupils, to maximise their effort on task and, finally, to judge what is an appropriate outcome. In assessing your pupils, attitudes are as important as cognitive skill.

Grouping pupils: wide ability vs. setting and streaming

Until recently, many schools grouped their pupils in wide (mixed) ability classes for teaching purposes. This decision was based on a belief that the backgrounds, aptitudes and abilities of pupils, which, coupled with differences in interest and motivation, can lead to large differences in achievement between pupils. At the secondary level, these differences grow larger as pupils get older. Recognising these differences without prematurely labelling pupils was regarded as an essential prerequisite for organising the teaching of secondary pupils. The moves towards de-streaming were most strongly evident in the 1960s, following the Plowden Report (DES, 1967) into primary schooling, some of the recommendations of which spilled over into secondary schooling. The abandonment of selection in schools by the introduction of comprehensive schooling in the 1950s and 1960s caused mixed ability grouping to be seen as the logical way to group pupils in secondary school thus avoiding the labelling which selection implied.

Nevertheless, there was strong opposition to this form of grouping especially from parents and teachers concerned with able pupils. Evidence accumulated in the 1970s suggested that differences in the academic performance of pupils in mixed ability groups, compared with those in other groupings, could not be attributed solely to the differences in grouping, especially given the other variables affecting pupil performance (HMI, 1978; Newbold 1977). The Newbold study and a later one (Postlethwaite and Denton, 1978) both identified gains for low ability pupils in the mixed ability setting and that, at the same time, the performance of able pupils was not reduced. The research into grouping pupils by ability carried out over many years has been reviewed by Hallam and Toutounji (1996).

Despite the uncertainty in the research evidence concerning the factors affecting the academic performance of pupils, there was evidence that all pupils gained socially from working in wide ability groups. Such groupings allowed pupils from a variety of backgrounds, as well as abilities, to work together, strengthening social cohesion. Such arguments were strongly supported in inner city environments where selection processes often led to separation of pupils along class and ethnic dimensions.

Recently, a comparative study of pupils in two comprehensive schools has rigorously documented their differences in knowledge and understanding of mathematics and their motivation and attitude towards the subject (Boaler, 1997). The 'progressive' school, which offered more open-ended project work, linked mathematics to the lives of the pupils and encouraged pupils to identify problems in which they were interested, achieved outcomes as good as, and in many cases better than, the school which adopted 'traditional' rule learning and application as the main teaching strategy. The 'progressive' mathematics department did not group pupils in streamed sets, unlike the department working on 'traditional' lines (Boaler, 1997, Chapter 10). There was evidence that in the traditional teaching structure able pupils were anxious, especially those in the top set, and under-performed in the GCSE examination. Many girls were disadvantaged by the traditional teaching approach of this school (Boaler, 1997, Chapter 9). The author points out that the current dismay in government circles at the low standard of mathematics performance by English pupils in international comparative studies has occurred when most mathematics teaching in classrooms is of the 'traditional' type, citing inspection reports as evidence (OFSTED, 1994b).

In the 1990s, following the introduction of the Education Reform Act (ERA, 1988) mixed ability grouping has been in retreat. Indeed, government advice from both left and right of the political spectrum has advocated a return to grouping by ability, together with increased whole class teaching. The response of the late 1990s under the new labour government has been to lay down policy on grouping for the next century. The White Paper 'Excellence in Schools' (DFEE, 1997b) states that mixed ability grouping has not proved capable of playing to the strengths of every child (p. 38, par. 3) and that by setting, advantage can be taken of whole class teaching to maintain pace and challenge of lessons. Furthermore, that by 2002 'we will have all schools setting pupils by ability' (p. 7, par. 4).

The White Paper introduces the idea of 'target grouping' (p. 39) in which pupils are grouped by ability for part of the week and the composition of the groups are changed in line with regular assessment. It is not clear what type of grouping is expected for the remaining part of the week. The consequences of moving pupils in and out of groups as the result of regular testing are not discussed. Movement of pupils between groups has implications for teachers setting appropriate work for pupils, which is based on their knowledge of pupils built up over time. Target grouping may also have implications for pupil friendship grouping; meeting friends is a powerful incentive for many pupils to go to school.

Teachers are required to organise teaching to maximise the potential of all pupils in their classes and that work should be differentiated to meet the needs of pupils and ensure progression in learning. Such demands in effect require teachers to acknowledge that their classes, however grouped, are mixed ability but clearly, when 'setted', classes contain a narrower spread of ability than when organised around wide-ability groupings. It is said to be less demanding on teachers to prepare lessons for a narrow spread of ability but this judgement may apply only to classes comprising able pupils. In addition, the pressures on schools to maximise performance can lead to streamed classes taught as though the pupils are a homogeneous set, defeating the purpose of streaming.

Streamed classes, however they are formed, are usually based on achievement not, for example, on potential, ability or motivation and so contain pupils with a range of attitudes and approaches to learning. However, some classes must contain many pupils who, for one reason or another, underachieve and are likely to contain a disproportionate number of pupils with learning difficulties, behavioural difficulties or other special needs. Teachers working with classes formed in this way may have a daunting task. Indeed, the existence of such classes in the 1960s was one reason why wide ability grouping was first introduced.

The best ways to group pupils has been a vexed question for many years. The raising of the school leaving age in 1972 required schools to cater for a wide range of ability, behaviours and motivation in pupils up to 16 years of age and, more recently, beyond 16 as more pupils sought post-16 education. The emphasis on schools and their teachers to raise standards, coupled with the use of SAT and GCSE results as the yardstick of the quality of those standards, has led to greater demands for setting or streaming and whole class teaching. Although standards of achievement may rise for some, but not all pupils (DFEE, 1998b, appendix), one wonders whether the achievements of pupils taught in this pressured way will have any lasting effect on the educational standards and the capacity of future adults to participate in the 'learning society' (DFEE, 1998a). For further discussion on this topic see Bourne and Moon (1994).

Task 4.1.7

How are pupils grouped in your school?
These inquiries could form the basis for written coursework, assignments or portfolio entries.

1 How are pupils grouped in your school for National Curriculum subjects? You may need to look at school documents and talk to senior staff. If possible find out:

- is there a school policy about the way pupils are grouped?
- how decisions are made about grouping pupils; that is, the criteria used for directing individual pupils into groups;
- do all subjects use the same or similar criteria for grouping pupils? If appropriate, what justification is given for applying different criteria?
- do different criteria apply for grouping pupils at KS3 and KS4?
- how do the results of tests for pupils on entry to the school relate to their later membership of classes formed by setting or streaming?

2 Respond to these questions.

A Is there any evidence that pupils gain academically, socially or in other ways from the grouping policy in your school?
B Are any pupils disadvantaged by the policy?
C Is the potential to achieve on entry to the school borne out by later performance? And is this performance related to the setting?

Compare the composition of the groups and identify any obvious differences between the membership of the groups?

DIFFERENTIATION AND AIMS

The introduction of the National Curriculum within the 1988 Education Reform Act required schools to address afresh the question of standards. The National Curriculum represents an entitlement; despite changes in its structure and some erosion of the notion of entitlement in the wake of revisions (Dearing, 1994), there remains for all pupils a substantial curriculum entitlement; see also Unit 7.3.

How can this entitlement be realised given the diversity of performance, experience and motivation displayed by young people? Schools either establish broad groups of pupils of similar attainment or work towards treating pupils as individuals. Establishing broad groups of pupils by streaming leads to a class of low-attaining pupils in each year group. Such groups may be taught on a regular basis using a restricted syllabus, less rich, narrow in focus and may lack balance. On the other hand, if pupils are treated more as individuals, their needs have to be diagnosed and their teaching structured to take account of those needs within the framework of a common syllabus.

Whichever policy is adopted, however, at the heart of the problem there lies a deeper question. This is:

> Do the same basic goals apply to all
> pupils across the whole ability range?

In the course of their review of and research into the educational provision for raising the attainment of pupils, the National Foundation for Educational Research identified very broad differences between schools which, in relation to the question above and by reference to their day-to-day practice, could be said to have answered as either YES! or NO! (Stradling *et al.*, 1991).

It was found that some schools made the same curriculum provision for all their pupils. This decision implied a common core timetable. Modification of the common core course in these schools might, for example, include a modular course with a common core of modules. Options outside the common core might include pre-vocational work, enrichment activities and units of work of a cross-curricular nature.

By contrast, schools which focused on differentiation by grouping pupils by ability were seen to be less sure whether the same goals of education applied to all pupils. Different tasks set to different groups of pupils frequently reflected different content and curriculum aims. Breadth and balance in the curriculum was less likely to be found for streamed pupils. For low-achieving pupils the thinner curriculum was justified by insisting that retaining breadth and balance might drive some 14–16-year-old pupils away from school. Allowing pupils to specialise successfully in a few activities will encourage them, it was said, to attend, raising their interest in school and lowering truancy rates.

Whichever route was developed within the common curriculum, many schools emphasised the importance of a regular review of progress, often by means of teacher–pupil discussion. Regular assessment and its outcome featured prominently in such dialogue.

In the same review (Stradling *et al.*) its findings were summarised by means of a diagram, shown in Figure 4.1.2. This shows the broad trends in several features of school policy and practice as detected across schools reflecting different aspects of differentiation. Two models are shown: one model in which differentiation is by classes; another by individuals.

The top half of Figure 4.1.2 identifies the broad features of a school which separates its pupils into streams or bands, i.e. differentiation by groups. The striking characteristic of this model is difference in the goals set for different groups of pupils. By contrast, in the second model in which differentiation is achieved by concentrating on the individual, goals remain the same but differences appear in teaching approaches and the pace of learning. The greatest difference lies in the review of pupils' work (see right-hand side of the diagram). For the schools which 'differentiate by groups', a common method of reviewing progress is used, i.e. the same for all pupils, whereas 'differentiation by individual' leads to attention being given to individual pupils in the review of their work.

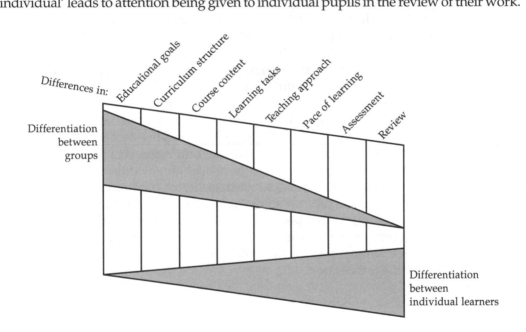

Figure 4.1.2 Forms of differentiation
Source: Stradling, Saunders and Weston (1991)

However, Figure 4.1.2 indicates trends and is not meant to imply that the practice of schools is one of either of the two extremes. It identifies in both models the overlap in the emphasis on learning tasks and teaching approaches. Whichever method of grouping pupils is adopted, the choice of task and the range of teaching strategies are seen to be important for the successful implementation of a differentiated approach to the curriculum.

Aims

At the heart of the debate about standards and differentiation of work for pupils are educational aims. See also Unit 7.1. Is it desirable for all pupils to work towards a curriculum in which common goals are shared for most of the pupils' time in school? Or should the differences between pupils as measured by their performance and achievement in the school be acknowledged and used as a basis for structuring curricula appropriate to their needs? Both courses of action can be justified educationally. Different curricula for pupils of different achievement allow clearly defined but separate goals to be set. This course of action limits the horizon of some pupils. Maintaining common goals for all through a common curriculum requires appropriate teaching methods so that individuals can reach out to those goals to the best of their ability.

The willingness of society to structure and resource these alternative curriculum decisions is a political decision, resting on values and beliefs. When the comprehensive system was introduced, in the 1960s, much of the educational system responded by developing mixed ability teaching methods and resourced-based learning. However, that policy has changed, largely as the result of the Education Reform Act, 1988. Setting by achievement is the expectation, with differentiation to be exercised within that context. Target setting is the new language of differentiation (DFEE, 1997a; SCAA, 1997). At the heart of the proposed changes lies a tension. On the one hand, teachers are expected to set targets for pupils based on regular testing; on the other hand, whole class teaching is advocated to maintain the pace and challenge of lessons. Thus teaching methods and class organisation is directed at groups while target setting is aimed at the individual.

The educational response to differences in ability hinges on the introduction of appropriate teaching strategies and tasks suited to the pupil; work needs to be differentiated, progression must be monitored and assessment made. The choice of educational aims for our pupils is a political one but the implementation of those aims through the curriculum, choice of teaching methods and the grouping of pupils in a school must be an educational one. We are in danger of more and more decisions being made for teachers outside the school.

> **⁞ Summary and key points**
>
> Children learn in different ways at different speeds; many pupils have learning needs related to emotional, behavioural and cognitive difficulties. It is abundantly clear that teachers need to plan their lessons to take account of those differences, as far as is practically possible. Schools have responded to these differences by grouping pupils in various ways: setting, streaming, banding and wide (mixed) ability classes. We have discussed the swing away from wide ability classes and attention to the individual pupil, to an emphasis in the late 1990s, by ministers and the inspectorate, on grouping pupils by setting, whole class teaching and target-setting. These movements in grouping need to be set against thin evidence from research into the effects on performance of pupils when grouped in different ways. In their review of research evidence, Hallam and Toutounji suggest that attention should be placed on encouraging effort and promoting motivation in pupils rather than setting pupils by ability. There is little evidence that a return to selection methods can change the culture of under-performance exhibited by some of our pupils (Hallam and Toutounji, 1996, pp. 23–4).
>
> Whatever grouping policy is adopted by a school, classes remain a collection of individuals for which you need to adopt a differentiated teaching approach. We have identified ways in which differentiation can be achieved, but you need to recognise the limitations of what can be achieved in large classes with heavy workloads. Nevertheless, the role of the teacher in supporting and motivating pupils in their work is crucial to their success.
>
> Your ability to respond to the needs of your pupils is a skill which develops over time as you get to know your pupils. Monitor your own progress throughout the course against the Standards expected of NQTs. In doing so you should recognise that this ability is made up of many skills found under the headings in the Standards of 'Planning, teaching and class management' and 'Assessment'.

FURTHER READING

Bourne, R., Davitt, J. and Wright, J. (1995) *Differentiation: Taking IT Forward*, Coventry: National Council for Educational Technology.

A useful book which identifies ways in which IT can support teachers introducing differentiation into their lessons.

Dickinson, C. and Wright, J. (1993) *Differentiation: Practical Handbook of Classroom Strategies*, Coventry: National Council for Educational Technology.

A set of practical resources which addresses issues of differentiated learning under the headings of resource, task, support and response. There are clearly identified discussions with examples taken from subject-specific work. There are many ideas for in-service teacher education. Student teachers as a start might usefully tackle the Diamond Nine exercise, page 33.

Hallam, S. and Toutounji, I. (1996) *What do we Know About the Grouping of Pupils by Ability? A Research Review*, London: Institute of Education, University of London, p. 40.

Contains an extensive bibliography (approx. 250 references) which reviews the research carried out in this country and overseas into the effects of pupil grouping on academic performance. Covers mainly the last 40 years but extends back further in time. Essential reading for those seeking to understand arguments about grouping pupils in school. See also Hallam (1996).

Hargreaves, D.H. (1984) *Improving Secondary Schools: Report of the Committee on the Curriculum and Organisation of Secondary Schools*, London: ILEA.

This report was a landmark in the development of strategies for the improvement of London schools. Its suggestions have wider implications for the raising of achievement of pupils in all schools. See, for example, the sections on pupil grouping (3.5) and independent learning (3.8).

Hart, S. (ed.) (1996) *Differentiation and the Secondary Curriculum: Debates and Dilemmas*, London: Routledge.

For those wishing to dig deeper into the purposes and practice of differentiation.

HMI (1978) *Mixed Ability Work in Comprehensive Schools*, London, HMSO.

An in-depth study of a key issue in the development of the comprehensive school in the 1970s. As well as dealing with school organisation, there are sections dealing with the use of mixed ability grouping in most subject areas.

Lambert, D. (1994) *Differentiated Learning*, London: University of London, Institute of Education, Initial Teacher Training (Occasional papers in teacher education and training. Resources).

A short, 24-page, booklet specially written for the student teacher which addresses the issues met by a new teacher attempting to put differentiation into practice.

National Commission on Education (1993) 'Innovation in learning', in *Learning to Succeed: A Radical Look at Education Today*, London: William Heinemann for the Paul Hamlyn Foundation.

Makes the case for the importance of the wider implementation of new methods of learning. These methods will involve raising the expectation of teachers and pupils, promoting study skills, independent learning and 'thinking skills'. Technology is seen as important in this process.

4.2 Growth and development

None of the teachers in our school have noticed that I am an intellectual. They will be sorry when I'm famous. There is a new girl in our class. She sits next to me in Geography. She is all right. Her name is Pandora, but she likes being called 'Box'. Don't ask me why. I might fall in love with her. It's time I fell in love, after all I'm 13 3/4 years old.

(from: Townsend, 1982), p. 17)

INTRODUCTION

Adolescence is a period of growth and physical, mental and emotional change. Sue Townsend's book, quoted above, offers an often amusing but insightful commentary on the pains of growing up. The onset of these changes in adolescence comes at a time when society demands that young people attend school and be in continual close contact with their peers where they are reminded constantly of the differences between themselves and others. This places a great strain on the adolescent's perception of themselves.

These physical and emotional changes take place against a background of family life, within a particular society and culture that itself has expectations of its young people. Young people bring to school a knowledge and expectation derived from their family; some young people bring not only the advantages, but some of the disadvantages of society. These disadvantages include parents living on low wages or are unemployed; or instability within the family, all or some of which portend poor career prospects; (see Child, 1993, p. 302). Yet others bring pressures to succeed and a burden of expectation; while others have disabilities, some mild and supportable by technology, e.g. wearing glasses, others carry more serious disadvantages, such as dyslexia, less easily overcome.

Most young people want to be normal, to conform to what they see others doing and being. This gives rise to pressure to conform to peer norms and to question or reject family norms. Conforming, in part, concerns appearance; personal appearance becomes a highly sensitive consideration during adolescence for two reasons; one concerns the notion of normality, shape, size etc., the second concerns their sexuality and emerging relationships.

Many adolescents are trying to 'find their feet', develop an identity and develop new relationships with adults, especially parents. Within this context the academic pressures of school demand that pupils make far reaching choices about careers. Pressures to make this choice come from home and school, such as through questions: 'what do you want to do when you leave school?' Many young people, often with good reason just don't know how to respond, or how to choose.

Schools have a vital part to play in this period. They unequivocally exist to further the development of the pupil and must try to provide the environment in which personal autonomy can grow. At the same time, but in order to cope with several hundred young people in a confined space, schools must provide a disciplined context for the healthy growth of not just the individual, but for everyone. In this sense of course, having so many young people all together means that conditions for the growth of the individual are not necessarily compatible with those for the emergence of the autonomous individual.

Balancing family and peer pressures is important during adolescence. Parents are anxious that any physical shortcoming should be treated properly whereas pupils are likely to shy away from drawing attention to themselves. Thus, wearing spectacles or dental braces become issues for teenagers at this period of their life, because the image they give to others is one of 'difference' and, perhaps, defect. Teachers need to be aware of these disabilities in order to respond sensitively in the classroom.

This unit enables you to consider through the eyes of pupils in your school first the phenomenon of physical growth and development and then to look at the range of behaviours that accompany young people at this period of their lives. It considers, too the possible effect of adolescence on personality and offers a theory to explain how pupils may begin to make subject choices in relation to their need to confirm their own emerging personality and identity.

OBJECTIVES

At the end of this unit you will be able to:

- discuss the meaning of normal growth and development in relation to adolescence;
- describe and understand some of the physical and emotional differences between school-age pupils;
- identify implications of these differences for teaching and learning;
- appreciate the effect of external pressures and influences on pupil behaviour.

ABOUT PHYSICAL GROWTH AND DEVELOPMENT

Variation in the height and weight of children depends largely on genetic, health and nutritional factors. Information about the growth and health of individuals is best obtained by a study of the changes in body measurements of the individual and comparing those with reference standards. Recent data on the height and weight of the population are shown in Figures 4.2.1–4.2.4 (Coles and Turner 1994). These data include measurements on young people across the ages 5 to 15 +.

The data are based on observations of large numbers of individuals in different age groups, i.e. a cross-sectional study, and presented in the form of several graphs on the same axis. Each graph is related to numbers of individuals having the same measurements, using percentiles (or centiles). The 50th centile on the height graph means that 50% of all individuals at that age were taller than this; and 50% were shorter. The 97th centile means that 3% of individuals were taller than this height. The value of using the

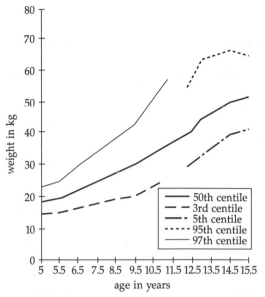

Figure 4.2.1 Weights of girls from 5 to 16 years
Source: Coles, A. and Turner, S. (1995)

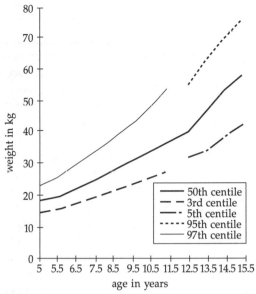

Figure 4.2.2 Weights of boys from 5 to 16 years
Source: Coles, A. and Turner, S. (1995)

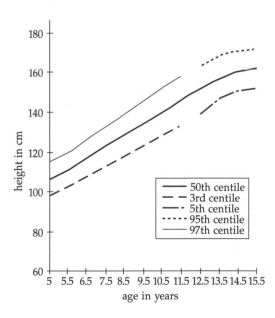

Figure 4.2.3 Heights of girls from 5 to 16 years
Source: Coles, A. and Turner, S. (1995)

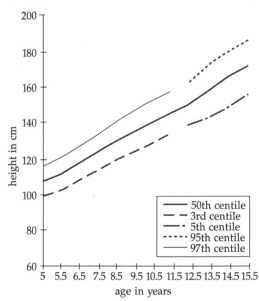

Figure 4.2.4 Heights of boys from 5 to 16 years
Source: Coles, A. and Turner, S. (1995)

50th percentile is that it corresponds to the mean value. Children who receive enough energy and nutrients in their diet should grow adequately; the growth curve of such a person should fit onto one of the centile curves, Figures 4.2.1–4.2.4, very closely. Sudden departures usually have a simple explanation, related to illness or nutritional change.

The data displayed show that there is considerable variation in the height and weight of individuals. Children tend to have growth spurts, particularly after puberty (puberty is the point at which the sex glands become functional). There are differences in growth rates between boys and girls at certain periods, girls showing a spurt at an earlier age than boys. Thus most girls mature physically earlier than most boys of the same age. Height increases appear earlier than weight increases and this has implications for physical activity, e.g. physical education. This is the origin of clumsiness and awkwardness of many adolescent boys. These differences can affect pupil's performance. Boys who develop late often cannot compete with their peers in games in early adolescence; and girls who mature earlier than their friends can feel embarrassed.

In the past one hundred years the average height and weight of children and adults has increased. At the same time the age at which puberty arrives has decreased. Such average changes are due in part to increased nutritional standards, better conditions of health and sanitation as well as better economic circumstances for the majority. The nutritional status of most children in England and Wales does not appear to be a cause for concern. However there is suggestion in some research that faster physically maturing children score better on mental tests than slower developing children. Of course, girls develop faster than boys on average; it was because of this factor that the 11+ examination of the 1940–1950s was adjusted to give equal opportunities for boys to gain places in grammar schools in the face of girls' earlier maturation.

There is other evidence accumulating (Tanner, 1991) that environmental factors affect growth. These include:

- the size of the family; many larger families have children of below average height;
- where the pupil is raised; urban-reared children are often taller and heavier than those raised in a rural society;
- the socio-economic status of the family (parents); lower social class, defined by the employment status of the parents, correlates with having shorter children;
- prolonged unemployment has a similar effect to socio-economic factors.

Such factors by themselves do not have a direct causal relationship but reflect complex underlying influences on growth and development.

Problems experienced by pupils because of early or late onset of puberty were mentioned earlier. It is of interest to consider that any 12-year-old girl might be in a pre-pubertal, mid-pubertal or post pubertal state; and any 14-year-old boy similarly. Thus it is not sensible to talk of a 14-year-old group of children as though they represented a homogeneous cohort.

Task 4.2.1

WHAT WILL YOUR PUPILS BE LIKE?

Some of the statements above may not fit in with your own experience of school as a pupil, or as you recollect your own school-days. You may not, for example, have considered the effect of socio-economic status on physical development or academic performance. This task is designed to open up that focus.

In what ways do the pupils in your practice school resemble or differ from:

- pupils from your own school days;
- your expectations prior to this course?

You might consider:

- family sizes, extended families in the school;
- physical appearance – height, weight, physical maturity;
- socio-economic classes into which pupils may fit;
- employment rates in the families, or the local area.

You may wish to compare, too, such additional details as:
- dress, uniform, well dressed, etc.;
- self-confidence, willing to talk to teachers and to each other;
- attitude to authority, respect for other pupils, respect for teachers.

Collect your own impressions for discussion with other student teachers and with a tutor. It may be interesting to repeat this exercise much later in your PGCE year and see how familiarity with the pupils and school has altered first impressions.

Task 4.2.2

GROWTH AND DEVELOPMENT

Use the graphs of Figures 4.2.1–4.2.4 to identify the possible range of heights and weights of pupils in Years 7, 9 and 11 and to contrast the different rate of weight increase between boys and girls; and identify the probable ages at which these are most obvious.

| Task 4.2.3 | PUPILS IN YOUR SCHOOL 1 |

PUPILS IN YOUR SCHOOL 1

Collect data on the height and weight of pupils in one or more classes for Years 7 through to Year 11. The school records hold that data and you must get permission to gain access to this confidential data; ask your tutor in the first instance. This is best carried out as a group task with other student teachers, sharing the tasks. Ensure that individual pupil records are not exposed.

Present the data in a way that allows you to compare them with norms of development, as shown in Figures 4.2.1–4.2.4. Consider in what ways the pupils in your school tend towards the norm. Discuss any variation in the following terms:

- Does the school data suggest a normal distribution of heights or weights across the sample? Look up, as needed, the meaning of 'normal distribution curve' in a mathematics, statistics or psychology text.
- What evidence is there that pupils are above or below an average height or weight?
- Does the cultural diversity of pupils in your sample contribute to any variation in your data? Consider both gender and ethnic group differences when discussing the data.

How will your findings affect your teaching or influence your lesson planning?

Task 4.2.4

DIFFERENCES OF CLASS MANAGEMENT: SOME QUESTIONS TO CONSIDER (WORK WITH OTHER STUDENT TEACHERS OR TUTORS)

What does the variation in the physical development of pupils in one year cohort imply for the management of secondary school classes? These questions are to start you thinking:

- different rates of growth and range of 'pupil size' in games, drama;
- apparent clumsiness of pupils in activities which require substantial psychomotor skills, e.g. PE and games, art and design, technology, science, computing;
- is there any relation in your teaching practice school between the growth data and free school meal provision, or, for example, the provision and take-up of breakfast?
- should pupils be grouped in classes by age, as they are now, or should some other method be used to group pupils for teaching purposes, e.g. in mixed age classes by academic performance?

Task 4.2.5	PUPILS IN YOUR SCHOOL 2: CLASSROOM OBSERVATION OR OTHER SCHOOL-BASED ENQUIRY

Arrange to follow a class for a day to see it in a variety of subject settings, with different teachers, and collect information about that class. Some of this information may be obtained in Task 4.2.3. The following list of suggestions (A to D) gives a range of information that it is possible to collect. Select from this list an appropriate focus, i.e. useful now to you and other student teachers. Remember to respect the confidentiality of information in written and oral reporting.

Devise a way of collecting this information. Some information can be obtained while watching a class while other pieces of information can be gained direct from the class or form teacher. The whole task may be shared among several people and information pooled for discussion. Your tutor can direct you to appropriate sources. The school PE staff may well be a good source of information on physical development. You will need a week or two to collect, collate and work up the information for presentation and discussion. If you concentrate on a class, start with a list of class names.

When you visit classrooms get permission from the teacher and tell them what you are doing, what is to happen to the information and what is expected to emerge.

A Register and attendance

- Numbers of boys and girls.
- Ethnic minority pupils; check the way the school reports ethnicity. If there is no guide to this available, then use the guide on p. 158 adapted from the Graduate Teacher Training Registry (GTTR) and used by them to collect statistical evidence about the ethnicity of applicants for teacher training.
- Any particular religious or culturally significant-sized group in the class, e.g. Seventh Day Adventist, travellers' children.
- Ask the form teacher to let you see the class register. Obtain a class list.
- Use the class register to identify any pattern of absences and whether absences are supported by notes from parents or guardians.
- The mark register may show the regularity and quality of homework.

B The physical characteristics of pupils   Collect information about pupils using this list of suggestions:

- The height and weight of pupils; see Task 4.2.3. Compare the data by gender.
- How many wear spectacles all the time?
- How many use spectacles for reading, or board work (it can be instructive to find out, perhaps from the form teacher, those who should use spectacles, but don't; young people don't usually wear contact lenses but ask about this as well)?

Table 4.2.1 A guide to reporting ethnicity

unplaced (not willing to state)
white
black – African
black – Afro-Caribbean
black – Asian
black – other
Asian – Indian
Asian – Pakistani
Asian – Bangladeshi
Asian – Chinese
Asian – other
other (i.e. ethnicity not recognised in above categories)

Source: adapted from GTTR Annual Report 1993

• Those that use a hearing aid; some pupils may be seated near the front of the class for this reason. Find out if any should wear a hearing aid, but don't.
• Any pupils undergoing dental treatment, e.g. wearing tooth braces.
• Ask about the number of pupils who suffer from anorexia nervosa, asthma, diabetes or epilepsy.
• Any other disabilities.

C Special needs   Probably best collected outside the lesson. Find out the number of pupils in the class who have

• specific learning difficulties, e.g. dyslexia;
• statements of special needs and the reason for this;
• a support teacher, and why;
• no support teacher, but need one and why.

D School meals   How many pupils in the class are entitled to free school meals? This information is confidential and may be obtained from your tutor. Reports should not quote names.

Using the information

The data should focus on a particular area of interest. Before meeting to discuss it, you should:

- have a copy of all the data collected;
- have read it through;
- note at least two points of interest, or which need clarification.

A group discussion could then focus on the collective information. Questions to address include:

- how representative is the information of the class or group investigated; does the sample you have used represent the school or does it only represent one section of the school; in what way is your sample biased?
- how does the revealed data compare with your impressions of the class; what has been added?
- how is this information useful in lesson preparation; classroom organisation and management; individual pupil management; pastoral care, e.g. form tutor roles?
- being alert to signs of pupils at risk, those lacking care, or are anorexics or subject to physical abuse.

The collected data could be worked up individually into a short report for the tutor. It could form the focus of a piece of coursework, and/or added to your portfolio of achievements. Finally your personal response to doing the work and its consequences could be recorded in your diary.

Personality development and response to school subjects

By personality we refer to those features of a person – physical, emotional and psychological – by which they are recognised. For children one aspect of their personality emerges out of their family relationships, as the daughter of . . . Physical characteristics emerge from birth and, although important, most are not affected by the environment. Weight is, however; it is very much dependent on diet and lifestyle. On the other hand, height is genetically determined but a maximum height is not realised unless the person receives a suitable diet. Other characteristics emerge because of the way young people are treated. Parental treatment in terms of discipline, control and affection affects the development of behaviour, which contributes to the development of personality. A warm, loving relationship accompanied by inflexible application of rules of conduct and behaviour, although giving security, may at the same time lead to lack of self-confidence. A lack of self-confidence or self-esteem can in turn lead to difficulties in adolescence when personal decision making arises. A sense of personal worth is needed when young people are required to make decisions about their future.

Excessive control and discipline can threaten the pupil's development of autonomy, self-confidence and self-reliance. Studies have suggested that where the discipline is flexible, but firm and consistent, and exerted only for the pupil's betterment (rather than in the interest of the parents' peace of mind or as an expression of hostility) then a good balance is achieved between conformity and personal autonomy. Such balance would include co-operative, responsible, disciplined behaviour on one hand and expressions of self-confidence, personal autonomy, self-reliance and freedom on the other.

Such are ideals; in practice pupils come to us from a range of backgrounds and climates of control. Parents act as best they can, sometimes under pressure, nearly always in the child's interest as they see it but occasionally with a touch of self-interest. Schools should be different. They exist only to educate pupils and with no other major agenda. The difficulty is to balance the needs of the individual with the greater good (needs) of all pupils.

It is possible, and a priority, for schools to create a climate of security and discipline which allows most pupils to achieve the balance between conformity and autonomy. In addition, such a balance defines to some extent personality; and it is the extent of personality development that affects the way pupils behave and respond to both school subjects and teachers. It is only when pupils have a measure of self-esteem that sensible choices, i.e. real choices, about their futures may be made. One example is subject choice at 13+.

The reading below is taken from a text which examines the role of personality and type in the response to school and choice of subjects, particularly as it affects the choice between arts and sciences. The author recognises that both physical and emotional changes at adolescence contribute to the development of personality; and that personality, in turn affects initial subject and career choice (Head, 1985).

The author attempts to construct a theory of how pupils make choices of subjects, and to some extent career choices, in terms of their imperative of seeking personal identity in the transition from pupil to adult. Pupils, it is argued, move from an identity based largely on their parents to one of their own definition. In this process, they may confirm earlier identities, or they may repudiate them. In this extract from the text three routes in this process of identity determination are defined.

Task 4.2.6

PERSONALITY AND CHOICE AT 13+

Read the passage through once to get the general sense of it. Read it a second time using the following questions to help focus your thoughts. A good way to follow this up is through discussion between student teachers from a range of subjects. It might be informative to consider your own choice of subject for study at A level and subsequent university course in this context.

- Identify three features of the process of 'foreclosure' – highlight them perhaps on a *photocopy* of the text. (See paragraph 2.)
- It is suggested that some adolescents adopting the foreclosure route to identity and career choice may rethink their decision at some later date. Do you think this is unlikely, as the author claims? Why? (See paragraph 4.)
- To what extent does the moratorium phase identify with the reality of adolescent behaviours? Is it, in fact, a mature route to decision making? (See paragraph 3.)
- The author uses the model of routes to identity acquisition to discuss the different responses of boys and girls to subject choice in schools. List the differences between boys and girls described in this passage. (See paragraphs 5 and 6.)
- To what extent does the model relate to your own personal experience? Does it fit in with your emerging knowledge of young adolescents in this situation?

From Head (1985, pp. 67–8):

1 It has been argued that the making of these choices (between, e.g. arts and science at 13+) relating to a personal identity involves two processes. The first is that of commitment: individuals have to make a choice and cannot go on indefinitely hedging their bets and changing their mind from hour to hour. The second process is to give full thought to all the factors involved in the decision making, including a recognition of their own limitations and strengths. A firm commitment reached after a full consideration of the full issues represents a mature choice, in which a sense of personal identity has been achieved.

2 There are less satisfactory outcomes to adolescence. Some adolescents may try to avoid the discomfort of self-examination by clutching at solutions ready-made by others. The process of active thought is avoided and such a person is said to 'foreclose' on the decision. Commitment reached without adequate thought is likely to be accompanied by a rigidity in thinking, as questioning the decision opens up areas of doubt and uncertainty which have been avoided in making the 'foreclosure'.

3 Another possibility is that the adolescent, at least for a while, is somewhat overwhelmed by uncertainties and possibilities, so that there is considerable thought and self-examination but little sense of decision and commitment. That uneasy period, described as a moratorium, can often be observed in adolescence: a period of uncertainty about their own destiny, a concern with all the problems and ideals of the world, a scrutiny of a range of ideologies in search of assistance. The period of moratorium is an uncomfortable one for parents and friends as well as adolescents, and therefore tends to provide motivation to make decisions and thus acquire a personal identity. In contrast, however, such motivation does not exist with the person who has undergone foreclosure, and as noted previously, might resist further consideration of the issues.

4 These ways of handling the decision making process of adolescent identity acquisition are summarised in Figure 4.2.5. See the note under Figure 4.2.5 for further explanation.

5 How does this description of adolescence relate to subject choice? For girls, the decision to specialise in science almost inevitably involves both considerable thought and firm commitment. It is not an easy choice, as it involves running counter to some of the norms of the peer group in studying a subject associated with boys, so that the girl making the choice must have debated the issues and have some sense of purpose. One might consequently expect those girls who opt for science to be mature and confident in their decision, an expectation borne out by studies reported in the last chapter.

6 With boys the situation is more complex. Some will similarly have thought through all the issues and reached a mature decision after due thought. Others, however, make the choice by foreclosure. Science with its masculine image and obvious vocational uses is an easy choice for a boy to justify. It does not involve running counter to peer group norms. Above all, its apparently objective, instrumental character can appeal to boys by providing an emotionally

undemanding area to work in. Studying science is less likely to raise questions about one's emotions, sexuality, the purpose of life, interpersonal relationships, and so forth than studying the arts or the social sciences.

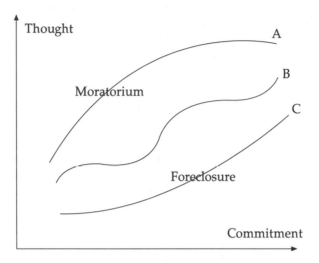

Figure 4.2.5 Routes to identity acquisition

Note: Some adolescents make a fairly even progress towards achieving adult identity (Route B), where others experience a period of moratorium (Route A). Those who tend to foreclose on difficult issues may later develop a mature identity (Route C) but the motivation to do so may not be strong.

Source: Head (1985, pp. 67–8)

Summary and key points

Adolescence sees dramatic physical changes in young people. Accompanying these changes are personality developments during which elements of personal autonomy appear. These changes can cause nervous introspection: 'Am I growing normally, am I too tall, too short, too fat? Will I be physically attractive to others?' Comparison with others becomes the main yardstick of development; young people want to be normal and this includes conforming to group norms about such things as behaviour, body shape and size. Personal appearance assumes a growing importance and sensitivity. In addition, muscles are flexed in relation to contemporaries, to teachers and to parents.

Tensions are often created for the adolescent when established family norms conflict with peer group norms (whether real or imaginary). Such tensions are revealed by the behaviour patterns of those involved, especially by their response to authority. Teachers represent authority; classroom difficulties can arise when pupils feel that their personal identity and respect is under challenge in front of their peers.

While individualism becomes an important concern for many pupils, many schools impose pressures of conformity of personal behaviour, of dress, of appearance and above all pressures on academic performance to succeed. Careers begin to loom over the horizon and parents and teachers start to ask 'what do you want to do when you leave school?' This question may well be linked to 13+ choices to be made in the curriculum, such as whether to choose another language or to take double sciences. Such a question may be the last thing on many pupils' minds, being more concerned with personal relationships within and between groups, both in and out of school, or with activities planned with contemporaries for the next day, week or month. For some, sporting activities assume much greater importance than long-term issues of careers.

However actively schools try to support the individual, much of their input must be through group work, in classes or other groupings. There is little time, unfortunately, for interaction at the individual level, except after school or on rare occasions, e.g. careers counselling, parents' evenings. Whereas many young people turn to their parents for support and guidance, a significant minority have no such support.

At the time of subject choice, pupils need to be helped to make decisions by teachers giving space and time for discussion and by providing them with information. Opportunities should be found to talk with pupils on their own, such that peer pressure is minimised and personal wishes allowed to surface without fear of ridicule and discussed non-judgementally. For the teacher, a knowledge of the possible routes (Task 4.2.6) by which young people come to decisions about subject choice may be helpful.

The National Curriculum introduced into England and Wales sought to minimise choice at 13+ (ERA, 1988) but aspects of that proposal have proved unworkable such that subject choice at the end of Key Stage 3 has been re-introduced for many subjects. A further important development affecting subject choice is the emergence of the vocational route as an alternative to the academic pathway at 14+ (DFEE, 1996). This development is a government response to an earlier review of the school curriculum (Dearing, 1994). An equally important factor is the development of study support for pupils in school which may have important effects on pupil choice of subject and career pathways (DFEE, 1998b). We have suggested that girls mature physically faster than boys, but the range of development of both sexes is wide. Adolescence involves physical, mental and emotional changes. However, the range of physical and emotional differences between pupils affects the way pupils of the same age cope with common tasks in school, as well as with each other.

To teach a class you need to know something of pupils' backgrounds, common features and differences; this is particularly hard on a student teacher taking over a class from the established teacher.

Pupils often have to make subject choices at 13+ which have a strong influence on career choices later in life, which causes decisions to be made in the middle of an often turbulent period of their life. We suggest that the way schools organise teaching and learning makes a difference to pupils' performance and life chances.

FURTHER READING

Coles, A. and Turner, S. (1995) *Diet and Health in School Aged Children*, London: Health Education Authority.

An up-to-date work written as a result of a survey of recent research findings of diet and health of the nation's children. Discusses the work of schools in Health Education, their provision of meals and what might be done to improve the diet of young people.

Head, J. (1985) *The Personal Response to Science*, Cambridge: Cambridge University Press.

Written with the teaching of science in secondary schools in mind, it explores how pupils respond to science teaching. Within that context it relates those responses to personality and discusses pupil attitudes and motivation to a range of school subjects. It explores, too, how pupils might come to choose arts or science and relates that to adolescence. Issues of gender arise naturally within that framework.

Rutter, M. *et al.* (1981) *Fifteen Thousand Hours*, London: Open Books. See page 66, 'School outcomes, attendance, behaviour and attainment'.

A research report which describes in detail how schools affect teaching and learning. The case is made that 'how schools are organised matters for pupils' success'. Worth reading in this context are Chapter 3, 'Schools and the area they serve'; and Chapter 8, 'Ecological influences'.

Tanner, J.M. (1991) *Foetus to Man (revised and enlarged edition)*, Cambridge, MA: Harvard University Press.

A fundamental resource for those interested in the detail of growth and development of humans. The chapters on 'Puberty' and 'Heredity and environment' are particularly valuable in the context of this unit.

4.3   COGNITIVE DEVELOPMENT

INTRODUCTION

Our everyday common-sense experience tells us that individuals differ in their capacity to cope with problems. Some children are more advanced than others from an early age. Some learn to walk before others; some children, not necessarily the same ones, learn to talk before others. Some children learn to read earlier than other children and appear, at least temporarily, to benefit more from school. We often refer to this ability as intelligence. Such differences are real for parents who are concerned that their child is developing normally and is able to respond to the demands of school work.

By **cognition** we mean the exercise of skills with understanding, such as map reading or following instructions to make something or carry out a task or to assess evidence. Thus cognition is distinguished from conditioned learning or reflex actions.

Intelligence is one aspect of cognitive or intellectual development and includes the capacity for logical reasoning, as in legal, moral, mathematical or scientific contexts. Many school subjects require the exercise of such skill, e.g. of handling evidence, making judgements, untangling moral dilemmas or applying theories. Imagination and imaginative thinking play a part in the capacity of individuals to solve intellectual problems. A pupil's ability to develop such skills demands particular **attitudes**. By attitude we include the wish to engage with tasks, perseverance as well as open-mindedness, willingness to withhold judgement in the face of inadequate evidence. In this unit we consider some ways in which pupils' cognitive abilities develop and are identified. It is, in a sense, a continuation of Unit 4.2 which considered physical and emotional development.

A description of intelligence by Gardner has proposed that humans have a number of intelligences (Gardner, 1994). Known as the 'theory of multiple intelligences', some of the ideas behind the theory have been adopted by some teachers and advisers but it is by no means widely accepted; see, for example, White (1998). In this unit we concentrate on some examples of logical reasoning in some aspects of the school curriculum.

OBJECTIVES

By the end of this unit you should:

- be able to appreciate the differences in academic performance of pupils in terms of intelligence and development;
- have met some tests of pupil attainment and tried them out with pupils;
- have contrasted ideas of 'specific intelligence' with a notion of 'general intelligence';
- have considered the implication for curriculum planning of a developmental model of learning;

- have entered the 'nature–nurture' debate concerning intelligence;
- have identified this aspect of understanding pupil attainment with the standards expected of NQTs.

DIFFERENCES BETWEEN PUPILS

Differences in young children, often siblings, are usually noted through play and games, e.g. cards, board games, etc. Games help children to socialise, learn to take turns, appreciate others' viewpoints. Success encourages greater participation, enhances skills and encourages the winner. In families with more than one child, it soon becomes evident that some children learn, e.g. to play board games, more quickly than others. It may result in some children being labelled brighter than others from an early age. Such children may be more intelligent than others, have greater drive or both.

It can be argued that school work is a game which pupils have not chosen to play, but which others, teachers and society, have chosen for them. If this assumption is correct, then it is likely that pupils are not highly motivated by the content and focus of lessons and, therefore, not all pupils succeed. In other words, the only motivation that is a spur to them is extrinsic such as praise, good examination results or even avoidance of unpleasant consequences of failure. It is well documented that both young and adult learners work best at tasks which they themselves identify as worthwhile. It would appear that they have the intrinsic motivation that accompanies self-chosen tasks. A key task for teachers is to generate motivation in pupils; see Unit 3.2.

From the pupils' first day in primary school, both parents and teachers are able to recognise that some pupils are better at school tasks than others. Their daily achievement is better than that of other pupils; they produce more work or achieve better quality of writing, tackle harder tasks or are able to read a wider range of books. Some pupils may be able to solve harder sums or achieve higher scores in tests.

From a young age it is clear that some pupils are more advanced than others. It might be said that some pupils are 'more intelligent' than others, or, more accurately, display more **intelligent behaviour**. A different way of describing such differences is that some pupils have **developed cognitively** faster than others. One description suggests that there is a factor or factors, called intelligence, which allows some pupils to respond to tasks and challenges in a different way to other pupils. The other description looks upon mental alertness as a developing quality which 'grows faster' for some pupils than for others. Intelligence, however that is measured, is perhaps something that, in part, limits the performance of its possessor.

Development carries with it the potential for change, which teaching can do something about. The capacity for intelligent behaviour may be imagined as something with which we are born; performance is the response of the individual to the environment, including school.

The appearance of intelligent behaviour requires situations in which these skills can be revealed, as well as the opportunity to exercise and hone them. Intelligent behaviour is the product of genetic factors and environmental factors. The extent to which one dominates the other or is the governing factor in determining final performance, is an age-old debate, referred to as the 'nature–nurture debate'. Nevertheless, much evidence has accumulated to suggest that lack of stimuli in early childhood limits the capacity of pupils to profit from school and other learning situations.

By means of tasks for you to carry out, we consider now some evidence obtained from tasks set to pupils which allow us to learn something about how pupils think and respond to problems and thereby gain insight into their cognitive development. In considering the information we gain about pupils as a result of doing these tasks, we should bear in mind that the final performance relates only to the context in which they were set; whether that judgement can be generalised to other situations is less certain.

Task 4.3.1

SORTING VARIABLES 1

Try out the following problem on your own; then share with other student teachers how you set about solving the problem.

When Amy, Bill and Clare eat out, each orders *either* chicken or fish, according to these rules:

a If Amy orders chicken, Bill orders fish;
b Either Amy or Clare orders chicken, but not both;
c Bill and Clare do not both order fish.

Who could have ordered chicken yesterday and fish today? (See Appendix 4.3.1 for the answer.)

The problem is essentially about handling information according to rules. It is the type commonly found in puzzle books and intelligence tests. It is of the type 'If A occurs, then B happens.' The rules are arbitrary and it is not a real life problem in the sense that people don't behave in this way. The problem cannot be solved by resort to practical activity; abstract thinking is required. It can be done in the head, but most people would need to devise a recording sheet (matrix) against which to check solutions.

Task 4.3.2

SORTING VARIABLES 2: WHICH FACTORS (VARIABLES) AFFECT THE SWING OF A PENDULUM; ABILITY TO HANDLE A COMPLEX SITUATION

This is a commonly set school problem; it concerns understanding and how that knowledge is gained, rather than knowing the answers.
A pendulum is essentially a rod pivoted vertically at one end and free to swing from side to side. A grandfather clock contains a pendulum, with a heavy weight at one end.
A simple example of a pendulum is a piece of string suspended at one end and a metal weight or bob, at the other. See sketches below.
From a developmental point of view the interesting features of this problem are:

- for a given pendulum, the time period remains the same whether the swings are small or wide; intuitively pupils do not expect this; it is not common-sense;
- those factors which may affect the time period of the pendulum, the length of the pendulum, mass of the bob or the position of release (high or low). The mass of the bob and small differences in position of release do not affect the time period. These results are not in tune with common-sense.

Pupils are sometimes expected to use experimental data to deduce 'rules of the pendulum'; some data contradict common sense and may therefore cause cognitive conflict. The extent to which pupils can rationalise the data into rules explaining how a pendulum is controlled is one measure of their intellectual development. The task is not to learn the rules, but to understand how the rules derive from observation.

What follows is an example of an experimental situation set up by a teacher with pupils and the information obtained by the pupils. Some limited deductions can be made from the data. The exercise is to work out what can or cannot be deduced from the data.

The task: Two pupils were given a task to find out which factors affected the time period of a pendulum. They were not told exactly what to do; they decided to measure the number of swings made by a pendulum in half a minute; see Figure 4.3.1. They changed aspects of the pendulum each time, by varying:

- the length of the pendulum; they had one short pendulum and one long pendulum;
- the size of the bob on the end of the pendulum – one heavy and one light;
- the height it was raised to set it going; one high up, the other low down.

Note: all long pendulums were the same length and all short pendulums were the same length. All heavy bobs were the same mass, as were all light bobs.

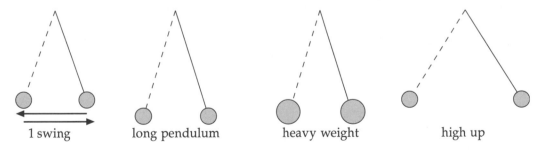

1 swing   long pendulum   heavy weight   high up

Figure 4.3.1 The pendulum

Sometimes they changed one thing at a time but occasionally changed more than one variable at a time. They collected some readings (Table 4.3.1) and then tried to sort out what the readings meant.

From this evidence alone what do you think the data tell you, separately, about the effect of length, of weight and of position of release on the number of swings per half minute of the pendulum?

See Appendix 4.3.2 for background information.

Table 4.3.1 Data on different pendulums

Investigation number	Length of the pendulum	Size of weight on the end	Position of release	Swings in $\frac{1}{2}$ minute
1	long	heavy	high	17
2	short	heavy	high	21
3	long	light	low	17
4	short	light	high	21

Task 4.3.3 SORTING VARIABLES 3: WORKING WITH PUPILS

If you want to try the pendulum task with pupils, details can be found in *Science Reasoning Tasks* (Wylam and Shayer, 1978) or the *CASE* materials (Adey *et al.*, 1989). The latter are important because the effects of using them suggest that cognitive change can be brought about by the same intervention strategies for pupils in English and mathematics as in science (Adey, 1992).

Task 4.3.4 PUPILS' UNDERSTANDING OF RATIO

A different sort of cognitive skill, for example, is how to calculate and use the concept of ratio. Percentages are a special aspect of ratio and part of current adult life. It is an area where considerable confusion reigns for both pupils and adults. One common confusion is financial inflation; many adults confuse cost of living with percentage inflation; they expect the cost of living to come down when the inflation rate is reduced but still positive. There is evidence, too, that not all adults can calculate real costs when sales advertising offers percentage discounts. Is performance in ratios and percentages a measure of intelligence or teaching? Consider the following test data.

Pupils were given a number of questions on percentages, together with an introduction which explained the meaning of '%'; the questions and the number of pupils getting the right answer (the success rate) for each year group are shown in Table 4.3.2 (Hart, 1981).

Carry out a survey to sample pupils' understanding of ratio. By sharing the work, Years 7, 9 and 11 in your school could be sampled. Analyse the results of your survey by:

- seeing how many succeed;
- seeing what sort of wrong answers you obtained and how they might be explained;
- interviewing some pupils to ask them to show you how they did the sum;
- using the discussion below (Appendix 2) to help interpret the pupils' responses.

A popular answer to question b was 192. You might like to speculate on how this figure was obtained. Common wrong answers to question c were 15 or 16 (40% of 13 year olds and 27% of 15 year olds). See also Task 6.1.9.

Table 4.3.2 Pupils' performance on questions involving ratio

Q.8 % means *per cent* or *per 100*, so 3% is 3 out of every 100			
a 6% of pupil in school have free dinners. There are 250 pupils in the school. How many pupils have free dinners?			
age/year	13	14	15
success rate/%	36	45	57
b The newspaper says that 24 out of 800 Avenger cars have a faulty engine. What percentage is this?			
age/year	13	14	15
success rate/%	32	40	58
c The price of a coat is £20. In the sale it is reduced by 5%. How much does it now cost?			
age/year	13	14	15
success rate/%	20	27	35

Source: Hart (1981, p. 96). For further studies on the performance of pupils in science and mathematics see Keys, Harris and Fernandes (1996).

IMPLICATIONS OF A SKILL DEVELOPMENT MODEL – DISCUSSION

The results of activities such as these suggest that as pupils get older there is a corresponding development in understanding. This may suggest that as pupils mature they are capable of an increasingly higher level of thinking (cognitive processing). Such a model of progressive development may be the result of biological maturation, of the quality of teaching, or both. The results may suggest, too, that some older pupils may not be able to solve such problems. The data accumulated by these and other tests of performance all point to the fact that a considerable number of pupils are unable to cope with such demands. However, such a result may be attributed to faulty teaching or lack of motivation, as to any lack of intelligence. It may be due to lack of biological maturation.

In this context you might wish to find out how pupils cope cognitively with moral dilemmas (i.e. work it out for themselves rather than an appeal to higher authority); or if they can solve murder mysteries in the popular genre of 'who dunits' of films or books.

Biological maturation may be another way of saying that the full genetic potential of the pupil becomes available. It implies, we suggest, that the conditions for the emergence of potential, the maximum intelligent behaviour of which the individual is capable, have been realised. What might those conditions be? It implies a home life in which the pupil has been encouraged in her play and schooling; where the emotional, linguistic and cognitive needs of the pupil have been met as the child grows and develops. It means, perhaps, exposure to good nursery and primary schooling and supportive parents who recognise and support the needs of the growing child. In other words, to what extent has the nurturing of the child allowed the child full expression of his potential? The performance we see in school, in class, on tests such as those above is at least a balance between nature and nurture, referred to earlier. This balance is unique for each child;

knowledge of the individual child's progress and background is essential before we can discuss the intelligence or otherwise of individuals.

Two ideas have been introduced so far: one suggests that performance is a product of inheritance and nurture – the nature–nurture debate; the second is that as pupils grow and develop so does their capacity to handle complex situations. If this second model is accepted it provides a rationale for structuring learning experiences for pupils or classes, i.e. it directs curriculum planning. Thus if the demand made by a piece of work is carefully analysed and the current performance of the pupil or a group of pupils is identified by reference to relevant skills needed to do the task, then the next learning activities for a pupil could be identified so as to guarantee some success for the pupil. Curriculum development, in this model, becomes a process of matching the curriculum demand to pupil development.

The following issues arise from proposing such a model. You may wish to add your own to this list:

- The efficiency of the model depends on being able to analyse teaching material sufficiently accurately in order to match material to pupil.
- Does the cognitive demand made by the teaching material depend on its 'intrinsic' concepts or does it depend on the way the material is presented? Put another way, can most concepts be taught to most pupils if suitably packaged and presented?
- Records of pupil performance and development are needed in order to match material to pupil. How might such records be kept?
- If matching 'curriculum to pupil' is the goal of the exercise, how might you build in development, going beyond the current level of performance? How would pupils progress? Is there a danger that fear of failure means removing challenges?
- If each pupil develops differently, how can a teacher cope with a class full of pupils at different stages of development? See Unit 4.1, 'Beyond task and outcome', p. 141.
- If pupils cannot cope with certain concepts because they are **not yet ready for them**, does this mean that some areas of the curriculum cannot be taught? Is rote learning an acceptable way to overcome this problem? See Unit 4.1 for more about differentiated learning and Unit 5.2 on active learning.
- If pupils perform well at some tasks, can they be expected to perform well at other tasks? Can the demonstration of one set of skills be used to predict success at new skills? Do the same pupils perform well at most subjects at school? You might investigate this hypothesis in your school. Can we speak of a 'generalised cognitive skill'? For further discussion see 'Describing and measuring cognitive development' in Adey and Shayer (1994, Chapter 2).

Task 4.3.5	**DISCUSSION** Discuss with other student teachers the evidence that pupils in your class(es) perform well in most subjects at similar tasks.

ANOTHER WAY OF LOOKING AT COGNITIVE SKILLS

Children can produce ready-made solutions to problems if given the appropriate conditions; sometimes the solutions are unusual, even impractical, but they give us insights into their understanding of the world. One such collection of children's responses to problems set by adults is by Edward de Bono (1972). His book is a collection of spontaneous work by pupils (upper primary, lower secondary) in response to problems related to everyday events. The responses show much imagination and insight into the world. The tasks selected by the author included:

- 'how would you stop a cat and a dog fighting?';
- 'design a machine to weigh an elephant';
- 'invent a sleep machine';
- 'how would you build a house quickly?';
- 'how would you improve the human body?';
- 'design a bicycle for postmen'.

Your choice of task should consider the pupils' environment; urban pupils may not see postmen on bicycles.

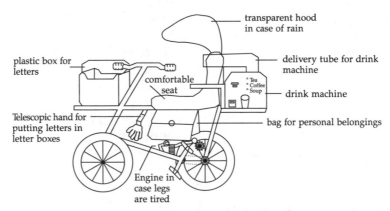

Bicycle - 6

Further refinements such as a transparent hood over the rider so that he doesn't get wet in the rain, and also a drink machine, where you put a coin in the slot and then choose whether you are going to have tea, coffee or soup. To save the postman's energy there is a telescopic hand for putting letters in letter-boxes. There is also an engine in case his legs get tired, but if there is going to be an engine it is hard to see why the postman should not use it all the time. But perhaps the designer thought that, if the bicycle was motorized throughout, then it would no longer be a postman's bicycle but a postman's motorcycle, so the engine is only provided as a sort of reserve, just as yachts have little reserve engines without ceasing to be yachts.

Figure 4.3.2 A bicycle for postmen
Source: De Bono (1972, p. 183)

Task 4.3.6 **DESIGN A BICYCLE FOR POSTMEN**

Ask pupils in one of your classes to do one task or invent your own related to a topic you are teaching. It may give you an insight into children's thinking as well as providing an imaginative homework task. It is important that the task is seen to be relevant to the topic, otherwise it may not be treated seriously. You should consider how you deal with the product, how is it to be marked and what are the criteria for your response? A good way to respond to such work is to display it around the class and to invite pupils to identify the interesting, imaginative and useful solutions generated. The pupils could develop the criteria for assessing the work.

Listed below is the brief and rationale for 'design a bicycle for postmen' together with the author's comments on children's products.

Brief: Design a special bicycle for postmen. Pupils were asked to write and/or draw their answer in any way they liked (you could provide pupils with a sheet of sugar paper, say 1/2m square).

Rationale: Bicycles are very familiar objects to pupils and the purpose of giving this problem was to see how pupils would alter what was already a familiar object in order to make it better. The question was how would pupils decide to improve the bicycle? What would be added? The problem was posed in such a way as to direct the improvements towards the postman's bicycle and not just bicycles in general.

Example: See Figure 4.3.2 on page 172.

General discussion Children quickly identified what the postmen's problems were. They included nasty dogs; getting wet; getting the bike up steep hills. Children recognised that postmen spent a lot of time getting on and off the bike; so solutions were directed to delivery in the saddle. In addition pupils acknowledged that postmen spent a lot of time outside delivering the post so some solutions provided the postman with food and drink, even hot drinks.

The solutions were usually additive, leading to complexity, without elegance or aesthetic appeal. The important criterion was effectiveness.

'MEASURING' COGNITIVE DEVELOPMENT

Much work has been carried out to measure (largely) children's responses to problem situations, as a means of 'getting a handle' on cognitive development. Much of it owes its origins to the studies by Piaget (see, for example, Donaldson, 1978; Child, 1993).

In order to say that someone has developed mentally in some way, something is measured in order to make that judgement. Thus at the heart of discussions about cognitive development there has to be some specific skill that is used as a yardstick. This gives rise to a notion of **specific cognitive skill**. Individuals may be able to display a number of such skills and display a range of specific skills, leading to a deeper idea of generalised cognitive skill.

Whenever an individual is tested or performance measured in some way, the information gained is, in fact, only about the individual's ability to perform that skill. This is what is measured when assessment is made by teachers or researchers. In the examples in this unit the specific cognitive skills were about logical thinking and understanding sums involving ratio. More generalised skills were revealed in Task 4.3.5 (Design a bicycle for postmen) in which pupils were given greater freedom of expression.

INTELLIGENCE AND COGNITIVE DEVELOPMENT

We mentioned intelligence earlier in this unit. Most people know in a common-sense way what is meant by intelligence. We can give examples of intelligent behaviour. We can talk about intelligent behaviour in non-human animals, such as food seeking in primates, maze learning in rats as well as the intelligent behaviour of humans. When we discuss pupils excelling at some board games we are likely to say 'she's intelligent' meaning that she is better at the game than other pupils. We would, if pushed, be able to give an example of her intelligence drawn from incidents in the game. That example would probably be chosen because the other players did not display that skill. Intelligence often, then, is revealed by outstanding performance in some skill by an individual. Cognitive development and intelligence are both described by reference to specific behaviours in the same way we discussed cognitive development in terms of specific examples, i.e skills.

INTELLIGENCE TESTS

The only sure fact is that 'intelligence is what intelligence tests measure'. Since these tests are constructed in different ways, e.g., verbal, non-verbal, numerical, then the 'intelligence' being measured can be said to be different in each case.

The study of intelligence and intelligence testing has been the focus of study all this century. It assumed great importance in the UK after 1944 when pupils were selected for grammar, technical or 'modern' schools by means of intelligence tests, the 11+. Despite being developed into a reliable sophisticated tool, IQ testing for selection purposes failed to take account of late developers or the variation in the social background of pupils. The tests favoured pupils with good linguistic skills, those who had a good vocabulary and were familiar with middle class culture, and girls. It was shown, too, that performance on the tests could be improved by training, which suggested that in part at least, learned skills were being tested rather than any innate intelligence. In the event, the IQ test was rejected by arguments of justice and equity.

IQ testing is used now by educational psychologists to assist in monitoring pupil progress and to assess pupils who, in various ways, find school difficult. It is also used in various selection procedures outside education. Many different sorts of tests exist, both general tests and tests which explore specific skills, e.g. spatial skills. Some test use non-verbal methods to identify intelligent behaviour. IQ tests, like most tests, are not culture free; that is, they make assumptions about the testee's familiarity with the society in which the tests are to be applied (Gould, 1984).

Testing is a skilled process and tests cannot be used by anyone. For example, if your school uses NFER tests to measure pupil abilities, usually they have to be carried out by approved persons. Your school may use these tests to help identify the abilities of pupils as part of a monitoring process. Find out about these tests in your school and see how they are applied. In the first instance seek the advice of the Special Educational Needs co-ordinator or the Examination officer in the school. For more information, see, for example, Child (1993). One test used widely is the Cognitive Abilities Test (CAT) (NFER-Nelson, 1996). The CAT is used to predict grades at GCSE. Pupils are tested on entry to secondary school and again at the end of KS3. Data are provided on groups and individuals. The CAT is one means of monitoring progression and 'Value Added'.

Intelligence testing is used to measure people's ability to carry out certain tasks. Usually the reporting is in terms of comparison of one group with another; or of one person against a standardised sample. This method of reporting intelligence is very different from that adopted by developmental psychologists who are interested in the type and sequence of thought process adopted by learners; see, for example, Piaget (Donaldson, 1978). Nevertheless both types of study lead to notions of norm referencing for comparison purposes, whether it be scores on an intelligence test or quality of thought processes revealed by interview.

THEORIES OF COGNITIVE DEVELOPMENT

There has been considerable research into cognitive learning; some researchers favour a stage theory of learning (Inhelder and Piaget, 1958; Bruner, 1986), often linked to bio-logical development (Piaget). See Unit 5.1. Other research has led to a focus on ways in which learners construct meaning for themselves; all pupils bring to school some knowl-edge, skills and understanding which interact with the new knowledge. Learning, then, becomes a process of relating existing knowledge with new knowledge. Sometimes this common-sense knowledge is in tune with accepted knowledge; on other occasions it con-flicts. In the circumstances where common-sense knowledge conflicts with taught knowl-edge, teaching has to provide a powerful reason to replace old knowledge or views of the world by the new. This applies to explanations for catching a cold (virus or getting wet in the rain); to standards of honesty (because stealing is wrong as opposed to danger of being caught); or reporting an offence such as bullying (justice as opposed to 'telling tales is wrong').

The theories of cognitive learning are not sufficiently developed to provide a coherent basis for teaching or curriculum construction in school. All research points, however, to the fact that learners must themselves engage with new knowledge or material in an active way if learning is to take place. Further, that experiences must be provided to support learning; that the way new material is presented is vital, e.g. in terms of the context, the language used; and that learning can be enhanced by teachers who recognise these requirements. Teachers cannot learn for the pupil, but can provide the context, activities and atmosphere in which meaningful learning, as opposed to rote learning, can take place. See Unit 5.1 and 5.2 on active learning.

It is hoped that by starting with the study of some pupils in your school, together with your developing teaching skills, this experience will provide the basis for considering theories of learning. Many theories have been alluded to in this unit. For further reading see the reference list. A useful place to start is 'Concept formation and cognitive development' in Child (1993, p. 152), listed below, which gives an overview and an entrance to the field of cognitive development. For a good discussion of Piaget's work, see Donaldson (1978, 1992); for an example of its application to curriculum and teaching see Adey *et al.* (1989) and Adey and Shayer (1994).

⠸ Summary and key points

The examples used in this unit have been selected from mathematics and science; to what extent are such situations reflected elsewhere in the school curriculum? What are the corresponding cognitive demands in geography, English, technology, etc.?

Consider the different ways of punctuating the following phrase and the meanings that result:

The constable said the manager was not doing his job

Many pupils have difficulty punctuating such sentences and identifying the different meanings to sentences thus punctuated. What is the cognitive demand of this task and in which ways does it compare with Tasks 4.3.2 and 4.3.4?

In the same way that pupils develop ways of understanding the natural world so do pupils show a range of ways of tackling number problems. There is a variation in abilities of pupils at the same age as well as some increase in the numbers of those successful with increasing age. As pupils mature there is an increased capacity to carry out more cognitively complex tasks. However, by the time pupils leave school many pupils have not shown the ability or willingness to attempt such problems. By listening to pupils and studying their responses to tasks and problems we can understand more about their understanding and help to match tasks to help their development. We need to adopt ways to encourage pupils' thinking and to motivate them to develop their thinking skills. One way to achieve this is to link their work in school more closely to their daily lives. Other units look at ways to encourage learning, e.g. active learning in Unit 5.2 and motivation in Unit 3.2.

FURTHER READING

Child, D. (1993) *Psychology and the Teacher*, London: Cassell.

The 5th edition of a classic text. Excellent review of cognitive development, theories of learning and intelligence. Includes research into classrooms, practice, management and special needs. Excellent source of references.

Donaldson, M. (1978) *Children's Minds (1st edition)*, Glasgow: Collins/Fontana.

Essential reading for anyone interested in developmental psychology and Piaget's work on cognitive growth. Excellent review of work of Piaget. See also *Human Minds* by the same author (Donaldson, 1992).

Gardner, H. (1994) 'The theory of multiple intelligences', in B. Moon and A. Shelton Mayes (eds) *Teaching and Learning in the Secondary School*, London: Routledge for the Open University.

Readers interested in this model of intelligence might read this short introductory paper before reading *Frames of mind*, 2nd edition' (Gardner, 1993). A contrary view is put by White (1998).

APPENDIX 4.3.1

Task 4.3.1 Sorting variables 1: the logical puzzle

From rules a and b, if Amy orders chicken, Bill orders fish and Clare orders fish. This contradicts rule c. So Amy orders only fish. Then from rule b Clare can order fish or chicken. Clare orders chicken, then Bill orders fish or chicken. If Clare orders fish then Bill can order only chicken. So Clare could have chicken yesterday and fish today. (Adapted from Brandeth, G. (1981) *The Puzzle Mountain*, Harmondsworth: Penguin Books.)

APPENDIX 4.3.2

Commentary on Task 4.3.2 Sorting variables 2: the pendulum

The time period of a pendulum depends on the length of the pendulum; neither the magnitude of the weight nor the position from which the pendulum starts swinging (– high or low –) affects the time period. The longer the pendulum, the fewer the number of swings per half minute, i.e. the longer the period.

From the pupil readings, Table 4.3.1, it follows:

- Investigations 1 and 2 tell you the length has an effect on the time period, since only length was changed, weight and position of release being held the same.
- Investigations 2 and 4 tell you that weight has no effect on the time period, since length and position of release are held the same.
- Finally, from 1 and 3, if weight has no effect, then since the length is constant, the position of release has no effect on the number of swings per half minute.

Research again suggests that many pupils in secondary school do not acquire the skills necessary either to sort out the data or to plan and carry out such an activity. This is not to say that, if told, they cannot understand the factors controlling the swing of a pendulum, rather it is that they have difficulty in generating evidence for themselves and analysing the evidence to prove it. It is the difference between learning and recall (which we, as teachers, do a lot of) and understanding what we have learned (which we do less of). In addition, when faced with the need to get evidence for themselves, pupils frequently choose trial and error methods rather than logically constructed enquiries. Trial and error methods often lead to data which do not provide clear-cut answers to questions.

Recognising that no clear inference can be made is also a measure of cognitive maturity.

Pupils and adults find some evidence harder to accept than other evidence. Thus evidence that the magnitude of the weight at the end of the pendulum has no effect on the time period is often rejected intuitively or put down to error. Common-sense notions are in powerful opposition to logical thinking. Some pupils do not accept that, if two variables are changed at the same time, then it is not possible on that evidence alone to make a deduction. Sometimes pupils bring in evidence external to the investigation to support their argument, instead of using the data they have and afterwards relating that to other situations they have met. In addition, there is a powerful expectation by pupils and many adults, that 'experiments' yield positive information and that saying 'this enquiry tells us nothing about the question' is not an acceptable answer, especially if the teacher sets up the enquiry. Such feelings are powerful motivating forces: and attitudes of persistence and honesty are critical for the generation of real understanding.

Such studies as these suggest that, without training, handling situations which contain several variables is a difficult task for many pupils. That pupils can achieve some success has been shown by the CASE Project (Adey *et al.*, 1991).

Commentary on Task 4.3.3 Sorting variables 3: percentages

In the example of questions about percentages the sample of questions shown here were part of a battery of questions designed to investigate children's ability to handle ratio and to investigate the strategies used by pupils. The author of this report (Hart, 1981) concluded that when faced with ratio or proportion sums:

- pupils can often handle problems that involve doubling or halving;
- some pupils can handle harder problems which use doubling or halving strategies to construct an answer – the building up approach to number problem solving;
- if doubling and halving and then adding bits on don't work, then a subtractive strategy is used (see question c in Table 4.3.2 where the answer 15 can arise from calculating $(20 - 5)$; and 16 as an answer from working out $(20 - 20/5)$.
- only a minority of pupils can handle ratio in terms of multiplying by a fraction;
- when additive strategies give nearly right answers then there is seen to be little need for a new strategy. Being nearly right is often seen as acceptable (Hart, 1981).

4.4 RESPONDING TO DIVERSITY

INTRODUCTION

In a recent report from the Organization for Economic Co-operation and Development (OECD, 1994, p. 1) it was stated that:

> Fifteen to thirty percent of pupils and students in many countries of the OECD are at risk of failing school.

The term 'at risk' was identified in the following ways: it would lead to

> low educational attainment and self esteem, dwindling participation in school activities, truancy, dropping out, behavioural problems and delinquency.

The authors of the report tried to identify factors which could be used to predict some or all of these outcomes. They acknowledged that many of the factors are interactive and do not act in isolation. Nevertheless, the factors include:

> family poverty; ethnic minority status; single parenthood, uneducated parents, cramped housing, no relations between home and school, physical and mental abuse; poor grasp of the language of instruction; the type and location of the school and community failings.

Such a list makes depressing reading. However, the report made an encouraging, positive statement by identifying education as a way of tackling the 'at risk' population and that:

> Schools can cope with the diverse demands and expectations presented by multi-cultural and pluralistic communities.

The OECD report echoes the findings of an influential report on school effectiveness in the UK which, although dated, is still highly relevant. It concluded that 'schools make a difference' to the life chances of pupils (Rutter *et al.*, 1979). Recent studies confirm this view, e.g. Myers (1996); Mortimore and Whitty (1997).

Equality of opportunity has long been the aim of educators. In the last two decades, rapid strides have been made in identifying the cultural issues which affect the academic performance of pupils. Cultural issues include factors such as family background, social class, gender and ethnicity. These factors rarely operate in isolation; performance and behaviour is the result of a set of influences on the child. The OECD report indicates that social class is not a useful predictor of disadvantage unless other causative factors are identified. Looking at these causative factors it is easier to consider them separately even though we know the overall effect on children is due to a combination of factors. In this unit we address issues of gender and ethnicity in schooling. We consider the different school performances of boys and girls as well as those of pupils from different ethnic groups in the community and ways you might respond to this diversity in school.

OBJECTIVES

At the end of this unit you should be able to:

- understand some of the cultural pressures on boys and girls which influence achievement;
- assess the power of teachers and schools to increase or ameliorate those pressures;
- discuss issues of discrimination and bias in relation to gender and ethnicity;
- review classroom procedures to promote better opportunities for learning in all pupils;
- consider school policies which can be adopted to promote equality of access to the curriculum;
- relate these skills and attitudes to the standards expected of an NQT.

LANGUAGE AND DEFINITIONS

The language of race relations sometimes, wrongly, uses the term 'ethnic' to refer to minority groups, often black. However, everyone belongs to an ethnic group; it has been customary to refer to numerically smaller ethnic groups as ethnic minorities, such as people of Afro-Caribbean origin in the UK. However, for some citizens that origin is perhaps distant, particularly if they are second or third generation British nationals. In this context, the term ethnic minority is offensive to some people, implying minority rights. Similarly it makes no sense to talk of ethnic foods, for example, unless you include fish and chips and black pudding alongside jerk pork and dhal.

Nevertheless, for many purposes, e.g. in a National Census or an application form to enter a PGCE course, the ethnicity of all candidates is requested. One such list of ethnic categories is in Unit 4.2, Task 4.2.5.

At the heart of much discussion about cultural and gender issues lie notions of discrimination. We shall use the following definitions of 'discrimination' and 'prejudice' in this unit.

Discrimination can be defined as:

- to perceive or note the difference in or between; to distinguish;
- to make a distinction, especially on grounds of race or colour or sex; to select for unfavourable treatment.

Prejudice can be described as:

- a feeling, favourable or unfavourable, towards any person or thing, prior to or not based on, actual experience. An unreasoning predilection or objection.

(Adapted from Klein, 1993, p. 13)

With these ideas in mind we first look at issues of equal opportunities.

Why do equal opportunities matter?

For many people it is self-evident as a reflection of basic human rights. It is a waste of human talent that deprives the individual of the satisfaction of realising their full potential as well as society of their skills. Of equal importance, the discrimination that lies beneath unfulfilled ambitions of many children sours families and communities and leads to anger and frustration. Such feelings are increasingly evident in our multiethnic society, in school, in the workplace and on the streets. Although much progress has been made in the last two decades as regards equal opportunities for men and women in the workplace and boys and girls at school, there remain substantial differences in the perceived role of men and women in society (Myers, 1987; 1990). In the 1980s and earlier there was concern about the underachievement of West Indian pupils (Short, 1986). In the 1990s there is growing concern about the low performance of many white working-class boys.

Some background and legislation

The understanding and awareness of the role of bias and discrimination in work, education, law, taxation, etc. has been growing in the past two decades. The concerns of society for the opportunities for all pupils to be realised have been supported by national legislation, all of which applies to schools and schooling. The Sex Discrimination Act of 1975 made both direct and indirect sex discrimination illegal. An example of direct discrimination would be refusing to allow a pupil to study a subject because of their gender. Indirect discrimination might be where a condition was applied which made it unlikely that boys (or girls) could comply. There is no national policy on anti-racist education. The legal protection for anyone who feels discriminated against because of their ethnicity is the Race Relations Act, 1976. As regards employment it is unlawful for a person, in relation to employment by him at an establishment in Great Britain, to discriminate against another

- in the arrangements he makes for the purpose of determining who should be offered that employment; or
- in the terms on which he offers him that employment; or
- by refusing or deliberately omitting to offer him that employment.

(The male pronoun is used here to denote both men and women.)

Section 17 of the Act specifies that discrimination in education is unlawful. It is concerned with the access to educational institutions in the terms on which pupils are offered admission; it is unlawful to refuse or deliberately omit to accept an application on the grounds of race.

Further, if limited, support for equal opportunities practices in school is the Children Act of 1989. Although it applies to the protection of children up to 8 years of age it sets a precedent for further legislative protection. It has been described as a genuine advance in providing child care and an education service founded upon anti-discriminatory practice and principles of race equality (Klein, 1993, p. 99). The 1989 Act asserts the children's 'right' to an 'environment which values the religious, cultural, racial and linguistic background of the child and which is free of racial discrimination'.

Furthermore the Act describes a fit person to care for the children to include one who has

- 'knowledge of and a positive attitude to multicultural issues and people of different racial origins';
- 'commitment and knowledge to treat all children as individuals and with equal concern'.

It is to be hoped that similar appropriate legislation can follow for schools and colleges. For further discussion on the legal issues, see Klein (1993, Chapter 6).

The real problems in society are much more subtle than this; overt discrimination is relatively easy to recognise and, often, to confront. Attitudes of parents, peers, teachers and others all influence behaviour, choice and hence performance. Attitudes are hard to identify and explain and are more difficult to change and thus less responsive to legislation. Attitudes have been shown to be responsible for discrimination in the curriculum, e.g. Wright (1994). In her study of subject choices made by pupils at 13 years old, it appeared that teachers directed pupils into lower achieving sets on behavioural grounds, in spite of the fact that these pupils had good enough examination results to enter the top sets. Such practices in this case prejudiced the chances of black pupils.

If, for example, girls are not allowed to opt out of science or mathematics before 16 years of age or boys are required to study home economics as well as a foreign language, then at least, hopefully, gender divisions are delayed until 16+. This is one reason why the National Curriculum was welcomed by many people because it was an entitlement for all pupils. Removing choice in this way eventually gives a wider educational opportunity to all. The recent softening of the demands of the National Curriculum has re-introduced the opportunity for schools to offer options at the end of KS3, in many ways a return to pre-National Curriculum practice.

DISCRIMINATION AND PREJUDICE

Secondary schools can have a positive effect in countering pupils negative attitudes towards themselves and others. A clear-cut secondary school policy has over 6000 hours in which to counteract the prejudices of the environment and earlier conditioning. This can be achieved through curriculum planning and the development of good practice. This approach can be used to tackle racism in school. It needs to be borne in mind, however, that getting it wrong means that 6000 hours is used to ignore or, worse, to consolidate and perpetuate prejudicial attitudes.

Deep-seated prejudice contains the dimension of insularity; that is, although new facts might become available to a person which logically should change their views, the basic prejudice is maintained. In other words, the belief is held in the face of evidence to the contrary. When such prejudice occurs in a situation between unequal partners and concerns differences in ethnicity then this leads to a definition of racism as 'prejudice plus power'. The teacher–pupil relationship is one such position of inequality and contains the potential for racist behaviour.

Anti-racist education attempts to address not just discrimination, but the power relations involved. Equally, any antipathy between the sexes is exacerbated in a power relationship; such situations occur widely in our society, e.g. some marriages. Sexist behaviour can occur as a result of stereotypical views about gender roles, e.g. career guidance when an officer directs boys or girls into stereotyped jobs; or headteachers encouraging girls to study biology rather than another science.

ACHIEVEMENT

Girls have been steadily improving their performance in school examinations over the past twenty years. They now outperform boys in many subjects at GCSE and have caught

	England GCSE, Grades A–C		Scotland SCE Ordinary and Standard Grades 3		Wales GCSE Grades A–C	
Subject	females	males	females	males	females	males
English	158.7	120.5	19.3	15.1	9.3	6.4
Mathematics	98.0	108.1	12.2	12.9	5.4	5.5
Biology	31.5	25.3	8.3	3.5	2.5	1.7
French	72.0	47.6	9.4	5.3	3.6	1.8
History	53.6	45.6	5.1	3.6	2.5	1.7
Chemistry	25.2	33.5	7.9	8.9	1.6	1.9
Physics	18.6	39.5	5.4	10.8	1.1	2.2
Computer Studies	12.4	15.9	2.0	3.7	1.2	1.6

	England GCE A Level, Grades A–E		Scotland SCE Higher* Grades A–C		Wales GCE A Level Grades A–C	
Subject	females	males	females	males	females	males
English	26.3	11.8	11.8	8.2	2.3	0.7
Mathematics	11.3	20.5	5.5	6.4	0.6	1.1
Biology	12.2	7.4	4.7	2.5	0.8	0.6
French	12.4	5.0	3.1	1.2	1.0	0.2
History	11.7	10.3	3.4	2.4	1.0	0.7
Chemistry	8.8	13.0	3.6	4.3	0.6	0.8
Physics	4.7	16.6	2.3	5.0	0.3	0.9
Computer Studies	–	–	0.3	0.9	0.1	0.4

Figure 4.4.1 School examination results, 1990–1991. Numbers in thousands
Notes: *The Scottish Higher award is similar to, but not directly equivalent to, the English GCE A Level: see Scottish Qualification Authority 1998.
Source: Department for Education, England; Examination results 1990/91: Scottish Examination Board; Welsh Joint Education Committee: Welsh Office. Data available in Equal Opportunities Commission (1992) *Some facts about women*, Manchester: Equal Opportunities Commission.

up at A Level. The subjects that they study often follow traditional lines, however, and their career aspirations, opportunities for promotion and likely earnings are all far lower. See Figures 4.4.1, 4.4.2, 4.4.3, 4.4.4 and 4.4.5.

	England GCSE Grades A–C		Scotland SCE Ordinary Standard Grades 1–3		Wales GCSE Grades A–C	
Subject	females	males	females	males	females	males
English	172.9	126.8	24.2	19.8	13.9	10.1
Mathematics	122.7	125.6	16.2	16.0	7.8	7.4
Science single award	7.2	4.7	1.9	2.7	0.2	0.1
Science double award	106.9	104.5	–	–	3.1	3.1
Biology	13.4	19.5	12.5	5.0	0.8	1.0
Chemistry	12.5	19.8	10.7	10.4	0.6	0.9
Physics	11.5	20.1	6.4	12.4	0.7	1.1
Design and Technology ^	39.9	30.8	1.4	4.9	4.7	4.1
Home Economics	30.9	3.0	3.7	0.4	2.4	0.1
French	92.2	61.4	13.1	8.4	4.3	2.3
History	64.1	54.3	7.2	4.9	3.1	2.2
Computer Studies	2.6	2.5	3.9	6.3	–	–

	England GCE A Level Grades A–E		Scotland SCE Higher* Grades A–C		Wales GCE A Level Grades A–E	
Subject	females	males	females	males	females	males
English	50.0	21.7	13.6	9.7	2.2	0.7
Mathematics	17.7	31.2	6.6	7.1	0.5	0.7
Biology	23.6	15.8	5.5	2.4	0.5	0.4
Chemistry	13.8	17.4	4.2	4.4	0.5	0.6
Physics	5.4	19.9	2.8	5.6	0.2	0.5
French	14.5	6.6	2.8	0.9	1.3	0.3
History	17.8	14.8	3.2	2.1	1.1	0.8
Computer studies±	1.8	6.9	0.7	2.0	0.2	0.6

Figure 4.4.2 School examination results, 1995–1996. Numbers in thousands
Notes: ^Craft and Design in Scotland – not available
± Technology in England
* The Scottish Higher Award is similar to, but not directly equivalent to, the English GCE A Level; see Scottish Qualification Authority, 1998.
Source: Department for Education and Employment, Scottish Examination Board, Welsh Joint Education Committee. Data available through EOC Fact sheet

Task 4.4.1

EXAMINATION PERFORMANCE AND JOB OPPORTUNITIES, BY GENDER

Examine Figures 4.4.1 to 4.4.5. Discuss with other student teachers the implications of these data for the education of boys and girls. How should schools respond?

Occupational Group	females	% of group	males	% of group	Total
1　Managers and administrators	1,118	30.7	2,527	69.3	3,645
bank, building society and post office managers	23	21.9	83	78.1	106
2　Professional occupations	915	38.4	1,470	61.6	2,385
medical practitioners	32	32.3	67	67.7	99
solicitors	17	23.3	57	76.7	74
3　Associate Professional and Technical occupations	1,112	49.3	1,146	50.7	2,258
computer analysis/programmers	41	20.6	157	79.4	19
nurses	397	89.7	46	10.3	443
4　Clerical and secretarial	3,047	75.2	1,007	24.8	4,054
computer operators	146	70.1	62	29.9	20
5　Craft and related	414	10.7	3,462	89.3	3,876
bakers, flour confectioners	16	35.5	29	64.5	45
6　Personal and protective services	1,530	65.4	809	34.6	2,349
police officers (Sgt and below)	17	12.1	124	87.9	14.1
hairdressers, barbers	100	86.7	15	13.3	115
7　Selling	1,242	62.0	760	38.0	2,002
sales assistants	867	76.6	251	22.4	1,118
8　Plant and machine operatives	570	22.1	2,011	77.9	2,581
assemblers, line workers	113	48.8	119	51.2	232
9　Other occupations	1.178	51.8	1,079	48.2	2,277
postal workers, mail sorters	32	17.6	150	82.4	182
cleaners, domestics	709	87.4	103	12.6	812
Inadequately described/not stated	19	34.5	35	65.5	54
ALL OCCUPATIONS	11,145	43.8	14,324	56.2	25,479

Figure 4.4.3 Employment by occupation: Great Britain 1991. Numbers in thousands
Source: Labour Force Survey, 1991

Occupational Group	females	%age of group	males	%age of group
1 Managers and administrators	1,318	33	2,700	67
bank, building society and post office managers	30	29	72	71
company secretaries	52	76	17	24
2 Professional	1,088	40	1,633	60
medical practitioners	44	31	97	69
primary and nursery school teachers	296	85	52	15
3 Associate Professional and Technical	1,227	50	1,215	50
computer analysis/programmers	36	18	162	82
nurses	445	88	58	12
4 Clerical & secretarial	2,782	75	933	25
storekeepers and warehouse persons	45	13	289	87
computer and office machine operators	80	63	46	37
5 Craft and related	299	10	2,806	90
textiles, garments and related trades	159	69	72	31
electrical/electronic trades	11	2	457	98
6 Personal and protective services	1,764	66	920	34
police officers (sergeant and below)	19	13	123	87
care assistants and attendants	391	92	35	8
7 Sales	1,282	64	721	36
technical and wholesale sales reps	40	18	187	82
retail cash desk and check out operators	188	86	30	14
8 Plant and machine operatives	494	20	1,948	80
drivers of roads goods vehicles	10	2	454	98
assemblers, lineworkers of electrical and	68	59	47	41
electronic goods 9 Other occupations	1,048	51	1,011	49
postal workers, mail sorters	23	15	128	85
counterhands, catering assistants	176	84	34	16
ALL OCCUPATIONS*	11,320	45	13,905	55

*includes those not stating occupation.

Figure 4.4.4 Employment by occupation: Great Britain 1996. Employees and self-employed over age 16 years. Numbers in thousands
Source: Labour Force Survey Spring 1996, Office for National Statistics. Data available through EOC Fact sheet

Turning to the performance of secondary school pupils from ethnic minority groups, the evidence accumulated by the Swann Inquiry (DES, 1984b) suggested that such pupils were underachieving. However, closer analysis of these data showed that different ethnic minority groups performed differently in public examinations or in school; see also Gillborn and Gippa (1996, p. 17). Underachievement in school may be more to do with school expectations, tradition and ethos than with any intellectual inadequacy (Wright, 1994; Eggleston, 1985, p. 219). Data on the performance of pupils in public examinations has not been gathered nationally by ethnic grouping, although some LEAs do so.

More recently, evidence has shown that young people from ethnic minority groups are more likely to stay on in full-time education after the age of 16 than young whites (National Commission on Education, 1993). For example, one reason that pupils from ethnic minority groups have a high profile in further education may be poor examination results, especially Afro-Caribbean boys. This situation may lead them to seek qualifications outside school. The numbers involved suggest that such people are determined and value education. This echoes earlier in-depth studies in a small number of schools in

	Hourly earnings, pence per hour			
	1976	1996		
	All	All	Manual	Non-Manual
Females•	122	750	472	814
Males§	167	939	651	1,187
Differential	44	189	179	373
Female earnings as % of male earnings	73	80	73	69
	Weekly earnings, £ per week			
	All	All	Manual	Non-Manual
Females•	46.2	283.0	195.2	302.4
Males§	71.8	391.6	301.3	464.5
Differential	25.6	108.6	106.1	162.1
Female earnings as % of male earnings	64	72	65	65

• females aged 18 and over; § males aged 21 and over.

Figure 4.4.5 Earnings: 1976, 1996. Average gross hourly earnings, excluding the effects of overtime, and weekly earnings of full-time employees on adult rates
Source: New Earnings surveys 1976 and 1996, Office for National Statistics. Data available through EOC Fact sheet

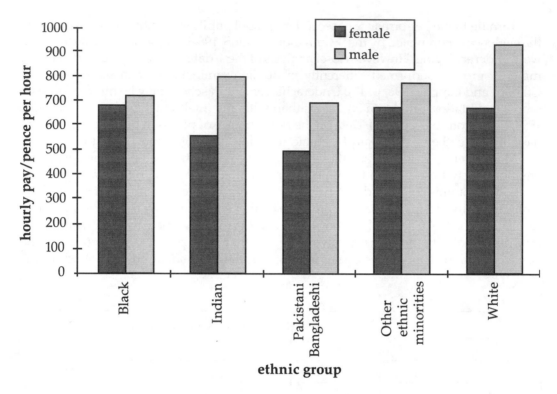

Figure 4.4.6 Hourly pay of ethnic groups, Great Britain 1994–1995
Source: Labour Force Survey 1994–95 in *Social Focus on Ethnic Minorities* (1996). Also available from EOC as Fact sheet

England of the educational and vocational experiences of pupils from ethnic minority groups (Eggleston, 1985).

Among young people in the age group 16–24 people from ethnic minorities are more likely than whites to have a degree or other higher education qualification. There is no marked difference in the availability of job-related training for people from ethnic minority groups as compared with whites, though in general the former are more exposed to unemployment (National Commission on Education, 1993, p. 11). Such evidence raises questions about what goes on in school and why for example, ethnic minority groups are under-represented in positions of responsibility; for example, recently the Law Society wrote to all firms of solicitors about discrimination against black applicants to train as solicitors (Dyer, 1994; Institute of Policy Studies, 1994).

The different cultural traditions of ethnic groups influence educational outcomes, as do factors associated with different social class, e.g. attitudes to learning and school. One important outcome of the Swann Report (DES, 1984b) was the realisation that no single causal factor was responsible for the underachievement of pupils from ethnic minority groups in school. Nevertheless, the same report identified racism and racist practices as one contributing factor.

A review of recent research into the performance of ethnic minority pupils has been carried out by OFSTED. Their commissioned review (Gillborn and Gipps, 1996) shows that since the Swann Report (DFE/WO, 1984b) considerable progress has been made in achievement in public examinations by pupils from many ethnic minority groups. The evidence is patchy because the collection of statistics nationally from examinations by ethnic grouping was discontinued in the early 1990s. Much of the evidence comes from LEA reports especially of those in inner cities. A continuing concern is the under performance of boys of Afro-Caribbean origin, which finds links with the low achievement of many white working-class boys in some areas of the country. The summary of the findings of the review is in Task 4.4.2, to which you are referred. In this Task you are invited to collect data in school which could be sensitive. You should discuss any proposed inquiry with your tutor before undertaking the Task.

ASPECTS OF SCHOOL PRACTICE

There is a great difference between intention and practice. However good the intentions, policies are only as effective as the extent to which people understand them and put them into practice. The tasks below are designed to enquire into the equal opportunities policies in your school.

There follows a collection of tasks from which you can select. Each task suggests collecting some facts during your school experience, using the ideas below as a starting point. A tactful summary of your thoughts on any of these matters might well be of interest to the school. However, you should seek the advice and guidance of your school tutor for **both** the enquiry and the format and distribution of any subsequent report. Inevitably the work that you do in this unit touches only the surface of the issues involved. Any one area could be explored in greater depth to form the basis for an academic assignment.

Task 4.4.2

ETHNIC MINORITY PERFORMANCE IN SCHOOLS

Some conclusions of a review of recent research into the performance of pupils from ethnic minority backgrounds is given below. Read them and, if necessary, refer to the survey for evidence; see Gillborn and Gipps (1996) in 'Further Reading'. Then respond to one or more of the questions and suggestions below. The review says (p. 78)

The encouraging developments since the Swann Report (DFE/WO, 1984b) include:

- generally higher levels of achievement, year on year;
- improving levels of attainment among ethnic minority groups in many areas of the country;
- dramatic increases in the examination performance of certain minority groups, even in LEAs where there is significant poverty;
- in higher education, people of ethnic minority background are generally well represented among those continuing their education to degree level.

However, the review identified areas of continuing concern. These included:

- the gap is growing between highest and the lowest achieving ethnic groups in many areas;
- African Caribbean young people, especially boys, have not shared equally in the increasing rates of attainment; in some areas their performance has actually worsened;
- the sharp rise in the number of exclusions from schools affects a disproportionately large number of black pupils;
- even when differences in qualifications, social class, and gender are taken into account, (minority) ethnic groups do not enjoy equal chances of success in their application to enter university.

Questions for discussion or action.

1   How do you account for the increasing achievement of all pupils as suggested in the review?
2   Suggest reasons why some groups of pupils are not maintaining the progress made by the majority, e.g. some Afro-Caribbean pupils.
3   How do you account for the differences in performances of pupils from various ethnic groups; see Gillborn and Gipps (1996, pp. 10–47).
4   Collect data in your school or LEA about the achievement of pupils in public examinations, including SATs. Analyse the data by gender and ethnic grouping (see Unit 4.2 for suggestions for categorising ethnic groups). How does your data compare with the national picture described in the review above. Is there evidence of the increase in achievement, year on year, of any groups of pupils in your school? What explanations are there for any changes observed?
5   Collect data in your school, or LEA, about the pupils who *either* are suspended or excluded from school *or* play truant. Analyse your data by gender and ethnic grouping. Relate your findings to the national picture (see Gillborn and Gipps, 1996, p. 48; Gillborn, 1996).
6   Have there been any changes in your school or LEA in the number or pattern of suspension of, or truancy by, pupils in recent years? How do you account for the pattern of suspension or truancy you find?

Task 4.4.3   SETTING AND STREAMING BY GENDER

If the school operates a streaming, setting or banding system collect the numbers of boys and girls in different teaching groups by ability and selected school subjects. You may find it helpful to focus on one year group, e.g. the transition from Year 9 to Year 10, when GCSE option choices are made.

> **Task 4.4.4**
>
> **SETTING AND STREAMING BY ETHNIC GROUP**
> Similar data on setting and streaming may be collected on the distribution of pupils from ethnic minority groups across classes. Several student teachers could share the work, enabling a wider picture of one year group to emerge. Collect the data in a form that allows comparison between pupil groups.

> **Task 4.4.5**
>
> **WHO IS RECRUITED TO POST 16 COURSES?**
> If the school has a sixth form, examine the relative number of pupils in the first year academic and vocational courses, by gender and ethnicity and compare those numbers with the numbers in the previous year's Year 11 cohort. Identify the subject preferences.
> How many pupils left school to carry on education in another institution and what are their gender and ethnic characteristics?

SCHOOL POLICIES

Many schools have developed policies concerning aspects of equal opportunities, including gender and anti-racism; there may be policies about behaviour, including bullying, which carries with it issues of equal opportunities of a different nature. In addition many equal opportunity issues are central to other policies, such as assessment or pastoral care. In the following tasks we focus on two aspects of school life: equal opportunity policies and pastoral care.

> **Task 4.4.6**
>
> **POLICIES TOWARDS EQUAL OPPORTUNITIES (EO)**
> Obtain a copy of the EO policy in your school. Read it and try to identify:
>
> * Who wrote the policy? Were parents or pupils involved?
> * How old is it?
> * Are there any later documents, e.g. Working Party Reports?
> * What areas of school life does it cover, e.g. curriculum, playground behaviour, assembly, etc.? Are there any areas omitted?
> * What is the focus of the policy? Is it gender, ethnicity, social class, disabilities?
>
> Who knows about the policy? Devise a way of sampling knowledge, understanding and opinion of pupils and staff about the policy. For example:
>
> * are copies of the policy displayed in the school?
> * how many staff know about it; have read it?

- how many pupils know about it; have read it?
- who is the member of staff responsible for EO in the school?

Is the policy treated seriously in the school? For example:

- has any in-service programme been devoted to equal opportunities issues?
- does the school EO policy influence departmental policy and hence classroom practice?

You could widen the study by examining another school's policy on equal opportunities. Try to obtain one from a nearby school or from another student teacher. An example of a recent policy from a school, called Nonesuch School, is given in Figure 4.4.7.

- In what ways is this policy different to your own school policy?
- In what ways does the policy correspond to that in your own school?
- Do the policies of either school go beyond intentions to practice? How can they be implemented? Read 'School policies' in Klein (1993, pp. 103–10).

Nonesuch School is a comprehensive school; that means it is for everybody. In this school we believe that everyone has a right to equal chances and each individual is valued and respected for who they are.
– There are at least 15 languages spoken in the homes of students and staff at Nonesuch.
– Students' families and staff have links with many parts of the world.
– People at Nonesuch are glad that it is a multicultural school.
– You will study many different cultures and countries.
– You also find out and discuss why people pre-judge others often through their own ignorance or lack of understanding.
– If anyone tries to offend you because of your race or colour, religion, nationality, language or culture the school supports you.
– At Nonesuch, all subjects are equally important; there are no 'girls' subjects and no 'boys' subjects.
– In the first year, everybody studies the same subjects. After that there is a choice. When choices are made for subjects or careers, you are given help; this will make sure that boys and girls all have the same opportunities.
– Many people grow up thinking that women are not as good as men; at Nonesuch you learn that this is not true.
– If anyone tries to offend or limit you because of your sex, the school supports you.
– Please report sexist comments or behaviour to a teacher or Head of Year or the Head (teacher).
No one should suffer prejudice or discrimination against them.

Figure 4.4.7 Equal opportunity policy of Nonesuch School

HOW ARE POLICIES IMPLEMENTED IN YOUR SCHOOL?

No matter how concerned the school is to promote equal opportunities through good policies, implementing them in the classroom is not an easy matter. It is instructive to use lesson observation time to look at a specific aspect of teaching and then to report back to your group. Some ideas are listed below in Tasks 4.4.7 and 4.4.8. Negotiate with a class teacher to observe a lesson or two.

When you first start teaching your concern is to conduct a well-ordered lesson and promote learning; as soon as you feel confident to consider these wider issues ask a colleague, class teacher or other student teachers to conduct an observation of your lesson.

Task 4.4.7

RESPONSES TO GENDER: CLASSROOM OBSERVATION

Keep a tally of the frequency of attention to and the time given to, boys and girls. Devise a recording sheet to collect information about one or two of the following behaviours:

- who puts their hand up to answer a question?
- who does the teacher select?
- in class activities, how much time is spent by the teacher with boys; with girls?
- whether the teacher responds to a pupil with praise, criticism or further questioning;
- when pupils are reprimanded, is there any difference in
  - the nature of the misdemeanour; that is, what is tolerated or not, by the teacher?
  - the action taken by the teacher?

You might consider if different messages are conveyed by the teacher to boys or girls, through such classroom interactions.

Task 4.4.8

RESPONSES TO ETHNICITY: CLASSROOM OBSERVATION

Redesign the record sheet used in Task 4.4.7 to collect data about teachers' response to pupils of different ethnicity. Use the same questions as listed under Task 4.4.7 and add:

- did racist behaviour occur in the class?
- what was the nature of the racism? Was it name calling, inappropriate language or metaphors, stereotyping, inappropriate book or other visual resources? (See Task 4.4.9.)
- how was the racist incident dealt with?
- Read 'Race and racism as a classroom topic' in Klein (1993, pp. 139–45).

BOOKS AND ATTITUDES

Equal opportunity policies must influence the material placed in front of pupils. Pupils, like us, are heavily influenced by the words and pictures, particularly moving ones.

Task 4.4.9	**BIAS IN BOOKS**

Interrogate books, worksheets, wall charts and video material for bias and stereotyping. Some questions you could use include:

- how accurate are the images shown of people and of places?
- are women and girls shown in non-traditional roles?
- are men shown in caring roles?
- who is shown in a position of authority? Who is the employer, the decision maker, the technologist? Is it always men? What are the roles of women?
- are people stereotyped, e.g. black athletes, male scientists, female social workers?
- how are people in the developing world depicted? Are they used to illustrate malnutrition; living in mud huts; technologically backward?
- what assumptions are made concerning under-development in the Third World? Read 'Printed and published materials in schools' in Klein (1993, pp. 167–80).

THE PASTORAL ROLE

In many schools new teachers are often expected to act as form tutors to a class. In this role it is likely that they will be asked to deal with a number of problems of relationships including issues of gender and race. You should take the opportunity to work alongside a form teacher throughout your Initial Teacher Education year so as to become aware of the demands on and responses by form teachers. Many schools expect that involvement of the student teacher, including participation in aspects of Personal and Social Education courses. Some examples of situations met by teachers have been identified in Unit 4.5. You will, no doubt, in a short time in school have begun to gather examples of incidents rooted in sexist or racist issues; you might wish to discuss these in a tutor group.

Task 4.4.10	**THE ROLE OF THE FORM TUTOR: SOME DILEMMAS**

Here are a few situations which teachers have had to tackle. If in a group, agree that one of you outline their reactions to the rest of the group. Then allow time for all to read through the chosen example and formulate your own reaction. Take it in turns to make the first response. As a group, identify the wider implications for the school of any one incident.

1 A pupil tells a racist joke during tutor time. How do you react? What are the limitations of your reaction? If this had happened either in a lesson or in the playground would you have behaved differently? If so, how and why?
    If it were a sexist joke how would it alter your response?
2 A girl in your class is crying. She tells you, eventually, that a group of boys in the class have been calling her names and tried to 'touch her up' on the way to school. She does not tell you who is involved. What do you do?
3 A group of girls in your form are making a young, male teacher's life misery by calling out after him, following him around and never leaving him in peace. What would you do?
4 Graffiti, calling a girl in your class a 'slag', have appeared in the girls' toilets. The person you think might be involved denies all knowledge of it. What might you do next? How would you tackle the issue with the whole class?
5 One of your class finds slogans saying 'Pakis go home' and the like written on his books and on bits of papers passed to him during lessons. The pupil is upset and asks you to do something about it. What course of action might you take?
6 You are a PE teacher and you want to introduce a dance unit into the curriculum for boys. In spite of the requirements of the National Curriculum your suggestion meets with disbelief from some of your colleagues as well as the boys concerned. What would you do?

Other examples of problem situations appear in Unit 4.5, Task 4.5.5.

Task 4.4.11

PERSONAL AND SOCIAL EDUCATION

Examine your school Personal and Social Education (PSE) programme; in what ways does it address relations with and attitudes towards the opposite sex? Does it suggest ways of identifying and combating bias, stereotyping and discrimination. How is the programme related to whole school policies, such as equal opportunities and anti-racism? In what contexts are these issues raised?

Write a short report on your findings and show it to your tutor. For further reading see, e.g. Klein (1993, Chapter 7).

RESPONDING TO DIVERSITY IN THE CLASSROOM

At this stage of your development as a teacher your concerns are focused on the classroom. However, much of what goes on in the classroom has its origins outside the classroom. These origins include the school's policy and practice, its ethos; the culture imported into the classroom by the pupils; and the teachers' expectations of pupils. Expectations of academic performance are often built upon both evidence of what the pupil has done in the past **and** their social position: male/female; white/black; Irish/ Afro-Caribbean; working/middle class; stable/unstable family background. The perceived social position is sometimes, if unconsciously, used by teachers to anticipate pupils' progress and their capacity to overcome difficulties. For example, 'Jimmy is always near the bottom of the class, but what do you expect with his family background?' Or 'The trouble with Verma is her attitude, she often seems to have a chip on her shoulder and doesn't respond well to discipline even when she is in the wrong. She never gives herself a chance; I'm always having a go at her.'

The interaction of the teacher with pupils in the classroom often reveals subconsciously the expectations of the teacher. By observing the behaviour of the teacher you can reveal if they favour asking boys to answer questions or girls. If this is so, then you need to ask why. Is it that the teacher does not expect girls to know the answer? A comparison of teacher behaviours in different lessons might reveal such influences, e.g. in science and English.

Other factors about teacher expectations include the way the teacher responds to answers. Whereas one pupil might make a modest and partly correct response to a question to which the teacher's response is praise and support, to another pupil, offering the same level of response, a more critical attitude is adopted by the teacher. Are these different responses justified? Is the pupil who received praise gaining support and encouragement from praise; or is the pupil being sent a message that low-level performance is good enough? It is teacher expectations that direct and control such responses. If, as has been documented about the performance of girls, the praise is implicitly saying 'you have done as well as can be expected because you are a girl' and the critical response is implying 'come on now, you're a boy; you can do better than this', then there is cause for concern. Such interpretations depend very much on the context, i.e. the subject and the teacher. You might get very different patterns of teacher response in a physics lesson compared with an English literature lesson.

MAXIMISING ASPIRATIONS

Equal opportunities are about maximising the aspirations of all pupils. They are not about trying to make pupils of all ethnic backgrounds more like each other, anymore than they are about trying to make girls behave like boys. **The task of the school is to create learning opportunities in which all pupils can thrive**. Such opportunities are recognised by not being 'gender blind' or 'colour blind'. Sometimes you hear a teacher say 'I didn't notice their colour, I treat them all the same'. We suggest that not recognising pupil differences, including culture, is as an inadquate response to teaching demands as is stereotyping pupils. Pupils learn in different ways and a key part of the differentiated approach to learning is to recognise those differences without placing limits on what can be achieved (see also Unit 4.1 and Unit 4.2). This brings us back to expectations of the teacher. If you expect most Asian girls to be quiet and passive and good at written work, then that is not only what they do, but also perhaps all they do. Individuals respond in different ways to teachers; we should try to treat each person as an individual and respond to what they do and say, irrespective of their gender, ethnic background, etc.

⁝ Summary and discussion

This unit has addressed issues of gender and ethnicity as part of its brief to address issues of equal opportunity. We have discussed the idea of an entitlement curriculum, as the National Curriculum promised, as well as linking this work with that of a differentiated approach to teaching and learning; see Unit 4.1. Gender and ethnicity are part of those important differences between pupils that need to be considered when planning lessons.

Finally, what can student teachers try to do in order to come to grips with some of the issues in the classroom? As a new teacher in school you might expect to:

- be aware that you are educating pupils to live in a culturally diverse society;
- promote respect and understanding between boys and girls, men and women;
- be aware of the main features of school policies on equal opportunities, including those on gender, multiculturalism and/or anti-racism;
- be aware of the main cultural groups in your school, e.g. by mother tongue, religious practice or cultural norms;
- be able to recognise the different cultural groups amongst pupils in the classes you teach;
- know the names of the pupils in your classes;
- know which pupils are bilingual and those that need English as a second language support in your class;
- show an understanding of the importance of language in teaching and learning and display that understanding in lesson preparation;
- prepare lessons that recognise the gender balance in your classes;
- prepare lessons that recognise the diversity of cultures in your class;
- be able to choose appropriate resource materials for your teaching subject and be helped to monitor them for bias and stereotyping;
- be sensitive to the opportunities to oppose sexism and racism in your lessons;
- seek to diminish bias and stereotyping in the classroom by monitoring classroom interactions. (Adapted from Turner and Turner, 1994.)

You may wish to apply this checklist to the classes that you teach at the end of your first period of school experience and again at the end of your course in order to monitor your development. If you can introduce all these skills into your teaching then you have gone a long way to meet the standards or competences required of an NQT. It would be useful to return to this checklist again during your first post.

FURTHER READING

Equal Opportunities Commission (1991) *Sex Discrimination in Schools: Guide for School Governors*, London: Equal Opportunities Commission.

Contains guidelines for a consideration of equal opportunity issues for both staff and pupils.

Gillborn, D. and Gipps, C. (1996) *Recent Research on the Achievements of Ethnic Minority Pupils,* London: HMSO (OFSTED: reviews of research)

The first major review since the Swann Report. The report identifies improving levels of attainment nationally as well as by some ethnic minority groups. Striking improvement has been achieved by some groups. Ethnic minority groups are well represented in those students continuing their education to degree level. The report draws attention to the growing gap in achievement between the top and the bottom groups; to the fact that boys have not shared in the overall rise in achievement especially those of Afro-Caribbean origin. Exclusions by schools of Afro-Caribbean pupils is disproportionately high.

Johnson, D. (ed.) (1997) *Minorities and Girls in Schools: Effects on Achievement and Performance,* London: Sage Publications.

A report of research findings into factors affecting the achievement of girls and ethnic minorities in American schools. The four reports address desegregation, economic status, curriculum and personal aspirations in career choice and are briefing papers for members of US Congress by four educational psychologists. The findings identify the progress made towards equal opportunities in US schools and charts future need. A particular focus is the poor representation of these groups in science, engineering and mathematics.

Klein, G. (1993) *Education Towards Race Equality,* London: Cassell.

An important book which gives an up-to-date review and overview of issues of race and anti-racism in schools. It tackles the issue of all-white schools. Considerable attention is given to the role of subject teaching in equal opportunities issues and is useful to the classroom teacher.

Myers, K. (1990) *Sex Discrimination in Schools,* London: Advisory Centre for Education.

This booklet provides a succinct and useful summary of the legal situation and the main issues in sex discrimination.

4.5 MORAL DEVELOPMENT AND VALUES

INTRODUCTION

Schools have always had a broad vision of their purpose, beyond the delivery of subject knowledge. This vision is expressed in a number of ways, ranging from the school motto to the publication of a set of school aims. Within such aims are personal targets for pupils – to do with the whole person and developing their skills and talents and social aims, such as concern for others, responsibility to and for others – and contributing to the welfare of society.

Manifestations of these aims are often found in the policies of the school, e.g. on equal opportunities, dress codes and behaviour, and ways in which parents contribute to the school. A key factor in the affirmation of aims is the way the teachers behave with pupils and respond to pupils in both subject work and the wider pastoral role, as well as through the many extra-curricular activities of school. The teacher sets the example; if the school is concerned for punctuality, then teachers must be punctual.

The way a school conducts itself, the standards it sets and the relationships it nurtures are sometimes referred to as the ethos of the school. Ethos is often intangible; it can be a feeling you get when you spend time in the school; or the way parents are welcomed into the school; or the relationship of teacher to pupil outside as well as inside the classroom. Other authors refer to the hidden curriculum: the values a school implicitly upholds and nurtures in all its dealings with young people. It is as much the ethos of a school that contributes to values education as does the prescribed curriculum of subjects.

Schools are concerned with developing young people who value themselves and have a good personal self-image. This includes self-confidence, willingness to tackle new ideas and problems, to feel that their contribution is valued and to be able to listen to the contribution of others. Values are about self and one's relation to other people.

All societies have a code of conduct which was, in the past, frequently related to a belief system. Thus moral development is linked for many with religious belief. Humanists and agnostics would argue otherwise. By moral development we refer to changes in the individual in relation to their personal and social behaviour. Such development is reflected in their response to authority, first through blind obedience, then through conforming to accepted standards because of understanding the need for rules; through to a personal code of behaviour generated by logical argument within a framework of personal autonomy.

Study of how moral judgement develops has been made by Piaget and Kohlberg; see, for example, Kohlberg (1984). Piaget linked the development of moral judgement with cognitive capability, i.e. mature moral judgement is dependent on a capacity to reason logically. Both writers describe the features of the development of moral judgement. They point out that not everyone appears to attain the higher levels of moral judgement and, moreover, if they do, may not practise them. Whereas these researchers place emphasis on maturational factors, others focus on moral development through social learning. Theories about the origin, as opposed to a description, of moral judgement have been attempted by Freud, in Child (1993).

This unit does not address either the theories of moral development or their origin but readers might wish to, using the references quoted. The focus in this unit is on the opportunities in our daily work with pupils and in the life of the school, to foster and develop moral judgement and values and to show pupils the need for society to have a set of common values.

OBJECTIVES

By the end of this unit you should:

- know the legal responsibility of the school towards pupils in the area of moral, spiritual and cultural development;
- be aware of the opportunities in school to promote these aims;
- be able to try out some methods of teaching towards these aims and evaluate them;
- be able to place moral and values education in a subject and school contest;
- be able to relate these aspects of a teacher's role to the standards and competences expected of an NQT.

A FRAMEWORK FOR VALUES EDUCATION

The development of moral judgement and a system of values is, ultimately, a personal choice. However, it is not simply a matter of personal choice. Both the development and exercise of moral judgement and personal values are influenced by home and school, culture and faith, people and society. The school has a potential for influence and may, for many pupils, be the only place where value systems are raised to consciousness, debated and challenged.

The 1988 Education Act (ERA, 1988) ushered in the National Curriculum for England and Wales. The broad principles of the Act were stated as follows:

(a) promote the spiritual, moral, cultural, mental and physical development of pupils at the school and of society; and
(b) prepare such pupils for the opportunities, responsibilities and experiences of adult life.

Dearing restated them like this:

Education is not concerned only with equipping students with the knowledge and skill they need to earn a living. It must help our young people to: use leisure time creatively; have respect for other people, other cultures and other beliefs; become good citizens; think things out for themselves; pursue a healthy life style; and, not least, value themselves and their achievements. It should develop an appreciation of our cultural heritage and of the spiritual and moral dimensions to life.

(Dearing, 1994, p. 18, para. 3.11)

The 1992 Education Act required OFSTED to inspect the contributions which schools make to pupils' spiritual, moral, social and cultural education (House of Commons, 1991). OFSTED has published guidelines for teachers to be responsible for the moral education of pupils (DFE, 1993a, 1993b). Schools have always paid attention to moral education but recent developments have created an overloaded curriculum, in which opportunities to develop such values have been limited and they have been taught implicitly rather than explicitly. Pupils don't just acquire the capacity to make moral judgements, it needs to be nurtured, displayed and practised.

We turn now to consider opportunities to develop a sense of moral judgement in school and ways to help young people integrate values into a personal philosophy; and to consider the roles of teachers and the curriculum in this process. This approach is presented as suggestions for activities. Select those appropriate to your school and your needs; it is not intended that all activities be undertaken.

Task 4.5.1 **AIMS OF THE SCHOOL AND HOW THEY ARE INTERPRETED**

There follows a number of activities which focus on the aims of the school. Carry out the tasks, either alone or in pairs and discuss your findings with other student teachers or your tutors.

1 Collect together the aims of your placement school and, if possible, those of several other schools. Compare and contrast the aims of different schools.
   - Does the school express in its aims a responsibility for the moral development of pupils?
   - How are these expressed and in what ways do the several school statements differ?
   - How do they meet the aims of the ERA identified above?

2 Consider these statements of broad aims for the curriculum:
   - pupils should be able to make decisions and act on them;
   - expose pupils to situations in which their contribution is necessary for the success of a project;
   - fosters pupils' self-image, or self-esteem;
   - pupils should develop independently but without losing contact with their peers;
   - enable pupils to interact with teachers as young adults with adults;

and respond to them using these headings.

A   In what ways do they contribute to the moral and values education of pupils?

B   How might the aims of the school curriculum be translated into opportunities for the pupil to achieve them?

3 Do the books, videos, films and other resources of your department reflect a moral dimension to the subject curriculum? Explore and discuss. This could be tackled by individual student teachers on a subject basis, later pooling and comparing

information. For example, choose a topic for which you have to prepare lesson plans and consider what might be the moral dimensions of that topic. What resources are there to support that topic in that way?

4 In what ways do the Personal and Social Education (PSE) or Personal, Social and Health Education (PSHE) programmes contribute to the moral education of pupils? Consider one or more of these topics:
   • practices and attitudes towards marriage;
   • acceptable and unacceptable food and the different practices for its preparation;
   • the celebration of festivals and holidays across cultures and nations;
   • preparation for careers, job application and interviews;
   • identifying bias and stereotyping and developing strategies to deal with them (e.g. personal relations, media, school textbooks).

5 How does school assembly contribute to the moral education of pupils?
   • Does the school have a programme for assemblies? Who takes assembly and how is the content and approach agreed?
   • Does the assembly have a Christian bias, a requirement of the 1988 Education Act (DFE, 1994d)?
   • How does the content and message of assemblies relate to the cultural mix of the school?
   • Does assembly develop a sense of community or is it authority enhancing?
   • What is made of the achievement of individuals?
   • Attend assembly; keep a record of its purpose, what was said and the way ideas were presented. Interview some pupils afterwards and compare your perception of the session with theirs. Did they understand the message or believe the message? In what way is it relevant to their life and their family?
   • Help plan an assembly with a teacher or with other student teachers.

6 Is any part of school in-service education (INSET) for staff devoted to moral, ethical and values education? How is such work focused and by whom? Your school tutor can direct you to the staff responsible for INSET. See also, for example, Cowie and Sharp (1992); Haydon (1997).

> **Task 4.5.2**
>
> **THE PLACE OF SUBJECT WORK IN PROMOTING MORAL DEVELOPMENT**
>
> Identify an example of a social, ethical or moral issue that would form part of teaching in your subject. Prepare and bring an example to a seminar meeting for discussion. You might include:
>
> - a statement of what the subject matter is and how it relates to your curriculum;
> - any issues and the moral focus for pupils; e.g. the decriminalisation of drugs; use of animals for research purposes; road building through the green belt;
> - a sample of the teaching material;
> - your outline teaching strategy, draft lesson plan perhaps, for discussion;
> - the problems that you anticipate teaching it;
> - any questions that the seminar might help you resolve.

CLASS MANAGEMENT

We have spoken earlier about the importance of teachers setting an example for pupils. If values are preached but not practised, pupils attach little significance to them much less uphold them. The task below contains three such examples. See also Unit 3.3 on classroom management.

> **Task 4.5.3**
>
> **CLASS CONTROL**
>
> Pupils dislike being punished for offences which they did not commit or being punished for the misdemeanours of others. It is easy to respond, under stress, to a misdemeanour by a few pupils by threatening to keep back the whole class.
>
> > A class is reading from a set text; from time to time there is a pause in the reading in order to discuss a point. As the lesson progresses, some children get bored and seek distraction by flicking pellets at other pupils seated towards the front. The teacher knows it is happening but is unable to identify the culprit. One or two pupils take offence at being hit by pellets and object noisily. The teacher asks for the action to stop but it continues; noise rises and the teacher threatens to keep the person in when they are identified. The lesson is stopped and the culprit asked to own up. No one volunteers; the class is given five minutes to sort this out; no one owns up and the whole class is kept in after school for fifteen minutes.
> >
> > Some pupils object on the grounds that they did not offend. Some walk out of the detention and refuse to stay.
>
> How might the teacher:
>
> - deal with this situation for those left in detention?
> - deal with those who walked out?
> - deal with any complaint of unfair practice?
> - have responded differently to the whole incident?

Task 4.5.4

CHEATING IN CLASS

Cheating in tests, for example, is rare but when spotted involves either collusion (with other pupils) or answers being hidden on the person. This may be recognised by direct observation during the test; by comparing pupil scripts; or by recognising a familiar phrase likely to have been copied.

A cause of cheating is fear. The fear may be of the teachers' wrath or punishment in response to poor marks. Some teachers may, for example, give a roll call of marks when the scripts have been marked or make public comment on individual performances.

If mistakes are treated with anger, with punishment or by humiliation, pupils are not encouraged to think freely or attempt solutions. Cheating often means the pupil gets the task correct, instead of wrong. This denies the pupil access to feedback from the teacher about the source of error and learning from mistakes.

Another cause of anxiety may be by trying to maintain personal esteem. This might occur when trying to 'keep their end up' at home. Some parents regularly ask their children how they got on and a pupil does not like admitting to low marks. On the other hand, the source of anxiety could be about being moved to a lower set. Where streaming is the method of grouping pupils, failure may lead to demotion, losing friends and having to make new ones; or to meet a new but unpopular teacher.

Cheating may be a sign that the pupil cares. It may not be their fault. Children who don't care are unlikely to cheat. The 'don't care' attitude is a different issue to contend with.

How might teachers respond to a pupil caught cheating? It is not possible to condone it but at the same time pupils are not mature adults.

Draw up some school guidelines to:

- prevent cheating;
- publicly deal with cheating;
- help the pupil concerned.

Check if there are guidelines in your school about cheating in school work or public examinations. How do they relate to your views?

DEALING WITH INCIDENTS

Many incidents which arise in school have at their heart moral judgements. How we respond to them taxes our notions of right and wrong; our decisions may guide pupils towards establishing their own position. Here are two examples; your experience in school will furnish you with others.

The examples attempt to show different aspects of moral judgement that need to be exercised by the teacher and the pupil. The first concerns personal morality; the individual has to wrestle with their own conscience and decide what to do. In the second case the teacher is put into a public position where their decision will be known to all. The situation has, in addition, a conflict of responsibilities between parents and pupils.

Task 4.5.5

CRITICAL INCIDENTS

Read through the following extract and respond to the questions below.

1   Wayne is in school during break in order to keep an appointment with a teacher. On the way, he has to walk past his own form room. As he does so he sees a pupil from his class, whom he recognises, going through the desk of a classmate. The pupil is not facing Wayne but it seems obvious to him that items are being removed from the desk and pocketed, but he can't identify the items. Wayne walks away unseen by the other pupil. Wayne decides to tell his class teacher.

2   Serena is 15 years old, the daughter of practising Muslim parents and attends the local girls' comprehensive school. Her parents do not approve of her mixing, at her age, with other pupils outside school hours and expect her to return home promptly after school.

Nevertheless, in the company of other girls, Serena sometimes walks home part of the way with boys from the adjacent boys' school. Under pressure from peers, she agrees to meet one boy after school. She arranges for an alibi with another girl. On the proposed day of the meeting, the girlfriend panics at the prospect of having to lie to Serena's parents and backs out of the agreement. That afternoon the two girls argue in class to the extent that they are kept back by the teacher after school. The teacher becomes unwittingly privy to the arrangements.

These examples have implications for both the pupil and the teacher. Identify the issues in each case.

What advice would you give in each situation to:

• teacher?
• pupils?

You may wish to prepare your response to these situations, prior to talking with other student teachers and your tutor. This may help you get a focus on the legal responsibilities of the teacher in these circumstances.

| Task 4.5.6 | **RESPONDING TO ETHNIC DIVERSITY** |

Read the following extract which is a statement of principle about the importance of educating pupils for life in an ethnically diverse society.

> If children see only white people around them in their school and locality, they are in danger of acquiring the outdated, inaccurate and racist view that only white people are of account. Schools that do not actively counteract such an impression are misleading and misinforming their pupils, neglecting the cross-curricular themes in the National Curriculum of 'multicultural issues' and 'citizenship', and are failing to prepare them for their place in multicultural Europe and in a shrinking and interdependent world in which most people are not white. And the learning materials selected for the school are a major source of information.
>
> (Klein, 1993, p. 169)

Use some or all of the following questions, as appropriate, to respond to this statement. We suggest that you consider this extract on your own and, if appropriate, bring your responses to a seminar with other student teachers or with your tutor.

1 What evidence do you have in your daily life that people living in an all-white community develop the views described above in the first sentence?
2 What evidence do you have in your school experience school that pupils recognise the views expressed in the first sentence of the quotation above? You will need to relate your response explicitly to the ethnic mix in your school.
3 How do the aims of your school meet the challenges posed by this statement?
4 What evidence do you have that your school adopts a positive approach to ethnic diversity advocated in this extract?
5 To what extent do, for example, assemblies, PSHE and extra-curricular activities in your school contribute towards fostering positive cross-cultural attitudes?
6 How does the teaching of your subject allow you to contribute to the development in pupils of positive attitudes towards people of other cultures?
7 How do you select teaching materials for pupils which contribute to the development in your pupils of positive attitudes towards people of other cultures?

MORAL DEVELOPMENT, VALUES AND CURRICULUM

Moral judgement, moral behaviour and the values they represent derive from personal, social, cultural, religious and political viewpoints. Societies have norms which are essential for its continuity. They guide interpersonal behaviour and national attitudes towards others. Societies in which the norms of some groups of people differ from the main group have the potential for friction and, perhaps, unrest. Very largely, moral standards come from parents, peers and teachers. Eventually some individuals are able to make their own judgement about values, to see the broader picture and consider all the variables in a situation. When individuals reach this stage of development, many may view justice as problematic, i.e. to be worked at, not just as the acceptance of authority.

This leads to the idea that the values they have grown up with are not necessarily useful for all time. They need to be reviewed periodically and changed if no longer valid. One purpose of education is to enable young people to work towards that level of response in their private lives and public faces.

Nevertheless, some young people (and not a few older ones) have not reached this stage; they may refer to rules for authority as a means of avoiding difficult issues; or flout agreed rules or conventions because the rules interfere with personal freedom or wants of the moment. Such a response may show a lack of concern for others.

It can be argued that values are relative, subjective and subject to change with age. Values alter with the generations and practice has to be re-examined in order that the values remain appropriate to the culture. Society changes, not least by different cultures entering and leaving the society, by processes of immigration and emigration. Our views change, e.g. through exposure to science, spiritual experience, developing technology, legislation, extended travel, interaction with others and, hopefully, through education. It is possible to see rules and conventions changing as we follow and contribute to debates about behaviour (homosexual rights, abortion), about improving humans (genetic engineering to prevent disease); our views about the environment (saving animal species, plant conservation in sites of special interest); and balancing the good of society with that of the individual (road building programmes). We referred in an earlier section to the Dearing Report. In its reiteration of the aims of the 1988 Education Reform Act it says that the goals for pupils are achieved through GCSE performances (paragraph 3.14) and that

> the levels of achievement underlying these targets will be realised only if we can ensure that all pupils master the knowledge, understanding and skills required by the National Curriculum Orders for the core subjects.
>
> (Dearing, 1994 paragraph 3.15)

It has never been made clear how a subject-based curriculum is expected to achieve the broad aims related to the spiritual, moral and ethical development of young people (O'Hear and White, 1991). It is supposed to be self-evident that the realisation of these aims is best achieved by the traditional route of English, mathematics, science, etc. The additional dimension of the National Curriculum, the cross-curricular themes and issues, was a late attempt to integrate its 'broad aims' into the fabric of subject-specific Attainment Targets (see National Curriculum Council, NCC, 1988, *The Whole Curriculum*). Schools have found it difficult to address cross-curricular issues while implementing so many other changes demanded of them. They remain as valuable guidelines for development. See National Curriculum Guidance, numbers 3–9 (NCC, 1988 et seq.).

In 1996 the School Curriculum and Assessment Authority (SCAA, now the Qualifications and Curriculum Authority (QCA)) began some work on values education. It set up a 'National Forum for Values in Education and the Community' to see if a consensus could be reached on certain values across the whole society. The forum produced a list of values – phrased in broad terms, under the categories of 'self', 'relationships', 'society' and 'environment' (Smith and Standish, 1997). The next stage in this work was to produce guidance for schools; this, while taking the results from the forum into account, was structured around the OFSTED inspection categories of 'spiritual, moral, social and cultural development'. At the time of writing, this guidance is being piloted in selected schools. Meanwhile, the White Paper *Excellence in Schools* (DFEE, 1997b) indicated that education in citizenship and education in parenthood should be among the tasks of schools. Whereas the National Curriculum in 1988 made little attempt to show how aims concerning values would be pursued, it seems likely that the revised National Curriculum after the year 2000 will build in some content relating to moral values and citizenship.

The situations described in this unit have used a variety of contexts. They include interactions which are teacher–teacher; student teacher–student teacher; student teacher–pupil, student teacher–class and student teacher–school. The most common interaction is the student teacher–class relationship. Whereas many situations involve decision making with an underlying implicit moral agenda, e.g. dealing with tale telling, there are occasions when moral and ethical issues provide the explicit aim of the lesson. Simulation is one way of introducing issues (see Glossary); your subject work may have given rise to others (Task 4.5.2).

HANDLING DISCUSSION WITH CLASSES

A common technique for raising moral and ethical issues is through discussion. Discussion activities have great potential as a vehicle for moral development through sharing ideas, developing awareness of the opinion of others, promoting appropriate social procedures and profitable debate. It can be a vehicle for learning. On the other hand, discussion can be the mere pooling of ignorance, the confirmation of prejudices and a stage for showing off.

Young people can be taught the protocols of discussion. It is necessary to help them realise that discussion may not end in a clear decision or agreement, but can lead to a deeper understanding of the issues and the position of others. For the teacher, discussion is one of the more difficult strategies to implement. Perhaps that is why it is not often used. See also Unit 3.1 on communicating with pupils. Advice about handling discussion is given in Appendix 4.5.1 to this unit.

> ## Summary and key points
>
> Schools have a responsibility in law for the development of spiritual, moral, social and cultural values in pupils. In school there are many opportunities for developing these qualities within both subject and pastoral work. At heart, this process is about values education.
>
> To be effective, however, you need to plan carefully for the introduction of such issues or to consider in your lesson planning whether such issues are likely to arise. From time to time, the teacher may deliberately plan to raise controversial issues in her lessons; the planning of that discussion is a high-level teaching skill.
>
> Nevertheless, situations and dilemmas occur constantly in school which call for the exercise of moral judgement, the resolution of which often has a profound effect on pupils. On occasions, it is difficult to know how to respond and, as a student teacher, you can refer matters to qualified staff. If you are called on to deal with racist and sexist issues, then it is important to know about the school policies and how such matters are treated in your school. See Unit 4.5. The national forum for values in education is expected to produce guidance for teachers by the end of this decade.

FURTHER READING

BBC (1993) 'The joy of teaching sex education', a video in the Teaching Today series, on *Sex Education*; with notes.

See the section on teaching methods, a session led by Janet Millward on handling difficult issues through discussion, a clip of 2 1/2 minutes. Useful for looking at rules for talking, use of video, assumptions about pupils, their attitudes and assumed knowledge. All the material in this video is useful to teachers.

Child, D. (1993) *Psychology and the Teacher*, London: Cassell.

The 5th edition of a classic text. Good review of cognitive development, moral development and Freud's theory of the mind. A useful source of references.

Haydon, G. (1997) *Teaching about Values: A New Approach*, London: Cassell.

Sets moral education in the broader context of educational aims and values. Part 5 reviews different conceptions of values education.

Smith, R. and Standish, P. (eds) (1997) *Teaching Right and Wrong: Moral Education in the Balance*, Stoke-on-Trent: Trentham.

Includes a discussion of the work of the School Curriculum and Assessment Authority (SCAA, now Qualification and Curriculum Authority (QCA)) 'Values forum' and arguments for alternative approaches to values education.

Wellington, J. (ed.) (1986) *Controversial Issues in the Curriculum*, Oxford: Basil Blackwell.

Contains sound advice concerning handling difficult moral issues in school. Examples from across the curriculum, with background information. Good chapters on theoretical underpinning of the place of controversial issues in the curriculum.

APPENDIX 4.5.1 HANDLING DISCUSSION

Four factors need to be considered. They are:

* Rules and procedures for discussion
* Provision of evidence – information
* Neutral chairperson
* Outcomes expected.

Rules and procedures   You need to consider:

* choice of subject and length of discussion (young pupils without experience may not sustain lengthy discussion);
* physical seating; room size; arrangement of furniture so that most pupils have eye contact;
* protocols for discourse; taking turns; length of contribution; abusive language;
* procedures for violation of protocols, e.g. racist or sexist behaviour;
* how to protect the sensitivity of individuals; pupils may reveal unexpected personal information in the course of a discussion;
* stance of the chairperson.

Provision of evidence   In order to stimulate discussion and provide a clear basis for argument, you need to:

* know the age, ability and mix of abilities of the pupils;
* know what information is needed;
* know sources of information;
* decide at what point the information is introduced (before, during).

Neutral chairperson   A neutral stance may be essential because:

* authority of the opinions of the chair should not influence the outcome;
* the opinions of pupils are to be exposed, not those of the teachers;
* the chairperson can be free to influence the quality of understanding, the rigour of debate and appropriate exploration of the issues; and
* pupils will understand the teacher's stance if it is made clear at the start.

Possible outcomes   The strategy is discussion not instruction. Pupils should:

* learn by sharing and understand the opinion of others;
* be exposed to the nature and role of evidence;

- realise that objective evidence is often an inadequate basis for decision making;
- come to know that decisions often rely on subjective value judgements;
- realise that many decisions are compromises.

Action   Try out these rules by setting up a discussion on the topic of

> **Equal opportunities for girls enables them to join the power structure rather than challenge it**

For further help on running discussions and other ways of introducing moral issues see Tarrant (1981), Wellington (1986), Jennings (1995) and BBC (1993).

4.6   AN INTRODUCTION TO PUPILS' SPECIAL EDUCATIONAL NEEDS

INTRODUCTION

The term special educational needs (SEN) encompasses a multitude of different learning and emotional and behavioural factors which may prevent pupils achieving their full potential. The Warnock Report (DES, 1978) suggests that one in five pupils requires special educational provision at least for some time during their education. The implementation of the National Curriculum (NC) from the late 1980s onwards is characterised – among other things – by the challenge it presents to teachers to address the wide-ranging needs of **all** pupils at 'a realistic but challenging level' (HMI, 1992, p. 1). Increasing your understanding of the special educational needs which different pupils might have is an essential part of your professional development.

OBJECTIVES

We would expect you, as a student teacher, simply to be beginning to develop an understanding of pupils' SEN. By the end of this unit you should:

- have an understanding of recent legislation in this area in particular teachers' responsibilities at stages 1 to 3 of the *Code of Practice for the Identification and Assessment of SEN* (DFE, 1994f);
- know that the term **special educational needs** spans a continuum ranging from the needs of pupils with multiple and profound disabilities to those of exceptionally able pupils;
- be aware of the possibility that teacher attitudes may limit pupils' achievement of their potential;
- be developing your knowledge of teaching strategies which may be used with pupils with different SEN.

We suggest that you review the competences/standards related to your course to see what is required of you in the area of SEN.

DEFINITIONS

There are differing views on the appropriate terms to use to describe SEN. In this unit, we use the terminology adopted by the National Curriculum Council (1993c, p. 1) which grouped pupils' **special educational needs** under four main categories:

1   Pupils with exceptionally severe learning difficulties including those with

- profound and multiple learning difficulties . . .
- exceptionally severe learning difficulties resulting from, for example, multi-sensory impairment; these pupils may not be considered as having profound and multiple learning difficulties.
2 Pupils with other learning difficulties including those with:
  - mild learning difficulties;
  - moderate learning difficulties;
  - specific learning difficulties;
  - emotional and behavioural difficulties.
3 Pupils with physical or sensory impairment.
4 Exceptionally able pupils.

Pupils in category 1 include those with 'severe autistic characteristics; multisensory impairment particularly pupils who are deaf–blind, pupils with extreme physical difficulties which may mask their potential' (NCC, 1993c, p. 4). Pupils in this category are not usually in mainstream secondary school classes.

You can expect a number of the pupils you teach to be included in category 2. Pupils' needs might be temporary – a child may be emotionally distressed because of home circumstances which are eventually resolved – or they might be long term such as specific learning difficulties (e.g. those described as 'dyslexic').

Category 3 includes hearing-impaired pupils as well as visually impaired and physically disabled pupils. The needs of pupils in this category pose a variety of challenges for subject teachers. Often it is the lack of curricular adaption or appropriate provision (e.g. wheelchair access to laboratories or libraries) which prevents pupils with these SEN having access to the curriculum rather than the disability itself.

Pupils do have differing mental and physical capabilities; the teacher's job is to ensure that each pupil is provided with the opportunity to develop their capabilities as fully as possible within the resources available.

REPORTS AND LEGISLATION RELATING TO SEN

The 1944 Education Act defined eleven categories of disability for which provision should be made in special or ordinary schools. The Act focused on the 2% of pupils educated in special schools, units or classes.

The Warnock Report on Special Education (DES, 1978a) defined SEN more broadly, estimating that about one in five pupils require some form of special educational provision at some time during their school careers. It recommended removing the eleven categories of disability and instead focusing on the needs of the individual pupil. The report recommended the early identification and annual review of needs.

The Warnock Report (paragraph 1.4, p. 5) also defined **common goals** and a **common purpose** for education for **all** pupils although it stopped short of recommending entitlement to a common curriculum which came with the 1988 Education Act.

The implication of this ideal is that if the purpose and goals of education are the same for all pupils, including those with SEN, then the special educational provision for pupils should enable them to achieve these goals. The report recognised that the continuum of

SEN across a range of abilities must be reflected in a continuum of provision, services and support to meet the needs of these pupils. It also recognised that the needs of most such pupils can be met through education in a mainstream school, with outside specialist help if necessary. Thus, many pupils with SEN were to be educated in ordinary classes in mainstream schools. To support this in practical terms, the report recommended that all initial teacher education courses should contain an element on special education, that teachers in mainstream schools should take short in-service courses on SEN and that LEA support and advisory services should be expanded. Further recommendations included the appointment of more educational psychologists, better co-ordination between health, education and social services and a continuing role for voluntary organisations. Units 4.1 and 2.2 discuss issues relating to the provision of work within lessons which is **differentiated** to take account of the varying capabilities of pupils.

The thinking behind the Warnock Report formed the basis for the 1981 Education Act. The changes in the law brought about by this Act included specific duties being imposed on Local Education Authorities (LEAs) and school governors to make provision for SEN, defining responsibilities and procedures for SEN and the establishment of parents' participation in special educational assessments, along with a right of appeal. The powers of the Secretary of State for Education were defined, enabling him or her to make regulations and perform certain procedures under the Act. All previous legislation on SEN was repealed. Governors were to ensure that 'teachers are aware of the importance of identifying and providing for SEN'. The teacher was said to be 'directly responsible for his pupils' and 'in a key position to observe their response in the classroom, to recognise the child who is experiencing difficulties in learning and to try out different approaches to help meet the child's needs'. Teachers were to 'be encouraged to keep full records of their pupils' progress and to include information about professional consultations and assessments' (DES, 1983, p. 3, paragraph 11).

The provisions of the 1981 Education Act provided the foundation for the Education Reform Act of 1988. This stated that

> The National Curriculum applies to all pupils, including those with SEN other than those for whom it has been disapplied under any arrangements. . . . The Secretary of State believes that these provisions for modification or disapplication of National Curriculum provisions should be applied sensitively and positively. The pupils concerned should obtain the maximum benefits they can from the National Curriculum. Positive alternatives should be offered in all cases.
>
> (DES, 1989, pp. 1–2)

Thus, the National Curriculum is firmly established as an entitlement curriculum. All pupils have the same statutory entitlement to a broad and balanced curriculum, including access to the National Curriculum, although adaptations and special arrangements may be necessary for pupils with SEN (DES, 1989, section 8).

The *Code of Practice on the Identification and Assessment of SEN* (DFE, 1994f) was introduced in the 1993 Education Act. It came into effect on 1 September 1994 and builds on the principles and practices established in the 1981 and 1988 Education Acts. An extract from this code is provided in Appendix 4.

This is a statutory code of practice which cannot be ignored by anyone to whom it

> **Task 4.6.1**
>
> **THE *CODE OF PRACTICE ON THE IDENTIFICATION AND ASSESSMENT OF SPECIAL EDUCATIONAL NEEDS* AND THE SCHOOL'S POLICY**
>
> Ask for a copy of the school policy on SEN provision and read this and the extract from the code of practice in Appendix 4. If you can, refer also to the code of practice itself (available in libraries). Discuss the implementation of the code of practice and school policy with your tutor and the SEN co-ordinator in your school experience school. Has this code of practice changed what is happening in the school? How does the school ensure that the requirements of the code of practice are met? How are all teachers in the school involved in implementing the code of practice? Discuss your findings with those of another student teacher who has undertaken the same exercise in another school.

applies. The statutory duty lies with the governing body of the school. They are responsible for the provision for pupils with SEN. One of the governing body's statutory duties is to publish information about and report on the school's policy on SEN. The code indicates that all teaching and non-teaching staff should be involved in the development of the school's SEN policy and be fully aware of the school's procedures for identifying, assessing and making provision for pupils with SEN. As part of its inspection procedures, OFSTED looks at the effectiveness of a school's practices for identifying, assessing and making provision for pupils' SEN in the light of the school's policies and code.

The code indicates that provision for pupils in mainstream schools should be subject to the views and wishes of parents. Partnership between schools, parents, LEAs, health services, social services, voluntary organisations and other agencies is essential in order to meet effectively the needs of pupils with SEN. The code provides practical guidance to LEAs and governing bodies of all maintained schools on their responsibilities towards pupils with SEN. It outlines a five-stage approach in order to match the needs of pupils with the special education provision available to them. These stages are outlined in paragraph 1.4 in Appendix 4. Here we discuss the first three stages which particularly relate to the teacher's responsibilities.

THE TEACHER'S RESPONSIBILITIES

Teachers are involved particularly in the first three stages, as at stages 4 and 5 outside specialist help is involved in assessing whether the child meets criteria for statutory assessment by the LEA. For example,

- At **Stage 1**, 'the child's class teacher or form/year tutor:
  - identifies a child's special educational needs
  - consults the child's parents and the child
  - informs the SEN co-ordinator, who registers the child's special educational needs
  - collects relevant information about the child, consulting the SEN co-ordinator

- works closely with the child in the normal classroom context
- monitors and reviews the child's progress' (DFE, 1994f, pp. 21–22).
- At **Stage 2** the SEN co-ordinator becomes involved and 'working closely with the child's teachers
- marshals relevant information, including, as appropriate, information from sources beyond the school
- ensures that an individual education plan is drawn up
- ensures that the child's parents are informed
- monitors and reviews the child's progress
- informs the head teacher' (DFE, 1994f, p. 22).
- At **Stage 3**, 'the SEN co-ordinator continues to take a leading role, again working closely with the child's teachers and
- keeps the head teacher informed
- draws on the advice of outside specialists, for example educational psychologists and advisory teachers
- ensures that the child and his or her parents are consulted
- ensures that an individual education plan is drawn up
- with outside specialists, monitors and reviews the child's progress' (DFE, 1994f, p. 22).

In carrying out their responsibility for identifying the special educational needs of pupils many schools routinely carry out tests to establish a baseline of the pupil's ability on starting secondary school.

Task 4.6.2	**PUPIL ASSESSMENTS ON ENTRY TO SCHOOL**

Ask what, if any, assessments are carried out on pupils on entry to the school and if you can see examples of them. The National Foundation for Educational Research (NFER) specialises in providing educational tests and these are widely used.

PROVISION FOR PUPILS WITH SEN

Arrangements for the education of pupils with SEN vary between schools and between LEAs.

Schools are required to have policies setting out their approach to SEN and to appoint an SEN co-ordinator who oversees provision throughout the school. They have access to resources, information and support agencies such as educational psychologists and educational welfare officers (EWOs). Pupils' needs may be supported in several ways – most commonly through allocation of extra teaching time in the form of in-class support for the pupil, although in some circumstances pupils may be withdrawn from a class.

Where other adults are supporting pupils in your classroom, you need to liaise closely with them to ensure the pupil gains maximum benefit from this support. The support staff should have the lesson plan well in advance and you need to check that the materials you are providing are appropriate for the particular child.

Task 4.6.3	WORKING WITH SUPPORT TEACHERS IN THE CLASSROOM

For a pupil with SEN to be fully supported in the classroom, the classroom teacher and the support teacher must develop an effective working relationship. Ask some support teachers for advice about how you can best work together. Observe support teachers working in classrooms and consider what has to be done to ensure the pupils make maximum progress.

Nationally there is a variety of special school provision with schools catering for pupils with moderate learning difficulties (MLD), emotional and behavioural difficulties (EBD), severe learning difficulties (SLD). Schools may have special units attached to them; there may be special units within schools. Some schools are day schools, others provide boarding accommodation. The Warnock Report (DES, 1978) recommended that pupils in special schools might, where appropriate, attend classes in ordinary schools and/or have social contact with pupils in ordinary classes. Tuition at home is also provided for some pupils. Staff working in special schools usually have additional qualifications.

HELPING CHILDREN WITH SEN TO LEARN

In this section we provide some guidance on working with pupils with SEN which you are most likely to teach in mainstream classrooms, i.e. specific learning difficulties ('dyslexia'), emotional and behavioural difficulties, hearing impairment and exceptional ability. We provide only a brief overview. As each pupil has individual needs, you should consult with the SEN co-ordinator (SENCO) about effective strategies to use with the pupils whom you are teaching. Many of the strategies listed will produce positive results with children without SEN as well. The SENCO forum on the Virtual Teacher Centre web sites provides a virtual space for teachers to discuss SEN issues (see p. 47 Unit 1.4, also Leask and Pachler, 1999 for advice about using ICT with pupils with SEN).

Specific learning difficulties (including dyslexia)

Pupils with specific learning difficulties experience some of the following problems:

- difficulty in sequencing
- difficulty with spelling
- inability to memorise a series of sound units
- difficulty with repeating items in serial order
- poor recall of tables and number bonds

- inability to follow a series of instructions in the correct order
- handwriting problems.

Walker (1989) describes a pattern of classroom behaviour which you are likely to come across a number of times in your teaching career.

> There are children in our classrooms who have serious problems with written language who cannot be said to suffer from a severe learning difficulty. In the absence of any evidence of overall learning difficulties the child may be branded 'careless' or 'lazy'. . . . Yet he may make a valuable oral contribution in classroom discussions, showing insight and a clear grasp of the concepts but be unable to communicate this understanding by means of the written work. He may be able to explain in graphic detail that he just made a model aircraft carrier describing the guns, the flight deck, the radar scanning equipment but when asked to write, he is unable to express all this and so merely writes, 'I made a bote.' This is the child with a specific learning difficulty. I will use the pronoun '**he**' throughout as the description is three times as likely to apply to boys as to girls.
>
> Besides reading and spelling very badly it is most likely that he will have difficulties in the areas of short term memory, organisation and sequencing. He shows evidence of this in that he is unable to recite the days of the week.
>
> It is unlikely that the busy class teacher will be able to give the close individualised, structured, multi-sensory language teaching which the child with specific learning difficulties needs to order/improve his reading and spelling. However the teacher can do a great deal to improve the memory, organisation and sequencing skills of such a child.
>
> (Walker, 1989, p. 41)

Do you recognise this pupil's work?

Task 4.6.4 **FOCUSING ON PUPILS' ACHIEVEMENT**
Check the work of pupils you teach against this description of an orally competent pupil who has difficulty with written language or number. Where you identify pupils causing concern, discuss appropriate teaching strategies with your tutor or the SEN co-ordinator.

Some pupils who have such problems have gone on to gain first class degrees at university. Software is available to help pupils with these difficulties (Leask and Pachler, 1999). A supportive teacher can make a difference to the pupil's understanding, self-esteem and ultimate achievement. Examination boards often make special arrangements for these pupils.

Emotional and behavioural difficulties (EBD)

The causes of disruptive pupil behaviour are numerous including family environment as well as physical and sensory impairments. The school and teachers' responses to certain behaviours should be carefully thought through as they can exacerbate the situation or help to resolve it. Pupils who are withdrawn in themselves are as much a cause for concern as those whose behaviour is disruptive. DFE Circular 9/94 defines the behaviour of pupils with EBD as 'on a continuum'. 'Their problems are greater than sporadic naughtiness or moodiness and yet not so great as to be classed as mental illness' (DFE, 1994e, p. 4). Behavioural problems are discussed elsewhere in this book and tasks are set to develop your skills in this area so we suggest you refer back to those sections (see, for example, the differentiation case studies in Unit 4.1).

Points to consider when you are working with pupils with EBD are:

- appropriate school and teacher responses make a difference;
- behaviour may improve if pupils' self-esteem is enhanced;
- the teacher needs to be constructive and positive as well as specific about what is and is not acceptable;
- parental involvement is to be encouraged;
- early identification of problems is likely to lead to improvements;
- stages 1–3 of the code of practice describe school-based strategies which can help;
- pupils should be given short-term goals which stretch but which do not overwhelm them;
- the curriculum should be relevant;
- behaviour policies should indicate clear boundaries of acceptable behaviour, should be clear, well understood, provide rewards and commendations where possible;
- sanctions should not include educational activities as punishment;
- corporal punishment is illegal for publicly funded pupils.

(Adapted from DFE, 1994e, Circular 9/94.)

Hearing impairment

Hearing-impaired pupils often attend mainstream schools. Sometimes it is difficult to identify a pupil with a hearing impairment; if such impairment is recognised, you can teach these pupils more effectively if you:

- give visual cues to topics being discussed, e.g. using visual aids, pointing;
- use notes on the board to reinforce what you are saying;
- make sure the pupil is watching your face when you speak;
- seat the pupil within 3 metres of you so they can lip read and perhaps hear you;
- give the pupil an unobscured view of your mouth;
- let your face reflect your mood – smiling can provide important feedback;
- explain something several different ways if you have not been understood the first time;
- talk to the pupil whenever possible;

- repeat what classmates say in discussion or question and answer sessions (in any case, others in the class may not have heard);
- don't draw attention to a pupil's hearing impairment;
- avoid using more than normal gestures.

Pupils can help you understand them if they show you what they want or draw or write what they want if you don't understand.

Hearing aids do distort sound so you may not be heard clearly even if the child is wearing one.

Attention deficit disorder (ADD)

This is a syndrome which usually comprises three principal behaviours: inattentiveness, impulsiveness and overactivity. What distinguishes pupils with ADD is the considerably greater degree and frequency with which these characteristics are displayed. The problem is much less marked in one-to-one situations. If overactivity is a major component, the term Attention Deficit Hyperactivity Disorder may be used. Associated behaviours include:

- insatiability
- social clumsiness
- poor co-ordination
- disorganisation

Points to note when working with pupils with ADD are:

- they usually act without malice, but also without deliberation;
- the first aim of treatment should be to create calm;
- respond to major behaviours, and try to disregard those that are irritating but unimportant;
- provide routine by running each day in a predictable way;
- gain eye contact, and speak clearly and simply;
- offer pupils frequent rewards.

Medication by means of stimulants is a widely used treatment, but this is controversial. Progress apparently made in occupational or cognitive behavioural therapy does not usually transfer well to the classroom. However, multi-disciplinary support is vital, as is co-operation with parents. A central action plan (such as an IEP) should include clear targets and criteria for the evaluation of all action taken. Further information may be found in *Attention-Deficit/Hyperactivity Disorder – A Practical Guide for Teachers* by Cooper and Ideus (1996).

Asperger's syndrome – one dimension of autism

The core features of this syndrome are:

- speech delay;
- cognitive delay;
- problems with non-verbal communication such as eye contact;
- poor phasing of thinking and feeling;
- repetitive activity such as echolalia;
- difficulty in re-focusing (i.e. challenging behaviour);
- excellence in particular skills, such as drawing (good eidetic memory);
- clumsiness or odd gait;
- absorbing interests (such as train timetables).

These children are similar to autistic pupils in some ways, but they cope with their difficulties much more effectively. They are also able to make a partial recovery. A pupil with Asperger's syndrome is often able to express complex ideas orally. Coping with their difference is a particular problem at adolescence. The syndrome affects nine times as many boys as girls.

Points to note when dealing with a pupil with Asperger's syndrome are:

- stress management is vital – the pupil cannot tolerate interruption to a ritual, or an object out of place;
- making little noises is normal for the child as a way of relieving tension. Other pupils have to be tolerant;
- choose winnable battles, and be assertive but not aggressive;
- force eye contact, calmly state what you want the pupil to do and ask the child to repeat this;
- be realistic – for example, is the child's very limited diet medically or socially threatening?
- ensure consistency with the child's parents' management strategies;
- the child can learn intellectually what behaviours he/she must change.

Like an autistic pupil, the child with Asperger's syndrome lacks 'mentalisation', i.e. the ability to picture what another person is thinking. The core problems can be modified by maturation, motivation, experience and compensation. (Further information may be found in *Asperger's Syndrome: A Practical Guide For Teachers* by Cumine *et al.* (1998).) The National Autistic Society can be contacted on 0171 833 2299; see also web site on p. 229.

Dyspraxia

Dyspraxia may be defined as difficulty in planning and carrying out skilled, non-habitual motor acts in the correct sequence. The difficulty lies more in the formulation of a plan of action than in poor motor co-ordination, though this difficulty often results in clumsiness. Dyspraxia is often developmental, i.e. it begins early in a pupil's life, and is not the result of injury or illness. The terms 'sensory integrative dysfunction' and 'developmental co-ordination disorder' are also used. Assessment by a speech and language therapist and an occupational therapist may be needed, though the Educational Psychologist plays a key role.

Common difficulties of dyspraxic pupils include:

- problems in learning new and unfamiliar tasts;
- awkward movements, with frequent falls and bruising;
- poor work habits;
- delays in attainment of life-skills such as dressing;
- apparent laziness – 'he could do it if he tried'.
- poor self-image, because they cannot perform as expected.

Points to note when dealing with a dyspraxic pupil are:

- provide seats, pegs, lockers etc. at the end of a row and preferably in a corner;
- help him to make lists of equipment and write instructions for common tasks;
- set up an effective system for communicating with parents;
- ensure that there is consistency between support methods used at home and at school;
- take care that suggestions made are appropriate to the pupil's age group;
- the problems are inconsistent – on some days they may appear to have vanished;
- the demands of secondary school life may call for fresh support with personal organisation;
- as with a pupil who is dyslexic, special examination arrangements may be needed.

Further information may be found in *Dyspraxia: A Guide for Teachers and Parents* by Ripley, Daines and Barrett (Fulton, 1997). The Dyspraxia Foundation's address is 8 West Alley, Hitchin, Herts, SG5 1EG.

The pupil with language difficulties

Pupils who are failing to reach their potential may have receptive or expressive language difficulties. These may initially be indicated by an inconsistency between language and other developmental levels. Such pupils often have a family history of problematic language development, and may have suffered from inflammation of the middle ear (*otitis media*). Areas of receptive language difficulty include:

- vocabulary;
- comprehension of syntax;
- accuracy of phonological awareness, e.g. auditory discrimination;
- memory for statements which are not simple, active and declarative;
- understanding inferences.

Expressive language difficulties include:

- formulating statements which are beyond the simple/active/declarative;
- poor ability to define words or give synonyms;
- stammering;
- articulation disorder;
- word-finding.

If a child appears to have difficulties in several of the above areas, assessment by a speech and language therapist is indicated. The following should be kept in mind in intervention with such children:

- speech disordered children often have emotional and relationship difficulties;
- goals should include communication as well as specific skills;
- carers at home must be involved in achieving goals;
- teachers should speak calmly and evenly, and try to look straight at the child;
- for stammerers, intervention should begin as early as possible.

Further information may be found in *Developmental Disorders of Language* by Adams, Brown and Edwards (1997).

Visual problems which may pass unnoticed in a busy classroom

All pupils are tested for visual acuity, i.e. normal vision for daily life. Literacy tasks involve the eyes in working 'at near' and require the following:

- accommodation (focusing);
- convergence (the eyes slightly 'turned inwards');
- fixation (the ability to remain focused on one item, often in rapid sequence as in reading);
- tracing (both eyes following a moving object);
- fusion (the ability of the brain to blend the images from each eye);
- binocular vision (the vision of one eye must not be suppressed).

Writing and drawing also require hand/eye co-ordination.

Difficulties with these eye functions may not be reported by a pupil who assumes that everyone's experience is the same as hers. This is also frequently the case with 'pattern glare', where blurring, swirling or vibrating of print is experienced, followed by head-ache. Such symptoms are often particularly marked in the case of black print on white paper, and in fluorescent light.

The pupil who covers one eye when reading, or suppresses one eye by means of head and/or arm position, may be having vision problems. The use of coloured plastic overlays or tinted spectacles may help. A specialist optometrist can assess the need for this by using an 'intuitive colorimeter', but preliminary trials using light-coloured plastic folders can often be revealing.

Further information may be found in *Supporting Children with Visual Impairment in Mainstream Schools* by Miller (1996). The web site for the Royal Institute for the Blind is on page 229 (3).

Exceptionally able pupils

Whilst schools and educational authorities usually provide support for pupils in most categories (as outlined earlier), support for exceptionally able pupils and their teachers is more variable. For this reason, we have included a more substantial section on this area in this unit. The terms exceptionally able, very able and high ability are used inter-changeably in this section. The web site for the National Association for Gifted Children provides further advice (see Unit 1.4).

There are a number of reasons that the needs of very able as well as less able pupils should be properly identified – for example,

- to meet the stated requirement of the NC, schools must cater for the needs of pupils with different abilities;
- to raise overall achievement;
- to empower children to contribute to society in the best possible way (see e.g. McLeod and Cropley, 1989, pp. 11f); and above all
- for pupils to be stretched to their full potential and to gain maximum satisfaction from their schooling.

For the subject teacher, working with pupils of high ability can present a welcome challenge and can result in a partnership between very able pupils and the teacher. In the modern languages classroom, for example, very able pupils often assume the role of interpreters for the teacher to the rest of the class and can therefore contribute to the teacher's maintenance of the target language (i.e. the speaking of the foreign language throughout the lesson).

Very able pupils present the teacher with the challenge of providing more demanding work to stretch them academically; this challenge in turn can reward the teacher with satisfaction. Supporting very able pupils to do well and to reflect their ability, knowledge and understanding of a subject in exam situations – by which teachers increasingly find their professional standing judged – can provide as much satisfaction for the teacher as the 'value-added' achievement of less able pupils, which is often difficult to quantify and frequently goes (formally) unrecognised. It seems therefore sensible and highly desirable to give further thought to the issue of adequate provision for exceptionally able pupils.

One of the main findings of the HMI review of the education of very able pupils in 1992 (HMI, 1992) is that 'very able pupils in maintained primary and secondary schools are often insufficiently challenged by the work they are set' (p. vii). Not only can subject teachers be involved in addressing the issue of very able pupils at the level of whole school policy making (e.g. as a member of the special needs working group) but they can also make an important contribution to catering for the needs of the exceptionally able pupils in the classes they teach.

Identifying exceptionally able pupils

The first step in appropriately catering for the needs of very able pupils is that of identification. Useful methods for the identification of exceptionally able pupils include monitoring of achievement and attainment in assessment situations and general teacher observation. In addition there are intelligence tests, pupils' self-evaluation and parent evaluation (see e.g. George, 1992; Callow, 1980; Weeks, 1993). A very common tool in the identification of able pupils is the checklist (Clarke, 1983: the 'Essex and Rapid' checklists; Hoyle and Wilks, 1990: the 'Laycock' checklist). Denton and Postlethwaite (1985, p. 31ff) put forward the following non-subject-specific checklist as a possible means of identification of very able pupils:

Exceptionally able pupils:

1 Possess superior powers of reasoning, of dealing with abstractions, of

generalizing from specific facts, of understanding meaning and of seeing into relationships.

2 Have great intellectual curiosity.
3 Learn easily and readily.
4 Have a wide range of interests.
5 Have a broad attention-span that enables them to concentrate on and persevere in solving problems and pursuing interests.
6 Are superior in the quantity and quality of vocabulary as compared with pupils their own age.
7 Have the ability to do effective work independently.
8 Have learned to read early (often well before school age).
9 Exhibit keen powers of observation.
10 Show initiative and originality in intellectual work.
11 Show alertness and quick response to new ideas.
12 Are able to memorize quickly.
13 Have great interest in the nature of man and the universe (problems of origins and destiny, etc.).
14 Possess unusual imagination.
15 Follow complex directions easily.
16 Are rapid readers.
17 Have several hobbies.
18 Have reading interests which cover a wide range of subjects.
19 Make frequent and effective use of the library.
20 Are superior in mathematics, particularly in problem solving.

Subject teachers can use lists of this nature as an *aide-mémoire* to help them in confirming their professional judgement in identifying exceptionally able pupils in their (mixed ability) classes.

Task 4.6.5

IDENTIFICATION OF EXCEPTIONALLY ABLE PUPILS
Evaluate the checklist approach to identifying exceptionally able pupils in the light of your own subject expertise; what additional subject-specific skills, knowledge and understanding do, in your view, denote specific aptitude and high ability? Discuss these issues with other student teachers.

The contribution of subject teachers towards meeting the needs of exceptionally able pupils

The teaching styles and classroom techniques you adopt can enable you to cater for your able pupils. McLeod and Cropley (1989) suggest that in addition to general principles like 'establishment of an appropriate atmosphere, encouragement of self-directed learning and evaluation, use of diagnostic teaching' you should:

- provide opportunities for independent work on challenging activities;
- place stress on the importance of completing difficult tasks;
- foster discussions among students of different approaches to the solution of such tasks (p. 156).

Observations made and evidence collected on (inspection) visits to schools prompt HMI (1992, p. 10, p. 16) to report on the following three further teaching strategies and class-room techniques:

- enabling pupils 'to work at their own pace with others of similar ability';
- 'pupils being encouraged to think for themselves, to ask questions, to take some responsibility for their own learning and to contribute ideas;
- variation in pace, teaching style and classroom organisation'.

Moreover, the strategy of differentiated activities in the classroom and as homework tasks is promoted by the DFEE in the framework of the NC and widely considered to be effective in working with both able and less able pupils.

These strategies and techniques require considerable experience, professional training and – on an everyday basis – careful lesson planning and preparation all together reflecting professional commitment.

The following further general points are frequently reiterated in the debate on how to raise achievement of pupils:

- high expectations of parents and teachers;
- high level of self-esteem;
- adequate support at home (HMI, 1992, p. 5).

This brief examination of aspects of the teaching of exceptionally able pupils in mainly mixed ability classes suggests that teaching styles and classroom techniques such as differentiated teaching activities, development of learner autonomy, use of flexible learning styles, variety in working modes (group work, pair work, independent study) as well as problem solving and a target setting approach can all have an important role to play in challenging exceptionally able pupils. Above all the importance of working in an environment of high expectations appears to be an important factor in achieving high standards.

ACCESS TO THE CURRICULUM

Teachers have a duty to act promptly when they consider that a pupil may have a particular special educational need which cannot be met within the resources available to the teacher.

Task 4.6.6

ANALYSING THE NEEDS OF INDIVIDUAL PUPILS

Identify, with the help of your tutor, pupils with whom you have contact who have SEN of different types. Draw up a table similar to the one below in your diary and complete it – drawing on the expertise of different staff as necessary.

Description of pupils' needs	Pupil's strengths and weaknesses	Adaptations to classroom work in specialist subjects	The role of the school/SEN co-ordinator	The role of outside agencies (LEA, educational psychologists, educational welfare officers)
Paul has almost complete hearing loss. He can lip read reasonably well and his speech is fairly clear.				

Use fictional names to preserve confidentiality and compare practice in your school with student teachers from different schools.

Task 4.6.7

WHAT DOES 'STATEMENTING' MEAN?

You will hear staff using the term 'statemented' with reference to pupils with SEN. Arrange a convenient time with the SEN co-ordinator to discuss the procedure by which a statement of special educational need is drawn up for a child.

> ▌ **Summary and key points**
>
> Every child is special. Every child has individual educational needs.
>
> Teachers need to ensure that all their pupils learn to the best of their abilities and that pupils with SEN are not further disabled by the lack of appropriate resources to support their learning.
>
> In your work as a student teacher, we expect you to develop your understanding of the teacher's responsibilities for pupils' SEN so that, when you are in your first post, you are sufficiently aware of your responsibilities that you ensure that your pupils' special educational needs are met. The basic rule for you to remember is that you cannot expect to solve all pupils' learning problems on your own. You must seek advice from experienced staff.
>
> A major problem pupils with SEN have is with the attitudes of others to them. For example, children who have obvious physical disabilities such as cerebral palsy often find they are treated as though their mental abilities match their physical abilities when this is not the case. How will children with special educational needs find you as their teacher?

FURTHER READING

Cumine, V., Leach, J. and Stevenson, G. (1998) *Asperger Syndrome: A Practical Guide for Teachers*, London: David Fulton.

Department for Education (1994e) *Circular 9/94: The Education of Children with Emotional and Behavioural Difficulties*, London: DFE.

A copy of this circular will have been sent to the school. It discusses the application of the *Code of Practice for the Identification and Assessment of SEN* to the management of pupils with emotional and behavioural difficulties.

Leask, M. and Pachler, N. (1999) *Learning to Teach using ICT in the Secondary School*, London: Routledge. See, for example, the chapter in this text on the use of ICT with pupils with SEN.

National Curriculum Council (1992a) *Curriculum Guidance 9: The National Curriculum and Pupils with Severe Learning Difficulties*, York: NCC.

This booklet provides advice for staff working with pupils with profound and multiple learning difficulties – many of whom are working at the earliest levels of the National Curriculum, i.e. at levels well below that expected of pupils of their chronological age. For the student teacher, the booklet provides an introduction to ways of working with these pupils and the bibliography provides lists of subject-specific materials to support this work.

OFSTED (1996) *The Implementation of the Code of Practice for Pupils with Special Educational Needs: A Report from the Office of Her Majesty's Chief Inspector of Schools*, London: HMSO.

This is a report on monitoring by OFSTED of the implementation of the Code of Practice on the Identification and Assessment of Special Educational Needs (DFEE, 1994). This report contains twelve key issues for schools to consider and some future developments. It supplements a report of OFSTED (1996a) *Promoting high achievement for pupils with special educational needs in mainstream schools* (London: HMSO) which was based on a survey undertaken during the gradual implementation of the code of practice.

Partnership with Parents (1998) *Dealing with Dyslexia in the Secondary School*. Shepway Centre, Oxford Road, Maidstone, Kent, ME15 8AW, tel. 01622 755515.

Reiser, R. and Mason, M. (1992) *Disability Equality in the Classroom: A Human Rights Issue (2nd edition)*, London: ILEA/Disability Equality.

This book provides case studies and covers a wide range of disabilities. It confronts the prejudice of able-bodied people.

Widlake, P. (1989) *Special Children Handbook: Meeting Special Educational Needs within the Mainstream School*, London: Hutchinson.

This book contains contributions from a range of people working in the field as well as case studies. Although it is focused on primary practice, ideas applicable across the age range are included. It covers behavioural policies, difficulties with reading, writing and language as well as sections on maths, art, science and information technology.

The following texts provide further guidance on the education of exceptionally able pupils:

Clarke, G. (1983) *Guidelines for the Recognition of Gifted Pupils*, Harlow, SCDC Publications, Longman.

This text has useful information about the use of checklists, in particular the 'Essex' checklist and the 'Rapid' checklist (p. 19ff).

Denton, C. and Postlethwaite, K. (1985) *Able Children: identifying them in the classroom*, Windsor: NFER–Nelson.

George, D. (1992) *The Challenge of the Able Child*, London: David Fulton Publishers

Her Majesty's Inspectors (1992) *The Education of Very Able Children in Maintained Schools*, London: HMSO.

Useful web sites:
1. *Special Educational Needs Service* in Swansea http://www.sens.demon.co.uk/index.htm

2. *National Autistic Society* http://www.sens.demon.co.uk/aut./htm

3. *Royal National Institute of the Blind* http://www.rnib.org.uk

4. See also Unit 1.4, p. 47 for web address.

5 HELPING PUPILS LEARN

This chapter is about teaching and learning. As you work through these units we hope that your knowledge about teaching and learning increases and that you feel confident to try out and evaluate different approaches.

Unit 5.1 introduces you to a number of theories of learning. Theories about teaching and learning provide frameworks for the analysis of learning situations and a language to describe the learning taking place. As you become more experienced, you develop your own theories of how the pupils you teach learn and you can place theories in the wider context.

In Unit 5.2 teaching methods which promote learning are examined. How you use these methods reveals something of your personal theory of how pupils learn. At this point in your development we suggest that you gain experience with a range of teaching methods so that you are easily able to select the method most appropriate to the material being taught.

Unit 5.3 provides you with details about teaching styles. Again we suggest that as you gain confidence with basic classroom management skills you try out different styles so that you develop a repertoire of teaching styles from which you can select as appropriate.

We have talked at various points in this book about the characteristics of effective teaching. Unit 5.4 is designed to provide you with information about methods for finding out about the quality of your own teaching and that of others – through the use of reflection using action research techniques. These techniques include, for example, the use of observation, pupils' written work and discussion. During your initial teacher education course you are using action research skills in a simple way when you observe classes. In this unit we explain some aspects of action research.

5.1   WAYS PUPILS LEARN

INTRODUCTION

You, as a teacher, have responsibility for presenting information, ideas, concepts and knowledge in a way that helps pupils learn. Your ability to do that is gained from your course and from experience – from watching others and from evaluating your own work. Your introduction to different ways of teaching and learning is also anecdotal, e.g. short conversations with experienced teachers over coffee or between lessons. Unless the knowledge gained from these experiences is evaluated by trying out ideas and reflecting on their value to you, their impact will be superficial. What is required is a systematic and reflective view of what constitutes learning in the classroom in order that teaching styles can be altered in a way that is beneficial to the pupil. Psychology helps to explain human behaviour and the thinking processes which influence the learning outcomes from teaching/learning situations.

Pupils learn in many different ways and studies from educational psychology may provide insights into possible conditions and experiences that apply with your own classes. It is important to try to understand basic learning processes, the factors which affect them and why individuals differ in their capability to learn. **Learning has cognitive, social and emotional dimensions**. Pupils' learning can be affected as much by their relationships with teachers as by the content and methods of the learning situations those teachers organise. It is therefore essential to develop a theoretical framework which allows us to consider all the components of a child's learning.

OBJECTIVES

By the end of this unit you should have a clear understanding of:

- teaching and learning frameworks;
- what is meant by learning;
- a variety of theories of how children learn.

Your management of the learning process is a thread linking a number of the standards/ competences required of NQTs. Identify these standards/competences from your coursebook and, at the end of this unit, review how your understanding of how pupils learn relates to what is required of you.

A TEACHING AND LEARNING FRAMEWORK

In the classroom teachers are constantly making professional judgements as to how much learning is going on and the value of that learning. These judgements rely on the interplay between the teacher's **subject and pedagogic knowledge**, their **knowledge of the pupils** and their **personal theories about how learning happens**. In Diana Burton's experience if you are to ensure that effective learning takes place you need a theoretical framework of how children learn within which to test your classroom experiences and thus develop your professional knowledge.

Let us imagine that you have spent 10 minutes carefully introducing a new concept to your class but a few pupils unexpectedly fail to grasp it. You will test the reasons for their lack of understanding against what you **know about the pupils'**:

- prior knowledge of the topic;
- levels of attention;
- interest and motivation;
- physical and emotional state of readiness to learn;

and so on.

You can also consider factors relating to the topic and the way you explained it – **subject and pedagogic knowledge**:

- the relevance of the new material to the pupils;
- how well the new concept fits into the structure of the topic;
- the level of difficulty of the concept;
- your clarity of speech and explanation;
- the accessibility of any new terminology;
- the questioning and summaries you gave at intervals during your explanation;

and so on.

Finally you can draw on explanations from educational psychology which have informed your **personal theories about learning** and provided you with questions such as:

- does the mode of presentation suit these pupils' learning styles?
- has sufficient time been allowed for pupils to process the new information?
- does the structure of the explanation reflect the inherent conceptual structure of the topic?
- do these pupils need to talk to each other to help them understand the new concept?

A teacher's theoretical framework of learning usually derives from a number of psychological ideas rather than from one specific theory. This is fine because it allows for a continual revision of ideas as more experience is gained. This is known as reflecting on theory in practice. We will now focus on the range of psychological theories from which these ideas are drawn.

Key areas which will be addressed are:

- what we mean by learning and the types of learning which can be identified;
- what we can learn from psychological theories of learning;
- how concept development works;
- how pupils' learning styles and strategies differ.

WHAT DO WE MEAN BY LEARNING?

Kyriacou (1986, p. 34) defines learning as a change in pupils' behaviour which takes place as a result of being engaged in an educational experience'. He bases this definition on Gagnè's (1985) conditions of learning which highlight five main areas of pupils' learning that need to be considered in a teaching/learning framework. They include:

- Intellectual skills which Gagnè classifies as 'knowing how' rather than 'knowing that'.
- Verbal skills: knowing names, principles and generalisations.
- Cognitive strategies: which are the ways in which pupils manage the mental processes, e.g. thinking and memorising.
- Attitudes: pupils' emotions and social/cultural approaches to subjects.
- Motor skills: physical tasks a pupil may be involved in – playing volleyball, keyboard skills, handwriting, sawing wood.

Each of these types of learning is involved in all subjects of the curriculum, interacting in complex ways. It can be helpful to consider them separately so that a particular pupil's learning progress and needs can be monitored and so that teachers can plan lessons which foster all types of learning. Stones (1992) has discussed the need to employ different pedagogical strategies depending on the type of learning planned.

Task 5.1.1

ANALYSING LEARNING ACTIVITIES

Draw up a table like the one below. Choose a topic you are observing the teaching of or are teaching yourself. Complete the learning activity involved in each of the five areas. An example from the science curriculum has been provided to guide you.

Activity	Intellectual skills	Verbal skills	Cognitive strategy	Attitudes	Motor skills
E.g. science; a group activity using particle theory of matter	Discussing how to set up the activity to test an hypothesis	Defining solids, liquids and gases	Recalling previous knowledge about particles	Listening to and sharing ideas	Manipulating equipment

---

WHAT WE CAN LEARN FROM PSYCHOLOGICAL THEORIES ABOUT LEARNING

Building on prior knowledge

A number of theories seek to explain how learning takes place but one premise which is widely accepted is that of David Ausubel, an American psychologist: **'The most important single factor influencing learning is what the learner already knows; ascertain this and teach him (her) accordingly'** (Ausubel, 1968, p. 36).

Psychologists have suggested various ways to interpret this premise with learners:

1 New material is assimilated more meaningfully if the learner can be helped to recall prior concepts first (Ausubel, 1985).
2 Find the subskills that a learner has and then plan his/her learning to start from these subskills (Gagnè and White, 1978).
3 Find the alternative viewpoints possessed by the pupil and provide material in such a way as to encourage the pupil to reconsider or modify these viewpoints (Driver, 1983).
4 Create cognitive conflict by confronting the pupil with an event which can't be explained using her current conceptual framework (Adey, 1992).

Burton's Ph.D. research on differentiation indicates that it can often be difficult in secondary schools for teachers to determine precisely the prior knowledge of their pupils. You observe that good teachers cue learners in to their prior knowledge by asking questions about what was learned last lesson or giving a brief resumé of the point reached in a topic. Such strategies are very important because, if previous learning has been effective, information will be stored by pupils in their long-term memories and needs to be retrieved.

Psychologists suggest that learning is more effective, i.e. more likely to be understood and retained, if material is introduced to pupils according to the inherent conceptual structure of the topic (Gagnè 1985; Ausubel, 1968; Stones, 1992). This is because information which is stored using a logical structure is easier to recall because the brain can process it more easily in the first instance, linking the new ideas to ones which already

Task 5.1.2   **STRUCTURING TOPICS FOR EFFECTIVE LEARNING**
Choose a topic from your subject area. Brainstorm some of the ideas contained within it for a couple of minutes, jotting them down haphazardly on paper. Now think about how those ideas fit together and whether, in teaching the topic, you would start with the general overarching ideas and then move to the specific ones or vice versa. See also 'concept maps', Figure 5.2.1. You can organise your topic by drawing up a conceptual hierarchy of it like the one started below for a PSE topic. This one moves from the general to the specific.

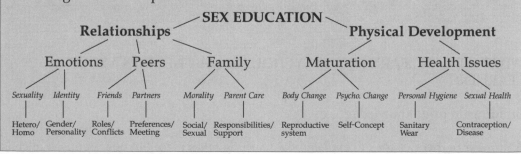

exist in the memory. As a teacher, this requires you to have thought through the structure in advance, and to know how the concepts fit together; hence the importance of spending time on schemes of work even where these are already produced for you.

This emphasis on structure and sequence can be found most readily perhaps in the teaching of Modern Foreign Languages and mathematics. Mitchell *et al.* (1994) found that MFL teachers use a 'bottom-up' language learning theory, encouraging recognition and acquisition of vocabulary first, followed by the construction of spoken and written sentences. This approach might be described as moving from the general to the specific but in most subjects the process is the other way around. Chyriwsky (1996) has stressed the importance of working hierarchically through mathematical knowledge. It might be argued that in mathematics we start with the general concepts of addition, subtraction and multiplication, moving to more specific computations like calculating area, solving equations, or estimating probabilities.

Learners constructing knowledge

The prior knowledge of learners is, by definition, individualised because each pupil's experiences of, attitudes towards and methods of processing prior knowledge are distinct. We now look at how learners actively construct this individualised knowledge or 'meaning'.

Learning and knowledge are inevitably discussed together but the nature of knowledge is a discussion in its own right. Psychological theories offer different notions about what constitutes knowledge.

Information-processing theories view knowledge as pieces of information which the learner's brain processes systematically and which are stored as abstractions of experiences (Klahr and Wallace, 1976; Gagnè, 1985; Ausubel, 1985; Anderson *et al.*, 1996).

Social constructivism explains that learners actively construct their individual meanings (or knowledge) as their experiences and interactions with others help develop the theories they hold (Vygotsky, 1962; Bruner, 1966; Rogoff, 1990; Brown, A.L. 1994).

The relatively new theory of **situated cognition** does not recognise knowledge as existing outside of situations, but rather as 'collective knowledge', i.e. the shared, ongoing, evolving interaction between people (Lave and Wenger, 1991; Greeno, Smith and Moore, 1993; Davis and Sumara, 1997).

Inevitably a great deal of our work in the classroom revolves around the way in which knowledge (principally that which constitutes the content and context of the school curriculum) is presented, received, shared, controlled, understood or mis-understood by teachers and pupils in their classrooms. In examining psychological theories you can consider alternative ways of construing both knowledge and learners. A comparison of three central theories can be seen in Table 5.1.1. A broad grouping of the ideas of different psychologists is helpful, but this is not to suggest that their ideas were identical. What we are looking at is sets of theories within each group which deal with similar explanations for learning. You need to read more deeply if you intend to write an assignment in this area (see references for suggestions).

Table 5.1.1 Comparison of three theories of learning. A comparison is made of three theories of learning and thinking. Theories that offer very different accounts of the way in which children think and learn also lead to alternative views on what is involved in teaching them. The way in which you use the different theories in your own teaching is based on your professional judgement of the factors affecting your own situation. (Adapted from Nicholls, G. (1995).)

Cognitive Developmental Theory (CD) (Piaget and Inhelder, 1969; Flavell, 1982)	Social Constructivist Theory (SC) (Vygotsky, 1962; Bruner, 1966)	Information-Processing Theory (IP) (Klahr and Wallace, 1976; Gagnè, 1985; Ausubel, 1985; Anderson, 1993)
All children pass through a series of stages before they construct the ability to perceive, reason and understand in mature, rational terms.	Shares some important areas of agreement with Piagetian theory, particularly activity as the basis for learning and for the development of thinking.	Develops elements of CD (sequences, activity) and SC theory (experience) but emphasises cognitive strategies rather than structures.

Central Aspects

1 Children's thinking is different in kind from that of more mature individuals.	1 Relationships between talking and thinking.	1 Fundamental processes and strategies underlie all cognitive activity.
2 All children develop through the same sequence of stages before achieving mature rational thought.	2 Role of communication, social interaction and instruction in scaffolding thinking and cognitive development is crucial.	2 Brain's systematic processes of perception, memory and problem-solving process information in the short-term memory and store it as abstractions in the long-term memory.
3 Structures of children's thinking at each stage are distinctive, i.e. the same for all children at the same stage and differ from the children and adults at other stages.	3 Learning involves search for patterns, regularities and predictability (Bruner).	3 Processes are the same for all individuals but speed and efficiency vary from learner to learner.
4 Development is **not** a continuous accumulation of things learnt step by step but 'intellectual' revolutions are marked by a change in structure of intelligence.	4 'Zone of proximal development' (Vygotsky) is the gap that exists for an individual between what she can do on her own and what she can achieve with help from a more knowledgeable or skilled person.	4 Cognitive development is the process of learning more and more helpful strategies of analysing, remembering and problem solving.
5 Active, experiential learning encouraged.	5 'Guided discovery' learning is encouraged.	5 Concrete examples and experiences are important in developing abstractions. Instruction important in strategy development.

Cognitive developmental theory

Piaget

Piaget put forward a theory of child development which has made his potential influence on education of vital importance. His work is supported by clinical case studies with children (Inhelder and Piaget, 1958). He saw children as actively constructing their own development through their interactions with the environment. Thinking is seen by Piaget as 'internalised action'. Within this framework the teacher's role becomes a rather indirect one which provides the optimum experience and environment to foster the pupil's natural capacity to develop and learn. One aspect of Piaget's theory is that development is stage-like. It involves a progression through three main stages or periods, each of which is characterised by the development of logical underlying mental structures and increasing organisation. A consequence of this notion was that children are seen as qualitatively different types of thinkers from adults and their adolescent peers. The thinking of young children relies mainly on what is termed **concrete operations**, being dominated by the everyday experiences and intuitions. The implication here is that the young child is not only less knowledgeable but also sees his world differently depending on the limitation of the mental structures governing thinking at any one time (Piaget, 1962). As children mature they become more able to cope with the more abstract concepts of life and can begin to think about more than one concept at any given time. During adolescence there is a gradual shift towards **formal operational** thinking; this type of thinking is considered to be the ability to use forms of logical reasoning, which supplements intuitive approaches to problem solving. These distinctive areas of thought are often referred to as stages of development (Unit 4.2 explores the area further).

The influence of stage theory

Burton suggests that Piaget's work influenced the way in which some other psychologists developed their views. Kohlberg (1976) saw links between children's cognitive development and their moral reasoning, proposing a stage model of moral development. Selman (1980) was interested in the way children make relationships, describing a set of stages or levels they go through in forming friendships.

Stage models were also conceptualised in personality development quite independently of Piaget's work. Influenced by Freud's psychoanalytic approach, Erikson's stages of psycho-social development explain the way in which an individual's self-concept develops, providing us with important insights into adolescent identity issues such as role confusion (1980). Harter's research (1985) has since indicated the significance of teacher–pupil relationships for pupils' feelings of self-worth in relation to learning competence.

You are already aware of the fragility of an adolescent's self-concept, of the fundamental but often volatile nature of adolescent friendships and of the increased interest adolescents show in ethical issues. It is essential to consider these issues when planning for learning since they impact so heavily on pupils' motivation for, and capacity to engage with, lesson content.

The stress on the idea of 'stages' in Piaget's theory has thus been quite far-reaching but the value of the stage idea itself has less currency than the features of development the various stage theories describe. Piaget's ideas have often been interpreted as giving support to the notion of learning 'readiness', i.e. that children only learn effectively if their educational experiences are suitably matched to their current level of understanding. Piaget's stages have often been used to indicate the limits of children's thinking but more recent research has shown this to be misleading (Donaldson, 1978).

Flavell (1982), a former student of Piaget, has argued that, while stage notions of development are unhelpful, Piaget's ideas about the sequences learners go through are still valid. They can help teachers to examine the level of difficulty of topics and curriculum material as a way of deciding how appropriate they are for particular age groups and ability levels. Teachers need to set work for pupils which enables them to experience success and yet gives opportunities for extending their understanding. Some topics may be too difficult for all the class, other topics inappropriate for other reasons, e.g. lack of relevance to previous work or experience.

The notion of 'readiness' cannot, therefore, be applied as a generalised principle. The key task for teachers is to examine the progress of individuals in order to determine readiness to deal with increased intellectual demand. Bruner (1966) argued that difficult ideas should be seen as a challenge and that, if properly presented, can be learned by most pupils. Adey and colleagues have developed a system of cognitive acceleration in science education (CASE) which challenges pupils to examine the processes they use to solve problems (Adey, 1992). In doing so it is argued that pupils are enhancing their thinking processes. The process of coming to know more about one's own learning strategies, i.e. strategies for remembering, ways of presenting information when thinking, approaches to problems, etc. is known as **metacognition**. If pupils are helped by their teachers to become more metacognitively aware, they are more able to take control of their learning.

Social constructivist theories

The importance of the ideas of Vygotsky and Bruner has been increasingly recognised by educators.

Vygotsky

Nicholls suggests that Vygotsky's approach allows for a relation between spontaneous common sense and formal school-based concepts. Vygotsky sees school-based learned concepts as conscious, reflective, originating in the classroom (or informal educational setting) and systematic. His understanding of intelligence is radically different from Piaget's. Vygotsky views the capacity to learn through instruction as central. He argues that intelligence is determined not only by a capacity to learn but also by a capacity for being taught and he introduces the concept of a **'zone of proximal development'** in his theory of learning. This concept refers to the gap between what an individual pupil can do alone and what they can achieve with the help and instruction of a more knowledgeable person.

What a child can do today in co-operation, tomorrow he will be able to do on his own.

(Vygotsky, 1962, p. 67)

Burton's reading of more recent research in this area (Topping, 1992) has indicated that reciprocal peer tutoring can also promote learning. Crucially, however, children need to be given specific preparation and guidance by the teacher in order to work effectively.

Brown, A.L. (1994) has developed the idea of learning communities where group-work and seminars provide the main vehicle for learning. Rogoff (1990) found that homogeneous student grouping and pairing, such as setting provides, has advantages in promoting argument and sharing complex ideas. However, Doise (1990) found that, in pairwork, a slight difference in the intellectual functioning of partners was best because it promoted cognitive conflict. Unit 5.2 provides information about active learning strategies which support a Vygotskyan approach to learning.

Bruner

Bruner formulated a theory of instruction, central to which is the notion of systematic, structured pupil experience. He concentrates on the different processes individuals use in **creative problem solving** and lays great emphasis on the point that language, communication and instruction are paramount to the development of knowledge and understanding. He argues that individuals develop different types of thinking strategies depending on their knowledge, the situation and the learning materials. For Bruner, learning involves the search for patterns, regularity and predictability. One aspect of the teacher's role is to assist pupils in the formulation and discovery of such patterns and rules – thus enhancing and expanding their knowledge.

Bruner described three stages in learning which refer to the way people think about the world:

- **Enactive representation** is the memories of actions which become stored in our muscles, enabling actions to become automatic, e.g. we can walk, eat, drive etc. without consciously thinking about what we are doing. The implications for teaching are to provide opportunities for practice or 'learning by doing', e.g. repetition of pronunciation, practice in craft and game skills, etc.
- **Iconic representation** is thinking about something through concrete images in order to understand or remember it, e.g. we might think about the idea of 'nature' pictorially – a field or landscape; pupils might be aided in understanding fractions by thinking about how a cake is divided into pieces.
- **Symbolic representation** is thinking abstractly about things, where there is no apparent connection between the object or idea and the way it is represented, e.g. language uses words to stand for objects but they have no visual correspondence – the word 'door' does not describe the physical manifestation of a door, it just stands for it. This is the most advanced form of thinking and we strive to help pupils use it in our lessons through, for example, the use of scientific formulae or grammatical terms.

Unlike Piaget's stages, learners do not pass through and beyond Bruner's different stages of thinking. Instead, the stage or type of representation used depends on the type of thinking required of the situation. It is expected, however, that as pupils grow up they will make progressively greater use of symbolic representation.

The influence of social constructivist theories

Burton identifies the importance of 'talk' in classrooms as being highlighted by the ideas of Vygotsky and Bruner. Essentially, it is argued that, in order to learn, pupils must discuss what new ideas mean to them with others. In so doing, further thinking is generated with more complex links between ideas afforded. The role of the teacher in facilitating learning situations involving talk is of critical importance.

Bruner's ideas about the power of systematic and well structured pupil experiences to promote cognitive development are fundamental to this approach. Maybin, Mercer and Stierer (1992) have used Bruner's (1983) ideas of 'scaffolding' in relation to classroom talk. The ideas of pupils emerging through their talk are scaffolded or framed by the teacher putting in 'steps' or questions at appropriate junctures. For example, a group of pupils might be discussing how to solve the problem of building a paper bridge between two desks. The teacher can intervene when he hears an idea emerge which will help pupils find the solution, by asking a question which requires the pupils to address that idea explicitly.

Bruner argued that the scaffolding provided by the teacher should decrease in direct correspondence to the progress of the learner. Wood (1988) has developed Bruner's ideas, describing five levels of support which become increasingly specific and supportive in relation to the help needed by the pupil:

- general verbal encouragement;
- specific verbal instruction;
- assistance with pupil's choice of material or strategies;
- preparation of material for pupil assembly;
- demonstration of task.

Thus, having established the task the pupils are to complete, a teacher might give general verbal encouragement to the whole class, follow this up with specific verbal instruction to groups who need it, perhaps targeting individuals with guidance on strategies for approaching the task. Some pupils will need physical help in performing the task and yet others need to be shown exactly what to do, probably in small stages.

We turn now to a theory which actually bears the name 'Constructivism'. Whilst sharing a Brunerian and Vygotskyan emphasis on the social construction of meaning, Constructivism places much more importance on the conceptions of learners and gives them responsibility for directing their own learning experiences. Less emphasis is placed on the role of instruction.

Task
5.1.3

SCAFFOLDING PUPILS' LEARNING

Wood's ideas can help you think systematically about the nature of the support you should prepare for particular pupils, and to keep a check on whether the level is becoming more or less supportive. This has obvious relevance for differentiation in your classroom, workshop or gym.

For a topic you are planning to teach, use Wood's five levels to prepare the type of support you think might be needed during the first lesson. Once you start teaching the topic choose two particular pupils who need different levels of support. Plan the support for each one, lesson by lesson, noting whether they are requiring less or more support as the topic progresses. What does this tell you about the way you are teaching and the way the pupils are learning?

Constructivism

Nicholls suggests that constructivism has been a dominant approach in the last decade especially with respect to science education. Constructivism explains conceptual change as the product of interaction between existing conceptions and new experiences. Driver and Bell (1986) list six features of a constructivist perspective that could have an impact on teaching/learning situations in school:

- Learners are not viewed as passive but are seen as purposeful and ultimately responsible for their own learning. They bring their prior conceptions to the learning situation.
- Learning is considered to involve an active process on the part of the learner. It involves the construction of meaning and often takes place through interpersonal negotiation.
- Knowledge is not 'out there' but is personally and socially constructed, its status is problematic. It may be evaluated by the individual in terms of the extent to which it fits with their experience and is coherent with other aspects of their knowledge.
- Teachers also bring their prior conceptions to learning situations in terms of not only their subject knowledge but also their views of teaching and learning. These can influence their interaction in the classroom.
- Teaching is not the transmission of knowledge but involves the organisation of the situations in the classroom and the design of tasks in a way which promotes learning. The curriculum is not that which is to be learnt, but a programme of learning tasks, material and resources from which pupils construct their knowledge.
- Constructivism generates a different view of what constitutes teaching/learning and how it might be carried out in the classroom. It is consistent with the National Curriculum requirements which state that:

    children's ideas will change as their experience widens . . . There is an essential role for the teacher as enabler in this process: the teacher may interact with the pupil, raise questions, build in appropriate challenges and experiences and offer new ways of thinking.

(DES, 1988)

The role of the teacher is:

- to encourage pupils to be involved and own the purpose of the lesson or task;
- if pupils are to take responsibility for their learning, to design learning experiences that allow pupils to investigate processes and outcomes;
- allowing and valuing pupils' own descriptions and hypotheses of what has taken place or assumed learnt.

The teacher's role is to facilitate learning. For pupils simply to acquire a body of knowledge or set of facts is not a constructive approach nor adequate achievement for the pupil.

Task 5.1.4

APPLYING THEORIES OF LEARNING

Vygotsky (1962) advocates that when adults help children to accomplish things that they are unable to achieve alone, they are fostering the development of knowledge and ability. Constructivism advocates pupils being actively involved in their learning. We suggest you spend some time exploring how these ideas can help you in your teaching.

1 During a class observation period identify a pupil who appears to be having difficulty in certain areas of a given topic or subject area. With the teacher's help establish what you think the learning difficulties are and list them.
2 Interview the pupil and identify what the pupil (a) knows about the topic in terms of facts, relationships, relevance, (b) misunderstands, i.e. the misconceptions the pupil holds in terms of facts, relationships processes and (c) is ignorant of.
3 Devise a short lesson to improve the pupil's learning; define your objectives for the pupil carefully.
4 Arrange to take this pupil aside during a lesson and teach the pupil. Test for understanding against your objectives.

Review your success against Vygotsky's ideas and constructivist ideas.

Information-processing theories

Bruner's ideas about learning processes can be seen as an early form of the information-processing approach to understanding how learning happens. This approach originated within explanations of perception and memory processes and was influenced by the growth of computer technology. The basic ideas of the I-P approach are represented diagrammatically in Figure 5.1.1 below.

Psychologists saw the functioning of computers as replicating that of the brain in relation to the processing of information. Information is analysed in the short-term memory (STM) and stored with existing related information in the long-term memory (LTM). This process is more efficient if material can be stored as abstractions of experience rather than as verbatim events.

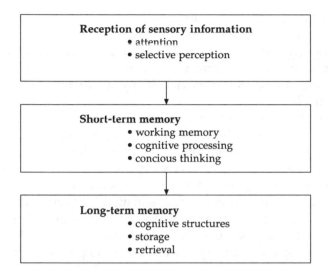

Figure 5.1.1   A basic interpretation of an information processing model which is associated with active learning
Source: Nicholls, 1995

Burton applies these ideas in the following example: if I ask you to tell me the six times table, you recite 'one six is six, two sixes are twelve' and so on. You do not explain to me the mathematical principle of multiplication by a factor of six. On the other hand, if I ask you the meaning of the term 'economic enterprise', it is unlikely that you will recite a verbatim answer. Instead, your STM searches your LTM for your 'schema' or idea of enterprise. You then articulate your abstracted understanding of the term, which may well be different from that of the person next to you.

In terms of intellectual challenge, articulating the second answer requires greater mental effort, although knowing one's tables can be a very useful tool. Thus teachers need to be absolutely clear that there is a good reason for requiring pupils to learn something by rote because rote learning is not inherently meaningful so cannot be stored in LTM with other related information. Rather it must be stored in its full form, taking up a lot of 'disk' space in the memory. Stored in this way, it is only analysed superficially in STM – the pupil does not have to think hard to make connections with other pieces of information.

The rest of this unit draws on the work undertaken for Burton's Ph.D.

Concept development

Since I-P theory is concerned with processing information it is helpful to consider briefly how that processing relates to concept development. The material held in the long-term memory is stored as sets of ideas known as 'schemata' ('schema' is the singular). A schema is a mental structure abstracted from experience. It consists of a set of expectations with which to categorise and understand new stimuli. For example, our schema of 'school' consists of expectations of pupils, teachers, classrooms, etc. As teachers, our school schema has been refined and developed as more and more information has been added and categorised. Thus it includes expectations about hierarchies, pupil culture, staffroom behaviour and so on. It is probable that our school schema is different from, and more complex than, the school schema held by a parent, simply because of our involvement in schools.

When children are young their schemata do not allow them to differentiate between pieces of information in the way that those of older pupils do. A one year old's schema of dog might include expectations about cats too because she has had insufficient experience of the two animals to know them apart. As she experiences cats as furry, dogs as hairy, cats miaowing, dogs barking, etc., greater differentiation is possible. Since the object of school learning is to promote pupils' concept differentiation in a range of different subjects, teachers should encourage comparison between objects or ideas and introduce new ideas by reference to concrete examples. Even as adults, whilst we can think abstractly, we find new ideas easier to grasp if we can be given concrete examples of them.

Critical thinking

Teaching in the context of I-P theories involves guiding pupils to apply knowledge and think things out for themselves, in other words, to think critically. This type of thinking requires pupils to locate relevant pieces of information, examine their interrelationships, and make connections which are not immediately obvious, e.g. a word learnt in English may be used to understand a concept in mathematics, for instance, 'graphs'. The ability to carry out such mental operations becomes greater with age and experience. The teacher's role is to help pupils find new ways of recalling previous knowledge, solving problems, formulating hypotheses and so on. Montgomery (1996) advocates the use of games and simulations because they facilitate critical thinking and encourage connections to be made between areas of subject knowledge or experience.

Within all three sets of theories about how learning occurs, there has been an emphasis on the individual and the differences between them. Looking at what is known about how learners' styles and strategies differ equips us further to understand individual differences.

Learning styles, strategies and approaches

There is often confusion between what is learning style and what is learning strategy. Psychologists argue that a cognitive or learning style is considered to be a fairly fixed characteristic of an individual, which may be distinguished from learning strategies, which are the ways that may be used to cope with situations and tasks. Strategies may vary from time to time and may be learned and developed. Styles, by contrast, are static and are relatively in-built features of the individual (Riding and Cheema, 1991).

Learning style

Understanding how in-built style features of learners affect the way they process information is important for teachers. Many researchers have worked in this area but Riding (1997) has proposed that the various conceptualisations may be grouped into two principal cognitive styles:

Wholist-Analytic Style – whether an individual tends to process information in wholes or parts;

Verbal-Imagery Style – whether an individual is inclined to represent information during thinking verbally or in mental pictures.

The styles operate as dimensions so a person may be at either end of the dimension or anywhere along it.

Think about what your own style might be:

do you approach essay writing incrementally, step by step, piecing together the various parts or do you like to have a broad idea of the whole essay before you start writing?

do you experience lots of imagery when you are thinking about something or do you find yourself thinking in words?

Riding explains that these styles are involuntary so it is important to be aware that classes of children consist of learners whose habitual styles vary. Teachers need then to ensure that they provide a variety of media in which pupils can work and be assessed. It would not be sensible to present information only in written form; if illustrations are added, this allows both Verbalisers and Imagers easier access to it. Similarly, Wholist pupils are assisted by having an overview of the topic before starting whilst Analytics benefit from summaries after they have been working on information.

This is not to suggest that you must determine the style of each pupil, but that there must be opportunities for all pupils to work in the way which will be most profitable for them. Unlike intelligence quotient, style measurement does not imply that one way of processing is better than the other. The key is in allowing learners to use their natural processing style. It is important for you to be aware of your own style because teachers have been found to promote the use of approaches which fit most easily with their own styles.

Learning strategy

Kolb's work (1976; 1985) describing two dimensions, perceiving and processing, is the most widely known in the area of strategy theory. Kolb argued that these dimensions interact so that four types of learner can be identified:

- **'divergers'** who perceive information concretely and process it reflectively, needing to be personally involved in the task;
- **'convergers'** who perceive information abstractly and process it reflectively, taking detailed, sequential steps;
- **'assimilators'** who perceive information abstractly and process it actively, needing to be set pragmatic problem-solving activities;
- **'accommodators'** who perceive information concretely and process it actively, taking risks, experimenting and needing flexibility in learning tasks.

Kolb believed that, although learners have these preferred 'styles', they could be trained to develop aspects of the other styles through experiential learning. He envisaged a cyclical sequence through four areas of learning mode arising from the interaction of the two dimensions (see Figure 5.1.2).

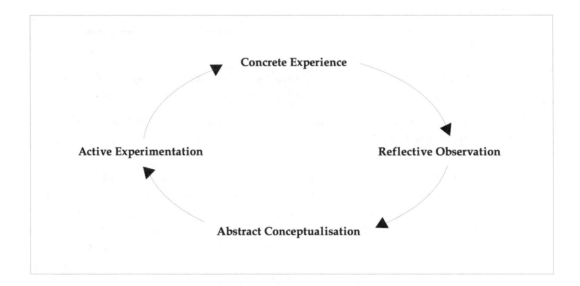

Figure 5.1.2 Kolb's experiential learning cycle (1985)

Thus Kolb suggests that learners need, at the Concrete Experience stage, to immerse themselves in new experience. This will then be reflected upon from as many perspectives as possible at the Reflective Observation stage. This reflection enables the learner to create concepts which integrate their observations into logically sound theories at the Abstract Conceptualisation stage, which are then used to make decisions and solve problems at the Active Experimentation stage (Fielding, 1996).

Learners have a predilection for one of the stages, hence the description of the four 'types'. It can be argued that learners should be provided with experiences that ensure their use of stages in the cycle additional to their preferred one in order to extend their learning strategies (McCarthy, 1987).

Task
5.1.5

DETERMINING TYPES OF LEARNER

Try to work out which stage of Kolb's cycle describes the way you learn yourself most of the time.

You first need to match the four types of learner (**diverger**, **converger**, **accommodator, assimilator**) to the four sectors of the diagram.

Next you need to think about how you process information, e.g.

- are you more comfortable reflecting on ideas where you have experienced lots of concrete experience?
- do you prefer to draw from abstract theory and experiment with it to solve problems?

Do you think Kolb's ideas could help you to process information differently? Would it be helpful to 'practise' different ways? What are the implications for your work with pupils?

Learning approaches

Biggs (1978; 1987; 1993) and Entwistle (1981) both researched learners' approaches to study. Entwistle described four orientations to learning: **'meaning'**, **'reproducing'**, **'achieving'** and **'holistic'**. Combinations of these orientations with extrinsic factors, such as the need to pass examinations or the love of a subject, were thought to lead to learning strategies which characterised certain approaches to study, from **'deep'** to **'surface'** levels of thinking.

Biggs (1993) explained that a student's approach is a function of both motive and strategy and that motives influence learning strategies. Thus, a student with an instrumental (surface) motive is likely to adopt reproducing or rote-learning (surface) strategies. Deep motive results from an intrinsic desire to learn and can inspire the use of deep strategies wherein understanding and meaning are emphasised. An achieving motive might be an egotistical need to pass examinations; from this can derive achieving strategies which stress time management, well-ordered resources and efficiency.

Do you recognise any of these motives and strategies in relation to your own learning? Do your motives and associated learning strategies stay the same over time or do they depend on the task and the reason you are learning it?

Pupils whose motives and strategies are compatible with the learning tasks are likely to perform well. Pupils are likely to be less successful where these do not tally, for instance if a pupil with a deep approach is constrained by superficial task design such as a requirement for short answers, or if a pupil with an achieving motive is set very long-term, vague objectives. Successful learning, if defined in terms of understanding and permanence, is linked with deep and deep-achieving approaches which can be taught. The achievement-driven context within which secondary school pupils in England currently learn, however, could militate against the possibility of teaching deep approaches because of time constraints.

There is a range of interesting work on learning style, strategy, approach and preference which we cannot go into here. The main thing to remember, as a teacher, is to maintain variety in the learning experiences you organise for your pupils, variety in the ways you present information, in the tasks you prepare for pupils, in the resources pupils use and in the ways you assess their progress. This variety gives pupils a greater chance of using their most effective strategies and approaches, thus increasing the potential for learning. See, e.g. Unit 5.1.

Summary and key points

We have said that the development of a teacher's personal framework of ideas about learning is enhanced by an understanding of psychological theories. The framework enables you to consider the significance and validity of new ideas you encounter. For instance, there has recently been a growing interest in what Daniel Goleman (1996) has called 'emotional intelligence'. The media have helped to publicise Goleman's theory such that there are now calls for teachers to help develop pupils' 'emotional literacy' in schools. When you come across this or other theories you will want to ask questions about how it fits with what you already know about pupils' learning and what it has to offer you in terms of moving on pupils' learning. Discussing such ideas with other students and teachers is a good way of doing this because it enables you to develop your thinking further.

Key points covered in this unit are:

1 Your teaching and learning framework consists of **subject and pedagogic knowledge, knowledge of the pupils** and **theories about how learning happens**.
2 Learning can be divided into five main types: **intellectual skills, verbal skills, cognitive strategies, attitudes** and **motor skills**.
3 School learning stresses cognitive types of learning but this cannot be planned for in isolation from what we know about pupils' **self-esteem, motivation, peer pressures and social situation**.
4 Effective learning depends on **relating new material to what is already known**.
5 Retention and recall is likely to be much greater if **information has been taught and learned according to its inherent conceptual structure**.
6 **Concept development** is enhanced where pupils are introduced to new ideas via **concrete examples** and given opportunities to **compare and contrast new stimuli**.
7 Three sets of theories currently have greatest influence on our thinking about learning: **Cognitive Developmental, Social Constructivism** and **Information-Processing**.
8 Learning is likely to be more effective where learners are **actively involved** with the material through **critical thinking, discussion** and an **awareness of their own learning strategies**.
9 The **role of the teacher** in structuring learning experiences is of critical importance; instruction should be **facilitative** and **interventionist** with transmission methods rarely used.
10 Developing **variety** in relation to **teaching approach, presentation of information, resources** and **assessment methods** will enhance opportunities for learners to use their **habitual learning styles** and extend their range of **learning strategies**.

FURTHER READING

Bee, H. (1992) *The Developing Child (6th edition)*, New York: Harper Collins.
Child, D. (1997) *Psychology and the Teacher (6th edition)*, London and Washington: Cassell.

Both of these excellent books will take you further into theories of learning and child development.

Norman, K. (ed.) (1992) *Thinking Voices: The Work of the National Oracy Project*, London: Hodder & Stoughton.

This book provides a host of information on techniques for learning through talk. The work of Maybin *et al.* referred to in this unit appears in this book.

Riding, R.J. (1998) *Cognitive Styles and Learning Strategies*, London: David Fulton.

This book provides very readable information about the research into learning styles and strategies and its implications for teachers and learners.

Wood, D. (1988) *How Children Think and Learn*, Oxford: Blackwell Press.

This book provides detailed information to extend some of the work discussed in this unit.

5.2   ACTIVE LEARNING

INTRODUCTION

> As we know from investigations of the process of concept formation, a concept is more than the sum of the certain associative bonds formed by memory, more than a mere mental habit; it is a complex and genuine act of thought that cannot be taught by drilling but can be accomplished only when the child's mental development itself has reached the requisite level.
>
> Practical experience also shows that direct teaching of concepts is impossible and fruitless. A teacher who tries to do this usually accomplishes nothing but empty verbalisation, a parrot like repetition of words by the child, simulating a knowledge of the corresponding concepts but actually covering up a vacuum.
>
> (Vygotsky, 1986, pp. 149–150)

Vygotsky uses the term concepts to mean 'word meanings'. This extract suggests that the teacher cannot do the learning for the pupil and that in order for understanding to occur the pupil has to be active in the learning process. Active learning is then meaningful learning, in which something of interest and value to the learner has been accomplished and understood. Some writers use the term 'deep learning' instead of meaningful learning; by contrast to 'shallow learning' which is learning without understanding. This unit is about some of the ways in which teachers help pupils to engage in meaningful learning.

OBJECTIVES

At the end of this unit you should be able to:

- explain the term active learning methods and discuss the advantage of active learning methods to the teacher and learner;
- be aware of ways of promoting active learning;
- be able to use some visual aids to their best advantage; and
- be prepared to link these teaching skills to the competences and standards expected of an NQT.

WHAT IS ACTIVE LEARNING?

Active learning occurs when the pupil has some responsibility for the development of the activity. Supporters of this approach say that a sense of ownership and personal involvement is the key to successful learning. Furthermore, that unless the work that pupils do is seen to be individually important to them and is seen to have purpose, that their ideas, contributions and findings are valued, little of benefit will be learned. Active learning can also be defined as purposeful interaction with ideas, concepts and phenomena and can involve reading, writing, listening, talking or working with tools, equipment and materials, such as paint, wood, chemicals, etc.

Active learning strategies benefit both teachers and pupils. As a teacher it enables you to spend more time with groups or individuals, which allows better quality assessment to take place (see formative assessment in Unit 6.1). Active learning can also enhance your access to special needs pupils. For the pupils the methods encourage autonomous learning and problem-solving skills, important to both academic and vocationally based work. There is, of course, an extra demand on you in the planning and preparation of lessons.

The advantages of active learning to pupils include greater personal satisfaction, more interaction with peers, promotion of shared activity and team work, greater opportunities to work with a range of pupils, and opportunities for all members of the class to contribute and respond. It encourages mutual respect and appreciation of the viewpoint of others. Active learning is supportive of co-operative learning, not competitive learning.

ACTIVE LEARNING AND MOTIVATION

You can often persuade pupils to learn by identifying a clearly defined task which has purpose and is relevant to them. That relevance may arise because of personal interest, i.e. it is intrinsic; or the motivation may be extrinsic if the task is set by the teacher. Outside interests become increasingly important as the pupils get older. If the school task links with some future occupation, employment training or higher education motivation is increased and engagement promoted. Motivation is considered in greater detail in Unit 3.2.

Upper school secondary curricula (Years 10 and 11) often aim to promote higher order thinking. Teaching to promote higher level intellectual skills, however laudable and desirable, cuts no ice with pupils unless the task engages with their need to know. If the task does not meet these needs then learning is on sufferance, leading to problems. Such problems may include poor recall of anything learned or rejection of learning tasks. The latter response often leads to behaviour problems, ranging from disruption to non-attendance.

LEARNING HABITS

Learning how to learn is a feature of active learning. By promoting activities which engage pupils and require them to participate in the task from the outset, you foster an approach to learning which is both skill based and attitude based. Active learning methods promote habits of learning. Teachers expect that some of what is learned in school to be of use in the workplace, the home and generally enhance pupils' capacity to cope with everyday life.

School can be a place where pupils learn to do things well and in certain ways. Some skills are developed which are used throughout life. For example, pupils learn to consult dictionaries in order to find meanings or to counteract poor spelling. These skills become habits, capable of reinforcement and development. Reinforcement leads to improved performance. Many of our actions are of this sort, like dressing and eating. Attitudes are learned as well, such as 'to question statements' or to believe that problems can be solved and not to be put off by difficulties.

Many professional people depend, in part, on habits and routines for their livelihood; these include the concert pianist who may well practise time and time again a piece of music already well established in her repertoire. Practice enables the playing to be second nature, leaving time to concentrate on expression. Actors, too, depend on related routines for skilful performance.

Task 5.2.1   WHAT MAKES FOR A GOOD PERFORMANCE?

Discuss the performance of skilled people in terms of habits, routines and performance of their job or role. You might wish to consider:

- what constitutes a good (public) performance or display of skill;
- the low-level skills (sub-routines) which contribute to the overall performance;
- the high-level skills (criteria for excellence) which characterise the skilled practitioner;

by comparing and contrasting the work of two or more of the following: a surgeon; racing driver; teacher; or accountant.

In addition, identify the sub-routines of teaching which are necessary in order for you to be a good teacher. If the sub-routines of a pianist are concerned with practice and high level skills with flair, such as the interpretation of a musical score, what are the equivalents of practice and flair for teachers?

ACTIVE LEARNING, ROTE LEARNING AND LEARNING BY DISCOVERY

Active learning is sometimes placed in opposition to **rote learning** in order to suggest that rote methods do not require the learner to understand what is learned. Nevertheless, rote learning is an active process and often hard work.

Rote learning may occur when pupils are required to listen to the teacher. It is a fallacy to assume that pupils can learn everything for themselves, by themselves, by, for example, discovery. Teachers are specialists in their fields of study; they usually know more than pupils and one, but not all, of their functions is to tell pupils things they otherwise might not know but need to know. The choice of teaching methods requires you to consider what you want to achieve and choosing the appropriate method with a purpose in mind.

Pupils need to be told when they are right; their work needs supporting. On occasions you need to tell pupils when they are wrong and how to correct their error.

How this is done is important but teachers should not shirk telling pupils when they underperform or make mistakes. See Unit 3.2 on motivating pupils, which includes a section on giving feedback.

There are occasions when you need to talk directly to pupils, e.g. to give facts about language, of spelling or grammar; about formulae in science; or health matters such as facts about drug abuse or safe practice in the gymnasium, etc. Other facts necessary for successful learning in school include recalling multiplication tables; or remembering vocabulary; or learning the reactivity series of metals; or to recall a piece of prose or poetry. Many of these facts may need to be learned by heart, by rote methods. There is nothing wrong with you requiring pupils to do this from time to time, providing that all their learning is not like that. Such facts are necessary for advanced work; they are the sub-routines which allows us to function at a higher level. Habits of spelling, of adding up, of recalling the alphabet are vital to our ability to function in all areas of the curriculum and in daily life. Frequently pupils need to apply a routine in order to carry out a more important task but they do not understand fully that routine. You may decide that the end justifies the means and that, later, as a result of maturation through experience and the further use of the routine in different contexts, understanding is achieved. Many of us learn that way.

Discovery learning is an example of active learning; in its 'pure form' it occurs when pupils are left to discover things for themselves. It is difficult to imagine when or where such learning ever happens.

Much more common is the use of a structured framework in which learning can occur, i.e. guided discovery. However, is it the intention of guided discovery that pupils come to some pre-determined conclusion, i.e. the answer is known in advance; or is it the intention that some learning in the topic should take place but that the outcomes vary from pupil to pupil? Guided discovery as a method of teaching is an important component of 'differentiated learning' strategies. Guided discovery allows differentiation to be achieved by monitoring the outcome, i.e. the task allows for pupils to get to different end points.

You need to be clear, however, about your reason for adopting guided discovery methods. If the intention in discovery learning is that pupils get to a particular end point, then as discovery it could be termed a sham. This might preclude, for example, considering other knowledge that surfaced in the enquiry. At the same time, if discovery focused on how the knowledge was gained, then the activity is concerned with processes, i.e. how to discover. The central question with discovery learning is purpose: is it the means or the end? Are discovery methods concerned with:

- discovery as 'process' – learning how to learn?
- discovery as motivation – a better way to learn pre-determined knowledge and skills?

AIDS TO ROTE LEARNING

Learning facts by heart usually involves a coding process. For example, recalling telephone numbers is easier if it is broken into blocks like this

Task 5.2.2   **ROTE LEARNING**

Describe three occasions when you would expect to adopt a rote learning method in your teaching. For each occasion, identify the age group, content and reason(s) for adopting this method. Copy and complete the following table.

	Age group	Content/material/topic	Occasion and reason for adopting method
1			
2			
3			

Compare your lists with other student teachers from:

a. the same subject group;
b. different subject groups.

What do each set of lists have in common? Discuss the lists in terms of:

- content or process;
- low-level knowledge or high-level knowledge;
- essential sub-routines underlying higher level skills.

    0171 612 6780   and not as   01716126870

Another strategy is the use of a mnemonic to aid recall of the musical scale notation:

    E G B D F can be recalled by the phrase 'Every Good Boy Deserves Fun'.

What other mnemonics do you know? What other ways are there of helping learning by rote?

CONSTRUCTING AIDS TO RECALL

Sometimes information cannot easily be committed to memory unless a structure is developed around it to help recall. That structure may involve other information which allows you to build a picture. In other words, recall is constructed. Structures may include other words, but often tables, diagrams, flow charts or other visual models are used.

Other ways of helping learners to remember ideas or facts are to **construct** summaries in various forms. Both the *act of compiling* the summary and the *product* contribute to learning.

Task 5.2.3

CONSTRUCTING A FLOW CHART TO HELP RECALL

The sequence of events and actions can be imagined by reference to events and by the help of a flow chart.

For example, helping a visitor to the UK to understand the 'correct' way to make a cup of tea might be summarised like this:

Making English tea

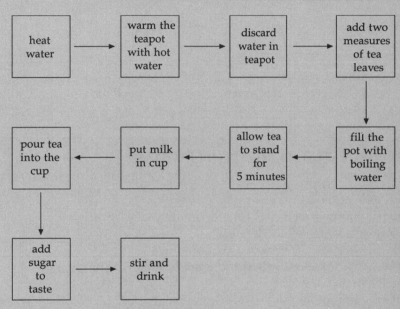

Now devise ways of helping pupils recall:

- the causes of the Second World War;
- the electronic structure of the first twenty elements in the Periodic Table;
- the differences and similarities between Islam and Christianity.

Alternatively, choose examples from your own subject area.

Constructing spider or burr diagrams

It is often helpful to pupils and teachers to 'brainstorm' as a way of exploring their understanding of an idea. One way to record that event is by either a spider diagram (in which the 'legs' identify the ideas related to the topic) or a burr diagram – ideas attached to the central word.

Here is a burr diagram of pupils' meaning of fruit:

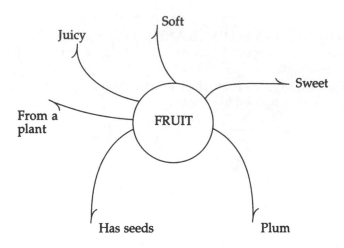

| | |

Task 5.2.4

REFORMULATING OTHER PEOPLE'S IDEAS

Below is a list of statements which describe features of 'active learning':

co-operation with other learners
curriculum development (choice of content) involves the learner
greater variety of teaching methods used
group work
learner 'owns' ideas for investigation and is interested in the product
learner is active in own learning
process skills are important
resource-based learning methods used frequently
responsibility for learning shifted from teacher to learner
self-discipline needed by learner
teacher is a guide, not a provider.

Discuss with other student teachers the use of this list as a way of summarising the meaning of active learning. Identify the value and limitations of this list. Suggest and carry out ways of improving this list; for example, by:

- shortening the list;
- adding to the list;
- regrouping the list;
- replacing a list with another visual device, e.g. a table.

You may wish to add ideas about active learning to this list as a result of regrouping the given ideas. Discuss ways in which your understanding of the meaning of active learning has been enhanced by this exercise.

How would you use this idea of reformulating information in teaching your subject? Develop an example and share this with other student teachers or your tutor.

> **Task 5.2.5**
>
> **ACTIVE LEARNING METHODS**
>
> With other student teachers construct a burr diagram identifying as many different active learning methods as you can, such as problem solving, project work, using multimedia resources: CD ROM, etc.
>
> When you have completed your brainstorming activities and developed a master list, compare it with the list in Table 5.2.1 at the end of this unit and combine the two lists.
>
> Work now with the combined list. As a group, discuss this list and then reconstruct the list in one or more of the following ways.
>
> Separate the learning methods into two sets:
>
> - those where the teacher has a central role, e.g. discussion of a controversial issue;
> - and those where the teacher is in a supportive role, e.g. pupils making a poster summarising evidence for the causes of the Plague.
>
> Does the teaching of your subject favour one set of methods over the other? If so, why do you think this situation occurs. Share your ideas with other student teachers or your tutor.

Concept maps are examples of spider diagrams and are used to display important ideas or concepts which are involved in a topic or unit of work and, by annotation, show the links between them. An example is shown in Figure 5.2.1; see also Unit 5.1, Task 5.1.2.

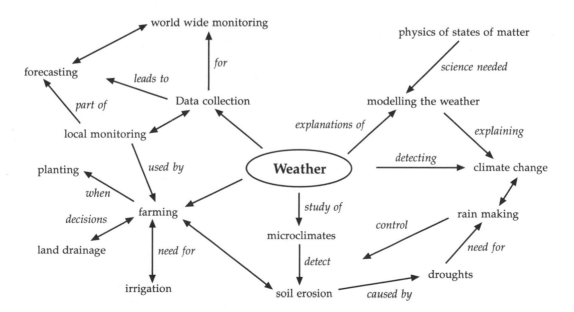

Figure 5.2.1 Concept map: weather

Concept maps can be made by pupils as a way of summarising their knowledge of a unit of work. The individual map reveals some of the pupil's understanding and misunderstandings of the topic. The task could also be given at the start of a unit in order to find out the pupils' prior knowledge of the subject. In either case, you need to provide a list of ideas with which pupils can work and to which they can add their own ideas.

Concept mapping is useful in your lesson preparation when beginning a new unit of work. Concept mapping enables you to gain an overview of the unit, to consolidate links between several ideas and may reveal weaknesses or gaps in your own understanding. Your tutor may ask you to prepare a concept map for a Unit of Work as part of your preparation for teaching, using your school's scheme of work. Concept mapping is a useful way of linking aspects of the National Curriculum in your subject. For further discussion on this topic see White and Gunstone (1992) or Novak and Gowin (1984); and for the use of concept mapping by science teachers see Willson and Williams (1996).

DARTS ACTIVITIES

In the list of active learning methods in Table 5.2.1 (p. 265) is the term 'DARTS'. This is an acronym for 'Directed Activities Related to (the use of) TextS'. It is in fact more than the use of textbooks, but takes in ways of using a variety of written materials.

The DARTS activities are ways of involving pupils in active reading, writing and listening. For example, a reading exercise may require pupils to learn from a textbook; then a DARTS activity suggests ways of interacting with that text, e.g. by underlining certain types of word; listing important words; or drawing diagrams or changing a labelled diagram into continuous prose.

In the same way a listening DARTS activity may be designed to help pupils understand instructions given by the teacher. The techniques involved in this interactive process are known as DARTS activities (Gilham, 1986, p. 164ff; also see Davies and Greene, 1984).

Some examples of DARTS activities are discussed below.

1 Giving instructions   This includes activities like making bread, preparing to carry out a traffic survey, gathering information on and making a summary of the effects of the Black Death in Europe.

A common complaint by teachers is that pupils do not read instructions or if they do, are unable to comprehend them. The language level may be too difficult or pupils may understand each step but not the whole. Most often it is because pupils do not have any investment in the project; it is not theirs. Ways of alleviating such problems include:

- **Make a list of the instructions** on a sheet and give to each pupil; then read it out. As the instructional steps are completed pupils could be asked to tick off that step.
- Instructions could be **written on numbered cards**. A set of cards can be given to a group who are instructed to put the cards into a working order. The final sequence can be checked, discrepancies discussed and the order checked against the purpose. The acceptable sequence can be distributed which pupils write or paste in their books.
- Instructions can be matched to sketches of events; pupils are expected to read

instructions and select the matching sketch and so build a sequence.
- A more demanding task is to discuss the enquiry or task and then ask pupils to **draft their own set of instructions**. After checking by the teacher the pupils' order can be used.

The same approach can be applied to **how things work**. For example, helping pupils explain how:

- ice erodes rock;
- a newspaper is put together;
- to interrogate a database;
- to use a thesaurus.

2 Listening to the teacher   Sometimes you may wish pupils just to listen and enjoy what is being said to them. There are other occasions when you want pupils to listen and interact with the material and **keep some sort of record**. It may be:

- explanation of a phenomenon, e.g. a riot;
- description of an event, e.g. a bore in a river;
- account of a process, e.g. making pastry;
- demonstration of a phenomenon, e.g. distillation;
- account of personal experience, e.g. of work experience or a visit to a gallery.

There are a number of ways you can help pupils. For example:

- Identify key words and ideas as you proceed, signalling pupils when to record them.
- Identify key words and ideas in advance on a worksheet and ask pupils to note them, tick, underline, highlight. These words can be written, in addition and for reference, on the board or overhead projector.
- Adopt the above strategy, but develop as a game. Who can identify these ideas? Call out when you hear them.
- By using a diagram which pupils annotate as the lesson proceeds. This might be used to:
  - label parts;
  - describe functions;
  - identify where things happen.
- Pupils could keep their own notes and then be asked to make a summary and presentation to the class. Alternatively pupils could be given a list of words to aid them.

Another way to effect learning is to give pupils a depleted summary and ask them to complete it. The degree of help is a matter of judgement. For example:

- You can write out the summary with some key words missing and ask pupils to add the missing words.
- The depleted summary could have an additional list of words from which to choose; the task then is to put them in the appropriate place.
- The focus of the depleted text could be on key words or concepts or focused on meanings of words, e.g. on connecting words or verbs, etc. (Sutton, 1981, p. 119).

3 Characterising events   You may wish to help pupils associate certain ideas, events or properties with a phenomenon. For example, what were the features of the colonisation of the West Indies; or what are the characteristics of a Mediterranean-type climate?

As well as reading about them (below) or making notes,

- You can list ideas on separate cards, some of which are relevant to the topic and others not relevant. Ask pupils to sort the cards into two piles, those events relevant to the phenomenon and those not directly related. Pupils can compare sorting and justify their choice.
- A more complex task is to mix up cards describing criteria related to two phenomena and ask pupils to select those criteria appropriate to each event. For example, compare the characteristics of the Industrial Revolutions of the eighteenth and twentieth centuries.

4 Interrogating books or reading for meaning   Learners often feel that if they read a book they are learning. Pupils don't always appreciate that they have to work to gain understanding. Learners need to **do something with the material** in order to understand it. There are a number of ways of interrogating the material in order to assist with learning and understanding.

There are first some general points to be considered. It is important that pupils:

- are asked to read selectively – the length of the reading should be appropriate;
- understand why they are reading and what they are expected to get out of it;
- know what they are supposed to be doing while they read, what to focus on, what to write down or record;
- know what they are going to do with the results of their reading; for example, write, draw, summarise, reformulate, précis, tell others, tell the teacher, carry out an investigation.

Teachers sometimes give homework such as 'read through this chapter tonight and I will give you a quick test on it tomorrow'. This is not helpful to learning because the focus and purpose is unclear. The following notes suggest ways of helping pupils read texts, worksheets and posters with purpose.

Getting an overview

Using photocopies of written material is helpful; pupils can annotate or mark the text to aid understanding. Pupils could be asked to read the entire text quickly, to get an overview and to identify any words they cannot understand and to clarify them by asking an adult or using a dictionary.

Asking pupils to read it a second time with a purpose, they could:

- list key words or ideas;
- underline key ideas;
- highlight key words.

Reformulating ideas

In order to develop understanding further, pupils need to do something with what they have read. They could:

- make a list of key words or ideas;
- collect similar ideas together, creating patterns of bigger ideas;
- summarise the text to a given length;
- turn prose into a diagram, sketch or chart:
  - a spider or burr diagram,
  - flow chart, identifying sequence of events, ideas, etc.,
  - diagram, e.g. of a process or of equipment with labels;
- turn a diagram into prose, by telling a story or interpreting meanings;
- summarise using tables, e.g. relating
  - structure to function (organs of body),
  - historical figures' contribution to society (emancipation of women),
  - form to origin (landscapes and erosion).

Where appropriate, pupils could be given a skeleton flow chart, burr diagram, etc., with the starting idea attached and asked to attach further ideas to that.

Reporting back

A productive way of gaining interest and involvement is to ask pupils to report their findings, summaries or interpretation of the text to the class.

The summary could take one of the forms mentioned above. In addition, of course, the pupil could use the board or overhead projector or make a poster. Pupils need to be prepared for this task. They cannot be expected to do this if not given time to prepare.

Public reporting is demanding on pupils. It is helped if groups draft the work and support the reporter. For example, a piece of narrative could be used or a poem could be the focus of the work. A possible sequence of events might be:

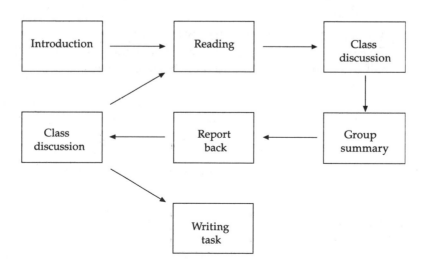

The process could continue by further reading or by a final class task, based on the class discussion. These types of learning activity emphasise the importance of language in learning. For further discussion on the role of language in learning, see Barnes (1976), Barnes *et al*. (1972) and Bennett and Dunne (1994).

COMMUNICATING WITH PUPILS

Throughout your teaching and by whichever methods you adopt you will use a number of resources to interact with the pupils. To get the best out of what you are doing it is necessary to consider how best to use them and to incorporate them into your lesson planning. The board and the overhead projector are used extensively by teachers as active teaching and learning devices. We consider in turn their use.

1 Using the board   Both blackboards and whiteboards are used extensively by teachers and hopefully by pupils. Writing on the board is not easy because we stand up to do it, whereas most writing is done sitting down. A few rules may help pupils follow your work on the board.

Handwriting: It is better to use joined up script, not capital letters or printing, when writing on the board as this is what pupils are used to. Most books use lower case letters in their words as we do here. You should practise handwriting on the board before you start teaching.

If you want a clear style, that known as the Marion Richardson style is a useful model to work from. This style of handwriting avoids loops and the 'thick and thin lines' associated with italic or cursive script. An example of clear handwriting influenced by the Marion Richardson style is given below.

Teaching in the secondary school.

Practise keeping your writing on a straight line and big enough to be seen at the back of the class. Go to the back of the class and check; better still, ask someone else to check it. Use white chalk but colour sparingly and only then colours that can be seen, e.g. red and yellow.

Prepare board work in advance, for choice of words, layout and headings. If you know you are going to elicit ideas from the class and build a set of ideas on the board, think in advance about how you are going to organise the board.

Advance planning can be done by writing on the board beforehand in coloured chalk that is **not easily** read, e.g. blue; then in class go over it in white as you develop the ideas, e.g. annotating diagrams.

2 The overhead projector   Much the same advice applies as to the board except of course that it is not a board or a book.

Some points to consider when writing a transparency include the following:

- Don't fill up your transparency with words – it is usually not read.
- Use large writing or, better, use 'point size' 18 on a word processor at least for all transparencies.

- The word processor allows good quality overheads to be made quickly. Most photocopiers will produce a transparency starting from a paper master; you should ask which type of clear acetate is suitable for your school photocopier.
- Margins of transparencies need attention; make sure you do not lose material off the screen; draw a margin round the acetate before you start making a transparency.
- Where to stand; do not stand where you block half the screen.
- If you are left handed, think where to stand to write.
- Use colour and underlining for emphasis.
- Use a marker (pencil) to indicate relevant text on the OHP; do not point at the screen or look at the screen as you talk. The great advantage of the instrument is that you face your audience.

The overhead projector is interactive and can be used to:

- stimulate pupils by listing ideas;
- record ideas;
- make summaries;
- bring in prepared ideas, diagrams, etc., to speak to but not read from;
- build ideas, models, diagrams, sequences, events, etc.

Another advantage of the overhead projector is its flexibility. Transparencies can be prepared which:

- use colour as highlight, by using coloured acetate;
- have overlays, successive sheets of acetate which successively add information as wanted;
- use windows; parts of the acetate are covered with an opaque material and subsequently revealed in the desired sequence.

Many transparent objects can be displayed on an overhead projector. By projecting a transparent ruler on the screen, you can discuss how to use the ruler. Similarly with protractors and other instruments involving scales. Many science phenomena can be demonstrated using the OHP, such as a compass, the pattern of a magnetic field using iron filings and a magnet; the motion of millipedes' legs, etc. Also, changes in a transparent liquid can be displayed using, for example, a transparent dish.

3 The video; and the worksheet   The place of both these resources in your teaching needs to be considered and planned so that effective learning can take place. In task 5.2.6 we suggest that you ask a number of experienced teachers about their use of video and worksheets.

4 The microcomputer   The computer can be used to support teaching and learning as a word processor, to display multi-media resources, to interrogate databases and use spreadsheets. It is also used to monitor and collect data from the environment. For further help you should refer to Unit 1.4 in this book as well as to subject books in the series 'Learning to teach (subject name) in the secondary school' which accompany this text; see the front of the book for details.

Task 5.2.6	DEVELOPING GUIDELINES FOR THE USE OF VIDEO AND DRAFTING A WORKSHEET

Draw up a set of guidelines for

- using a video with a class;
- constructing a worksheet. A useful way to start is to collect a number of worksheets used in your school in different subjects and to develop a set of criteria for good practice (Lloyd-Jones, 1988).

For each visual aid, identify a broad set of guidelines and illustrate their use by means of an example. Compare and contrast the different ways each of these resources are used in several subject areas by discussing these with other student teachers.

Summary and key points

Learners learn and teachers teach; teachers enable pupils to learn but cannot do the learning for them. Pupils need to engage actively, i.e. mentally, with a task if learning is to take place; thus your work as a teacher is to enthuse and motivate pupils and give purpose to learning tasks and provide active learning experiences. This unit is also about study skills. Preparing your pupils, e.g., for public examinations, requires them to develop such skills; see also Balderstone and King (1997).

This unit has focused on reading, writing, listening and talking and how to help pupils get the most out of such experiences. There is much activity in practically based subjects, such as art and design, home economics, science and technology. However, the mere act of doing something using the hands does not guarantee that learning takes place. Hand and brain need to be involved. Pupils need to be involved in the design, execution and evaluation of practical work in the same way as we have discussed their involvement in reading and listening. Concepts grow and develop by means of continuing purposeful interaction with them; this is what active learning is about. Active learning helps you to monitor pupil progress because it enables you to gain information about the learner from a variety of sources. Such activities can reveal much about pupils' understanding. Active learning has been contrasted with rote learning. The latter is a small but important part of active learning. It makes available to the learner skills that are needed for higher level learning.

The key to good teaching is preparation; it is even more important for active learning strategies and methods where good preparation and clear purpose are of the essence. The use of active learning is a key part of your repertoire as a teacher and contributes to your Career Entry Profile. You should check the range of teaching methods expected of you as an NQT in the list of competences and standards for your course. For further ideas and advice see the reading list at the end of the unit.

Table 5.2.1 Active learning methods (for use with Task 5.2.5)

case studies	games
creative writing	drama
DARTS	diaries
debating	brainstorming
experiments	role play
fieldwork	CD ROM
problem solving	interviewing
reports	designing
simulations	visitors
small group discussion	teacher demonstration
surveys	CAL
visits	formal presentations
developing multimedia representation	

FURTHER READING

Bennett, N. and Dunne, E. (1994) 'How children learn: implications for practice', in B. Moon and A. Shelton Mayes *Teaching and Learning in the Secondary School*, London: Routledge, pp. 50–6.

Centre for Science Education, Sheffield (1992) *Active Teaching and Learning Approaches in Science*, London: Collins Educational.

A detailed discussion of active learning methods, copiously illustrated with examples. Useful to all teachers, not just science teachers.

Child, D. (1993) 'Learning theories and teaching children', in *Psychology and the Teacher (5th edition)*, New York: Holt, Rinehart and Winston, p. 101.

A useful introduction to the ways in which learning can occur and their application to the classroom.

Sutton, C. (ed.) (1981) *Communicating in the Classroom*, London: Hodder and Stoughton.

An old but valuable book illustrating ways of supporting pupils in their own learning. Full of practical classroom ideas and suggestions for lesson planning.

5.3 | TEACHING STYLES

INTRODUCTION

In Chapter 1, you were asked to consider what kind of teacher you would like to become. In working through this unit, we hope you take the opportunity to analyse your teaching to see what has to happen if you are to achieve your goals. Everyone's 'natural' teaching style varies but you also need to be able to use other teaching styles which are more appropriate to particular lesson objectives and particular characteristics of the pupils. Thus building your repertoire of teaching styles is a necessary part of your professional development.

OBJECTIVES

By the end of this unit you should:

- understand how teacher behaviour and teaching strategies combine to produce a teaching style;
- understand the importance of using a range of teaching styles;
- have experimented with different styles of teaching and evaluated their effectiveness.

We suggest you check the competences/standards for your course to see what is required in the area of teaching styles.

WHAT DO WE MEAN BY A TEACHING STYLE?

Teaching style is the term used to describe the way a learning experience is conducted. It is built from the **behaviour** of the teacher and the **strategy** chosen to ensure that the planned learning takes place, that the lesson objectives are achieved. Table 5.3.1 illustrates this point.

By **teacher behaviour** we mean the demeanour of the teacher and the way the teacher relates to pupils; for example, a teacher may choose to be distant, to be more friendly or to convey enthusiasm for their subject. The teacher indicates their expectations to pupils through their behaviour when teaching the class. Teachers also adopt particular forms of

Table 5.3.1 Defining a teaching style

teaching style = teacher behaviour + teaching strategy

behaviour to foster certain types of learning. For example, the teacher may see themselves as a **facilitator of learning** in a situation where group discussion has been chosen as the teaching method and the teacher's role is both to help individuals to contribute fully and to ensure the group functions effectively. Or the teacher may take the role of **transmitter of knowledge** where knowledge acquisition is the desired outcome.

By **teaching strategy**, we mean the choice and range of teaching methods used for a lesson; for example, a teaching strategy for a drama lesson might include the methods of individual enquiry (pupil research), discussion and pupil demonstration. Unit 5.2 provides examples of a range of methods which might be used when you are devising your teaching strategies. Discussion, role play, investigational work and demonstrations are among the methods from which a teacher may choose. The method chosen influences decisions about assessment, routines, grouping, choice of materials.

In any lesson you are likely to use a range of styles in order to achieve your objectives. It is, for example, common to start with a didactic style, setting out what is to be done in the lesson and then move on to a facilitator/pupil-centred style as pupils tackle the work set then return to a more formal style at the end of the lesson to check that the learning intended has taken place.

Precisely defining the teaching style of a particular teacher is a difficult if not impossible task as in each teaching and learning situation there are many individual variables operating.

Some of the terms often used to describe ways of teaching are: **experiential, didactic, chalk and talk, teacher-directed, pupil-centred, practical, theoretical, traditional, progressive, transmission, content-based, process-based, whole-class-based**. But these are general descriptions which at best give an indication of how a teacher might conduct a lesson or part of a lesson and the boundaries between the styles implied are blurred. On their own, these descriptions provide just part of the picture of how a teacher teaches. For example, two teachers could both use 'chalk and talk' as a teaching strategy but their behaviour would influence their overall style and thus the pupils' learning. If one was very formal, the learning of pupils in that class may be more passive than for pupils of a teacher who was enthusiastic, interested in them and actively engaged them in the material.

LEARNING OUTCOMES AND TEACHING STYLE

Teaching styles are chosen to suit the characteristics of the pupils (i.e. their attitudes, abilities, preferred learning styles) and specifically to help you achieve your lesson objectives. For example, an 'instructional' style is particularly appropriate in achieving certain types of learning – when you want to develop particular skills such as explaining how a piece of equipment is to be used. It may not be the most effective approach in other instances such as learning about colour mixing in art which may best be done through practical activities which reinforce the learning taking place. In choosing objectives for a particular lesson, you need to decide which of a whole range of potential learning outcomes are to be the focus of the lesson. The style you choose should be one which best enables those objectives to be realised. Table 5.3.2 provides examples of learning

Table 5.3.2 Examples of learning outcomes from a lesson

Aspect 1 Acquisition of knowledge and ability to demonstrate this, e.g. through focusing on knowledge retention, memorisation, written expression, acquiring theoretical knowledge, individual achievement
Aspect 2 Ability to apply knowledge: through developing communication skills, oral skills, investigative skills, transferability of knowledge, ability to research, organise, select material
Aspect 3 Increased personal and social skills such as self-confidence, leadership skills, accepting responsibility, initiative, ability to work with other people
Aspect 4 Improved attitudes to learning demonstrated through increased motivation, perseverance, commitment, self-reliance

Source: Adapted from ILEA (1984, p. 2)

outcomes. These are based on the aspects of achievement defined later on in Table 6.2.2.

If you always use a particular style then there is a danger that the learning outcomes for your pupils may be restricted to a narrow band. Your pupils may be high achievers in one aspect of achievement but low achievers in another aspect. Of course, pupils do not depend on their learning in one subject for their overall development; a school needs to ensure that across the whole curriculum there are opportunities for pupils to achieve in the areas outlined in Table 5.3.2.

FACTORS AFFECTING CHOICE OF TEACHING STYLES

As well as taking account of the **characteristics** of the pupils and the desired **learning outcomes**, your choice of teaching style is a matter for your professional judgement. Any judgement you make about appropriate teaching styles is based on:

- your professional knowledge;
- the environment in which you teach;
- your personal qualities.

Extent of your professional (pedagogic) knowledge

This book provides a brief introduction to the body of pedagogic knowledge available. Teacher education is considered to fall into three phases: initial teacher education, induction – which is the education and training you are given during your first year of teaching; and in-service education and training (INSET – see Unit 8.2 for further information) which should be available during your teaching life.

Your choice of teaching style is affected by your beliefs, views and assumptions as well as professional knowledge in, for example, the following areas:

- *Your theories of how teachers should teach and how pupils learn.* For example, teachers hold differing views about pupil choice, the place of negotiation in the classroom, appropriate teacher/pupil interaction, appropriate pupil/pupil interaction, the teacher's role (purveyor of knowledge, interpreter of knowledge, facilitator of learning) and the use of questions. Decisions you make about the balance in your lessons between the process of learning and the content influence your style. By a 'process' approach to teaching and learning we mean an approach that focuses on teaching through activities like problem solving, skill-based learning, experiential learning, role play, simulations, collaboration. At the other end of the spectrum, content focused teaching means that mastery of content is the focus and it is achieved through, for example, a transmission style, chalk and talk, rote learning or didactic teaching. Your theories about learning reveal themselves in a number of ways: for example, whether you make subject matter relevant to pupil experiences and interests, in the variety of resources you use or in the way you group the pupils.

- *Your approach to classroom management.* Your views on maintenance of discipline, including noise, movement and talk, influence the way you teach (see Unit 3.3).
- *Your confidence and competence* with the subject matter and with classroom management affect your behaviour and hence your teaching style.

The environment in which you teach

There are many environmental issues which affect your teaching – physical and mental state of the pupils, school/department decisions about pupil grouping (setting/ streaming/mixed ability), type and layout of room and the range and availability of teaching materials and equipment. Resources are usually limited and you need to adjust to the circumstances in which you find yourself. Two other influential factors are class size and your assumptions and knowledge about the pupils.

- *Class size.* There are some government ministers and officials who argue that class size has no effect on achievement. It is a convenient argument for those who allocate resources to education as the theory supports the limiting of resources. However, we believe that class size inevitably influences your choice of teaching style and so affects what can be achieved. Teaching a large group of pupils where a significant majority are demotivated is not the same as teaching the same size group of highly motivated pupils. Similarly, developing oral skills in a class of thirty is a different matter to developing them with a class of six.
- *Your assumptions and knowledge about the pupils.* Teacher expectations have a significant effect on pupil self-esteem, motivation and achievement and it is too easy for teachers to make damaging assumptions about pupils from backgrounds different to their own. This can lead to discrimination and so needs to be avoided. This can be done by increasing your knowledge and understanding of the social and cultural influences on the pupils. Educational researchers such as Feuerstein, Vygotsky and Bruner have written extensively on the impact of social context on learning and their work is referred to in the texts listed at the end of the unit.

Your personal qualities

Your imagination, enthusiasm, energy, ability to form positive relationships with pupils as well as prejudices and assumptions about gender and race all contribute to your classroom behaviour and thus influence your teaching style. Your communication skills such as body language, voice and the other issues outlined in Chapter 3 also significantly affect your teaching style.

IDENTIFYING TEACHING STYLES

The findings of research on teaching styles used by teachers involved in the Technical Vocational Education Initiative is reported in Table 5.3.3 and the framework used to analyse styles may provide you with an approach to analysing your own styles. Three broad bands of style were identified:

Table 5.3.3 Pupil participation and teaching styles

	The participation dimension		
	Closed ───────	Framed ───────	Negotiated ───────
Content	Tightly controlled by the teacher. Not negotiable.	Teacher controls the topic, frames of reference and tasks; criteria made explicit.	Discussed at each point; joint decisions.
Focus	Authoritative knowledge and skills; simplified, monolithic.	Stress on empirical testing; processes chosen by teacher; some legitimation of pupil ideas.	Search for justifications and principles; strong legitimation of pupil ideas.
Pupils' role	Acceptance; routine performance; little access to principles.	Join in teacher's thinking; make hypotheses, set up tests; operate teacher's frame.	Discuss goals and methods critically; share responsibility for frame and criteria.
Key concepts	'Authority': the proper procedures and the right answers.	'Access' to skills, processes, criteria.	'Relevance': critical discussion of pupils' priorities.
Methods	Exposition; worksheets (closed); note giving; individual exercises; routine practical work. Teacher evaluates.	Exposition, with discussion eliciting suggestions; individual/group problem solving; lists of tasks given; discussion of outcomes, but teacher adjudicates.	Group and class discussion and decision making about goals and criteria. Pupils plan and carry out work, make presentations, evaluate success.

Source: Adapted from Barnes *et al.* (1987, p. 25)

closed – which was a more didactic and formal way of teaching with little pupil involvement in the material of the lesson;

framed – where the teacher provided a structure for the lesson within which pupils were able to contribute their own ideas and interpretations; and

negotiated – where the direction of the lesson was to a considerable extent dependent on pupil ideas and contributions.

As an aim of TVEI was to develop pupils' initiative and involvement in their own learning, participation in the lesson was a focus for the analysis of teaching styles. In the table, the choices that teachers made about teaching styles are analysed under the headings: content, focus, pupils' role, key concepts and methods.

Task 5.3.1 PUPIL PARTICIPATION AND TEACHING STYLES

Look at the continuum of styles identified by Barnes *et al.* in Table 5.3.3

———— CLOSED ———— FRAMED ———— NEGOTIATED ————

and consider what the level of pupil participation in your lessons is. Check, through discussion with your tutor or other student teachers, that you understand and would recognise these different styles. With the agreement of the teacher or student teacher concerned, use the framework provided by the table to analyse the teaching styles in some lessons or parts of lessons which you are observing.

Mosston's continuum of teaching styles

Mosston and Ashworth (1994) carried out careful analytical work on teaching styles and their ideas are worthy of much more detailed consideration than is possible here. They define the components of different teaching styles in considerable detail and use a framework (the 'anatomy of a teaching style') as a basis for analysis and comparison for each one. Table 5.3.4 provides a brief outline of the styles they define. Like Barnes *et al.*, they see these styles as being part of a continuum – moving from teacher-controlled and directed learning experiences through to more independent learning.

Mosston and Ashworth describe the links between 'teaching behaviour, learning behaviour and the objectives of each style' – the T–L–O approach to use their terms. They point out that there are two aspects to objectives: intended objectives and the actual objectives observed. They also describe in detail the decisions made by teacher and learner during three phases of learning: pre-impact ('preparation'), impact ('execution and performance') and post-impact (or 'evaluation' which is ongoing throughout the lesson). A number of the styles above require the teacher to teach the pupils the style of learning they are expected to be undertaking. Developing such awareness on the part of the pupils can be seen as one of the objectives for learning.

Table 5.3.4 Mosston's continuum of teaching styles

The command style This style is often described as autocratic or teacher centred. It is appropriate in certain contexts, e.g. teaching safe use of equipment, learning particular routines in dance.

The practice style Whilst similar to the command style, there is a shift in decision making to pupils and there is more scope with this style for the teacher to work with individuals whilst the group are occupied with practice tasks such as writing for a purpose in English or practising skills in mathematics.

The reciprocal style The pupils work in pairs evaluating each other's performance. Each partner is actively involved – one as the 'doer' and one observing, as the 'teacher partner'. The teacher works with the 'teacher partner' to improve their evaluative and feedback skills. This style provides increased possibilities for 'interaction and communication among students' and can be applied when pupils are learning a foreign language or learning routines in gymnastics. Pupils learn to judge performance against criteria.

The self-check style This style is designed to develop the learner's ability to evaluate their own performance. The teacher sets the tasks and the pupils evaluate their performance against criteria and set new goals in collaboration with the teacher – for example, some mathematics programmes are organised to allow this type of personal development. All pupils start at the same level and move up when the teacher deems them ready.

The inclusion style In this style, differentiated tasks are included to ensure that all pupils gain some feeling of success and so develop positive self-concepts, e.g. if an angled bar is provided for high jump practice, all pupils can succeed as they choose the height over which to jump. They decide at what level to start.

Guided discovery Mosston sees this as one of the most difficult styles. The teacher plans the pupil's learning programme on the basis of the level of cognitive development of the learner. The teacher then guides the pupil to find the answer – reframing the question and task if necessary. Pupils with special educational needs are often taught in small groups and this approach might be used by the teacher to develop an individualised learning programme for each pupil.

Divergent style The learners are encouraged to find alternative solutions to a problem, e.g. in approaching a design problem in art.

The individual programme: learner's design The knowledge and skills needed to participate in this method of learning depend on the building up of skills and self-knowledge in earlier learning experiences. A pupil designs and carries out a programme of work within a framework agreed and monitored by the teacher. Pupils carrying out open-ended investigations in science provide an example of this style.

Learners' initiated style This style is more pupil directed than the previous style where the teacher provided a framework. At this point on the continuum, the stimulus for learning comes primarily from the pupil not wholly from the teacher. The pupil actively initiates the learning experience. Giving homework which allows pupils freedom to work on their own areas of interest in their own way would fall into this category. The teacher acts in a supportive role.

Self-teaching style This style describes independent learning without external support. For example, it is the type of learning that adults undergo as they learn from their own experiences.

Source: Adapted from Mosston and Ashworth (1994)

Task 5.3.2

MOSSTON'S CONTINUUM OF TEACHING STYLES

Consider Mosston's continuum. Think back to a recent lesson you taught which did not go as well as you had planned. Was the dominant teaching style you used the most suitable, i.e. did it achieve the objectives of the lesson? How else could you have tackled the lesson material? Discuss Mosston's work with other student teachers. Are his categories useful in providing you with alternative approaches? If not, why not?

ANALYSING YOUR TEACHING STYLE

One of our student teachers, who carried out an analysis to establish the level of her interaction with pupils during a lesson, found that over a twenty minute period she spent only about ninety seconds supporting the work of individual pupils. For most of the rest of the time she was addressing the class as a whole. What surprised her was that she had intended her lesson to be much more pupil centred and thought she had gone some way to achieving that. Unit 5.4 gives examples of ways in which you can evaluate your work. This student used another student to observe and record interactions. An observation sheet was used which required the observer to note every five seconds whether the teacher/pupil interaction was at a group level, an individual level or a whole class level. Such observation sheets need to be designed with the particular purpose in mind. Recording every five seconds is rather too often for some purposes but it worked in this case as the observer had to remember only three codes: G – group, I – individual, W – whole class. Table 5.3.5 shows the format these students used.

Table 5.3.5 An observation grid

Time (min)	Type of interaction (G = group, W = whole class, I = individual) at five second intervals										
5	G	G	G	G	G	G	G	W	W	W	W	W
6	W	W	W	G	G	G	I	G	G	G	I	I

Task 5.3.3 ANALYSING ASPECTS OF YOUR TEACHING STYLE

Arrange for another student teacher to observe two of your lessons where you try out contrasting styles. Ask them to focus on particular aspects of your work which interest you, e.g. the use of open ended questions or giving praise. You probably need to devise your own observation schedules to record the findings. In the discussion afterwards you may find it useful to answer the following questions. Did you achieve your objectives? How successful were you in varying your teaching style? What factors influenced your success? How could you have done things differently? What could you try next? If you can repeat this exercise regularly, you will build up your repertoire of styles and your responsiveness to changing classroom situations.

> ## ❗ Summary and key points
>
> In this unit, we have tried to identify factors which influence teaching style and asked you deliberately to structure some lessons in ways which allow you to explore factors influencing your teaching style. Acquiring knowledge of different teaching strategies and becoming aware of your own behaviour in the classroom are two steps on the ladder to effectiveness. However, you need to move from knowing about how these aspects influence teaching style to being able to apply this professional knowledge to your classroom teaching so that effective learning can take place. Applying a reflective approach to your teaching helps you develop your skills. The following unit provides details of reflective strategies which will help you in the further analysis of aspects of your own teaching.

FURTHER READING

Coles, M.J. and Robinson, W.D. (1991) *Teaching Thinking: A Survey of Programmes in Education (2nd edition)*, Bristol: The Bristol Press.

This is a book which will challenge your views about what you should teach and how you should teach it. It describes a number of *Thinking Skills/Critical Thinking* programmes in the UK as well as discussing international developments such as the *Philosophy for Children* programme which was started in the USA by Mathew Lipman and Feuerstein's *Instrumental Enrichment* programme which originated in Israel.

Dennison, B. and Kirk, R. (1990) *Do, Review, Learn, Apply: A Simple Guide to Experiential Learning*, Oxford: Blackwell Education.

This is a very practical book. It includes an introduction to the theory supporting the experiential learning approach as well as a host of ideas and practical activities which may be used in experiential learning situations.

Gibbs, G. and Habeshaw, T. (1992) *253 Ideas for your Teaching (3rd edition)*, Bristol: Technical and Educational Services Ltd.

Gibbs and Habeshaw have published a range of books which provide practical ideas for teachers – this is just one from their range.

Joyce, B. and Weil, M. (1996) *Models of Teaching (5th edition)*, Boston and London: Allyn and Bacon.

Joyce and Weil identify models of teaching and group them into four 'families' which represent different philosophies about how humans learn. This is a comprehensive text designed for those who have knowledge of teaching and learning issues. See also:

Joyce, B., Calhoun, E. and Hopkins, D. (1997) *Models of Learning – Tools for Teaching*, Buckingham: Open University Press.

Mosston, M. and Ashworth, S. (1994) *Teaching Physical Education (4th edition)*, Colombus, OH: Merrill Publishing.

This text describes a continuum of teaching styles. Although written for physical education teachers, the styles decribed are applicable to different extents in all subjects.

Waterhouse, P. (1983) *Managing the Learning Process*, Maidenhead: McGraw-Hill.

Chapter 7 'The management of individual and small-group learning' provides ideas about effective learning strategies for use in the classroom.

5.4   IMPROVING YOUR TEACHING: AN INTRODUCTION TO ACTION RESEARCH AND REFLECTIVE PRACTICE

INTRODUCTION

How do you know your lesson went well?

This is a question you can expect to be asked from time to time and you need to be able to provide answers. The purpose of teaching pupils is that they learn. The fact that pupils are quiet and look as if they are working industriously is no guarantee that the learning you have intended is taking place.

Children should not be able to pass through your class unaffected by the experience!

In this unit, we introduce you to simple techniques which may help you find answers to your questions about your teaching. In carrying out the tasks in this book you are engaging in 'reflective practice'. **Action research** is a term used to describe 'reflective practice'. Action research is the investigation of professional practice by practitioners themselves. Action research methods encompass the methods you have been using – of observation, keeping a diary, obtaining the perspectives of different interested parties (pupils, staff) and examining documentation. The work in this unit provides a brief introduction to this area and we suggest that once you are qualified, you extend your knowledge and understanding of the tools of action research as part of your further professional development.

OBJECTIVES

By the end of this unit you should:

- be able to demonstrate an understanding of the action research process;
- be able to discuss characteristics of effective teaching and learning;
- know about different forms of evidence which you could draw on in answer to the question 'How do you know your lesson went well?'
- have applied action research strategies to evaluate and improve aspects of your teaching;
- understand that acquiring a high level of professional knowledge and professional judgement is a long-term learning process which can be developed by the use of reflection based on evidence gained from action research.

Check the competences/standards for your course to see which in particular relate to this unit.

THE PROCESS OF ACTION RESEARCH

Action research describes a process which teachers use to find out about the quality of teaching and learning taking place. It is based on a simple process.

In your classroom observations, you may have **started with a clear focus** or a question to answer (e.g. what routines does the teacher use in managing the work of the class?) and you may have **collected evidence from various sources** to answer that question. You may have observed and made notes about what the pupils and the teacher actually did during the lesson; you may have looked at the pupils' work and the teacher's lesson plans; you may have cross-checked your perceptions with those of the teacher as a way of eliminating bias, improving accuracy and identifying alternative explanations. So, like any action researcher, you have **gathered data from different sources, checked for alternative perceptions/explanations and drawn on all of this in making your conclusions** so as to **improve your work** in the future.

Table 5.4.1 sets out the process in more detail.

Table 5.4.1 An action research framework

1   What do we want to know? It is important to define the question clearly – perhaps breaking the question down into several sub-questions. 2   Who has or where are the data needed to answer the question? 3   How much time and what other resources can be devoted to exploring this issue? 4   How are we going to collect the data? 5   When do we need to collect the data? 6   What ethical questions arise from the collection and use of these data? 7   How are we going to analyse and present the data? 8   Are we prepared and able to make changes in the light of the findings?

HOW DO YOU KNOW YOUR LESSON WENT WELL?

To help you answer this question, we provide you with a set of criteria (see Tables 5.4.2 and 5.4.3) to use in a small action research project in which you evaluate some aspects of teaching and learning.

Task 5.4.1	FOCUSING ON EFFECTIVENESS

Look at the criteria listed in Tables 5.4.2 and 5.4.3 and identify those that you feel competent with already. Now consider those with which you have had difficulty. Choose one or two of these issues for further investigation. Later in this unit, you are given a task that asks you to plan a strategy for investigating these issues in the classroom.

Table 5.4.2 Criteria for evaluating teaching

Teaching quality is to be judged by the extent to which:
- teachers have clear objectives for their lessons;
- pupils are aware of these objectives;
- teachers have a secure command of the subject;
- lessons have suitable content;
- activities are well chosen to promote learning of that content;
- activities are presented in ways that engage and motivate and challenge all pupils, enabling them to make progress at a suitable pace.

Source: OFSTED (1993, Part 2, p. 27)

Table 5.4.3 Some characteristics of effective learning

The learners
- clearly perceive the purpose of the lesson
- see a practical application for what they are learning
- solve genuine problems
- have an active role in the processes of learning
- use their initiative, exercise imagination and think for themselves
- acquire knowledge and develop skills
- develop good habits of work, including perseverance and a concern for correctness
- derive enjoyment and satisfaction from a job well done and realise that these are related to the amount of effort they put in
- discuss their work
- receive constructive assessment of their efforts from the teacher and from fellow students
- learn from their mistakes
- perceive their own progress
- change their ways of thinking about a subject or issue
- improve their confidence and image of themselves.

The teaching
- has a clear purpose and a strategy for achieving it
- is firmly structured with a beginning, a middle and an end, yet with the possibility of being varied to take advantage of opportunities which arise unexpectedly
- takes account of differences in learners' abilities
- offers variety of activity and strikes a good balance between oral, practical and written work
- involves effective use of learning aids and resources
- proceeds at a brisk pace without sacrificing rigour
- covers a good deal of ground in a challenging way
- demands high standards and provides the learner with the opportunities and encouragement to achieve them
- generates a dynamic atmosphere in which the individual can experience a shared sense of achievement.

Source: DES Conference N213, September 1988

Having listed criteria for effective teaching and learning, we move on to the question: what evidence can be collected to show that effective teaching and learning are taking place? The collection and evaluation of evidence should enable you to answer with some confidence. But what counts as evidence?

SOURCES OF EVIDENCE ABOUT TEACHING AND LEARNING

The evidence available for drawing conclusions about teaching and learning can be divided into two types:

- **qualitative data** which is collected through observation, interview, questionnaires (especially open-ended questions), analysis of documents, diaries, video, photographs, discussions;
- **quantitative data** which is collected from, for example, statistical returns, questionnaires or other sources which can be reduced to numerical form.

Both of these forms are used in action research. You simply choose forms most appropriate for the issue under investigation.

ACTION RESEARCH TECHNIQUES

You have already been using diaries, observation, discussions and documents to inform your thinking about teaching and learning. Here we provide further advice about two areas which you may find particularly useful during your initial teacher education: **observation schedules** and **paired observation**.

Observation schedules

Unit 2.1 (Observing classrooms) provides an example of an observation schedule as does Unit 5.3 (Teaching styles). You should by now have used forms of these to observe classroom routines. Hopkins (1993) and others listed in the further readings provide other detailed examples of observation schedules. However, Hopkins suggests that you devise your own observation schedules to suit your particular purpose. It is not possible to record everything that happens in a classroom so you need to focus on, for example, a particular group or pupil or aspect of the teacher's work and record behaviour over time. The observation schedule provides a useful framework for recording classroom behaviours.

Paired observation

This is a streamlined procedure which enables you to obtain feedback on aspects of your work which are difficult for you to monitor. The example in Unit 5.3 of two students working together with one providing feedback on the topic chosen by the other is an example of paired observation in practice. Paired observation works in the following way.

Two colleagues pair up with the purpose of observing one lesson each and then giving feedback about particular aspects of the lesson or the teaching of the person observed. The person giving the lesson decides what the focus of the observation should be. The three stages of a paired observation are:

Step 1: **You both agree the focus of the observation and what notes, if any, are to be made.**
Step 2: **You each observe one lesson given by the other. Your observations and notes are restricted to the area requested.**
Step 3: **You give each other feedback on the issue under consideration.**

And you can repeat the cycle as often as you like.

Task 5.4.2	**A MINI-ACTION RESEARCH PROJECT**

Look at an issue you identified in Task 5.4.1 for further investigation:

- Describe how the issue relates to your own teaching and the concerns you have about your teaching.
- List the behaviour related to the issue which you would expect to see displayed by a teacher successfully exercising this skill.

For example, if you select 'clear objectives', identify

- what is meant by clear and to whom is it clear?

Discuss with your tutor how you can improve your work in this area and then evaluate your success using action research strategies described in this unit.

There is a wealth of information about your teaching which could be collected each lesson. However, you need to focus on specific aspects or you could be so swamped with information that you might feel unable to proceed. The goal is to become a more effective teacher through regular reflection to check your skills as well as to develop your professional knowledge and judgement.

Ethical issues

A word of warning! There are ethical considerations to be taken into account when you are collecting data from pupils and teachers. You must have agreement from those who are in a position to give this – your tutor may advise you to get the permission of the headteacher. You need to take your responsibility in this area seriously. Table 5.4.4 outlines the key areas to consider.

If you intend to develop your action research skills, then we suggest that you read several of the set texts and consult with experienced colleagues.

Table 5.4.4 An ethical approach to action research

You must take responsibility for the ethical use of any data collected and for maintaining confidentiality. We suggest that you should as a matter of course:

1   Ask a senior member of staff as well as the teachers directly involved with your classes for permission to carry out your project.
2   Before you start, provide staff involved with a copy of the outline of your project which includes
    • the area you are investigating
    • how you are going to collect any evidence
    • from whom you intend to collect evidence
    • what you intend to do with the data collected (e.g. whether it is confidential, whether it will be written up anonymously or not)
    • who the audience for your report will be
    • any other factors relevant to the particular situation.
3   Check whether staff expect to be given a copy of your work.
4   If you store data electronically, then you should check that you conform to the requirements of the Data Protection Act. For example, you should not store personal data on computer discs without the explicit authorisation of the individual.

Summary and key points

Developing your teaching skills is one important aspect of your professional development. But other important attributes of the effective teacher which we stress in this book are the quality and extent of your professional knowledge and judgement.

Skills can be acquired and checked relatively easily. Building your professional knowledge and judgement are longer term goals which are developed through reflection and further professional development.

In this unit, we have opened a door on a treasure-trove of strategies which you can use to reflect on the quality of your work. We suggest that you come back to this work during the year and again, later in your career, when you have fully mastered the basic teaching skills. The application of action research to your work at that stage opens your eyes to factors influencing your teaching and learning which you didn't know existed.

Over the early years of your teaching you acquire many teaching skills – they become part of what you could think of as your professional tool kit. But teaching skills, like tools, can become rusty or are perhaps not suitable for the job in the first place. Critical reflection aided by action research, by individuals or by teams, provides the means by which the quality of teaching and learning in the classroom can be evaluated as a prelude to improvement.

If, through studying this section, you were hoping to find an easily adopted method which ensures that you will be a good teacher, then we're afraid you will have been disappointed. If, however, you are seeking to understand an approach which provides you with tools to evaluate your own professional work, then we hope this has helped. You should now have ideas of how to evaluate the quality of your teaching through using a continuous cycle of critical reflection so that you can plan improvement based on evidence.

FURTHER READING

The following texts all provide a grounding in aspects of action research.

Bell, J. (1993) *Doing Your Research Project: A Guide for First-Time Researchers in Education and Social Science*, Milton Keynes: Open University Press.

Dillon, J.T. (1994) *Using Discussion in Classrooms*, Buckingham: Open University Press.

Hopkins, D. (1993) *A Teacher's Guide to Classroom Research (2nd edition)*, Milton Keynes: Open University Press.

Lewis, I. and Munn, P. (1987) *So You Want to do Research! A Guide for Teachers on How to Formulate Research Questions*, Edinburgh, Scotland: The Scottish Council for Research in Education with the General Teaching Council for Scotland.

McKernan, J. (1991) *Curriculum Action Research: A Handbook of Methods and Resources for the Reflective Practitioner*, London: Kogan Page.

Munn, P. and Drever, E. (1990) *Using Questionnaires in Small Scale Research: A Teacher's Guide*, Edinburgh, Scotland: The Scottish Council for Research in Education with the General Teaching Council for Scotland.

Wragg, E.C. (1994) *An Introduction to Classroom Observation*, London: Routledge.

Yin, R. (1994) *Case Study. Design and Methods (2nd edition)*, London: Sage.

6 ASSESSING AND RECORDING PUPILS' WORK

Assessment and its reporting has become a central issue in teaching and learning in the 1990s. The 1988 Education Reform Act in England and Wales introduced statutory subjects into the curriculum for the first time, together with statutory assessment procedures. The introduction of national testing is to monitor standards on a national basis. This chapter includes discussion about the way the results of national testing are being used.

Assessment is needed for a number of purposes, such as to provide information about individual pupil's progress, help the teacher devise appropriate teaching and learning strategies, give parents helpful information about their child's progress and compare pupils and schools across the country. This chapter discusses to what extent one test can provide all this information and the relationship between national testing and other forms of testing. It considers the design and application of tests in relation to their purpose.

Thus Unit 6.1 gives an overview of the principles of assessment, taking into account formative and summative assessment, diagnostic testing and important ideas of validity and reliability. In addition, the difference between norm-referenced testing and criterion-referenced testing is introduced and the nationally set tests discussed in the light of these principles.

The second unit in this chapter focuses mainly on testing and the classroom teacher, with an emphasis on how to use the results of testing to assess progress and diagnose problems. The unit connects assessment with lesson planning and schemes of work.

The third unit shifts focus to consider external assessment as exemplified by the GCSE and GCE Advanced Level. This is, of course, a vital area of the teachers' work because it grades pupils on a nationally recognised scale and exercises some control over both entry to jobs and higher education. Unit 6.3 addresses how standards are maintained and national grades are awarded. In addition, recent developments in vocational education are discussed and contrasts made with the assessment methods used for these courses and those used for the traditional academic course.

6.1   AN OVERVIEW OF ASSESSMENT: PRINCIPLES AND PRACTICE

INTRODUCTION

Assessing children's work is not a recent development. Tests and examinations have existed in various forms since the latter half of the nineteenth century when a national education service became established. As you know, from your own school experience, 'marking' is commonplace and goes with the job of teaching. Yet assessment is sometimes described by experienced teachers as a new concern and an extra pressure.

One reason for this is the new structure for assessment which resulted from the 1988 Education Reform Act and the National Curriculum Attainment Targets. Another reason is the sharper critical analysis to which assessment is now subjected. This has grown out of an increasingly sophisticated and refined assessment 'industry' which, for example, now sees examination syllabuses described in terms of 'assessment objectives' and 'specification grids' rather than merely a list of contents to be learned.

The broad aim of this unit is to provide a framework and introduce you to a number of concepts concerning assessment in schools today. This should help you become an informed contributor to the important professional debate concerning the assessment of children's learning.

OBJECTIVES

By the end of this unit you should have:

- begun to analyse categories of what to assess, when to do it and for what purpose;
- some understanding of some key elements for any assessment scheme;
- gained increased insight to the inherent tensions which exist in collecting and using assessment data;
- identified the competences and standards for your course related to assessment.

ASSESSMENT AND LEARNING

As all pupils know, most teachers mark their work. Teachers who do not manage to mark regularly or who mark cursorily or carelessly are often perceived to be deficient, certainly by their peers and by parents. Research shows that for many younger pupils **marking** provides the **only** form of communication between them and the teacher.

Pupils who do not receive feedback on their work quickly lose motivation and become unsure of the basis of their success or failure.

Most teachers acknowledge that marking is important. Sometimes a chore, sometimes a source of great pressure as the days and weeks of term pass by, it is nevertheless seen as an essential professional task.

The Task Group on Assessment and Testing (TGAT) (the expert group appointed by the government of the day, whose task was to devise an assessment framework for the national curriculum) was the originator of the principle of the ten level scale. This scale applies now only to KS3 and up to Level 8. This was to underpin the curriculum reforms under the 1988 Education Reform Act, which also recognised the teacher's role by its influential analysis of the way assessment should be an integral part of teachers' work. For example,

> The assessment process itself should not determine what is to be taught and learned. It should be the servant, not the master, of the curriculum. Yet it should not simply be a bolt-on addition at the end. Rather, it should be an integral part of the education process, continually providing both 'feedback' and 'feedforward'. It therefore needs to be incorporated systematically into teaching strategies and practices at all levels. Since the results of assessment can serve a number of different purposes, these purposes have to be kept in mind when the arrangements for assessment are designed.
>
> (DES/WO, 1988, paragraph 4)

Some schools have institution-wide policies on marking. In others, responsibility is devolved to departments. The National Curriculum gave impetus to reconsider marking as a component of what has become known as 'teacher assessment', which itself is a part of the arrangements designed to measure children's progress against National Curriculum **attainment targets**. To put this rather more bluntly: not only is assessment (including marking) an essential professional responsibility, it has also become a mandatory duty which falls to all teachers of National Curriculum subjects.

Task 6.1.1 **YOUR EXPERIENCE OF ASSESSMENT**

Think back on your own experiences of being assessed as a student. Compile two lists to show ways in which assessment was, for you,

(a) a positive experience
(b) a negative experience.

Share and discuss your list with a wider group of teachers or other student teachers.

HOW TO THINK ABOUT ASSESSMENT: IDENTIFYING CONTRADICTIONS

Assessment, it seems, is self-evidently a worthwhile activity. If we are to plan appropriate work for children, work which is enjoyable, motivating and which takes children forward in some way, then we need to know something about these children: what they can do, for example, or the kinds of work they find difficult.

And yet, it is controversial. Arguments continue about the **purposes** of assessment, the kinds of assessment teachers should undertake and even when to do it. Assessment is a matter of professional judgement; however, is it an 'art', relying on experience and being essentially qualitative in nature, or is it a 'science', relying on the application of tried and tested techniques and being essentially quantitative? Yet scratch just beneath the surface and we quickly see that **what** to assess is no easy matter to resolve. For example, consider these questions:

- Do I wish to assess my pupils' **knowledge** or **understanding**? How do I distinguish these from **recall**? Or, am I more interested in my pupils' level of **skills** development?
- Did I find out what my pupils can do (their **positive achievement**) or was the assessment experience essentially negative with low levels of success demonstrated by pupils?
- Are my assessments capable of showing individual **progress**, based on measurable **performance**, or do my assessments simply rank my pupils against each other?

Assessment is a field full of contradictions or tensions and it is helpful to think of it in this way.

> **Task 6.1.2**
>
> **WHY ASSESS?**
> Examine the three questions above.
> - Identify and discuss the contradictions they contain.
> - Select any one of these tensions or contradictions. Explore how it may be resolved.

> **Task 6.1.3**
>
> **A PUPIL'S VIEW OF ASSESSMENT**
> Spend a minute or two reading the cartoon (Figure 6.1.1) entitled 'Assessment: A view from the receiving end'. Make a list of some issues which you feel the cartoon raises. Compare these with a colleague or group of colleagues.
>   Discuss:
>
> - The kind of assessment information that perhaps Billy needs.
> - The measures the teacher could introduce to improve the effectiveness of her marking.

ASSESSMENT AND 'RAISING STANDARDS'

The only reason why teachers or the education service in general would wish to engage in the time-consuming business of assessment is because it improves learning. Apart from any legal requirement to do so that is.

   Is 'improving learning' the same thing as 'raising standards'? This is a difficult

Figure 6.1.1 This cartoon portrays the characteristics and some deficiencies of traditional 'marking'
Source: Lambert (1991a, p. 30). © Cambridge University Press 1991

Table 6.1.1 High stakes and low stakes assessment

A High stakes assessment	B Low stakes assessment

• The result or score **matters** because it can decide:
  – future educational pathways;
  – job opportunities.
• The result also matters because it contributes to the:
  – school's overall score;
  – school's league table position.
• The result is **public**. It has a high stake attached to it.
	• The result or score **in itself**, has little effect on future groupings, opportunities, etc.
	• The result is understood for what it is – an aggregate score which in itself says little about how it was achieved.
	• Individual performances need analysing.
	• The result and the analysis is **private** between the teacher and student.

question because it depends on what we mean by these two categories. However, for the sake of argument, we assume that they are practically the same. The question now is **how** assessment improves learning or raises standards. There are different views on this claim.

As a result of your own experience, you may have realised that educational assessment usually has to serve more than one purpose at the same time. Furthermore, these purposes are often contradictory. All progress may ultimately be concerned with 'raising standards' but purposes differ significantly on the basis of beliefs concerning how this progress can be achieved. This becomes problematic when, in any assessment **system**, one set of assumptions dominates at the expense of another; the assessment system can become unbalanced which may, in turn, lead to distorted learning.

For example, Table 6.1.1 sets out the features of two broad categories of assessment which can be associated with quite different and opposing views on how assessment can 'raise standards'.

In the context of 'raising standards' the belief underlying high stakes assessment is that competition to raise scores is the motivation to spur higher achievement. In low stakes assessment, it is the creative use with children of assessment information and evidence in supporting future learning that raises the standard of achievement.

The notion of 'standards' is important and is returned to on a number of occasions in this unit but especially in the discussion of criteria in the section on applying and using criteria and Task 6.1.8.

Task 6.1.4

ASSESSMENT AND THE NATIONAL CURRICULUM

The National Curriculum and its assessment arrangements were introduced under the 1988 Education Reform Act. It can be seen as part of the government's policy to raise educational standards. Elements of the reform proved to be and have remained controversial; this is discussed further in Unit 7.3.

Read the two extracts (see Figure 6.1.2) which appeared at the time.

1 To what form of assessment do the writers appear to be objecting?
2 What is the basis of their objection?
3 Why is the notion of 'standards' controversial?

The Growth of the Assessment Industry

... The exponential growth of the assessment industry must be questioned, despite its seeming inevitability ... This diversion of energy and resources from the classroom can be justified only if student attainment improves.

Unfortunately ... it is technically impossible to show that education is better or worse from one year to another ...

... A 'standard' is an artificial construction ... Nothing more is measured than variation around a norm on a particular test or aggregation of tests ...

... The ultimate, and circular logic of the scheme is that the tests, at 7, 11, 14 and 16, will improve students' work and simultaneously generate the data to prove the 1988 Act a success.

Bernard Barker in *The Independent*,
5 January 1989

'Tests or Jests'

... Built into this cornucopia of quizzes are two assumptions which do not bear too close an inspection. The first is that a huge diet of tests will raise standards ...

... Like many other notions in education, the idea of asking children a few questions to see how much they have learned, or what they do or do not understand, is in itself relatively neutral. What is wrong with the present proposals is the principle of doing this at a ritualised national, rather than local level, with children as young as seven, the use of resulting scores for school league tables, and the belief that written tests based largely on short-term memory will in themselves truly measure and eventually raise standards.

Ted Wragg in *The Times Educational Supplement*, 15 January 1988

Figure 6.1.2 The assessment industry
Source: Lambert (1991b, p. 6)

FORMATIVE AND SUMMATIVE ASSESSMENT: THE NATIONAL ASSESSMENT SYSTEM

The fundamental tension revealed in the brief discussion on standards in the previous section is that between **formative** and **summative** assessment. This distinction goes to the heart of what we see are the main purposes of assessment in education. It may be helpful to think of these as the opposite poles on a continuum, as in Figure 6.1.3. Expressed in this way we can see that formative assessment is designed primarily to serve the needs of teachers supporting individual learners and is thus identified with **professional** purpose. Summative assessment can be associated more closely with **bureaucratic** purpose, serving the needs of the system as a whole, the administration and politicians (see, e.g. the section on assessment and raising standards).

Both purposes are important, of course and in reality the assessment **system** needs to

Assessment	
Formative	**Summative**
During course:	End of course:
• to diagnose learning needs	• to measure and report learning outcomes
• to describe progress in learning and identify future progress	• to enable comparisons to be made between children, class groups, schools
• can utilise the full range of assessment opportunities ranging from the formal to the informal.	• emphasis on formal methods which are efficient and reliable.

Figure 6.1.3 Characteristics of 'formative' and 'summative' assessment

serve both. It was the attempt to bridge this divide, by means of a combination of externally devised Standard Assessment Tasks or 'SATs' and internal 'Teacher Assessment', which made national curriculum assessment initially so difficult to implement. Different purposes were **combined** rather than **distinguished**, as this quote from the TGAT Report demonstrates:

> Some purpose may, however, be served by combining in various ways the findings of assessments designed primarily for a different purpose.
>
> (DES/WO, 1988, paragraph 25)

It was this lack of clarity which, in the opinion of some, led ultimately to the teachers' boycott of Standard Assessment Tasks in 1993 and to the Dearing Review of the National Curriculum completed in 1994. See Unit 7.3 for further information about the Dearing Review.

Task 6.1.5

CHARACTERISTICS OF FORMATIVE AND SUMMATIVE ASSESSMENT

Consider this list of the purposes of assessment and carry out the two exercises below. Assessment is to:

(a) motivate learners
(b) motivate teachers
(c) measure or control 'standards'
(d) check learning outcomes against teaching objectives
(e) create a rank order of students
(f) diagnose learning needs and learning difficulties
(g) find out and report what children know, understand and can do
(h) derive quantitative data on which to base comparisons of schools
(i) select students
(j) support children in their learning.

The list is not exhaustive and you may wish to add to it

1   Place each purpose into one of the two categories, 'formative' and 'summative'. The division is not necessarily clear cut and you may decide that some items belong to both categories.
2   In what ways could the distinction between formative and summative assessment be helpful to pupils? How could the distinction be made clear to young secondary school pupils?

Task 6.1.6

CRITERIA FOR ASSESSMENT: THE TGAT MODEL
Examine Figure 6.1.4, which shows the four fundamental criteria which guided the writing of the TGAT Report.

1   Examine the TGAT criteria and make sure you have an understanding of each of the four categories.
2   (a) Discuss an appropriate assessment strategy for each of the four categories.
    (b) Is it possible to identify a single assessment strategy which satisfies all four criteria?
3   When deciding how to assess pupils' learning, choices usually have to be made. The assessment strategy employed depends on what kind of information we want, for whom and for what purpose. In other words the assessment strategy needs to be fit for purpose.

Now read the letter written to the *Times Educational Supplement*, reproduced as Figure 6.1.5 (Gipps, 1991). This letter provides another insight into the assessment debate in the years following the Education Reform Act. It concerns the testing of reading SATs for 7 year olds.

Identify two or three general points made by the letter. Consider whether similar or parallel points can be made within your own subject area; discuss the issues with other student teachers with different subject specialisms.

Four fundamental criteria of the TGAT Report

Assessment should be:

- Formative   (supporting learning; planning next steps in learning)

- Diagnostic   (identification of learning difficulties)

- Summative   (systematic recording of attainment at 7, 11, 14 and 16 years old)

- Evaluative   (assessment scores to feed into the evaluation of schools and local authority performance – published league tables)

Figure 6.1.4 The guiding criteria for the national assessment system
Source: The Task Group on Assessment and Testing: A Report (DES/WO, 1988)

Reading SATs cannot be made to serve two purposes

In all the debate about reading standards and methods of teaching reading we seem to have lost sight of a few basic realities of assessment:

- Tests can only give us an approximate measure of children's attainment.
- No test is perfect.
- The old NS6 (*Guardian*, January 22) is so out of date in terms of its content (words) and style of task that pupils taking it now would find it a much harder test than children did in 1978, so scores would show a decline whatever had happened to their reading attainment.

Teaching to the test is not always bad – if all our seven-year-olds read the prescribed set of books (whether at home, because their parents bought them or at school) at least we would know they had had a good diet of basic children's literature. The task in the seven-year-old reading SAT is much more valid than traditional standardised reading tests.

There are rumblings that the SATs won't tell us whether reading standards are going up or down – because they will only give us gross indications of the percentage of children at levels 1, 2 and 3. This is true. And remember that the levels are supposed to cover two years so any change in standards would have to be pretty big to be noticed. But equally significant is the effect of the choice of texts: the more choice there is, the less comparability there is among scores. By having a choice – which is one factor which lends the SAT assessment its validity – we lose on reliability.

So hundreds of thousands of pounds have been spent on a national assessment programme which should be of great help to teachers in their formative assessment of children but which won't do what the Government really wants it to do: tell us about standards.

The moral of the story is that you can't have one test that serves two purposes. Measuring national standards requires:

- precise measures in order to show the fairly small shifts in performance that there are only ever likely to be;
- tests which do not date (difficult);
- full-standardised procedures (not particularly suitable for seven-year-olds) or widespread moderation of less standardised tasks (time consuming);

but, you do not need to test every child.

Perhaps the Department of Education and Science had better revive the Assessment of Performance Unit surveys – which did have a reading assessment which was valid and also standardised – and extend them down to the seven-year-old age group.

Dr CAROLINE V GIPPS
Institute of Education and British Education Research Association
University of London

Note: The context of this letter is the early attempts to implement Standard Assessment Tasks (SATs) in accordance with the TGAT recommendations *and* widely reported concern over supposed falling standards of reading (as measured by a particular commercial test available since 1978).

Figure 6.1.5 Letter to the *Times Educational Supplement*
Source: Gipps (1991)

THE NATIONAL CURRICULUM ASSESSMENT SYSTEM

The TGAT proposals attempted to describe an overall assessment strategy. Each National Curriculum subject was to be delineated by a number of **Attainment Targets** divided into **ten levels**; see Figure 6.1.6. The national assessment system, serving the range of purposes as expressed in Figure 6.1.4, was to consist of:

Teacher Assessment; continuous, comprehensive assessment of each student, devised and administered by teachers using a range of methods from the informal (e.g. conversations with pupils) to the formal (e.g. short tests).

Standard Assessment Tasks ('SATs'); a variety of centrally produced tests, activities and observations to indicate level of attainment. They were to be administered by teachers in accordance with instructions laid down by the testing agency, a government organisation.

Moderation; a process by which the results of Teacher Assessment and SATs could be combined – the key, according to the TGAT Report, to producing national standards.

Those involved directly with the TGAT group have argued that this system was never given a chance to work (see for example Black, 1993). It is true that Teacher Assessment was not, initially, given adequate support by the government and moderation (a very expensive activity because it involves taking teachers away from their classes so that they can talk to each other) was never seriously contemplated for the whole education system.

Others have argued that the system simply was not clearly enough articulated. Specifically, that the proposal that the different purposes of assessment could be served by a single system was a fundamental flaw. However, in 1993 the government was forced to review the system with the onset of the teachers' boycott of SATs. After wide consultation, Sir Ron Dearing presented a report to the government at the end of 1993, which was immediately accepted. It recommended retention of the ten level scale for most subjects in a simpler and more manageable form. Some subjects, e.g. Physical Education, do not have levels. This change was to be achieved by a respecification of the National Curriculum subjects into fewer Attainment Targets (ATs) and the replacement of the 'Statements of Attainment' (SOA), which purported to define the levels, with more holistic 'level descriptions'. In addition, the Dearing Review tried to clarify and separate the main purpose of assessment; and the profile of **Teacher Assessment** was raised with a restatement of the importance of teachers' professional judgement in making assessments.

However, Teacher Assessment information is still required for summative **as well as** formative purposes and so the tension within the system remains. One issue, which the Dearing Review fully acknowledged, is the practical difficulty of an 'age-free' scale; that is, a level 4, say, is the 'same' whether for a bright 7 year old or for a low attaining 14 year old. It is difficult to see how this can be the case in some subjects in which twice the life experience must count for something!

The problem of levels, plus the other issues we have discussed, is important for you to keep under review when the National Curriculum is revised.

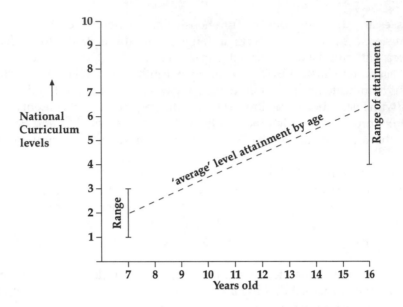

Figure 6.1.6 The 'TGAT Graph' against which the attainment of all pupils in National Curriculum subjects (England and Wales) was to be calibrated
Note that the dashed line is not showing the progress expected from individual students; it does show that the range of attainment expected in a cohort of students is expected to increase with age. The system of level attainment was retained after the Dearing Report (1994) although it now effectively terminates at 14 years and uses a scale of 1–8; the GCSE is the main assessment route for pupils of 14–16 years.

RELIABILITY AND VALIDITY

The letter in Figure 6.1.5 is concerned with the difficulty in reconciling the different purposes of assessment within one assessment system. In expressing this concern the author introduced two important concepts, namely **reliability** and **validity**, both of which are closely related to the notion of **fitness for purpose**. For any teacher involved in the assessment of pupils' work and specifically how they should undertake this, these concepts become key elements for guiding practice. These terms are explained in Table 6.1.2.

Just as the question of purpose in assessment is the source of considerable tension, validity and reliability are requirements which usually **pull in opposite directions**. In other words, if validity is maximised, it is often at the expense of reliability and **vice versa**, as Figure 6.1.7 suggests.

This figure illustrates another tension which can only be resolved by teachers exercising professional judgement. What guides this judgement is the main purpose they attach to the particular assessment; in other words, what is the assessment for?

Table 6.1.2 The key elements for any assessment strategy

Definitions:

Fitness for purpose: Assessment can be used for a range of purposes. Choices need to be made in order to fit an appropriate assessment strategy to the purpose to which the assessment is to be put.

Validity: The assessment strategy chosen should have validity. This means we should have confidence that it is assessing what we intend it to assess. To maximise validity the assessment should closely resemble the pupils' learning experience both in terms of content and process.

Reliability: The assessment strategy chosen should also be reliable. This means that all external variables are minimised so that we have confidence that our assessments are comparable. **Standardised** tests are designed to reduce all possible sources of variance – most importantly, the conditions in which the test takes place and the different interpretations or judgements applied by the marker or rater.

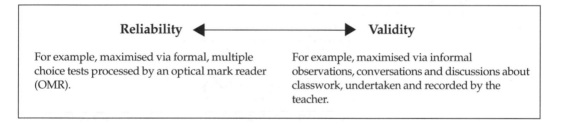

Reliability ◄——————► **Validity**

For example, maximised via formal, multiple choice tests processed by an optical mark reader (OMR).

For example, maximised via informal observations, conversations and discussions about classwork, undertaken and recorded by the teacher.

Figure 6.1.7   Reliability and validity pull in opposite directions

> **Task 6.1.7**
>
> **LEARNING ACTIVITIES AS ASSESSMENT OPPORTUNITIES**
> 1 Conduct a brainstorm of the types of learning activities which take place over, say, your school experience or over a school year. You may wish to compile lists under these headings:
>
>   Oral   Writing activities   Graphic activities   Other
>
>   If you find it difficult to get started, Table 6.1.3 may help you.
> 2 Examine your lists. How many of the learning activities on your list could also be thought of as potential assessment opportunities?

Table 6.1.3 **Learning activities presenting potential evidence on which to base assessment**

Oral evidence	Written evidence	Graphic evidence	Products
questioning	questionnaires	diagrams	models
listening	diaries	sketches	artefacts
discussing	reports	drawings	games
presentations	essays	graphs	photographs
interviews	notes	printouts	
debates	stories	overlays	
audio recording	newspaper articles		
video recording	scripts		
role play	short answers to questions		
simulation	lists		
	poems		
	descriptions		

Consider:

- Which of these are produced frequently in your classrooms?
  Which are produced infrequently?
  Why does this difference occur?
- Are any of the above underused in your classrooms?
- Can you add to this list?

INTEGRATING ASSESSMENT WITH THE CURRICULUM

This way of thinking about assessment, linking 'learning activities' with 'assessment opportunities', can be referred to as **curriculum-integrated assessment**. It maximises validity and places value on a greater range of activities than traditional tests or examinations. This is one reason why 'coursework' (introduced in the mid-1980s with GCSE) became popular with teachers, despite the fact that it places additional demands on both pupils and teachers.

It is perhaps ironic that in the early 1990s the government introduced strict limits on coursework in both GCSE and A level examinations and remains convinced of the need to introduce simple pencil and paper tests for the National Curriculum core subjects at Key Stage 3. Such a policy is much cheaper than a fully 'curriculum-integrated' one but the government's concern was also the need for **reliable** assessment data for the purposes of **league tables** and such like. However, at the same time there was a lively interest being shown by educators from the United States of America in those very aspects of assessment the British government wished to curtail. Widespread agreement has emerged in the USA about how short, standardised tests have resulted in 'measurement driven instruction' which has done nothing to raise levels of achievement because the emphasis falls on coaching for tests, by contrast with broader notions of teaching and learning. Many states are now trying to develop assessment strategies which

> use terms such as 'authentic', 'direct' and 'performance' assessment to convey the idea that assessments must capture real learning activities if they are to avoid distorting instruction

(Shepard, L.A., quoted in Black, 1993)

USING CRITERIA

Basing the assessment of children's attainments – and progress – on explicit **criteria** represents a fundamental shift in education practice over the last decade or so. The next task should give you practice in working to given criteria and should help reveal the significance of using criteria in practice.

Task 6.1.8	**APPLYING CRITERIA** At least six people are required for this exercise.

Awarding damages: compensation levels*

1 Participants in pairs or small groups need to examine all the information on pages 299–300 'Using criteria: compensation levels'. A recording sheet is provided (Figure 6.1.8).
2 Select one person to be the convenor of the exercise who should record the judgements of each pair or small group on a copy of the blank recording sheet (Figure 6.1.9).
3 The *whole group* should now compare:
   (a) the rank order of size of damages decided by each pair or small group;
   (b) the absolute size of the damages awarded.
   An exemplar is shown in Figure 6.1.10.
4 The whole group should discuss a small number of generalisations which they feel they can support on the basis of this exercise. For example,
   • Deciding on rank orders is relatively straightforward and uncontroversial.
   • Assigning individual value is more difficult and can lead to wide disagreement.
   • Using criteria assists in the process of assigning value.
   • Discussing criteria usually results in agreement about their meaning and application.

*The author acknowledges Alison Wolfe at the Institute of Education, University of London, who originated the materials on which this exercise is based.

Record your decisions here.

Rank	Case (A–F)	Scale of award

Figure 6.1.8 Record sheet for use with Task 6.1.8

Rank	Group 1	Group 2	Group 3	Group 4	Group 5	Group 6	Group 7	Group 8
1								
2								
3								
4								
5								
6								
Awards								
1								
2								
3								
4								
5								
6								

Figure 6.1.9 Compensation levels: blank recording sheet for use with Task 6.1.8

Rank	Group 1	Group 2	Group 3	Group 4	Group 5	Group 6	Group 7	Group 8
1	A	F	D	D	A	D	D	D
2	D	E	C	A	D	C	A	C
3	B	A	A	C	C	A	B	A
4	C	C	B	B	B	B	C	E
5	E	D	F	E	E	F	F	B
6	F	B	E	F	F	E	E	F
Awards								
1	100,000	30,000	40,000	80,000	150,000	100,000	100,000	100,000
2	60,000	25,000	200,000	500,000	100,000	100,000		100,000
3	40,000	20,000	150,000	50,000	75,000	80,000	75,000	75,000
4	40,000	20,000	100,000	30,000	35,000	60,000		40,000
5	6,000	15,000	100,000	30,000	10,000	20,000	35,000	16,000
6	4,000	8,000	40,000	30,000	6,000	10,000		15,000

Figure 6.1.10 Exemplar: a completed recording sheet for Task 6.1.8 (awards in £)

Using criteria: compensation levels

1 Recently there has been public concern abut the low level of damages that are awarded by the courts to accident victims. This concern relates to damages for pain, suffering and loss of quality of life ('general damages'). It does NOT concern damages for past or present loss of earnings or for the cost of disability, aids or for the conversion of a dwelling for someone crippled or for nursing care. These items are called 'special damages' and their cost can normally be calculated empirically.

2 Sums awarded as general damages are necessarily arbitrary figures. The courts are guided in their awards by previous cases. Because the sums are based on legal precedent the figures do not always reflect the public's view of the appropriate sum to compensate someone for the pain and suffering endured through loss of a leg, an eye or a relative. Your views are sought on the level of general damages.

3 Below are listed six cases on which courts have been asked to decide the appropriate compensation. You should now consider what if any sum is appropriate in each of these cases. In deciding a sum please remember that you are ONLY concerned with monetary compensation for pain, suffering and the loss of quality of life. You should award one single figure for each case.

Loss of an eye

Case A   Boy aged 9 at date of injury. Left eye wounded and had to be removed. Replaced with an artificial eye, which caused cosmetic disfiguration. The socket remained painful especially in the mornings. He suffered severe emotional upset and educational retardation. As a result of teasing by fellow pupils he regularly played truant from school. He had taken comfort in eating, which resulted in him being grossly overweight and further increased his difficulties at school. He became increasingly difficult to manage at home and eventually it was decided to send him to a special school for maladjusted children. Recently his behaviour has improved and he has started to come to terms with his disability, but he still attends a special school.

Case B   A woman aged 53 was injured in a car accident. Her right eye was injured and part of the iris was destroyed. Although the eye was operated upon at once, a cataract developed which had to be removed by a subsequent operation. As a result of the accident the pupil in the right eye was missing and the eye had an outward squint of 20 degrees. The plaintiff also had a bad cut from her nose across the right upper eyelid which caused permanent scarring.

   As a result of her injuries the plaintiff's sight was permanently affected. She had good sight in her left eye but her right eye was useless. Due to squint the plaintiff could not tolerate a contact lens which would have given the eye a very limited amount of useful vision. The permanent visual function of the right eye without a contact lens was assessed at 30% of normal functions. Because of the restriction of part of the iris and the absence of the pupil more light than was natural was admitted to the right eye and this caused such discomfort that the victim had to wear dark glasses at all times except in bed. The deficiency in the right eye meant that the left eye became tired. Lack of full use of both eyes impeded the victim from playing tennis which she had formerly enjoyed and caused difficulty with her housework.

Loss of limb

Case C   The victim was a 64-year-old milkman who was injured when a car hit his moped. His right leg was amputated at the mid-thigh. The injury altered his whole life with regard to his occupation, mobility and leisure activity. He had difficulty getting in and out of the bath. He occasionally suffered from phantom limb pains. When the stump felt stiff he could not lie on his right side. He was depressed. It took him fifty minutes each day to put on the artificial leg. When it was well healed there was a tendency for the bone to project where the muscles did not fully cover the bone. In effect every conceivable activity in his daily life was affected by the amputation. His lifespan had not been reduced.

Case D   A man aged 23 was injured when an iron gate fell on him injuring his left leg which had to be amputated below the knee. He suffered weakness in the right foot and a 50% loss of sexual functions. He could walk without a stick but could not resume his pre-accident work or take part in outdoor activities. The loss of sexual function was very serious. His chances of marriage were slender and he would never be able to have a family.

Case E   An 18-year-old man was injured in an accident. He was right handed, the accident was to his left and his middle, ring and little fingers were dismembered. He was left with a significant reduction in grip, was unable to lift heavy weights and his ability to type was impaired. The stumps of the fingers were tender especially in cold weather and occasionally he was embarrassed by the appearance of his hand. His pre-accident hobbies of cricket, rowing and horse riding were adversely affected.

Case F   A 32-year-old right-handed man was injured. His right index finger was amputated and his right ring finger was injured. He was left with some scarring and sensory loss of tip of the ring finger. He had severely limited movement of the joints of the middle and index finger and severe impediment of gripping objects and in particular of handling small objects. He was a well-motivated man who had adapted well to his disability.

ASSESSMENT CRITERIA AND STANDARDS

1   One outcome of Task 6.1.8 should be to realise that in assigning values we are making judgements. This is a similar process to applying 'standards' in educational assessment. In assigning a mark or a level to pupil's work we are giving it a certain value. This is ultimately a matter for professional judgement as no two pieces of work

are exactly the same. Using criteria helps the process as criteria can guide our judgements, but no criteria can be all-inclusive, exactly matching the pupil's work we are assessing.

2 The previous point leads us to consider the potential danger of any criterion-referenced assessment system: the tendency to define criteria on an ever increasing level of detail in the understandable desire to make the assessment process reliable. This is a 'holy grail', a trap into which, initially, many National Curriculum subjects fell. The result was that primary teachers especially found themselves chasing literally hundreds of criteria (in the form 'Statements of Attainments') in order to assess the National Curriculum progress of each pupil in their care.

3 Carrying out Task 6.1.8 can help you see that 'standards' in education are created by those who have the responsibility of applying them: that is, teachers. 'Standards', in this sense, cannot be imposed by the government or by any other external agency. The 1994 Review of the National Curriculum (Dearing, 1994) demonstrated that for the National Curriculum and assessment system to work several of the subject Orders needed 'simplification' with less emphasis on prescribing, point by point, what should be taught and learned (and assessed) and more emphasis on guiding teacher judgement by way of 'best-fit' **level descriptions**. In the assessment of geography, for example, 183 Statements of Attainment were replaced by just eight level descriptions.

These level descriptions, together with **exemplars** of pupils' work, allow teachers to create for themselves a clearer picture of what constitutes success and progress in geography. Draft new National Curriculum guidelines for some subjects were published at the end of 1994, with the expectation that no further changes would occur in the next five years, the 'Dearing moratorium', which has been realised.

Task 6.1.9	AN ASSESSMENT TASK

The data in Figure 6.1.11 show three ways in which 11-year-old pupils could be tested on their ability to read correctly information presented in the form of a pie chart. The criterion being measured may be stated as:

the ability to read correctly information presented in the form of a pie chart

The percentage figure beneath each case is the success ratio, in percentages, when groups of Year 7 pupils were given the questions stated. Look through the questions and responses and then discuss questions 1 to 3 below.

Assessment: pie chart

1 Why does the success ratio vary?
2 Is it possible to say which is the most appropriate question: A, B or C?
3 Is it possible to agree with other student teachers which is the most appropriate way to ask the question?

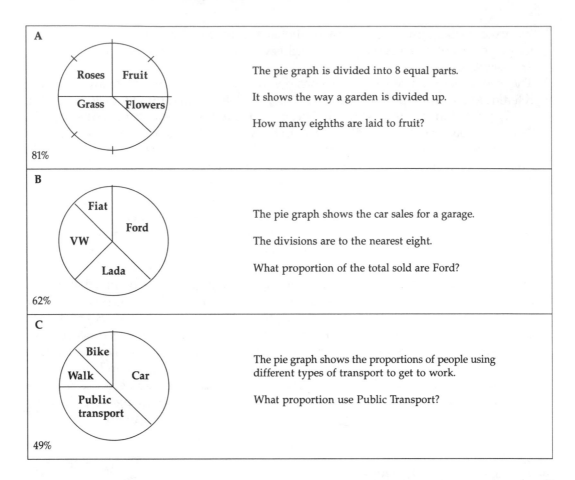

A

The pie graph is divided into 8 equal parts.

It shows the way a garden is divided up.

How many eighths are laid to fruit?

81%

B

The pie graph shows the car sales for a garage.

The divisions are to the nearest eight.

What proportion of the total sold are Ford?

62%

C

The pie graph shows the proportions of people using different types of transport to get to work.

What proportion use Public Transport?

49%

Figure 6.1.11 To test the ability of pupils to read a pie chart: Task 6.1.9

Summary and key points

This unit has guided you in examining a number of principles concerning the design and implementation of procedures to assess pupils' work. Without a grounding in such matters as

- the technical advantages and problems associated with criteria,
- the significance of reliability and validity in designing assessment strategies,
- the impact of assessment on teaching and learning,

teachers are ill-prepared to make principled judgements and decisions about developing their practice in this essential aspect of their work.

For Further Reading see the end of Unit 6.2.

6.2 ASSESSMENT AND IMPROVING THE QUALITY OF PUPILS' WORK

INTRODUCTION

Educational assessment is a broad field which incorporates a potentially conflicting range of purposes. These were explored in the previous unit. In the present unit we adopt a more focused approach to the question of how assessment can be used by teachers to improve the quality of pupils' work. This unit, therefore, identifies assessment as an essential professional task; the focus is on assessment in its formative role. Whenever educationalists think about the assessment of pupils' work fundamental questions arise such as what to assess, how to assess and when. Guiding our answers to these questions are principles whose origins lie in our response to yet other questions: Why are we assessing pupils? What purpose do our assessments serve? Such discussions dominated the previous unit (6.1). In this unit we focus on **formative assessment**.

The unit does not address the marking of written work or practical exercises or even tests set by a class teacher in a lesson. These issues are very subject specific. This unit does lay some groundwork for helping you think about what is involved in setting work and responding to it.

OBJECTIVES

By the end of this unit you should have:

- acquired perspectives on the issue of **what** to assess, **when** to do it and **how**;
- begun to build assessment into various levels of **planning** including lessons and schemes of work;
- discussed the question of **manageability** in day-to-day assessment practice including the storing and using of **evidence** and the production of meaningful records of achievement.

As you read through this unit refer to the competences and standards expected of NQTs related to assessment.

ASPECTS OF ACHIEVEMENT OR ELEMENTS OF LEARNING?

In this unit we have, for the sake of argument, assumed that our day-to-day assessments are formative and are undertaken within the context of improving the quality of pupils' work. Immediately, we come to the 'what to assess' question. Even when we have agreed that it is desirable to have clearly declared learning objectives for a topic or a series of lessons – expressed perhaps in terms of the 'elements of learning' (see Table 6.2.1) – the

Table 6.2.1 The elements of learning

KNOWLEDGE	knowing, recall
UNDERSTANDING	application
SKILLS	doing, techniques
VALUES	opinions, motivations

'what' question has still not necessarily been fully answered. It is partly through this realisation that the Inner London Education Authority (ILEA) Committee on the Curriculum and Organisation of Secondary Schools developed in 1984 a broader view of pupil achievement (see Table 6.2.2). In the words of the committee:

> We do not feel that we should be bound by psychologists' measures of achievement, such as tests of numerical or verbal attainment or by the popular measures of achievement, such as performance in the 16+ public examinations. By no means do we dismiss such definitions, but we believe it would be unwise to be restricted by them. Most people and certainly a large majority of those who submitted evidence to us, question the extent to which public examinations are capable of measuring the whole range of knowledge, skills and qualities which the secondary school seeks to develop in its pupils.
>
> (Hargreaves, 1984, p. 2)

These elements of learning are difficult to separate out completely. Take, for example, a role play in which pupils are exploring the decision making involved in the siting of a major new dam:

'**Values**', in terms of the different beliefs or attitudes displayed by the various 'players' in such an environmental dispute, can be seen as a component of:

> '**Understanding**': the conflict can only be understood by reference to different perspectives;
> '**Knowledge**': pupils need to be able to identify accurately the attitudes or ways of seeing the issue from the point of view of several protagonists;
> '**Skills**': to come to a knowledge and understanding the pupils need to be able to analyse categories and generalise from a range of information in printed, graphical and audio-visual formats, using information technology.

Nevertheless, the identification of the elements in terms of learning objectives helps focus teaching and learning. Teachers can assess the success of both the pupils and themselves by testing the learning outcomes. There is still legitimate controversy over how this is done; if, for example, our aim is to test 'understanding', how can we be sure we are not (merely?) testing recall?

The ILEA committee mentioned above devised an alternative way to categorise learning. Broader 'aspects of achievement', shown in Table 6.2.2, were advocated. These categories are analytical; literally, categories to help teachers analyse their work with pupils. In other words, we cannot assume that these categories are any more amenable to clear distinction for the purposes of practical pupil assessment in classrooms than the

Table 6.2.2 Aspects of achievement

'We offer these four aspects (of achievement) in order to clarify our own and our readers' thinking about achievement and we believe that such a scheme is appropriate to the educational aims of comprehensive schools and secondary school teachers.'
Aspect I That aspect most strongly represented in GCSE: written expression, capacity to retain propositional knowledge and select from it in order to answer questions. Examinations tend to emphasise knowledge more than skills; memory more than problem solving or investigation; writing more than other forms of communication; speed more than reflection; and individual more than group achievement.
Aspect II The capacity to interpret and apply knowledge. The emphasis here is practical rather than theoretical; oral rather than written; investigation and problem solving rather than recall. This aspect forms one part of public examinations, but which is rarely important. It is more time consuming and expensive to assess than Aspect I.
Aspect III Personal and social skills. The capacity to communicate with others face to face; to work co-operatively in the interests of a wider group; initiative, self-reliance and skills of leadership. This is not an element assessed directly by traditional public examinations, including the GCSE.
Aspect IV Motivation and commitment; the willingness to accept failure without destructive consequences; readiness to persevere and the self-confidence to learn despite the difficulty of the task.   This is often seen as a prerequisite of achievement rather than achievement in its own right and yet motivation can be seen as an achievement in most walks of life. It is in many ways the most important aspect as it can affect outcomes in the other three.

Source: Hargreaves (1984, p. 2)

clear distinction for the purposes of practical pupil assessment in classrooms than the 'elements of learning'. Nevertheless, these aspects can help us counter the tendency to overplay the achievements acknowledged by the public examination system at the expense of others of at least equal importance.

NORM-REFERENCED MARKING

Reacquaint yourself with the cartoon of Billy's story, Figure 6.1.1, Unit 6.1. Billy had no idea what was being assessed and neither, possibly, did the teacher other than in vague terms such as 'the quality of the work' or 'or how well the pupils have answered the questions'. Now read the extract in Task 6.2.1.

Task 6.2.1	A TEACHER'S VIEW OF MARKING WORK

Read the following passage. It is by an experienced teacher reflecting back on his practice at the beginning of his career. Then respond to the questions in the box below it.

We had very little training in assessment and marking. Everyone knew you had to do it but it was something like a 'black box' – difficult to penetrate and almost impossible to find anyone to give you advice.

So how did I mark? Well, I could draw from my experience as a pupil: marking seemed simply to be a process which resulted in a number out-of-ten accompanied sometimes with a comment. The number was important: it enabled you to compare your work but I remember feeling that the comment was potentially even more valuable. I resolved, therefore, to write lengthy comments on pupils' work before returning it to them. But the problem remained of what mark to give. In the end the solution (which survived for some years) was simple. I gave 7/10 for work I deemed to be satisfactory, 8 if it was better than satisfactory and 6 for deficient work. Occasionally I strayed beyond these limits for outstanding or particularly shoddy work but basically I had invented for myself a 3 level assessment system. It was easy to operate, gave me rough information about my pupils and seemed to satisfy their desire for me to give them marks.

Responding to the text:

1 List the strengths of the assessment strategy described by the teacher and in the accompanying commentary.
2 Write another list, this time of the weaknesses.
  You may wish to categorise your lists into two columns headed 'for the teacher' and 'for the pupil'.
3 Share your list with other student teachers. Agree a composite list among yourselves.
4 With other student teachers discuss an alternative to such a norm-referenced assessment strategy.
5 When you have identified your alternative assessment strategy, analyse it in a similar manner to that in 1 above. That is, audit your alternative in terms of strengths and weaknesses for both pupils and teachers.

Commentary

The extract used in Task 6.2.1 illustrates what is deficient about an assessment strategy which is ill-defined or unfocused. The marks were awarded on the basis of a norm which was implicit. Such **norm-referenced** assessment essentially sorts the pupils' work into three piles: 'average', 'below average' and 'above average'. The norm or yardstick may remain hidden – even from the teacher – until the work itself is received for marking; it is on the basis of the overall 'quality' of the work that the norm (7/10) is set. It is quite possible that different definitions of 'quality' are applied to different pupils and it is likely that the teacher's comments or descriptive assessment of the work addressed to the pupil reflect this.

Towards criterion-referenced assessment

Task 6.2.1 probably re-emphasised the powerful case supporting criteria-referenced assessment. The advantages of moving from an essentially norm-referenced assessment strategy to one guided by criteria lie principally in the act of formulating or agreeing the criteria. This helps the teacher to specify what she wants to achieve with a group of pupils and to articulate these expectations or targets to the pupils.

There are dangers, however. Simply defining 'the what' does not automatically ensure their successful completion. Dangers lie in the technical difficulties inherent with criteria referencing:

- Can all desirable learning be defined by a set of 'assessable' criteria?
- Once defined, a detailed set of criteria can render the assessment process overly complex.
- Does teaching (or learning) become distorted by those criteria which happen to be readily 'measured'?

Charles Dickens warned us about this in *Hard Times*:

> Now what I want is, Facts. Teach these boys and girls nothing but Facts. Facts alone are wanted in life. Plant nothing else and root out everything else. You can only form the minds of reasoning animals upon Facts: nothing else will ever be of any service to them. This is the principle on which I bring up these pupils. Stick to Facts, sir!

(Dickens, 1989, p. 1)

This passage is sometimes taken to show the perverting effect of 'teaching to the test', although the speaker attempts to make some educational justification in terms of what is considered to be the needs of the child!

Guided by attempts to analyse the 'elements of learning' and broader notions of 'achievement', the education service has evolved a more sophisticated view of learning than in Dickens' time. Educational assessment needs to reflect and support this development, to give it credence.

Task 6.2.2	ASSESSMENT AND DEPARTMENTAL POLICIES

ASSESSMENT AND DEPARTMENTAL POLICIES

Obtain a copy of the school's and several departments' assessment policies. Scrutinise each policy by using the following questions to get started. You may wish to generate further questions. For question 5 you have to ask teachers their opinions about the policy.

1 Is the policy written down?
2 Who was responsible for devising the policy?
3 Does the policy 'fit in' with a school-wide assessment policy?
4 Is the policy intelligible: is the purpose of pupil assessment clearly defined, as well as the detail of who does what, when and how?
5 Is the policy understood, agreed and used by departmental staff?
6 In what ways is pupil achievement defined as described in the policy?

DIAGNOSTIC ASSESSMENT

'Diagnosis' has a medical ring to it; your doctor diagnoses illness on the basis of evidence which she observes or has brought to her attention. The quality of the diagnosis depends very largely on the professional skills of the doctor: her medical knowledge and training, for example and the various aids (including past records) which can be brought into play. Above all it depends on how well 'tuned in' the doctor is to the patient in question.

There is a sense in which this analogy is useful to teachers. Think of the pupil who thinks of himself as 'no good at maths'. There is no doubt that some people have greater gifts in the field of 'logical–mathematical intelligence' (Gardner, 1983) than others, but the apparent finality of this self-judgement could be deeply worrying. At least it should be of some concern to the teacher, either simply to understand more fully (make a better diagnosis) or to correct (make better).

The origin of the pupil's negative self-image in maths could be relatively simple. **Consider the contrast** in the teacher's practice in the examples which follow. Both concern just one aspect of mathematics, namely the multiplication of fractions (e.g. 3/8 * 1/4 = ?), where * means multiply.

> **A** The pupil consistently fails to come to the correct solution in a long series of examples set in class and for homework.
>
> The teacher marks them conscientiously and accurately, makes some written comment to concentrate harder on the explanation – to 'try harder' – and records in her mark book a series of low marks. This builds a picture of low attainment in mathematics.
>
> **B** The pupil consistently fails to come to the correct solution in a long series of examples set in class and for homework.
>
> The teacher marks them conscientiously and accurately. The teacher decides to 'have a chat' with the pupil during the next lesson. The three minute conversation

reveals that the pupil had been using the wrong algorithm for the task. This is corrected (the 'penny drops'), the homework is repeated with much more success and the mark book records this improvement.

In the second example, the assessment has more than one facet. It consists of marking the work (a formal and sometimes quite impersonal activity), but also the informal, often snatched, conversation with the pupil. The aim of the conversation can be expressed very simply as a 'getting to know' activity. In large classes containing a wide range of individual differences this can be an exhausting business. But it is vital as it enables the teacher to step beyond the 'diagnosis' of this pupil being 'no good at maths', which is no more effective a statement than the medical diagnosis that the patient is ill.

Diagnostic assessment, then, is designed to find out how to help pupils in their learning. It is usually multifaceted as we have seen and takes a complex view of the human mind which resists the tendency to reduce the pupil's potential to a single dimension such as 'intelligence'. Intelligence tests are accurate predictors of a pupil's success **at school** but have a far less impressive track record in predicting performance later in life. Task 6.2.3 provides an opportunity to explore this notion a little further.

Task 6.2.3 WIDENING THE FOCUS OF ASSESSMENT

This is a discussion activity for a group of student teachers and is designed to encourage further exploration of the dangers of depending on too narrowly focused assessments in education.

Read this extract, then consider the questions on page 310:

Contrasting points of view

Two 11-year-old children are taking a test of 'intelligence'. They sit at their desks labouring over the meanings of different words, the interpretation of graphs and the solutions to arithmetic problems. They record their answers by filling in small circles on a single piece of paper. Later these completed answer sheets are scored objectively: the number of right answers is converted into a standardised score that compares the individual child with a population of a similar age.

The teachers of these children review the different scores. They notice that one of the children has performed at a superior level; on all sections of the test, she has answered more questions correctly than did her peers. In fact, her score is similar to that of a child three or four years older. The other child's performance is 'average' – his scores reflect those of other children his age.

A subtle change in expectations surrounds the review of these test scores. Teachers begin to expect the first child to do quite well during her formal schooling, whereas the second should have only moderate success. Indeed these predictions come true. In other words, the test taken by the 11 year olds serves as a reliable predictor of their later performance in school.

(Gardner, 1994)

Discuss with other student teachers the following questions:

1 Concentrate on the events in the third paragraph of the passage. Generate a number of hypotheses to explain what happens.
2 In what ways can this case study support the notion of the educational 'self-fulfilling prophecy'? (See Unit 3.2 on motivating pupils for further information about this.)
3 Suggest reasons why the IQ tests taken by these 11-year-old pupils fail to predict accurately performance and achievement later in life.
4 In what ways can you learn from this example within the context of your own subject teaching?

Bias and testing

It could be that one reason for the observation above concerning the deficiency of standard IQ tests is that they contain bias. They may be biased against recognising and rewarding certain kinds of 'intelligence'. They may also be biased against certain groups of the population such as those which, for some reason, are not well prepared to answer the questions. Take for example the following question from a reading test. Over half the pupils who had English as their second language did not select what was judged to be the correct response. Researchers who examined this case concluded that this was a significantly atypical performance by this group of pupils which could be explained by their lack of knowledge of the colloquialism 'jump' rather than their lack of reading ability. Unless the word 'jump' is known in its colloquial sense then **on** makes no more or less, sense than **by** or **at**.

Finally, the form of the questions which dominate the test can lead to biased results, as is the case with multiple choice questions which consistently seem to favour boys over girls.

An example from the reading test:

The man was very late and just managed to jump .... the bus as it was pulling away from the stop.
1 at
2 up
3 on
4 by

(from Hannon and McNally, 1986, quoted in Murphy, 1994, p. 287)

The potential which bias in assessment has in reinforcing assumptions or prejudices about, say, girls' achievement in science or mathematics is considerable. Bias can work in other ways too but it is difficult to draw firm conclusions as to what the root cause of the problem may be or what action teachers can or should take. For example, does the tendency for girls to outperform boys in GCSE coursework (even in subjects in which boys are ahead in the written papers) indicate something significant is being measured which improves the fairness and balance of the examination as a whole or does it demonstrate a bias based upon (as has been suggested) the coursework being a 'softer' option distorting the more 'objective' written examination performance?

Multifaceted diagnostic assessment of the kind being proposed in this section puts assessment on an individualistic basis in which individual differences can be recognised. This provides a strong foundation for reducing bias – at least most forms of **group** bias – in the assessment process.

Task 6.2.4 is an experiment in assessment which needs careful preparation and setting up. The aim of the experiment is to provide an activity and data to stimulate further discussion of a range of assessment issues introduced in earlier sections of this unit on 'aspects of achievement' and 'diagnostic learning'.

Task 6.2.4

A MARKING TASK: SIX OR MORE PEOPLE

To accomplish the following 'experiment' in marking the group needs to generate from a class of, say, KS4 pupils a set of twenty-five to thirty essays to mark. The essays should be handwritten by the pupils on lined paper but they should not put their real names on the scripts. In order to standardise the activity it would be helpful if the class were able to write the essay in class time, a 'timed essay'.

An essay title should be selected which enables your group (who may have varied subject specialisms) reasonably to pass judgement on the work. For example: 'Imagine a future world without cars.'

Form a group of six or more people and identify a convenor, a tutor perhaps, first to organise the generation of the work as described and secondly to orchestrate the following:

1 Divide the essays randomly into three sets of around eight to ten scripts per pile. Number the scripts A1, A2, . . ., A10; B1, B2, . . ., B10; C1, C2, . . ., C10. The numbers should be unobtrusive.

   Give one set of scripts each to three colleagues and give them five to ten minutes in which to award a mark to each script (marks out of 10). They are not to deface or write on the scripts in any way.

2 On photocopies of the numbered essays print names clearly on the top of the work. Set A is to have boys' names, set B girl' names and set C a mixture of the two chosen from the following lists:

Boys			Girls	
A1	David		B1	Marilyn
A2	Timothy		B2	Frances
A3	Christian		B3	Jasmine
A4	Josh		B4	Jessica
A5	Kevin		B5	Fathom
A6	Gary		B6	Rebecca
A7	Ahmed		B7	Christine
A8	Elvis		B8	Harriet

Table 6.2.3 Recording form for Task 6.2.4

(a) Numbered scripts   Mark recording sheet

script number	first marker	second marker	third marker	script number	first marker	second marker	third marker	script number	first marker	second marker	third marker
A1				B1				C1			
A2				B2				C2			
A3				B3				C3			
A4				B4				C4			
A5				B5				C5			
A6				B6				C6			
A7				B7				C7			
A8				B8				C8			
A9				B9				C9			
A10				B10				C10			

(b) Named scripts   Mark recording sheet

script number	Name	first marker	second marker	third marker	script number	Name	first marker	second marker	third marker	script number	Name	first marker	second marker	third marker
A1					B1					C1				
A2					B2					C2				
A3					B3					C3				
A4					B4					C4				
A5					B5					C5				
A6					B6					C6				
A7					B7					C7				
A8					B8					C8				
A9					B9					C9				
A10					B10					C10				

Assessing and recording pupils' work 313

| A9 | Graham | B9 | Tracy |
| A10 | Abdul | B10 | Sharon |

Give a set of scripts each to three other colleagues and give them ten to fifteen minutes in which to award a mark to each script (mark out of 10). They are not to write on the scripts.

3 Both activities under 1 and 2 can be repeated on a circus basis and the resulting marks recorded on a copy of Table 6.2.3 by the convenor. It is important that successive markers are not influenced by the judgements of others at this stage.

4 When complete, all participants should have a copy of Table 6.2.3. This provides data which may reveal patterns.

   Your discussion could focus upon these issues:

- how did you arrive at a mark?
- did you change your mind on some scripts under the influence of other scripts?
- what criteria emerged or did you decide upon to guide your marking?
- are there any apparent differences
  (1) between markers
  (2) between numbered scripts, Table 6.2.3(a) and named scripts, Table 6.2.3(b)?
- can you speculate on influences which may explain any variations you have identified?

5 Finally, in your groups or with other student teachers, list ways in which clearly expressed assessment objectives or expressions of what we are aiming to assess in pupils' work may:

- help teachers plan work;
- help pupils learn through supporting diagnostic assessment;
- reduce bias in assessment.

PLANNING WITH ASSESSMENT IN MIND

Read this short extract taken from a Report entitled *Learning to Succeed* :

> We commissioned a survey of the views of pupils in the early years of secondary school. It found that 44% of year 7 pupils and 45% of year 9 pupils indicated that they never talked individually to their class teachers about their work and 42% of year 7 pupils and 41% of year 9 pupils indicated that they never talked individually to other teachers about their work. Only 55% of year 7 pupils and 50% of year 9 pupils indicated that all or most of their teachers praised them when they did their work well. (National Commission on Education (1993), p. 205.)

In defence of this apparently shocking state of affairs, teachers might draw attention to the challenging management issues which may explain why pupils do not feel individually catered for. What seems certain is that this matter is not one that can safely be left to

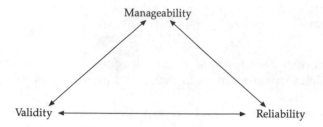

Figure 6.2.1 Assessment tensions?

chance. In other words, such are the management problems inherent in 'getting round' the whole class that this is an aspect of teachers' work which requires careful planning.

As the experience of National Curriculum assessment has shown us, particularly in the early 1990s and particularly in primary schools, it is sometimes difficult to avoid attempting to introduce an assessment system which, in our quest to satisfy all professional and bureaucratic requirements, becomes unwieldy or unworkable. This, of course, serves nobody's interests and least of all the pupils'. Thus **manageability** becomes another competing consideration which itself could be seen to be in tension with those other basic touchstones, reliability and validity, as Figure 6.2.1 illustrates. See Unit 6.1 (p. 294–5) for an explanation of these terms.

Task 6.2.5 is an invitation to explore further the management issues of **curriculum-integrated** and **individualised** formative assessment.

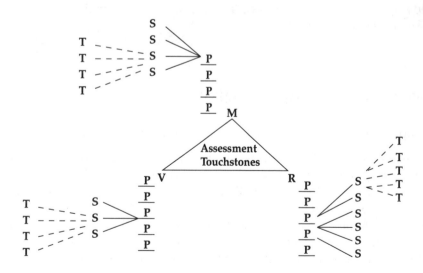

Figure 6.2.2 An effects-chain brainstorm
The terms P refer to primary statements; S top secondary statements; and T to tertiary statements; see Task 6.2.5

> **Task 6.2.5**
>
> **ASSESSMENT AND CLASSROOM PRACTICE**
>
> 1 On a large piece of paper or on a blackboard, reproduce the diagram shown in Figure 6.2.1. Brainstorm each word. Write down the 'key characteristics' of each word. These are primary statements, 'P'.
>
> 2 The intention now is to examine 'effects' and 'links'. You can do this in discussion with other student teachers, via one of two routes, (a) small group or (b) for a larger group.
>
> (a) Continue on your piece of paper (or on the blackboard). After discussion focusing upon effects and links write labels to the arrows on the diagram.
>
> (b) If you are part of a large group break into pairs or threes. Each pair select one of the 'primary statements' written onto your copy of Figure 6.2.1 under either 'validity' or 'reliability'.
>
> (1) Run a second mini-brainstorm, based on your chosen word. This should be focused by the following: The effects of this on classroom practice are. . . . We can refer to the outcomes of this brainstorm as 'secondary statements' (S).
>
> (2) Select one of your 'secondary statements'. Run a further mini-brainstorm on this statement. You should focus this by the following: The further effects of this on classroom practice are. . . . We can refer to these outcomes as 'tertiary statements' (T).
>
> (3) Come back as a large group. Pairs take turns to share their outcomes. You have created a structured brainstorm which we can refer to as an 'effects chain', as shown in Figure 6.2.2.

MANAGING ASSESSMENT

It is impossible to provide a rounded discussion of **your** brainstorm here. But hopefully you have identified some of the ways in which certain forms of assessment can result in significant manageability issues. This is not to say that such approaches to assessment are therefore unavailable to us. It is to say that the issues need to be understood and then acted upon. As in Figure 6.2.3, there are certainly some cases in which unnecessarily elaborate methods have been introduced and simplification is a solution. But there is, surely, an alternative to classroom chaos without compromising on the individual attention that pupils need from time to time.

PLANNING LESSONS

To find possible alternatives we need to **plan**.

As we plan lessons, schemes or units of work and plan for effective discipline and well-managed classrooms, we should also incorporate assessment considerations. Unless we plan with assessment in mind it tends to slip down the long list of day-to-day tasks which teachers face. At worst, it may simply become a 'bolt-on extra'.

Q. What do the rest of the class do when I'm assessing one person......?
A. .....it's obvious really!

Q. How does one carry out careful and structured observation?
A. .....!

Some National Curriculum questions explained!

Figure 6.2.3 Assessment!
Source: Balderstone, D. and Lambert, D. (1992) *Assessment Matters*, Sheffield: Geographical Association

Planning is a multistage process (see unit 2.2). Assessment considerations can be built in at each layer of planning. For example,

National Curriculum: National Curriculum subjects are set out within a national assessment framework. In this sense we have a curriculum which is assessment driven.

Scheme of work: ensure a balanced and valid assessment programme and steps to raise reliability levels over the Key Stage. Meetings with colleagues are essential.

Unit: identify a suitable range and variety of assessment opportunities providing an appropriate range of evidence.

Lesson: identify specific assessment opportunities; ensure that materials are available, pupils are prepared and appropriate circumstances prevail. It is helpful to think of lessons consisting of 'episodes': most lessons can contain at least one episode during which the class are 'getting on' and the teacher is available for individual (or small group) work.

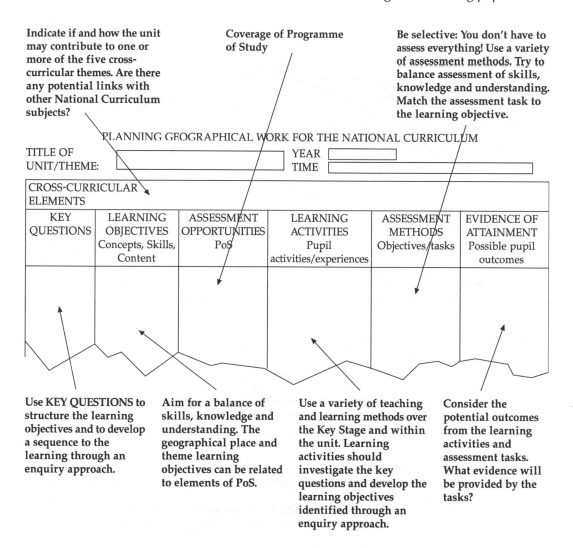

Indicate if and how the unit may contribute to one or more of the five cross-curricular themes. Are there any potential links with other National Curriculum subjects?

Coverage of Programme of Study

Be selective: You don't have to assess everything! Use a variety of assessment methods. Try to balance assessment of skills, knowledge and understanding. Match the assessment task to the learning objective.

PLANNING GEOGRAPHICAL WORK FOR THE NATIONAL CURRICULUM

TITLE OF UNIT/THEME: YEAR
  TIME

CROSS-CURRICULAR ELEMENTS

KEY QUESTIONS	LEARNING OBJECTIVES Concepts, Skills, Content	ASSESSMENT OPPORTUNITIES PoS	LEARNING ACTIVITIES Pupil activities/experiences	ASSESSMENT METHODS Objectives/tasks	EVIDENCE OF ATTAINMENT Possible pupil outcomes

Use KEY QUESTIONS to structure the learning objectives and to develop a sequence to the learning through an enquiry approach.

Aim for a balance of skills, knowledge and understanding. The geographical place and theme learning objectives can be related to elements of PoS.

Use a variety of teaching and learning methods over the Key Stage and within the unit. Learning activities should investigate the key questions and develop the learning objectives identified through an enquiry approach.

Consider the potential outcomes from the learning activities and assessment tasks. What evidence will be provided by the tasks?

Figure 6.2.4 A planning grid for a scheme of work
Source: Balderstone and Lambert, 1992, pp. 3–7.

It is very important to emphasise what is **not** being said here. In putting assessment at the heart of curriculum planning is **not** to have the assessment tail wagging the curriculum dog.

Without planning, however, **assessment opportunities** which give rise to a range of assessment methods and evidence are likely to be squandered. And, once the opportunities have been identified, the teacher's time 'moving around the room' can become highly focused. The teacher's time is controlled by **her** agenda, not by the *ad hoc* demands of the pupils.

Simple devices exist to ensure that the planning takes place as in Figure 6.2.4.

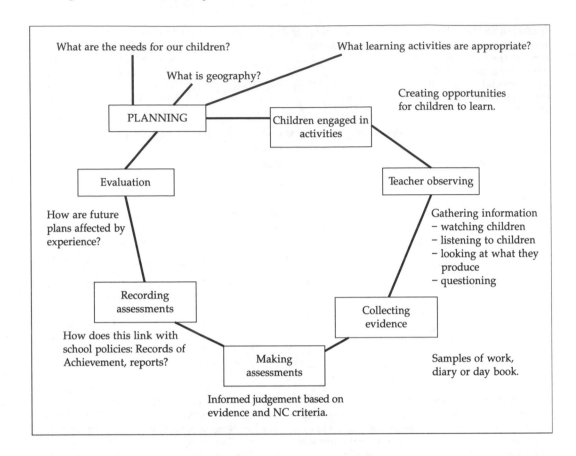

Figure 6.2.5 An ideal planning cycle
Source: Lambert (1991d). (Based upon ideas in *Teacher Assessment: Making it Work for the Primary School*, Association for Science Education)
Note: This is a professional process – implying much dialogue with colleagues within and between schools at all stages, particularly on questions such as 'What counts as evidence?' and 'What constitutes attainment?'

Using devices such as this helps the 'ideal' planning cycle come to fruition, such as that shown in Figure 6.2.5 and become part of our day-to-day professional lives.

Task 6.2.6	**PLANNING CYCLES: INDIVIDUAL OR GROUP TASK**

Examine the diagram of an ideal planning cycle in Figure 6.2.5.

1 Discuss how closely this cycle represents a school planning activity which you have either experienced directly or observed. You may prefer to begin this discussion in pairs before moving into the larger group.
2 Identify reasons for any divergence from the 'ideal' introduced into your discussion.
3 How important is it in your view that the 'ideal' planning cycle accurately reflects individual practice?

RECORDS OF ACHIEVEMENT AND PROFILING

Profiling is a widespread activity both in schools and the world of work. You are required to prepare a profile of your teaching performance as an element of your initial teacher education course.

Profiling is a **process** involving assessment and the recording of assessment outcomes. It is in essence a formative process. It often results in a summative **product** known as the profile or record of achievement. The 'philosophy' or ethos of records of achievement and profiling has been memorably expressed in Figure 6.2.6.

An example of a subject profile is given in Figure 6.2.7. However, it is likely that your school has its own version(s) which fits into its system of **reporting** which may or may not involve a form of Record of Achievement which goes beyond the legal minimal requirement (namely, reporting National Curriculum level by Attainment Target). All the contents of the units on assessment in this book are designed to contribute towards operating a profiling system for pupils in school. Task 6.2.7 is designed simply to prepare the ground in readiness for taking forward the assessment of pupils' work into the related realms of recording and reporting.

A Profile is

…a

Personal and
ositive record which reflects a
articular
hilosophy of assessment that is both
rocess and
roduct resulting in a

Portrait which serves as a
assport

It must not be only a caricature
a label
a silhouette
a shadow
a 'photograph' for the album

After G. Pearson, reprinted in P. Broadfoot (1987)
Introducing Profiling: a practical manual, Macmillan, p. 11

Figure 6.2.6 A profile
Source: Lambert (1990b)

Chesham High School

Subject Profile HISTORY

NAME: Lucy Ambrose   **FORM:** 3ii   **DATE:** Dec. 88

ASSESSMENT: USE OF EVIDENCE During the course of this term the above named pupil has shown the ability to make use of historical evidence at one of the following skill levels. Each level assumes mastery of the skills of the previous level or levels.

LEVEL ONE	LEVEL TWO	LEVEL THREE	LEVEL FOUR
Can point to basic similarities and contrasts in evidence; can offer a basic evaluation of the evidence without specific reference to the evidence presented;	Able to make a simple evaluation of the evidence by reference to information in the evidence;	Can point to gaps and bias in the evidence; able to evaluate the evidence by reference to more than one source;	Able to evaluate the evidence by cross-referencing sources and making conclusions which go beyond the evidence presented.

TEACHER ASSESSMENT

Academic skills (Assessment: top level 3)

This was a capable effort by Lucy. The last question let her down because she did not make precise enough reference to the source she was using. This is mostly a matter of technique which Lucy can easily improve on.

Personal and Social skills

Lucy is one of the liveliest and keenest contributors to class discussions. Sometimes her search for "a different angle" does lead her to go off the point but she remains confident of her views and is not easily discouraged.

signed: N. deMards.

PUPIL SELF - ASSESSMENT (Comment on your work, behaviour, contributions to the lessons, homework; suggest how you might improve your standard)

I think that I can work quite well when I try. I find it easy to say my finding but difficult to write well. I try to see things from a different angle but and sometimes it works, sometimes and it doesn't.

signed: Lucy Ambrose

Figure 6.2.7 A history subject profile
Source: Lambert (1990c)

Task 6.2.7

PRINCIPLES FOR RECORDING AND REPORTING
This activity is best carried out in groups

Stage 1 In pairs

The technique to be used is one of *brainstorming*.

Each member of the pair should write down privately any answers that occur to her or him. (You should not spend more than 2 minutes on each question.)

1 *Who* requires information concerning student progress and achievements?
2 *Why* do these respective groups or individuals require information?
3 *What* information do these different audiences require?
4 *How* might this information be passed?
5 *When* is the optimum time for this information to be passed?

Pairs should share their answers. Each pair draw up a composite list.

Stage 2

The whole group should return to each question in turn. Any unclear answers should be clarified.

Any answers which then do not have the agreement of the whole group should be removed.

Create a list of agreed answers to each question. Determine which answers should form part of a school policy for assessment, recording and reporting.

Stage 3 Implications

If the size of the whole group is large, arranging smaller subgroups may be advantageous for this final stage; subgroups will, of course, need to report back in some way.

Consider these questions:

1 What are the implications of the discussions in stages 1 and 2 for the departmental recording and reporting systems?
2 What specific changes to existing procedures ought to be made?
3 How does the (existing or proposed) departmental recording and reporting system link with whole-school arrangements?
4 Are there specific ways in which whole-school reporting arrangements may need to change?

Source: Lambert (1990d)

Summary and key points

In this unit we have linked assessment with planning and teaching. The unit has raised issues concerning the nature of assessment – what is it we wish to assess, why and how will it be recorded? The unit has emphasised the multidimensional nature of assessment and that identifying what to assess is problematic if promoting learning is a goal. The point was made that assessment is much easier to undertake if you simply wish to assess knowledge and recall, rather than for higher level skills such as analysis and synthesis. Teachers assess all the time, mostly for diagnostic purposes and, to be effective, assessment must be planned and built into lesson plans. The manner of reporting assessment is increasingly descriptive and supportive of pupil achievement, via profiles and Records of Achievement.

FURTHER READING

Black, P. and Wiliam, D. (1998) *Inside the Black Box: Raising Standards through Classroom Assessment*, London: King's College.

A short, twenty-one page, concise and pithy discussion about the role of teachers in assessment. One of the authors (PB) was the chair of the Task Group on Assessment and Testing (TGAT) which devised the system for assessment of pupils and reporting for the National Curriculum. This paper is important reading for all student teachers.

Brown, S. (1994) 'Assessment: a changing practice', in B. Moon and A. Shelton Mayes (eds) *Teaching and Learning in the Secondary School*, London: Routledge.

This is a short, clear overview of how the notion of educational assessment has developed in recent years; why certain practices have been questioned; and the nature of the major currents of innovation.

Daugherty, R. (1995) *National Curriculum Assessment: A Review of Policy 1987–1994*, London: The Falmer Press.

For those who want a clear, blow by blow account of how national curriculum assessment came to be as it is, from the first blueprint of the Task Group on Assessment and Testing to the Dearing review. The book also offers analysis and commentary and a firm platform from which to view future developments in National Curriculum assessment.

Gipps, C.V. (1995) *Beyond Testing: Towards a Theory of Educational Assessment*, London: The Falmer Press.

This is a very readable and teacher friendly overview of the contemporary assessment scene. The author describes the need to reconceptualise educational assessment in the 1990s in order to take into account the steady shift in emphasis from a 'testing and examinations culture to an assessment culture'.

Harlen, W., Gipps, C., Broadfoot, P. and Nuttall, D. (1994) 'Assessment and the improvement of education', in B. Moon and A. Shelton Mayes (eds) *Teaching and Learning in the Secondary School*, London: Routledge

This is a very accessible summary which was prepared originally for the National Commission On Education.

6.3 EXTERNAL ASSESSMENT AND EXAMINATIONS

INTRODUCTION

Previous units, 6.1 and 6.2, concentrated on the fundamentals of assessment, what it was for and the different purposes for which assessment could be used. In addition, Unit 6.2 discussed ways in which assessment is linked with day-to-day classroom teaching. In this unit we shift focus to the external examination system and how that has developed and relates to the National Curriculum.

There are two fundamentally different modes of assessment: the classroom mode which teachers are very familiar with in its various forms; and the external mode. This is what has been referred to as 'the two disciplines of educational assessment': classroom assessment and externally designed tests (Stiggins, 1992). In the United Kingdom, teachers in particular have often responded to the external element by substituting the external syllabus for the school curriculum (Harlen *et al.* 1992). This has placed enormous power and responsibility on those agencies in charge of the examinations and the associated syllabuses. This unit explores their role and that of other agencies within the system.

The question of the reliability of examinations is central to the discussion. Examinations perform a variety of functions, but in the end they depend for their credibility on user groups feeling confident that the tests achieve what they set out to achieve (Black, 1998). It has been found that two factors greatly affect the reliability of examinations. The greater the emphasis on testing subject knowledge, especially in a different context from that in which it was taught and learnt, and the greater the requirement to synthesise, analyse and evaluate information, then the greater is the unreliability of the examination (Brown, 1994).

Examination Boards, however, have developed structures which attempt to minimise the unreliability of examinations. This unit discusses such structures and then goes on to suggest techniques which might be applied to the teaching of a course which is externally examined.

Finally the unit looks at the vocational pathway, which is increasingly being introduced alongside the academic. This development in turn presents challenges and opportunities to teaching and assessment of which any teacher entering the profession must be aware.

OBJECTIVES

At the end of the unit you should:

- be aware of the functions of external assessment;
- understand some ways in which the reliability of an examination is maximised;
- become aware of the influence of external examination syllabuses on the school curriculum;
- have had practise in applying criteria to the marking of work;
- have been introduced to the assessment of vocational courses and their potential influence on traditional examination assessment methods.

You should refer also to the competences and standards related to the assessment of pupils expected of an NQT.

THE FUNCTIONS OF EXTERNAL ASSESSMENT

Pupil assessment can generally be classified as being formative or summative (see Unit 6.1). This section concentrates on summative assessment although it is virtually impossible to separate the two completely. Within the classroom there is often a strong sense of the formative being driven by the summative.

The three main functions of summative assessment are to:

- categorise candidates;
- certify candidates;
- encourage learning.

Categorising candidates

The most obvious function of summative assessment is to **categorise**. At its simplest this is the notion of pass or fail. It may also be **normative**, that is to say candidates are compared with each other's performance and a certain quota allowed through. So for any year group the condition might be arranged such that 80% of all those sitting the examination will pass and 20% will fail. For example, examinations for entry into some professions operate in this way in order to limit the supply of those allowed to practise, and, thus, to maintain salary levels.

In the case of the school population such a system might seem very unfair, since the quality of the candidates varies from year to year. Although not a justification of the practice, a large enough sample population approximates to a normal distribution of performance and so ensures relatively little difference each year in the quality of those passing.

Most external examinations go a great deal further in their categorisation function.

Pass or fail says very little about precise skills and so candidates are graded in a variety of ways, sometimes with such subtlety as to amaze an outside observer.

The grade performance for General Certificate in Education (GCSE), for example, lies between A* and G. Below that grade candidates are 'unclassified'. From its inception, however, it was recognised by user groups, including schools and colleges, that only grades A–C were **really** passes – a situation tacitly accepted following the introduction of differentiated papers. In effect, this situation is a return to the days prior to 1988 when GCE O levels existed for the most able and Certificate of Secondary Education (CSE) for almost all the remaining pupils. This situation left teachers with the unenviable task of deciding which pupils should sit which paper.

The National Curriculum had, in 1988, introduced a further complicating twist to the grading system by the development of a ten point scale at Key Stage 4. Nevertheless the 1994 review of the assessment of the National Curriculum stated:

> The GCSE is well established and understood. There has been too much change in recent years and I see no good reason to upset this understanding. I recommend, therefore, that the decision to maintain the GCSE grading for 1995 should . . . be confirmed for subsequent years.
>
> This raises the question of whether the ten-level scale is needed at all in Key Stage 4. It is confusing and unhelpful to have two grading systems in existence. On the other hand, if the scales were to be abandoned, then there would, at present, be no means of accrediting the achievement of pupils who have not obtained a Grade G at GCSE. Some, moreover, have argued that it is worth giving more thought to the mapping of equivalencies between National Curriculum levels and GCSE grades in order to achieve an objective definition of what GCSE grades actually mean in terms of specific pupil achievement.
>
> (Dearing, 1994, p. 70)

In 1998, the GCSE uses a grading system A*–G while at KS3 the National Curriculum assessment is reported using an eight-point scale, 1–8.

The final sentence of the quotation hints at the notion of **grade-related criteria**. That is to say, each grade must have quite specific outcomes or criteria, which candidates must meet in their examination responses in order for that grade to be awarded. Identifying such criteria is essential in order to move away from normative testing, because this enables each candidate to be assessed on an absolute rather than a relative scale.

In some tests, particularly related to vocational curricula, these criteria can be relatively easily defined. Thus the driving test specifies that a criterion for a successful hill start is that the vehicle does not roll backwards. This is a demonstrable outcome which the test inspector can see for herself.

The translation of grade-related criteria for the assessment of school subjects into a written examination is not so straightforward. Indeed, in the case of a driving test, the specification of the criterion for a Grade A hill start as opposed to, say, a Grade C hill start might well cause similar difficulties. When GCSEs were introduced to replace General Certificate in Education Ordinary Level examinations in 1987 it was felt that a wonderful opportunity presented itself to set grade-related criteria which would move examinations away from norm referencing. Subject working parties were established, not only at GCSE but also at GCE Advanced Level (A Level). However, they failed to achieve their objectives and were abandoned. With hindsight, this sobering experience might perhaps have been used to inform assessment work in the National Curriculum (refer to Unit 6.1 for further detail).

Task 6.3.1 below develops work already undertaken in Unit 6.1, but focuses more specifically on the difficulties and potential pitfalls of external tests designed to classify pupils.

Task 6.3.1

SETTING AND MARKING WORK AT KS4

Work with another student teacher from the same subject.

Most subjects at KS4 and A Level require candidates to write either essays or, more often, some form of extended prose. Set a piece of writing from your subject area and then each of you write an answer to it yourself in about twenty minutes. Now exchange your answers and discuss the factual content which you feel should be included in the responses. It is important to emphasise that this knowledge is baseline material and there is no advantage in having huge lists of factual points: three or four are usually quite sufficient.

Your next task is to decide how you are going to award marks. In other words, what are your criteria? Mark the work out of 20. Identify four 'levels' of five marks which demonstrate increasing attainment as you move to the next level. When this is done, mark each other's essay, making notes as you go along on a separate piece of paper. Swap your essays and your criteria and mark your own work. You now have two pieces of work, both of which have been marked twice.

Now answer the following:

1 How did the two sets of marks for the same piece of writing compare? Use your notes which you made as you went along to justify the marks given. Remember the key justification is whether the work matches the criteria.
2 Now multiply the difference in the marks by five and then relate the result to a situation where, at A Level for instance, it is not untypical for less than a 10% shift in marks to alter a grade.
3 To what extent did the marks differ because you were working with someone who would know what mark you had given them? What does this say about internally and externally marked work? Now agree marks. This is the process of moderation which all teacher-assessed work has to go through if it is used as part of an external examination.
4 Did the question allow or encourage a response which would match the criteria? If it didn't, how would you change the wording to make it more effective?
5 Were the marking criteria precise enough or did they contain words which were too vague? If they were too vague, how might they be tightened up?

Certifying candidates

Another function of assessment is the role of certifying pupils or **Certification**. It is connected with the categorising function, but subtly different. If you hold a certificate it is evidence that competence in particular skills has been achieved. If you hold a driving licence you have proof that, on the day of the test at least, you could demonstrate your ability to perform a hill start, carry out a three point turn, make an emergency stop and so on, regardless of whether or not the previous ten or twenty candidates could or could not do the same.

If you hold an A Level or GCSE certificate it says very little about the precise nature of the skills which are thus guaranteed (see Task 6.3.2). This was best demonstrated in the past by those university departments who saw holding an A Level in the subject which was to be studied there as almost a disadvantage, since the knowledge content was regarded as being at best too trivial or at worst positively misleading. Nevertheless, holding **other** A Levels remained a necessary condition for entry, which suggests that the certificates did and do indicate something about the skills of the people involved; for instance, that they could and can acquire, process and synthesise information under pressure. Somewhat ironically, the same phenomenon occurs after university. Many post-graduate job offers are made not on the basis of the degree subject studied; rather it is the holding of the degree itself, **any** degree (and perhaps from where it was obtained), which is the important factor in employment opportunities.

Encouraging learning

Few people would deny that tests and examinations act as an incentive to acquire knowledge. Whether that is the same as learning is debatable, but examinations undoubtedly focus the minds of pupil and teacher alike.

Examinations perform a monitoring role as well, in that it is possible to judge whether pupil performance is rising over time or not. The monitoring role presupposes that examinations maintain the same standard year by year. Most people have believed this to be the case; an A Level pass in 1960 is generally accepted as having identical currency to one in 1990. However, in the past few years this assumption has been called into question, as the quotations in Task 6.3.2 indicate.

Following the furore over the standards of the 1992 GCSE results, the government banned those syllabuses containing 100% coursework and introduced a 'Code of Practice' which all the Examination Boards are now required to follow. It imposes a 20% maximum on coursework. At the time of writing (1998) this limit is once again under review.

THE INSTITUTIONS INVOLVED IN EXTERNAL ASSESSMENT

The GCSE and GCE A Level examinations are administered and run by Examination Groups and Boards. The Examination Boards have existed for many years, generally linked to the older universities such as Oxford, Cambridge and London. Prior to 1998

Task 6.3.2	RISING STANDARDS?

Discuss with another student teacher the implications of the evidence presented below. You may wish to consider the effect of ever improving grades. What does it say about teachers, pupils, the Examination Boards and what is the role of government in all this? Try to debate the issue without adopting a party political stance.

Study the following evidence paying particular attention to the dates:
In the last year of O Levels (1987) fewer than 40% of candidates achieved A–C grades. *Source:* Wiltshire County Council (1988), *National Consortium for Examination Results.*

In 1993 52.4% of candidates achieved grades A–C of the GCSE. *Source:* DFE (1994), *Statistical Bulletin,* July.

In 1993 the percentage of candidates getting GCSE A grades increased from 12.5% to 12.7% over the previous year. *Source:* (ibid.)

'Record numbers take and pass GCSE examinations'
Record breaking GCSE results, which today sees most entrants achieving the equivalent of an O Level pass, have brought calls for the government to reconsider plans to limit marks for coursework.

(O'Leary, J., *The Times,* 27 August 1992, p. 1)

The changing proportions of children gaining five or more higher grade GCSE passes (grades A–C) in the period 1988–94 are shown below.

Year	1988	1989	1990	1991	1992	1993	1994
Proportion (%) of pupils gaining five or more GCSE passes (A–C)	30	–	34	37	38	41	43

Source: Gillborn and Gipps (1996, Figure 2.2)

they were responsible for Ordinary and Advanced Levels, whilst the Examinations **Groups** administered the Certificate of Secondary Education (CSE).

When O Levels and the CSEs were abolished and replaced by GCSEs, the Examinations Groups and the Boards combined. They already had very close links. So, for instance, the Southern Examining Group (SEG) became a part of the Associated Examining Board (AEB) and the Midland Examining Group (MEG) became a part of the University of Cambridge Local Examinations Syndicate (UCLES).

These amalgamations were painful for the organisations concerned. The importance placed by government on vocational qualifications led to further reorganisations following the review of the 14–19 curriculum (Dearing, 1996). In 1997, the University of London Examination Board (ULEAC) combined with the Business and Technician

Education Council (BTEC) to form a board (EdExcel Foundation) which set examinations for both academic and vocational routes to qualifications. The 'Royal Society of Arts' and 'City and Guilds' retained their role as awarding bodies for vocational courses.

Overseeing the work of the examination boards is the Qualifications and Curriculum Authority (QCA). This government quango was formed by the amalgamation in 1997 of the School Curriculum and Assessment Authority (SCAA) and the body responsible for vocational qualifications, the National Council for Vocational Qualifications (NCVQ). This merger provided one body which, in theory, might provide a coherent framework in which to develop the dual track to qualification – the academic (the GCSE and GCE) and vocational (GNVQ and NVQ). Similar bodies to QCA operate in Northern Ireland, Scotland and Wales (see *Qualifications Framework*, DFEE 1998 website on the Internet for up-to-date information).

In 1997, the joint academic and vocational body (QCA) published proposals for consultation for a new framework of qualifications called National Certificates and National Advanced Diplomas. Achievement is recognised at four levels: Advanced, Intermediate, Foundation and Entry. These four levels can be gained by achievements in academic, general vocational or vocational courses. For example, it is proposed that the National Award at Advanced Level can be gained by *either*

- a GCE AS levels (Advanced Subsidiary) or GCE A levels. The AS level award provides a foundation for A level and a useful exit point for those leaving an A level course. The AS level can be taken by students on GCE or GNVQ courses. For those students going on to full A level, the AS course contributes 40% of the A level marks. It was due to begin in September 1998;
- General National Vocational Qualifications (GNVQ) at Advanced Level;
- National vocational qualifications at level 3;

or

- a mixture of the above qualifications.

For further discussion on vocational qualifications see the section 'The vocational pathway' p. 000.

Examination syllabuses prepared by the boards have to be approved by the QCA and must contain a specified subject core laid down by the QCA. The GCSE core is the National Curriculum. At Advanced Level the specified core for a subject comprises 50% of the total examination, which gives examination boards freedom to experiment with the remaining 50% of the syllabus.

The QCA has identified some components of the testing procedure. Most importantly, at GCSE there is a 20% limit on coursework which applies to all subjects. Boards have, however, freedom to use different styles of testing, say by introducing oral examinations in addition to written ones.

The five-year period of stability introduced by Dearing in 1994 following his review of the National Curriculum is nearly at an end. By the year 2000 a new National Curriculum will be developed and the place of the subjects in that curriculum is to be re-examined. Your subject associations will be responding to this challenge and you should refer to your subject course notes or subject association publications for such details. You may wish to read Unit 7.2 on the *Aims of Education*, which discusses how a curriculum might respond once the aims, or purposes, are clearly defined.

THE PROCESSES INVOLVED IN EXTERNAL ASSESSMENT

The Examination Boards' experiences over many years have taught them the value of systems which as far as possible eliminate inconsistencies. They rely heavily on internal back-up support for the teams of teachers who set and mark the papers and this requires time, money and a clear commitment to excellence.

The entire examination process involves a number of key players. Firstly there is a Chief Examiner who sets the papers, devises the mark scheme and oversees the marking. She is also responsible for any appeals which may be lodged after the examination is sat.

Supporting the Chief Examiner is a Reviser who looks at the draft questions and offers advice and suggestions before they are sent to a committee. Like the Reviser, this committee also has a reviewing function, so, as far as possible, the final papers are fair, accessible to candidates and unambiguous. This process can take several weeks and is often subject to much negotiation on the form and content of questions. Increasingly, boards send papers to teachers who attempt to answer the questions set, again as a safeguard for candidates.

Following final approval by the committee the paper goes through the normal pro-cesses of publishing to eliminate any errors which may have evaded the scrutiny procedures. Inevitably, but fortunately very rarely, mistakes do still slip through and when this happens the Board may, after the examination has been sat, exclude a question from the final marking.

A day or so after the exam all the examiners have their marking 'standardised' to that of the Chief Examiner so that, in theory at least, they are clones of her. This process is designed to ensure reliability and any who fail to maintain consistency are removed and their scripts re-marked. The process of identifying poor or inconsistent markers is achieved through rigorous sampling.

'Borderlining' occurs after grade boundaries have been set. 'Borderlining' is the re-marking of papers whose mark is on the boundary between two grades. Again, even at this late stage, if inconsistencies are found, scripts are re-marked. Defining grade boundaries differs between Boards in that statistics plays either a greater or lesser role, but all Examination Boards rely on the professional judgement of committees comprising experienced subject specialists.

Finally, there is an appeals procedure where candidates who feel aggrieved can have their work re-marked. Candidates may also request a written report to identify areas of strengths and weaknesses. The same facility is given to schools and colleges, who can request feedback and advice about the performance of all candidates sitting at their Centre. All appeals attract a fee. Despite this fee, the number of appeals has risen recently, which has caused some concern since it suggests a reduction in public confidence in the examining system and especially in the reliability of the markers.

In the past, the entire examination process was shrouded in mystery and there were areas which perhaps the Boards had little to be proud of. However, procedures and practices have changed and are changing for the better and can only improve further as public accountability and competition increase.

TEACHING EXTERNALLY ASSESSED COURSES

If the weight of responsibility lies heavily on the shoulders of teachers in normal circumstances, how much heavier is that burden when it comes to teaching externally examined classes? In some ways it is an exciting challenge since the final examination results give some indication of performance which is theoretically free from subjectivity and therefore bias.

On the other hand, teaching towards public examination is a little like playing a team game where the rules are known in detail only by the referee and the line judges. In recent years the Examination Boards have become increasingly sensitive to accusations of this sort and so, for instance GCSE and A Level marking schemes are available to teachers for a nominal charge. Examination Boards provide INSET and related sessions when teachers can meet the Chief Examiner. Also, reports on the previous series of examinations, which are provided to all Centres that entered candidates, are now more informative and helpful rather than consisting of bland generalisations.

Of course many teachers become examiners so that they can learn the rules from the inside and anyone can apply to be an examiner after teaching the subject for two or three years or more. In fact obtaining such a post is a good idea for a number of reasons other than learning about how the system works. Firstly, the experience usually has a profound effect on what you teach and how you teach. For instance, it usually results in less time being spent accumulating and regurgitating 'facts'. Secondly, it provides a measure of standards against which you can judge your own pupils. Thirdly, it can provide a network of fellow subject specialists which can become very useful and broadening. Fourthly, it is possible to develop a 'mini-career' in assessment and rise through the ranks to become a Chief Examiner and set the papers themselves. There is also a career advantage in the broader sense, in that when applying for head of department posts such experience is usually counted very highly. Finally, there is the money, which, whilst being by no means generous, is usually enough to pay for a good summer holiday, which of course is especially needed as a result of all the extra work involved in the marking!

Becoming an examiner is a powerful INSET tool for personal development. A teacher writes in the following way in the context of A Level teaching:

> Teachers are inevitably specialists and one of their cherished ambitions is to produce a new generation of geographers or chemists who surpass them in their own subject. They transmit their interest and enthusiasm for their subject and prepare their pupils for working in a polytechnic or university. The teachers' excitement in their own subject is an important part of the A Level process. Much of the energy occurring in the A Level development goes on within subjects. The choice of a new syllabus can be the sign of a whole new area of educational provision bringing in new skills and relevance.

(al Qadhi, 1991, p. 23)

Other than becoming a marker, there are ways of deducing the rules of the examination game from available evidence. Examination 'law', so to speak, consists of two parts: statutory law (the syllabus) and case law (past papers). The older the syllabus the more important are past papers because the Chief Examiner keeps the subject up to date, as best she can within the constraints of the syllabus, by writing contemporary questions. This gives rise to what is called 'syllabus bend'; that is, the way the syllabus is translated into papers becomes less clear cut. This is a good reason for avoiding older

---

Task 6.3.3

EXPLOITING PAST PAPERS IN YOUR TEACHING

Contact the Examination Board used in your school and obtain a syllabus for your subject which is relevant to your pupils in the year they sit the examination. Copies of the syllabuses may also be available in school. At the same time purchase as many of the most recent past papers as you can afford, both the winter series as well as the summer series of papers if they are available.

Construct a chart similar to the one below for your particular subject. Write down the syllabus concept in the left-hand column and then enter the dates and the papers when each appeared in those on the right; a model using an economics syllabus is shown below.

CONCEPT	DATE				
	91	92	93	94	95
Opportunity cost	P1		P2	P1	P1
Market economies		P1		P2	
Command economies	P2				P1
Sole traders			P1		
Multinationals	P1			P2	P1

You may have to break down the syllabus into more detail than is supplied by the Examination Board and you need to spend some time on this part of the exercise. You may wish to seek advice from a subject teacher in the school. For instance, in the example above, an economics syllabus might say 'Forms of business organisation' and that has to be broken down into sole traders, partnerships and so on.

When the chart is completed you see a pattern emerging. Some topics invariably turn up in the examination, others do so less frequently. Some tend to be examined in a particular way, perhaps by short answer questions rather than by extended writing and so on. Most Chief Examiners have a chart similar to this one for their own purposes and while it is never a good idea to guess which areas of the syllabus are coming up in the next examination, it can help your teaching by indicating, for example, the particular weight a topic should be given.

syllabuses, unless of course you feel that the 'bend' is exactly the direction in which the syllabus should 'go'.

The Examination Board's syllabus is not a curriculum and it is dangerous practice to assume that it is when setting out to teach one. Syllabus developers are aware of this danger and so they invent ingenious designs to encourage teachers to be imaginative and creative in the way they deliver the material. For example, instead of writing the syllabus line by line, some are written in the shape of a wheel or a clock. Predictably and unfortunately, some teachers then simply start at 12 o'clock and work their way around!

When studying any syllabus another vital point is to recognise that the teacher's role is as much or more about imparting skills as it is knowledge. Many syllabuses are related to a taxonomy of educational objectives, such as that of Bloom (1956). Thus the way for pupils to succeed in their examinations is for them to reveal the higher level skills of analysis, synthesis and evaluation, rather than simply to regurgitate factual information; such high level skills are demanded particularly at Advanced Level. On the other hand, it would be wrong to assume that remembering facts is in any sense 'easy', especially when faced with eight or nine different subjects. (For further information, see Unit 5.2 on active learning.)

The important point to make is that classroom time is precious – some would argue far too precious to waste on mere facts! Textbooks are available to help with facts and the creative use of homework to help acquire the essential details often enhances lessons which follow. For further advice on preparing your pupils for examinations see Balderstone and King (1997).

THE VOCATIONAL PATHWAY

We turn now from the well-established academic pathways leading to a certification of A Level and GCSEs to a consideration of assessment of the vocational pathways.

In 1992 GNVQs were introduced into schools and colleges. Originally they were specified in levels, in the same way as National Vocational Qualifications (NVQs), but in 1993 the Secretary of State renamed the ones taught in the secondary and tertiary sectors as Foundation, Intermediate and Advanced. These corresponded to grades C–G and A–C at GCSE and A Level. The rationale of this move for government was to encourage parity of esteem between the semi-vocational route and the academic.

In his final report on the assessment of the National Curriculum, Dearing opened up the possibility of providing GNVQs alongside academic courses:

> A major new option for the medium term for Key Stage 4 is the GNVQ, which is currently being piloted pre-16 in a number of schools. The GNVQ is designed to offer courses which combine some general education with study of a broad vocational area. It is designed as a middle pathway between academic and occupational (NVQ) provision.
>
> (Dearing, 1994, p. 48)

Shortly after the review of the National Curriculum, Sir Ron Dearing was asked to review the 14–19 curriculum with a brief to identify pathways to further and higher education which might bring together the academic, general and vocational courses. His report (Dearing, 1996) included the following recommendations:

- calling Advanced GNVQs 'Applied A levels';
- introducing a new GCE A level in core skills;
- certification of core skills within the GCE and GCSE assessment;
- reducing the number of GCE A level syllabuses;
- making GCE A/S level part of GCE A level;
- creating National Certificates at each level so that 'mixing' can take place between GCE A levels, GNVQs and NVQs.

Meanwhile there are fourteen vocational areas on offer at GNVQ at Foundation, Intermediate and Advanced Levels, of which two are in the pilot stage, 'Land and Environment' and 'Performing Arts and Entertainment Industries'. For further details of current vocational courses, see DFEE website 'General National and Vocational Qualifications: a brief guide' (http://open.gov.uk/dfee/gnvq/gnvq.htm). For a more detailed discussion on the background and evolution of the merging vocational and academic pathways, see Lucas (1997).

The reason why GNVQs are discussed in this chapter is that the assessment is accompanied by an element of external testing. The assessment takes the form of multiple choice tests which occur several times per year and offer candidates the opportunity to resit if they are not successful. However, their role is quite different from that of GCSEs or A Levels. The background of vocational qualifications is such that its assessment is carried out by means of coursework related to criteria. The criteria for assessment are written in behavioural terms and thus the skills can be demonstrated to the examiner by the pupil. Nevertheless, multiple choice tests were imposed on GNVQs in order to offer quality assurance and counter similar criticisms of coursework which were aimed at GCSE.

The multiple choice tests themselves are designed to **confirm** knowledge rather than test it in the way conventional examinations do, but they have been highly controversial. Such tests carry a very high pass mark and they have not correlated well with the work that pupils have done in class.

In addition, the multiple choice tests themselves have been subject to criticism. They are run by the three **awarding bodies** – the Business and Technical Council (BTEC), the City and Guilds of London Institute (known as City and Guilds) and the Royal Society of Arts (RSA). Mainly because of time constraints but also, some would argue, as a result of inexperience of external testing, the checks and balances which operate within the traditional Examination Boards are not yet in place with the new awarding bodies.

Early critics of the GNVQ system identified another negative factor, namely the role of the National Council for Vocational Qualifications (NCVQ), which was the equivalent controlling body to SCAA. NCVQ appear to have a quite different relationship with the awarding bodies from that which SCAA have with the Examination Boards. The merger of NCVQ with SCAA to form the QCA may ameliorate these problems.

However, there are other problems of a structural kind which must be addressed and which require strategic decisions by NCVQ. For instance, there appears to be a glaring inconsistency between GNVQ courses, which are mainly teacher assessed through coursework with tests acting as confirmation of the underpinning knowledge and GCSE, and A Level courses, which are allowed only a 20% teacher-assessed coursework element. In addition, GNVQs are specified by outcomes, GCSE and A Levels by syllabuses; GNVQs emphasise process, GCSE and A Levels emphasise subject skills and so on.

In 1997, following the formation of QCA, and the formation of a new bigger examining board (EdExcel Foundation) to provide examinations for both vocational and academic courses, the government launched a consultation exercise on measures to improve standards across qualifications. Through the consultation process the government hoped to find ways to improve flexibility and breadth across the qualifications framework. This consultation exercise was due to be reported in the spring of 1998. There is a growing interest in the results of this consultation, feeding into the review of the National Curriculum. Of particular interest and importance are the core skills developed by GNVQ and it is likely in the future that all students studying post-16 will be expected to include an element of such work in their course. In addition, from 1997 onwards the traditional Examination Boards were allowed to set external tests for GNVQs, just as from 1996 the awarding bodies for the GNVQs were allowed to enter candidates for GCSE. The increased competition in an already crowded assessment market has major implications for the future development of both vocational and academic qualifications and may well be the cause of further change.

Summary and key points

Much criticism is aimed at summative assessment, but it is very often the vehicle – A Level examination papers, GNVQ tests, multiple choice tests and so on – rather than the principle of assessment itself which is the real target of the critics. Change is inevitable and the next few years are more likely to be ones of fluctuation than of consistency. To teachers this prospect offers the inevitable feelings of uncertainty and insecurity, but, more positively, also the potential for fresh challenges and new opportunities.

The key points of this unit are:

*   Public examinations are very largely about summative assessment, whose purpose is to grade or certify those examined; or to provide a means of controlling access to a next stage of education or entry to a profession.

*   The means by which grades are arrived at is 'traditionally' through a norm-referenced system; increasingly and under pressure from bodies awarding vocational qualifications, criterion-referenced systems of awarding grades are under discussion.

*   The National Curriculum, through its SATs, sought to develop criterion-referenced testing, but to date this goal has proved elusive. The link between grading and standards is not clear cut. It has proved notoriously difficult to show conclusively whether standards are rising or falling. In that context, the rise in the number of people gaining academic qualifications may be grounds for satisfaction and praise for teachers.

- The formation of a government body responsible for all qualifications (QCA) and the merger of BTEC and ULEAC to form a large examining body (EdExcel Foundation) serve to identify possible ways forward for the broadening of the qualifications pathway. The results of the consultation exercise by QCA on the future of National Certificates and National Advanced Diplomas are part of that movement.

- The preparation of your pupils for external examinations is an important part of your teaching skills. You should refer now to the knowledge and skills demanded by your course to meet the competences and standards required of a Qualified Teacher and review your progress.

FURTHER READING

Black, P. (1998) *Testing: Friend or Foe? Theory and practice of assessment and testing*, London: The Falmer Press.

Black, P. and Wiliam, D. (1998) *Inside the Black Box: Raising Standards through Classroom Assessment*, London: King's College.

A short, twenty-one page, concise and pithy, discussion about the role of teachers in assessment. Paul Black was the chair of the Task Group for Assessment and Testing (TGAT) for the National Curriculum. This book examines areas of contention involved with assessment, particularly with those associated with reform of assessment practices.

Brown, S. (1994) 'Assessment: a changing practice', in Moon, B. and Shelton Mayes, A. (1994) *Teaching and Learning in the Secondary School*, London: Routledge.

A short discussion about the ways in which assessment practice has changed and is undergoing further change. The factors that are driving that change are reviewed.

Dearing, R. (1996) *Review of 16–19 Qualifications: Issues for Consideration*, London SCAA.

A follow up from an earlier report of a similar title (HMSO, 1995). An important document setting out proposals for the development of broader course of study for pupils post 16.

Gipps, C. (1994) *Beyond Testing: Towards a Theory of Educational Assessment*, London: Falmer Press.

This book takes a challenging position in relation to the established assessment 'paradigm' which, it is argued, has damaging effects on education. This book provides a vision of what assessment might be and provides criteria by which it may be judged. A readable and accessible text.

Lucas, N. (1997) 'The changing sixth form', in Capel, S., Leask, M. and Turner, T. (1997) *Starting to Teach in the Secondary School: A Companion for the Newly Qualified Teacher*, London: Routledge.

A review of the changing scene at sixth form. The chapter describes vocational education and the advantages and shortcomings of traditional routes to higher education and training. It discusses the different teaching and assessment styles of academic and vocational courses.

7 THE SCHOOL, CURRICULUM AND SOCIETY

This chapter takes you away from the immediacy of teaching to consider the purposes of education. It is easy to push the 'why' into the background and simply get on teaching the syllabus; after all, you might say, that is what pupils have got to learn, so let's get on with it.

Some parents do question the judgement of others who insist that their children go to school from '9 to 4', five days a week for 42 weeks for 11 years and have to do homework (see, for example DFEE, 1998c). Pupils will bring you to a halt when, say in the middle of a lesson on the Great Depression of the 1920s and 1930s, they say, 'Why have I got to learn this? My mum says that if I'm going to work in "Asda" down the road, knowing the economic reasons for the depression won't help me in my job, will it?' As a prospective teacher you need an answer to such questions.

The 1944 Education Act was a landmark in education in this country. It gave a new framework for teaching and learning and it was introduced in the middle of a national crisis – The Second World War. In a speech marking the fiftieth anniversary of the 1944 Education Act, the current Secretary of State for Education identified three key qualities which need to be fostered in schools in order for pupils to get the best out of education (Patten, 1994). These qualities were:

- **determination**
- **self-discipline**
- **(the) competitive spirit.**

How do these qualities fit with the aims of the 1988 Education Reform Act (see Unit 7.1, p. 348)?

The aims of education are a key issue in the review of the school curriculum by the Qualification and Curriculum Authority (QCA) which began in 1997. In the first unit, 'Aims of education', a comparative and analytical approach will be taken to examine assumptions about education. The second unit examines the school curriculum, and finally, we examine the structure and effectiveness of the 1988 Education Reform Act, which, for the first time in the England and Wales, gave schools a statutory curriculum for a large part of the school day.

Within the general standards laid down for Newly Qualified Teachers in England (DFEE,1997c) it is not expected that NQTs know about the aims of the National Curriculum. Neither are they expected to be aware that the aims of education are a matter of debate and political decision. We believe that teachers should be aware of the foundations on which national policy on the school curriculum is based if only because young people, beween the ages of 5 and 16, spend a substantial part of the formative period of their lives in school; hence this chapter. If education is "what is left after most of what you have learned in school is forgotten', then what is education for and who decides?

7.1   AIMS OF EDUCATION

INTRODUCTION

Education is very much a value-laden activity; this unit is designed help you to reflect on your own values and on the values which you encounter in your work. People's ideas about the aims of education may partly be simply 'read off' from the educational traditions of their own society, which incorporate certain shared values; or they may partly be formed through individuals' own reflection on their personal values. Not surprisingly, then, in a complex society there is room for many differences in views about educational aims. Individuals with different educational experience, different religious groups and cultural traditions, or different political tendencies may all differ in their ideas about the aims of education. What may at first sight seem rather an abstract question – What should the aims of education be? – is in fact an unavoidable part of the context in which you are working as a teacher.

OBJECTIVES

This unit should help you to:

- be aware of the variety of aims in education;
- reflect on and formulate your own aims in being a teacher;
- discuss aims in education with other teachers and with parents.

The social and political context of aims

One difference between education systems is that the aims which teachers are expected to pursue may be decided at different administrative levels. Most countries today have a national education system, at least partly state-funded and state-controlled. In some cases, as once in the Soviet Union, a clearly defined ideology sets aims which the whole education system is meant to promote. Even in a more decentralised system, such as the American one, while much is left to local level, there seems to have been a national sense earlier this century that the education system should function to make a single nation out of diverse communities.

In Britain, both historically and at the present day, the picture is mixed. For much of the twentieth century, schools had a good deal of autonomy, from a legal point of view, in setting and pursuing their aims, though in many cases the aims of a particular school were not made explicit. There was also room for variation at local authority level; for instance, in the 1970s and 1980s, there have been cases in which particular Local Education Authorities have pursued more radical equal opportunities policies than were supported centrally.

The question of how far there is to be scope for diversity in aims between different localities and different schools is still being played out in Britain in the late 1990s. On the one hand, with a political emphasis on parental choice and local management, there is encouragement to each school to make its own aims clear, and perhaps to present itself as being in some way distinctive from other schools at the level of aims. On the other hand, there has been a strong tendency recently towards central legislation, at least as regards the curriculum and a tendency for politicians to make statements about the aims of education. When, for instance, politicians say that schools should be inculcating moral standards or enabling Britain to compete economically with other nations, they are in effect recommending certain aims as being more important than others.

As a student teacher, then, you are working in a context in which many expectations about aims are already in place, at least at a general level. And even if you were able to pursue some idiosyncratic aims of your own, you would have to recognise that other teachers, your pupils, their parents and the wider society all have a legitimate interest in what you are doing. So you are working within constraints not of your own making. Nevertheless, your own thinking about aims is relevant in at least two ways:

1 Within the constraints, it influences how you approach your own task as a teacher (see for instance section 'Aims and the curriculum' pp. 347–8);
2 As a citizen, you have the same right as any other citizen to your view on what the broad aims of education should be (because this is a question of values and therefore, on a public level, a political question), and as a member of the teaching profession you have a special responsibility to be as clear as you can what your aims are and to be prepared to argue for them.

The following tasks give you some insight into the nature and variety of aims in education, as well as some experience in thinking about and discussing aims and their implications.

Task 7.1.1   **SCHOOL AIMS: A COMPARISON**

If you can, carry out this task and discuss your findings with other student teachers.

The two schools for comparison are:

1 The school in which you received your own secondary education (or if you experienced more than one school, the one in which you spent most time between the ages of 11 and 16).
2 Your school experience school.

For the first school, your data are wholly or largely from your own memory. Answer the following questions as far as you can:

Did your school have an explicit statement of aims?
Were you as a pupil aware of the school's aims?
In what ways did the particular aims of your school impinge on your experience as a pupil?

For your school experience school, ask:

Does your school have an explicit statement of aims – if so, what does it say?
Are the pupils you are teaching aware of the school's aims?
In what ways do these aims impinge on the pupils you are teaching?

If you are a parent, then identify the aims of the school your children attend, using the schools' documentation and, perhaps, by discussion with staff.

Answering these questions in the case of your present school experience school gives scope for some empirical research. Depending on your subject, you may be able to incorporate this into your teaching, e.g. in a discussion about school aims or through pupils themselves conducting a survey into how far their fellow pupils actually know the school aims.

Compare your findings for the two schools. Do you find that aims have a higher profile in your school experience school? Is there any evidence that the existence of an explicit policy on aims enhances the education the school is providing?

Task 7.1.2 **THE GOVERNING BODY: AIMS FOR A NEW SCHOOL**
This is a group task involving role play. This task is only suitable in circumstances when several student teachers are placed in a school or as part of a tutor-led tutorial session in an IHE.

With other student teachers, role play a governors' meeting which is intended to come up with a statement of aims for a new school (imagining that it is a new school allows you to start with a relatively clean sheet). Within the allotted time (say, one hour) you must try to produce a statement of aims to be included in the school's prospectus, to help show prospective pupils and their parents what is distinctive about the new school and its educational priorities.

Before you start the role play, you should agree on any special characteristics of the area in which the school is located. It may be best to make it a school which has to serve a wide range of interests, i.e. a comprehensive mixed school with a socially and ethnically varied intake.

Depending on the number in your group, you can assign individuals to some of the following roles as governors. (There is some stereotyping in the brief descriptions of these roles; if you have experience of role play, you should be able to distance yourself from the stereotypes.)

A Conservative-voting company director
A Labour-voting trade union leader
A Church of England vicar
A spokesperson for the main local ethnic community
A parent of a bright child, with high academic ambitions for the child
A parent of a child with learning difficulties
A teacher–governor
The head teacher.

One of you should be elected to chair the meeting. Another, without taking part in the discussion, takes notes on the points made and writes down anything which is agreed.

After the role play, if you have not arrived at an agreed statement, talk about what it was that prevented agreement. In what ways does the disagreement within your group reflect the actual diversity of cultures and interests within your society?

Task 7.1.3

THE PROSPECTUS: COMMUNICATING AIMS TO PARENTS

This is a two-part task, with an individual stage followed by a group stage, which could be undertaken on different days.

You are role playing only to a limited extent, since you are still speaking for yourself, as a teacher of your own subject (or another subject of which you have experience) and from your own standpoint. If possible, individuals should agree with each other in advance with which subjects they are going to identify, covering as wide a range of subjects as the group can manage.

Your task is again to contribute to a school prospectus (if you have done Task 7.1.2, you can use the same imaginary school). Assume the school already has agreed aims which are stated in the prospectus. If you have an agreed statement as an outcome of Task 7.1.2, use that; otherwise, you could borrow from the statement of aims in the Education Reform Act (see section 'Aims and the curriculum' pp. 347–8).

Your individual task is to write a paragraph of fifty to seventy-five words explaining to parents the major aims of the teaching of *your subject*, and how these aims relate to the general aims of the school. For example, if you consider that the main point of teaching history is to promote empathy, which contributes to the moral development of your pupils, this is what you have to try to get across. (Remember that some parents – and pupils – may wonder what is the point of studying a particular subject at all.)

For the group task, you and your fellow student teachers are a working party with responsibility for making sure that the individual subject statements fit together so as to complement each other and support the general aims, without contradicting or competing with each other. Discuss the subject statements, ask their authors to defend them if necessary and see if there are any modifications you agree on.

Task 7.1.4	**AIMS AND DEMOCRACY**

Decisions made in generating a National Curriculum are decisions made on behalf of the whole nation. Does this mean that these decisions, including the formulation of the aims which the curriculum is meant to promote, should be arrived at democratically?

One writer (White) accepts the link between aims and democracy, but argues that instead of aims being arrived at by consensus, they should be directly derived from an understanding of democratic values (Aldrich and White, 1998).

Individual task: read White's article 'New aims for a new National Curriculum' in Aldrich and White (1998) (see Further Reading). (Pages 22 to the end contain White's positive proposals.)

Answer these questions:

1 Do you think that White's position, in which aims can be established by philosophical argument, gives enough weight to what ordinary citizens want the aims of education to be?
2 Do you think his argument gives enough – or too little, or too much – responsibility to teachers in deciding on aims and how to carry them out? See pages 38–40 of the recommended article for White's view on this.

WHY BOTHER WITH AIMS?

> *Education as such has no aims. Only persons, parents and teachers, etc., have aims, not an abstract idea like education.*
>
> (Dewey, 1916, Chapter 8, Aims of education)

Your experience in doing the tasks may have backed up Dewey's point. You may have realised that different people can have different aims for education. You may also have considered how much difference aims make. A statement of aims on paper does not, of course, make any difference by itself. But what people do and how they do it is certainly influenced by what they are aiming at. Aims, at their different levels, can affect:

* How a whole school system is organised. (For example, the movement beginning in the 1960s towards comprehensive education was driven at least partly by explicit aims of breaking down class barriers and distributing opportunities for education more widely.)
* How an individual school is run. (For example, various aspects of a school's ethos and organisation may be motivated by the aim that pupils should respect and tolerate each other's differences.)
* How curriculum content is selected and taught (see section below on aims and the curriculum).

MAKING SENSE OF THE VARIETY OF AIMS

Because aims can be so many and varied, it is useful in thinking about them to be able to group them in some way. There is no single right way of dividing different aims into categories; in fact it is more helpful to be able to work with different categorising schemes.

Some approaches assume that education is aiming to develop personal qualities and capacities of one sort or another and therefore divide aims up into the categories of knowledge, attitudes and skills. A distinction between academic, personal and vocational aims is related to this, but does not exactly coincide with it. The importance in practice of the academic/personal/vocational division is that it can to some extent be recognised in ways in which different types of school historically have conceived their task.

But even if you are clear that education should be promoting certain qualities or capacities in individuals, there is the wider question – still one of aims – of why this should be done. Is it for the benefit of each individual, or for the general good of society?

This question introduces another distinction which has its uses, but which, like any categorisation, can be misleading if not used carefully. If you had to make a sharp choice, say between developing in people the capacities which enable them to lead fulfilling lives and giving them the skills and attitudes which fit them to be cogs in an impersonal machine, then there would be a real divide between aiming at the good of the individual and aiming at the good of society. But it is not necessarily like that. If, for instance, your view of a good society is that it is the kind of society in which all individuals can lead fulfilling lives and nobody prevents anyone else from leading a fulfilling life, then there is no contradiction between aiming at the good of the individual and aiming at the good of society.

In fact, even without being idealistic, many aims do cut across the individual/social division. Giving people skills which enables them to get productive jobs, for instance, is in many cases of benefit both to the individuals concerned and to others within society. Other cases may be more difficult. Certain types of academic knowledge might benefit the individuals who have that knowledge – if only because they find an inherent interest in it – without having any spin-off for others. Certain types of moral training – getting people to adhere to a moral code – might benefit others without doing anything positive for the individual concerned.

JUSTIFYING AIMS

In your role plays and discussions people have been trying to defend their own conceptions of what the aims of education should be. What sorts of argument have they been using?

One approach which used to be favoured by philosophers was to say that certain aims are incorporated into the **concept** of education. So, if someone aimed at inculcating in pupils particular religious or moral beliefs which they would adhere to without question, this could be rejected as an aim for education on the ground that inculcating unquestioned beliefs is simply not part of our concept of education. In fact it is part of our concept of **indoctrination**, whereas the concept of **education** implies the promotion of rationality and critical thinking.

You may agree with this. Its limitation as an argument, though, is that it does not allow you to meet on their own ground people who might argue that what they want teachers and schools to do **is** to inculcate unquestioned beliefs. They may not mind if you don't **call** this education; it is what they want you to aim at.

At bottom, argument about aims of education is not about concepts – how we use words – but about values – about what is important in life. It is a search for aims that promote the quality of life and in particular about the responsibilities of adults and of the whole society towards each of its members as they grow up. It is also about the distinctive contribution that teachers and schools can make to promoting what is important in life, which other people and institutions cannot make. Health, for instance, is important in everyone's life, but teachers and schools cannot promote people's health in the same way as doctors and hospitals can. But there is a lot that teachers and schools **can** do; that is why many people would want to see health education in the curriculum. And there may be some sorts of knowledge and experience which would probably not be promoted at all if teachers and schools did not do it.

The individual/social dimension affects the issue of justification. If some aspect of education is seen as being of value only for (some) individuals, there may be questions about why society – people in general – should support it; if some aspect is seen as being of value only for society at large, there may be questions about whether, if not freely chosen by the individual, it should be imposed. Such questions, though, may often stem from a simplistic contrast between society and individual. John Dewey is worth reading in this respect (Dewey, 1916).

EQUAL AIMS FOR EVERYONE?

Through much of the history of education, it would have been an unquestioned assumption that the aims of education should be different for different people. Plato built his theory of an ideal state (*The Republic*) on his argument that the rulers would need a much more thorough education than anyone else. A similar position was apparent in Victorian Britain, where the expansion of education was driven in part by the aim that the mass of the population should be sufficiently educated to form a productive workforce but not so well educated that they might rebel against the (differently educated) ruling classes. Through much of the twentieth century, differences in aims were apparent between the major independent public schools, maintained grammar schools and secondary modern schools; between boys' and girls' schools; and between religious foundations and more or less secular schools.

Today the unquestioned assumption is often the reverse: that the basic aims of education are the same for everyone, even if some people go further in the process than others. This assumption underlies many important developments in the promotion of equal opportunities. One of the basic reasons for being concerned with equal opportunities is that, if what you are aiming at is worthwhile, no one should be excluded from it because of factors, like race or gender, which are irrelevant to achieving these worthwhile aims. But this basic assumption is still not without its problems.

In the area of special needs, the Warnock Committee, which was set up in the late

1970s to look into the education of children with physical and mental disabilities, argued that the fundamental aims of education are the same for everyone (DES, 1978a). This was part of the thinking which led in the 1980s to the integration of an increasing proportion of children with special educational needs into mainstream schools, rather than their segregation in special schools.

On gender, few people would now suggest that the aim of education for girls should be to produce wives and mothers while the aims of education for boys should be to produce breadwinners. But there are those who would argue, recognising reality, that the education of girls does need some special aims; for instance, it may need to develop assertiveness in girls. Few would argue that there should be any fundamental difference in aims for children of different ethnic backgrounds, but some would argue, in the cause of equal opportunities, that there should be a special element in the aims of education for some ethnic groups, in order to give their members a sense of their own cultural inheritance.

Questions of equal opportunities show the difficulty of keeping a distinction between aims for individuals and aims for society. To try to ensure that fundamental aims are realised equally for all is one thing; does it need to be complemented by aiming (as far as education can do this) to create the kind of society which keeps opportunities equal for everyone in other ways as well?

AIMS AND THE CURRICULUM

So far as teaching your own subject is concerned, being clear about its aims, in relation to broader aims for education generally, can make a difference to how you approach your teaching. In mathematics and science, for instance, what is the balance between trying to give pupils certain technical skills which they can put to practical use, and trying to show them something of the sheer fascination which mathematics and science hold for some people quite apart from their applications? In history, what is the balance between trying to promote a sense of a common British inheritance and exploring the history which has led to Britain being the multicultural society it now is? What are the similar questions you could ask about your own subject if it is not one of these?

However, questions can be raised about the content of the whole school curriculum. If the aims of education are to be the same for everyone, one would expect that, at some level of generality, the curriculum would be the same for everyone (though there might be local or individual variation in details). In Britain, one of the ideas behind the introduction of the National Curriculum in 1988 was that all children, even if they moved between different schools, were entitled to and would in fact receive a common curriculum.

However, the early 1990s saw moves towards greater differentiation again, driven in part by teachers' widespread concern that the detailed and extensive requirements laid down by the National Curriculum in its original form were unmanageable. The trimming down of common requirements effectively reintroduced a greater degree of choice into the curriculum, especially for over 14 year olds. For example, history and geography, which in the original conception of the National Curriculum would have been compulsory for all children until the age of 16, became options. What is noticeable about such changes is that they seemed to stem more from practicalities than from reference to any underlying conception of the aims of education. If there had been a greater consensus about the aims of education, perhaps there would have been greater agreement about which areas of learning should or should not be compulsory for everyone.

Logically, you might expect that broad aims for education would come first, and that the content of the curriculum would be worked out with reference to these. In practice, this has not always happened. For instance, the 1988 Education Reform Act, which introduced the National Curriculum into England and Wales, included in its preamble a rather broad and open-ended statement of aims which required each school to:

(a) promote the spiritual, moral, cultural, mental and physical development of pupils at school and society;
(b) prepare such pupils for the opportunities, responsibilities and experiences of adult life.

(Education Reform Act, 1988, section 1.2)

However, there was no attempt to show that the subjects included in the National Curriculum would promote these aims; the actual list of subjects appears to have been arrived at quite independently.

By the mid-1990s it was widely accepted that there should be no further major changes to the National Curriculum until the year 2000, but in the meantime a more thorough review of the Curriculum should be undertaken. This time, the Qualifications and Curriculum Authority (QCA), charged with carrying out the review, acknowledged that there needed to be 'a much clearer statement about the aims and priorities of the school curriculum as a necessary preliminary to any review'. So the QCA, in the winter of 1997, started a consultation exercise to try to establish a broad consensus on the aims of the curriculum, which would be fed into the QCA's recommendations to the Secretary of State for Education for changes in the National Curriculum (for more on these developments, see Aldrich and White, 1998). At the time of writing, it remains to be seen whether the National Curriculum at the beginning of the twenty-first century will be systematically derived from an underlying policy on the aims of education.

Summary and key points

The aims of education are, in the end, about why we send our children to school. Society has a right to influence and determine the way in which our schools are run and the purposes they serve. Different sections of society have differing views about the aims of education, teachers included. Schools have to serve the aims set for them by society and interpret those aims when they implement the agreed curriculum.

However, the question of what aims to pursue is one of values and it may never be settled to everyone's satisfaction; hence, across a whole society, it is inevitably a controversial political question.

This unit has tried to suggest that:

- aims do make a difference – not if they are just written on paper, but if people have thought through their aims and are consciously trying to put them into practice;
- you have your own aims as a teacher but that you can only pursue these within the agreed aims of the school set by the governing body;
- other people – including parents and politicians – also have their aims for education. Such views are exercised, e.g. through the ballot box and acts of Parliament respectively;
- different aims can be variously classified, articulated, defended and debated;
- aims can be set at different levels, such as national government, local government, different schools, individual teachers. This factor is often what distinguishes the educational systems of different societies. In England and Wales aims have been set for the first time this century at national level.

FURTHER READING

Aldrich, R. and White, J. (1998) *The National Curriculum beyond 2000: The QCA and the Aims of Education*, London: Institute of Education.

An argument for basing the curriculum on a consideration of aims and for deriving the aims of the curriculum from democratic values.

Dewey, J. (1916) Democracy and Education, New York: Free Press.

A classic which is still well worth reading. Dewey is often recognised simply as an advocate of child-centred education. In fact his educational theory is part of a well worked out theory of the relations between individual and society and of the nature of knowledge and thought. See especially Chapters 1 to 4, 8 and 9.

Haydon, G. (1997) *Teaching about Values: A New Approach*, London: Cassell.

Chapter 2, 'Education and aims', is a brief and wide-ranging consideration of possible aims, raising a series of questions to be posed about any suggested aims for schools.

White, J. (1982) *The Aims of Education Restated*, London: Routledge.

A philosophical argument which first reviews some accounts of aims which, in White's view, are unsatisfactory and then develops the author's own view (at that time), which puts heavy weight on individual autonomy. White also looks at the practical implications of his account.

Wringe, C.(1988) *Understanding Educational Aims*, London: Unwin Hyman.

An introductory text, reviewing a variety of positions about aims in education concerned with (i) the development of qualities and capacities in the individual for the individual's own good; (ii) what is good from the point of view of society; (iii) the pursuit of aims seen as intrinsic to education and valuable in their own right.

7.2 THE SCHOOL CURRICULUM

INTRODUCTION

This unit invites you to think about the specific aims of your own teaching subject and its place in the curriculum. Many subjects appear to be in the curriculum just because they have always been in the curriculum and, therefore, perhaps need no justification. In addition, you begin to examine the relationship between the academic and pastoral roles of a teacher.

The background information is designed to help you address the key issues of:

What is the school curriculum?
Why is the curriculum as it is?
How does the curriculum work?

OBJECTIVES

By the end of this unit you should:

- be able to understand aspects of the processes involved in curriculum change;
- have explored some of the relationships between curriculum policy and practice;
- have considered the contribution of your subject to the whole curriculum;
- appreciate the overall curriculum experience of the pupil.

WHAT IS THE SCHOOL CURRICULUM?

The curriculum is often referred to as though it were all those subjects that appear on the timetable or as all those planned events on the timetable that occur during school hours. Yet another way of looking at the curriculum is as all those experiences to which a child is exposed. The National Curriculum in England and Wales has been written in such a way as to suggest that it is a number of subjects, some more important than others (the core subjects) together with cross-curricular themes. Furthermore, these themes link subjects and provide a vehicle for the study of topics which do not fit neatly into subject work, but nevertheless are important. These include the environment, health, etc.; see the list of cross-curricular elements below. The National Curriculum of England and Wales is discussed in more detail in Unit 7.3.

Since the 1970s there has been an emerging consensus that the whole curriculum includes the following elements:

the subject curriculum: the knowledge, skills and processes associated with each subject;

the cross-curricular elements: economic and industrial understanding; health education; careers education; environmental education; citizenship; information technology;

pastoral curriculum: equal opportunities; personal and social education; form and year groupings; the 'house' system;

the hidden curriculum: attitudes, values and relationships; the reward and discipline system;

the extra-curricular curriculum: opportunities to develop individual talent; clubs, societies and events; community service; residential trips, etc.

Task 7.2.1   COMPARING SCHOOLS – THE LEAGUE TABLES AND OFSTED REPORTS

Collect reports from the Internet which describe comparisons between schools – the league tables and OFSTED reports (find these on the Internet at the DFEE and OFSTED local sites. See Unit 1.4, p. 47). Compare the features of schools which are identified in those comparisons, with those of interest and importance to parents choosing their child's secondary school. What did you value the most from your own secondary school?

Task 7.2.2   YOUR SCHOOL PROSPECTUS/WEB SITE

Look at your own school's prospectus/web site and try to identify the features of the school which are cited as attractive to prospective parents. Use the list above to help you; compare and contrast what you find in the prospectus/web site with the list above. If there are several of you in a tutor group, attending different schools, compare the information provided by those schools.

WHY IS THERE A SCHOOL CURRICULUM?

The most visible part of the school curriculum, especially from the point of view of parents and pupils, is the subject curriculum. Given that the aims of the school are achieved best through the medium of academic disciplines, then a timetable of subjects inevitably follows. That assumption is not universally accepted, despite its widespread practice; see Unit 7.1, in particular Task 7.1.4.

The pattern, frequency and timing of the subject components of the timetable reflect a view about the nature of knowledge and the ways pupils learn; they respond, as well, to constraints in the system, such as the availability of suitably qualified teachers. The organisers of National Curriculum 'Technology' suggested incorporating Home Economics and Business Studies into its programme; this is a good example of traditional subjects being viewed in a new way, in this case as examples of process-based problem-solving skills related to design and realisation. The school makes timetable decisions based on these views through the staff and the governing body. These decisions include the way pupils are grouped (see Unit 4.1); whether to include or not certain subjects, e.g. what constitutes a modern foreign language; the way subjects are organised (integrated studies such as humanities or history, geography and social studies). Another factor is whether a school operates through a subject departmental structure or a faculty structure.

Faculty structures enable subjects with features in common to share timetable space and to plan and implement their teaching within a shared framework of ideas. The identification of faculty groupings is itself a reflection of underlying educational assumptions. By identifying features in common between two or more subjects, decisions have to be made about those features which are worthy of emphasis and those which are not. Is mathematics a science or is it a means of communication better linked with, for example, English teaching?

Such decisions respond to perceived aims of education and to priorities established within those aims. A further set of curriculum issues is the balance between the proportion of time given to developing the academic, physical and emotional potential of pupils. What part does the school play in fostering the moral, ethical and spiritual values and where is that reflected in the school curriculum?

It is of interest to note that as parents, employers, neighbours and customers we value people who are courteous and considerate; who promote as well as display honesty and

| Task 7.2.3 | **AIMS AND GCSE SYLLABUSES** |

Most GCSE syllabuses set out their content to respond to a set of aims. Some aims are assessed through the examination; others are not but are perceived, nevertheless, as important features of the course. Examine the aims of the GCSE syllabus for your teaching subject used in your school.

Classify the aims initially into three groups, as follows:

* knowledge
* processes and skills
* attitudes.

Now subdivide further the aims in each group into those aims which are

* assessed
* not assessed.

Discuss the groupings that evolve in terms of aims which are attitudinal (have a moral, ethical or social dimension) and the value placed on these dimensions by the examination syllabus.

This enquiry could be developed further by:

* comparing syllabuses from different Examination Groups within your subject;
* comparing different subject syllabuses in your school.

are reliable and punctual. In whatever role, we value these virtues as well as those of professional knowledge, skill and understanding. Many of these virtues are attitudinal and not directly measured, praised or acknowledged in public statements of what is a 'good school'.

To return to the issue of pupil grouping, organising the timetable forces schools to address the question to what extent should the learning experiences be common to all pupils, both between and within schools? Should the curriculum reflect, respond to and promote the differences between pupils? Unit 4.1 addresses this issue in more detail.

Should the organisation of schooling and pupil grouping be planned for progression by developmental stage (or level) or by age? It is a tradition in schools in England and Wales and elsewhere in Britain that classes are grouped by age. There is no tradition of holding pupils back until they have reached an acceptable level of performance before entering the next stage. Many other countries, however, adopt performance as a basis for progression. Issues of differences in the development of pupils have been discussed in Units 4.2 and 4.3.

All these considerations are educational in the sense that they require decisions concerning the best way in which to set about teaching adolescents in secondary school. However, these issues have a strong social and political dimension. The questions are, in the end, philosophical ones in that they involve beliefs about our humanity, what it means to be educated and how best that can be achieved. They are social questions in that decisions are made which enable the education system to respond to the trends in society.

Two such trends are the growth of computer technology and the perceived rising crime rate. The microprocessor has led to questions about the age at which information communication technology (ICT) is introduced into the curriculum and in what form. Should ICT be a subject in its own right? Or should it be a tool for learning? The increase in some crimes, especially violent ones, has led to renewed emphasis by some politicians on the role of team games in sport in school. The latter trend, if consolidated, is a reaffirmation of values of a previous century whereas the former, by contrast, is the anticipation of the next millennium.

The issues are political in that they determine the ways in which power is distributed; whether the responsibility for decision making belongs to the subject specialist, the head of department, the headteacher, the governors or the Secretary of State.

HOW DOES THE CURRICULUM WORK?

The majority of teaching and learning takes place formally within the framework of the school timetable. In maintained schools, the responsibility for creating an effective teaching and learning environment is shared by all the teaching staff, both pastoral and academic. In the front line, so to speak, are the subject teachers who have increasing responsibility for the appropriateness and effectiveness of the programme taken up by heads of department, curriculum and pastoral co-ordinators through finally to the headteacher. The headteacher carries the ultimate responsibility.

The role of the headteacher is to ensure that the Local Education Authority's (LEA's) curriculum policies are implemented. In the case of a locally managed school (LMS), the governing body has the responsibility to ensure that this duty is carried out. In the case of grant-maintained schools, the governing body has to ensure that statutory government policies are enforced, without reference to the LEA. There are variations in the responsibility of different schools according to their status, both in the maintained and independent school systems.

Government legislation changes the extent to which responsibility for planning, implementation and monitoring of the curriculum is devolved to individual schools and to individual teachers. Since the 1988 Education Reform Act (ERA), school governors have had increasing responsibility for the curriculum, for the appointment of staff, for the management of the budget and for monitoring the implementation of legislation related to the curriculum, equal opportunities, special educational needs, sex education and religious education and collective worship; see also Unit 7.3. These circumstances identify the heavy responsibility devolved to governors to identify and construct the whole curriculum and to monitor that the aims of the school are being achieved within the statutory framework. In practice, of course, the responsibility is normally delegated to the headteacher by the governing body of the school.

LEGISLATION AND THE SCHOOL CURRICULUM

The role of government is to respond to the changes in society in order to provide an appropriate education system. Examples of that response include, in the 1960s, recognising the inadequacies of selection and the tripartite system of schooling, and the provision of support teachers for increasing numbers of pupils from the New Commonwealth whose mother tongue was not English (Section 11 Teachers).

In addition, however, the government must lead by providing a framework and climate for change which recognises growing or potential demands on people. In recent times, the development of vocational courses, both in post-16 institutions and the upper secondary school, has required closer links between school and the workplace. Such links provide relevance and motivation to schooling as well as upgrading the skills of the working population.

Throughout the period between the two major Education Acts of 1944 and 1988 some important legislation was enacted, framing and shaping our educational system. We identify in Table 7.2.1 some key pieces of legislation.

GOVERNMENT INQUIRIES, REPORTS AND SURVEYS ON THE CURRICULUM

Government policy very often depends upon the recommendations of government committees responsible for offering guidance on aspects of educational policy and practice. Such bodies often commission research or inquiries which, in some cases, have had great influence on decision making. We identify here (Table 7.2.2) some influential reports and their main spheres of interest, many of which continue to shape thinking and decision making. The full details of these reports may be found in the Bibliography at the end of this book.

Table 7.2.1 Some important educational legislation, 1944 to 1994; a summary

1944 Education Act (The Butler Act)
Appointed a Minister of Education under whose control and direction the LEAs in England and Wales were to ensure that each child received an 'efficient and full time education suitable to his age, aptitude and ability', by regular attendance at school or otherwise. The school leaving age was to be raised to 15 (implemented in 1947). The existing division between 'elementary' and 'higher' education was replaced by 'a continuous process conducted in three stages – the primary, secondary and further education'. The only mandatory subject was religious education for all pupils and included a daily, collective act of worship.

1980 Education Act – the Parents' Charter
This Act placed more teachers and parents on to governing bodies of schools. Information about a school had to be published in order to make schools more accountable to parents and guardians and to aid them in their choice of school.

1986 Education Act
This increased the numbers of parents and community representatives on the governing body. It extended the powers and responsibility of the governors. These included monitoring the provision in the school of sex education, Christian worship and ensuring that political education is non-partisan.

1988 Education Reform Act (the ERA)
The biggest piece of legislation since the 1944 Education Act. It is still being enacted. The ERA introduced a National Curriculum and testing for pupils at ages 7, 11 and 14 with the intention of testing at 16 but using GCSE in the interim. Membership of government policy making committees (National Curriculum Council (NCC), Curriculum Council for Wales and the Schools Examination and Assessment Council (SEAC)) was by appointment of the Secretary of State, i.e. members were not elected. In England, SCAA replaced both the NCC and SEAC. The content and assessment of the school curriculum was nationalised whilst responsibility for management, finance and resourcing for school was localised to school governors (LMS and GMS). See also Unit 7.3.

1991 Children Act
This came into force in October 1991. It is concerned with public law rights (e.g. LEA care) and private rights (e.g. divorce). It concerns the duty of the state to intervene in parental rights and for the rights of parents in relation to their children. The Act gives the children formal rights to express an opinion about decisions affecting their lives.

1993 Education Act
New requirements for religious education and collective worship; also new arrangements to strengthen the provision of sex education in schools (see Circulars 1/94 and 5/94 respectively).

Table 7.2.2 Influential reports concerning the school curriculum

A language for life; the Bullock Report: Recommended a language policy across the school curriculum.
DES (1975)

Curriculum 11–16: A discussion document which covered ways of developing a school curriculum. Important for identifying a philosophical basis for organising the curriculum.
HMI (1977)

The Warnock Report: Made recommendations about the provision of education for pupils with special educational needs. Led to the 1981 Act and now consolidated in special needs legislation (see Appendix 4).
DES (1978a)

Aspects of secondary education: A very important survey of Year 10 pupils in a sample of schools across the country. It exposed inadequacies in provision, revealing, for example, evidence for gender stereotyping in the curriculum of schools. Its findings were, in part, evaluated against the criteria set out in Curriculum 11–16, see above.
HMI (1978)

Mathematics counts (The Cockcroft Report): A report into the teaching of mathematics which recommended widespread changes in the way pupils were taught.
DES (1982)

The Swann Report: Addressed the implications of education for pupils in a pluralist society and the concern for the failure in school of some pupils from ethnic minority groups. The final report adopted a multicultural stance, as opposed to an anti-racist stance, by contrast with the extensive discussion within the report on the influence of racism on the life chances of pupils.
DES (1984b)

Task 7.2.4

THE CURRICULUM AS AREAS OF EXPERIENCE

In 1977, HM Inspectors of Schools produced a definitive document which described the experiences that pupils should have in their schooling in terms that went beyond the subject boundaries. It was an effort to rethink the curriculum in a different way. The Inspectorate suggested that all pupils should be exposed to experiences in the following areas of human endeavour and behaviour and that subjects should be taught in a way that contributed to those experiences (HMI, 1977; 1994). HMI identified the following areas of experience:

aesthetic and creative
linguistic
scientific
social and political

ethical
mathematical
physical
spiritual

Discuss these ideas in the following ways. Which areas of experience:

1 contribute to personal development?
2 contribute particularly to the role of pupils as members of society?
3 contribute to the understanding of the place and purpose of human life?
4 would your own teaching subject contribute to?

These ideas are developed further by HMI: see HMI (1977) and HMI (1994) and Unit 7.1 on aims of education.

SOME IMPORTANT CONSULTATIVE DOCUMENTS

In addition to legislation and commissioned reports, government agencies produce discussion documents to promote further thinking on issues of current importance. A great many of these reports were produced in the 1980s, in the debate about the nature and purpose of the school curriculum. Despite the intense cerebral activity and extensive publication in this field in this period, the National Curriculum, which emerged quite quickly in 1988 as part of that year's Education Reform Act, does not appear to bear any of the hallmarks of those efforts. Indeed, as published, the National Curriculum is remarkably like many school curricula which preceded it. It differs fundamentally, however, in two ways, because it applies now to all pupils in maintained schools and is subject to extensive testing arrangements.

An important consultative document which influenced both the framing and the introduction and development of the National Curriculum was *Better Schools* (DES, 1985). This document concentrated on the planning and management of the school curriculum. It provided four principles on which the National Curriculum was based: breadth, balance, relevance and differentiation. These are discussed in Unit 7.3.

Another major development in the 1980s was the introduction of better and more informative reporting procedures. The consultative paper *Records of Achievement* (DES, 1984a) was aimed at providing a systematic process of profiling in order to provide pupils, parents and employers with an open document of individual qualifications and achievements. Its aim was to motivate pupils to develop their potential, to encourage them to take responsibility for their progress and to involve them in assessing and recording many aspects of personal development. This process is now firmly established in many schools.

LINKING CURRICULUM POLICY TO PRACTICE

During the 1980s there was a growing recognition that subject knowledge was part of a wider curriculum and that learning did not happen in isolation from the whole experience of being at school. In addition to assessing the quality of subject teaching, inquiries and reports identified the key influences and opportunities of the pastoral curriculum, cross-curricular elements, extra-curricular activities and the hidden curriculum of the school environment and ethos. Consequently, those responsible for managing the curriculum promoted the introduction of timetabled 'Personal and Social Education' (PSE), records of achievement, residential experience and work experience. There was 'necessarily' an increase in documentation concerning: statements of school aims; declarations of intentions concerning gender stereotyping; multicultural and anti-racist policies; procedures for counselling and referral; integrated support for pupils with special educational needs; revised systems of reward and punishment; consultation with parents concerning home learning (homework).

In other words, there evolved a process to ensure that curriculum practice correlated to curriculum policy. Curriculum policy was to be cohesive and comprehensive; for maintained schools it had to be publicly presented as the consensus of the school, LEA and governing bodies. There had to be improved communication between those who could influence the education of the child, although the practitioners (teachers) were less involved in the processes of making policies whilst the structure and content of the curriculum became more prescribed and more the responsibility of non-professionals.

CURRICULUM PRIORITIES AND THE CLASS TEACHER

As a teacher you contribute to the subject curriculum, the cross-curricular elements, the pastoral curriculum, the extra-curricular activities and to the 'hidden curriculum'. In some schools, for example, there is a declared commitment to one or more of these elements of the school curriculum above others, which may be stated in the school's prospectus.

In other schools there is an implicit priority, such as when in public statements about the success of the school, importance is placed on, for example, examination results or extra-curricular activities.

Confusion and frustration can arise when the school procedures seem to contradict the school philosophy. For example, a school brochure may state its aim to promote individual talents whether they be in sport, art or music and to promote social and personal skills, but the school's timetable squeezes out PSE, staff cuts are made in the creative arts and the allocation of the school's budget favours science laboratories rather than sports equipment or musical instruments.

There have been debates about whether there is a false distinction between the subject curriculum and the pastoral curriculum. This debate has centred on the provision of PSE in the school. Should it be a discrete subject taught by specialists or does it belong to the pastoral or tutorial system? On the other hand, should each teacher be responsible for the personal and social development of pupils as part of their subject teaching? One way in which to assess whether a school believes in separation or integration of subject, pastoral and hidden curricula is to identify the functions and working of the management structures. For example, do heads of department meet alongside the heads of year or house heads or are their priorities considered to be quite different?

In teaching your subject you need to be conscious of the explicit and implicit messages you give to pupils about:

- the relative value of academic achievement, personal development and social development. For example, what kind of feedback do you give pupils, what is the focus of that response and is it verbal or written?
- equal opportunity issues concerning gender, social class, cultural group, mental abilities and physical capability. For example, do you challenge stereotypes in your choice and discussion of images in texts, worksheets, illustrations, etc.?
- the hidden messages of the way you teach? How do you respond to:
  - language used by pupils with each other or with you?
  - the way pupils enter and leave the classroom?
  - the organisation and maintenance of 'who sits with who'?
  - pupils' work? Do you display pupils' work; is it properly mounted and attractive?
  - your own feelings? How does your body language match with your spoken language?

Task 7.2.5	**HIDDEN MESSAGES IN YOUR TEACHING**

Ask another student teacher to watch your lesson and report on agreed aspects of your teaching. You might include in this task:

- Where do you stand during the lesson? Take spot checks at three-minute intervals. Map the resulting data onto a plan of the class floor area. Do you keep your distance from pupils or are you 'in amongst them'?
- Do you look at pupils when you speak to them? Do you hold their attention, eye to eye?
- Does your facial expression match your words? Do you smile when you punish pupils? Do you look bored when urging pupils to get on with their work?
- How do you use your hands? Do you use them expressively; clasp them tightly; put them in your pockets? Do you fold your arms defensively across your chest? Do you carry anything with you as you walk about? Why?
- When you discipline pupils, do you follow it up by ensuring that they carry out the punishment or attend detention? Do you check excuses, talk to the form teacher? Do you show that you both care about them and mean business?

Discuss together the information gleaned during this task and the implications for your teaching. See also Unit 3.1 on verbal communication.

Task 7.2.6	**YOUR SUBJECT AND THE SCHOOL CURRICULUM**

In pairs, give a ten-minute presentation on 'the place of your subject in the whole curriculum'. This could be given live or prepared in advance on video tape. You might consider using the following questions as a prompt:

- how is your subject distinct from other subject areas?
- how does it complement other school subjects?
- how does it contribute to the personal and social development of pupils?
- in what ways is it relevant to the everyday lives of pupils?

You should find your school's documentation helpful, such as the departmental syllabus and the school PSE programmes.

THE HIDDEN CURRICULUM

In the National Curriculum, statutory orders are concerned with the subject curriculum because the cross-curricular dimensions cannot be formally assessed. These non-statutory elements remain, however, as principles for which schools are answerable; they are inspected by OFSTED under such section headings as 'Pupils' spiritual, moral, social and cultural development'; 'Equality of Opportunity'; 'Pupils' Welfare and Guidance'; 'Provision for Pupils with Special Educational Needs'.

The significance of the 'hidden curriculum' has always been understood by teachers and has been acknowledged by LEAs:

> the attitudes, values, aspirations, expectations, pressures and constraints and the spirit and atmosphere of a school all express messages that are variously perceived by the child or student. In many ways these messages may be more influential and more significant than the stated avowed curriculum.
>
> (Northamptonshire County Council (April 1985) The School Curriculum: A Framework of Principles – The Northamptonshire View)

The hidden curriculum and extra-curricular activities are also obviously considered to be important to parents:

> they want a place where their children are happy and secure, but they also want their children to realise their abilities. Good music and drama, lively out-of-hours sporting activities, warm community links, all count as strongly as top GCSE grades. Firm but friendly discipline is viewed as being as vital as winning trophies.
>
> (Hughes, C. (1993) 'Parents' choice', *The Independent*, 4 July, p. 2)

Task 7.2.7

DEPARTING FROM YOUR PLANS

This a group task. The aim of the activity is to apply the principles of a whole curriculum to the practice in confronting a common occurrence in the teaching and learning situation. What do you do when pupils want to talk about something not on your lesson plan? Imagine an individual who wants to share some good or bad personal news; or the whole class enters bubbling with excitement or anger about a new event.

Discuss the following dialogue:

Pupil: I've got to tell you about . . .
Teacher: What do you say first?
Pupil: Sorry I'm late, but it's about . . .
Teacher: Why are you late? And take your coat off and where's your . . .
Pupil: But I've got to tell you about . . .
Teacher: Hurry up, you've got work to do.

Observe how teachers in your school deal with such occasions and discuss the effect of possible responses with other student teachers and tutors.

Summary and key points

As a teacher you are expected:

- to be a subject specialist;
- to integrate cross-curricular elements into your teaching;
- to contribute towards the pastoral structures of the school;
- and to foster links with the local community and with industry.

Your role as a subject specialist is to:

- communicate the special relevance and rewards of your subject;
- support and stretch all pupils in learning the knowledge, skills and processes of your subject areas;
- achieve the best possible examination results; contribute to your subject department; sustain your own subject expertise and enthusiasm.

In showing awareness of cross-curricular elements you are also expected to challenge prejudices and stereotypes concerning minority groups; to avoid preferential treatment of any individual or type, especially concerning gender, race, class and ability; in your own language and treatment of pupils, to encourage mutual tolerance, understanding and respect; to develop a range of teaching strategies which give equal opportunities to all pupils; to incorporate information technology into your subject.

As a pastoral tutor you are expected to uphold the school's procedures of reward and discipline; to engender a sense of belonging and security in your tutor group; to raise awareness of social and personal issues; to know the individual backgrounds, personalities and potential of your group.

FURTHER READING

DFE (1993c) *School Governors: A Guide to the Law*, London: HMSO.

This is essentially a guide to governors, explaining clearly the respective roles of the headteacher, LEA and governing body. It aims primarily to outline the legal responsibilities of governors in matters of the curriculum, staffing, equal opportunities, buildings and information to parents. It has useful lists of legislative documents and associated publications. It would be valuable for new teachers in understanding the reasons underlying much of the paperwork which they are required to submit and it acquaints them with their rights and responsibilities in the law.

Gilham, B. (ed.) (1986) *The Language of School Subjects*, London: Heinemann.

Although the focus is on language across the curriculum, the essays on specific subjects raise awareness about the hidden assumptions within different disciplines. It is valuable reading for a subject specialist considering the wider experience of pupils and the contributions of their subject to the whole development of the pupil. Case studies are used to look at the language of textbooks, interactive talk between the teacher and the group and the relationship between language, thinking and learning.

Lawton, D. (1989) *Education, Culture and the National Curriculum*, London: Hodder and Stoughton.

This is an enlightening account of the educational changes from Butler (1944) to Baker (1988). It is highly informative and analytical in its clear presentation of events and the educational and social implications of curriculum changes.

National Curriculum Council (1988) *Curriculum Guidance 3: The Whole Curriculum*, York: NCC.

Part 1 gives a clear and brief description of whole curriculum policy in terms of what is taught. Part 2 is a series of questions which schools need to address. These concern development plans, subject overlaps and links and cross-curricular elements. Suggestions are made about identifying responsibilities and about regular reviewing of curriculum implementation. (See also National Curriculum Council (1990) *Curriculum Guidance 2: A Curriculum for All* which claims to 'move from principles to practice' in examining provision for pupils with disabilities and learning difficulties. A useful bibliography.)

Taylor, P.H. and Richards, M. (1985) *An Introduction to Curriculum Studies*, Windsor: NFER/Nelson.

A comprehensive analysis which also stimulates further enquiry into curriculum theory and practice. It gives plentiful references for further research and reading. Aimed at the teacher in training, it elucidates ideologies of curriculum design and interprets different models of curriculum practice.

The following provide detailed information about the development of the school curriculum.

AMMA (1992) *The Children Act and the Teacher*, London: Assistant Master and Mistresses Association (February) (Note: AMMA is now the ATL.)
DES (1975) *A Language for Life*, London: HMSO (The Bullock Report).
DES (1978) *Special Educational Needs*, London: HMSO (The Warnock Report).
DES (1979) *Aspects of Secondary Education: A Survey by HM Inspectors of Schools*, London: HMSO.
DES (1982) *Mathematics Counts*, London: HMSO (The Cockcroft Report).
DES (1984a) *Records of Achievement: A Statement of Policy*, London: DES and the Welsh Office.
DES (1984b) *Education for All*, London: HMSO (The Swann Report).
DES (1985) *Better Schools*, Cmnd 9469, London: HMSO.
DFE (1994d) *Circular 1/94*, London: DFE.
HMI (1977) *Curriculum 11–16, Working Papers*, London: DES.

HMI (1994) 'The entitlement curriculum', in B. Moon and A. Shelton Mayes (eds) *Teaching and Learning in the Secondary School*, Milton Keynes: Open University Press, pp. 232–240.

O'Hear, P. and White, J. (eds) (1991) *A National Curriculum for All: Laying the Foundations for Success*, London: Institute for Public Policy Research.

O'Hear, P. and White, J. (eds) (1993) *Assessing the National Curriculum*, London: Paul Chapman.

7.3 THE NATIONAL CURRICULUM

INTRODUCTION

This unit is designed to provide information concerning the introduction, modification and terminology of the National Curriculum for England and Wales. It should also help you to develop a theoretical framework within which to analyse and interpret the principles behind the changes in the National Curriculum. You are encouraged to learn from other student teachers about the impact of the National Curriculum on other subjects. Importantly, you should know how to respond to the requirements of the National Curriculum in your own specialist subject.

OBJECTIVES

By the end of this unit you should be:

- able to understand the principles of a national curriculum for all pupils;
- informed about developments in the implementation of the National Curriculum;
- able to consider the implications of the National Curriculum for the individual pupil, for teachers, schools and society.

BACKGROUND: EDUCATION REFORM ACT

The Education Reform Act (ERA) (1988) changed the education system in England and Wales in three major aspects. The major points of the ERA were:

- To provide for the establishment of a national curriculum comprising foundation subjects for all pupils of compulsory school age in maintained schools. The curriculum identified subject matter to be assessed and stated when the assessment would be implemented. The National Curriculum Council (NCC) was set up in England and a Curriculum Council for Wales (CCW).
- To require that information concerning schools' performance and examination results be reported.
- To create a new category of self-governing (grant-maintained) schools.

These points are considered in reverse order.

Grant-maintained (GM) schools (now called Foundation Schools)

These schools 'opted out' of Local Education Authority (LEA) control and received their funding direct from the Secretary of State for Education. The decision to apply for GM status was made through a ballot by the parents. In GM schools, the governing body is responsible for the management of the school's affairs and ensuring that the school abides by all legislation. This status was changed by the Labour Government elected in 1997. The schools were renamed Foundation Schools and reintegrated into their local authority.

Publication of examination results

This is now a requirement in Section 22 of the ERA. The main features are:

- the publication of GCSE and A Level results in the governing body's annual report to parents and in school prospectuses;
- the availability of information on individual pupils' achievements;
- the publication of comparative tables of school performance.

The Parents' Charter (1993) (DFE Circular 4/93) required the publication of comparative or 'league tables' of GCSE, A and A/S Levels, International Baccalaureate Diplomas and results in courses leading to vocational qualifications. It demanded more and better performance indicators in the governors' annual report and the school's prospectus.

'More and better' meant the percentage of pupils entered for examinations, information on examination performance according to gender and ethnicity and the school's performance in relation to LEA and national tables.

For an OFSTED inspection, schools must provide data of GCSE results in all National Curriculum core subjects. The LEA may also undertake analyses which give evidence of the 'value added' for pupils in a particular school in its area. The concept of 'value added' recognises that the academic backgrounds and performance of pupils at the point of entry into a school differ between schools; these differences need to be taken into account when analysing examination results. The results of each school are available on the DFEE web site (see Unit 1.4, p. 47).

THE NATIONAL CURRICULUM

The ERA gave the Secretary of State for Education, LEAs and governing bodies of maintained schools in England and Wales a duty to ensure that each school provided a broadly based and balanced curriculum which:

a) promotes the spiritual, moral, cultural, mental and physical development of pupils at the school and of society
   and
b) prepares such pupils for the opportunities, responsibilities and experiences of adult life.

(Education Reform Act, 1988, Chapter 40 1.(2))

The National Curriculum was presented as the working version of the ERA. It outlined the principles for the curriculum which concerned the entitlement for all pupils:

- The principle that each pupil should have a broad and balanced curriculum which is also relevant to his or her particular needs is now established in law.
- That principle must be reflected in the curriculum of every pupil. It is not enough for such a curriculum to be offered by the school: it must be fully taken up by each pupil.
- That curriculum must promote development in all the main areas of learning and experience which are widely accepted as important.
- The curriculum must also serve to develop the pupil as an individual, as a member of society and as a future adult member of the community with a range of personal and social opportunities and responsibilities.

(DES, 1989)

The declared rationale of the National Curriculum was to:

- provide teachers with clear objectives for their teaching; children with identifiable targets for learning; parents with accurate, accessible information about what their children can be expected to know, understand and be able to do and what they actually achieve

and that

- the result would be higher expectations and more effective progression and continuity throughout the years of full-time education.

(NCC, 1989)

Teachers and parents mostly welcomed the introduction of a national curriculum which provided a common learning experience for all pupils. The concept of a learning continuum meant that a pupil's education need not be impaired by changing schools. The National Curriculum Council aimed to extend the good practice observed in many areas to all schools. The National Curriculum would ensure that HMI reports and government inquiries could be responded to by schools across England and Wales. It would also safeguard against overspecialised or idiosyncratic teaching and reduce the incidence of incompetent teaching.

Core and foundation

The fundamental aims of the National Curriculum, as listed on p. 366 under headings a) and b), were to be achieved through the teaching of **three core** subjects:

- English (and Welsh in Welsh speaking schools)
- Mathematics
- Science

and a further set of subjects, called **foundation subjects:**

- History
- Geography
- Technology
- Music
- Art
- Physical Education
- a modern foreign language (in secondary schools).

Religious Education had to be in the basic curriculum for all pupils; the syllabus should be locally agreed and had to reflect the fact that religious traditions in England and Wales are in the main Christian. A local standing advisory council (SACRE) had to include representatives of 'such Christian and other religious denominations as will appropriately reflect the principal religious traditions of the area'.

The subject curriculum was expected to constitute no more than **80%** of the whole curriculum, in order to leave space for curriculum flexibility within schools. The concept of a whole curriculum was reinforced in subsequent publications and an acknowledgement of the importance to pupils of personal development:

> The whole curriculum of a school, of course, goes far beyond the formal timetable. It involves a range of policies and practices to promote the personal and social development of pupils, to accommodate different teaching and learning styles, to develop positive attitudes and values and to forge an effective partnership with parents and the local community.
>
> (NCC, 4 October 1989, Circular 6. *The Whole Curriculum Context*)

Cross-curricular themes, skills and dimensions were added later to the subject-based curriculum. The notion of 'Themes' embraces all those important ideas which sometimes slip between the subject planks; the NCC identified these as:

> Economics and Industrial Understanding; Careers Education and Guidance; Environmental Education; Health Education; Citizenship.

The term 'Skills' includes communication, problem solving and study skills.

The concept of 'Dimensions' is concerned with the intentional promotion of personal and social development, which includes positive attitudes towards cultural diversity, gender equality and people with disabilities.

In order to consolidate and affirm the importance of progression and the testing associated with monitoring progress, the concept of **Key Stages** was introduced. A Key Stage (KS) represents an age cohort of pupils arranged according to the pupil ages and, importantly, to the stages of national testing:

KS	Age of the majority of pupils at the end of the school year	New description of groups
*	5	Reception (R)
KS1	6	Year 1 (Y1)
	7	Year 2 (Y2)

KS2	8	Year 3 (Y3)
	9	Year 4 (Y4)
	10	Year 5 (Y5)
	11	Year 6 (Y6)
KS3	12	Year 7 (Y7)
	13	Year 8 (Y8)
	14	Year 9 (Y9)
KS4	15	Year 10 (Y10)
	16	Year 11 (Y11)
**	17	Year 12 (Y12)
	18	Year 13 (Y13)

('Key stages, ages and year groups', National Curriculum Council, 1992b, p. 5)
Note: * and **: no Key Stage designation is given officially to these periods before and beyond compulsory schooling.

Attainment Targets

The curriculum was structured differently for each Key Stage, but written to provide continuity and progression from one stage to the next. The content of each subject was divided into Attainment Targets (ATs) or characteristic content and processes associated with the subject. For example, the ATs for English are:

Speaking and Listening
Reading
Writing

The ATs were supported by syllabus guidance, called Programmes of Study (PoS), described as compulsory and illustrative learning experiences and activities. Listed within each AT were statements of content which formed the basis of what was to be tested by means of Standard Assessment Tasks.

It was envisaged originally that teachers would assess pupils' work as a continuing process, with some statutory tests at the end of the four key stages (see table above). Grading would be on a ten level scale, showing the appropriate levels reached for each Key Stage and the average level of attainment. Modifications and amendments to the original intention occur regularly. You need to check the specific requirements for your subject with your tutor or mentor.

Task 7.3.1	**YOUR SUBJECT AND THE IMPACT OF THE NATIONAL CURRICULUM** Give a ten to fifteen minute presentation on 'The National Curriculum and the teaching of your subject at KS3 or KS4 or both'.

The aim of this task is to find out the content of the National Curriculum in your subject and to explain it to student teachers of other subjects. In addition to knowing the content of the Attainment Targets and Programmes of Study, you need to know the extent to which they have been implemented, the nature of the assessment and the recording. You could also read about how it has changed the nature of your subject and the implications for the subject teacher. (A good place to find information is your subject association journal.)

Policy into practice

The nationally prescribed curriculum was never intended to constitute the whole curriculum. The original intention of the NCC and CCW was to ensure a common experience for 80% of the curriculum and, further, that forms of assessment would monitor the continuity and progression within and between schools. The government's introduction of Standard Assessment Tasks (SATs), the reporting of test and examination results in league tables, ostensibly to raise standards, did not take into account regional and social diversity. The emphasis on examination performance through complex procedures of recording, testing and reporting meant that assessment dominated and determined the curriculum, whilst non-assessed subjects such as home economics, PSE and music were undermined. The introduction of tiered examination papers forced some schools into grouping by ability and consequently towards whole school streaming.

Although cross-curricular elements were included, the increase in prescribed subject content and the threat of league tables meant that there was an inevitable privileging of aims and objectives which could be evaluated (subject knowledge) and a relegation of what could not be evaluated, such as relationships, creativity and attitudes. The cross-curricular themes and dimensions did not receive much attention in schools because of the pressure of reorganising the subject curriculum and attending to KS3 testing. Together with league tables, the introduction of the self-financing of schools (through LMS) and the development of GM schools combined to encourage a 'marketplace' mentality and competition between local schools for the brightest pupils.

Although the original National Curriculum framework was ostensibly designed for flexibility, the pressures upon the timetable to incorporate all foundation subjects and the pressure within each subject to cover the prescribed content of the National Curriculum meant that, in practice, there was negligible room for flexibility. In order that students could have maximum opportunity to achieve their best results in the tests, the individual teacher found little space to introduce their own enthusiasms, to draw upon local events, to foster the interests of the pupils or to develop cross-curricular issues.

The form and intensity of testing, especially at KS3, led rapidly to teacher unrest. For example, in 1993, teachers of English boycotted the first cohort of KS3 tests on the following grounds:

- lack of adequate preparation time;
- the objection to tiered papers which required teachers to forecast pupils' results without due evidence and to segregate pupils according to this forecast of their ability to perform in the tests;
- inappropriate question and answer examinations;
- impossible demands on teacher time which would detract from effective classroom teaching.

The National Union of Teachers won an appeal against the accusation by the DFEE of being in breach of their legal duties. The verdict was that the SATs involved an unreasonable workload; consequently all teachers were relieved of the obligation to undertake the tests. In 1994, tests in English, mathematics and science were boycotted by large numbers of schools. Some pupils took the tests in some schools but very few schools sent their results to SCAA as required by law.

Task 7.3.2

CURRICULUM PLANNING: INTRODUCING ICT

This situation should be addressed through Group role play.

Situation: The school governors have recommended that pupils in Year 9 be given one lesson per week for information communication technology and cross-curricular projects. The deputy head in charge of curriculum planning is to chair a meeting of heads of department. The heads of department must decide how to make provision for this additional lesson.

The school week consists of 25 x 1 hour lessons. Each head of department gives a brief speech in order to safeguard or to increase the current lesson allocation (given in parentheses) in their subject:

PSE (1)   English (3)
RE (1)   Mathematics (3)
Careers   Science (3)
Citizenship (1)   Modern Foreign Languages (3)
PE (2)   Humanities (3)
Creative arts – Music, Dance, Drama – (2)
CDT – Design, Home Economics, Technology (3)

Activity: Take on the role of the head of department and prepare your speech. You may need to obtain copies of a department's aims and syllabus. Hold the committee meeting: someone needs to take on the role of the deputy head and act as chairperson (this could be a student teacher or a tutor).

Additional activity: Write a short report of the meeting for the governors with the response to their recommendation. Give a full explanation and justification of your position concerning changes to the timetable, identifying key issues and decisions.

Modifying the National Curriculum: the new orders – The Dearing Report (Dearing, 1994)

By 1993 the National Curriculum was proving to be unacceptable and unworkable in schools. At this time, Sir Ron Dearing was appointed by the Secretary of State to review the National Curriculum Statutory Orders, and to revise the National Curriculum, taking into account the views of teachers. John Patten, Secretary of State for Education, set out four key targets for the review:

- to slim down the mandatory curriculum;
- to review the ten level scale of Statements of Attainment;
- to simplify the SATs;
- to improve the administration arrangements for the National Curriculum Orders and assessment.

In July 1993, an interim report was produced, for comment by teachers and the government, followed by the Final Report (Dearing, 1994). This was followed by a further review stage in July in which all ten National Curriculum subjects were revised by government-appointed subject teams and published for consultation with teachers and other educationalists. The revised National Curriculum Statutory Orders were to be finalised in October/November 1994, distributed to schools for January 1995 and implemented from September 1995. It was agreed that there then would be no further curriculum changes for five years. The next review is underway.

The Dearing Report – key features

In 1993, the new assessment council, the School Curriculum and Assessment Authority (SCAA) in England (now the Qualifications and Curriculum Authority), replaced both the NCC and SEAC which hitherto were separate government quangos. SCAA and The National Council of Vocational Qualifications (NCVQ) had the responsibility for implementing the proposals and overseeing all assessment arrangements. The Final Report showed a commitment to streamlining and simplifying the content, delivery and assessment of the National Curriculum subjects. The new Orders allowed more flexibility for the individual subject teacher and for a school's curriculum. The requirements within each syllabus were reduced so that there could be more time for non-prescribed aspects of a subject and for academic and vocational options. The intention was that time should be freed to develop both academic options and a range of vocational courses. The recommendation was for the introduction of vocational pathways from the age of 14, from which students could progress post 16. In accordance it proposed three pathways:

- The Academic Pathway – leading to GCSE;
- The Vocational Pathway – leading to General National Vocational Qualifications or vocationally oriented GCSEs;
- The Occupational Pathway – leading to NVQ or other occupationally specific certification, e.g. City and Guilds.

The underlying principles of the revised Orders were presented as 'Baseline principles' and the proposed practices of these were termed 'Curriculum features' (SCAA, 1994, Consultative document). The implications of vocational courses are discussed further in Unit 6.3.

The report underlined the primacy of the **Programmes of Study** in the planning and day-to-day teaching of each subject. The complex table of Statements of Attainment was reduced to ten simplified Level Descriptions (LDs) in each Attainment Target. The function of LDs was to assist in the making of summary judgements about pupils' achievements as a basis for reporting at the end of the Key Stage.

Further details of the proposals included the following:

Key Stages 1–3 (implemented from September 1995)   Twenty per cent of a school's time should be freed for discretionary teaching. Schools are accountable to governors for the proper use of the 'discretionary' time. This time should concentrate on literacy, oracy and numeracy and then extension work in the National Curriculum subjects. Importance is given to increasing competence in the use of information technology (IT).

The **'baseline' principles** which informed the slimming down at **KS3** were concerned with:

- breadth, depth, access, entitlement;
- need for opportunities to build on KS2 experiences and achievements to acquire, develop and apply a range of more advanced knowledge, understanding and skills;
- need for informed decisions at KS4;
- pupils' greater independence and need to motivate in different ways.

Each subject was charged with incorporating three curriculum features:

- a requirement for at least one aspect of the subject to be studied in depth;
- flexibility of approach within the statutory content;
- sufficient breadth and depth to enable pupils to make informed choices about post-14 study and also to provide a sound basis for pupils' future study and life outside school.

Key Stage 4 (implemented from September 1996)   The mandatory subjects, which might only take up 60% of the curriculum, were English; mathematics; single science; short courses in a modern foreign language and information technology; PE; religious education; sex education.

The **'baseline' KS4 curriculum principles** were that the curriculum should:

- continue to develop knowledge and skills in key subject areas;
- motivate all students and ensure high expectations;
- develop a range of talents and thereby raise standards;
- provide recognition of progress and attainment at age 16;
- keep open a range of education and training options and provide progression through education and training post 16.

The **KS4 curriculum features** recognised:

- the need for the revised Orders to be assessed through public examinations;
- the need to provide double award and single award science options;
- the need to establish Programmes of Study and suitable accreditation arrangements for short courses in modern foreign languages and design and technology;
- the potential relationship between Programmes of Study in English, mathematics and IT and corresponding GNVQ core skills;
- the relationship between the Programmes of Study for PE and IT and GCSE in these subjects.

A further important statement was that the A–G grading scale (instead of the ten level scale) would be retained for GCSEs. Level Descriptions were to be devised which would relate to the GCSE grades and, where relevant, the equivalent for other appropriate qualifications. Consequently, the purpose of levels 8–10 was open to discussion now that KS4 is assessed through GCSE.

The Dearing Report emphasised that schools must continue to provide information about progress and achievement for parents. In addition, the curriculum should facilitate the achievement of National Education and Training Targets (NETTs); these targets are set by the government and aim to produce an improvement in educational qualifications as registered by a rise in the average national qualifications at 16. The revised Orders also set out in detail the requirements of the provision for pupils with special educational needs and emphasised the importance of IT throughout the Key Stages and across the curriculum.

Special educational needs (SEN)

A national SEN advisory group was established; it comprised specialist teachers and headteachers, with representatives from each subject and Key Stage advisory group. They reviewed the method of assessing and recording achievement by pupils with SEN in order to provide a means of registering small steps of progress which may not show on the respective Level Descriptions. The following principles were established and published in the Dearing Report:

1 Where programmes of study require a pupil to communicate, any means of communication, including technological aids, signing, symbols or lip reading, are acceptable.
2 Unless the skill of handwriting is being developed, the use of technical aids in producing written work is acceptable.
3 Physical aids to help with manipulation of equipment or resources are acceptable whenever a particular physical skill is not being developed.
4 Pupils should be allowed to acquire information in any non visual or non aural way necessary e.g. Braille, taping of text.
5 Where programmes of study require the use of specific senses such as sight, alternative approaches may be used to gain knowledge or acquire skills where needed. This should be indicated in the Orders.
6 At each key stage, programmes of study should be written so that age

appropriate activities can be planned at every level. Planning work at Levels 1 to 3 for older pupils is particularly important in this respect.

(SCAA, 1994, Consultative document)

In addition, SCAA published an overall 'Enabling Statement' which advised teachers to select material from earlier or later Key Stages if necessary to enable individual pupils to progress and demonstrate achievement, as long as it was in contexts suitable to the pupil's age. There were also Subject Specific Access Statements which give guidance concerning the particular challenges and opportunities for SEN pupils in different subjects. SCAA was replaced by the Qualifications and Curriculum Authority (QCA) in 1998).

INFORMATION TECHNOLOGY (IT)

All National Curriculum subjects contain a reference to IT. At Key Stages 1 and 2, it was assumed by Dearing that IT would be taught through all curriculum subjects. At KS3 there would be some time for separate IT classes for the teaching of new skills, but these skills would be practised across the curriculum. At KS4 there would be some development of IT in all areas of the curriculum whereby pupils should consolidate and augment prior learning. The phrase Information and Communication Technology (ICT) is now used, as access to e-mail and the Internet is available to schools.

Task 7.3.3	SCHEMES OF WORK AND CROSS-CURRICULAR ISSUES (INDIVIDUAL TASK)

Plan a scheme of work (or bring a scheme of work which has already been prepared) for a mixed ability Year 9 group. It should last for six to eight fifty-minute lessons. Identify the relevant Programmes of Study, points for assessment, Level Descriptors, cross-curricular links and teaching strategies. Accompany it with sample resources and an explanation of the decisions concerning content, delivery and outcomes with a view to equal opportunities.

Summary and key points

As with the original Orders for the National Curriculum (1989), the principles of the Dearing Review maintained the spirit of ERA:

> Education ... must be concerned to serve all our children well, whatever their background, sex, creed, ethnicity or talent.
>
> (The Dearing Report, 1994)

There is evidence in this report that the views of teachers had been sought in the attempt to reduce the prescription of subject content and testing of the National Curriculum at Key Stages 1–3. The streamlining of the ten level scale and fewer test papers were improvements on the previous models of assessment. There was agreement about the principle that Programmes of Study, not Standard Assessment Tasks or Level Descriptions, should drive the teaching and learning of a subject.

The content of the initial Orders had been broad and balanced, but the procedures of reporting and assessment had minimised the proportion of coursework and teacher assessment. In other words, assessment is driven largely by external examinations (SATs) and much less by teacher assessment. The purpose of assessment has shifted, therefore, from formative and diagnostic (teacher-based) to summative and grading (reporting by level grading). In addition, there were still extensive demands upon the syllabus, an over-emphasis upon examinations and undue workload on the teachers.

FURTHER READING

Hargreaves, A. (1989) *Curriculum and Assessment Reform*, Milton Keynes: Open University Press.

Drawing upon sociological and educational research, Hargreaves analyses modern initiatives and illustrates the contradictions between theories concerning teaching and learning and methods of testing and recording. He offers both a critique of current practices and constructive examples of alternative strategies. See also:

Hargreaves, A. and Evans, R. (1997) *Beyond Education Reform: Bringing Teachers Back In*, Buckingham: Open University Press.

Kelly, A.V. (1990) *The National Curriculum: A Critical Review*, London: Paul Chapman Publishing.

A succinct outline and critique of the concepts and introduction of the National Curriculum. Statistical evidence and empirical research are used to evaluate the first stages of implementation and to project the further implications of a nationalised curriculum. See also:

Blenkin, G., Edwards, G. and Kelly, A.V. (1992) *Change and the Curriculum*, London: Paul Chapman.

Matthews, J. (1989) *Curriculum Exposed*, London: David Fulton.

This book is intended as an introduction to the language and concepts of curriculum structures. It is an analytical guide which identifies characteristics, defines terms and explores the implications of curriculum structures. Policies and practices are discussed in their local and wider contexts in order to unveil the practical and political aspects of change. The introduction and impact of the National Curriculum forms the centre of debate in each chapter.

Moon, B. (1996) *A Guide to the National Curriculum (3rd edition)*, Oxford: Oxford University Press.

O'Hear, P. and White, J. (eds) (1993) *Assessing the National Curriculum*, London: Paul Chapman Publishing.

The book provides an excellent basis for discussing and responding to the National Curriculum. All but one of the contributions were papers at a conference entitled 'The National Curriculum – Which Way Now?' It builds on the controversial paper *A National Curriculum for All: Laying the Foundations for Success* by O'Hear and White (1991). The approach to the National Curriculum is in the form of a debate which centres on the structural features of and possible alternatives to the existing framework.

The subject-specific texts in the *Learning to Teach* series provide specific advice for each subject.

The following books provide more detailed information:

Dearing, Sir Ron, (1994) *The Final Report*, London: SCAA.
Lawton, Dennis (ed.) (1990) *The Education Reform Act, Choice and Control*, London: Hodder and Stoughton.
Moon, B. and Shelton Mayes, A. (1993) *Teaching and Learning in the Secondary School*, Milton Keynes: Open University Press.
National Curriculum Council (1993a) *A Curriculum Perspective: 14–19 Education in Schools and Colleges*, York: NCC.

8 YOUR PROFESSIONAL DEVELOPMENT

In this chapter we begin to consider life beyond your student teaching experience. The chapter is designed to prepare you for applying for your first post and to be aware of the opportunities available to further your education as a teacher after you have completed your initial teacher education course. It contains three units.

Getting a job at the end of your initial teacher education course is very important, time consuming and worrying for student teachers. Unit 8.1 is designed to help you at every stage of the process of getting your first post. It takes you through the stages of deciding where you want to teach, looking for suitable vacancies, sending for further details of posts that interest you, making an application, attending an interview and accepting a post.

Unit 8.2 considers the transition from student teacher to newly qualified teacher, immediate induction into the school and the job, ongoing induction throughout the first year and your further professional development. Part of the unit focuses on the development of your professional portfolio, which you should start as a student teacher (see the introduction) and how this may be used to aid your further professional development. At the end of your initial teacher education course it is used to inform and illustrate your career entry profile, which is mandatory for those gaining qualified teacher status in England.

Unit 8.3 is designed to give you an insight into the system in which many of you will be working as teachers. We look briefly at the structure of the state education system and then at teachers' accountability: professional, moral and contractual. This leads into a slightly fuller consideration of the legal and contractual requirements and statutory duties that govern the work of teachers.

8.1 GETTING YOUR FIRST POST

INTRODUCTION

Obtaining your first teaching post may be one of the most important decisions of your life, so it needs to be taken carefully. Obtaining a post involves a number of stages, each of which is equally important. The stages are:

- deciding where you want to teach;
- looking for suitable vacancies;
- selecting a post which interests you and sending for further details;
- making an application;
- preparing for and attending an interview;
- accepting a post.

Before you apply for your first post you need to decide where you want to teach, prepare your curriculum vitae (CV), write a generic letter of application, contact potential referees to make sure that they are prepared to act for you and to confirm their address, and undertake a mock interview. This unit is designed to help you with that process.

OBJECTIVES

At the end of this unit you should:

- understand the procedure for and process of applying for your first teaching post;
- be able to make a written application which is received favourably;
- be prepared for an interview for a teaching post.

DECIDING WHERE YOU WANT TO TEACH

If you are committed to living in one place because, for example, you have family commitments, you need to consider the distance it is possible to travel to a job in order to determine the radius in which you can look for jobs. You need to think about the travel time to and from school, as you probably will not want a long journey in your first year of teaching when you are likely to be tired at the end of each day or when you have had school commitments in the evening.

For other students, deciding where to apply is your first major decision. If you opt for a popular area it could be difficult to obtain a post. The reasons for popularity may be that there are few schools, turnover from schools is low or there are a number of applications from students at a local higher education institution. It is therefore worth considering if your preferred areas are popular areas and if so, whether there are other areas to which you could go or whether you could be totally flexible as to where you teach. It is worth doing some research about other areas of the country rather than basing your decision on assumptions about certain areas.

Task 8.1.1	**WHERE DO YOU WANT TO TEACH?**

WHERE DO YOU WANT TO TEACH?
Think about where you would like to teach and how flexible you are able to be in where you can look for a post. List all areas you would consider working in and find out something about those areas. If you know anyone from the area, talk to them about it. Visit the area if at all possible to get a general 'feel of the place' and further information about the area.

Also think about the type of school in which you want to teach. There are different types of school. In most areas there are primary schools catering for pupils in Years 1–6 (ages 5 to 10) and secondary schools catering for pupils in Years 7–13 (ages 11 to 18) or in some cases Years 7–11 (ages 11 to 16), with pupils going to a sixth form college for Years 12 and 13. Other areas have middle schools catering for pupils in Years 4–7 (ages 8 to 11) or 5–8 (ages 9 to 12) and upper schools starting at Year 8 or 9 (age 12 or 13) and generally catering for pupils up to Year 13. In some areas middle schools operate on a secondary model, employing subject specialists, in others, on a primary model, employing class teachers and in yet others they operate on both a primary and secondary model, with class teachers for the first one or two years and then subject specialists.

Schools can be either maintained or private. Maintained schools are funded through the Local Education Authority (LEA) and supported by services from the LEA. Grant-maintained schools have opted out of LEA control and receive their money directly from the government, using some of this to buy in services that the LEA would normally provide. Other types of school include voluntary aided, e.g. some Church schools and special schools. (There are proposals to change the status and names of schools to Community, Aided and Foundation schools; see DFEE, 1997b, pp. 66–8.) You would also be qualified to teach in a sixth form college or further education college. Alternatively, you may want to teach abroad, either in a paid or voluntary capacity, such as Voluntary Service Overseas (VSO). Some teaching jobs abroad require you to have teaching experience before you can apply.

You probably have a list of criteria for the type of school you would be happy to teach in. However, it is advisable not to close your mind to other options. During your school experiences you see or hear about a range of types of school and you may surprise yourself by enjoying teaching in a type of school which you had not previously considered.

| Task 8.1.2 | **WHAT TYPE OF SCHOOL DO YOU WANT TO TEACH IN?** |

List criteria for schools you would be happy to teach in. Find out about different types of school and discuss these with other student teachers or teachers in your school experience school who have gone to or taught in these different types of school. Find out what types of school there are in those areas in which you would like to teach. You can start by looking at the *Education Authorities Directory and Annual* and the *Education Year Book* (see the further reading at the end of this unit). If you visit the area(s) in which you would like to teach, try to arrange to visit some schools.

LOOKING FOR SUITABLE VACANCIES

The majority of advertisements for teaching posts are for specific posts in specific schools. Advertisements generally start around January or February. However, the majority of advertisements are around April or May because teachers who are leaving at the end of the academic year are not required to hand in their notice until the end of May. Independent schools often advertise earlier, from December onwards.

Teaching posts are advertised in a number of different places. Advertisements are generally placed in the **national press**, sometimes the **local press** (especially for part-time posts) and sometimes **sent directly to your institution**. The major source of information about teaching posts is the *Times Educational Supplement* (published every Friday). However, jobs are also advertised in:

- the *Guardian* (the Tuesday edition);
- the *Independent* (the Thursday edition);
- the *Daily Telegraph* (the Thursday edition) (mostly for jobs in independent schools);
- the *Teacher* (published weekly).

There are also advertisements in **religious and ethnic minority newspapers** such as:

- the *Asian Times*;
- *Catholic Herald*;
- *Church Times*;
- *Jewish Chronicle*;
- the *Voice*.

Letters from headteachers are often sent to teacher education institutions. These give advance notice of posts about to be advertised and information about making applications.

LEAs sometimes advertise posts themselves. Sometimes information is sent by subject inspectors or advisers to institutions which have courses offering that specific subject. Some LEAs produce lists of vacancies which they send on request, some send information and guidance about applications for posts to teacher education institutions. Some (although a decreasing number) advertise for general applications to the LEA rather than to an individual school. Many LEAs produce recruitment literature, e.g.

brochures and/or videos, which are designed to show what it is like to work for the authority. Practices vary; therefore check current practice in LEAs in which you might be interested.

The procedures for applying for teaching jobs in Scotland and Northern Ireland are different. If you are interested in teaching in Scotland or Northern Ireland, you should obtain further information from your institution, the Scottish or Northern Ireland Office (addresses are in Appendix 5).

Task 8.1.3   FINDING INFORMATION ABOUT TEACHING POSTS

Find out where in your institution (e.g. the careers office or library) books which are useful in applying for a teaching post and information sent to the institution about specific jobs are held and made available to interested student teachers. Find out specific procedures for applications to LEAs in which you are interested. Read the *Times Educational Supplement* regularly.

SELECTING A POST WHICH INTERESTS YOU AND SENDING FOR FURTHER DETAILS

If an advertisement interests you then write for further details. Write briefly and to the point. For example:

Dear Sir/Madam (or name if given in advertisement)

I am interested in the vacancy for a (subject) teacher (quote reference number if one is given) at ABC School, advertised in (publication, e.g. the *Times Educational Supplement*) of (date) and would be grateful to receive further details of this post.

Yours faithfully (if you use Sir/Madam or Yours sincerely if you use a name)

MAKING AN APPLICATION

As you read details of all posts to which you are interested in applying, underline key words and phrases which indicate whether the post is suitable for you as a first post, e.g. whether you have the knowledge, skills, qualities and experience the school is looking for and whether the school meets some or all of your requirements.

If you decide to apply, remember that first impressions are very important and applications are the first stage in the selection process. You need to present yourself effectively on paper. Plan the content of your application before you complete an application form or CV or write a covering letter for a specific post. You use the same basic information for all applications. However, you cannot have a standard application form, CV or letter of application which you use for every application. Each application needs to be slightly different as you want to match your experience and qualifications to the requirements of the post, highlighting different points and varying the amount of detail you provide according to specific requirements of the post and the school. A personalised application shows that you have taken the time to find out about a specific post in a specific school. An application which fails to explain why you are interested in the specific post in the specific school is unlikely to be considered further.

Thus, completing an application form for each post takes time. Two hours is probably the minimum time to complete an application properly without rushing it if you have prepared beforehand and have all the information available, longer if you have not.

Referees

When applying for teaching posts you are normally asked to supply the names and addresses of at least two referees. Before you complete an application, contact potential referees to make sure that they are prepared to act for you, to confirm their address and if there are any dates when they are away and unable to respond should a request arrive.

Your first referee is normally someone associated with your teacher education course. Some institutions indicate who you should name as the referee, e.g. the course director or your personal tutor, others leave this to the student. Check if there is one particular person who you should name as the first referee and if not, decide who you would like this to be and then ask that person. This reference covers all areas of your work on the course and represents the assessment of a large number of staff, including lecturers, professional tutor and mentor. It is often helpful for the person compiling your reference to have additional information about you which might be included in a reference, e.g. other activities you are involved in. Therefore, check whether it would be helpful for your referee to have a copy of your CV.

Your second referee should be someone who knows you well and is able to comment on your character, qualities, achievements and commitment to teaching as a career. This may be someone with whom you have worked in a permanent or vacation job, someone from your degree course, your school or institution tutor or other member of staff of a school where you have been on school experience.

It is not normal practice to include open testimonials with your application as schools or LEAs value confidential references more highly. Some LEAs have a policy of open references, i.e. the reference is shown to the applicant in certain circumstances. The referee knows this at the time of writing the reference.

Methods of application

Schools normally require job applicants to submit a letter of application and completed application form or a CV.

1 Letter of application   A letter of application should clearly state your reasons for applying for the post, matching your qualifications, experience, particular skills and personal qualities to the post as described in the information sent to you from the school. The letter is normally between one and two sides of A4 in length, on plain white notepaper. A suggested format for a letter of application is given below:

Address
(at top right hand side)

Date

Name of headteacher
Address

Dear Sir/Madam or Name of headteacher

Paragraph 1
In reply to your advertisement in (name of publication) of (date) I would like to apply for the post of (subject(s)) teacher (quote reference number if one is given) at (name of school).
Or
I have been informed by my University/College that, in September, you will have a vacancy on your staff for a teacher of (subject(s)) and I would like to apply for this post.

Paragraphs 2/3
This section should begin by explaining why you are applying for this particular post. It should then carefully match your qualifications, experience, particular skills and personal qualities to those required by the school, indicating what you could contribute as a teacher of the subject(s) specified.

Paragraphs 3/4
These might begin:
The enclosed curriculum vitae provides details of the content of my teacher education course. I would also like to draw your attention to . . . (here outline any special features of your course and your particular interest in these, anything significant about your teaching and any other work experience, anything else you have to offer above that required specifically by the post, including being able to speak a language other than English, extra-curricular activities, a second subject etc. that you wish the school to be aware of and any other information about interests and activities related to the post or to you as a teacher, including additional qualifications, awards and positions of responsibility you have held).

If you are unavailable for interview on any days, this is the point to mention it. You might indicate this by including a statement something like 'It may be helpful to know that my examinations (or other event) occur on the following date(s) (quote actual dates). Unfortunately this means that I am not able to attend for an interview on those dates. I hope this does not cause inconvenience as, should you wish to interview me, I could come at any other time.'

Yours faithfully (or Yours sincerely if you use the headteacher's name)
Name

---

2 An application form The information required on an application form closely matches that identified for a CV (below). Read through any application form before you write anything on it. We recommend that you make a photocopy of the blank form and complete this in pencil as a practice before completing the original form. This both helps you focus on what you are going to write and enables you to see whether it fits into the space provided. Follow exactly any instructions given. Check that there is no missing information, dates or other detail or questions which have not been answered. Do not leave any sections of the form blank. If there are sections which you cannot complete write N/A (not applicable). You might find it helpful to check your draft with your tutor.

One page of the form is often blank and in the space provided you are required to explain why you are applying for the post and to elaborate on the skills and experience that equip you for it. This section should be written in continuous prose as if it is a section of a letter, following the suggested format and containing the type of information given for a letter of application (above). It is usually acceptable to use additional sheets of paper and staple them to the form. This section requires information that would otherwise be included in a letter of application; therefore a letter of application with such an application form is normally very brief, indicating that you have included your application for the post of (subject) teacher as advertised in (publication). A longer letter of application would be needed if the application form does not include such a section.

3 CV A CV should always be accompanied by a longer letter of application. A CV summarises your educational background, qualifications, teaching and other work experience, interests and activities and any other relevant qualifications and information. A sample format for a CV is provided below.

CURRICULUM VITAE

Name: Date of birth:
Term time address: Home address:
Telephone number: Telephone number:

(indicate dates when you are at your term time address and when your home address should be used)

Academic qualification(s): (your first degree and above, with subject, institution and class)

Professional qualification (for initial teacher education): If you are yet to qualify write 'I am currently on a PGCE/BEd (or other) course and expect to qualify in July 200?.'

Previous relevant experience:

(provide only very brief details here to highlight the most important points to help the reader; expand on these later in the CV)

EDUCATION
(list institutions from Secondary School on, in reverse chronological order)

Institution   Dates attended
(you might want to include some detail about your degree and/or teacher education course, particularly emphasising those aspects of your course which match the requirements of the post)

QUALIFICATIONS
(list qualifications from 'O' levels/GCSEs on, in reverse chronological order)

Qualification gained   Date awarded
(with subject(s), grades or classification)   (or date to be awarded)

TEACHING EXPERIENCE
(list any prior teaching experience and the school experiences on your course, in reverse chronological order)

School and subject(s) taught   Year(s) and length of practice

OTHER WORK EXPERIENCE
(list permanent full- or part-time jobs and holiday jobs separately, each in reverse chronological order)

Job   Dates (start and finish)
(include anything special about each job, particularly where it relates to children and/ or teaching)

INTERESTS AND ACTIVITIES
(e.g. membership of Clubs or Societies, details of offices held, achievements, e.g. sport, music, hobbies; group these together if appropriate, with the most relevant first and if giving dates, in reverse chronological order)

ADDITIONAL QUALIFICATIONS
(e.g. ability to use (ICT), additional languages, music grades, coaching or first aid awards)

OTHER INFORMATION
(include anything else that you think is important here in relation to the post for which you are applying)

REFERENCES
First referee   Second referee
Position   Position
Address   Address
Telephone number: Telephone number:

Notes about applications

1 Applications should be laid out well and presented clearly, completed neatly, with legible writing and without using jargon. Check your application to ensure that there are no basic errors such as typing errors, mistakes in spelling, grammar or punctuation; and that the information is accurate and consistent. We recommend that you use black ink as applications are often photocopied for members of an interview panel.

2 Indicate clearly any dates that you will not be able to attend for interview, e.g. because you have an examination. Examinations must normally take precedence over interviews. However, holidays do not take precedence and most schools will not wait until you return from holiday to interview you; therefore do not book holidays at times when you are likely to be called for interview.

3 Remember that if you put down additional skills or experiences, e.g. that you can sing, you may be invited to use those skills in school, e.g. in the school choir. Do not, therefore, make exaggerated claims about your skills or additional experiences.

4 Always send the original application, but keep a copy of every letter of application, application form or CV so that you can refresh your memory before an interview.

> **Task 8.1.4** **YOUR CURRICULUM VITAE**
> Draft a specimen letter of application and CV and obtain and complete an application form. Ask your tutor to check these for you. Use these as the basis for all your job applications.

ATTENDING AN INTERVIEW

If you are offered an interview, acknowledge the letter at once, in writing if there is time, indicating that you are pleased to attend for interview on that date. If you are offered two interviews on the same day, you probably have to choose which one you attend, unless they are at different times and close enough together to enable you to attend both. Write and decline the interview you decide not to attend.

   If there is a problem with an interview date, e.g. it coincides with an examination, let the school know immediately.

Preparing for the interview

Prepare for an interview in advance. Read through the advertisement, job description and any other information about the school and post again. Also try to find out if there is anyone at your institution or school experience school who knows the school. If possible, visit the school beforehand to find out more about it and about the local area. Most schools welcome this as long as you ask, as this enables them to arrange a suitable time.

Do not just turn up at the school and expect to look round. Decide what to look for when shown round the school. If possible, talk to a newly qualified teacher in the school.

You might find it helpful to reflect on why you applied for this particular post so that you can put across the relevant information convincingly at the interview. Read through your application again so that you can communicate effectively the information and evidence you consider to be relevant to the post. It also helps you avoid any contradictions between what you say and what you wrote in your application, as each member of the interview panel has a copy of your application and so can compare answers.

If you are not reading the *Times Educational Supplement* on a regular basis, we recommend that you do so before your interview so that you can talk about and answer questions on the latest educational issues and debates.

It is useful to have a portfolio of, for example, good lessons, worksheets, evaluations, review of resource(s), word processing skills. This is derived from the professional portfolio you have been keeping throughout your initial teacher education course (see Unit 8.2 for further information). From this professional portfolio you also develop your career entry profile.

If you are learning to teach a subject which requires you to take a portfolio of your work, e.g. art or design technology, begin to prepare this early in the year, gathering examples of work from school when you are on school experience. Subject books addressing student teachers on initial teacher education courses often include advice on interviews.

Plan what you are going to wear to the interview as your appearance is important. Knowing something about the school is useful, e.g. if the staff dress formally you should dress formally. If you are unsure, it is advisable to be conservative in your dress.

Attending the interview

It is difficult to generalise about interviews because these vary considerably. In many schools, all people invited to interview arrive at the school at the same time, are shown round the school, sit and wait while everyone is interviewed, for a decision to be made and for the successful candidate to be told. In other interviews, candidates are invited at different times so that they do not meet.

The format for interview days varies. It may, for example, comprise a tour of the school, an informal talk or interview with the head of department or a senior teacher, lunch and a panel interview. You may be asked to teach a lesson. If asked, make sure that you know the age and size of the class, what you are expected to teach and the pupils' prior knowledge, i.e. all the information you require before teaching any class. You should be told this on the letter of invitation to the interview. If not, telephone and ask.

As the format for interview days varies so does the panel interview. In some interviews you are faced by a panel comprising anything between two to three and six to seven people, in others you have a series of interviews with different people. In either case these people normally include some of the following: the headteacher, a governor, another senior member of the school staff, head of department and possibly LEA subject adviser. The length of time for a panel interview can vary from about half an hour to one and a half hours.

An interview is a two-way affair. At the same time as being interviewed you are, in effect, interviewing the school and deciding if this is a school you could work in and therefore if this is a post for you. Therefore, take the opportunity to learn as much as you can about the school, the post and the working environment. This requires you to be alert to what is being said and being prepared to ask as well as to answer questions at all times. If not included as part of the interview day, be firm in requesting an opportunity to look round the school prior to interview, including sitting in on a subject lesson if appropriate.

The initial impact you make is very important as interviewers tend to form an overall impression early. The interview starts as soon as you walk into the school and you are assessed throughout the day. Your performance, including your verbal and non-verbal communication, in each activity is therefore important and could make the difference between being offered the job or not.

Particular attention is paid to the impression you create in the formal interview. For example, do not sit down until you are invited to do so and then sit comfortably on your chair looking alert; do not sit on the edge of your chair looking anxious or slouch in your chair looking too relaxed. Look and sound relaxed and confident (even if you are not). Try to be yourself. Try to smile and to look at the panel during discussion. Do not talk too much. If you are unsure about how much information to give when answering questions it is probably better to keep an answer brief and then ask the panel if they would like further information. Avoid repeating what you say but do not worry if you repeat information included in your application, as long as you do not contradict what you wrote. Interviewers have various degrees of specialist knowledge and understanding. Avoid jargon in explanations but assume interviewers have some knowledge and under-standing of your subject area. Aim to provide a balanced picture of yourself and your course, being on the whole positive and emphasising your strengths, but constructively criticising where appropriate.

Interviewers are trying to form an impression of you as a future teacher and as a person and have a number of things they are looking for. These include:

- your knowledge and understanding of your subject and your ability to teach it. Interviewers assess your ability to discuss, analyse, appraise and make critical comment about ideas, issues and developments in your subject and subject cur-riculum, your personal philosophy about and commitment to the teaching of your subject(s);
- your professional development as a teacher. This is based partly on your school experiences. Interviewers assess your ability to analyse observations of pupils' behaviour and development, your involvement in the whole life of the school on your school experiences, your development on school experiences and your ability to discuss, analyse, appraise and make critical comment about educational issues;
- your ability to cope with the post. Interviewers assess how you would approach your teaching, e.g. your understanding of the different roles you are required to undertake as a teacher, how you have coped or would cope, in a number of different situations, e.g. disciplining a difficult pupil or class, dealing with a difficult parent or with teaching another subject;
- your ability to fit into the school and the staffroom and to make contact with and relate

to colleagues and pupils. Interviewers assess your verbal and non-verbal communication skills (your written communication skills have been assessed from your application);

- your commitment to living in that particular area and to the specific post. Interviewers assess the interest and enthusiasm you show for the post to try to find out if this is a post you really want or whether you see this post as a short-term stop-gap before you can find a post in an area where you really want to teach.

After introductions and preliminaries, most interviews focus on the information in your application, including your personal experiences, your education, qualifications, teaching skills gained from school experiences and other teaching and/or work experience, your interests and activities and other qualifications. You are normally also asked what you feel you can contribute to the school and why you are interested in and want this particular post and general questions about professional or personal interests, ideas, issues or attitudes. Therefore, think about areas you want to emphasise or any additional evidence of your suitability for the post that you did not have room to include in your application. Draw on your experiences both from your teacher education course and school experience and other experiences, e.g. other work with children such as Camp America, Sunday school teaching, work in a youth club or with organised groups such as boys' brigade or guides or voluntary work. These demonstrate your commitment to working with children.

You also need to show that you realise you still have things to learn (you should be able to talk about your weaknesses here) and that you are committed to continuing your development as a teacher. It is helpful to have a career plan, but not to appear so ambitious that you leave the school with the impression that you will leave at the first opportunity (you may want to think of committing yourself to two years in your first post, provided that you and the school are happy with your development).

Questions asked at interview vary considerably; therefore it is not possible for you to prepare precisely for an interview. However, it is helpful if you identify possible questions in your preparation and prepare some possible outline responses to such questions. Some questions which might be asked are:

Your commitment to teaching

Why did you choose teaching as a career?

Why did you choose to teach the secondary (middle/upper) age range?

Tell me something about your teacher education course.

Why did you choose this particular course?

Tell me something about your school experiences.

Which school experience was most successful/did you enjoy most and why?

What have been the most difficult aspects of your school experiences and why?

How do you know that a lesson is going well?

Recall a lesson that went well and/or one that went badly. Describe why this lesson went well or badly. How would you improve the lesson that went badly?

Have you used computers in your teaching? If so, how and if not, how do you think you might incorporate them into your teaching?

What do you consider to be your strengths and weaknesses as a teacher? How are you working to overcome your weaknesses?

Tell me about any other experiences of working with children which you think are relevant. What have you learned from these?

Your knowledge and understanding of your subject and subject application

What experience do you have of teaching your subject(s)?

Which aspects of your subject have you taught on school experience and to what years?

How would you introduce topic X to a Year 9 class?

How would you deal with, say, three boys misbehaving during a lesson in which there are safety implications?

Do you think that your degree subject prepares you to teach A Level?

How has your development in your subject during your course contributed to your work in the classroom?

How do the theory and practice on your course relate?

How can you tell if pupils are learning in your subject?

Can you describe one incident where a pupil was not learning and what you did about it?

What experience have you had of setting targets for pupils?

What other subjects could you teach and to what level? What background/teaching experience do you have in these subjects?

Your views about education, philosophy of education and educational ideas

Do you view yourself as a teacher of children or of X subject?

Why should all pupils study X subject?

What do you think education is about (individual development or to acquire skills to get a job)?

What do you think the aims of secondary (middle/upper) education should be?

What type of school would you like to work in and why?

What are your views about streaming, setting or mixed ability teaching?

How did you set about planning differentiated learning for a class you have taught recently?

How do you think your subject can contribute to the education of less able pupils?

What are your views about the way that the National Curriculum should develop?

What are your views on assessment?

Should pupils' achievements be based on test results or classwork/homework?

Your ability to cope as a teacher

What do you think are the qualities of a good teacher?

What are your strengths as a teacher at this stage in your career?

How would you maintain good discipline in the classroom?

What are your views about noise in the classroom and how would you keep it at an acceptable level?

How would you motivate a group of Year 9 pupils who do not have much interest in your subject?

Other roles you may be asked to undertake
What experience do you have of being a form tutor?
How do you feel about taking on the responsibilities of a form tutor?
How do you feel about taking extra-curricular activities after school, in the lunch times or on a Saturday morning?
What experience do you have of dealing with parents?

Your future development as a teacher
What are your targets for development during your first year of teaching?
How do you see your career developing?
How do you think you will go about achieving your career goals?
How long do you expect to stay in this school?
How do you aim to widen your experience as a teacher?

Other interests, activities etc.
What has been your greatest/worst achievement to date?
What interests or hobbies do you have and how involved are you in these? Do you see yourself being involved with any of these at the school?
Have you taken any positions of responsibility in any organisations you belong to?

Other questions
At the end of the interview you may be asked:
If you were to be offered this post would you be in a position to accept it?

At some interviews you may be asked this question earlier. You can say that you decline the offer to respond at that point but will respond after the interview.

At the end of the interview you are normally asked if you have any questions. Asking one or two questions shows a genuine interest in the school and the post; therefore do ask questions (not too many), if you have any. You are likely to forget the questions you wanted to ask when you are nervous; therefore, do not be afraid to take a checklist of questions with you to an interview. It is quite acceptable to refer to this during the interview itself. You should enquire what arrangements there are for induction of newly qualified teachers in the school and what you might expect. However, do not ask questions just to impress. If all your questions have been answered during the course of the day and you do not have any questions, just say politely that all the questions you wanted to ask have been answered during the day (or in the interview).

At some point you may want to ask about your starting salary. In a private school and in some situations in the state sector you may have to negotiate your salary. In the state sector you are on a national rate of pay, but your starting point on the scale depends on your degree classification. Any previous relevant experience may also be taken into account. Student teachers with prior relevant experience may be offered different starting points on the scale in different schools and different LEAs. If you have left school, gone straight through a degree and then completed a teacher education course, you probably cannot negotiate a starting point on the scale. However, if you have previous relevant experience, you may want to negotiate your starting salary. If you feel you are in a strong position, you may want to negotiate your starting point on the scale during your interview and ask for confirmation of this before you accept a post. In other situations, e.g. if you feel you are not in a very strong position to be offered the post, but really want the post, it may be appropriate to discuss the starting salary at a later date. How you describe experience in an application and at interview is therefore very important as it may be used to support any claim for increments above the starting salary.

> **Task 8.1.5**   **MOCK INTERVIEWS**
>
> Arrange for a mock interview with your tutor or another student teacher. If possible, either have an observer or video the interview so that you and the interviewer can use this to analyse your verbal and non-verbal communication after the interview. If, on analysis, you or the interviewer feel that there is a great deal on which you can improve, arrange for another interview after you have worked at improving your weaknesses.

ACCEPTING A POST

Where all candidates are invited for interview at the same time, you may be offered a post on the same day as the interview. You are normally expected verbally to accept or reject the offer at that time. Schools will rarely give you time to think about an offer. It is therefore important that you consider all the implications of accepting the post before you attend the interview. On rare occasions it may be that you feel you really need some time to think about the offer. You may want to ask if you can think about the offer overnight and telephone first thing in the morning. If your request is refused, you have to make a decision there and then or be prepared for the post to be offered to another candidate. Your decision depends on how much you want a particular job and how strong a position you think you are in.

If candidates are invited for interview at different times, you may have to wait for a few days before being offered a post. However, normally you do not know which format an interview is going to take until you arrive at the school, so you cannot rely on being able to do this.

It is normal practice to be asked to confirm your verbal acceptance of a post in writing. It is unprofessional to continue to apply for other teaching posts after you have verbally accepted a post, even if you see one advertised that you prefer.

Expenses (including basic overnight accommodation where necessary) are usually paid for attending an interview. However, rules vary between schools and LEAs and you might want to check in advance whether expenses are paid, whether receipts are needed and whether a claim for meals and/or overnight accommodation will be approved. You should receive a travel and expenses claim form with the letter notifying you of the interview or at the interview itself.

As you have access to children and young people, you are required to disclose all previous criminal convictions under the Rehabilitation of Offenders Act. After you have been offered a post you will be asked to complete a form detailing any criminal convictions and to give your consent to the school or LEA to verify your responses with the police.

You may also be asked to have a medical before you start a job. You will be sent the details of this from the school or the LEA.

Summary and key points

There is no point in you learning to become effective teachers if you do not obtain a teaching post at the end of your teacher education course. This unit is therefore designed to help you realise that, just as with your teaching, you must prepare for obtaining your first post; you cannot leave it to chance or rely on your innate ability to perform well at an interview. In this unit we have tried to lead you through the steps, skills and techniques you need to prepare actively for obtaining your first post. We hope it serves you well as you apply for your first post.

FURTHER READING

Crane, C.D. (1993) *The Key to your Success: Applying for a Secondary School Post*, Weymouth, Dorset: The Education Appointments Council.

This book provides information and examples, where appropriate, about job selection, CVs, letters of application and interviews to help you in applying for jobs.

National Union of Teachers (annually) *Your First Teaching Post*, London: NUT.

This guide is designed to answer some of your questions about where to look and what to look for in your first teaching post. It contains information supplied by education authorities and can be obtained from the NUT.

The Education Authorities Directory and Annual, (annual) Redhill, Surrey: The School Government Publishing Company Ltd and
The Education Year Book, (annual) London: Longman.

These books list all the LEAs in England and Wales, along with the names, addresses and telephone numbers of secondary schools, sixth form colleges and grant-maintained schools in their areas.

Times Educational Supplement (annually, around the middle of January) *First Appointments Supplement*, TES.

This supplement is published yearly. It contains articles and features on processes and procedures to help you get your first post and what to expect when you start your first post. It also contains many advertisements from LEAs about general applications.

ACKNOWLEDGEMENT

In preparing this unit, we would like to acknowledge the work by Gay Humphrys at the University of Greenwich published in a booklet entitled *Getting a Teaching Job*, sponsored by the Teaching as a Career Unit (TASC).

8.2   DEVELOPING FURTHER AS A TEACHER

INTRODUCTION

The success of any school depends on its staff. At the end of your initial teacher education (ITE) course you are recognised as having qualified teacher status (QTS). However, you still have a lot to learn about teaching. In Scotland, teachers serve a two-year probationary period. Up until recently, in England and Wales, your first year of teaching was considered to be a probationary year. The probationary year no longer exists in England and Wales, but you should not be 'thrown in at the deep end'. You should receive induction, which is part of your continuing professional development (CPD). CPD helps you continue to learn and develop professionally throughout your career in order to increase your effectiveness. Induction includes immediate induction into the post and ongoing induction throughout the first year. The agenda for ongoing induction should be derived largely from the issues identified by you in your career entry profile. Thus, induction is the first part of your CPD. This can be shown as follows:

Although school managers should recognise your need for further professional development, you must take responsibility for your own professional development. Your career entry profile is the beginning of active planning of your future career, identifying appropriate areas for development and activities and learning or experience to get you there. Professional accountability includes a commitment to keeping abreast of changes in education, in order to develop your knowledge and teaching skills.

This unit considers life beyond your student teaching experience to the transition from student teacher to newly qualified teacher, induction into the school and the job and during the first year of teaching and CPD beyond the first year. It also considers aspects of the work of the school that provide valuable developmental experiences.

OBJECTIVES

By the end of this unit you should:

- understand the need to undertake continuous learning and development; and
- be beginning to recognise the induction and CPD opportunities available to you.

The competences/standards about further professional development identified for your course form the basis for this unit. You should identify these now.

PROFESSIONAL PORTFOLIO

You should develop, throughout your ITE course, a professional portfolio or portfolio of achievement. This portfolio contains evidence of your developing professional knowledge and judgement to complement your subject knowledge. Specifically, it documents your performance in relation to the competences/standards identified for newly qualified teachers on your course, documents other strengths and successes, identifies areas for development and gives examples of your work as part of your ITE course (e.g. reports, observations on you made by teachers, lesson plans, assignments and notes and records contained in your diary of reflective practice). The diary of reflective practice is a record of the outcomes of tasks undertaken as you work through aspects of this book and other tasks undertaken as part of your course. It should help you to reflect on your school experiences and provide useful information for assignments undertaken.

Towards the end of your course you need to make sure that this information is gathered together. The evidence in the portfolio can be used to develop a portfolio to take to interview (see Unit 8.1 for further information about interviews). For those of you learning to teach in England it is also used to develop your career entry profile which you take into your first teaching post to inform your induction and which you build on throughout your career.

Many ex-student teachers of ours have commented that they did not see the relevance of certain information, theories or activities while they were student teachers but began to see their relevance as they developed as teachers. They then referred back to the notes they took or work they did as student teachers. Therefore, the information included in the portfolio is useful in its own right. However, many higher education institutions now recognise and accredit learning that has resulted from experience (this is called accreditation of prior experiential learning (APEL)) as entry to or exemption from part of a higher degree or professional qualification. In order to claim this exemption you

Task 8.2.1	**DIARY OF REFLECTIVE PRACTICE AND PROFESSIONAL PORTFOLIO** If you are reading this unit near the beginning of your course, start keeping a diary of reflective practice for tasks you undertake as you read through this book and as part of your ITE course. If you are near the end of your course and have not been developing a diary, collect together evidence from the tasks and assignments you have undertaken on your course. Reflect on and write down what you perceive to be your strengths and your weaknesses as a student teacher. Try to identify ways of reducing your weaknesses (if you cannot do this now, do it after you have gained ideas from this unit).

must provide evidence. This is normally requested as a portfolio. Therefore, if you get into the habit of keeping your portfolio up-to-date, you will have evidence ready to hand for consideration for APEL for a further qualification.

CAREER ENTRY PROFILE

A career entry profile is completed by all newly qualified teachers in England (Teacher Training Agency, 1998). The purpose of the career entry profile is to provide a summary of information about your strengths and priorities for your further professional development from ITE to your first teaching post, in relation to the standards required for gaining QTS. This information is intended to help you to target and address your development needs and to build on your strengths in your first year of teaching and to take responsibility for your own professional development from as early as possible in your career, by establishing the practice of target setting and review, in order to provide a good foundation for appraisal and your CPD.

It is also designed to help your first teaching post school to deploy newly qualified teachers effectively, taking account of the strengths and development needs which were identified as priorities at the end of your ITE course. It enables the school to draw up an action plan for induction which takes account of your own targets, targets identified by the school and any nationally identified objectives for induction. It also enables targeted monitoring and support to be provided during your induction.

The career entry profile has four sections:

- Section A contains a summary of your ITE, including any distinctive features of your course (as agreed between you and your ITE provider);
- Section B identifies your strengths and priorities for your further professional development during induction (as agreed between you and your ITE provider);
- Section C enables you to identify your own targets for your induction period:
- Section D identifies targets and an action plan for the induction period as agreed between you and your first teaching post school.

Sections A and B are completed near to the end of your ITE course. Section C is completed after you have finished your ITE course, but before you take your career entry profile to your first teaching post school. Section D is completed in conjunction with the member of staff responsible for your induction in your first teaching post school.

TRANSITION FROM STUDENT TEACHER TO NEWLY QUALIFIED TEACHER

When you successfully complete your course and get your first teaching post you will probably feel immense relief at having 'made it'. You may feel very confident and believe that you are going to be able to solve any problem you are faced with, e.g. motivating an unmotivated pupil or class or changing the teaching methods in the department so that much more active learning takes place. You may also fear failing in your new job. Different people have different fears, e.g. fear of not being able to control the pupils, of being thought to be lacking skill or ability, of not being accepted by other members of staff, of not liking the school or the people you work with. The transition from student teacher to newly qualified teacher is considered further in Capel, Leask and Turner (1997).

As the new person in a school and department, you may not be sure of how to behave or of the rules or procedures to follow. You will have some successes and some failures and will soon realise that you cannot solve every problem or change the world. As a result, your confidence may decrease and you may not be fully effective until you are settled in the school and the job. A well-structured induction programme should help you make this transition. A chapter on your immediate professional needs is included in Capel, Leask and Turner (1997).

INDUCTION

In England since September 1998 all schools are required to provide an induction programme for newly qualified teachers (see DFEE, 1997b, pp. 47–8).

Induction can be divided into two main parts: immediate induction into the job, which gives you vital information to help you through the early days; and ongoing induction, which continues throughout the year, providing the link between ITE and CPD. We consider immediate induction first.

Immediate induction

The Department of Employment (1971) defined induction as:

> arrangements made by or on behalf of, the management to familiarise the new employee with the working organisation, welfare and safety matters, general conditions of employment and the work of the department in which he is employed. It is a continuous process starting from the first contact with the employer.

Induction should, therefore, help you to understand, as quickly as possible, how you fit into the school and the department, building on information gained previously from literature, your interview or any further visits to the school after you were appointed. ACAS (1984) produced an induction checklist (summarised below) which you can use to check the content of an induction programme that you receive:

- reception, including completing paperwork required by the school, tour of the school, introducing you to key members of staff you have not previously met, management and administrative arrangements;
- layout of school, including cloakroom and toilets, first aid room, entrances and exits to be used, canteen, notice boards;
- the school, including structure and departments, future developments, brief historical comments;
- the department, including its function, supervision, colleagues and standard of work expected;

- conditions of employment, including contract of employment, reporting, salary and deductions, holidays, sickness and medical statements, sick pay, pension scheme;
- education, training and promotion, including school or LEA training schemes, policy on release for courses, assistance with fees, appraisal;
- safety procedures, including behaviour, fires, location of fire-fighting equipment, location of exits, use of extinguisher, first aid, how to get medical help;
- rules, regulations and procedures, including misconduct, disciplinary procedures, involvement of employee representatives, grievance procedures, appeals;
- employee involvement and communication, including employee representatives, dispute procedures, consultative arrangements, communication and briefing arrangements (e.g. morning staff meetings);
- physical facilities, welfare and employee benefits/facilities, including canteen facilities, protective clothing, lockers, medical services, suggestions scheme, sports/social facilities, telephone facilities, transport arrangements.

The immediate induction programme applies only to the first few days and weeks of any job. It should be supported by ongoing induction throughout your first year of teaching, which is linked to CPD beyond the first year.

Ongoing induction

In our experience many newly qualified teachers report that school experience gave them an indication of the demands of teaching, but had not prepared them fully for the demands of a full-time post. They had felt that as they would not be constantly observed, evaluated and assessed, stress and tiredness would reduce. However, they discovered that the first year of teaching was just as, if not more, tiring and stressful as their school experience.

In one way being a newly qualified teacher in your first teaching post is not much different to being a student teacher: you are still a beginner, albeit a beginner with more experience. In other ways, however, your first teaching post is a very different experience from school experience as a student teacher. You may feel differently about yourself as a 'real' teacher. This may influence the way you behave. Further, staff and pupils may treat you differently as a full member of staff.

ITE courses cannot adequately prepare student teachers for all aspects of teaching in the time available. All newly qualified teachers still have a lot to learn and inevitably feel unprepared for some aspects of the teacher's role. It is likely that as a student teacher you do not undertake all the activities that teachers undertake, e.g. student teachers are unlikely to be involved with developing schemes of work for a year or a key stage or for administering examinations. In your first year of teaching you undertake a greater range of responsibilities than as a student teacher, e.g. you have your own groups and classes and can establish your own procedures and rules for classroom management right from the beginning of the school year. You therefore undertake the full role of the teacher in your classroom.

During the first few weeks or first term in your new post, you probably find that you concentrate mainly on becoming confident and competent in your teaching so as to establish yourself in the school. You are busy getting to know your classes, planning units of teaching from schools' schemes of work, lesson plans, teaching, setting and marking homework, undertaking pastoral activities with your form and getting to know the rules, routines and procedures of the school.

Over the course of the first year you face situations that you did not experience as a student teacher. This includes undertaking activities for the first time, e.g. discussing progress with pupils as part of their Record of Achievement, setting questions for examinations or undertaking supervisory duties and activities that you have not had to sustain over such a long period of time previously, such as:

- planning and preparing material for a year to incorporate different material, teaching strategies and approaches to sustain pupil interest and motivation;
- adapting your planned course to meet the needs of different groups of pupils. As you should be aware from your school experiences, you cannot plan one set of material and deliver it in exactly the same way to different groups of pupils. This adaptation requires careful planning and being able to think on your feet in order to meet the needs of particular pupils and classes;
- encouraging progress, target setting and maintaining learning over the period of a year;
- maintaining discipline over a whole year. This is very different to maintaining discipline over a short period of time on school experience. You cannot 'put up with' things which you may have been able to put up with for a relatively short period of time on school experience.

Although taking extra-curricular activities may be expected of you, particularly of physical education teachers, we advise you not to take on too many (certainly not every lunch time and evening as many physical education teachers do). In your first year you need to concentrate initially on developing into an effective teacher.

However, as a newly qualified teacher, you may not be expected to undertake the full range of roles and responsibilities of teachers, e.g. you may not be expected to deal with some of the more serious pastoral problems or undertake the full range of administrative demands. Marland (1993, p. 191) said that this:

> therefore confirms and contradicts the assertion that probationers are invariably thrown in at the deep end of teaching. They might be thrown in, but it is a rather smaller pool in which they have to swim, since most of the administrative and managerial responsibilities do not come their way. Nonetheless, to continue the metaphor, it is possible to drown in a very small pool and . . . the classroom is notoriously hazardous. The major consolation is that much of the classroom-based work will have been encountered during the teaching practice term.

Thus, you may feel that teaching is more difficult than you first thought and realise that you still have a lot to learn. As a result, you may become frustrated, have doubts about whether you can teach and what you are achieving with the pupils. You may need help and understanding from other members of staff to overcome these doubts and continue to develop as a teacher.

Newly qualified teachers should be allocated an experienced member of staff to act as a mentor during their first year of teaching. You may be given a lighter teaching load during your first year of teaching to enable you to spend time with your mentor and also to account for the fact that everything is new and therefore takes you longer to do. You can draw on your mentor's experience to help you to answer the numerous questions you have as new situations arise and to overcome problems with aspects of your teaching. Your mentor can help you to learn as part of your normal job, by identifying and using opportunities available in your everyday work to develop further your skills, knowledge or understanding. You may discuss a problem and then go away and try to put some of the suggested possible solutions into practice. Your mentor should observe a lesson, discuss it with you, give you feedback and constructively criticise your performance, suggesting alternative approaches if appropriate. This type of learning (often called coaching) is generally effective because you learn by doing, you get feedback on your performance and the learning is relevant. This is especially important in an activity or situation in which it is very difficult to simulate the experience.

In an ideal world a mentor is proactive, making a conscious effort to look for opportunities for development. However, your mentor is busy and you spend much of your time in a classroom on your own with pupils; therefore there may be limited opportunities for coaching. You may therefore use coaching reactively by identifying areas where you feel you would benefit most from further development or where something has gone wrong. You can set up a situation where your mentor can help you address or correct that particular issue, e.g. ask your mentor to observe a lesson and comment on a particular aspect of your teaching, observe a lesson taken by your mentor or another member of staff or team-teach particular topics in which you lack confidence. A chapter on working with your mentor is included in Capel, Leask and Turner (1997).

> **Task 8.2.2**
>
> **THE ROLE OF THE MENTOR TO NEWLY QUALIFIED TEACHERS**
> Find out who is/has been a mentor for a new member of staff recently. Discuss with that member of staff their role and responsibilities and what they expect from a newly qualified teacher. Record this in your diary. It may form the basis of answers to questions at interview or help you in your first post. Alternatively, talk to a newly qualified teacher about the role and responsibilities of their mentor.

Most other members of staff are also helpful and understanding, especially if you establish good relationships with them. Relationships take time to develop and you need to be sensitive to the environment you are in. You will not get off to a very good start if, for example, you sit in someone's usual chair in the staffroom, try to impress everyone with your up-to-date knowledge, ideas and theories, try to change something immediately because you think things you have seen in other schools could work better, either ask for help before you have tried to solve a problem yourself or do not know when to ask for help or do not operate procedures and policies and enforce school rules. If you do not operate procedures and policies or enforce these rules, you undermine the system and create tensions between pupils and teachers and between yourself and other members of staff.

However, as you settle into the job and work with your classes and learn the procedures, rules and routines, other staff may forget that you are new. As they become ever more busy with their own work as the term and year progress, they treat you as any other member of staff and do not offer help and advice. If you need support, approach staff and talk to them about your concerns and ask for help.

You may form a support group with other newly qualified teachers. You can share your concerns and problems, support and learn from each other and remind each other that despite the amount you still have to learn, you also have much to offer and are enthusiastic.

CPD (BEYOND THE FIRST YEAR)

New teachers spend the first couple of years in teaching establishing themselves. There are some activities which teachers undertake which you need to develop after you have established yourself in the teaching role. As you develop you will probably want to take on posts of responsibility, either within the department or the school. It is important to recognise that, just as when you started your first post, when you take up a new post later in your career, you will go through a period of transition as you adjust to the new situation. You are likely to adjust more quickly if you have identified the range of new responsibilities required in the post, identified areas for development through reflection and planning as recorded in your professional portfolio, through the appraisal process or analysis of critical incidents and undertaken appropriate, continuing professional development. Your career entry profile should have been the beginning of a professional development scheme which you continue to work on throughout your career. There are many ways you can develop new areas of expertise (as well as improve on any areas of weakness), e.g. short or long courses, a higher degree or a further professional qualification and being involved in development and change activities in the school. In England, all new heads of department and head teachers are required to undertake training for their responsibilities (see Teacher Training Agency, 1998).

Initiating development and change through the school development plan

Involvement in development and change processes, most often through school development planning, is a valuable form of CPD. Following an inspection by OFSTED, all schools must produce a development plan to address issues raised in the OFSTED report. Further, you are more likely to effect change through being involved in this process. You are unlikely to effect change if you 'jump in with both feet' as a new teacher because you are unlikely to understand the particular school context, its politics, rules, routines, procedures and policies and the reason that these are in place, to have developed effective channels of communication and working relationships with established staff.

A school development plan enables a school to:

organise what it is already doing and what it needs to do in a more purposeful and coherent way . . . it brings together, in an overall plan, national and LEA policies and initiatives, the school's aims and values, its existing achievements and its needs for development. By coordinating aspects of planning which are otherwise separate, the school acquires a shared sense of direction and is able to control and manage the tasks of development and change. Priorities for development are planned in detail for one year and are supported by action plans or working documents for staff. The priorities for later years are sketched in outline to provide the longer term programme.

(Hargreaves *et al.*, 1989, p. 4)

School development plans should start from where the school is now, developing whole school, departmental and other plans covering all aspects of school life, e.g. teaching, curriculum and assessment, management and organisation, resources, staff development and finance. Development planning comprises four processes. These are:

audit: a school reviews its strengths and weaknesses;
plan construction: priorities for development are selected and turned into specific targets;
implementation: of the planned priorities and targets;
evaluation: the success of implementation is checked.

(Hargreaves *et al.*, 1989, p. 5)

This is illustrated in Figure 8.2.1.

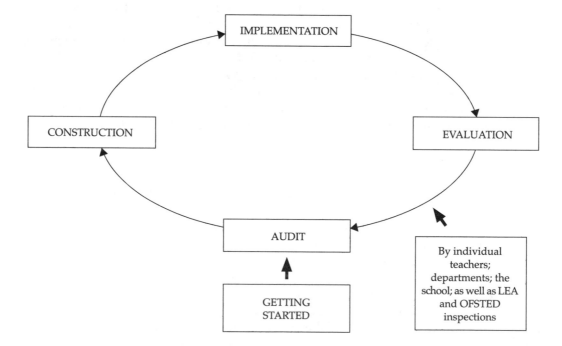

Figure 8.2.1 The planning cycle for school development planning
Source: adapted from Hargreaves *et al.* (1989, p. 50)

School development plans work best when all staff are involved. This requires consultation so that the views of all staff are considered, including support staff and any parent–teacher association. To work best, everyone needs to know how they can contribute and what they are expected to do. Different processes and activities are shared out; for example, governors, the head, senior managers, the CPD co-ordinator, curriculum leaders, departments and teams of staff may be responsible for different aspects of the plan. You may be involved at different stages of school development planning in a number of different ways, depending on the foci of the plan for any one year. Take the opportunity to be fully involved in all appropriate aspects of the plan in order to initiate development and change within the school and to further your professional development.

Professional development is part of your professional accountability as a teacher. You should therefore monitor your progress as a teacher and your professional development.

Monitoring and evaluation

You should already be familiar with the process of monitoring and evaluating in your work with pupils, e.g. monitoring the attainment of pupils, evaluating the effectiveness of lessons or of different teaching strategies. In order to continue to learn in the teaching situation, as well as get the most out of your professional development activities, continue the active, reflective approach to learning which you started during your ITE course. Monitor and evaluate your teaching and your development activities against specific objectives you have identified for development, as you would a lesson, and continue to question what you are doing and identify alternative approaches. Record your progress in your portfolio.

You can also benefit from discussing your development as a teacher and your professional development activities. You can, of course, do this informally, but appraisal gives you the opportunity to discuss this formally.

APPRAISAL

Teacher appraisal is part of making explicit teacher accountability. Appraisal normally consists of observation of your teaching and an appraisal interview. The appraisal interview may start with discussion of your observed teaching performance. It may then progress to your performance in the job over the past year, your strengths, areas for development and professional development undertaken to address these. In doing this, there are a range of topics which may be discussed, e.g. your teaching, pastoral work, curriculum development work, management and administrative activities and membership of committees and working parties. Your career entry profile should be used to provide a focus for this discussion in your first appraisal. An appraisal interview should provide you with valuable dialogue, resulting in the identification and confirmation of areas for development and ways in which any identified needs might be met, e.g. by attending conferences, studying for a higher degree, further involvement in the school development plan or other opportunities for CPD within the school.

> ## Summary and key points
>
> This unit has considered the sequence of development as a teacher through:
>
>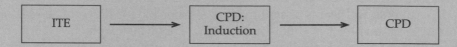
>
>   You are already on the professional development road and it is your professional responsibility throughout your career to seek opportunities for development. Your career entry profile helps you to target and address your development needs and to build on your strengths in your first year of teaching. It also helps you to take responsibility for your own professional development from as early as possible in your career, by establishing the practice of target setting and review, in order to provide a good foundation for appraisal and your CPD. Your targets may include targets for wider aspects of your role as a teacher. For example, do you know what to do if a pupil has an epileptic fit or an asthma attack? Would you feel more in control if you knew how to deal with such situations in your teaching? If so, would you benefit from undertaking a first aid course? Similarly, although competence in information and communications technology (ICT) is a requirement if you are learning to teach in England (DfEE, 1998), do you, for example, need to develop further the use of ICT in teaching and learning or are there aspects that you need to update?
>   There are many areas in which you could probably benefit from education and training. For example, your career plans may be to progress to a management post. Although you may be identifying CPD needed to make such a move, you will want to ensure that you are fully established as a teacher first. It is important not to take on too much at once. Your first year of teaching is very demanding and therefore it is important that you pace yourself when planning for your further professional development.

FURTHER READING

Dean, J. (1993) *Managing the Secondary School*, London: Routledge.

This book was written for people in management positions in secondary schools and therefore gives a broad perspective on the life of the school. For any new teachers looking to management as a possible future career path, this text is very helpful in highlighting the range of managerial activities undertaken.

Dunham, J. (1995) *Developing Effective School Management*, London: Routledge.

This book is designed to help teachers to identify and develop knowledge and skills to become effective middle managers. The first chapter addresses the importance of whole school management and following chapters address different aspects of management, including effective management styles, management theories, the management of teams and meetings, key management skills, CPD, managing change, time management, stress management.

Hargreaves, D.H., Hopkins, D., Leask, M., Connolly, J. and Robinson, P. (1989) *Planning for School Development: Advice to Governors, Headteachers and Teachers*, London: DES.

This short booklet provides information about school development planning, but should provide useful information for any planning process in which you might be involved and therefore should be of interest whether or not you are working on a school development plan.

OFSTED (1993b) *The New Teacher in School: A Survey by Her Majesty's Inspectorate in England and Wales, 1992*, London: Department for Education.

This report should help to put your training and preparation into context as the first stage in your career. It should help you to realise that many other new teachers share your feelings of having a lot to learn as a teacher or doubts about being inadequately prepared for teaching. It therefore should be encouraging.

8.3   ACCOUNTABILITY, CONTRACTUAL AND STATUTORY DUTIES

As a newly qualified teacher in the state system your work is controlled by the requirements of national and local government, school, subject, parent and pupils – so you are accountable to a whole range of interested parties for the quality of your work.

To help you understand the context in which teachers work, we have provided a description of the system within which teachers in the state system operate.

OBJECTIVES

By the end of this unit you should:

- understand the structure of the state education system;
- be aware of the legal and contractual requirements that govern the work of the teacher.

WHERE DO TEACHERS FIT WITHIN THE EDUCATION SYSTEM?

The structure of the education system in England and Wales is set out in Figure 8.3.1 to show the relationships between classroom teachers and the rest of the education system.

The Secretary of State, ministers and staff at the DFEE do not usually have teaching experience. They are provided with professional advice by advisory bodies such as the Qualifications and Curriculum Authority (QCA) (previously the School Curriculum and Assessment Authority (SCAA)) which have some members with a wide range of expertise in the profession. However, Local Education Authority officers and professors and lecturers in education normally start their careers as classroom teachers.

Whilst the responsibilities within the school, listed in Figure 8.3.1, are shared out differently in different schools, the structure is not usually too dissimilar. In Scotland and Northern Ireland, the structures are similar but the terminology used is in some cases different.

There are also numerous support staff whose contribution to school life is essential to the smooth running of the school: caretaker (school's premises' officer); nurse; secretarial staff; technical staff; cleaners; lunch time supervisors. Staff from other professions are also linked with the school, e.g. the education welfare officer, school psychologists and some pupils have social workers who are responsible for overseeing their progress.

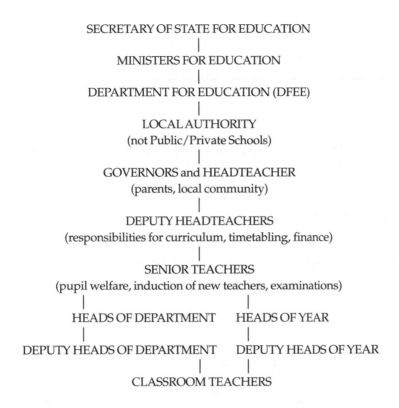

SECRETARY OF STATE FOR EDUCATION
|
MINISTERS FOR EDUCATION
|
DEPARTMENT FOR EDUCATION (DFEE)
|
LOCAL AUTHORITY
(not Public/Private Schools)
|
GOVERNORS and HEADTEACHER
(parents, local community)
|
DEPUTY HEADTEACHERS
(responsibilities for curriculum, timetabling, finance)
|
SENIOR TEACHERS
(pupil welfare, induction of new teachers, examinations)

HEADS OF DEPARTMENT   HEADS OF YEAR

DEPUTY HEADS OF DEPARTMENT   DEPUTY HEADS OF YEAR

CLASSROOM TEACHERS

Figure 8.3.1 Structure of the education system

Accountability

Within the structure of the education system and individual schools, teachers are accountable for what they do and the Office for Standards in Education (OFSTED) plays a major part in monitoring the work in schools. As an individual teacher though, you are also accountable – to parents, to colleagues, to pupils, to your employer.

Bush (in Goddard and Leask, 1992, p. 156ff) identifies three ways in which a teacher experiences accountability. Bush calls these:

Moral Accountability
Professional Accountability
Contractual Accountability.

Moral accountability is related to your conscience about how you should carry out your work. You are 'morally accountable' to students, parents and to society.

Your professional accountability relates to your responsibility to your colleagues and to the teaching profession, to do your work to the highest standard of which you are capable.

Contractual accountability is defined by legal requirements set down by your employer as well as in legislation passed by Parliament.

Whilst this may seem an oversimplification of a teacher's accountabilities these three aspects provide a useful framework for developing your own understanding of your accountability. However, the way moral and professional accountability is personally perceived depends on the values of the individual teacher and on the standards they set themselves.

Task 8.3.1	**MORAL ACCOUNTABILITY AND PROFESSIONAL ACCOUNTABILITY** Consider what being morally and professionally accountable means for you and for the way you approach your work. Discuss this with other student teachers or your tutor.

The following section sets out in some detail your legal duties, both contractual and statutory.

Legal duties

You have various legally binding contractual responsibilities and statutory duties. In addition you also have, as do all citizens, 'common law duties' which mean, among other things, that you have a duty of care towards other people. Teachers, again as citizens, are subject to criminal law. One aspect of criminal law you should note is that if you hit a pupil or if a pupil hits you this constitutes assault. It also is common sense to protect yourself against allegations by ensuring that you do not spend time alone in closed environments with individual pupils. Talk to your tutor about these issues and about practice in your school experience school.

Contractual duties

Your contractual duties are negotiated between you and your employer. In the case of teachers employed in state schools in England and Wales, the document that sets out teachers' contractual duties in England and Wales is *School Teachers' Pay and Conditions* which is produced by the DFEE and updated annually. Additional conditions may apply in individual schools. There may also be 'implied terms' to your contract, i.e. terms which are not written down, e.g. that you will behave in a manner befitting your role – some schools operate a dress code. You can obtain detailed advice from one of the teachers' unions. *The Headteacher's Guide to the Law* (annually updated, Croner) is recommended further reading for those with a particular interest in this area.

In *School Teachers' Pay and Conditions*, guidelines are laid down for the exercise of your **professional duties** under the headings of **teaching, other activities (which covers pastoral work), assessment and reports, appraisal, review, further training and development, educational methods, discipline, health and safety, staff meetings,** cover (for absent colleagues), public examinations, management, administration and working time.

Statutory duties

Statutory duties are those which the government has established through legislation.

In Table 8.3.1, we provide a summary of those statutory duties of teachers in which you are most likely to be involved as a student and early in your career. A fuller version of the statutory duties of those involved in education is set out in the *Handbook for Inspection, Part 6 The Statutory Basis for Education* (OFSTED, 1994). Later editions of the handbook are less detailed) where information is provided covering the statutory duties of heads, governors and parents. Table 8.3.1 is taken directly from this handbook. In the handbook, the legislation related to each aspect is also listed.

Task 8.3.2	**STATUTORY DUTIES**

STATUTORY DUTIES
As you read the list of statutory duties, we suggest you think carefully about the responsibilities you are taking on and that you summarise these and record them in your diary. All of these statutory duties are part of the teacher's job. As a student teacher you gain experience of most of the statutory duties during your school experience. However, three areas which are easily neglected are report writing (7.2), special educational needs (7.4) and appraisal (7.6.1). We suggest that you occasionally check back to this list to see that you are gaining the required experience and that you ask if you are not.

Table 8.3.1 Statutory duties of teachers: this summary is taken from the OFSTED handbook (1994a, Part 6)

> **5.1 Pupils' spiritual, moral, social and cultural development**
> The curriculum of a maintained school must promote the spiritual, moral, cultural, mental and physical development of pupils and of society; and prepare pupils for the opportunities, responsibilities and experiences of adult life.
> . . . All pupils, unless withdrawn by their parents, must attend a daily act of collective worship.
>
> **5.2 Behaviour and discipline**
> The head is responsible for maintaining discipline taking the governors' views into account . . .
> Corporal punishment has been abolished for all pupils in maintained schools and for pupils in independent schools whose fees are wholly or partly met from public funds. Corporal punishment may be applied to privately funded pupils in independent schools with more than 50 boarders.
> Child Protection: parents, in effect, give schools the authority to act 'in loco parentis'. Schools should take independent action to deal with emergencies. They have a general duty to act independently in respect of suspected abuse at home.

Schools have a duty to protect children from harm. They are recommended to have designated teachers and procedures to notify Social Services Departments, NSPCC and police where they are concerned about a pupil's safety. The designated staff should be properly trained and be aware of the role of local Area Child Protection Committees.

5.3 Attendance
. . . All schools must keep an attendance register in which pupils are marked present or absent at the beginning of each morning and afternoon session. Schools must distinguish in their attendance registers between authorized and unauthorized absences of pupils aged 5–16 and must publish rates of unauthorized absence in prospectuses and annual reports . . .

6 Subjects of the curriculum and other curricular provision
This section of the OFSTED report outlines the legislation behind the curriculum. Religious education and ten other subjects have to be taught – English, Mathematics, Science, Technology, History, Geography, a Modern Foreign Language, Art, Music, Physical Education.

7.2 Assessment, recording and reporting

National Curriculum assessment
Schools are required to assess pupils in National Curriculum subjects at or near the end of each Key Stage for the purpose of ascertaining what they have achieved in relation to attainment targets for that stage . . .

Records
Schools must provide at least annually a written report to the parents of each pupil for their retention . . . The report must contain brief particulars of a pupil's progress in all subjects and activities studied as part of the school curriculum; details of a pupil's general progress; information on performance in all National Curriculum assessments and in public examinations; school and national comparative information about National Curriculum assessments and public examinations; an attendance record; and details of the arrangements under which the report may be discussed with teachers at the school.

Provision of Information
School must make available the results of pupils' achievements in examinations and ensure that they are published . . .

7.3.ii Equality of Opportunity
Schools have a general duty to ensure that facilities for education are provided without sexual or racial discrimination.
Pupils are entitled to efficient full-time education suitable to their ages, abilities and aptitudes and any special educational needs they may have.

7.4 Provision for pupils with SEN
Where a pupil has been assessed as having special educational needs, a statement of needs must be prepared and maintained in accordance with its provisions.
All pupils in maintained schools should follow the National Curriculum to the maximum extent possible, but the application of its provisions may be disapplied or modified in relation to pupils with statements of special educational needs.

7.6.i Teaching and non-teaching staff
All qualified teachers, except those in non-maintained schools, employed full-time or at least 40% full-time on contracts of not less than one year, are subject to appraisal of their performance on a two-year cycle . . .

7.6.ii Resources for learning
A local authority shall not intentionally promote homosexuality or publish material with the intention of promoting homosexuality.
Licences are required for reprographics and recording of broadcasts.
School must use resources safely, especially low level radioactive materials . . .

Summarised from OFSTED (May 1994a) *Handbook for Inspection, Part 6 The Statutory Basis for Education*, pp. 6–15; see also further OFSTED texts listed at the end of this unit

❗ Summary and key points

As a student teacher, you need to be aware of the full range of a teacher's duties. Whenever you are working in a school, you are acting with the agreement and support of qualified teachers. When you take over their classes, you are responsible to them for upholding the legal duties which guide their work.

We recommend that you return to this unit from time to time as you become more familiar with the work of the teacher so that you can check your practice against the requirements. Students and teachers who are union members will find that advice is readily available from their union. The addresses of teachers' unions can be found in the *Education Year Book* which is available in many libraries (or can be obtained from the addresses at the back of this book).

FURTHER READING

Croner (updated annually) *The Headteacher's Guide to the Law*, New Malden: Croner Publications.

Croner produce a range of publications which provide up-to-date advice for headteachers and other staff.

Department for Education and Employment (updated annually) *School Teachers' Pay and Conditions*, London: HMSO.

The provisions in this document are based on the statutory conditions affecting the employment of teachers (in all sectors primary, secondary, special) who are employed by Local Education Authorities or governing bodies of voluntary or most grant-maintained schools. It provides useful information about salary scales and conditions of work.

OFSTED (1996) *Arrangements for the Inspection of Schools from September 1997*, London: OFSTED.

OFSTED (1995) *Guidance on the Inspection of Secondary Schools: The OFSTED Handbook*, London: OFSTED

OFSTED (May 1994a) *Handbook for Inspection for Schools, Part 6 The Statutory Basis for Education*, London: OFSTED, pp. 6–15.

OFSTED publications such as those above set out the statutory basis for the work of teachers. The main requirements affecting the work of beginning teachers have been summarised in this unit. We suggest that you become familiar with the latest OFSTED publications for your subject.

9 AND FINALLY

Throughout this book, we have mixed enquiries and tasks with information and background. The tasks are intended to provide opportunities to examine the practice of other teachers, of yourself and the organisation of schools. The tasks which focus on enquiries generate the data or ideas upon which an understanding of and an explanation for the complex world of teaching and learning in schools is built.

The relationship between practice and explanation is a dynamic one; explanations are needed to make sense of experience and inform practice. Some explanations will be your own, to be tried and tested against the theories of others, often more experienced teachers and educators. At other times you may use directly the explanations of others. Explanations in turn generate working theories, responsive to practice and experience. Theory is important; it provides a framework in which to understand the complex world of the classroom and to direct further research into improving the quality of learning. It provides, too, a reference point against which to judge change and development, both of yourself and schools. It is the encompassing of these ideas, the interplay of theory and practice, which underpins the notion of the reflective practitioner.

We ask you, as one last task, to consider the message in the following poem which we have occasionally found displayed on staffroom walls:

CHILDREN LEARN WHAT THEY LIVE

If a child lives with criticism,
  he learns to condemn,
If a child lives with hostility,
  he learns to fight,
If a child lives with ridicule,
  he learns to be shy,
If a child lives with shame,
  he learns to feel guilty,
If a child lives with tolerance,
  he learns to be patient,
If a child lives with encouragement,
  he learns confidence,
If a child lives with praise,
  he learns to appreciate,
If a child lives with fairness,
  he learns justice,
If a child lives with security,
  he learns to have faith,
If a child lives with approval,
  he learns to like himself,
If a child lives with acceptance and friendship,
  he learns to find love in the world.
                Dorothy Law Nolta (date unknown)

As a teacher you will have an impact – beyond what you will ever know – on people's lives and thus on the community and society. We hope that what your pupils learn from you will help them make positive contributions to their world. We hope too that you will have helped pupils to build personal self-confidence and skills to cope with adult life and to become autonomous learners and caring members of society.

APPENDIX 1 GLOSSARY OF TERMS

All items with * are used with specific reference to England and are taken from: OFSTED (1994a) *Handbook for Inspection for Schools, Part 6 The Statutory Basis for Education*, London: HMSO.

All items with ** are taken from: Department for Education (1994f) *Code of Practice on the Identification and Assessment of Special Educational Needs*, London: DFE.

ACCAC

Awdurdod Cymwysterau, Cwricwlwm ac Asesu Cymru (Qualifications, Curriculum and Assessment Authority for Wales). The English equivalent is QCA (qv).

AEB

Associated Examining Board.

AQA

Assessment and Qualifications Alliance (of C & G) (qv), NEAB (qv) and AEB (qv), for GCSE (qv), A and AS levels and GNVQs (qv).

**Annual Review

The review of a statement of special educational needs which an LEA must make within twelve months of making the statement or, as the case may be, of the previous review.

*Attainment Targets (ATs)

Objectives for each core and foundation subject of the National Curriculum, setting out the knowledge, skills and understanding that pupils of different abilities and maturities are expected to develop within that subject area. See also Level Descriptions and Programmes of Study.

*Banding

The structuring of a year group into divisions, each usually containing two or three classes, on grounds of general ability. Pupils are taught within the band for virtually all the curriculum.

*Basic curriculum

Religious education plus the three core subjects and the seven other foundation subjects (six in Key Stages 1 and 2) of the National Curriculum.

BEd

Bachelor of Education (a route to QTS (qv)).

BTEC

Business and Technician Education Council. Joined with London Examinations (qv) on 24 April 1996 to form EdExcel Foundation (qv). The BTEC label is still used for certain purposes.

Career Entry Profile A document to help newly qualified teachers and their first teaching post schools to identify and address targets, to target monitoring and provide support during induction. All ITT (qv) providers in England are required to provide newly qualified teachers with a career entry profile produced by the TTA (qv).

CATE Council for the Accreditation of Teacher Education. Provided guidelines and codes of practice for teacher education institutions. Replaced by the TTA (qv).

CCW Curriculum Council for Wales; now ACCAC (qv).

CDT Craft, Design and Technology; a school curriculum subject.

C & G City and Guilds.

*Collaborative group work A way of working in which groups of children are assigned to groups or engage spontaneously in working together to solve problems; sometimes called co-operative group work.

*Combined course A course to which several subjects contribute while retaining their distinct identity (e.g. history, geography and RE within combined humanities).

*Comprehensive school A secondary school which admits pupils of age 11 to 16 or 19 from a given catchment area, regardless of their ability.

*Continuity and progression Appropriate sequencing of learning which builds on previous learning to extend and develop pupils' capabilities.

Core skills Skills required by all students following a vocational course, e.g. GNVQ (qv).

*Core subjects English, mathematics and science within the National Curriculum. Strictly speaking these are both core and foundation subjects.

Coursework Work carried out by pupils during a course of study marked by teachers and contributing to the final examination mark. Usually externally moderated.

CPD Continued professional development.

CRE Commission for Racial Equality.

Criterion-referenced assessment	A process in which performance is measured by relating candidates' responses to pre-determined criteria.
*Cross-curricular elements	These run across the whole curriculum and are not confined to one subject. They cover dimensions (e.g. equal opportunities); themes (e.g. economic and industrial understanding, health education, careers education and guidance, environmental education and citizenship); and relevant skills.
CTC	City Technology College.
*Curriculum guidelines	Written school guidance for organising and teaching a particular subject or area of the curriculum (see National Curriculum Programmes of Study).
D and T	Design and Technology (in National Curriculum Technology).
Dearing Report	A review of the 'National Curriculum and its assessment' (1994). Recommended review of subject orders and five year moratorium on further change.
DES	Department of Education and Science (became DFE (qv)).
DFE	Department for Education (formerly DES (qv)). (Now DFEE (qv).)
DFEE	Department for Education and Employment (formerly DFE (qv); DES (qv)).
*Differentiation	The matching of work to the differing capabilities of individuals or groups of pupils in order to extend their learning.
*Disapplication	Arrangement for lifting part or all of the National Curriculum requirements for individuals or for any other grouping specified by the Secretary of State.
DOVE	Diploma of Vocational Education (was the Certificate of Pre-Vocational Education (CPVE)).
*EBD	Emotional and behavioural difficulties and disorders. Used with reference to pupils with such difficulties or schools/ units which cater for such pupils.

EdExcel Foundation

An examining body formed on 24 April 1996 from BTEC (qv) and London Examinations (qv) (previously ULEAC (qv)).

*Education Welfare Officer (EWO)

An official of the LEA concerned with pupils' attendance and with liaison between the school, the parents and the authority.

EOC

Equal Opportunities Commission.

ERA

Education Reform Act (1988).

*ESL

English as a second language.

Examination Group

Public examination bodies which have agreed to work together to provide a range of syllabuses for examination.

*Exclusion

Under Section 22 of the Education (No2) Act 1986 the headteachers of county, voluntary and maintained special schools are empowered to exclude pupils temporarily or permanently when faced with a serious breach of their disciplinary code. The Act sets out procedures relating to the three categories of exclusions: fixed term, indefinite and permanent. Similar responsibilities are placed on GM schools by their articles of government.

Formative assessment

Assessment linked with teaching; describes pupils' progress and used to identify the next stage of teaching and learning; it uses diagnostic approaches, employing a wide range of methods, including formal and informal methods.

*Forms of entry (FE)

The number of forms (of thirty pupils) which a school takes into its intake year. From this can be estimated the size of the intake year and the size of the school.

*Foundation subjects

English, mathematics and science are both core and foundation subjects. The remaining foundation subjects are technology, history, geography and physical education in all Key Stages; music and art in Key Stages 1, 2 and 3 and a modern foreign language in Key Stages 3 and 4.

*GCSE

General Certificate of Secondary Education. National external qualification usually taken at age 16 after a two-year course. This replaced GCE 'O' level.

GMS	Grant-Maintained School. It receives funding direct from DFEE (qv) and is not under LEA (qv) control.
GNVQ	General National Vocational Qualifications.
Grade-related criteria	The identification of criteria, the achievement of which are related to different levels of performance by the candidate.
Graduate teachers training scheme:	see QTS.
*Group work	A way of organising pupils where the teacher assigns tasks to groups of children, to be undertaken collectively although the work is completed on an individual basis.
HMI	Her Majesty's Inspectors (of schools).
HOD	Head of Department.
*House system	A structure for pastoral care/pupil welfare within a school in which pupils are grouped in vertical units, i.e. sections of the school which include pupils from all year groups.
HOY	Head of Year.
IB	International Baccalaureate. A post 16 qualification designed for university entrance.
ICT	See Information and Communications Technology.
*In-class support	Support within a lesson provided by an additional teacher, often with expertise in teaching pupils with special educational or language needs, in the classroom.
Independent school	A private school which receives no state assistance but is financed by fees. Often registered as a charity. See also public school.
Information and Communications Technology (ICT)	Computer hardware and software which extend beyond the usual word-processing, databases, graphics and spreadsheet applications to include hardware and software which allow computers to be networked across the world through the world wide web, to access information on

the Internet and which supports other communication activities such as e-mail and video-conferencing.

Information Technology (IT)
Methods of gaining, storing and retrieving information through microprocessors. Covers a range of micro-computers, both portable and desktop; generic or integrated software packages, such as word processors, spreadsheets, databases and communication programmes, and inter-facing equipment; input devices such as keyboards, overlay keyboards, specialised access switches and touchscreens; output devices such as monitors, printers and plotters; storage devices such as CD ROM, and microelectronics control devices such as a floor turtle. Often encompassed within Information and Communications Technology (qv).

INSET
In-service Education and Training.

Integrated course
A course, usually in a secondary school, to which several subjects contribute without retaining their distinct identity (e.g. integrated humanities, which explores themes which include aspects of geography, history and RE, for example).

Integration
Educating children with special educational needs together with children without special educational needs in main-stream schools wherever possible and ensuring that children with special educational needs engage in the activities of the school together with children who do not have special educational needs.

IT
See Information Technology.

ITT
Initial Teacher Training.

Key Stages (KS)
The periods in each pupil's education to which the elements of the National Curriculum apply. There are four Key Stages, normally related to the age of the majority of the pupils in a teaching group. They are: Key Stage 1, beginning of compulsory education to age 7; Key Stage 2, 7–11; Key Stage 3, 11–14; Key Stage 4, 14 to end of compulsory education. The equivalent year groups are Years R (Reception), 1 and 2; Years 3–6; Years 7–9; Years 10 and 11.

Language support teacher
A teacher provided by the LEA or school to enhance language work with particular groups of pupils.

LEA	Local Education Authority. LEAs have a statutory duty to provide education in their area.
*Learning support	A means of providing extra help for pupils, usually those with learning difficulties, e.g. through a specialist teacher or specially designed materials.
Level Description	A statement describing 'types and range of performance that pupils working at a particular level should demonstrate'.
Levels of Attainment	Eight different levels of achievement are defined within the National Curriculum Attainment Targets. These stop at KS3 (qv) (before 1995 there were ten levels, which continued until KS4 (qv)).
*LMS	Local Management of Schools. The arrangements by which LEAs delegate to individual schools responsibility for financial and other aspects of management.
London Examinations	An examining body previously known as ULEAC (qv) which joined with BTEC (qv) on 24 April 1996 to form EdExcel Foundation (qv).
**Maintained school	For the purposes of the *Code of Practice on the Identification and Assessment of Special Educational Needs* (DFE, 1994f), any county school, grant-maintained school, grant-maintained special school, voluntary school or maintained special school.
MEG	Midland Examining Group (of examination boards).
Middle school	A school which caters for pupils aged from 8 to 12 or 9 to 13 years of age. They are classified legally as either primary or secondary schools depending on whether the preponderance of pupils are under or over 11 years of age in the school.
*Minority ethnic groups	Pupils, many of whom have been born in the United Kingdom, from other ethnic heritages, e.g. those of Asian heritage from Bangladesh, Pakistan, India or East Africa, those of African or Caribbean heritage, or of Chinese heritage. The groups are often closely associated with countries in the British (New) Commonwealth, although non-Commonwealth refugee pupils are also to be found in schools.

*Mixed ability group	Teaching group containing pupils representative of the range of ability within the school.
Moderation	An exercise involving teachers representing an examination group external to the school to check that standards are comparable across schools and teachers. Usually carried out by sampling coursework or examination papers.
*Module	A definable section of work of fixed length with specific objectives and usually with some form of terminal assessment. Several such units may constitute a modular course.
NATs	New Attainment Targets (1991 of National Curriculum).
*National Curriculum (NC)	The core and other foundation subjects and their associated Attainment Targets, Programmes of Study and assessment arrangements.
NCC	National Curriculum Council. Merged with SEAC (qv) in October 1993 to form SCAA (qv).
NCVQ	National Council for Vocational Quyalifications. Joined with SCAA (qv) on 1 October 1997 to form QCA (qv).
NEAB	Northern Examinations and Assessment Board (of examination groups).
NFER	National Foundation for Educational Research. Produce educational diagnostic tests.
*Non-contact time (NCT)	Time provided by a school for a teacher to prepare work or carry out assigned responsibilities other than direct teaching.
Norm-referenced assessment	A process in which performance is measured by comparing candidates' responses. Individual success is relative to the performance of all other candidates.
Normative assessment	Assessment which is reported relative to a given population.
NQT	Newly Qualified Teacher.
NSG	Non-Statutory Guidance (for National Curriculum). Additional subject guidance for the National Curriculum but which is not mandatory; to be found attached to National Curriculum Subject Orders.

NVQ National Vocational Qualifications.

OCEAC Oxford and Cambridge Examination and Assessment Council (see OCR).

OCR Oxford, Cambridge and RSA Examinations (a merger of MEG (qv), OCEAC (qv) and RSA (qv) examinations groups).

OFSTED Office for Standards in Education. Non-Ministerial government department established under the Education (schools) Act (1992) to take responsibility for the inspection of schools in England. Her Majesty's Inspectors (HMI) form the professional arm of OFSTED. See also OHMCI.

OHMCI Office of Her Majesty's Chief Inspector (Wales). Non-Ministerial government department established under the Education (schools) Act (1992) to take responsibility for the inspection of schools in Wales. Her Majesty's Inspectors (HMI) form the professional arm of OHMCI. See also OFSTED.

**Parent This is defined in section 114 (1D) of the Education Act 1944, as amended by the Children Act 1989. Unless the context otherwise requires, parent in relation to a child or young person includes any person:

- who is not a natural parent of the child but who has parental responsibility for him or her, or
- who has care of the child.

Section 114 (1F) of the 1944 Act states that for the purposes of subsection (1D):

- parental responsibility has the same meaning as in the Children Act 1989, and
- in determining whether an individual has care of a child or young person any absence of the child or young person at a hospital or boarding school and any other temporary absence shall be disregarded.

**Parental responsibility Under section 2 of the Children Act 1989, parental responsibility falls upon:

- all mothers and fathers who were married to each other at the time of the child's birth (including those who have since separated or divorced),

- mothers who were not married to the father at the time of the child's birth, and
- fathers who were not married to the mother at the time of the child's birth, but who have obtained parental responsibility either by agreement with the child's mother or through a court order.

See *Code of Practice on the Identification and Assessment of Special Educational Needs* (DFE, 1994f) for further details.

*Partnership teaching An increasingly common means of meeting the language needs of bilingual pupils in which support and class teachers plan and implement together a specially devised programme of in-class teaching and learning. It is used as a criterion for the allocation of Section 11 grants. See also Support teacher.

*Pastoral care Those aspects of a school's work and structures concerned to promote the general welfare of all pupils, particularly their academic, personal and social development, their attendance and behaviour.

PGCE Post Graduate Certificate in Education. The main qualification for secondary school teachers in England and Wales recognised by the DFEE (qv) for QTS (qv).

*Policy An agreed school statement relating to a particular area of its life and work.

PoS Programmes of Study (of National Curriculum).

*Pre-vocational courses Courses specifically designed and taught to help pupils to prepare for the world of work.

Profile Samples of work of pupils/students, used to illustrate progress, with or without added comments by teachers' and/or pupils/students.

*Programmes of Study (PoS) The subject matter, skills and processes which must be taught to pupils during each Key Stage of the National Curriculum in order that they may meet the objectives set out in Attainment Targets.

*Project An investigation with a particular focus undertaken by individuals or small groups of pupils leading to a written, oral or graphic presentation of the outcome.

*PSE courses   Personal and Social Education courses are sometimes provided in Years 9, 10 and 11. They deal with cross-curricular elements (qv) and are mainly concerned to promote pupils' personal and social development, and to help educate them for life outside and following school. See also PSHE courses.

PSHE courses   Personal, Social and Health Education courses. See PSE courses.

*PTA   Parent–Teacher Association. Voluntary grouping of parents and school staff to support the school in a variety of ways (financial, social, etc.).

*PTR   Pupil:Teacher Ratio. The ratio of pupils to teachers within a school or group of schools (e.g. 17.4:1).

Public school   Independent secondary school not state funded. See also independent school.

QCA   The Qualifications and Curriculum Authority. The QCA came into being on 1 October 1997 as a result of the Education Act 1997. Its remit is to promote quality and coherence in education and training. It brings together the work of NCVQ (qv) and SCAA (qv), with additional powers and duties that give it an overview of the curriculum, assessment and qualifications across the whole of education and training, from pre-school to higher vocational levels. QCA advises the Secretary of State for Education and Employment on all matters affecting the curriculum in schools, the assessment of pupils and publicly funded qualifications offered in schools, colleges and workplaces. The Welsh equivalent is ACCAC (qv).

*QTS   Qualified Teacher Status. This is usually attained by completion of a Post-Graduate Certificate in Education (PGCE) or a Bachelor of Education (BEd) degree or a Bachelor of Arts/Science degree with Qualified Teacher Status (BA/BSc (QTS)). **The registered teacher training scheme** is a route to QTS (qv) for people in posts as unqualified teachers and who have 240 credits at higher education levels. The final 120 credits at level 3 required for a degree can be accrued during the period of training. **The graduate teacher training scheme** is a route to QTS (qv) for people in posts as unqualified teachers who are graduates and with degree content relevant to the subject(s) being taught.

*Record of Achievement (ROA)	Cumulative record of a pupil's academic, personal and social progress over a stage of education.
Registered teacher training scheme:	see QTS.
Reliability	A measure of the consistency of the assessment or test item; that is, the extent to which the test gives repeatable results.
RSA	Royal Society of Arts.
*SACRE	The Standing Advisory Council on Religious Education in each LEA to advise the LEA on matters connected with religious education and collective worship, particularly methods of teaching, the choice of teaching materials and the provision of teacher training.
SATs	See Standard Assessment Tasks.
SCAA	School Curriculum and Assessment Authority. Joined with NCVQ (qv) on 1 October 1997 to form QCA (qv).
*School Development Plan (SDP)	A coherent plan, required to be made by a school, identifying improvements needed in curriculum, organisation, staffing and resources and setting out action needed to make those improvements.
SEAC	School Examination and Assessment Council. Merged with NCC (qv) in October 1993 to form SCAA (qv).
*Section 11 staff	Teachers and non-teaching assistants additional to the school's staffing establishment whose specific function is to provide language and learning support for pupils of New Commonwealth heritage. Funded, in response to LEA or school bids, up to 75% of cost by the Home Office under the Local Government Act 1966.
SEG	Southern Examining Group (of examination groups).
*SEN	Special Educational Needs. Referring to pupils who for a variety of intellectual, physical, social, sensory, psychological or emotional reasons experience learning difficulties

which are significantly greater than those experienced by the majority of pupils of the same age. *The Warnock Report* (DES, 1978) envisaged support for very able pupils but this is excluded from the definition of SEN and is rarely provided.

*Setting

The grouping of pupils according to their ability in a subject for lessons in that subject.

*Short course

A course in a National Curriculum foundation subject in Key Stage 4 which will not by itself lead to a GCSE or equivalent qualification. Two short courses in different subjects may be combined to form a GCSE or equivalent course.

Sixth Form College

A post-16 institution for 16 to 19 year olds. It offers GCSE, GCE A Level and vocational courses.

SLD

Specific Learning Difficulties.

SOA

Statements Of Attainment (of National Curriculum subjects).

**Special school

A school which is specially organised to make special educational provision for pupils with special educational needs and is for the time being approved by the Secretary of State under section 188 of the Education Act 1993.

*Standard Assessment Tasks (SATs)

Externally prescribed National Curriculum assessments which incorporate a variety of assessment methods depending on the subject and Key Stage. This term is not now widely used, having been replaced by 'standard national tests'.

*Statements of Attainment

More precise National Curriculum objectives than the broader Attainment Targets. They were related to one of ten levels of attainment on a single continuous scale, covering all four Key Stages. They were removed from the National Curriculum in the Dearing Review (1994).

*Statements of Special Educational Needs

The provision of Statements of Special Educational Needs under the 1981 Education Act to ensure appropriate provision for pupils formally assessed as having SEN (qv).

*Statutory Order

A statutory instrument which is regarded as an extension of an Act, enabling provisions of the Act to be augmented or updated.

*Streaming

The organisation of pupils according to general ability into classes in which they are taught for all subjects and courses.

Summative assessment

Assessment linked to the end of a course of study; it sums up achievement in aggregate terms and is used to rank, grade or compare pupils, groups or schools. It uses a narrow range of methods which are efficient and reliable, normally formal, i.e. under examination conditions.

Supply teacher

Teachers appointed by LEAs (qv) to fill vacancies in maintained schools which arise as a result of staff absences. Supply teachers may be attached to a particular school for a period ranging from half a day to several weeks or more.

*Support teacher

Teachers who give additional support for a variety of purposes, e.g. ESL (qv), general learning support for SEN (qv) pupils; most support is now given in-class although withdrawal (qv) does still occur.

*Teacher's record book

A book in which a teacher plans and records teaching and learning for his or her class(es) on a regular basis.

*Team teaching

The teaching of a number of classes simultaneously by teachers acting as a team. They usually divide the work between them, allowing those with particular expertise to lead different parts of the work, the others supporting the follow-up work with groups or individuals.

TES

Times Educational Supplement. Published weekly and contains job vacancies.

TGAT

Task Group on Assessment and Testing (of National Curriculum). Produced the *TGAT Report* (1988) which led to assessment procedures for the NC.

*Travellers

A term used to cover those communities, some of which have ethnic minority status, who either are or have been traditionally associated with a nomadic lifestyle, and include gypsy travellers, fairground or show people, circus families, New Age travellers, and bargees.

*Traveller education

The development of policy and provision which provides traveller children with unhindered access to and full integration in mainstream education.

TTA	Teacher Training Agency. Established in 1994, the TTA is responsible for teacher education and educational research in England. This has taken over the work of CATE (qv).
*Tutor group	Grouping of secondary pupils for registration and pastoral care purposes.
*TVE/TVEI/TVEI(E)	Technical and Vocational Education/Technical and Vocational Education Initiative/Technical and Vocational Education Initiative (Extension).
ULEAC	University of London Examinations and Assessment Council (was LEAG) (of examination groups) (became London Examinations (qv)).
Validity	A measure of whether the assessment measures what it is meant to measure. Certain kinds of skills and abilities are extremely difficult to assess with validity via simple pencil and paper tests.
Voluntary school	School which receives financial assistance from the LEA, but which is owned by a voluntary body, usually religious.
*Withdrawal	Removal of pupils with particular needs from class teaching in primary schools and from specified subjects in secondary schools for extra help individually or in small groups. In-class support is increasingly provided in preference to withdrawal.
WJEC	Welsh Joint Education Committee (of examination groups).
*Work experience	The opportunity for secondary pupils to have experience, usually within school time, of the world of work for one or two weeks, during which a pupil carries out a particular job or range of jobs more or less as would regular employees, although with emphasis on the educational aspects of the experience. It may only take place after Easter in Year 10 (i.e. in the final year of statutory schooling).
*Year system	A structure for pastoral care/pupil welfare within a school in which pupils are grouped according to Years, i.e. in groups spanning an age range of only one year.
Years 1–11	Year of schooling. Five year olds start at Year 1 (Y1) and

progress through to Year 11 (Y11) at 16 years old. This comprises four Key Stages (KS) (qv): KS1 = Y1 to Y3; KS2 = Y4 to Y6; KS3 = Y7 to Y9; KS4 = Y10 to Y11.

APPENDIX 2 GUIDANCE FOR WRITING AND REFLECTION

INTRODUCTION

In order to gain qualified teacher status at the end of your initial teacher education course you are required to meet the competences/standards for newly qualified teachers which apply for your course. You are also required to pass written assignments. These assignments may include:

- reports or enquiries undertaken in school;
- reviews of educational research and practice;
- answers to traditional essay questions.

The purpose of this appendix is to provide guidance for this work.

You are likely to have written many essays and other assignments as part of your degree course. In this case you will be very familiar with the conventions for, and requirements of, writing for academic purposes. However, if you have had little or no experience of writing essays as part of your degree course, or have been away from formal study for a period of time, you will need to (re)familiarise yourself with the conventions and requirements of academic essay writing. These conventions and requirements are important.

However, it is also important for you to understand the contribution that your written assignments make to your development on your initial teacher education course. Your assignments are aimed at helping you to identify features of your growing development as a teacher and actively to promote that development through reflection: that is, they are aimed at helping you to become a reflective practitioner. Becoming a reflective practitioner requires you systematically to review what you and other teachers do and to plan future action based on that review, i.e.

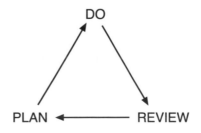

This appendix is designed to:

- remind you of the conventions of academic writing;
- introduce you to features of reflective practice in your work in schools.

PREPARATION FOR WRITING AN ASSIGNMENT

Before you begin an assignment, you need to be very clear about what you are writing about, i.e. the title and focus of the assignment. You may be given a title or you may have to choose your own topic or focus. In either case, you should be very clear about the topic and focus before you start. Otherwise you can waste a lot of time at all stages of completing the assignment. It is often helpful to have a short title which clearly focuses on the issue you are going to address. The title can be written as a problem or a question and may be intentionally provocative. Phrasing the title in this way clarifies and reminds you of the focus when you are writing the assignment. Ask yourself 'what are you seeking to find out by writing this assignment?'

You should then note down all ideas and references that will help you to address the topic. You may want to use a spider diagram (see Unit 5.2 for further information about spider diagrams) or similar device to organise your thoughts. When you have identified a number of relevant aspects of the topic, you should collect together all the information that you need. You will be used to identifying and collecting together relevant notes from higher education institution based sessions, books and articles from journals. However, you should make sure that you have also collected together information gathered in school, such as lesson plans and evaluations of lessons you have taught or observed and records of observations or interviews conducted in school, so that your written work can refer to, and link, published sources and your developing practice in school.

Make sure that you are familiar with the library system at your institution. You will probably have an induction. If not, find out what books and journals are available to support your course. Ask what databases for education are available (e.g. BEIndex) and find out how to use them.

Once you have collected the relevant information, you can use this to refine your thoughts further, and to develop an assignment plan that meets the requirements of the title or focus of the assignment. The plan can be developed into a specific structure for the assignment, which identifies the sequence of material, the arguments and supporting evidence from practice. This level of planning will help you to construct the assignment so that it flows logically from one section to the next.

Plan a timescale to complete your assignments, leaving adequate time for redrafting and editing and stick to it. Your work in school as part of your course is very time consuming and there may be a temptation to leave your written assignments to the last minute.

You should check whether the assignment is supported by tutorials or if you are expected to prepare it alone. Ask your tutor what help can be expected.

CONVENTIONS IN ACADEMIC WRITING

As with all writing for academic purposes, a clear structure is needed throughout the assignment, based on your earlier preparation. The assignment should begin with an *introduction,* which identifies the focus of the assignment and outlines the structure of what is to follow, i.e. the sequence in which material will be presented in the assignment.

The *main body of the assignment* presents the content in the order you have planned. The quality of the assignment largely relies on the content of this section. In this section you should go beyond description or examples of what is or has been the case to provide a critical analysis of the issues raised by the assignment title/focus.

Ideas, descriptions and explanations should not be taken for granted, even if everything you have read about the issue seems to provide a consensus. The ideas, assertions, descriptions, explanations or arguments should be supported by evidence from the work of others – from research and theory, appropriately referenced (e.g., you might say, that the research undertaken by Bloggs (1997) suggests that . . . This supports/ contradicts the findings of Smith (1994). However, alongside references to the work of others, the research and theory from texts or articles, you should draw on your own teaching or observations in school, giving examples of activities or events you have observed or participated in to provide evidence from practice, where appropriate. Thus, although it is generally true that the more evidence from the work of others and your own practice, the stronger your argument, you should not over rely on the work of others, but should make sure that you include your own work as well. Your tutors should be able to provide examples of what their expectations are.

By 'the work of others' and 'theory' we mean explanations of teaching and learning, descriptions of research and any theories which have been developed from such work. You should use the evidence of others and your own evidence to advance your own understanding and formulate your own theories. Your own theories evolve by bringing your critical faculties to bear on the work of others and what has been happening in your teaching.

When referring to other research or to texts, a reference should always be given, together with a page number if quotations are used. It is important to show, by appropriate citation, what is your work and what is the work of others. Direct quotations should be used sparingly, otherwise they disrupt the flow of the assignment. Do not put in a quotation for the sake of it: only use quotations with a clear purpose. You need to explain whether a quotation is being used as evidence which supports or disagrees with your point of view. If you are not clear why you are using a quotation, you may be better to paraphrase the point.

Use of sub-headings, though not too many, throughout the assignment can help you to keep to the structure you have planned to use and can help the reader grasp the structure and direction of your discussion.

The assignment should end with a *conclusion:* a brief summary or set of conclusions; and, in some assignments, some recommendations. A summary or any conclusions should draw out, or derive logically from, the key points you have made in the main body of the assignment. If your assignment has focused on improving your practice or practice within a school, the conclusion may also include a set of recommendations which you (or others) could implement. Whatever the focus of the conclusion, it should provide a sound conclusion to the assignment.

References cited in the text must be included in a *bibliography* at the end of the assignment. Your higher education institution will give you information about how to present your bibliography. This may be different to the way you were required to present bibliographies on your degree course. If you are not given information, ask the library which system is used in the institution to present bibliographies. Otherwise use a recognised system such as the Harvard system. Details of this should be available in the library.

The structure of an academic piece of work is summarised in Figure A.2.1 below.

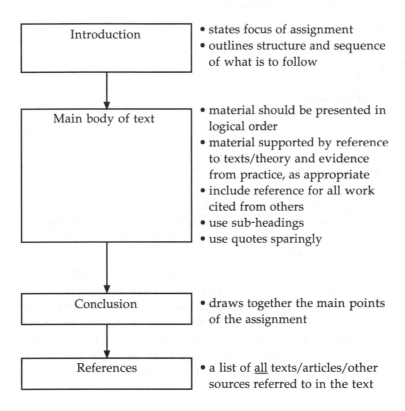

Figure A.2.1 Structure of an academic piece of work

Refer to the ways your course or higher education institution requires work to be presented and references to be written and follow that format.

Spelling, grammar, punctuation, sentence construction and paragraph formation all require the same high level of accuracy as for written assignments on your degree course. The conventions are too numerous to identify here, although a few examples of what to do and what not to do in writing are given at the end of this appendix. You should refer to specialist support, packages or texts to help you if needed. Your institution may have a study support unit or package to help you develop your writing skills. There are texts which are designed to help you develop your writing skills; some of them are listed in the further readings at the end of this appendix. Alternatively, you may have a friend, family member or tutor who can help you. What is most important is that if you need help, you seek help as early as possible in your course.

You should, however, spell check any word processed work. Lack of spell checking is probably one of the most frequent mistakes, but also one of the most easily corrected. You should get into the habit of spell checking your work. It certainly helps if you leave yourself time to complete the assignment and are not rushing to write the last sentence two minutes before the deadline for submitting the work.

You should check your work before you hand it in to ensure that you have:

- answered the question you set for yourself;
- expressed what you want to communicate;
- made your meaning clear;
- not been ambiguous;
- spelled words correctly.

These stages of writing are shown in Figure A.2.2.

REFLECTIVE WRITING

One of the aims of your initial teacher education course is your development as a reflective practitioner. But what does this mean? It means that you think about/reflect on your experiences in school, your own teaching, your observations of or discussions with others, and your analysis of school documents or activities or events that occur in school, in order to reach a higher standard of awareness about your teaching and the ways in which children learn. The reflective process can be shown as follows:

Reflection requires you to stand back from the specific lesson, observation, activity or event and question it. You draw on your knowledge about and understanding of the work of others, research and theory, and consider it in relation to the practice on which you are reflecting. You should develop your skills of reflection as an integral part of your development as a teacher in order to achieve the competences/standards required of newly qualified teachers identified for your initial teacher education course. Reflection is as integral to your teaching as your ability to manage a class and control pupil behaviour. It is a process which continues into your first year of teaching and throughout your teaching career.

Evaluation of your teaching at the end of each lesson is an example of reflection. Evaluation can be carried out alone or with your tutor. When you evaluate a lesson, you question what went well as well as what did not go well, what might have worked better and what you might do next time that will enable you to improve what you are doing. As evaluation and reflection involve recall of what took place, you need to focus your evaluation and reflection in advance. So much is going on in a lesson that unless you select one or two things on which to focus you are unlikely to collect the detailed data necessary for an in-depth evaluation. You also need to write a few notes and identify

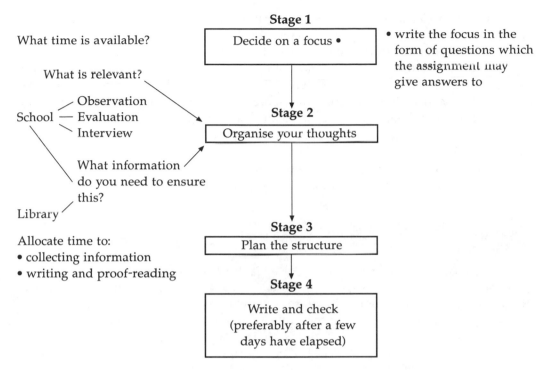

What time is available?

What is relevant?

School —
- Observation
- Evaluation
- Interview

What information do you need to ensure this?

Library

Allocate time to:
- collecting information
- writing and proof-reading

Stage 1

Decide on a focus •

• write the focus in the form of questions which the assignment may give answers to

Stage 2

Organise your thoughts

Stage 3

Plan the structure

Stage 4

Write and check
(preferably after a few days have elapsed)

Common errors to check for:

- typographical errors;
- lack of flow of ideas from one paragraph to the next or one section to the next. Ideas in one paragraph or section should lead naturally to the next paragraph or section;
- not explaining ideas fully Imagine your readers as interested people who do not know about the topic and write for them. Do not make assumptions about what the readers know because, e.g. your work may be sent to an external examiner;
- apostrophes (these denote possession, e.g. boys' book (the book of the boys); or abbreviations, e.g. don't, isn't;
- using paragraphs.

Figure A.2.2 The stages involved in producing a written assignment

points of relevance as soon as you can after the lesson or observation so that you record your perceptions when they are fresh in your mind. You might use the questions/points at the beginning of this paragraph to guide your initial reflections. Alternatively, there are checklists, guidelines and series of questions included in many of the texts concerned with helping teachers to develop into reflective practitioners (see some texts in the further readings at the end of Unit 5.4).

Your notes/reflections can then be used as the basis for explicitly linking the work of others to your practice in your assignments. You should aim to show how the work of others, research and theory, informs your practice and vice versa, rather than leaving the two separate, isolated from and not informing each other. Reflection allows you to put your points across and to give your own opinions, but you should underpin this with research/theory. An assignment title which requires you to reflect does not mean that you should not include theory; nor does it mean that you should not include references. Rather, it expects you to include examples from practice to support or challenge the research/theory.

When drawing on examples from your practice in assignments, you should not use the name of the school or any individual. All such references should be made anonymous.

❗ Summary and key points

To sum up, assignments set as part of your initial teacher education course require good academic writing, but are also designed to enable you to show that you are reflecting on the theory of teaching and are applying this to your own developing practice as a teacher, i.e. that you are developing as a reflective practitioner. You therefore need to combine academic writing and evidence of reflection in your written assignments.

Teachers need good writing skills. You write on the board, you write notices, you send letters to parents, write reports and undertake numerous other written communications. Whatever your subject, you have a responsibility to promote in your lessons the development of key literacy skills. Therefore, you need good spelling, grammar, punctuation, sentence construction and paragraph formation. If your writing skills are not as good as necessary to write effectively for a variety of audiences in school, you should seek help.

Good luck with writing your course assignments and the written communications you make as part of your teaching.

FURTHER READINGS

Burchfield, R. (ed.)(1996) *The new Fowler's Modern English Usage*, Oxford: Clarendon.
Greenbaum, S. and Whitcut, J. (1988) *Longman Guide to English Usage*, Harlow: Longman.
Palmer, R. (1996) *Brain Train: Studying for Success*, London: Spon.
Palmer, R. (1993) *Write in Good Style: A Guide to Good English*, London: Spon.

EXAMPLES OF WHAT TO DO/NOT TO DO IN WRITING

Although most of these points are, no doubt, familiar to you, we hope that the reminders given here are useful to you.

1   Check your spelling. Poor spelling makes your efforts to communicate to the reader less effective. Make sure that you use a spell check and, if necessary, consult a dictionary and/or ask a friend to help you with your spelling.

2   Generally, you should write your assignments in the third person. However, if you are reflecting on your own practice you may want to use the first person – I – when referring to your own practice. This helps to distinguish your practice and thoughts from those of other writer(s) to whom you refer.

3   Claims that you make in your assignment should always be backed by evidence from the work of others and, where appropriate, by reference to your own practice or the practice of others (e.g. from observations).

    To write reflectively you need to make links between the work of others and your own practice. Thus, your ideas and those of others, descriptions, explanations, arguments, research and theoretical statements should be exemplified from your own practice or practice that you have observed. Thus, important concepts or ideas are linked to concrete observations.

4   Be very careful about the use of words. The word 'the' tends to be overused in written assignments and should, therefore, be thought about especially carefully. A statement that includes 'the', e.g. 'the fact that' or 'the answer is', is a categorical statement that portrays certainty or definitiveness which may not be appropriate. Words such as 'a', 'one of', 'there is a suggestion that', or 'one possible answer is' may be better instead because they are less definite. Another overused word is 'very', e.g. 'very large', when 'large' would do.

5   Choose your words carefully. Do not use slang, jargon, colloquialisms, abbreviations or words that need to be put into quotation marks, unless quoting somebody else. For example, the use of 'kids' is slang.

6   Be careful about punctuation, e.g. full stops, commas, colons, semi-colons, dashes (e.g. for an aside) and brackets (e.g. for an explanation). By using punctuation appropriately, you help the reader to make sense of what you are saying. Under use of commas is probably the most common error. Leaving out a comma can alter the meaning of a sentence. Dashes or brackets (normally curved brackets), used at the beginning and end of a phrase or clause, may help the relative importance of different parts of the sentence to be better understood by the reader.

7   Write proper sentences. Do not try to put more than one thought into a sentence. Sentences which have more than one thought included in them should generally be split into two sentences. The two thoughts should not be joined together by a comma. Make sure that each sentence contains a main verb.

8 Paragraphs should be brief and should contain one, specific point. However, a paragraph should not be limited to one sentence. The first sentence of a paragraph usually identifies the main point of the whole paragraph. Generally, each paragraph should contain between five and ten lines. However, it helps the reader if paragraphs are of different lengths.

9 Throughout the writing of an assignment, keep in mind the title or focus of the assignment, the problem or question you have set or have been set, the arguments you are making and the structure to which you are working. This will help you to stick to the point of the assignment; to focus each sentence, each paragraph and each section on the title. This focus helps you to make each sentence, paragraph and section follow on from the previous one and to link to the next. It should also help you to achieve consistency throughout the assignment.

STRATEGIES FOR MAKING NEUTRAL REFERENCE TO GENDER

(Adapted from a paper produced by the Department of Language Studies, Canterbury Christ Church University College.)

Your writing is governed by social customs and conventions. One such custom and convention in Britain is to make sure that there is no gender bias in your writing, that men and women are regarded as equal. This translates into not making assumptions that certain jobs (e.g., lawyer, doctor, lorry driver, primary teacher, nurse) are either male or female and, therefore, not using words such as he, him, his or she, her, hers to refer to someone in one of these jobs.

Thus, in your writing you need to avoid such gender bias. Three methods of overcoming the difficulty have been identified: (i) *avoidance*; (ii) *disclaimer*; or (iii) *inclusion*. Unless your higher education institution prescribes one method for you to use, you may use any of the three methods. Avoidance is probably the most popular and effective of these methods; inclusion, the least popular method.

1 AVOIDANCE

'Avoidance' avoids using male or female words altogether when reference is made to a person who could equally be male or female. Some strategies for avoidance include:

Strategy	Example	
	Avoid this	by writing this
Change to plural	. . . when a teacher meets his class for the first time	. . . when teachers meet their classes for the first time
Change to an article	. . . so that every member of the group can give his opinion	. . . so that every member of the group can give an opinion
Recast the clause so that a different noun becomes the subject	if the student cannot understand his feedback . . .	If the feedback is difficult to understand . . .
Use neutral words like *the other, an individual, the author*	Each student must read what his partner has written	In pairs, each student must read what the other has written.
Omit the male/female word	. . . working with each individual to ascertain her needs	. . . working with each individual to ascertain needs

2 DISCLAIMER

A disclaimer is a statement at the beginning of the assignment that you are using words like he, him and his throughout without wanting to convey gender bias. In other words you claim that the male words are to be read as neutral in their reference. Alternatively you might state that you are using she, her and hers throughout the assignment for some particular purpose, without wanting to convey gender bias. This might be appropriate, for example, when referring to a primary teachers as most primary teachers are female. Thus, the statement disclaims that any gender bias is intended. Without such a statement, you are likely to offend others. Even with a disclaimer, some readers may find this strategy offensive.

3 INCLUSION

Some people prefer to get round the difficulty by using the phrase he or she, or he/she or s/he. If used occasionally, such phrases may be appropriate, but they affect the style and interrupt the flow of the assignment when used frequently. It may be best to avoid using this approach to avoid such difficulties.

APPENDIX 3 DISCIPLINE IN SCHOOLS (ELTON REPORT)

Extracts from: Department of Education and Science and the Welsh Office (1989) *Discipline in Schools: Report of the Committee of Enquiry Chaired by Lord Elton*, London: HMSO/DES and WO, pp. 20–53.

RECOMMENDATIONS

3 TEACHERS

Teachers and their trainees should recognise and apply the principles of good classroom management.

4 SCHOOLS

R21 Headteachers and teachers should, in consultation with governors, develop whole school behaviour policies which are clearly understood by pupils, parents and other school staff.

R22 Schools should ensure that their rules are derived from the principles underlying their behaviour policies and are consistent with them.

R23 Schools should strike a healthy balance between rewards and punishments. Both should be clearly specified.

R24 Pupils should learn from experience to expect fair and consistently applied punishments for bad behaviour which make the distinction between serious and minor offences apparent.

R25 Headteachers and teachers should ensure that rules are applied consistently by all members of staff, but that there is flexibility in the use of punishments to take account of individual circumstances.

R26 Headteachers and teachers should avoid the punishment of whole groups.

R27 Headteachers and teachers should avoid punishments which humiliate pupils.

R28 Headteachers and staff should:

R28.1 be alert to signs of bullying and racial harassment;

R28.2 deal firmly with all such behaviour;

R28.3 take action based on clear rules which are backed by appropriate sanctions and systems to protect and support victims.

R29 Pupils should tell staff about serious cases of bullying and racial harassment of which they are aware.

R30 All parties involved in the planning, delivery and evaluation of the curriculum should recognise that the quality of its content and the teaching and learning methods through which it is delivered are important influences on pupils' behaviour.

R32 Schools should not use rigid streaming arrangements to group their pupils by ability. They should take full account of the implications for pupil behaviour when reviewing their arrangements for grouping pupils.

R33 Schools should:

R33.1 distribute their teaching and other resources equitably across the ability range;

R33.2 provide a range of rewards accessible to pupils of all abilities.

R34 Schools should make full use of off-site learning as a means of motivating their pupils.

R36.2 Schools should also provide personal and social education programmes outside the National Curriculum.

R37 Secondary headteachers and teachers should base pastoral systems on the strengths of the traditional integrated academic, welfare and disciplinary role of the teacher.

R38 Secondary headteachers and teachers should identify clear aims for the use of tutorial time. These aims should include reinforcing the school's behaviour policy.

R39 Headteachers and teachers should:

R39.1 recognise the importance of ascertaining pupils' views;

R39.2 organise systems for doing so and for taking the information gathered into account in the management of the school.

R40 Headteachers should ensure that there is regular and effective communication between their staff and support services, and that these services are given early warning of developing problems.

R41   Headteachers and teachers should ensure that pastoral care in schools is characterised by a healthy balance between challenge and support for pupils.

R46   Headteachers and teachers should recognise the importance of displaying pupils' work in creating an attractive environment, increasing pupils' self-esteem and fostering a sense of ownership of the premises.

R51   Headteachers and their senior management teams should recognise the importance of efficient and sensitive timetabling as a management tool which can be used to reduce problems of circulation, supervision and classroom management. The annual timetabling cycle should involve thorough consultation with staff.

R52.1 Senior staff should be visible and strategically placed during mass circulation periods between lessons.

R52.2 Headteachers and teachers when moving about the school should be aware of and take responsibility for pupils' behaviour.

R56.2 Headteachers should use . . . (for funding lunchtime supervision) funds to devise schemes which meet the needs of their schools and encourage participation by teachers.

R57   Headteachers and teachers should ensure that parents receive positive and constructive comments on their children's work and behaviour as a matter of course.

R58   When disciplinary problems arise, headteachers and teachers should involve parents at an early stage rather than as a last resort.

R59   Teachers should recognise that pupils' behaviour at home may differ markedly from their behaviour at school. They should take this into account when discussing pupils with their parents.

R60.1 Headteachers and teachers should develop an active partnership with parents as an aid to promoting good behaviour.

R60.2 They should ensure that their schools provide a welcoming environment for parents.

R61   Headteachers and teachers should develop policies to secure easy access to them by parents and good communications between them and parents which go beyond the provision of formal parents' evenings.

R62   Schools should ensure that:

R62.2 where significant numbers of parents use first languages other than English, communications are in these languages as well as in English.

R66 In appropriate cases, LEAs and headteachers should make time available for home visits by teachers, who should consult with the education welfare service and other agencies where necessary.

5 PARENTS

6 PUPILS

R75 Headteachers and teachers should give pupils every opportunity to take responsibilities and to make a full contribution to improving behaviour in schools.

R76 Headteachers and teachers should encourage the active participation of pupils in shaping and reviewing the school's behaviour policy in order to foster a sense of collective commitment to it.

R77 The Secretaries of State, LEAs and schools should ensure that records of achievement give due weight to a wide range of achievements and personal qualities.

R79 Schools, LEAs and employers should increase their co-operation in developing means of increasing pupils' motivation, such as compacts.

R80 Pupil records should cover their pastoral as well as their learning needs. They should be in a format which could be adopted by schools and LEAs throughout England and Wales.

R83 All LEAs and schools should ensure that the special educational needs of pupils with emotional and behavioural difficulties are assessed and met.

R85 LEAs and schools should ensure that the learning needs of pupils involved in disruptive behaviour who may not be suffering from emotional and behavioural difficulties are properly identified as part of any plan for remedial action.

R89 Teachers should take account of the gender differences involved in pupils' behaviour, for example by not reinforcing attention-seeking and aggressive behaviour.

R90 Headteachers and staff should work to create a school climate which values all cultures, in particular those represented in it, through its academic and affective curricula.

R91 Teachers should recognise the potential for injustice and the practical dangers of stereotyping certain kinds of pupils as troublemakers.

R92 Teachers should guard against misinterpreting non-verbal signals and speech patterns of pupils from different cultural backgrounds.

R93 Teachers should avoid modelling any kind of insulting or discriminating behaviour.

R96 Teachers and parents should make active use of television as an educational resource, reinforcing the positive messages presented by programmes and encouraging children to become more discriminating and critical viewers.

7 ATTENDANCE

R99 Headteachers and teachers should make full use of education welfare officers to maximise attendance.

R100 Senior school staff should carry out frequent random attendance checks on individual lessons.

8 POLICE

R107 All LEAs and schools should recognise the practical and educational value of good relations with the police and promote the development of school–police liaison projects.

9 GOVERNORS

10 LOCAL EDUCATION AUTHORITIES

11 THE GOVERNMENT

APPENDIX 4 SPECIAL EDUCATIONAL NEEDS (CODE OF PRACTICE)

Extract from: Department for Education (1994f) *Code of Practice on the Identification and Assessment of Special Educational Needs*, London: DFE.

1. Introduction: Principles and Procedures

1.1 To enable pupils with special educational needs to benefit as fully as possible from their education presents teachers, and all the professionals and administrators involved, with some of the most challenging and rewarding work the education service can offer. Much had been achieved by schools and local education authorities (LEAs) in enabling children with special educational needs to lead full and productive lives. The purpose of this Code of Practice, which benefits from this experience, is to give practical guidance to LEAs and the governing bodies of all maintained schools – and to all those who help them, including the health services and social services – on the discharge of their functions under Part III of the Education Act 1993.

1.2 The fundamental principles of the Code are that:

- the needs of all pupils who may have special educational needs either throughout, or at any time during, their school careers must be addressed; the Code recognises that there is a continuum of needs and a continuum of provision, which may be made in a wide variety of different forms
- children with special educational needs require the greatest possible access to a broad and balanced education, including the National Curriculum
- the needs of most pupils will be met in the mainstream, and without a statutory assessment or statement of special educational needs. Children with special educational needs, including children with statements of special educational needs, should, where appropriate and taking into account the wishes of their parents, be educated alongside their peers in mainstream schools
- even before he or she reaches compulsory school age a child may have special educational needs requiring the intervention of the LEA as well as the health services
- the knowledge, views and experience of parents are vital. Effective assessment and provision will be secured where there is the greatest possible degree of partnership between parents and their children and schools, LEAs and other agencies.

1.3   The practices and procedures essential in pursuit of these principles are that:

- **all children with special educational needs should be identified and assessed as early as possible and as quickly as is consistent with thoroughness**
- **provision for all children with special educational needs should be made by the most appropriate agency. In most cases this will be the child's mainstream school, working in partnership with the child's parents: no statutory assessment will be necessary**
- **where needed, LEAs must make assessments and statements in accordance with the prescribed time limits; must write clear and thorough statements, setting out the child's educational and non-educational needs, the objectives to be secured, the provision to be made and the arrangements for monitoring and review; and ensure the annual review of the special educational provision arranged for the child and the updating and monitoring of educational targets**
- **special educational provision will be most effective when those responsible take into account the ascertainable wishes of the child concerned, considered in the light of his or her age and understanding**
- **there must be close cooperation between all the agencies concerned and a multi-disciplinary approach to the resolution of issues.**

1.4   The detailed guidance which follows in the rest of the Code is subject to these principles, practices and procedures, and must be read with them kept clearly in mind. The Code recommends the general adoption of a staged model of special educational needs. The first three stages are based in the school, which will, as necessary, call upon the help of external specialists. At stages 4 and 5 the LEA shares responsibility with schools:

Stage 1:   **class or subject teachers identify or register a child's special educational needs and, consulting the school's SEN coordinator (. . .), take initial action**

Stage 2:   **the school's SEN coordinator takes lead responsibility for gathering information and for coordinating the child's special educational provision, working with the child's teachers**

Stage 3:   **teachers and the SEN coordinator are supported by specialists from outside the school**

Stage 4:   **the LEA considers the need for a statutory assessment and, if appropriate, makes a multidisciplinary assessment**

Stage 5:   **the LEA considers the need for a statement of special educational needs and, if appropriate, makes a statement and arranges, monitors and reviews provision.**

1.5   There is scope for differences of definition of the stages in such a model and for variation in the number of stages adopted by schools and LEAs. The Code does not prescribe definitions and does not insist that there must always be five stages. But the Code does advise that the adoption of a model which recognises the various levels of need, the different responsibilities to assess and meet those needs, and the associated variations in provision, will best reflect and promote common recognition of the continuum of special educational needs. School and LEAs will need to be able to demonstrate, in their arrangements for children with special educational needs, that they are fulfilling their statutory duty to have regard to this Code. In the case of schools, OFSTED and OHMCI (Wales) inspection teams will consider the effectiveness of schools' policies and practices and the extent to which schools have had regard to the Code.

1.6   The ordering of the guidance reflects the consideration that it should be read as a whole, so that a full picture can be gained of the various parts of the processes, the roles of all concerned, and the particular considerations affecting the treatment of children at different stages in their lives and school careers. The format of the document is:

Part 1: Introduction: Principles and procedures
Part 2: Stages 1–3   School-based stages of assessment and provision
Part 3: Stage 4:   Statutory assessments
Part 4: Stage 5:   Statements
Part 5: Children under five with special educational needs
Part 6: The annual review of statements.

1.7   The Code thus starts with the school-based stages of assessment and provision since some general issues can most appropriately be addressed in this Part. That should not, however, be taken to diminish the importance of addressing needs as early as possible, such as at the pre-school stage when appropriate, as explained in Part 5. Nor should the emphasis on the work of mainstream schools be seen to diminish the importance of the work of or the relevance of the Code to special schools (see Glossary). Throughout, the law on which the Code offers guidance is summarised in lined boxes with the text in light blue: except where stated otherwise, references to 'the Act' are to the Education Act 1993; references to 'sections' are references to sections in the 'Act'; references to 'the Regulations' are to the Education (Special Educational Needs) Regulations 1994.

1.8   Bodies helping children with special educational needs and their parents in Wales should bear in mind that the Welsh Language Act 1993 (. . .) has the fundamental principle that the Welsh language should be treated on the basis of equality with the English language. All bodies serving the public in Wales are required to agree schemes setting out the services they provide, and intend to provide, through the medium of Welsh. In their dealings particularly with parents, those bodies should remember the requirements of the Welsh Language Act and the need to communicate in the language preferred by parents.

APPENDIX 5 USEFUL ADDRESSES

Department for Education and Employment   0171 925 5000
Sanctuary Buildings
Great Smith Street
London SW1P 3BT

Welsh Office Education Department   01222 825111
Government Buildings
Cathays Park
Cardiff CF1 3NQ

Scottish Office Education and Industry Department   0131 556 8400
Victoria Quay
Leith
Edinburgh EH6 6QQ

Department of Education for Northern Ireland   01247 279279
Rathgael House
Balloo Road
Bangor
Co Down BT19 7PR

The Qualifications and Curriculum Authority (QCA)   0171 509 555
29 Bolton Street
London W1Y 7PD

The Qualifications, Curriculum and Assessment Authority for Wales
 (ACCAC)   01222 375400
Castle Buildings
Womanby Street
Cardiff CF1 9SX

Scottish Consultative Council on the Curriculum (Scottish CCC)   01382 455053
Gardyne Road
Broughty Ferry
Dundee DD5 1NY

Northern Ireland Council for the Curriculum, Examinations and
Assessment (NICCEA)   01232 261200
29 Clarendon Road
Belfast BT1 3BG

EXAMINATION BOARDS

(Boards provide copies of syllabuses, past examination papers, and reports by subject. Some also produce support materials, particularly for teaching A level.) For addresses of Examination Boards, please refer to *The Education Authorities Directory and Annual* (see below).

SUBJECT ASSOCIATIONS

Council for Subject Associations   01757 706161
19 Green Lane
North Duffield
Selby YO8 7RR

For Subject Associations please refer to *The Education Authorities Directory and Annual* (see below), or consult appropriate staff.

OTHERS

Equal Opportunities Commission   0161 833 9244
Overseas House
Quay Street
Manchester M3 3HN

Commission for Racial Equality   0171 828 7022
Elliott House
10–12 Allington Street
London SW1E 5EH

National Society for the Prevention of Cruelty to Children   0171 242 1626
67 Saffron Hill
London EC1N 8RS

Health and Safety Executive   0181 594 5522
Maritime House
1 Linton Road
Barking
Essex 1G11 8HF

Voluntary Service Overseas   0181 780 7200
317 Putney Bridge Road
London SW15 2PN

Health Education Authority   0171 222 5300
Trevelyan House
30 Great St Peters Street
London SW1P 2HW

For further addresses please refer to: *The Education Authorities Directory and Annual*
(published annually), The School Government Publishing Company Ltd.

This includes addresses of Government Departments, Public Offices, LEAs,
Examinations Organisations, Schools, Teachers Centres, Further Education Colleges,
English Language Schools, Recognised Education and Educational Associations,
Teachers Unions, Subject Associations, Institutes/Colleges of Higher Education, University Departments of Education, establishments for pupils with special learning needs,
Social Services Departments, Educational Psychology Services, Careers Centres, Public
Library Authorities and other organisations concerned with education, and educational
publishers and equipment suppliers in England, Wales, Scotland, Northern Ireland,
Channel Islands and Isle of Man.

This is available from most public libraries.

BIBLIOGRAPHY

ACAS (1984) *Advisory Booklet Number 7: Induction of New Employees*, London: HMSO.

Adair, J. (1988) *Effective Time Management. How to Save Time and Spend it Wisely*, London: Pan Books.

Adams, C., Brown, B.B. and Edwards, M. (1997) *Developmental disorders of language*, London: Whurr.

Adelman, C. and Walker C. (1976) *A Guide to Classroom Observation*, London: Methuen.

Adey, P. and Shayer, M. (1994) *Really Raising Standards; Cognitive Intervention and Academic Achievement*, London: Routledge.

Adey, P. (1992) 'The CASE results: implications for science teaching', *International Journal of Science Education*, 14, 137–146.

Adey, P., Shayer, M. and Yates, C. (1989) *Thinking Science*, London: Macmillan.

—— (1991) *Better Learning: A Report from the Cognitive Acceleration Through Science Education (CASE) Project*, London: King's College, University of London, Centre for Educational Studies.

Aldrich, R. and White, J. (1998) *The National Curriculum beyond 2000: the QCA and the Aims of Education*, London: Institute of Education.

Allsop, T. (1994) 'The language of partnership', in M. Wilkin and D. Sankey *Collaboration and Transition in Initial Teacher Training*, London: Kogan Page.

al Qadhi, E. (1991) *Enhancing A Level Teaching*, London: University of London, Institute of Education, Department of Policy Studies, Centre Report Number 7.

Anderson, J. (1993) *The Architecture of Cognition*, Cambridge, MA: Harvard University Press.

Anderson, J.R., Reder, L.M. and Simon, H.A. (1996) 'Situated learning and education', *Educational Researcher*, 25, 5–11.

Anglin, J.M. (1973) *Beyond the Information Given*, New York: W.W. Norton.

—— (1977) *Word, Object and Conceptual Development*, New York: W.W. Norton.

Assistant Master and Mistresses Association (AMMA) (1992) *The Children Act and the Teacher*, London: AMMA (February) (Note: AMMA is now the ATL.)

Atkinson, J.W. (1964) *An Introduction to Motivation*, Princeton, NJ: Van Nostrand.

Ausubel, D.P. (1968) *Educational Psychology: A Cognitive View*, New York: Holt, Rinehart and Winston.

—— (1985) 'Learning as constructing meaning', in: N. Entwistle (ed.) *New Directions in Educational Psychology: 1. Learning and Teaching*, Lewes: Falmer Press.

Balderstone, D. and King, S. (1997) 'Preparing pupils for public examinations: developing study skills', in S. Capel, M. Leask and T. Turner (eds) *Starting to Teach in the Secondary School: A Companion for the Newly Qualified Teacher*, London: Routledge.

Balderstone, D. and Lambert, D. (1992) 'Some National Curriculum questions explained', in D. Balderstone and D. Lambert *Assessment Matters*, Sheffield: Geographical Association.

Barker, B. (1989) 'The growth of the assessment industry' in *The Independent*, 5 January.

Barnes, B. *et al.* (1987) *Learning Styles in TVEI: Evaluation Report No. 3*, MSC, Leeds University.

Barnes, D. (1976) *From Communication to Curriculum*, Harmondsworth: Penguin Education.

Barnes, D., Britton, J., Rosen, H. and the London Association for Teachers of English (LATE) (1972) *Language, the Learner and the School (Revised edition)*, Harmondsworth: Penguin Education.

Batchford, R. (1992) *Values: Assemblies for the 1990s*, Cheltenham: Stanley Thorne.

Bee, H. (1992) *The developing child (6th ed.)*, New York: Harper Collins.

Bell, J. (1987) *Doing Your Research Project: A Guide for First Time Researchers in Education and Social Science*, Milton Keynes: Open University Press.

Bennett, N. and Dunne, E. (1994) 'How children learn: implications for practice', in B. Moon and A. Shelton Mayes (eds) *Teaching and Learning in the Secondary School*, Milton Keynes: Open University Press.

Biggs, J.B. (1978) Individual and group differences in study processes, *British Journal of Educational Psychology*, 48, 266–279.

———— (1987a) *The Study Process Questionnaire (SPQ) Manual*, Hawthorne, Victoria: Australian Council for Educational Research.

———— (1993) 'What do inventories of students' learning processes really measure? A theoretical review and clarification', *British Journal of Educational Psychology*, 63, 3–19.

Black, P. (1993) 'The shifting scene of the National Curriculum', in P. O'Hear and J. White (eds) *Assessing the National Curriculum*, London: Paul Chapman Publishing.

———— (1998) *Testing: Friend or foe? Theory and practice of assessment and testing*, London: The Falmer Press.

Black, P. and Wiliam, D. (1998) *Inside the Black Box: Raising Standards through Classroom Assessment*, London: King's College.

Blenkin, G.P., Edwards, G. and Kelly, A.V. (1992) *Change and the curriculum*, London: Paul Chapman.

Bloom, B.S. (ed.) (1956) *Taxonomy of Educational Objectives. Handbook 1; Cognitive Domain*, London: Longman.

Bloom, B.S., Krathwohl, D. and Masica, B. (1964) *Taxonomy of Educational Objectives. Handbook 2: Affective Domain*, London: Longman.

Boaler, J. (1997) *Experiencing School Mathematics: Teaching Styles, Sex and Setting*, Buckingham: Open University Press.

Bourne, J. and Moon, B. (1994) 'A question of ability?' in B. Moon and A. Shelton Mayes (eds)*Teaching and Learning in the Secondary School*, London: Routledge for the Open University, pp. 25–37.

Bourne, R., Davitt, J. and Wright, J. (1995) *Differentiation: Taking IT Forward*, Coventry: National Council for Educational Technology.

Brandeth, G. (1981) *The Puzzle Mountain*, Harmondsworth: Penguin Books.

British Broadcasting Corporation (1993) 'The joy of teaching sex education', a video in the Teaching Today series, on *Sex Education*, London: BBC.

—— (1994) 'Simple minds', a video in the *Education Special: Understanding Science* series, London: BBC.

Broadfoot, P. (1987) *Introducing Profiling: a practical manual*, London: Macmillan.

Brown, A.L. (1994) 'The advancement of learning', *Educational Researcher*, 23, 4–12.

Brown, S. (1994) 'Assessment: a changing practice', in B. Moon and A. Shelton Mayes (eds) *Teaching and Learning in the Secondary School*, Milton Keynes: Open University Press.

Bruner, J. (1986) *Actual Minds, Possible Worlds*, Cambridge, MA: Harvard University Press.

—— (1960) *The Process of Education*, New York: Vintage.

—— (1966a) *The Process of Education*, New York: Vintage.

—— (1966b) *Towards a Theory of Instruction*, New York: W.W. Norton.

—— (1966c) *The Process of Education*, New York: Vintage.

—— (1971) *The Relevance of Education*, New York: W.W. Norton.

—— (1983) *Child's Talk: Learning to Use Language*, Oxford: Oxford University Press.

Bull, S. and Solity, J. (1987) *Classroom Management: Principles to Practice*, London: Croom Helm.

Burchfield, R. (ed.) (1996) *The New Fowler's Modern English Useage*, Oxford: Clarendon.

Buzan, T. (1984) *Use your Memory*, London: BBC Books.

Callow, R. (1980) 'Recognizing the exceptionally able child', in R. Povery, (ed.) *Educating the Exceptionally able Child*, London: Harper and Row.

Canter, L. and Canter, M. (1977) *Assertive Discipline*, Los Angeles: Lee Canter Associates.

Capel, S.A. (1992) 'Stress and burnout in teachers', *European Journal of Teacher Education*, 15, 3: 197–211.

—— (1993) 'Anxieties of beginning physical education teachers', *Educational Research*, 35, 3: 281–289.

—— (1994) 'Help – its teaching practice again!' Paper presented at the 10th Commonwealth and International Scientific Congress,' Victoria, BC, Canada.

—— (1996) 'Changing focus of concerns for physical education students on school experience', *Pedagogy in Practice*, 2, 2: 5–20.

—— (1977) 'Changes in students' anxieties after their first and second teaching practices', *Educational Research*, 39, 2: 211–228.

—— (1998) 'A longitudinal study of the stages of development or concern of secondary PE students', *European Journal of Physical Education*, 3, 2: 185–199.

Capel, S., Leask, M. and Turner, T. (1997) *Starting to Teach in the Secondary School: A Companion for the Newly Qualified Teacher*, London: Routledge.

Centre for Science Education, Sheffield (1992) *Active Teaching and Learning Approaches in Science*, London: Collins Educational.

Child, D. (1993) *Psychology and the Teacher (5th edition)*, London: Cassell.

—— (1997) *Psychology and the Teacher (6th edition)*, London: Cassell.

Chyriwsky, M. (1996) 'Able children: the need for a subject-specific approach', *Flying High*, 3, 32–36.

Clarke, G. (1983) *Guidelines for the recognition of gifted pupils*, Harlow: SCDC Publications, London.

Cohen, L. and Manion, L. (1989) *A Guide to Teaching Practice (3rd edition)*, London: Holt, Rinehart and Winston.

Cole, M. and Walker, S. (eds) (1989) *Teaching and Stress*, Milton Keynes: Open University Press.

Coles, A. and Turner, S. (1995) *Diet and Health in School Aged Children*, London: Health Education Authority.

Coles, M.J. and Robinson, W.D. (1989) *Teaching Thinking: A Survey of Programmes in Education*, Bristol: The Bristol Press.

Collins, J., Hammond, M. and Wellington, J. (1997) *Teaching and Learning with Multimedia*, London: Routledge,

Cooper, P. and Ideus, K. (1996) *Attention-deficit/hyperactivity disorder – a practical guide for teachers*, London: David Fulton.

Cowie, H. and Sharp, S. (1992) 'Students themselves tackle the problem of bullying', *Pastoral Care in Education*, 10, 4: 31–37.

Cox, M. (1997) *The Effects of Information Technology on Students' Motivation*. Final Report, London: NCET/King's College.

Crane, C.D. (1993) *The Key to your Success: Applying for a Secondary School Post*, Weymouth Dorset: The Education Appointments Council.

Croner (1984, updated fortnightly) *Head's Legal Guide*, New Malden: Croner Publications.

Crook, C. (1994) *Computers and the Collaborative Experience of Learning*, London: Routledge.

Cumine, V., Leach, J. and Stevenson, G. (1998) *Asperger Syndrome: a practical guide for teachers*, London: David Fulton.

Curtis, S.J. (1967) *History of Education in Great Britain*, Foxton, Cambs: University Tutorial Press.

D'Arcy, J. (1989) *Stress in Teaching: The Research Evidence*, Belfast: Northern Ireland Council for Educational Research, Occasional Paper Number 1.

Daugherty, R. (1995) *National Curriculum Assessment: A Review of Policy 1987–1994*, London: The Falmer Press.

Davis, B. and Sumara, D.J. (1997) 'Cognition, complexity and teacher education', *Harvard Educational Review*, 67, 105–121.

Davies, F. and Greene, T. (1984) *Reading for Learning in Science*, Edinburgh: Oliver and Boyd.

Dean, J. (1993) *Managing the Secondary School*, London: Routledge.

Dearing, R. (1994) *The National Curriculum and its Assessment. Final Report* (The Dearing Report), London: Schools Curriculum and Assessment Authority.

——— (1996) *Review of 16–19 Qualifications: Issues for Consideration*, London SCAA.

De Bono, E. (1972) *Children Solve Problems*, London: Penguin Education.

Dennison, B. and Kirk, R. (1990) *Do, Review, Learn, Apply: A Simple Guide to Experiential Learning*, Oxford: Blackwell Education.

Denton, C. and Postlethwaite, K. (1985) *Able children: identifying them in the classroom*, Windsor: NFER–Nelson.

Department for Education (1993a) 'Education for the whole pupil', *DFE NEWS*, 320/93.

——— (1993b) 'Schools must deliver spiritual and moral values rigorously', *DFE News*, 287/93.

—— (1993c) *School Governors: A Guide to the Law*, London: HMSO.

—— (1994a) *Circular 8/94: Pupil Behaviour and Discipline*, London: DFE.

—— (1994b) *Bullying: Don't suffer in silence. An anti bullying pack for schools*, London: DFE.

—— (1994c) *School Teachers' Pay and Conditions Document 1994*, London: HMSO.

—— (1994d) *Circular 1/94: Religious Education and Collective Worship*, London: DFE.

—— (1994e) *Circular 9/94: The Education of Children with Emotional and Behavioural Difficulties*, London: DFE.

—— (1994f) *Code of Practice on the Identification and Assessment of Special Educational Needs*, London: DFE.

Department for Education and Employment (1996) *Learning to Compete: Education and Training for 14–19 year olds*, London: Stationery Office (Cm. 3486).

—— (1997a) *Targets to Action: Guidance to Support Effective Target Setting in Schools*, London: Standards and Effectiveness Unit, Department for Education and Employment.

—— (1997b) *Excellence in Schools*, London: DFEE.

—— (1997c) *Circular 10/97: Teaching: High Status, High Standards*, London: DFEE.

—— (1998a) *University for Industry: Engaging People in Learning for Life* (Pathfinder Prospectus, the Learning Age), London: DFEE.

—— (1998b) *Extending Opportunity: A National Framework for Study Support*, Sudbury: DFEE Publications Office.

—— (1998c) *Homework: Guidelines for Secondary Schools (draft consultation)*, London: Standards and Effectiveness Unit, DFEE.

Department for Education and the Welsh Office (1992) *Circulars 9/92 and 35/92: Initial Teacher Training (Secondary Phase)*, London: HMSO.

Department for Education and Science (1967) *Children and their Primary Schools* (The Plowden Report), London: HMSO.

—— (1975) *A Language for Life* (The Bullock Report), London: HMSO.

—— (1978) *Special Education Needs* (The Warnock Report), London, HMSO.

—— (1979) *Aspects of Secondary Education: A Survey by HM Inspectors of Schools*, London: HMSO.

—— (1982) *Mathematics Counts* (The Cockcroft Report), London: HMSO.

—— (1983) *Circular 1/83: Assessments and Statements of Special Educational Needs* (joint circular with DHSS Health Circular HC(83)3 and Local Authority Circular LAC (83)2), London: DES.

—— (1985) *Better Schools*, London: HMSO, Cmnd 9469.

—— (1988) *The Report of the Working Party: Science*, London: DES.

—— (1989) *From Policy to Practice: the National Curriculum*, London: DES.

Department of Education and Science and the Welsh Office (1984a) *Records of Achievement: A Statement of Policy*, London: DES and the Welsh Office.

—— (1984b) *Education for All* (The Swann Report), London: DES and the Welsh Office.

—— (1988a) *National Curriculum Task Group on Assessment and Testing (TGAT Report)*, London: DES.

—— (1989) *Discipline in Schools. Report of the Committee of Enquiry Chaired by Lord Elton* (The Elton Report), London: HMSO.

Department of Employment (1971) *Glossary of Training Terms*, London: HMSO.

Dewey, J. (1916) *Democracy and Education*, New York: Free Press.

Dickens, C. (1989) *Hard Times*, Oxford: Oxford University Press World Classics.

Dickinson, C. and Wright, J. (1993) *Differentiation: Practical Handbook of Classroom Strategies*, Coventry: National Council for Educational Technology.

Dillon, J. and Maguire, M. (eds) (1997) *Becoming a Teacher: Issues in Secondary Teaching*, Buckingham: Open University Press.

Doise, W. (1990) 'The development of individual competencies through social interaction', in: H. Foot, M. Morgan and R. Shute (eds) *Children Helping Children*, Chichester, Wiley.

Donaldson, M. (1978) *Children's Minds (1st edition)*, Glasgow: Collins/Fontana.

———— (1992) *Human Minds: an Exploration*, London: Allen Lane.

Driver, R. (1983) *The Pupil as Scientist?*, Milton Keynes: Open University Press.

Driver, R. and Bell, J. (1986) 'Students thinking and learning of science: a constructivist view', *School Science Review*, 67, 240: 443–456.

Dunham, J. (1995) *Developing Effective School Management*, London: Routledge.

Dyer, C. (1994) 'Law Society warns solicitors to stamp out race discrimination', in *The Guardian*, 14 September 1994, p. 7.

The Education Year Book (annual) London: Longman.

Education Authorities Directory and Annual (annual) Redhill, Surrey: The School Government Publishing Company Ltd.

Eggleston, J. (1985) *Education for Some*, Stoke on Trent: Trentham Books.

Elton Report: see DES/WO 1989.

Entwistle, N.J. (1981) *Styles of Learning and Teaching (1st edition)*, Chichester, Wiley.

———— (1988) Understanding Classroom Learning, London: Hodder and Stoughton.

———— (1993) *Styles of Learning and Teaching (3rd edition)*, London: David Fulton.

Equal Opportunities Commission (1991) *Sex Discrimination in Schools: Guide for School Governors*, London: Equal Opportunities Commission.

ERA (1988) *Education Reform Act, 29 July 1988*; Section 1, 2, Aims of the School Curriculum, London: HMSO.

Erikson, E.H. (1980) *Identity and the Life Cycle*, New York: Norton.

Fielding, M. (1996) 'Delivery packages and the denial of learning', in H. Bradley, G. Southworth and V. Conner (eds) *Developing Teachers, Developing Schools*, London: Fulton.

Flavell, J.H. (1979) 'Metacognition and cognitive monitoring', *American Psychologist*, 34: 906–11.

———— (1982) 'On cognitive development', *Child Development*, 53: 1–10.

Fontana, D. (1993) *Managing Time*, Leicester: British Psychological Society Books.

Franklin, G. (1999) 'Using ICT for special educational needs' in M. Leask, and N. Pachler *Learning to teach ICT in secondary school*, London: Routledge.

Gagnè, R.M. (1985) *The Conditions of Learning and Theory of Institutions (4th edition)*, New York: Holt, Rinehart and Winston.

Gagnè, R.M. and White R.T. (1978) 'Memory structures and learning outcomes', *Review of Educational Research*, 48: 187–222.

Gardner, H. (1983) *Frames of Mind*, New York: Basic Books.
———— (1993) *Frames of Mind (2nd edition)*, New York: Basic Books.
———— (1994) 'The theory of multiple intelligences', in B. Moon and A. Shelton Mayes (eds) *Teaching and Learning in the Secondary School*, Milton Keynes: Open University Press.
George, D. (1992) *The Challenge of the Able Child*, London: David Fulton Publishers.
———— (1994) 'Provision and strategies for teaching more able children', in *Topic 11/1994*, Slough: NFER.
Gibbs, G. and Habeshaw, T. (1989) *253 Ideas for your Teaching*, Bristol: Technical and Educational Services Ltd.
Gillborn, D. (1996) *Exclusions from School*, London: Institute of Education. Viewpoint, No. 5, September. p. 8.
Gillborn, D. and Gipps, C. (1996) *Recent Research on the Achievement of Ethnic Minority Pupils*, London: HMSO (OFSTED: views of research).
Gilham, B. (ed.) (1986) *The Language of School Subjects*, London: Heinemann.
Gipps, C.V. (1991) 'Reading SATs cannot be made to serve two purposes', *Times Educational Supplement*, 1st February 1991, p. 22.
———— (1994) *Beyond Testing: Towards a Theory of Educational Assessment*, London: Falmer Press.
Goddard, D. and Leask, M. (1992) *The Search for Quality: Planning Improvement and Managing Change*, London: Paul Chapman Publishing.
Gould, S. (1984) *The Mismeasure of Man*, London: Pelican Books.
Graduate Teacher Training Registry (GTTR) (1993) *Annual Report*, Cheltenham, GTTR.
Greenbaum, S. and Whitcut, J. (1988) *Longman Guide to English Usage*, Harlow: Longman.
Greenhalgh, P. (1994) *Emotional Growth and Learning*, London: Routledge.
Greeno, J.G., Smith D.R. and Moore, J.L. (1993) 'Transfer of situated learning', in D.K. Detterman and R.J. Sternberg (eds) *Transfer on Trial: Intelligence, Cognition and Instruction*, Norwood, NJ: Ablex.

Hallam, S. (1996) Grouping Pupils by Ability, London: Institute of Education. Viewpoint, No. 4, July, p. 8.
Hallam, S. and Toutounji, I. (1996) *What do we Know about the Grouping of Pupils by Ability? A Research Review*, London: Institute of Education, p. 40.
Handy, C. (1993) *Understanding Organizations (4th edition)*, London: Penguin.
Hargreaves, A. (1989) *Curriculum and Assessment Reform*, Milton Keynes: Open University Press.
Hargreaves, A. and Evans, R. (1997) *Beyond Education Reform: Bringing teachers back in*, Buckingham: Open University Press.
Hargreaves, D.H. (1984) *Improving Secondary Schools: Report of the Committee on the Curriculum and Organisation of Secondary Schools*, London: ILEA.
Hargreaves, D.H. and Hopkins, D. (1991) *The Empowered School: The Management and Practice of Development Planning*, London: Cassell.
Hargreaves, D.H., Hopkins, D., Leask, M., Connolly, J. and Robinson, P. (1989) *Planning for School Development: Advice to Governors, Headteachers and Teachers*, London: DES.
Hargreaves, D., Molly, C. and Pratt, A. (1982) 'Social factors in conservation', *British Journal of Psychology*, 73: 231–234.

Harlen, W., Gipps, C., Broadfoot, P. and Nuttall, D. (1992) 'Assessment and the improvement of education', A paper prepared for the National Commission on Education, BERA Policy Task Group on Assessment, London: William Heinemann for the Paul Hamlyn Foundation.

Hart, K. (1981) *Children's Understanding of Mathematics*, London: Murray.

Hart, N.I. (1987) 'Student teachers' anxieties: four measured factors and their relationship to pupil disruption in class', *Educational Research*, 29, 1: 12–18.

Hart, S. (ed.) (1996) *Differentiation and the Secondary Curriculum: Debates and Dilemmas*, London: Routledge.

Harter, S. (1985) 'Competence as a dimension of self-evaluation: Toward a comprehensive model of self-worth', in R.L. Leahy (ed.) *The Development of the Self*, Orlando, FL: Academic Press, pp. 55–152 .

Haydon, G. (1997) *Teaching about Values: A New Approach*, London: Cassell.

Haydon, G. and Lambert, D. (1992) *Professional Studies: Tutor Support Pack*, London: University of London, Institute of Education.

Head, J. (1985) *The Personal Response to Science*, Cambridge: Cambridge University Press.

Her Majesty's Inspectors (1977) *Curriculum 11–16, Working Papers*, London: HMSO.

———— (1978) *Mixed Ability Work in Comprehensive Schools*, London: HMSO.

———— (1992) *The education of very able children in maintained schools*, London: HMSO.

———— (1994) 'The entitlement curriculum', in B. Moon and A. Shelton Mayes (eds) (1994) *Teaching and Learning in the Secondary School*, Milton Keynes: Open University Press.

Hogg, I. (1998) 'Using information technology in teaching and learning science' in T. Turner and W. DiMarco *Learning to teach science in the seconmdary school: a companion to school experience*, London: Routledge.

Hopkins, D. (1993) *A Teacher's Guide to Classroom Research (2nd edition)*, Milton Keynes: Open University Press.

House of Commons (1991) *Education (Schools) Bill*, London: HMSO.

Hoyle, E. and Wilks, J. (1990) *Exceptionally able Children and their Education*, London: HMSO.

Hughes, C. (1993) 'Parents' choice' in *The Independent*, 4 July, p. 2.

Humphrys, G. (1993) *Getting a Teaching Job 1994*, London: University of Greenwich.

ILEA (1984) *Improving Secondary Schools* (The Hargreaves Report), London.

Inhelder, B. and Piaget, J. (1958) *The Growth of Logical Thinking from Childhood to Adolescence*, London: Routledge.

Institute of Policy Studies (1994) *Entry to the Legal Profession: Discrimination: A Report*, London: Institute of Policy Studies.

Jennings, A. (1995) 'Discussion', in J. Frost (ed.) *Teaching Science*, London: Woburn Press.

Johnson, D. (ed.) (1997) *Minorities and Girls in Schools: Effects on Achievement and Performance*, London: Sage Publications.

Joyce, B., Calhoun, E. and Hopkins, D. (1997) *Models of Learning – Tools for Teaching*, Buckingham: Open University Press.

Joyce, B. and Weil, M. (1986) *Models of Teaching (3rd edition)*, London: Prentice Hall.

Kelly, A.V. (1990) *The National Curriculum: A Critical Review*, London: Paul Chapman Publishing.

Keys, W., Harris, S. and Fernandes, C. (1996) *Third International Mathematics and Science Study – First National Report – Part 1: Achievement in Mathematics and Science at Age 13 in England*, London: National Foundation for Educational Research.

Klahr, D. and Wallace, J.G. (1976) *Cognitive Development: An Information Processing View*, New Jersey, Lawrence Erlbaum.

Klein, G. (1993) *Education Towards Race Equality*, London: Cassell.

Kohlberg, L. (1984) *The Psychology of Moral Development: The Nature and Validity of Social Development: The Nature and Validity of Social Stages*, San Francisco: Harper and Row.

Kolb, D.A. (1976) *The Learning Style Inventory: Technical Manual*, Boston: McBer and Co.

—— (1985) *The Learning Style Inventory: Technical Manual (revised edition)*, Boston: McBer and Co.

Kyriacou, C. (1986) *Effective Teaching in Schools*, Oxford: Basil Blackwell.

—— (1989) 'The nature and prevalence of teacher stress', in M. Cole and S. Walker (eds) *Teaching and Stress*, Milton Keynes: Open University Press.

—— (1991) *Essential Teaching Skills*, Oxford Basil Blackwell.

—— (1995) *Essential Teaching Skills (2nd edition)*, Cheltenham: Stanley Thornes.

—— (1997) *Effective Teaching in Schools: Theory and Practice (2nd edition)*, Cheltenham: Staney Thornes.

Lambert, D. (1990a) *Geography Assessment*, Cambridge: Cambridge University Press.

—— (1990b) 'A profile is', in D. Lambert *Geography Assessment*, Cambridge: Cambridge University Press.

—— (1990c) 'A history subject profile', in D. Lambert *Geography Assessment*, Cambridge Cambridge University Press.

—— (1990d) 'Principles for recording and reporting', in D. Lambert *Geography Assessment*, Cambridge: Cambridge University Press.

—— (1991a) 'Assessment: a view from the receiving end', in *Geography Assessment Supplementary Pack*, Cambridge: Cambridge University Press.

—— (1991b) 'The assessment industry', in *Geography Assessment Supplementary Pack*, Cambridge: Cambridge University Press.

—— (1991c) 'A planning grid for a scheme of work', in *Geography Assessment Supplementary Pack*, Cambridge: Cambridge University Press.

—— (1991d) 'An "ideal" planning cycle', in *Geography Assessment Supplementary Pack*, Cambridge: Cambridge University Press.

—— (1994) *Differentiated Learning*, London: University of London, Institute of Education, Initial Teacher Training (Occasional papers in teacher education and training. Resources).

Lave, J. and Wenger, E. (1991) *Situated Learning: Legitimate Peripheral Participation*, Cambridge: Cambridge University Press.

Lawton, D. (1989) *Education, Culture and the National Curriculum*, London: Hodder and Stoughton.

—— (ed.) (1990) *The Education Reform Act: Choice and Control*, London: Hodder and Stoughton.

Leask, M. (1999) *Issues in the use of ICT in schools*, London: Routledge.

Leask, M. and Pachler, N. (1999) *Teaching and Learning with ICT in the Secondary School*, London: Routledge.

Lewis, I. and Munn, P. (1987) *So You Want to do Research? A Guide for Teachers on How to Formulate Research Questions*, Edinburgh, Scotland: The Scottish Council for Research in Education with the General Teaching Council for Scotland.

Lloyd-Jones, R. (1988) *How to Produce Better Worksheets*, London: Hutchinson Education.

Lucas, N. (1997) 'The changing sixth form', in S. Capel, M. Leask and T. Turner (eds) (1997) *Starting to Teach in the Secondary School: A Companion for the Newly Qualified Teacher*, London: Routledge.

McCarthy, B. (1987) *The 4Mat System*, Barrington: Excel.

McCelland, D.C. (1961) *The Achieving Society*, Princeton, NJ: Van Nostrand.

McCormick, R. and James, M. (1983) *Curriculum Evaluation in Schools (2nd edition)*, London: Croom Helm.

McGregor, D. (1960) *The Human Side of Enterprise*, New York: McGraw-Hill.

McKernan, J. (1991) *Curriculum Action Research: A Handbook of Methods and Resources for the Reflective Practitioner*, London: Kogan Page.

McLeod, J. and Cropley, A. (1989) *Fostering academic excellence*, Oxford: Pergamon Press.

Mager, R. (1990) *Preparing Educational Objectives (2nd edition)*, London: Kogan Page.

Marland, M. (1993) *The Craft of the Classroom*, London: Croom Helm.

Maslow, A.H. (1970) *Motivation and Personality (2nd edition)*, New York: Harper and Row.

Matthews, J. (1989) *Curriculum Exposed*, London: David Fulton.

Maybin, J., Mercer, N. and Stierer, B. (1992) 'Scaffolding learning in the classroom', in K. Norman (ed.) *Thinking Voices: The Work of the National Oracy Project*, London: Hodder and Stoughton, pp. 186–195.

Mercer, N. (1994) 'Classrooms, language and communication', in B. Moon and A. Shelton Mayes (eds) *Teaching and Learning in the Secondary School*, London: Routledge.

Miller, O. (1996) *Supporting children with visual impairment in mainstream schools*, Birmingham: Questions Publishing.

Mitchell, R. (1994) 'The communicative approach to language teaching: an introduction', in A. Swarbrick (ed.) *Teaching Modern Languages*, London: Routledge/Open University, pp. 33–42.

Moll, L.C. (ed.) (1990) *Vygotsky and Education: Instructional Implications and Applications of Socio-historical Psychology*, Cambridge: Cambridge University Press.

Montgomery, D. (1996) 'Differentiation of the curriculum in primary education', *Flying High*, 3: 14–28.

Moon, B. (1983) *Comprehensive Schools: Challenge and Change*, Windsor: NFER-Nelson.

Moon, B. and Shelton Mayes, A. (eds) (1994) *Teaching and Learning in the Secondary School*, London: Routledge for Open University Press.

Mortimore, P. and Whitty, G. (1997) *Can School Improvement Overcome the Effects of Disadvantage?* London: Institute of Education.

Mosston, M. and Ashworth, S. (1994) *Teaching Physical Education (4th edition)*, New York: Macmillan College Publishing.

Munn, P. and Drever, E. (1990) *Using Questionnaires in Small Scale Research: A Teacher's*

Guide, Edinburgh, Scotland: The Scottish Council for Research in Education with the General Teaching Council for Scotland.

Munn, P., Johnstone, M. and Holligan, C. (1990) 'Pupils' perceptions of effective disciplinarians', *British Educational Research Journal,* 16, 2: 191–198.

Murphy, P. (1994) 'Assessment and gender', in B. Moon and A. Shelton Mayes (eds) *Teaching and Learning in the Secondary School,* London: Routledge.

Myers, K. (ed.) (1987) *Genderwatch!* Cambridge: Cambridge University Press.

—— (ed.) (1996) *School Improvement in Practice: Schools make a Difference Project,* London: Falmer Press.

Myers, K. (1990) *Sex Discrimination in Schools,* London: Advisory Centre for Education.

National Commission on Education (1993) *Learning to Succeed: A Radical Look at Education Today,* London: Heinemann for the Paul Hamlyn Foundation.

National Foundtion for Educational Research (NFER) (1996) *Cognitive Abilities Test,* Windsor: NFER-Nelson.

National Curriculum Council (1988) *Curriculum Guidance 3: The Whole Curriculum,* York: NCC.

—— (1989) *An Introduction to the National Curriculum,* York: NCC.

—— (1990) *Curriculum Guidance 4: Education for Economic and Industrial Understanding,* York: NCC.

—— (1990) *Curriculum Guidance 5: Health Education,* York: NCC.

—— (1990) *Curriculum Guidance 6: Careers Education and Guidance,* York: NCC.

—— (1990) *Curriculum Guidance 7: Environmental Education,* York: NCC.

—— (1990) *Curriculum Guidance 8: Education for Citizenship,* York: NCC.

—— (1992a) *Curriculum Guidance 9: The National Curriculum and Pupils with Severe Learning Difficulties,* York: NCC.

—— (1992b) *Starting Out with the National Curriculum,* York: NCC.

—— (1993a) *A Curriculum Perspective: 14–19 Education in Schools and Colleges,* York: NCC.

—— (1993b) *Spiritual and Moral Development: a Discussion Paper,* York: NCC.

—— (1993c) *Special Educational Needs and The National Curriculum: Opportunity and Challenge,* York: NCC.

National Union of Teachers (annually) *Your First Teaching Post,* London: NUT.

NCET (1994) *Information Technology Works! Stimulate to Educate,* Coventry: NCET.

Newbold, D. (1977) *Ability Grouping: The Banbury Inquiry,* Windsor: NFER-Nelson.

Nicholls, G. (1995) 'Ways pupils learn' in S. Capel, M. Leask and T. Turner *Learning to teach in the secondary school: a companion to school experience,* London: Routledge.

Nicholls, J. (1992) 'Late' in R. Batchford (1992) *Assemblies for the 80s,* London: Faber.

Nisbett, J. and Schucksmith, J. (1986) Learning Strategies, London: Routledge.

Nolta, D.L. 'Children learn what they live'; source unknown; see page 415.

Norman, K. (ed.) (1992) *Thinking voices: The work of the National Oracy Project,* London: Hodder and Stoughton.

Novak, J.D. and Gowin, D.B. (1984) *Learning How to Learn,* Cambridge: Cambridge University Press.

OFSTED (1993) Working paper for the inspection of secondary initial teacher training, London: Office of Her Majesty's Chief Inspector.

——— (1993a) *Handbook for the Inspection of Schools, Revised Edition*, London: OFSTED.

——— (1993b) *The New Teacher in School: A Survey by Her Majesty's Inspectorate in England and Wales, 1992*, London: HMSO.

——— (1993c) *Achieving Good Behaviour in Schools: A Report from the Office of Her Majesty's Chief Inspector of Schools*, London: HMSO.

——— (1994a) *Handbook for Inspection of Schools, Part 6 The Statutory Basis for Education*, London: OFSTED.

——— (1994b) *Mathematics Key Stages 1, 2, 3 and 4*, London: HMSO.

——— (1996) *The implementation of the Code of Practice for Pupils with Special Educational Needs: A Report from the Office of Her Majesty's Chief Inspector of Schools*, London: HMSO.

——— (1996a) *Promoting High Achievement for Pupils with Special Educational Needs in Mainstream Schools*, London: HMSO.

O'Hear, P. and White, J. (eds) (1991) *A National Curriculum for All: Laying the Foundations for Success*, London: Institute for Public Policy Research.

——— (eds) (1993) *Assessing the National Curriculum*, London: Paul Chapman Publishing.

O'Leary, J. (1992) 'Record numbers take and pass GCSE exams', in *The Times*, 27 August, p. 1.

Olweus, D. (1993) *Bullying at School*, Oxford: Blackwell.

Organization for Economic Co-operation and Development (1994) 'Risk of failure in school', in *Innovation in Education*, 67 (February): p. 1.

Pachler, N. and Williams, L. in press (1999).

Palmer, R. (1993) *Write in Good Style: A Guide to Good English*, London: Spon.

——— (1996) *Brain Train: Studying for Success*, London: Spon.

Papert, S. (1993) *The Children's Machine: Rethinking School in the Age of the Computer*, New York: Basic Books.

——— (1996) *The Connected Family: Bridging the Digital Generation Gap (includes CD-ROM and Web-site links)*, Atlanta, GA: Longstreet Press.

Pateman, T. (1994) 'Crisis, what identity crisis?', *First Appointments Supplement, Times Educational Supplement*, 14 January, 28–29.

Patten, J. (Secretary of State for Education) (1994) 'Educational outputs', *Schools Update*, Summer: 8, London: DFE.

Perrott, E. (1982) *Effective Teaching*, London: Longman.

Piaget, J. (1932) *The Moral Judgement of the Child*, London: Routledge and Kegan Paul.

——— (1962) *Judgement and Reasoning in the Child*, London: Routledge and Kegan Paul.

Piaget, J. and Inhelder, B. (1969) *The Psychology of the Child*, New York: Basic Books.

Postlethwaite, K. (1993) *Differentiated Science Teaching: Responding to Individual Differences and Special Educational Needs*, Milton Keynes: Open University Press.

Postlethwaite, K. and Denton, C. (1978) *Streams for the Future? The Long-term Effects of Early Streaming and Non-streaming: The Final Report of the Banbury Enquiry*, Banbury: Pubansco.

Reeve, P. (1992) 'The average child' unpublished dissertation, De Montfort University, Bedford.

Reiss, R. and Mason, M. (1992) *Disability Equality in the Classroom: a Human Rights Issue*,

(2nd edition), London: ILEA/Disability Equality.

Riding, R.J. (1997) 'On the Nature of Cognitive Style', *Educational Psychology*, 17: 29–49.

Riding, R.J., and Cheema, I. (1991) 'Cognitive styles – an overview and integration', *Educational Psychology*, 11: 193–215.

Ripley, K., Daines, R. and Barrett, J. (1997) Dyspraxia: *A guide for teachers and parents*, Hitchen: The Dyspraxia Foundation.

Robertson, J. (1989) *Effective Classroom Control: Understanding Pupil–Teacher Relationships*, London: Hodder and Stoughton.

Rogers, C. (1982) *A Social Psychology of Schooling: The Expectancy Process*, London: Routledge and Kegan Paul.

Rogoff, B. (1990) *Apprenticeship in Thinking: Cognitive Development in Social Context*, Oxford: Oxford University Press.

Rutter, M., Maughan, B., Mortimore, P. and Ouston, J. (1979) *Fifteen Thousand Hours: Secondary Schools and their Effects on Pupils*, London: Open Books.

St John Ambulance (1994) *Emergency Aid for Schools (5th edition)*, London: St John Ambulance.

Sandholtz, J.H., Ringstaff, C. and Dwyer, C.D. (1996) *Teaching with Technology: Creating Pupil-centred Classrooms*, New York: Teachers College Press.

School Curriculum and Assessment Authority (SCAA) (1997) *Target Setting and Benchmarking in Schools: A Consultation*, London: School Curriculum and Assessment Authority (SCAA is now the Qualifications and Assessment Authority, QCA).

School Examination and Assessment Council (SEAC) (1990) *Post 16 Developments*, London: SEAC.

Scottish Qualification Authority (1998) *Where credit's due: how to compare Scottish Higher Qualifications and GCE A Level*, Glasgow: Scottish Qualifications Authority.

Selman, R.L. (1980) *The growth of interpersonal understanding: developmental and clinical analyses*, New York: Academic Press.

Shayer, M. and Adey, P. (1981) *Toward a Science of Science Teaching*, London: Heinemann.

Shepard, L.A. (1992) 'Commentary: what policy makers who mandate tests should know about the new psychology of intellectual ability and learning', in B.R. Gifford and M.C. O'Connor (eds) *Changing Assessments: Alternative Views of Aptitude, Achievement and Instruction*, Boston and London: Kluwer Academic.

Short, G. (1986) 'Teacher expectation and West Indian underachievement', in *Educational Research*, 27, 2: 95–101.

Skinner, B.F. (1953) *Science and Human Behaviour*, New York: Macmillan.

Smith, C.J. and Laslett, R. (1993) *Effective Classroom Management: A Teacher's Guide*, London: Routledge.

Smith, R. and Standish, P. (eds) (1997) *Teaching Right and Wrong: Moral Education in the Balance*, Stoke-on-Trent: Trentham.

Somekh, B. and Davis, N. (eds) (1997) *Using Information Technology Effectively in Teaching and Learning*, Routledge, London.

Stiggins, R.J. (1992) 'The two disciplines of educational assessment', Paper presented to the Educational Commission of the States Assessment Conference, Boulder, CO, USA (June).

Stoll, L. and Fink, D. (1996) *Changing our Schools*, Buckingham: Open University Press.

Stones, E. (1992) *Quality Teaching: A Sample of Cases*, London and New York: Routledge.

Stradling, R., Saunders, L. and Weston, P. (1991) *Differentiation in Action: A Whole School Approach for Raising Standards*, London: HMSO.

Sutton, C. (ed.) (1981) *Communicating in the Classroom*, London: Hodder and Stoughton.

Tanner, J.M. (1991) *Foetus to Man (revised and enlarged edition)*, Cambridge, MA.: Harvard University Press.

Tarrant, G. (1981) 'Social studies in the primary school: the place of discussion', *Social Studies Teacher*, 13, 3: 65–65.

Task Group on Assessment and Testing (TGAT) (1988) A Report, London: DES and Welsh Office.

Taylor, P.H. and Richards, M. (1985) *An Introduction to Curriculum Studies*, Windsor: NFER-Nelson.

Teacher Training Agency (1998) *Career Entry Profile for Newly Qualified Teachers*, London: Teacher Training Agency.

Times Educational Supplement (annual) *First Appointments Supplement*, TES.

Topping, K.J. (1992) 'The effectiveness of paired reading in ethnic minority homes' in *Multicultural Teaching to combat racism in school and community*, Volume 10, No. 2, Spring, pp. 19–23.

Townsend, S. (1982) *The Life of Adrian Mole*, London: Methuen.

Turner, A. and Turner, S. (1994) 'Multicultural issues in teacher education in science', in S. Thorp, P. Deshpande and C. Edwards (eds) (1994) *Race, Equality and Science Teaching: A Handbook for Teachers and Educators*, Hatfield: Association for Science Education.

Vygotsky, L.S (1962) *Thought and Language*, Cambridge, MA: MIT Press.

—— (1986) *Thought and Language (Revised edition)*, Cambridge, MA: The MIT Press. Translated by A. Kozulin.

Walker, J. (1989) in P. Widlake *Special Children Handbook: Meeting Special Educational Needs within the Mainstream School*, London: Hutchinson.

Warnock, M.: see DES 1978a.

Warren, A., Brunner, D., Maier, P. and Barnett, L. (1998) *Technology in Teaching and Learning: An Introductory Guide*, London: Kogan Page.

Waterhouse, P. (1983) *Managing the Learning Process*, Maidenhead: McGraw-Hill Series for Teachers.

Weeks, A. (1993) *Your Exceptionally Able Pupils in School. Meeting the Needs of the Exceptionally Able*, London: New Education Press.

Weiner, B.J. (1972) *Theories of Motivation*, Chicago, IL: Markham.

Wellington, J. (ed.) (1986) *Controversial Issues in the Curriculum*, Oxford Basil Blackwell.

White, J. (1982) *The Aims of Education Restated*, London: Routledge.

—— (1998) *Do Howard Gardner's Multiple Intelligences Add Up? Perspectives on Education Policy*, London: Institute of Education.

White, R.T. and Gunstone, R. (1992) *Probing Understanding*, London: Falmer Press.

Widlake, P. (1989) *Special Children Handbook: meeting Special Educational Needs within the mainstream school*, London: Methuen.

Willson, M. and Williams, D. (1996) 'Trainee teachers misunderstandings in chemistry: diagnosis and evaluation using concept mapping', in *School Science Review*, 77, 280: 107–115.

Wittrock, M.C. (1974) 'Learning as a generative process', *Educational Psychologist*, 11, 87–95.

Wood, D. (1988) *How Children Think and Learn*, Oxford: Blackwell Press.

Wragg, E.C. (ed.) (1984) *Classroom Teaching Skills*, London: Croom Helm.

Wragg, E. (1994) *An Introduction to Classroom Observation*, London: Routledge.

Wright, C. (1994) 'Black children's experience of the secondary system', in B. Moon and A. Shelton Mayes (eds) *Teaching and Learning in the Secondary School*, London: Routledge.

Wringe, C. (1988) *Understanding Educational Aims*, London: Unwin Hyman.

Wylam, H. and Shayer, M. (1978) CSMS *Science Reasoning Tasks: General Guide*, Windsor: NFER Publishing Co.

Yin, R. (1994) *Case Study. Design and methods (2nd ed.)*, London: Sage.

NAME INDEX

SUBJECT INDEX

schemes of work 49, 66–79, 283, 316–7, 376; planning cycle 30; *see also* lesson planning
School Curriculum and Assessment Authority (SCAA) 330, 335, 371–3, 375, 408
school development planning 14, 215, 351–64, 403–4; *see also* school policies
School Examination and Assessment Authority (SEAC) 330, 373
school experience 29, 341; concerns during 52, 83–9; *see also* role, student teacher, tutor,
school meals 158
school policies 13–5, 20, 128–9, 199, 216; assessment 308; behaviour 84, 219, 403; equal opportunities 182, 189, 191–3; sanctions and rewards 80; Special Educational Needs (SEN) 215–6; *see also* behaviour, school development planning, rules
school teacher pay and conditions 410
school web site 352
school-based course 1
school: ethos 14, 60, 151, 160, 162, 199–203, 344–5, 352, 359; prospectus 343–4, 352; success of 14, 179, 367, 370; types 380
science: 40; reasoning tasks 169, 177
SEAC; *see* School Examination and Assessment Authority
seating plans 74–5, 82
secondary modern schools 346
Section 11 teachers 355
selection 355
self discipline; *see* discipline
self esteem: pupils 111, 122, 129, 159–61, 270
self presentation 101–5
sequence of a lesson 55
server 38
setting 112, 134, 190–1; by gender 190; by ethnic grouping 191; *see also* banding, grouping, mixed ability, streaming
Sex Discrimination Act 181
sex education 9, 209, 234, 355–6, 412
sexism 183–8, 190–2, 197; *see also* bias, gender
shouting by teachers 87
silence 62, 80, 82; *see also* attention, routines
skills of pupils 67–8; *see also* cross-curricular
social class 179
social constructivism 235–42
social skills 231, 268, 354, 357; *see also* student teacher
special educational needs 39, 42, 133, 158, 212–29, 251, 272, 355, 358, 360–62, 375–6,

411–12; background case studies of pupils 137–9; identification and assessment of SEN 133, 212, 214–5, 228, 447–49; review (Dearing) 374–5; statements for testing 173; *see also* code of practice, Special Educational Needs (SEN) Co-ordinator, Warnock;
Special Educational Needs Co-ordinator (SEN) 215–7
special schools 217
specific learning difficulties 217
speech; *see* language, voice
spelling 217–8, 435–6, 439
spider diagram 433; *see also* study skills
spiritual and moral welfare 14, 353, 357, 366, 411; *see also* moral, pastoral
St John's Ambulance 15
stage theory (of development) 237; in learning 239–40
stages of development; *see* development, stage theory
Standard Assessment Tasks; *see* SATs
standards: for NQT 3, 9, 12, 29, 51–2, 64, 66, 93, 107, 121, 212, 231, 266, 276, 303, 325, 397; national 283, 286, 288–302, 329–30, 366, 370; personal 21–2, 128, 408; of pupils' work 303–23; *see also* competencies, OFSTED
statement of Special Educational Needs (SEN) 226–7, 412
Statements of Attainment (of National Curriculum) 352–3
status 123
statutory duties 9, 408–13
stereotyping 178–98; *see also* bias, equal opportunities, prejudice
streaming 111, 134, 143–49, 190–1, 370; *see also* grouping, mixed ability, setting
stress 6, 29–36, 88, 398–9; awareness of 29; causes of, in student teachers 33–5; management of 34–6, 87–8; prevention of 32, 35; prioritising activities 29
student teacher: common problems 83–6; concerns 2, 52, 83–9; confidence 23; feedback to 19; ICT competence 39, personal qualities 78, 81, 87–8, 101; phases of development 18, 22–7, 64; professional development 6; relationships with pupils 63, 78–9, 83, 86–8; role ambiguity 33–4; role and responsibilities 18–19, 23, 27, 33, 362, 411–3; school's expectations of 20; self image 22–4, 362; social skills 20
study skills 85–6, 252–62; aids to recall 252–8;